To my wife Bonni – it's a privilege to share m

Philip Yaeger, PhD, MBA, CPA, CGMA Owner, Editor-in-chief
Megan Lewczyk, MAcc, CPA Production Editor

This book was set in Calibri font designed by Lucas de Groot.
Cover Design: Larissa Jaster Design Studio
Cover Photography: Travis Rieth

The following items, copyright © the American Institute of Certified Professional Accountants, Inc., New York, NY 10036, are reprinted and/or adapted with permission:

1. Material from Uniform CPA Exam Selected Questions and Unofficial Answers © 2000–2017
2. Definitions, examples, etc. from The Code of Professional Conduct
3. Material from the Preparation, Compilation and Review Standards
4. Material from the Clarified Statements on Auditing Standards
5. Material from the AICPA Audit Guide over Audit Sampling

Material from the Certified Management Accountant Examinations, copyright © 2011–2014 by the Institute of Certified Management Accountants, Montvale, New Jersey 07645, are reprinted and/or adapted with permission.

The FASB material is copyrighted by the Financial Accounting Foundation, 401 Merritt 7, Norwalk, CT 06856, and is used with permission.

The information disclosed in this document, including all designs and related materials, is the property of Yaeger CPA Review. Yaeger CPA Review and/or its licensors, as appropriate, reserve all patent, copyright and other proprietary rights to this document, including all design, reproduction, use, and sales rights thereto. You may not reproduce or transmit in any form or by any means, electronic or mechanical, including photocopying, recording, and storage in an information retrieval system, nor may you modify or create derivative works based on the text of any file, or any part thereof, without the prior written permission of Yaeger CPA Review.

Limit of Liability/Disclaimer of Warranty: While the content development team has used their best efforts in preparing this book, they make no representations or warranties with respect to the accuracy or completeness of the contents of this book and specifically disclaim any implied warranties of merchantability or fitness for a particular purpose. No warranty may be created or extended by sales representatives or written sales materials. The advice and strategies contained herein may not be suitable for your situation. You should consult with a professional where appropriate. Neither the publisher nor author shall be liable for any loss of profit or any other commercial damages, including but not limited to special, incidental, consequential, or other damages.

Solicitation or disclosure of CPA Examination questions and answers is strictly prohibited.

ISBN: 978-0-9987002-4-3   *Yaeger CPA Review 2018 - Auditing and Attestation*
978-0-9987002-5-0   *Yaeger CPA Review 2018 - Business Environment and Concepts*
978-0-9987002-6-7   *Yaeger CPA Review 2018 - Regulation*
978-0-9987002-7-4   *Yaeger CPA Review 2018 - Financial Accounting and Reporting*

Copyright © 2018 Yaeger CPA Review. ALL RIGHTS RESERVED.

Second Edition: December 2017 (Version 2.8)

For additional information on our other products or for customer service, please call 1.800.824.2811.

Introduction: Preparing for the CPA Exam

A. Message from Phil Yaeger

On behalf of YAEGER CPA REVIEW, I thank you for purchasing our program, and I wish you the best success with the CPA EXAM! If you have questions during your studies, I will be very happy to speak with you personally at any time. I am here to help you and motivate you during your journey.

With warmest regards,

Philip S. Yaeger

B. CPA Exam Basics

The CPA (Certified Public Accountant) exam is a computer-based exam that according to the American Institute of Certified Public Accountants (AICPA), tests the knowledge and skills typically possessed by a person with two years of accounting experience, to protect the public interest. Experience requirements may be obtained before or after passing the CPA exam with some time limitations dependent on your state. Even though many students take the CPA Exam after graduating college, the AICPA has stated that this should not, and will not, impact the standard established regarding required knowledge and skills necessary for licensure as a CPA.

The CPA Exam must be passed to qualify for licensure as a CPA. The licensure can be obtained in any of the 55 U.S. jurisdictions, which includes all 50 states, Puerto Rico, Guam, District of Columbia, Commonwealth of Northern Mariana Islands, and the U.S. Virgin Islands.

Apply to take the exam through your state board of accountancy or NASBA (nasba.org), as applicable. It is best to apply to take the exam when you have met the educational requirements of the jurisdiction you plan to apply for the exam in. It is recommended to check the jurisdiction you plan to take the exam in to ensure you have met the requirements before commencing your CPA Exam preparation. Most states offer a self-assessment education evaluation worksheet which you can complete to determine your status.

The Uniform CPA Exam consists of four sections: Auditing and Attestation(AUD), Business Environment and Concepts (BEC), Financial Accounting and Reporting (FAR), and Regulation (REG). Each exam section is four hours, for a total of 16 hours of testing.

Examination Structure by Section				
Section	Item Type	Item Weighting	Testlet and Time Allocation Recommendation	
Auditing and Attestation (AUD)	72 MCQs 8 TBSs	50% 50%	No.1 36 MCQs - 1 hour No.2 36 MCQs - 1 hour No.3 2 TBSs - 30 min. No.4 3 TBSs - 45 min. No.5 3 TBSs - 45 min.	Time to complete – 4 hours
Business Environment and Concepts (BEC)	62 MCQs 4 TBSs 3 Written Communications	50% 35% 15%	No.1 31 MCQs - 1 hour No.2 31 MCQs - 1 hour No.3 2 TBSs - 30 min. No.4 2 TBSs - 30min. No.5 3 Written Communications - 60 min.	Time to complete – 4 hours

Financial Accounting and Reporting (FAR)	66 MCQs 8 TBSs	50% 50%	No.1 33 MCQs - 1 hour No.2 33 MCQs - 1 hour No.3 2 TBSs - 30 min. No.4 3 TBSs - 45 min. No.5 3 TBSs - 45 min.	Time to complete – 4 hours
Regulation (REG)	76 MCQs 8 TBSs	50% 50%	No.1 38 MCQs - 1 hour No.2 38 MCQs - 1 hour No.3 2 TBSs - 30 min. No.4 3 TBSs - 45 min. No.5 3 TBSs - 45 min.	Time to complete – 4 hours

Sections may be taken in any order; however, you must complete all four sections within 18 months of passing the first section. The passing score is 75 for each section.

The exam is administered at Prometric testing centers in the USA (and some international locations): https://www.prometric.com/en-us/clients/cpa/Pages/landing.aspx. The exam can be physically sat for in a different state to that in which you apply for your license in. Some states allow for candidates to sit the exam internationally in Japan, Brazil, Bahrain, Kuwait, Lebanon and the United Arab Emirates. Check your state board for more information.

Testing "windows" represent available months when a candidate can take the exam. The testing windows are the first two months of each calendar quarter (e.g., January and February). To accommodate candidate demand for more opportunities to take the exam, the testing windows have been extended through the 10th of the third month of each testing window and are applicable for all testing windows through December 2018. Additional information will be posted as it is announced by the AICPA.

Types of questions on the CPA Exam include:
1) **Multiple-choice questions**: These questions are in all four sections and are based on the content/topics outlined in the AICPA blueprint (discussed below).

2) **Task-based simulations:** These questions utilize the type of activities that replicate real-life work situations. The simulations may include tasks such as editing a document, searching databases, or completing worksheets. Task-based simulations appear in all four sections of the exam.

   Document Review Simulations (DRS) and *Research* simulations are two specialized types of task-based simulations. A *DRS* will present a primary document, as well as related source materials, for the candidate to review. Highlighted words, phrases, sentences or paragraphs in the DRS document may or may not be correct, requiring the candidate to select appropriate edits based on relevant source materials.

   Research simulations require candidates to locate authoritative guidance to answer the prompt and cite the location where he/she found the information.

3) **Written communications tasks**: Written Communication questions are found only in the BEC sections. They are like a case study that includes a writing skill exercise. The candidate must review a description of a situation and will then be asked to write a constructed response relating to the situation. The instructions will require that the CPA candidate write a letter or a memorandum providing the correct information about the situation in a clear, complete, and professional manner.

C. **CPA Candidate Checklist**
   ☐ **Complete your state's education requirements to sit for the CPA Exam**
   ☐ **Start studying with YAEGER CPA REVIEW**
   ☐ **Apply for your exam:**

   Option A (NASBA-supported state – see NASBA.org):
   ☐ Apply at https://cpacentral.nasba.org/ to sit for the exam
   ☐ Your application, fees, and transcripts must be sent to NASBA
   ☐ NASBA will send your authorization to test (ATT) to the National Candidate Database (NCD)
   ☐ If approved by NCD, you will receive a notice to schedule (NTS)

   Option B (non NASBA-supported state):
   ☐ Apply to your State Board of Accountancy directly to sit for the exam
   ☐ Your application, fees, and transcripts must be sent to the State Board
   ☐ The State Board will send your ATT to the NCD
   ☐ If approved by NCD, NCD will issue a Payment Coupon to notify you of remaining exam fees that must be paid to NASBA if you only were required to send the application fee to the State Board
   ☐ Once all fees are paid, you will receive your NTS

   After you receive your NTS:
   ☐ **Visit www.prometric.com to schedule your exam**
   ☐ **Sit for the scheduled exam** (*you MUST bring NTS and two forms of ID or you can't take exam*)
   ☐ **Wait patiently and receive your scores**
   ☐ **Complete the experience requirements for your state and submit application for licensure to state board**

D. **Exam Day**

	Testlet 1	Testlet 2	Testlet 3	Scheduled 15 Minute Break	Testlet 4	Testlet 5
AUD	36 MCQ	36 MCQ	2 TBS		3 TBS	3 TBS
BEC	31 MCQ	31 MCQ	2 TBS		2 TBS	3 WC
FAR	33 MCQ	33 MCQ	2 TBS		3 TBS	3 TBS
REG	38 MCQ	38 MCQ	2 TBS		3 TBS	3 TBS

Candidates must work each testlet in order and complete/submit the current testlet before access to the next testlet is permitted. Once you submit, you are **not** permitted to return and reopen a completed/submitted testlet.

E. **Current Version of the CPA Exam**
Beginning April 1 2017, an updated version of the CPA Exam will be administered to CPA candidates. According to the AICPA, professional content knowledge will remain fundamental to protecting the public interest. Also, the candidates must be competent in the following skills:
- Remembering and understanding: The perception and comprehension of the significance of an area utilizing knowledge gained.
- Application: The use of demonstration of knowledge, concepts or techniques.

- Analysis: The examination and study of the interrelationships of separate areas in order to identify causes and find evidence to support inferences.
- Evaluation: Examination of assessment of problems and use of judgment to draw conclusions.

To test these competencies, the new CPA Exam has increased the number of task-based simulations and the length of the CPA Exam increased from 14 to 16 hours (four hours for each section).

The material that the candidate should learn is now based on the **AICPA Blueprints**. In 2018, the CPA Exam is no longer based on content specification outlines (CSOs). The AICPA Blueprints can be found at https://www.aicpa.org/becomeacpa/cpaexam/examinationcontent.html

These are the maps that tell the candidate the areas that are tested and what tasks are required for the candidate to master the information. *If you just follow the blueprints, you will know exactly the required information to be successful on the exam.*

There are hundreds of specific "representative tasks" that indicate what a new CPA would typically be responsible for performing on the job.

> **Hint: At a glance -- what is the AICPA blueprint?**
> - Serves as an essential study tool for CPA candidates
> - Replaces OLD Content Specific Outline (CSO)
> - Demonstrates what is tested on exams (including specific tasks)
> - Outlines skills and knowledge needed for licensure (typically possessed by a person with two years of experience)

YAEGER CPA REVIEW textbooks, and all videos, follow the AICPA Blueprints. Each blueprint is mentioned, and the relevant material is discussed, along with any relevant journal entries. Not all courses in CPA REVIEW follow the blueprints, but YAEGER DOES!

YAEGER CPA REVIEW has aligned its review content with the blueprints and shows each representative task with this icon:

For example, below is a representative task from the AUDITING AND ATTESTATION (AUD) section blueprint, under:
- Area I — Ethics, Professional Responsibilities and General Principles
- Content Group/Topic: A. NATURE AND SCOPE
- 1. Nature and scope: audit engagements
- Representative Task: Identify the nature, scope and objectives of the different types of audit engagements, including issuer and nonissuer audits.

In the auditing and attestation YAEGER CPA REVIEW book, this representative task will look like this:

> **CPA Exam Blueprint Representative Task** | Identify the nature, scope and objectives of the different types of audit engagements, including issuer and nonissuer audits.

F. Exam Schedule

The CPA Exam schedule for 2018 will be posted on the AICPA website when announced. The AICPA website is www.aicpa.org. Candidates should **definitely** visit this site before scheduling their exam for the most recent updates and information.

G. AICPA Tutorial and Sample Tests

On the AICPA website (https://www.aicpa.org/becomeacpa/cpaexam/forcandidates/tutorialandsampletest.html) candidates can experience the user interface that they will see on exam day. It is also the best place to see AICPA constructed examples of multiple-choice and task-based simulations with full functionality. YAEGER CPA REVIEW highly recommends all CPA candidates complete the sample test prior to taking their exam.

H. Access to Professional Literature

A commonly tested task-based simulation involves answering a research question, where the candidate must search through professional literature databases to answer the question.

Candidates who have applied to take the exam and have received their NTS can access a **free six-month subscription to the professional literature** used in the computerized CPA Exam. The professional literature includes the AICPA Professional Standards, FASB Original Pronouncements, and FASB Accounting Standards Codification. Access to this authoritative literature will familiarize candidates with the use of online accounting resources with full search functionality. Candidates should test the use of the keyword search to make the best use of their time in the exam.

The following link will take you to the National Association of State Boards of Accountancy (NASBA) website where you can apply for the free six-month subscription to the professional literature package: https://nasba.org/proflit/

I. Examination Scoring

A score of 75 is required to pass each section of the exam. A score of 75, however, is not indicative of the percent of correct answers. Rather, the score represents the weighted combination of multiple-choice questions, task-based simulations and written communications (for BEC only). Each section uses a scoring scale from 0 to 99. The scaled scores take into consideration whether the question was answered correctly and the level of difficulty of each question. The CPA exam score was obtained using Item Response Theory (IRT) scoring and was calculated as a whole, taking into account all of your responses.

Fifty percent of a candidate's score in the AUD, FAR, and REG sections comes from multiple-choice questions with the remaining 50% from task-based simulations. In the BEC section, 50% of a candidate's score comes from multiple-choice questions, 35% comes from task-based simulations, and 15% from written communication tasks.

A Candidate Performance Report will be provided if you receive a non-passing score. An example of this report is below.

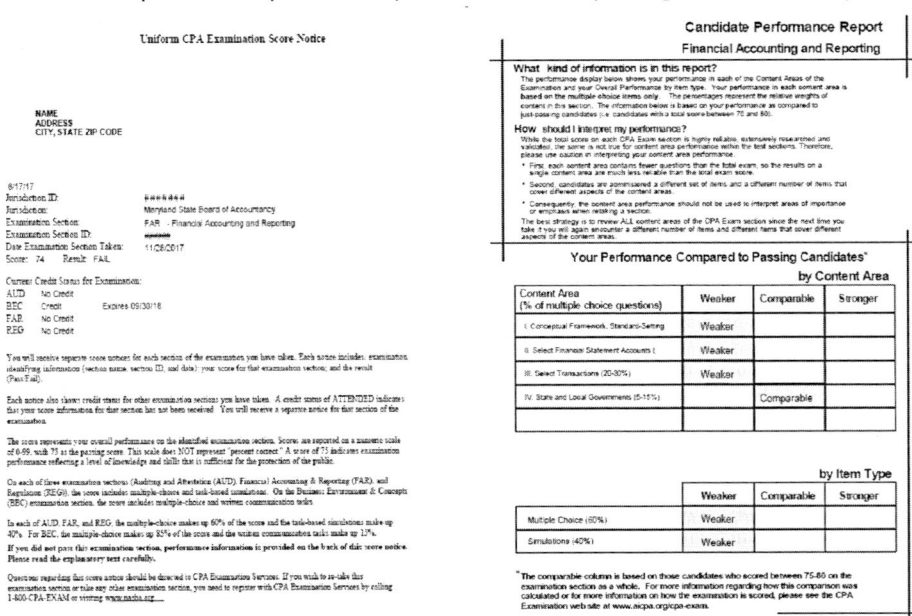

The Candidate Performance Report helps you determine what areas to focus on when you prepare to re-take an exam section. The Candidate Performance Report shows performance in each of the content areas of the exam and overall performance by item type and provides a comparison of your exam results to candidates who passed with a score between 75 and 80. According to the AICPA:

> *The relative performance scale (stronger, comparable, weaker) on the Candidate Performance Report is derived from the range between one-half of one standard deviation above and below the average score of candidates who earned scores between 75 and 80. Performance within the range is considered "comparable," below the range "weaker," and above the range "stronger."*

Candidates who received a weaker assessment for a particular content area should not focus only on that area when reviewing the material. It is always best to study everything. As no two exams are identical, if a candidate only studies their areas of weakness, they may do better in those areas, but worse on others when re-testing.

J. Yaeger's AdaptaPASS Technology

Since 1977, YAEGER CPA REVIEW has been following the philosophy that conceptual learning trumps memorization every time. And today is no different! YAEGER CPA REVIEW takes learning to the next level. With the most advanced technology in the CPA Exam Review industry, YAEGER CPA REVIEW combines traditional teaching and learning with an adaptive technology that determines what learning style works best for each individual CPA Exam candidate.

What is AdaptaPASS? It is an adaptive learning program that YAEGER developed to determine what learning style works best for each CPA candidate. Some students are visual learners, or auditory learners; others prefer to read and work a great deal of multiple-choice and/or simulation problems to reinforce a concept. Some have more time than others to prepare. It makes no difference. AdaptaPASS accounts for all different learning styles and creates a study program just for each individual candidate! The candidate begins by answering a few qualifying questions, then AdaptaPASS will deliver the optimal learning environment. This will include a blend of all study formats and content served in a way that takes the guesswork out of how the candidate is doing and what study method/format works best for them to succeed.

AdaptaPASS is not a "results" based platform like all others in the market. AdaptaPASS is the only program that creates a prescribed learning environment that adapts simultaneously with the candidate's progress. Proactively, the candidate will benefit from the "best" learning environment for them. Fully utilize the study plan that you will establish with YAEGER CPA REVIEW to stay on track for success on the CPA Exam.

K. Partnership with Dr. Marc Schoen

YAEGER CPA REVIEW is very excited to partner with Dr. Marc Schoen, a UCLA professor and leading performance psychologist to bring his expertise to you with a customized program designed specifically for CPA candidates.

The Performance under Pressure Audio Bundle teaches you how to properly control your fear response when faced with CPA Exam stress to boost your test score! Perform at your very best on exam day and tap into your brain's ability to problem solve with higher-order processing.

How? Using a gentle, but powerful technique that will reshape the way your brain responds to pressure. Train both your mind and body for CPA Exam success with an integrated study experience. Be reminded while using our AdaptaPASS software when to practice these research-based techniques founded in cutting-edge neuroscience.

We look forward to helping you on your CPA Exam journey. Best wishes for CPA Exam success from YAEGER CPA REVIEW!

REG 1 – Ethics, Professional Responsibilities, and Tax Procedures

A.	**Ethics and Responsibilities in Tax Practice**	**1A-1 – 1A-8**
	1. Regulations governing practice before the Internal Revenue Service	1
	2. Internal Revenue Code	4
	3. Regulations related to tax return preparers	5
B.	**Licensing and Disciplinary Systems**	**1B-1 – 1B-2**
	1. Role of state boards of accountancy	1
	2. Requirements of regulatory agencies	1
C.	**Federal Tax Procedures**	**1C-1 – 1C-8**
	1. Audits, appeals, and judicial process	1
	2. Substantiation and disclosure of tax positions	2
	3. Taxpayer penalties	4
	4. Authoritative hierarchy	6
	5. Tax research	8
D.	**Legal Duties and Responsibilities**	**1D-1 – 1D-8**
	1. Common law duties and liabilities to clients and third parties	1
	2. Privileged communications, confidentiality and privacy acts	7
Glossary: Ethics, Professional Responsbilities, and Tax Procedures		**Glossary 1-1 – 1-3**
Multiple Choice – Questions		**MCQ 1-1 – 1-7**
Multiple Choice – Solutions		**MCQ 1-8 – 1-14**

Ethics, Professional, and Legal Responsibilities

A. **Ethics and Responsibilities in Tax Practice**
   In light of famous scandals involving accounting profession, it has become increasingly obvious that technical competence alone is not sufficient in creating a quality accounting system. In practice, the right decision is not always obvious and clear-cut, and ethical sensitivity and professional judgment can be impacted by many factors, such as time constraints, and pressure related to job requirements, client demands, and personal needs. Therefore, a significant portion of the CPA Exam is devoted to testing a candidate's ability to identify situations that are unethical, perform appropriate research and consultations, and determine the appropriate course of action in each particular situation. Additionally, according to the American Institute of Certified Public Accountants (AIPCA), successful candidates should be able to recognize the potentially unethical behavior of clients and determine the impact on the tax services being performed.

   There is currently not one unified system that provides ethical and legal guidelines of the CPA's conduct. Accountants can be subject to the regulations developed by state boards of accountancy, American Institute of Certified Public Accountants (AICPA), Internal Revenue Service (IRS), Securities and Exchange Commission (SEC), Public Company Accounting Oversight Board (PCAOB), U.S. Congress, and others. CPA's civil liability is governed by the contract law, the law of negligence, fraud, the Securities Act of 1933, and the Securities Exchange Act of 1934. The goal of this chapter is to provide an overview of the main regulatory bodies and documents available to guide CPA's ethical decisions and to outline responsibilities placed on CPAs in private and public practice.

   1. Regulations governing practice before the Internal Revenue Service
      a. **Authority to practice**
         Treasury Department Circular 230 governs federal tax practice before the IRS by CPAs, enrolled agents (EA), attorneys, registered tax return preparers (RTRP), enrolled retirement plan agents, appraisers, and actuaries.

         Practice before the IRS comprehends all matters connected with a presentation to the IRS on behalf of the taxpayer. Those matters include, but are not limited to, preparing and filing documents on behalf of the clients, communicating with the IRS, and rendering written advice concerning a client.

      b. **Representation**
         Different levels of client representation are available to different tax practitioners. Enrolled agents, typically do not have restrictions as to which taxpayers they can represent, which IRS offices they can represent clients in, and the types of tax matters they can handle.

         A registered tax return preparer (RTRP) is limited to preparing and signing tax returns, refund claims, and other documents submitted to the IRS. Representation before the IRS is only allowed when the same RTRP had previously prepared and signed the return or claim for the refund for that year.

         A RTRP must not represent a taxpayer before the appeals officers or similar IRS employees. The scope of RTRP practice should not include providing tax advice besides that which is necessary to provide tax services.

         Individuals who are not registered tax preparers are allowed to represent themselves and other taxpayers, for whom a fiduciary duty is owed. For instance, family members can represent their immediate family, employers may represent their employees, and partners, estate executors, and trustees are allowed to represent their respective entities.

CPA Exam Blueprint Representative Task

> Recall the regulations governing practice before the Internal Revenue Service.

> Apply the regulations governing practice before the Internal Revenue Service given a specific scenario.

c. **Practice before the IRS – Duties and restrictions including key Circular 230 provisions**

1) Client requests for records
   Original records provided by the client must be promptly returned when requested by the client. A dispute over the fees does not constitute a valid reason for retaining client-provided records.

   Multiple Choice
   REG 1-Q1

2) IRS requests for records
   Records or information requested by the IRS must be promptly submitted by the practitioner unless there are good faith and reasonable grounds to believe that information requested is privileged.

   Multiple Choice
   REG 1-Q2

3) Errors, omission, and non-compliance with the law
   Clients must be promptly notified regarding any errors, omissions, and instances of non-compliance with the law discovered by the tax practitioner. Any legal consequences of errors, omissions, and non-compliance must be communicated to the clients.

   Multiple Choice
   REG 1-Q3 through REG 1-Q5

4) Due-diligence using client-provided information
   The tax preparer may rely on, in good faith, and without having to verify the information provided by the client. However, reasonable inquiries must be made about information furnished to the tax preparer that appears incorrect, incomplete, or inconsistent with other facts or assumptions.

   Multiple Choice
   REG 1-Q6

5) Due-diligence using the work of others
   Work of other people may only be used when reasonable care is utilized in the process of their engaging, supervising, training, and evaluation. Reasonable inquiries must be made about information furnished to the tax preparer that appears incorrect, incomplete, or inconsistent with other facts or assumptions.

6) Competence
   The tax preparer must have the necessary knowledge and skill in the area that the tax preparer has been engaged to work. Competence may be obtained by researching and educating oneself on the issue or by working with another tax professional that has competence in the field in question.

7) Conflicts of interest
A conflict of interest exists if representing a client will be directly adverse to another client. For example, a tax preparer performs tax preparation work and tax planning advice to a partnership, in addition to providing these services to the partnership the tax preparer also performs tax preparation and tax planning for several of the partners in the partnership. There could be a conflict of interest if the partnership was dissolved over a dispute among the partners and it was based on an asset valuation that the tax preparer performed on the partnership assets that was requested by the partnership.

8) Quality of representation and best practices
Best practices and high-quality standards must be followed while preparing tax returns or providing tax advice to clients. Under Treasury Circular 230, the responsibility of a tax practitioner, a CPA tax advisor, is to establish relevant facts, evaluate the reasonableness of assumptions and representations, and arrive at a conclusion supported by the law and facts in a tax memorandum.

Multiple Choice

REG 1-Q7

9) Unconscionable and contingent fees
Unconscionable and contingent fees must not be charged by the practitioner in preparing a client's original income tax return. Contingent fees may only be charged in connection with the IRS examination of the original or amended returns or claims for refund, or any judicial proceedings arising under the Code. The practitioner may publish written fee schedule outlining fixed and hourly rates, as well as an approximation of rates charged for specific services. The practitioner must not increase the rates for at least 30 days after the fee schedule is published.

Multiple Choice

REG 1-Q8

10) Misleading and deceptive claims
Practitioners should fairly represent their qualifications and expected outcomes of their work. A CPA cannot advertise in any manner that is false, misleading, or deceptive.

Multiple Choice

REG 1-Q9

11) Refund checks
No federal tax refund checks issued to a client by the government may be endorsed or negotiated by the practitioner.

Multiple Choice

REG 1-Q10

12) Reasonable basis
Practitioners should ensure that positions taken on the return have a reasonable basis. This standard requires at least 20% probability of a position being sustained on its merits. Willful attempts to understate tax liability or reckless disregard of rules and regulations by the practitioner are prohibited.

13) Frivolous tax positions
Practitioners must not advise clients to take positions that are not based in fact or law, or those that the courts have held to be frivolous or groundless, e.g., *frivolous tax positions*. Clients may not be advised about how to impede the administration of the tax law.

14) Communicating Potential Penalties
Potential penalties related to a tax position must be communicated to the client.

15) Overseeing the Work of Others
Reasonable steps must be taken by the management to guarantee that the firm established procedures to ensure compliance by all firm members, associates, and employees.

16) Rules for Written Advice
IRS applies reasonable practitioner standard in evaluating whether the advice given complies with the provisions of Circular 230, considering all facts and circumstances. General guidelines for the written advice are as follows:
   1. Advice should be based on reasonable factual and legal assumptions.
   2. All the facts that are known or should be known to the practitioner should be reasonably considered.
   3. Reasonable efforts should be made to identify and ascertain relevant facts.
   4. Applicable law and authorities to facts should be related to the client.
   5. The probability of the tax return not being audited or the matter not being examined should not be considered.
   6. Unreasonable representations, statements, findings, or agreements provided by the taxpayer should not be relied on.
   7. The advice of others can only be relied on if, considering all the facts and circumstances, the reliance was done in good faith and the advice was reasonable.

Multiple Choice

REG 1-Q11 through REG 1-Q12

2. Internal Revenue Code
   a. **Definition**
   The Internal Revenue Code (IRC) of 1986, as amended, represents a codification of the tax laws of the country and serves as a basic foundation of the tax law. It is passed by the U.S. Congress and enforced by the Internal Revenue Service (IRS), which is a collection branch of the U.S. Department of Treasury.

   b. **Evolution**
   The Internal Revenue Code was not passed all at once, and it is subject to a constant evolution and amendment. The last comprehensive re-organization of the Code occurred in 1986, and there have been many amendments since then.

   c. **Organization**
   The Internal Revenue code is located under title 26 of the U.S. Code. It is organized into Subtitles, Chapters, Subchapters, Parts, Subparts, Sections, and Subsection.

   1) Subtitles
   The IRC is comprised of 11subtitles, denoted with capital letters, A through K, relating to different areas of tax law. The most commonly encountered by the tax practitioner are Subchapter A - Income Taxes, Subchapter B - Estate and Gift Taxes and Subchapter C - Employment Taxes. Remaining subtitles relate to topics of Excise Taxes, Procedure and Administration, Trust Fund Code, Health Benefits and plans, etc.

   2) Chapters
   Each subtitle is comprised of the consecutively numbered chapters (1-6). For example, Subtitle A (Income Taxes) contains a portion of the Code dealing with "Normal Taxes and Surtaxes" (Chapter 1).

3) Subchapters, parts, subparts, and sections, and etc.
Chapters are further divided into subchapters, and each subchapter is then generally divided into parts and subparts, which are then divided into sections. Those sections are typically referred to as "Code Sections." Code sections may be further broken down into subsections, paragraphs, subparagraphs, clauses, etc.

d. **Citing the code**
Code sections are cited by detailed reference to the section, subsection, paragraph, and subparagraph (e.g., §453(e) (3) (A) (i)). In this example, § is used to denote the section, 453 relates to the number of the section itself, (e) to the subsection, (3) to the paragraph, (A) to subparagraph, and (i) to the Clause.

> Recall who is a tax return preparer.

e. **Tax preparer**
A tax preparer is defined as a person who prepares income tax returns, for compensation (implicit or explicit). Tax returns prepared by tax preparers include tax returns for, not-for-profit entities, for-profit entities, individuals, estates, and trusts.

To become a tax preparer, an individual should possess the necessary competence gained through practice, studying the applicable law, and consulting experts. The examination is required to become an Enrolled Agent (EA) or Registered Tax Return Preparer (RTRP) unless competency is demonstrated by prior service. All tax preparers must obtain Preparer Tax Identification (PTIN) from the IRS, which they are required to renew on an annual basis.

Multiple Choice

REG 1-Q13

3. Regulations related to tax return preparers

> Recall the situations that would result in tax return preparer penalties.
>
> Apply potential federal tax return preparer penalties given a specific scenario.

a. **Penalties for unreasonable tax positions**
1) Rules
Unreasonable tax position penalties are assessed on tax positions that are *not disclosed* and lack substantial authority. Tax positions have substantial authority when the weight of the authorities supporting the tax treatment is substantial compared to the weight of the authorities supporting the contrary treatment. At least 40% (50% for tax shelters or reportable transactions) of the probability of tax position being sustained on its merits may be required The 50% test having to do with substantial authority concerning tax shelters, is known as the higher-more-likely-than-not standard, it need not be disclosed.

Reportable transactions are transactions that the IRS believes have the potential for tax avoidance, but for which it lacks enough information to determine whether they should be identified specifically as tax avoidance transactions. A higher, more likely than not standard applies if the position has to do with a tax shelter and requires more than a 50% probability of it being sustained on its merits.

Multiple Choice

REG 1-Q14

2) Amounts
Preparers are subject to penalties equaling the greater of $1,000 or 50% of the income derived (or to be derived) from preparing the return, if any of the understatement of the liability with respect to the tax return is caused by an undisclosed position that was taken on the tax return, where there is not substantial authority. The substantial authority standard may require at least a 40% probability of it being sustained on its merits. A higher-more-likely-than-not standard applies if the position concerning a tax shelter, then the substantial authority standard requires a more than 50% probability of being sustained on its merits.

3) Defenses
Penalties may be waived if (1) there is an adequate disclosure of the questionable position on the tax return or, the claim for refund and (2) the taxpayer shows that there was a reasonable basis for the position, the penalty will be waived. The reasonable basis standard may require at least a 20% chance of tax position being sustained on its merits.

b. **Penalty for promoting abusive tax shelters**
   1) Rules
   A tax shelter is defined as any arrangement (e.g., trust, partnership, etc.) that is entered with the main purpose of avoidance or evasion of federal income tax.

   2) Amounts
   The penalty for a promoter of an abusive tax is equal to $1,000 for each organization or sale of an abusive plan or arrangement (or, if lesser, 100 percent of the income derived from the activity).

c. **Penalties for willful or reckless conduct**
   1) Rules
   Penalties are assessed when any part of a client's underpayment is a result of the tax preparer's deliberate actions to understate the tax liability. Penalties can also be assessed for a tax preparer's deliberate disregard for tax laws. Generally, the preparer is not always required to obtain supporting documentation from the client. However, reasonable inquiries should be made by the preparer when information provided appears to be incomplete, inconsistent or incorrect.

   2) Amounts
   When the understatement of a tax liability is a result of a tax preparer's deliberate action to understate the tax liability, or if there were deliberate actions to disregard the tax laws, the tax preparer is subject to a penalty, which is the greater of $5,000 or 50% of the income derived (or to be derived) from preparing the return.

d. **Unauthorized disclosure or use of client information**
   1) Rules
   Information obtained in connection with the tax return should be kept confidential and can only be disclosed for quality or peer review or in response to the administrative order by the regulatory agency.

   No information should be sent to or discussed with an unauthorized third party. Any unauthorized parties requesting information on behalf of the taxpayer should be notified in writing that the request cannot be met. All future communication should be sent directly to the taxpayer.

2) Amounts
The penalty is $250 for each unauthorized disclosure or use of information furnished for, or in connection with, the preparation of a return. The maximum penalty on any person shall not exceed $10,000 in a calendar year.

Additionally, the preparer can be found guilty of a misdemeanor for knowingly or recklessly disclosing information furnished in connection with a tax return or using such information for any purpose other than preparing or assisting in the preparation of such return. Upon conviction, a fine of not more than $1,000, imprisonment for not more than one year, or both, including the costs of prosecution.

e. **Other preparer penalties**
1) Penalties and rules
   i. Failure to provide a copy of tax return (or claim for a refund)
      A copy of the tax return or a claim for a refund should be provided to the taxpayer no later than the time the completed return or claim for a refund is presented for taxpayer's signature.

   ii. Failure to sign tax return (or claim for a refund)
       All returns prepared for compensation must be signed by the tax preparer.

   iii. Failure to furnish identifying number
        Tax preparer should list her preparer tax identification number (PTIN), as well as her federal identification number (FEIN) or social security number (SSN) on all tax returns prepared for compensation.

   iv. Failure to retain records
       The preparer must either keep copies of actual returns or lists containing names and IDs of all people for whom the returns were prepared for three years following the last day of the return period. When other tax preparers are employed, lists of those preparers and places of their employment should also be maintained for three years.

   v. Failure to file correct information returns
      Information returns should be filed on time, with all required or correct information, via correct channels (on paper or electronically when so required), and in a manner, that is available for future processing (no damaged and unreadable files).

   vi. Endorsing or negotiating a refund check issued to a taxpayer
       Preparers are not allowed to endorse or negotiate refund checks issued to taxpayers.

   vii. The preparer cannot disclose information having to do with the preparation of the tax return without the client's permission unless the return is given to a quality control review panel or, peer review. The preparer does not need the permission to disclose information from the tax return if the preparer is under an administrative order by the courts (subpoena).

2) Amounts
Most of the penalties listed above are assessed at $50 for each failure to comply, with the maximum penalty imposed on any tax return preparer not to exceed $25,000 in a calendar year.

3) Defenses
    Most of the penalties listed above do not apply if it can be shown that tax preparer acted in good faith, the failure to comply was due to a reasonable cause, and there was no willful neglect on the part of the tax preparer.

Multiple Choice

REG 1-Q14 through REG 1-Q16

B. Licensing and Disciplinary Systems
  1. Role of state boards of accountancy

> Understand and explain the role and the authority of state boards of accountancy.

State Boards of Accountancy are created to assist the state government in the licensing and regulation of the accounting profession. Within the United States and its territories, 55 licensing jurisdictions are providing regulatory oversight of CPAs.

   a. **Sole power to issue and renew CPA licenses and firm permits**
      1) Requirements for licensed activity
         Individuals and firms performing certain attest and compilation services or those that hold themselves out as CPAs must be licensed by the state. State boards of accountancy are the sole agencies with the power to issue CPA licenses and firm permits.

      2) Mobility rules
         Most states adopted mobility rules to allow licensed CPAs who are in good standing with their principal state, to practice outside of that state, without obtaining a new license. CPAs performing services through mobility may only perform the same level of services (attest or non-attest) in the mobility jurisdiction as they were permitted in the home jurisdiction.

      3) Licensure rules
         Although rules for licensure vary from state to state, common requirements include successful completion of the CPA examination and meeting certain thresholds of education and experience. Also, some states impose residency and citizenship requirements.

      4) Renewal rules
         Licenses and permits must be regularly renewed. Individuals are subject to continuing education requirements, and firms may be required to undergo peer reviews.

   b. **Power to discipline and suspend or revoke licenses**
      When members are found in violation of state board rules, depending on the severity of the offense, disciplinary actions may vary. The board may require members to take additional continuing education courses, place them on probation, formally reprimand, require to pay a monetary fine, temporarily suspend, or permanently revoke their licenses to practice in the state.

Multiple Choice

> REG 1-Q17

  2. Requirements of regulatory agencies
     a. **American Institute of Certified Public Accountants (AICPA) and state CPA societies**
        The AICPA is a non-profit organization that was founded to ensure that accountancy gained respect as a profession and that it was practiced by ethical and competent professionals. The AICPA is an advocate for the CPA profession before public interest groups, regulators, and legislators.

        State CPA societies are independent membership organizations serving all CPAs licensed in the particular state. Their mission is to provide professional development and training, as well as networking opportunities and public outreach. Although structurally they are unaffiliated with each other or AICPA, cooperative relationships are common.

1) **AICPA Code of Professional Conduct**
   All CPAs (not just AICPA members) must adhere to the code of professional conduct that outlines minimum levels of acceptable behavior while performing services as CPAs. This code of conduct is enforced by Professional Ethics Executive Committee (PEEC), which is a senior technical committee of the AICPA.

2) **AICPA Statements on Responsibilities in Tax Practice**
   The AICPA Statements on Responsibilities in Tax Practice include a source of accepted customs and practices of the CPA profession. These statements are intended to be educational and advisory, and are not enforceable under the AICPA Code of Professional Conduct.

3) **Ethics code of state CPA societies**
   All members of state CPA societies must adhere to their respective codes of ethics, which are very similar to those outlined in AICPA code of professional conduct. Many state societies incorporated AICPA code of professional conduct.

4) **Joint Ethics Enforcement Program (JEEP)**
   Because of the similarities between AICPA Code of Professional Conduct and ethics rules of state CPA societies, Joint Ethics Enforcement Program (JEEP) was created. The goal of this program is to save resources and promote uniformity of the two codes and their enforcement and implementation by conducting a single investigation and action.

b. **Disciplinary Actions**
   1) **No power to revoke licenses**
      AICPA or state CPA societies do not have the power to revoke CPA licenses. State boards of accountancy can only revoke licenses for violation of state board code. Because the state board codes are similar to those of AICPA, violation of AICPA code of conduct often leads to the state board disciplinary actions that may include revocation or suspension of licenses.

   2) **Suspension (up to 2 years) or termination of membership**
      Membership in AICPA and/or State society can be suspended or terminated for failure to pay dues or comply with membership-retention standards (e.g., continuing education).

      Membership can be terminated *without hearing* in the following situations:
      1. The member committed a crime punishable by imprisonment for more than one year.
      2. The member intentionally failed to file any of his or her required individual income tax returns.
      3. The member filed or assisted in filing a false or fraudulent tax return.
      4. The member's CPA license or permit is revoked by the licensing state as a disciplinary measure. Such suspension is usually lifted upon reinstatement of the revoked certificate, license, or permit.

   3) **Other disciplinary actions**
      Disciplinary actions for less severe conduct are as follows:
      1. Publication of formal admonishment
      2. Requirement for corrective action (e.g., additional continuing education courses)
      3. Monetary fines.

C. Federal Tax Procedures

In their day-to-day work, CPAs are expected to demonstrate excellent abilities to appropriately apply knowledge of existing federal tax processes, procedures, and planning. Solid understanding of those concepts is crucial in CPA's tax preparation and advisory services, as well as in performing other responsibilities as certified public accountants. The goal of this content group is to provide an overview of a federal audit and appeals procedures and learn about the options available to the taxpayers within each stage of the audit. An overview of any potential penalties associated with late or incorrectly filed tax returns, as well as requirements relating to the substantiation and disclosure of tax positions, will also be provided in this chapter.

1. Audits, appeals, and judicial process

> Explain the audit and appeals process as it relates to federal tax matters.

> Identify options available to a taxpayer within the audit and appeals process given a specific scenario.

   a. **Field, office, or correspondence examination**
   After the return is filed, any subsequent IRS questions could be addressed by correspondence (taxpayer receives a letter asking for additional information), at the IRS office, or at the taxpayer's place of business. For the in-office and correspondence examinations, the taxpayer can challenge the results by requesting a meeting with the supervisor.

   b. **Thirty-day letter – pay, ignore, or appeal**
   When the examination is conducted in the field (at the taxpayer's place of business) or in cases where the taxpayer does not reach an agreement with the supervisor, a thirty-day letter summarizing any proposed changes is sent by the IRS. If the taxpayer does not accept the deficiencies, a thirty-day window is allowed for filing an appeal.

   c. **Ninety-day letter -- pay or petition the court**
   In situations where the timely filed appeal is not accepted, or when the taxpayer ignores the thirty-day letter, a ninety-day letter is mailed by the IRS. From that moment, the taxpayer has ninety days to file a petition in the Tax Court. While the petition is filed, the payment is not required, and assessment and collections are prohibited during that time.
   If the petition is not filed, any of the tax deficiency not paid within 90 days is subject to collection.

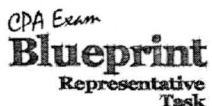

> Explain the different levels of the judicial process as they relate to federal tax matters.

> Identify options available to a taxpayer within the judicial process given a specific scenario.

   d. **Choose the court**
   The taxpayer can choose any of the three courts (U.S. Tax Court, U.S. District Court, or U.S. Court of Federal Claims).

   1) United States district court
   U.S. District Court is the federal trial court available in each district of the United States. It is the only court where a jury trial is available.

2) United States tax court
U. S. Tax court is a specialized court of law that hears and adjudicates only tax-related disputes and issues. This court has some unique characteristics, not applicable to other courts.

They are as follows:
1. It is the only court that does not require payment of assessed tax liability before the hearing.
2. The IRS adopts decisions reached by the Tax Court for all of the following cases with similar facts and circumstances.
3. If tax court is chosen, and the disputed amount does not exceed $50,000, taxpayers can represent themselves at its Small Tax Case Division. However, decisions reached at this level cannot be appealed.

3) United States Court of Federal Claims
U.S. Court of Federal Claims requires payment of the tax before taxpayer's filing the tax claim. A jury trial is not allowed. The court has nationwide jurisdiction, and trials are conducted at the locations that are most convenient and least expensive to taxpayers.

e. **Agree or appeal**
Court decisions can be appealed to the U.S. Court of appeals at taxpayer's place of residence or business. If the agreement is not reached at that level, and U.S. Supreme court wants to hear the case, its rulings are considered final and become the law of the land.

2. Substantiation and disclosure of tax positions

> Summarize the requirements for the appropriate disclosure of a federal tax return position.

> Identify situations in which disclosure of federal tax return positions is required.

A federal tax position is a position that is expected to be taken in a future tax return, or a position in a return that was filed previously, related to the implications of tax assets and tax liabilities. Tax positions include allocations of income among jurisdictions, whether or not to file a return and decisions on the planned transaction classification.

A tax position is a position reflected on a tax return on which an accountant has specifically advised a taxpayer on a position about which a CPA knows all material facts, and by those facts, has concluded whether the position is appropriate. When advising taxpayers about tax return positions, CPA should adhere to the rules outlined below.

a. **Frivolous positions (0% probability)**
1) Definition
A frivolous position is a position that is knowingly advanced in bad faith and is patently improper.

2) Advising
Frivolous tax positions should never be recommended by a CPA, as it is not a sufficient basis for avoiding any penalties, even if the tax position is disclosed on the return.

b. **Reasonable basis standard (20% probability)**
1) Definition
Reasonable basis standard requires that the position has at least 20% chance of being sustained on its merits.

2) Advising
Tax preparers are prohibited from signing a tax return or claim for a refund that contains a position that lacks reasonable basis.

3) Do not disclose
   1. To avoid negligence penalty (when understating tax that is not substantial).
   2. To avoid penalty for disregard of rules or regulations.

4) Disclose
   1. Disclose to avoid substantial underpayment penalty
   2. Disclosure will not help in cases of tax shelters.

c. **Substantial authority (33-50% probability)**
   1) Definition
   Tax position has substantial tax authority when its likelihood of being sustained on its merits is more than 33% but less than 50%. Substantial authority exists when the weight of authorities supporting the tax treatment of the item are substantial in relation to the weight of authorities supporting the opposing treatment.

   2) No disclosure requirement - *Avoids substantial underpayment penalty*
   The taxpayer is not required to disclose tax position to avoid a substantial underpayment penalty. If there is substantial authority for the tax treatment of an item, the item is treated as if it was shown properly on the return for the taxable year in computing the amount of the tax shown on the return.

d. **More-likely-than-not standard (greater than 50% probability)**
   1) Definition
   More-likely-than-not standard is met when there is greater than 50% of likelihood of the tax position being upheld, if challenged by the IRS.

   2) Undisclosed tax shelters
   When dealing with undisclosed tax shelters, positions based on the more likely than not standard
   1. Avoids negligence penalty (when understatement of tax that is not substantial).
   2. Avoids substantial understatement of tax penalty.

Identify whether substantiation is sufficient given a specific scenario.

e. **General substantiation requirements**
In addition to being aware of the tax positions and disclosures, taxpayers must also maintain proof of any deductions claimed on their returns. The burden of proof belongs to taxpayers, and documentary evidence required includes receipts, canceled checks, or bills. Additional evidence is required for charitable deductions, travel, entertainment, gifts, charitable, or auto expenses.

f. **Charitable deductions – substantiation**
   1) Substantiation is always required
   Regardless of the amount of charitable contribution deduction claimed by the taxpayer, all charitable contributions must be substantiated. To accomplish this, the taxpayer must obtain any of the following:

   1. A bank record
   Bank records may include bank or credit union statements, canceled checks, or credit card statements and should reflect the date when the contribution was paid or posted, the name of the charity, and the amount of the payment.

2. A written communication from the charitable organization.
3. A copy of W-2, pay stubs, or a pledge card (for payroll deductions).
4. Any other document furnished by the employer or the charity.
   This document should state the amount withheld for payment to charity.
5. Must obtain before filing
   All substantiation documents must be obtained no later than the date the taxpayer files the return for the year the contribution is made.

2) Contribution of $250 or more
   1. Written acknowledgment from the charity
      When claiming $250 or more in charitable contributions, the taxpayer is required to obtain a contemporaneous written acknowledgment from the organization.
   2. List value of considerations received (if any)
      The acknowledgment must state if any goods or services were provided in consideration for the contribution, and if so, estimate the value of those goods or services. Although there is no prescribed format for the written acknowledgment, it must provide sufficient information to substantiate the amount of contribution.

3) Property contributions of $500 or more
   For contributions exceeding $500 of noncash property, form 8283 must be filed by the taxpayer, listing certain information.

4) Property contributions over $5,000
   For claimed contributions over $5,000, a qualified appraisal prepared by a qualified appraiser must be obtained.

5) Out-of-pocket expenses
   For taxpayer's out-of-pocket expenses, the statement must describe the taxpayer's services and state whether the charity provided goods or services in consideration for out-of-pocket expenses.

3. Taxpayer penalties

| Recall situations that would result in taxpayer penalties relating to federal tax returns. |
| Calculate taxpayer penalties relating to federal tax returns. |

The Internal Revenue Service may assess a variety of taxpayer penalties, the severity of which can depend on such factors as the amount of taxes due, return filing (or not filing) dates, taxpayer intentions, and other facts and circumstances applicable to the situation.

a. **Failure-to-pay penalty**
   1) The base rate is 5% per month (or part of the month) of the unpaid tax.
   2) The penalty is not to exceed 25% of the tax due.
   3) No penalty is assessed if at least 90% of tax is paid by the original due date and the balance of the tax is paid by the extended due date.

b. **Late filing and failure-to-file penalties**
   1) Late filing and late payment penalties are calculated on net tax liability due with the return.
   2) The base rate is 5% of the amount of tax due for each month (or part of the month) the return is not filed.
   3) The penalty is not to exceed 25% of the tax due.
   4) The minimum penalty is the *smaller* of $135 or 100 percent of the unpaid tax if the return is filed more than 60 days after the due date or extended due date.

5) No penalty is assessed if a refund is due.
6) When both failure-to-file and failure-to-pay penalty applies, the failure-to-file penalty is reduced by the amount of the failure-to-pay penalty.
7) The failure-to-file penalty is usually more than the failure-to-pay penalty. Therefore, the taxpayer should file a timely tax return even if there is no way to pay his tax liability.

c. **Failure to make estimated tax payments penalty**
This penalty applies to all taxpayers who failed to disburse sufficient tax withholdings and estimated tax payments when those payments were due.
1) Penalty accrues from the date the estimated income tax must be paid until the original (not extended) tax return due date.
2) No penalty is due when net tax liability payable with the return is less than $1,000.
3) No penalty is due when a taxpayer paid at least 90% of the current or 100% of the prior year's taxes (110% if prior year AGI exceeds $150,000).
4) No estimated tax payments are required if the taxpayer had no tax liability for the prior tax year, was a U.S. citizen or resident for that entire year and the prior tax year was for a full 12-month period.

Multiple Choice

REG 1-Q21 through REG 1-Q22

d. **Negligence penalty**
Negligence is defined as any careless, reckless, or intentional disregard of rules or regulations, and any failure to make a reasonable attempt to comply with the provisions of the tax law.
1) Applies when understatement of tax is not substantial.
2) Negligence penalty is 20% of the understatement of tax.
3) No penalty is assessed if the taxpayer shows a reasonable basis for the tax position (even if the position is not disclosed).
4) If this penalty is applied by the IRS, penalties for substantial understatement of tax or substantial valuation misstatement cannot be assessed.

e. **Substantial understatement of tax penalty**
1) The penalty is 20% of the understatement of tax.
2) Applies when understatement is substantial.
3) Substantial understatement is defined as the amount exceeding the greater of 10% of the tax due or $5,000 ($10,000 for most corporations).
4) No penalty applies if the taxpayer shows reasonable basis *and* discloses her tax position on the return, assuming that the position disclosed is not a tax shelter.
5) No penalty applies if there is a substantial authority for the position (disclosure is not required in this case) and the position is not a tax shelter.
6) If this penalty is applied by the IRS, negligence or substantial valuation misstatement penalties cannot be assessed.

f. **Substantial valuation misstatement penalty**
1) Substantial valuation misstatement exists if the value of the property claimed on the return is at least 150% or more of its correct value.
2) The penalty is 20% of the understatement of tax.
3) The penalty is 40% if valuation exceeds 200% of the correct amount.
4) No penalty is applied if the resulting income tax underpayment does not exceed $5,000 ($10,000 for most corporations).
5) If this penalty is applied by the IRS, negligence or substantial understatement of tax penalties cannot be assessed.
6) If this penalty is not applied, negligence or substantial understatement of tax penalties can still be assessed.

g. **Tax shelter penalty**
   1) A tax shelter is defined as any entity, investment plan, or another arrangement that has federal tax evasion as its significant purpose.
   2) The penalty is 20% of the understatement of tax for the disclosed tax shelter positions (30% for not disclosed).
   3) The penalty can be avoided if there was a reasonable cause for the taxpayer's position, such as the position was adequately disclosed, was supported by substantial authority, and there was a reason to believe that the position was more-likely-than-not correct.
   4) The penalty cannot be waived if the position was not disclosed on the return.

h. **Fraud Penalty**
   1) Fraud penalties are applied in cases where an underpayment of taxes was due to the fraud.
   2) Other accuracy-related penalties would not apply to the portion of underpayment due to fraud.
   3) Civil fraud penalty is 75% of the understatement of tax attributable to fraud.
   4) Criminal penalties can apply.
   5) It is the only penalty where the burden of proof is on the IRS and not on the taxpayer.
   6) To prove civil fraud, the IRS must prove by *the preponderance of the evidence* that the taxpayer willfully and deliberately attempted to evade tax.
   7) To prove criminal fraud, the IRS must prove *beyond a reasonable doubt* that the taxpayer criminally, willfully, and deliberately attempted to evade tax.

i. **Accuracy-Related Penalty**
   There is an accuracy-related penalty in addition to the income tax of 20% of the portion for which the underpayment applies. A taxpayer must have an underpayment of tax, and the underpayment must be attributable to one of the specific conditions or behaviors including:
   1) Negligence or disregard of rules or regulations;
   2) Any substantial understatement of income tax;
   3) Any substantial valuation misstatement;
   4) Any substantial overstatement of pension liabilities; and
   5) Any substantial estate or gift tax valuation understatement.

Multiple Choice

REG 1-Q23 through REG 1-Q24

4. Authoritative hierarchy

Recall the appropriate hierarchy of authority for federal tax purposes.

a. The **U.S. federal tax law hierarchy** summarizes the weight of authority from highest to lowest for use in determining whether these sources can be relied upon for a tax position or tax planning and are as follows:
   1) U.S. Constitution
   2) Internal Revenue Code (IRC)
   3) Treasury Regulations
   4) U.S. Supreme Court
   5) U.S. Circuit Courts of Appeals
   6) Federal courts of original jurisdiction (decisions may be appealed to a Circuit Court of Appeals).

b. **Primary authorities**
   1) Internal Revenue Code (IRC)
      The Internal Revenue Code is the most authoritative source of tax law.

2) **Treasury Regulations**
Treasury Regulations provide the official interpretation of the Internal Revenue Code by the Department of Treasury. They are the second most important authoritative source.
   1. Legislative Regulations
   Legislative regulations have the force and effect of law. The Treasury issues them to prescribe the operating rules for a statute.
   2. Interpretative Regulations
   Interpretative Regulations do not have the force and effect of the law but still, carry substantial authority. They provide guidance regarding compliance with the statute.
   3. Proposed Regulations
   Proposed regulations do not carry the same authority as temporary and final regulations. They are issued to allow public comments (and possible changes) before regulations are made final.
   4. Temporary Regulations
   Temporary regulations carry the same weight as final regulations, up until their expiration date. Temporary Regulations provide interim guidance regarding recent tax legislation until final Regulations are issued.
   5. Final Regulations
   Final regulations are the second most important authoritative source of tax law. They supersede any existing temporary regulations.

3) **Internal Revenue Service Rulings**
IRS Rulings provide administrative interpretations of the IRC. They are issued in response to a specific issue with the purpose of uniform treatment of cases with similar facts and circumstances. Although IRS Rulings do not hold the same authority as Treasury Regulations, they may serve as precedents. However, the effect of subsequent legislation, regulations, court decisions and ruling should also be considered when consulting IRS Rulings.

4) **Tax court decisions**
Tax court decisions interpret tax law and can serve as precedents for cases with similar circumstances.

c. **Secondary authorities**
Secondary authoritative sources explain the primary sources. They include professional publications, textbooks, newsletters, tax research services, and IRS publications that interpret primary sources of authority. Although those interpretations of tax law can be very comprehensive and knowledgeable, primary sources should be consulted first, as neither IRS nor courts would give any authoritative weight to those opinions.

Multiple Choice

REG 1-Q25 through REG 1-Q26

5. Tax research
   When advising taxpayer about available tax positions and analyzing the necessity of tax disclosures, more weight should be given to the primary authoritative sources described above.

   The most authoritative current source of the tax law is IRC. Also, the list of "substantial authority" now includes the Joint Committee on Taxation's General Explanation of tax legislation, called the Blue Book, Internal Revenue Bulletins, regulation proposals, and private letter rulings.

   > *Hint*: CPA candidates are required to research federal tax issues in the Regulation simulations part of the CPA exam, and excerpts from the IRC will be included in the research database. When performing tax research, the issue at hand should first be identified. The search is then performed by typing corresponding keywords in the search tab. If the results of the search do not provide a satisfactory answer to the question at hand, different keywords should be tried in the search box until the correct answer is found.

D. **Legal Duties and responsibilities**
   1. Common law duties and liabilities to clients and third parties

> Summarize the tax return preparer's common law duties and liabilities to clients and 3rd parties.

> Identify situations which result in violations of the tax return preparer's common law duties and liabilities to clients and third parties.

Common law refers to the part of the law that is derived from the judicial precedent rather from the statutes. Tax preparer's responsibilities to clients under the common law can result from a breach of contract or commission of a tort. Under common law, a tax practitioner will sign a contract with the client called an engagement letter. If the tax practitioner violates any of the terms of the engagement letter, the tax practitioner can be liable for breach of contract.

   a. **Breach of contract**
      1) Engagement letter as a contract
         Contractual responsibility between the client and tax preparer is established upon signing of the engagement letter. This document should outline the nature and scope of the engagement and the procedures to be used.

      2) Contract privity
         Contract privity means that if one party of the contract breaches the terms of the agreement, the injured party can sue the offending party. In other words, if either the tax preparer or the client fails to perform under the terms of the engagement letter, the injured party can sue the offending party. Privity also generally means that only a party to the contract can sue the offending party for breaching the contract.

      3) Consequences of a breach
         In cases where a tax preparer is liable for a significant contract breach, he or she is not entitled to the compensation. Additionally, the client is usually entitled to recovering monetary (but not punitive) damages from the tax preparer, even if no compensation was received. In cases of minor errors, the client is allowed to reduce the accountant's fee for the damages caused by the breach.

Multiple Choice

REG 1-Q27

   b. **Commission of a tort**
      Tort refers to a negligent or intentional civil wrong not arising out of a contract or statute. Torts include ordinary negligence, actual fraud, and constructive fraud.

      1) Ordinary negligence
         Tax preparers must exercise a level of care, competence, and diligence commonly associated with other members of the profession. To prevail in action against a tax preparer for committing ordinary negligence, the plaintiff must prove:

         1) Tax preparer owed a duty to the taxpayer,
         2) A breach of that duty occurred,
         3) Plaintiff suffered a loss, and
         4) A relationship between the cause of the injury suffered and that duty.

Multiple Choice

REG 1-Q28

2) Defenses
Demonstrating that the CPA acted with "due care" is the best defense because it establishes the absence of ordinary negligence. If ordinary negligence is established, the CPA may be able to show that he could not foresee that the injured third party (the one not privy to the contract) would be relying on the results of his work. Additionally, contributory negligence, when the client's negligence prevented the CPA from adequately performing his work, can also serve as a defense in cases of ordinary negligence.

Multiple Choice
REG 1-Q29

c. **Liability to third parties**
Accountants face legal liability based on contract law, tort law, and statute law.

1) Who is liable?
Usually, not only the accountant but also the company's management can be found responsible for the resulting damages. In states with *joint liability*, the entire amount can be collected from either party. In states adhering to the several *liability concepts*, resulting damages are usually collected in proportion to the degree of responsibility each party had in causing such damages.

2) What needs to be proven?
To prevail in a lawsuit, the injured party should prove that the following elements took place:
- Negligence or fraud by the accountant
- Reliance on the accountant's work
- Damages resulting from the reliance on the accountant's work

3) To whom liability is owed?
   i. Ordinary negligence – to clients and primary foreseen beneficiaries
   A set precedent in Ultra-mares decision (minority view), accountants can be found liable only to persons in privity of contract with the CPA (clients) and intended third-party beneficiaries. However, most states expanded the Ultra-mares rule to foreseen users, and any foreseen class of users (majority view) that the accountant knew would rely on his work.

   ii. Fraud and constructive fraud – to all parties
   In cases of fraud and constructive fraud, accountants are liable to all parties who rely on their work. This holds true even when the accountant did not know or could not reasonably predict that the injured group of people would be relying on his work.

d. **Contract law liability to third parties**
An engagement letter defines an accountant's contractual obligations to a client and specifies the work to be done. The accountant implies that services provided to the client are equivalent to any other reasonably competent accountant. If not, the accountant has failed to provide due care and could be subject to the tort of ordinary negligence.

Third parties can sue for breach of contract if that specific 3rd party was mentioned in the engagement letter.

e. **Tort law liability to third parties**
The torts that deal with accountants' legal liability are (1) ordinary negligence and (2) fraud, either actual or constructive fraud.

1) Ordinary negligence
   If an accountant fails to exercise their duty of due care, the accountant has committed ordinary negligence.

   A plaintiff must show reliance (e.g., made a decision based on the information) and proximate cause (e.g., plaintiff's legal injury resulted from the accountant's actions) to prove ordinary negligence.

   If sued, the accountant's primary defense is he or she followed generally accepted accounting principles (GAAP) and/or generally accepted auditing standards (GAAS). An accountant who follows GAAP and GAAS is, in most cases, not be liable for ordinary negligence.

   i. Third party beneficiaries-Ordinary Negligence
      In most states (under the majority rule), an accountant owes a duty of due care to the client, and, also, to any third-party beneficiaries. Third party beneficiaries may be either explicitly named in the engagement letter or be part of a foreseeable class of users who the accountant knew will rely on their work.

      In a handful of states, as a precedent set in the Ultramares decision (minority view), accountants can be found liable only to persons in privity of contract with the accountant (e.g., named clients) and intended third-party beneficiaries.

      > *Hint*: The Ultramares case, limiting accountants' liability for negligent misrepresentation to the client or intended third party, was the majority rule until the court adopted a new rule called the Foreseeability Rule. This rule is now the majority position of the courts. It now states that if the accountant knew that the financials were to be given to banks to obtain a loan, then any third-party bank could sue for ordinary negligence, if they suffered a loss.

      Example: Financial statements were prepared for the client to get a loan from the XYZ Bank. XYZ Bank is named in the engagement letter.

      Assume that the accountant committed an act of ordinary negligence. Since XYZ Bank is mentioned as a third party intended beneficiary, it can sue the accountant for ordinary negligence.

      Now, assume that in addition to providing the financial statements to XYZ Bank, the client also provided the statements to ABC Bank to qualify for a loan. ABC Bank is a foreseen party, as would be any bank, and could sue for ordinary negligence under the majority view. Since the accountant knew that the financial statements were to be used to obtain a loan from a bank, any bank that received the financials for the determination of a loan can sue the accountant if the accountant committed ordinary negligence.

      However, in states that rely on the Ultra-mares (minority view), ABC Bank could **not** sue for ordinary negligence because ABC Bank is not either a named party or the third party intended beneficiary in the engagement letter.

Multiple Choice

REG 1-Q30 through REG 1-Q31

2) Fraud to third parties
Actual fraud consists of issuing false financial information with knowledge that it is false and with intent to deceive someone. This intent to deceive is called scienter, which is Latin for deceit. If the accountant is sued for actual fraud, the plaintiff must prove M S R I D.

M – Misrepresentation of the material fact
S – Scienter (deception) by the accountant
R – Reasonable reliance on the accountant's work
I – Intention of the CPA for the client to rely on this misrepresentation
D – Damages were suffered by the client or the relying party

3) Gross negligence (constructive fraud) to third parties
The last tort involves gross negligence or constructive fraud. In gross negligence, instead of scienter, there is a reckless disregard for the truth. This means that the accountant made a misrepresentation that he or she believed was true, but did not have an expert verify the representation. CPA acted recklessly, meaning that the CPA made the statement without knowing whether it was true or false. If the accountant is found to be negligent, then the loss is determined based on the loss that the plaintiff incurred. If the accountant is sued for gross negligence or constructive fraud, they must prove all of the following to prevail:

M – Misrepresentation of the material fact
R – Reckless disregard of the truth by the accountant
R – Reasonable reliance on the accountant's work
I – Intention of the CPA for the client to rely on this misrepresentation
D – Damages were suffered by the client or the relying party

When it comes to fraud, any third party can sue the accountant.

4) Defenses
Unlike in cases of ordinary negligence, client's contributory negligence (the lack of even slight care) is not a valid defense in fraud and constructive fraud cases. CPAs can be found liable not only for actual but also for punitive damages, and privity of contract is not required to be proved in order to win in a lawsuit.

Multiple Choice

REG 1-Q32

f. **Statute law liability when sued by third parties**
An accountant's most serious liability is statute liability. Statute liabilities can extend an accountant's liability to criminal liability. The main statues that promulgate this liability are the Securities Act of 1933, and the Securities Act of 1934. These acts were enacted to protect the buyers and sellers of securities by means of interstate commerce. As a result, these acts increased the liability of the accountants who work for and audit public companies.

The two sections in particular that can cause potential legal liability to accountants are Section 11 of the Securities Act of 1933 and Section 10b of the Securities Exchange Act of 1934.

1) Section 11 of the Securities Act of 1933
Section 11 of the Securities Act of 1933 deals with the issuance and sale of new securities, or Initial Public Offerings (IPOs). To issue new securities, unless exempt, a company must file a registration statement with the Securities Exchange Commission (SEC). If the registration

statement contains a material misstatement or omission, anyone who knowingly or unknowingly contributed to the misstatement or omission is presumed to be liable (e.g., the issuer, underwriter, and any experts such as accountants).

Normally, if a plaintiff brings a suit against an accountant, the plaintiff has the burden of proof. Under the SEC act of 1933, the burden of proof shifts over to the defendant, the accountant.

The plaintiff does **not** need to prove:
- The accountant was negligent or at fault
- Scienter or reckless disregard for the truth
- Reliance

All that is required by the plaintiff is to prove that he or she purchased the security, suffered a loss, and the registration statement contained a material misstatement or omission.

With the burden of proof now back to the accountant, the accountant has to prove that he or she was not at fault. This defense is called the due diligence defense.

Using this defense for ordinary negligence, the accountant needs to show that he or she exercised reasonable care and followed generally accepted auditing standards, and the statements in the registration statement were true.

2) Section 10b of the Securities Exchange Act of 1934
Section 10b also holds an accountant potentially liable for a shareholder's loss, but it does not deal with IPOs. Again, an accountant is liable for financial information that contains a material misstatement or omission.

If the security has a connection with interstate commerce (e.g., the stock certificate is mailed, or the security is traded on a national securities exchange) then Section 10b is applicable.

Unlike with Section 11, under Section 10b, the burden of proof is now back on the plaintiff. The plaintiff must now prove that the accountant acted with scienter, or reckless disregard for the proof. The plaintiff also has to show reliance now.

g. **The Sarbanes-Oxley Act of 2002**
The Sarbanes-Oxley Act of 2002 is an act passed by the Congress to safeguard the public from fraudulent corporate reporting by providing protection of whistleblowers and implementing more stringent regulations of the company's key employees, their auditors, and advisors.

In 2002, as the dust settled on the financial devastation caused by the demise of Enron and Arthur Andersen, Congress voted to enact Sarbanes-Oxley to bolster confidence in the financial reporting and improve corporate governance. The act has directly changed the corporate governance and regulatory environment for public companies in the United States. Sarbanes-Oxley requires greater separation between the external auditors and corporate officers (Sec. 301), increases corporate responsibility for financial reports (Sec. 302), emphasizes the importance of internal control with enhanced disclosure requirements (Sec. 404), proposes whistleblower protection (Sec. 806), and creates criminal penalties for corporate fraud (Sec. 802, 804, 906).

The Sarbanes-Oxley Act created the Public Company Accounting Oversight Board (PCAOB), a regulatory board that provides oversight of public company auditors and ensures high standards of audit quality. It is a private, nonprofit organization. The funding for the PCAOB comes from public companies, not from accounting firms that audit publicly held companies.

Before the Sarbanes-Oxley Act, the accounting was primarily self-regulated. The PCAOB can conduct inspections, set new standards, and punish violators. The board requires auditor independence and separated auditing functions from non-auditing functions. If a CPA firm performs the attest function (e.g., performs a financial statement audit) of a publicly held company, it cannot also perform non-attest functions for the same company. Non-attest functions include bookkeeping, advisory services, installation of computer equipment, financial information system work, appraisal or valuation, actuarial services, internal audit outsourcing, management or human resource services, investment banking, and legal work related to the audit.

The PCAOB has five members, appointed by the SEC for five-year terms. Of the five members, two must be or have been certified public accountants, and three must be non-CPAs.

The PCAOB may, in effect, audit the auditors. The PCAOB has strong oversight power. It can conduct inspections of accounting firms that perform audits on public companies. Large firms (who audit over 100 issuers) are inspected once per year. Smaller firms (who audit less than 100 issuers) are inspected at least every three years. The requirements for both large and small firms are equally stringent. Accounting firms must register with the PCAOB before performing audits of public companies.

If the inspection by the PCAOB reveals violations, an investigation may follow. The board can subpoena witnesses and documents to conduct these investigations. The PCAOB can take testimony from members of the firm or any person associated with the registered public accounting firm. If an accounting firm fails to cooperate with an investigation, the registration of the firm may be suspended or revoked.

Sarbanes-Oxley extended the statute of limitations for securities fraud to the earlier of 2 years after the discovery of the facts constituting the violation; or 5 years after such violation.

The Sarbanes-Oxley Act requires audit partner rotation. The audit partner must rotate off the audit after five (5) years of working for the same public company.

Companies and auditors are held accountable under Sarbanes-Oxley for destructing, altering, for falsifying records and could face either a fine, incarceration, or both if found guilty. A corporate officer (e.g., CEO, CFO) can be fined up to $5 million and could spend up to 20 years in prison.

Additionally, an auditor found guilty of altering client documents or failing to retain working papers for the required retention period (i.e., 7 years) could receive a sentence of up to 10 years in prison, a fine, or both.

Sarbanes-Oxley puts accountability on the CEO and CFO, or equivalent signing officer to be ultimately responsible for a financial statement's content. It is the CEO and CFO's job to affirm that the report does not contain misleading omissions or untrue statements of material fact. Based on the officer's knowledge, their signature certifies that the report fairly presents, in all material respects, the financial condition of the issuer for the periods presented in the report.

Finally, Sarbanes-Oxley establishes whistleblower protection to prevent retaliatory discrimination (e.g., termination, demotion, suspension, harassment) against employees who lawfully provide information to aid in an investigation by law enforcement, federal regulators, members of Congress, or other individuals with supervisory authority.

Remedies for such retaliatory discrimination against the whistleblower include compensatory damages such as reinstatement, back pay with interest, and compensation for damages arising from the discrimination (e.g., litigation costs, attorney fees). If found guilty of retaliation in a case of whistleblowing, criminal penalties can include prison sentences up to 10 years.

Multiple Choice

REG 1-Q33

2. Privileged communications, confidentiality and privacy acts

CPA Exam Blueprint Representative Task: Summarize the rules regarding privileged communications as they relate to tax practice.

Identify situations in which communications regarding tax practice are considered priveleged.

a. **Confidential communication**
On a federal level, and in most states, the accountant-client relationship is one of a confidential nature. This means that in most cases, the accountant cannot reveal confidential client information without client permission.

b. **No privileged communication**
Federal and most state laws do not recognize the accountant-client communication between the clients as privileged. This means that unlike doctors or lawyers, CPAs must disclose confidential client information when subpoenaed into a court, even if the client does not consent to those disclosures.

c. Exceptions to the privileged communication rule
1) When allowed by the state (few states only)
2) When acting as an agent for covered employer (e.g., lawyer or doctor)

When the accountant-client privilege exists, state (not federal) courts and agencies generally cannot require a CPA to reveal confidential client information. Note, however, that to be considered privileged, communication must be confidential and done in a jurisdiction that recognizes that type of communication. This privilege is meant to benefit the client and can be waived by him or her. If part of the privilege is waived by the client, the whole privilege is considered to be waived.

d. **AICPA rules applicable to workpapers**
Workpapers are confidential information that belongs to a CPA and consists of notes, calculations, and other information that the accountant accumulates during the engagement. CPAs are prohibited from showing workpapers to anyone except as outlined in situations below.

Multiple Choice

REG 1-Q34 through REG 1-Q35

1) Sale of a CPA practice
Confidential information cannot be revealed to a purchaser of a CPA practice without the client consent. However, samples of work conducted by the firm can be turned over to the purchaser as long as the purchaser keeps this information confidential.

2) Peer review
If a CPA firm is going through a peer review, a quality review, or a control review panel, no client permission is needed to disclose confidential client information required for such review.

3) Subpoenas
   In the absence of the accountant-client privilege, when an enforceable subpoena is served to an accountant, confidential client information must be revealed to the requesting court or government agency. Subpoenas should be specific in scope and purpose and can be rejected by the accountant for being too broad or unreasonably burdensome.

   Multiple Choice
   REG 1-Q36

4) Third-party service providers (TPSPs)
   Third-party providers are other tax return preparers. A CPA might be able to give third-party providers confidential client information without the client's consent if there is a contractual relationship between the CPA and the third-party provider and the CPA is reasonably assured that the third-party provider has appropriate procedures in place to safeguard confidential client information.

5) Other situations
   Accountants are allowed to disclose confidential client workpapers in response to a lawsuit brought by the client, to comply with the rules of GAAS/GAAP, or while responding to the AICPA ethics investigation.

   Multiple Choice
   REG 1-Q37

e. **Rules specific to tax preparers (IRC rules and Financial Modernization Act of 1999)**
   1) Prohibit disclosure of any non-public personal information without client permission.

   Multiple Choice
   REG 1-Q38

   2) Require accountants to develop, implement, and maintain a comprehensive information security program for protecting client information.

   3) Places responsibility for the confidentiality of outsourced client information on the accountant.

   4) Requires information to be used only for agreed-upon tax preparation or planning purposes. Allowable uses also may include peer-review, computer processing, and administrative orders.

   5) Prohibits tax preparers from "knowingly" and "recklessly" disclosing and using client tax information.

   Multiple Choice
   REG 1-Q39 through REG 1-Q40

This page is intentionally left blank.

Glossary: Ethics, Professional Responsibilities, and Tax Procedures

A

AICPA Code of Professional Conduct – document that outlines minimum levels of acceptable behavior while performing services as a certified public accountant

Alien – an individual who is not a U.S. citizen

American Institute of Certified Public Accountants (AICPA) – a non-profit organization that is integral to rule-making and standard-setting in the CPA profession, and serves as an advocate before legislative bodies and public interest groups

Arms length's standard – standard that requires affiliated organizations to conduct business as if they were dealing with an unrelated organization

B

Breach of contract – is a failure to fulfill the terms of the engagement

C

Calendar year – is an accounting period which follows the normal calendar year

Common law – the part of the law that is derived from the judicial precedent rather from the statues

Constructive fraud (gross negligence) – refers to the actions containing MRRID elements (misrepresentation of the material fact, reckless disregard of the truth, reasonable reliance, intention on the misrepresentation to be relied on, and damages)

Contract privity – the right of the injured party to sue the offending party for failure to deliver under the terms of contractual agreement

Corporation – a legal entity that is separate and distinct from its owners

Correspondence examination – is an IRS audit conducted via a written request to mail additional information directly to the IRS office

D

E

Engagement letter – a document that outlines contractual responsibility between the client and CPA

Enrolled agent (EA) – is the highest credential issued by the IRS, which authorizes an individual to have unlimited practice rights before the IRS

Estimated tax payments – protective tax payments towards current year's tax liability that some taxpayers are required to make in order to avoid IRS penalties

F

Failure to make estimated tax payments penalty – penalty that applies to all taxpayers who failed to disburse sufficient tax withholdings and estimated tax payments when those payments were due

Field examination – an IRS examination conducted at the taxpayer's place of business

Fiscal year – the company's natural year which ends on the last day of the month other than December.

Fraud – refers to the actions containing MSRID elements (misrepresentation of the material fact, scienter, reasonable reliance, intention for the misrepresentation to be relied on, and damages)

Fraud penalty – a penalty that applies in cases where underpayment of taxes was due to the fraud

Frivolous tax position – a tax return position that is not based in fact or law

G

Green card test – is a test which treats a foreign alien in possession of a valid alien registration card (aka green card) as a U.S. resident for the purposes of tax return filing

Gross negligence – see constructive fraud

H

I

Internal Revenue Code (IRC) – a codification of the tax laws of the country that serves as a basic foundation of the tax law.

J

Joint Ethics Enforcement Program (JEEP) – a collaborative program between AICPA and state CPA societies, which conducts a single investigation and action for the CPA ethical violations.

K
L
M
Mobility rules – rules that are adopted by most states to allow licensed CPAs in good standing from a substantially equivalent state to practice outside of their principal place of business without obtaining a new license.
More likely than not standard – standard that is met when there is greater than 50% likelihood of the tax position being upheld, if challenged by the IRS.
N
Negligence – any careless, reckless, or intentional disregard of rules or regulations, and any failure to make a reasonable attempt to comply with the provisions of the tax law.
Ninety-day letter – is an IRS letter providing taxpayer with a ninety-day window to file a petition in the Tax Court or satisfy any unpaid tax deficiency.
O
Office examination – an IRS examination of the taxpayer conducted at the IRS office.
Ordinary negligence – refers to the failure of a CPA to act with the due care and perform as a reasonable, prudent accountant.
P
Preparer tax identification number (PTIN) – a tax identification number that every tax preparer is required to obtain from the IRS and renew on an annual basis.
Primary tax authority – documents providing primary authority for the U. S. income tax, which consists of the IRC, Treasury regulations, IRS rulings, tax court decisions, private letter rulings, etc.
Private Securities Litigation Reform Act – legislation passed by the U.S. Congress to amend earlier provisions and prevent abuse in private securities litigation against accounting firms and issuers of securities under federal law.
Privileged communication – protected communication disclosure of which cannot be forced even in the court of law (e.g., lawyer and client communication).
Public Company Accounting Oversight Board (PCAOB) – a nonprofit corporation that was created to establish rules relating to the preparation of audit reports for issuers, and conduct inspections, investigations, and disciplinary proceedings concerning registered public accounting firms.
Q
R
Reasonable basis standard – is a substantiation standard which requires at least 20% probability of a position being sustained on its merits.
Recurring item exception – an exception to the economic performance rule that allows certain recurring items to be treated as incurred during the tax year even though economic performance has not occurred.
Registered Tax return preparer (RTRP) – an individual authorized to practice before the IRS, whose practice is generally limited to preparing and signing tax returns, refund claims, and other documents submitted to the IRS.
S
Sarbanes-Oxley Act of 2002 – act passed by the Congress to safeguard public from fraudulent corporate reporting by means of providing protection of whistleblowers and implementing more stringent regulations of the company's key employees, their auditors, and advisors.
S corporation – is a qualified small-business corporation that has between 1 and 100 shareholders, and elects to be taxed under the Subchapter S of the IRC.
Secondary tax authorities – professional publications, textbooks, newsletters, tax research services, and IRS publications that interpret primary sources of authority.
Securities Act of 1933 – legislation stating that publically-traded securities must be registered with the SEC and contain reliable information that is free from any material misrepresentation or material omission of a fact.
Securities Act of 1934 – legislation that pertains to the stock sold on national stock exchanges and requires reports and financial statements prepared by public accountants.
Sole proprietorship – is a business entity which consists of one individual who carries on the unincorporated trade of business.
State boards of accountancy – state organizations with the sole power to issue, revoke, renew or otherwise regulate CPA licenses within the specific state.

State societies of CPAs - independent membership organizations serving all CPAs licensed in the particular state by providing professional development, training, networking opportunities, and public outreach.

Substantial authority standard – a tax standard that requires the weight of the authorities supporting the specific tax treatment to be substantial compared to the weight of the authorities supporting the contrary treatment, and implies at least 40% (50% for tax shelters or reportable transactions) of the probability of the tax position being sustained on its merits.

Substantial presence test – a test for establishing a residency status of an alien taxpayer by calculating the amount of days she was physically present in the U.S. during the last three years.

Substantiation requirements – standards for supporting documentation that taxpayers are required to collect before claiming any tax deductions.

Substantial understatement penalty – a penalty that is imposed when understatement of tax exceeds the greatest of 10% of the tax due or $5,000.

Substantial valuation misstatement penalty – a penalty that applies when the value of the property claimed on the return is at least 150% or more of its correct value.

T

Tax position – a position in a previously filed tax return or a position expected to be taken in a future tax return that is reflected in measuring current or deferred income tax assets and liabilities for interim or annual periods.

Tax preparer – an individual who prepares for compensation (implied or explicit), or who employs one or more persons to prepare for compensation, any federal tax return.

Tax shelter – is any arrangement (e.g., trust, partnership, etc.) that is entered into with the main purpose of avoidance or evasion of federal income tax.

Thirty-day letter – an IRS letter that summarizes any proposed audit changes and provides the taxpayer with a 30-day window for filing an appeal.

Tort – a negligent or intentional civil wrong not arising out of a contract or statute.

Treasury Department Circular 230 – an IRS publication that provides guidelines for federal tax practice before the IRS for CPAs, enrolled agents, attorneys, registered tax return preparers, enrolled retirement plan agents, appraisers, and actuaries.

U

United States Court of Appeals – the court at the taxpayer's place of residence or business where the previous court decisions can be appealed.

United States Court of Federal Claims – the court with a nationwide jurisdiction, which conducts trials at the locations that are most convenient and least expensive to taxpayers, but requires payment of tax before the hearing and disallows jury trial.

United States District Court – is a federal trial court available in each district of the United States.

United States Supreme Court – is the highest federal court in the United States that has final appellate jurisdiction and has jurisdiction over all other courts in the nation.

United States Tax Court – is a specialized court of law that hears and adjudicates only tax-related disputes and issues.

V

W

Workpapers – confidential information which accountant accumulates during the engagement and which consists of CPA notes, calculations, and other information about the client.

X

Y

Z

This page is intentionally left blank.

Multiple Choice – Questions

REG 1-Q1 R322. According to the ethical standards of the profession, which of the following acts generally is prohibited?

A. Accepting a contingent fee for representing a client in connection with obtaining a private letter ruling from the Internal Revenue Service.
B. Retaining client records after the client has demanded their return.
C. Revealing client tax returns to a prospective purchaser of the CPA's practice.
D. Issuing a modified report explaining the CPA's failure to follow a governmental regulatory agency's standards when conducting an attest service for a client.

REG 1-Q2 R151. Which of the following actions by a CPA most likely violates the profession's ethical standards?

A. Using a records-retention agency to store confidential client records.
B. Retaining client records after the client has demanded their return.
C. Arranging with a financial institution to collect notes issued by a client in payment of fees due.
D. Compiling the financial statements of a client that employed the CPA's spouse as a bookkeeper.

REG 1-Q3 R51. A CPA prepares income tax returns for a client. After the client signs and mails the returns, the CPA discovers an error. According to Treasury Circular 230, the CPA must

A. Document the error in the workpapers.
B. Prepare an amended return within 30 days of the discovery of the error.
C. Promptly advise the client of the error.
D. Promptly resign from the engagement and cooperate with the successor accountant.

REG 1-Q4 R305. While preparing a client's individual federal tax return, the CPA noticed that there was an error in the previous year's tax return that was prepared by another CPA. The CPA has which of the following responsibilities to this client?

A. Inform the client and recommend corrective action.
B. Inform the client and the previous CPA in writing, and leave it to their discretion whether a correction should be made.
C. Discuss the matter verbally with the former CPA and suggest that corrective action be taken for the client.
D. Notify the IRS if the error could be considered fraudulent or could involve other taxpayers.

REG 1-Q5 R1168. While reviewing a new client's prior-year tax returns, a CPA became aware that the client did not properly file all required federal income tax returns. Under Treasury Circular 230, what should the CPA do in this situation?

A. Notify the AICPA of the situation and request a ruling of continuance.
B. Notify the Internal Revenue Service of the client's noncompliance.
C. Resign from the engagement.
D. Advise the client of the consequences of the noncompliance.

REG 1-Q6 R48. A CPA prepares a client's tax return containing business travel expenses without inquiring about the existence of documentation for the expenses. Which statement best describes the consequence of the CPA's lack of inquiry?

A. The CPA may be assessed a tax return preparer penalty.
B. The CPA may be charged with preparing a fraudulent return.
C. The client will **not** owe an understatement penalty if the return is audited and the expenses disallowed.
D. The client will **not** be subject to a fraud penalty.

REG 1-Q7 R439. Under Treasury Circular 230, which of the following actions of a CPA tax advisor is characteristic of a best practice in rendering tax advice?

A. Requesting written evidence from a client that the fee proposal for tax advice has been approved by the board of directors.
B. Recommending to the client that the advisor's tax advice be made orally instead of in a written memorandum.
C. Establishing relevant facts, evaluating the reasonableness of assumptions and representations, and arriving at a conclusion supported by the law and facts in a tax memorandum.
D. Requiring the client to supply a written representation, signed under penalties of perjury, concerning the facts and statements provided to the CPA for preparing a tax memorandum.

REG 1-Q8 R362. Which of the following fee arrangements generally would **not** be permitted under the ethical standards of the profession?

A. A referral fee paid by a CPA to obtain a client.
B. A commission for compiling a client's internal-use financial statements.
C. A contingent fee for preparing a client's income tax return.
D. A contingent fee for representing a client in tax court.

REG 1-Q9 R365. Which of the following statements best describes the ethical standard of the profession pertaining to advertising and solicitation?

A. All forms of advertising and solicitation are prohibited
B. There are **no** prohibitions regarding the manner in which CPAs may solicit new business.
C. A CPA may advertise in any manner that is **not** false, misleading, or deceptive.
D. A CPA may only solicit new clients through mass mailings.

REG 1-Q10 R18. A CPA prepared a tax return for a client who will receive a refund check. The client is traveling abroad and asked the CPA to pick up the check at the client's home address. Under Treasury Circular 230, any of the following actions, if taken by the CPA relating to the refund check, would be a violation of the rules of practice before the Internal Revenue Service, **except**

A. Endorsing the check and depositing it into the client's bank account.
B. Holding the check for safe keeping and awaiting the client's return.
C. Holding the check until the client is billed, then endorsing and depositing the check into the CPA's account as payment for the bill.
D. Endorsing the check and depositing it into an escrow account for the client's benefit.

REG 1-Q11 R50. Under Treasury Circular 230, in which of the following situations is a CPA prohibited from giving written advice concerning one or more federal tax issues?

A. The CPA takes into account the possibility that a tax return will not be audited.
B. The CPA reasonably relies upon representations of the client.
C. The CPA considers all relevant facts that are known.
D. The CPA takes into consideration assumptions about future events related to the relevant facts.

REG 1-Q12 R70. Joe is the trustee of a trust set up for his father. He does not receive compensation for preparing the annual trust tax return, Form 1041. Under the Internal Revenue Code, when Joe prepares the annual trust tax return, Form 1041, he

A. Must obtain the written permission of the beneficiary prior to signing as a tax return preparer.
B. Is not considered a tax return preparer.
C. May not sign the return unless he receives additional compensation for the tax return.
D. Is considered a tax return preparer because his father is the grantor of the trust.

REG 1-Q13 R1188. With respect to any given tax return, which of the following statements is correct?

A. More than one person may be deemed to be a preparer of a tax return.
B. The final reviewer of a tax return is automatically considered the preparer of the return.
C. Only one person may be deemed to be a preparer of a tax return.
D. The two individuals who have done the most work in preparing the return will be deemed to be the only preparers.

REG 1-Q14 R442. A CPA prepared a tax return that involved a tax shelter transaction that was disclosed on the return. In which of the following situations would a tax return preparer penalty **not** be applicable?

A. There was substantial authority for the position.
B. It is reasonable to believe that the position would more likely that not be upheld.
C. There was a reasonable possibility of success for the position.
D. There was a reasonable basis for the position.

REG 1-Q15 R33. Tax return preparers can be subject to penalties under the Internal Revenue Code for failure to do any of the following, except

A. Sign a tax return as a preparer.
B. Disclose a conflict of interest.
C. Provide a client with a copy of the tax return.
D. Keep a record of returns prepared.

REG 1-Q16 R1169. A tax preparer filed a return for a taxpayer and used the taxpayer's detailed check register containing both business and personal expenses. If the tax preparer knowingly included personal expenses as deductible business expenses on the taxpayer's business, then the

A. Tax preparer will be liable only for penalties for taking an unreasonable position that led to an understatement of tax liability.
B. Taxpayer will be liable for penalties for taking an unreasonable position that led to an understatement of tax liability.
C. Tax preparer will be liable for penalties arising from an understatement due to willful or reckless conduct.
D. Taxpayer will be liable for penalties attributable to transactions lacking economic substance.

REG 1-Q17 R205. Which of the following professional bodies has the authority to revoke a CPA's license to practice public accounting?

A. National Association of State Boards of Accountancy.
B. State board of accountancy.
C. State CPA Society Ethics Committee.
D. Professional Ethics Division of AICPA.

REG 1-Q18 R261. Professional rules and ethics for CPA tax practitioners that are merely advisory, rather than having formal administrative authority, include which of the following sources?

A. AICPA Code of Professional Conduct.
B. AICPA *Statements on Responsibilities in Tax Practice*.
C. Internal Revenue Code.
D. Treasury Department Practice Rules (Circular 230).

REG 1-Q19 R1170. To whom must a CPA pay license fees in order to maintain a CPA license?

A. The Public Company Accounting Oversight Board.
B. The American Institute of Certified Public Accountants.
C. The state board of accountancy of the CPA's state of licensure.
D. The state society of certified public accountants of the CPA's state of licensure.

REG 1-Q20 R1189. Which agency is responsible for determining the continuing professional education requirements for licensed CPAs?

A. The Securities and Exchange Commission.
B. The board of accountancy for the state in which the licensed CPA practices.
C. The American Institute of Certified Public Accountants.
D. The National Association of State Boards of Accountancy.

REG 1-Q21 R1141. Tom Young's adjusted gross income on his 2014 tax return was $180,000. The amount covered a 12-month period. For the 2015 tax year, Young may be able to not have a penalty for the underpayment of estimated tax if the estimated tax payments made timely, are equal the annual amount of

I. 90% of the tax on the return for the current year, paid in four equal installments.
II. 100% prior year's tax liability paid in four equal installments.

A. I only
B. II only
C. Both I and II
D. Neither I nor II

REG 1-Q22 R1142. Sue Campbell is an unmarried taxpayer whose income was made up solely of wages. As of December 31, 2014, Campbell's employer had withheld $17,000 in federal income taxes and Campbell did not make any estimated tax payments. On April 15, 2015, Campbell filed an extension to file her individual tax return and paid $300 of additional taxes. Campbell's income tax liability for 2014 was $17,500 at the time she filed her tax return on April 30, 2015. At that time, she paid the tax liability's remaining balance. What is the amount that is subject to the underpayment of estimated taxes penalty?

A. $0
B. $200
C. $500
D. $17,500

REG 1-Q23 R1143. Jason filed his income tax return after the due date, but did not file for an extension. The return Jason sent in showed a tax liability of $60,000 and taxes withheld of $55,000. What is the base amount that the penalties for late filing and late payment should be calculated?

A. $0
B. $5,000
C. $55,000
D. $60,000

REG 1-Q24 R1144. Accuracy-related penalties apply to the underpayment of tax amount attributable to

I. Any substantial gift or estate tax valuation understatement.
II. Any substantial income tax valuation overstatement.

A. I only.
B. II only.
C. Both I and II.
D. Neither I nor II.

REG 1-Q25 R9. Which of the following is **not** considered a primary authoritative source when conducting tax research?

A. Internal Revenue Code.
B. Tax Court cases
C. IRS publications
D. Treasury regulations

REG 1-Q26 R281. In evaluating the hierarchy of authority in tax law, which of the following carries the greatest authoritative value for tax planning of transactions?

A. Internal Revenue Code.
B. IRS regulations.
C. Tax court decisions.
D. IRS agents' reports.

REG 1-Q27 R266. Which of the following penalties is usually imposed against an accountant who, in the course of performing professional services, breaches contract duties owed to a client?
A. Specific performance.
B. Punitive damages.
C. Money damages.
D. Rescission.

REG 1-Q28 R342. A client suing a CPA for negligence must prove each of the following factors **except**

A. Breach of duty of care.
B. Proximate cause.
C. Reliance.
D. Injury.

REG 1-Q29 R95. A company engaged a CPA to perform the annual audit of its financial statements. The audit failed to reveal an embezzlement scheme by one of the employees. Which of the following statements best describes the CPA's potential liability for this failure?

A. The CPA's adherence to generally accepted auditing standards (GAAS) may prevent liability.
B. The CPA will **not** be liable if care and skill of an ordinary reasonable person was exercised.
C. The CPA may be liable for punitive damages if due care was **not** exercised.
D. The CPA is liable for any embezzlement losses that occurred at the time the scheme should have been detected.

REG 1-Q30 R94. Under the position taken by a majority of the courts, to which third parties will an accountant who negligently prepares a client's financial report be liable?

A. Only those third parties in privity of contract with the accountant.
B. All third parties who relied on the report and sustained injury.
C. Any foreseen or known third party who relied on the report.
D. Any third party whose reliance on the report was reasonably foreseeable.

REG 1-Q31 R280. An accounting firm was hired by a company to perform an audit. The company needed the audit report in order to obtain a loan from a bank. The bank lent $500,000 to the company based on the auditor's report. Fifteen months later, the company declared bankruptcy and was unable to repay the loan. The bank discovered that the accounting firm failed to discover a material overstatement of assets of the company. Which of the following statements is correct regarding a suit by the bank against the accounting firm? The bank

A. Cannot sue the accounting firm because of the statute of limitations.
B. Can sue the accounting firm for the loss of the loan because of negligence.
C. Cannot sue the accounting firm because there was **no** privity of contract.
D. Can sue the accounting firm for the loss of the loan because of the rule of privilege.

REG 1-Q32 R116. Able, CPA, was engaged by Wedge Corp. to audit Wedge's financial statements. Wedge intended to use the audit report to obtain a $10 million loan from Care Bank. Able and Wedge's president agreed that Able would give an unqualified opinion on Wedge's financial statements in the audit report even though there were material misstatements in the financial statements. Care refused to make the loan. Wedge then gave the audit report to Ranch to encourage Ranch to purchase $10 million worth of Wedge common stock. Ranch reviewed the audit report and relied on it to purchase the stock. After the purchase, Able's agreement with Wedge's president was revealed. As a result, Wedge stock lost half its value and Ranch sued Able for fraud. What will be the result of Ranch's suit?

A. Ranch will win because Able intentionally gave an unqualified opinion on Wedge's materially misstated financial statements.
B. Ranch will win because Able is strictly liable for errors made in auditing Wedge's financial statements.
C. Ranch will lose because Ranch is **not** a foreseen user of Able's audit report.
D. Ranch will lose because Ranch is **not** in privity with Able.

REG 1-Q33 R12. Which of the following statements is correct regarding the liability of a CPA for services performed?

A. A CPA's work is **not** guaranteed to be accurate even though the CPA acted in a reasonably competent and professional manner.
B. A CPA is negligent for exercising only that degree of care a reasonably competent CPA would exercise under the circumstances.
C. A CPA's liability for negligence extends only to the client and **no** further.
D. A CPA's liability for fraud extends only to the client and **no** further.

BEC 1-Q34 R177. Spinner, CPA, had audited Lasco Corp.'s financial statements for the past several years. Prior to the current-year's engagement, a disagreement arose that caused Lasco to change auditing firms. Lasco has demanded that Spinner provide Lasco with Spinner's working papers so that Lasco may show them to prospective auditors to help them prepare their bids for Lasco's audit engagement. Spinner refused and Lasco commenced litigation. Under the ethical standards of the profession, will Spinner be successful in refusing to turn over the working papers?

A. Yes, because Spinner is the owner of the working papers.
B. Yes, because Lasco is required to direct prospective auditors to contact Spinner to make arrangements to view the working papers in Spinner's office.
C. No, because Lasco has a legitimate business reason for demanding that Spinner surrender the working papers.
D. No, because it was Lasco's financial statements that were audited.

BEC 1-Q35 R408. Which of the following statements is correct regarding an accountant's working papers?

A. The accountant owns the working papers and generally may disclose them as the accountant sees fit.
B. The client owns the working papers but the accountant has custody of them until the accountant's bill is paid in full.
C. The accountant owns the working papers but generally may **not** disclose them without the client's consent or a court order.
D. The client owns the working papers but, in the absence of the accountant's consent, may **not** disclose them without a court order.

REG 1-Q36 R285. At a confidential meeting, an audit client informed a CPA about the client's illegal insider-trading actions. A year later, the CPA was subpoenaed to appear in federal court to testify in a criminal trial against the client. The CPA was asked to testify to the meeting between the CPA and the client. After receiving immunity, the CPA should do which of the following?

A. Take the Fifth Amendment and **not** discuss the meeting.
B. Site the privileged communications aspect of being a CPA.
C. Discuss the entire conversation including the illegal acts.
D. Discuss only the items that have a direct connection to those items the CPA worked on for the client in the past.

REG 1-Q37 R169. A CPA in public practice may **not** disclose confidential client information regarding auditing services without the client's consent in response to which of the following situations?

A. A review of the CPA's professional practice by a state CPA society.
B. A letter to the client from the IRS.
C. An inquiry from the professional ethics division of the AICPA.
D. A court-ordered subpoena or summons.

REG 1-Q38 R28. Which of the following statements is correct regarding disclosure of client working papers prepared by a CPA?

A. Working papers may **not** be transferred to another accountant without the client's permission.
B. Working papers may **not** be turned over to a CPA quality review team without the client's permission.
C. Working papers may **not** be disclosed under a federal court subpoena without the client's permission.
D. Working papers may **not** be disclosed to any third parties without the client's permission.

REG 1-Q39 R207. Which of the following acts by a CPA is a violation of professional standards regarding the confidentiality of client information?

A. Releasing financial information to a local bank with the approval of the client's mail clerk.
B. Allowing a review of professional practice without client authorization.
C. Responding to an enforceable subpoena.
D. Faxing a tax return to a loan officer at the request of the client.

REG 1-Q40 R1190. A husband prepared his own tax return as married filing separately. His wife hired a CPA to prepare her tax return as married filing separately and asked the CPA not to disclose the information to anyone. The CPA was not retained by the husband for any tax work. The husband believed that his wife's tax return was negligently prepared and that he was financially harmed. He hired an attorney, without his wife's consent, to pursue a negligence claim against the CPA. The CPA hired an attorney to defend against the negligence claim. To which party, if any, may the CPA disclose the wife's tax return information without the wife's consent?

A. The husband, for the evaluation of the negligence claim.
B. The CPA's attorney, for the evaluation of the negligence claim.
C. The husband's attorney, for the evaluation of the negligence claim.
D. No one, because all disclosures must be made with the wife's consent.

This page is intentionally left blank.

Multiple Choice – Solutions

REG 1-Q1 R322. The correct answer is B. According to the ethical standards of the profession, a CPA cannot retain the client's records after a client has demanded their tax return. Even if the client has not paid the CPA's fee, the CPA cannot retain the client's records.

Answer A is incorrect because a CPA is allowed to receive a contingent fee for representing a client in an examination by the IRS. Representing a client in connection with obtaining a private letter ruling from the IRS is an example of this.

Answer C is incorrect because a CPA is allowed to reveal both the working papers and the client's tax returns to a prospective purchaser of the CPA's practice without the client's permission, which would not violate the ethical standards of the profession. A prospective purchaser is a purchaser who it thinking of buying the practice and the CPA is showing the prospective purchaser a sample of the CPA's work. When a CPA sells his practice, he must get the permission from the clients to turn over their tax returns to the new purchaser and if not, the CPA would violate the ethical standards of the profession.

Answer D is incorrect because if a CPA fails to follow a governmental regulatory agency's standards when conducting an attest service for a client, issuing a modified report does not require the permission of the client and is therefore not a violation of ethical standards of the profession.

REG 1-Q2 R151. The correct answer is B because a CPA cannot retain the client records after the client has demanded their return. Therefore, the CPA must return the client records after the client has demanded their tax return records.

Answers A, C and D are not actions by the CPA that would violate the CPA's ethical standards.

REG 1-Q3 R51. The correct answer is C. Per Circular 230: If a CPA discovers an error on a tax return they have prepared after the client signed and mailed it to the IRS, the CPA must promptly advise the client of the error.

Answers A, B and D are incorrect because Treasury Circular 230 does not apply.

REG 1-Q4 R305. The correct answer is A. While preparing a client's individual federal tax return, the CPA noticed that there was an error in the previous year's tax return that was prepared by another CPA. The present CPA has the responsibility to inform the client of the error and recommend corrective action.

Answer B is incorrect because the present CPA is not required to notify the previous CPA, only the client.

Answer C is incorrect because the present CPA is not required to notify the previous CPA, only the client.

Answer D is incorrect because the present CPA cannot notify the IRS as it would be a breach of confidential relationship. If the IRS issues a subpoena to the CPA, the CPA must turn over the requested information to the IRS, and does not need the client's permission.

REG 1-Q5 R1168. The correct answer choice is D. Under Treasury Circular 230 the CPA would be required to advise clients promptly of errors or omissions of the preparer or client in any tax matter with respect to which the preparer is required.

Choice B and D are incorrect because to notify the IRS would violate their professional responsibilities to the client.

Choice C is incorrect because it is not appropriate for the CPA to resign from the engagement under these circumstances.

REG 1-Q6 R48. The correct answer is A. The CPA may be assessed a tax return preparer penalty if they fail to make reasonable inquiries about the existence of documentation. The CPA is not required to audit the client's records. The key words in this question are: *"without inquiring about the existence of documentation"* (this means the CPA did not make reasonable inquiries which may subject the CPA to tax return preparer penalties.)

Answers B, C and D are incorrect because they do not address the issue of failure to make reasonable inquiries.

REG 1-Q7 R439. The correct answer is C. Under Treasury Circular 230, the responsibility of a tax practitioner, a CPA tax advisor, is to establish relevant facts, evaluate the reasonableness of assumptions and representations, and arrive at a conclusion supported by the law and facts in a tax memorandum.

Answer A is incorrect because the CPA tax advisor does not have to request written evidence from a client that the fee proposal for tax advice has been approved by the board of directors.

Answer B is incorrect because as a tax practitioner, a CPA tax advisor's advice should be made orally only when, in the advisor's judgment, it is appropriate to do so.

Answer D is incorrect because, under Circular 230, the CPA is not required to advise the client to supply a written representation signed under penalties of perjury concerning whether the facts and statements provided to the CPA for preparing a tax memorandum are correct or incorrect.

REG 1-Q8 R362. The correct answer is C. The ethical standards of the profession prevent an accountant from charging a contingent fee for preparing a client's income tax return.

Answer A is incorrect because a referral fee paid by a CPA to obtain a client is not a violation of the ethical standards.

Answer B is incorrect because a commission for compiling a client's internal-use financial statements, which are solely for the client's own use and not given the public is permitted under the ethical standards of the profession.

Answer D is incorrect because an accountant may charge a contingent fee for representing a client in tax court as it is permitted under the ethical standards of the profession.

REG 1-Q9 R365. The correct answer is C. A CPA may advertise in any manner that is not false, misleading, or deceptive.

Answer A is incorrect because a CPA may advertise in any manner that is not false, misleading, or deceptive.

Answer B is incorrect because there are prohibitions regarding the manner in which CPAs may solicit new business as a CPA may advertise in any manner that is not false, misleading, or deceptive.

Answer D is incorrect because a CPA may advertise in other manners besides mass mailings. Answers with exclusive terms such as only, always and never are generally incorrect.

REG 1-Q10 R18. The correct answer is B. Any question that addresses federal tax refund checks issued to the client by the government, which was endorsed or negotiated by the tax practitioner, is subject to a tax preparer penalty. Holding the check for safe keeping and awaiting the client's return does not mention anything about the tax practitioner endorsing or negotiating federal tax refund check issued to the client.

Answer A is incorrect because it would be a violation of rules of practice for endorsing and depositing the check into the client's bank account.

Answer C is incorrect because it would be a violation for endorsing and depositing the check into the CPA's account as payment for the bill.

Answer D is incorrect because it would be a violation for endorsing the check and depositing it into an escrow account for the client's benefit.

REG 1-Q11 R50. The correct answer is A. The CPA cannot account for the possibility that a tax return will not be audited under Circular 230.

Answers B, C, and D are allowed under Circular 230.

REG 1-Q12 R70. The correct answer is B. Joe is not considered the tax return preparer because he has not received compensation to prepare the annual trust return Form 1041.

Answer A is incorrect because Joe is not a tax return preparer.

Answer C is incorrect. A trustee of a trust is not considered a preparer of a tax return even if the trustee receives additional compensation.

Answer D is incorrect because as stated earlier, Joe is not considered a tax return preparer.

REG 1-Q13 R1188. The correct answer choice is A. A preparer is any tax professional with a preparer tax identification number who is authorized to prepare federal tax returns for compensation. This answer choice is correct because it is true that more than one person may be deemed to be a preparer of a tax return. Enrolled agents, certified public accountants, and attorneys are examples of professionals who can be preparers and any combination of these professionals can prepare the same return.

Choice B is incorrect because the person who reviews the returns for possible errors is not automatically considered a preparer.

Choice C is incorrect because as stated in choice A, more than a single person can be a preparer.

Choice D is incorrect because the individual who does the most work is not necessarily the preparer.

REG 1-Q14 R442. The correct answer is B. As long as a tax shelter transaction meets the more-likely-than-not standard, it need not be disclosed on the return.

Answers A, C and D are incorrect because substantial authority, realistic possibility of success, and reasonable basis are less rigorous standards than the more-likely-than-not standard. A preparer penalty could be applicable in situations involving these standards, if the position is undisclosed.

REG 1-Q15 R33. The correct answer is B. If a tax preparer has a conflict of interest with the company whose return the preparer is filing, the preparer may disclose the conflict of interest and not be subject to a preparer penalty.

Answers A, C & D are required of tax preparers. Failure to do any one of those will subject preparer to tax preparer penalties.

REG 1-Q16 R1169. The correct answer choice is C. If the CPA deducted personal expenses, which are not deductible, this was done intentionally to understate tax liability, and the action done by the CPA was willful and reckless, then the CPA will be subject to preparer penalties.

Choice A and B are incorrect because the tax preparer is liable for taking unreasonable positions that are not disclosed and lack substantial authority, not those that lead to an understatement of tax liability.

Choice D is incorrect because the taxpayer will not be liable, the tax preparer is liable.

REG 1-Q17 R205. The correct answer is B. The state board of accountancy is the only governing body that issues CPA licenses and also has the authority to revoke a CPA's license.

REG 1-Q18 R261. The correct answer is B. This question deals with which of the choices are advisory vs. authoritative (issued by an organization in a position of authority).

Answer A is incorrect because the AICPA Code of Professional Conduct is issued by the AICPA, an organization in a position of authority.

Answer C is incorrect because the Internal Revenue Code is the law governing income taxes, issued by the government, an organization in a position of authority.

Answer D is incorrect because Circular 230 is issued by government, an organization in a position of authority.

REG 1-Q19 R1170. The correct answer choice is C. The CPA is licensed by the state, and the license fees are paid to the state board of accountancy.

Choice A is incorrect because the PCAOB oversees the Sarbanes Oxley Act and is charged with setting standards for publicly traded organizations.

Choice B and D are incorrect because they are only societies, they are not responsible for licensing CPAs. Societies are used for resources to support the profession.

REG 1-Q20 R1189. The correct answer choice is B. The state board of accountancy for each state determines continuing education requirements to maintain a CPA license in that state.

Choice A is incorrect because the SEC regulates the buying and selling of securities sold through interstate commerce.

Choice C is incorrect because the AICPA is the national professional organization for CPAs in the United States.

Choice D is incorrect because NASBA acts as a forum for the state boards of accountancy to discuss areas of common concern.

REG 1-Q21 R1141. The correct answer is A. No penalty is due when a taxpayer paid at least 90% of the current or 100% of the prior year's taxes (110% if prior year AGI exceeds $150,000).

Choices B, C, and D are incorrect as per the explanation above.

REG 1-Q22 R1142. The correct answer is A. No penalty is due when net tax liability payable with the return is less than $1,000. Because Campbell's' employer withheld $17,000 from her wages, the net amount left to be paid with the return was $17,500-$17,000 = $500.

Choices B, C, and D are incorrect as per the explanation above.

REG 1-Q23 R1143. The correct answer is B. Late filing and late payment penalties should be calculated on net tax liability due with the return of $5,000 ($60,000 - $55,000).

Answers A, C, and D are incorrect as per the explanation above.

REG 1-Q24 R1144. The correct answer is C. An accuracy-related penalty can apply to both (I) any substantial gift or valuation misstatement and (II) any substantial income tax valuation overstatement.

Answers A, B, and D are incorrect as per the explanation above.

REG 1-Q25 R9. The correct answer is C. Primary authoritative authorities are official sources of tax law, the internal revenue code (IRC), tax court cases and treasury regulations. Secondary sources are unofficial tax authorities that interpret and explain the primary sources. Examples of secondary sources are tax research services, professional periodicals and IRS publications.

REG 1-Q26 R281. The hierarchy of authority in tax law in descending order is:
1. U.S. Constitution
2. Internal Revenue Code (IRC)
3. Treasury Regulations
4. U.S. Supreme Court
5. U.S. Circuit Courts of Appeals
6. Federal courts of original jurisdiction (decisions may be appealed to a Circuit Court of Appeals).

The correct answer is A because according to the hierarchy of authority in tax law, the Internal Revenue Code (IRC) as the most authoritative.

REG 1-Q27 R266. The correct answer is C. In the course of performing professional services, if the accountant breaches contract duties owed to a client, the client may sue for monetary damages.

Answer A is incorrect because specific performance is a legal remedy available to the injured party if the subject of the contract is unique.

Answer B is incorrect because punitive damages are generally not awarded in contract disputes.

Answer D is incorrect because rescission is where both parties are released from the contract and are restored to their original position and this remedy rarely occurs in contract disputes.

REG 1-Q28 R342. The correct answer is C. For a plaintiff (client) to prevail when suing a CPA for ordinary negligence; the client must prove the following:
1. The CPA breached his duty of due care
2. The client suffered some type of injury
3. The injury was caused by the CPA's breach (proximate cause)

A client does not have to prove reliance.

REG 1-Q29 R95. The correct answer is A. Based on the facts of the question, you can only assume that the CPA committed ordinary negligence because nothing is said that the CPA committed any type of fraud. The best defense for a CPA when sued for ordinary negligence is that they adhered to generally accepted auditing standards (GAAS).

Answer B is incorrect because the answer must state the care and skill of an ordinary reasonable accountant and not an ordinary reasonable person.

Answer C is incorrect because punitive damages are rarely awarded to the plaintiff in a common law breach. Committing ordinary negligence by the CPA may cause a common law breach.

Answer D is incorrect because the CPA is liable for any embezzlement losses that occurred at the time the scheme was detected, not before the scheme was detected.

REG 1-Q30 R94. Answer C is correct because the majority of the courts state that any foreseen or known third party who relied on the report can sue the CPA for ordinary negligence. For example, a CPA knows that he is doing an audit to prepare audited financial statements where the client is going to use the financials to obtain a loan from a bank but does not mention the specific name of that bank. Then, any bank who relies on the financials to give a loan to the client can sue the CPA if they commit ordinary negligence in the preparation of the financial statements and the bank suffers a loss by extending the loan to the client based on the financials. This is the majority view of the courts dealing with third parties suing the CPA for ordinary negligence.

REG 1-Q31 R280. The correct answer is B If the third party knows the class of clients, such as banks, who will rely on the financial statements, then the CPA is liable for ordinary negligence to any banks that get the financial statements. The accounting firm knew that the client needed the audit report to obtain a loan from the bank. Even though no specific bank was mentioned in the agreement between the CPA and the client, any bank could sue the CPA if they relied on the financial statements to give a loan to the client. Since the financial statements contained materially overstated assets and the client declared bankruptcy, the bank can sue the accounting firm for the loss of the loan due to negligence. The word negligence means ordinary negligence and not gross negligence.

Answer A is incorrect because the statute of limitations is not relevant to this question.

Answer C is incorrect because lack of privity of contract is not relevant as long as the CPA knew that the financial statements were being prepared to be used to obtain loans from banks. Therefore, any bank using the financials can sue the CPA for ordinary negligence, should the bank suffer a loss due to materially misrepresented financial statements.

Answer D is incorrect because the relationship of the CPA and client is one of a confidential relationship in most jurisdictions, and not a privileged relationship. The relationship between the CPA and client is not relevant in whether the bank can sue the CPA for ordinary negligence due to a loss from materially misrepresented financial statements.

REG 1-Q32 R116. The correct answer is A. Ranch will win because Able intentionally gave an unqualified opinion on Wedge's materially misstated financial statements.

Answer B is incorrect a CPA does not have strict liability for errors made in auditing a client's financial statements. Strict liability means that if a plaintiff proves his case, the CPA has no defense. In this question, the CPA can use the defense of showing that the CPA did not commit fraud by proving lack of deceit.

Answer C and D are incorrect because any third party can sue a CPA for fraud. Whether a third party (Ranch) is a foreseen user or is not a party to the contract, if they can prove fraud, they will win the case.

REG 1-Q33 R12. The correct answer is A. A CPA's work is not guaranteed to be accurate as long as the CPA acts as a reasonably prudent accountant (reasonably competent and professional).

Answer B is incorrect because a CPA must also act in a professional manner.

Answer C is incorrect because a CPA's liability for negligence could extend to a third party who is named to get a direct benefit from the engagement.

Answer D is incorrect because a CPA is liable for fraud to not only the client but also the third parties. Please note that the definition of negligence in this question is ordinary negligence, not gross negligence.

REG 1-Q34 R177. The correct answer is A. Spinner is the owner of the working papers and may successfully refuse to turn them over.

Answers B, C, and D are incorrect because Spinner owns the working papers.

REG 1-Q35 R408. The correct answer is C. The accountant's working papers belong to the accountant, but the accountant cannot disclose information contained in the working papers without the client's consent or a court order.

Answer A is incorrect because the accountant may not disclose information in the working papers without the client's permission.

Answers B and D are incorrect because the client does not own the working papers.

REG 1-Q36 R285. The correct answer is C. Even though the relationship of the CPA and client is confidential, if the CPA was subpoenaed to appear in federal court, he must disclose the illegal actions of the client that the CPA is aware of.

Answer A is incorrect because the Fifth Amendment only applies to self-incriminating evidence. The CPA is not the one on trial and does not have to exercise the Fifth Amendment.

Answer B is incorrect because the relationship between the client and the CPA is confidential and not privileged.
Answer D is incorrect because the CPA would have to discuss ALL items that the CPA worked on with the client in the past and present due to the CPA receiving a subpoena from a federal court.

REG 1-Q37 R169. The correct answer is B. A CPA may not disclose confidential client information when there is a letter from the IRS and the IRS is requesting information about the client. If the IRS issues a subpoena, then the CPA does not need the permission of the client.

Answer A is incorrect because a CPA may disclose confidential information to a state CPA quality review panel (peer review) without the client's permission.

Answer C is incorrect because if there is an inquiry from the professional ethics division of the AICPA, the CPA does not need permission from the client to discuss confidential information.

Answer D is incorrect because if the CPA receives a court-ordered subpoena or summons, they do not need the client's permission to turn over confidential information from the audit they are performing.

REG 1-Q38 R28. The correct answer is A. The working papers may not be transferred to another accountant without the client's permission.

Answer B is incorrect because working papers may be turned over to a CPA quality review team without the client's permission.

Answer C is incorrect because working papers may be disclosed under a federal court subpoena without the client's permission.

Answer D is incorrect because working papers may be disclosed to any third parties without the client's permission. Examples of this include:
- No permission is required to turn over work papers to a quality review panel.
- No permission is required if a CPA is subpoenaed by the IRS or any court.

REG 1-Q39 R207. The correct answer is A. Releasing financial information to a local bank must have the approval of the client, not the approval of the client's mail clerk.

Answer B is incorrect because a CPA does not need permission to provide client information during a review of a professional practice board. This is known as a review by a quality control review panel or peer review.

Answer C is incorrect because when responding to an enforceable subpoena (i.e., court subpoena or an IRS subpoena), a CPA does not need the client's permission.

Answer D is incorrect because faxing a tax return to a loan officer at the request of the client is permitted.

REG 1-Q40 R1190. The correct answer choice is B. The husband is suing the wife's CPA for negligence because the husband believes that the CPA retained by his wife prepared her return negligently, which caused the husband to be financially harmed. The CPA hired an attorney to represent him in court. The CPA can show the wife's return (his client) to the attorney because the return is evidence to show that the CPA did not prepare a negligent return. Also, the attorney is a party to the lawsuit and has privity.

Choice A is incorrect because the wife expressly stated that the CPA must not disclose information in the tax return to anyone, including the husband in this case.

Choice C is incorrect because the CPA cannot disclose the information on the wife's tax return to anyone and the husband's attorney doesn't have legal grounds to view the return unless a subpoena is issued by the court.

Choice D is incorrect because the CPA can disclose information to the attorney who represents the CPA in the negligence lawsuit in order to support the CPA's defense.

This page is intentionally left blank.

REG 2 – Business Law

A.	**Agency**	**2A-1 – 2A-4**
	1. Authority of agents and principals	1
	2. Duties and liability of agents and principals	3
B.	**Contracts**	**2B-1 – 2B-18**
	1. Formation	1
	2. Performance	8
	3. Discharge, breach, and remedies	10
	4. Sales contracts	13
C.	**Debtor-Creditor Relationships**	**2C-1 – 2C-16**
	1. Rights, duties, and liabilities of debtors, creditors, and guarantors	1
	2. Bankruptcy and insolvency	5
	3. Secured transactions	13
D.	**Government Regulations of Business**	**2D-1 – 2D-9**
	1. Federal securities regulation	1
	2. Other federal laws & regulations	4
E.	**Business Structure**	**2E-1 – 2E-11**
	1. Selection and formation of business entity and related operation and termination	1
	2. Rights, duties, legal obligations, & authority of owners & managers	7
F.	**Property**	**2F-1 – 2F-4**
	1. Definition	1
	2. Personal property vs. fixtures	1
	3. Acquisition of personal property	1
	4. Real property deeds	2
	5. Co-ownership of property	3
	6. Mortgages & leases	3
	7. Bailments	4
Glossary: Business Law		**Glossary 2-1 – 2-5**
Multiple Choice – Questions		**MCQ 2-1 – 2-15**
Multiple Choice – Solutions		**MCQ 2-16 – 2-33**

Business Law

It is essential that CPAs understand business law so that they can properly audit various entities, as well as, understand a variety of legal concepts and their tax ramifications.

The term "business law" looks at the law, as it applied to the rights, relations, and conduct of individuals and businesses that are involved in commerce, trade, sales, and merchandising. Business law is often considered a branch of civil law as it looks at issues of both public and private law. As the law has become a more complicated issue over time, it is essential for business owners to have a basic understanding of these legal concepts and how they may affect their business.

A. Agency
1. Authority of agents and principals
    a. **Agency** is a fiduciary relationship between two parties whereby one party (the agent) agrees to work for, represent, and/or act for the other party (the principal).

    Examples of the Agency Relationship include:
    i. The employer-employee relationship is an example of one type of Agency Relationship.
    ii. A Power of attorney is a written authorization of agency. In this form of agency, the document only needs to be signed by the principal, not the agent, and typically limits the Agent's authority to specific transactions.
    iii. Only agencies formed to buy land and those that cannot be performed within one (1) year need to be in writing.

    b. **Agents** are individuals who have the authority to act on another party's behalf (typically the principal). Partners, corporate officers, and employees are thus, all agents. Additionally, minors are eligible to act as agents too.

    c. **Principals** are individuals who authorize an agent(s) to act on their behalf.

    > Identify whether an agency relationship exists given a specific scenario.

    d. **Agency formation**
    The agency relationship can be formed for any legal purpose and is typically created by either: agreement of the parties, ratification, estoppel, or operation of laws.

    1) Agency by agreement – an agency relationship that is formed through the express oral consent (either oral or written) agreement between the parties.

        > *Example*: The seller of home signs a contract with a real estate agent to have that individual act as his agent in the sale of his house.

    2) Agency by implication – an agency relationship that is formed through the implied acts (either oral or written) between the parties.

        > *Example*: The seller of a home meets with a real estate agent over the sale of his home. The seller of the home agrees to let the agent hold an open house and provides the agent with a key to his house.

3) Agency by ratification – an agency relationship that is formed either by act or by an agreement whereby the principal ratifies conduct of a person who is not their agent.

> *Example*: The seller of a home does not contract with a real estate agent to sell their house; however, the agent finds a buyer to purchase the house that is agreeable to the seller. If the seller ratifies the contract for the sale of the house, they are creating an agency relationship with the real estate agent.

4) Agency by estoppel (apparent authority) – an agency by estoppel is created when the principal causes a third party to believe that an agency relationship is present when dealing with the alleged agent. The principal is estopped from denying later that an agency relationship existed.

> *Example*: The seller of a home is at lunch with a real estate agent whom they have not "signed" with. At lunch, a prospective buyer approaches the seller about purchasing the home. If at lunch, the seller directs the buyer to speak directly with the real estate agent sitting at the table (even though no contract with the real estate agent has been created); the seller is later estopped from claiming that an agency relationship did not exist.

e. Termination of agency relationship
  1. Most agencies are terminable at will, but if you breach a contract, you must pay damages.
  2. Termination by agreement of the parties:
     i. Lapse of time – an agency relationship may be terminated when the agreement specifies the time period during which the agency relationship will occur.
     ii. Purpose Achieved – an agency relationship will be terminated upon the accomplishment of a specific objective called for in the original agreement.
     iii. Occurrence of a specific event – an agency relationship will be terminated upon the happening of a specific event called for in the agreement.
     iv. Mutual agreement – an agency relationship may be terminated by mutual agreement of the parties.
     v. Termination by one party – one of the parties may terminate an agency relationship by revoking the agency agreement.

  3. Termination by operation of law
     i. Death or insanity – the death or mental incompetence of either the principal or the agent will terminate the agency relationship.
     ii. Impossibility – when the specific subject matter of an agency relationship is destroyed or lost, the agency relationship will be terminated.
     iii. Changed circumstances – when an event occurs to impact the relationship's subject matter drastically, such that the agent can infer that the principal would not want to continue the agency relationship, the relationship will terminate.
     iv. Bankruptcy – if the principal files for bankruptcy protection, the agency relationship will terminate immediately. The bankruptcy of the agent does not terminate the agency.
     v. Failure to have or loss of a required license.
     vi. Agency coupled with an interest – Principal appoints an agent to grant that party the legal right to property or to pay a debt the principal owes to the agent.
        a) The principal cannot terminate this agency; however, the agent can.
        b) Death or insanity does not end this agency.
     vii. When an agent is terminated, the principal must notify current customers. Additionally, the principal must publish notice to inform potential new customers.

e. Agent's authority

Recall the types of agent authority.

1) Express authority – this is a form of authority that has been declared in clear and definite terms. This type of authority can be oral or in writing.
2) Implied authority – this form of authority permits the agent to do what is reasonably necessary to carry out their express authority and carry out the objectivities of the agency.
3) Apparent authority – this form of authority is only apparent and not real. The agent's apparent authority only arises when the principal causes a third party to believe that the agent has authority, even though the authority does not exist.
4) Ratification – an agent will be presumed to have authority to certain acts, if the principal accepts responsibility for an agent's unauthorized act(s).

f. Principal's authority
1) The principal has the authority to direct the course and nature of the agency relationship.

> *Hint*: Apparent authority or agency by estoppels, is where the agent appears authorized. (e.g., it was reasonable to believe the agent was authorized.)

2. Duties and liability of agents and principals

Explain the various duties and liability of agents and principals.

a. Agent's duties to a principal
1) Due care – the agent must use reasonable diligence and skill in completing tasks for, and on behalf of the principal.
2) Inform – the agent must notify the principal of all matters concerning the subject matter of the agency relationship, no matter how small.
3) Accounting – the agent has a duty to keep and provide to the principal an accounting of all property and funds that the agent has received and paid out on behalf of the principal.
4) Loyalty – the agent must act exclusively for the benefit of the principal. It is inappropriate for an agent to make decisions that solely benefits the agent or a third party. The agent cannot represent two principals in the same transaction unless both of the principals have been made aware and agreed to the amended relationship.
5) Obedience – the agent has a duty to follow both the stated instructions of the principal and all applicable laws of the jurisdiction.

b. Principal's duties to an agent
1) Indemnification – the principal has a duty to indemnify the agent for losses incurred while the agent is acting on behalf of the principal.
2) Compensation – the principal has a duty to pay the agent for services rendered on behalf of the principal. Such payment should be made in a reasonable amount of time, or as specified in the agency agreement.
3) Reimbursement for Expenses – the principal has a duty to reimburse the agent for expenses paid on behalf of the principal, and expenses paid in furtherance of the agency relationship.

c. Liabilities in the agency relationship

Identify the duty or liability of an agent or principal given a specific scenario.

1) Liability on contracts
   Liability for a contract formed by an agent will often depend on how the principal is classified at the time the contract is executed.
   i. Disclosed principal – this is a principal whose identity is known to a third party when a contract is agreed to by that party. In these types of contracts, the disclosed principal will be liable for the contract.
   ii. Undisclosed principal – this is a principal whose identity is unknown by a third party. The third party is unaware of an agency relationship, or the agent is acting on behalf of a principal when a contract is created. In these types of contracts, the principal will be liable. The agent has the same authority as an agent for a disclosed principal; however, the agent must not have apparent authority.
      a) The third party cannot get out of the deal because of an undisclosed principal.
      b) If there is a breach, both the principal and agent are liable.

2) Authorized acts
   If an agent acts within the scope of their authority, the principal is responsible for performing the contract and will be liable for non-performance.

3) Unauthorized act
   If an agent has no authority to contract with a third party, but contracts with the third party anyway, the agent will be liable for the contract.

4) Ratification
   The principal is not liable for unauthorized contracts unless the principal ratifies.
   i. Principal must know all material facts to ratify.
   ii. If principal accepts the benefits of the deal, the principal has ratified it.
   iii. Once the principal ratifies, the third party is bound by the deal.
   iv. For the principal to ratify, the agent must have indicated they were making the contract on behalf of the principal.

5) Liability for torts
   i. Agents are liable for their own tortious acts, either intentional or negligent.
   ii. Principals are liable for the tortious acts of their agents when
      a) The principal authorized the act.
      b) The agent acted on the belief that there was implied authority.
      c) There was innocent misrepresentation on the part of the agent.
      d) Per the doctrine of respondent superior, an employer is vicariously liable for negligent acts of their employees if committed during their employment.
   iii. Even if negligent, employees injured in the scope of employment are eligible to collect workers' compensation.

6) Liability for criminal acts
   i. Agents are liable for their own criminal acts.
   ii. Principals are liable for their own criminal acts, as well as acts performed in furtherance of the agency.

Multiple Choice

REG 2-Q1 through REG 2-Q8

B. Contracts
1. Formation

> Summarize the elements of contract formation between parties.

A contract is simply defined as an agreement between two or more parties where the parties make a set of promises, the breach of which the law provides a remedy. When creating a valid contract, six elements are required:
1) Offer
2) Acceptance
3) Consideration
4) Proper form
5) Lawful object, and
6) Two or more competent parties

a. **Offer**
When examining the elements of a contract individually, you have to start with the Offer. An offer is the presentation of terms and conditions made by one party (the offeror) to another party (the offeree). A valid offer to form a contract must contain three essential elements. These elements include: <u>be seriously intended</u>, in that a reasonable person would consider the offer to be serious, the offer <u>must be communicated to the other party</u> (either through words or actions), and the offer <u>must be definite in its terms</u> (including price). The absence of any of these elements will lead to an ineffective offer.

> *Hint*: Advertisements and price quotes are not usually offers, but are invitations to deal.

When looking at offers, it is important to remember that offers are only valid for limited periods of time. Offers can end either by actions taken by one of the parties, or by acts of law.

Offers terminate by actions of one of the parties, when a party of the offer takes specific actions. For example, if the offeree makes a counteroffer to an original offer presented by the offeror, the offeree is legally rejecting the original offer and making a new offer. This rejection of the original offer terminates the original offer for future consideration. This rejection and counteroffer are made official upon their receipt by the original offeror. In addition to the steps set forth above that an offeree can take to terminate an offer, the offeror also can revoke their offer at any point in time prior to acceptance of that offer by the offeree. There are three major exceptions to the offeror's ability to terminate an offer. These include:

1) The option contract
This is a type of offer where the offeree pays monetary compensation to the offeror in exchange for the offerors promise to keep an offer open for a defined period. As such, the offeree pays a fee to hold an "option" to accept the original offer.

2) The firm offer
In a UCC Sales Contract, a "Firm Offer" is an offer whereby a merchant makes an offer in writing and guarantees that the offer will remain open for a defined time period. It is irrevocable, without any additional consideration necessary, but the maximum period is three months.

3) Auctions
Once an auctioneer calls for bids on an item up for auction without reserve, withdrawing the item is prohibited unless no bid is made within a reasonable amount of time. In an auction

with a reserve, the auctioneer may withdraw the goods at any time before the completion of sale announcement.

Offers can also terminate through acts of law upon a variety of circumstances. An offer may expire or end at the time outlined in the original offer. If no specific time is stated in the offer, the offer is valid for a reasonable period. Additionally, the death or insanity of the offeror, or offeree will immediately terminate a contract offer. Finally, an offer may be terminated by the destruction of the subject matter. For example, if there is an offer to purchase "A"'s car, and the car is destroyed in a fire, the offer also terminates.

Multiple Choice

REG 2-Q9 through REG 2-Q10

b. **Acceptance**
The second element of a contract is acceptance. Acceptance is the agreement by the offeree of the terms and conditions presented by the offeror. To have a valid acceptance, the acceptance must include three essential elements. These include: the acceptance being <u>unconditional</u>, in that the acceptance must comply with all terms presented by the offeror. Additionally, the <u>acceptance must be communicated</u> by either words or actions to the offeror, and finally, the <u>acceptance must be made by the party to whom the offer is made</u>.

Acceptance of a contract typically occurs when the offeror receives acceptance by the offeree. While this is the general rule, two limited exceptions should be noted.

1) The mailbox rule
The mailbox rule states that acceptance of an offer will be valid when *sent* (not received) if the acceptance is properly addressed and the offeree uses the express means of communicating the acceptance, or a reasonable means of communication if no specific means are stated. Courts have inferred that this last requirement means that the offeree should use the same, or faster, means to make their acceptance as those used to make the offer. For example, if the offeror mails the offer to the offeree using US Mail, and no means of acceptance are stated, the offeree could accept the offer by mailing their response via US Mail (the means used to provide the original offer) or Federal Express (a faster method of acceptance then the one used by the offeror).

2) Offer states
If the offer states that the offer will not be effective until the acceptance is *received*, it is not effective until that acceptance is received. Furthermore, if the offer provides a specific means of communicating the acceptance, the acceptance will not be effective until that means is used.

In some situations, a party may originally agree to a contract, but later learn that that agreement was made improperly or under false pretenses. In these situations, the contract may be voidable by one of the parties.

3) Mistake
When a mistake occurs in the making of a contract, most of which have little to no effect on the contract.
   i. Mutual mistakes are mistakes that both parties make as to a material fact involved in the contract. When this occurs, because both parties make a mistake as to a material fact, the contract is void, as both individuals failed to have the capacity required to make an educated decision on entering into the contract.

Multiple Choice

REG 2-Q11

ii. Unilateral mistakes are mistakes that only one party made with respect to a material fact in the contract. When this occurs, the contract may be disaffirmed only if the non-mistaken party knew or should have known that the mistake was being made.

4) Duress
Duress is the forcing of an individual into a contract by force or threat of immediate force, violence, economic, or criminal action. A contract entered into under duress is voidable as the party entering into the contract lacked capacity to make a clear decision on the subject.

Multiple Choice
REG 2-Q12

5) Undue Influence
Under influence occurs when a party uses their position of love, confidence, or affection to overcome the other party's free will and have that individual agree to the terms of a contract. In this situation, the contract is voidable.

Multiple Choice
REG 2-Q13

2) Fraud
Fraud is the act of using deception to get another party to agree to the terms of a contract. At its core, there are two types of fraud, Actual Fraud and Constructive Fraud.

   i. The Elements of Actual Fraud – **MS RID.**

M	• Must have a **M**aterial **M**isrepresentation of fact or a deliberate concealment. In this case, there must a fact that was purposefully concealed, and that concealment was the basis of the decisions.
S	• Must have **S**cienter, or intent to deceive.
R	• Must have **R**easonable Reliance. The victim must have reasonably and justifiably relied on the misrepresentation.
I	• Must have **I**ntent to rely.
D	• Must have **D**amages. The aggrieved party must have incurred actual damages as a result of the misrepresentation.

   ii. Constructive Fraud
   This form of fraud is also known as gross negligence. Constructive Fraud is proven using the same basic elements of proving fraud; however, the Scienter requirement is met by simply having a reckless disregard for the truth – **MR RID.**

M	• Must have a **M**aterial **M**isrepresentation of fact or a deliberate concealment. In this case, there must a fact that was purposefully concealed, and that concealment was the basis of the decisions.
R	• Must have a **R**eckless disregard for the truth (making a statement without knowing if it is true or false).
R	• Must have **R**easonable Reliance. The victim must have reasonably and justifiably relied on the misrepresentation.
I	• Must have **I**ntent to rely.
D	• Must have **D**amages. The aggrieved party must have incurred actual damages as a result of the misrepresentation.

iii. Fraud in the execution occurs when the injured party enters into a contract not knowing that they have entered into a contract. In these circumstances, the contract entered into is void.

iv. Fraud in the Inducement occurs when the injured party knows that they have entered into a contract, but one or more terms in the contract have been misrepresented. When this occurs, the injured party has the option to either rescind the contract, or they can accept the contract and sue for monetary damages resulting from the fraudulent actions.

3) Innocent Misrepresentation is similar in nature to fraud; however, when an innocent misrepresentation occurs, there is no scienter or reckless disregard for the truth. When this occurs, the injured part can only rescind a contract, because the misrepresentation was innocent, they cannot sue for money damages.

   i. Elements of Innocent Misrepresentation – **MR ID.**

M	• Must have a **M**aterial **M**isrepresentation of fact.
R	• Must have **R**easonable Reliance. The victim must have reasonably and justifiably relied on the misrepresentation.
I	• Must have **I**ntent to rely
D	• Must have **D**amages. The aggrieved party must have incurred actual damages as a result of the misrepresentation.

c. **Consideration**

Consideration, the third element in forming a valid contract, is the giving up of a legal right that is either legally detrimental to the promisee, or legally beneficial to the promisor. For example, when a buyer gives money to the seller, the buyer is giving something to the seller that is to the detriment of the buyer (the buyer loses money). In contrast, if the buyer agrees not to do something (i.e. not to sue the seller) that is also consideration, because it is something that is to the benefit of the seller.

When looking at consideration, it is important to note that consideration must be present for both parties in a contract, must be mutually bargained for and must be legally sufficient to form the basis of the bargain. This often means that consideration is for something other than money. When looking at consideration, it is important to remember that there is no requirement that consideration be of "equal" value. Courts consistently have held that as long as the parties agree that the consideration is present and sufficient between the parties, a court will not get involved in determining if the consideration was "fair".

When looking at consideration, it is also important to remember cases where consideration is not present. Past consideration (consideration given for a previous action) is not and cannot be consideration for a future event. For example, if "A" paid "B" to paint their house, and "B" painted the house, "A" cannot come back to "B" five years later and argue that "B" is contractually obligated to paint the house again. Additionally, no consideration is needed if a party is already contractually obligated to perform a duty. For example, an individual cannot provide consideration to a police officer to arrest a criminal, as the police officer, as part of their job, already has a contractual obligation complete this task.

Under the doctrine of promissory estoppel, no consideration is needed on a promise to donate to charity.

An output contract is a contract where one party to the agreement agrees to buy all of the party's production of a particular commodity. Output contracts are covered in the UCC. Prior to the enactment of the UCC, many common law courts refused to enforce such agreements on the grounds that a failure to specify the quantity of goods produced, or purchased, rendered these contracts misleading. An output contract is supported by consideration because the seller agreed not to sell that output to any other party.

Multiple Choice
REG 2-Q14 through REG 2-Q15

d. **Proper Form**
The Statute of Frauds requires that certain contracts be in writing to be enforceable. Under this concept, the only contracts that need to be in writing to be enforceable include the following six **"GRIPE + MARRIAGE"** contracts:

G	1) Contracts for the Sale of **G**oods over $500. These are contracts governed by the Uniform Commercial Code where the goods involved in the contract are valued at over $500.
R	2) **R**eal Estate Contracts. This includes all contracts for the sale of real property.
I	3) Contracts that are **I**mpossible to perform in one (1) year. If by the terms of the contract, the contract cannot be performed within a year, the contract must be in writing.
P	4) **P**romise to answer for the debt of another.
E	5) **E**xecutor's promise to be liable for the debts of an estate.
Marriage	6) Contracts for **Marriage**.

Multiple Choice
REG 2-Q16 through REG 2-Q18

While these contracts need to be in writing to be enforceable, what needs to be included in the contract is very broad. The only items that need to be included in the writing are the quantity being sold, the name of the parties involved in the contract, the subject matter and description of the item(s) being sold, and the consideration involved in the sale. Any type of writing that states the major terms can satisfy the Statute of Frauds.
   1) Need only be signed by one party, but is only enforceable against the one who signed.
   2) The terms can be stated in more than one document.

In limited circumstances, the law allows for the writing requirement to be waived. Such circumstances include:
   1) A contract that has been fully performed by both parties will be considered enforceable when no writing exists where there should traditionally have been one.
   2) If one party has performed on an unwritten contract to perform services that are impossible to perform within one year, the contract will be considered enforceable without a writing. For example, if party "A" agrees to perform services for party "B" in 18 months, and party "B" pays party "A" for those services, but fails to sign a contract, because party "A" paid party "B", the contract will be enforceable without a written contract.
   3) Oral real estate agreements are enforceable without a writing if the buyer of the land is in possession and has made a substantial down payment or other improvements to a contract.

Multiple Choice
REG 2-Q19

e. **Lawful Object**
The subject matter for any contract must be legal. If not, the contract is considered void in that it is unenforceable on any parties to the contract. One item to consider concerning this requirement is that if a specific clause in a contract is illegal, but the balance of the contract is legal, a court can

remove the illegal clause, while at the same time enforcing the balance of the contract. One example of how this might work is if person A contracts to buy a gun from person B and uses that gun to commit a crime. While the first part of the contract (to purchase the gun) may be completely legal and enforceable, the second part of the contract (to commit a crime) is illegal and unenforceable.

f. **Competent parties**
The issue of competency looks at whether or not the parties have the mental ability to understand their rights and obligations in the contact. If the person is unable to understand these rights and obligations, they are considered not competent, not able to contract, and any contract that they execute will generally be considered unenforceable. A general rule is that individuals who are legally considered adults have the competency to enter into contracts; however, there are exceptions to this rule.

1) Minors and contracts
Minors are generally considered not competent to execute contracts, and contracts that they enter into can be disaffirmed by the minor at any time that the person is a minor, or for a reasonable time after that. To disaffirm a contract, the minor only has to return what they obtained as a result of the contract, and the contract will be voided. Once the minor has become an adult, they can ratify a contract, making it legally enforceable. In doing so, the ratification must be of the contract in its entirety.

In limited circumstances, minors are not permitted to disaffirm a contract entered into when they are a minor. Contracts entered into by a minor for essential services such as life-saving medical care cannot be disaffirmed by a minor. Additionally, if a minor commits a tort in the execution of the contract, such as lying about their age, then the minor will be responsible for the commission of the tortious act.

Multiple Choice

REG 2-Q20

2) Intoxication
Intoxicated individuals can argue that they were not competent at the time that they entered into the agreement. In this defense, the individual can disaffirm a contract by proving that they were so intoxicated at the time they entered into the contract that they were incapable of understanding what they were doing.

3) Insanity
Similar to intoxication, insanity is a defense to having entered into a contract. When this occurs, the insane individual has to show that not only are they adjudicated as insane (a court has rendered them insane), but also, this mental defect has caused them to be incapable of understanding the contract that they have entered into. Typically, once adjudged to be insane, the individual will be able to disaffirm the contract, but will not be able to execute any contract in the future legally. Any future contracts will be void.

Multiple Choice

REG 2-Q21

g. Illegal contracts
Illegal contracts are **void** – courts won't aid either party. Failure to have a required license makes all contracts **void** (exception: the contract is **not** void if the license was a mere revenue raising measure).

> **Identify whether a valid contract was formed given a specific scenario.**

> **Identify different types of contracts (e.g., written, verbal, unilateral, express, implied, etc.) given a specific scenario.**

Upon determining that a contract has been formed, it is important to determine what type of contract has been created. In contract law, there are several different types of contracts.

h. Bilateral and unilateral contracts
1) Bilateral contracts are those contracts that call for a promise in exchange for a promise. These contracts are the most common form of contract, as the promise alone is enough to create the contract.

> ***Example***: Billy promises to paint John's house, and John promises to pay Billy $500. The contract is made when Billy and John each make the promise.

2) Unilateral contracts are contracts that are created when there is a promise for an act. In this type of contract, the only way the contract can be accepted is when the act is completed.

> ***Example***: John promises to pay Billy $500 when Billy paints John's house. The contract can only be accepted by Billy painting John's house.

i. Void and Voidable Contracts
1) Void contracts are those contracts that are unenforceable by either party. These contracts are typically illegal and have no meeting of the minds between the parties. If a party was adjudicated incompetent by a court, having proper jurisdiction, all contracts subsequently entered into by that party are void.

> ***Example***: John promises to pay Billy $500, and Billy promises to kill Sarah. Since murder is an illegal act, this contract is void.

2) Voidable Contracts are contracts that are rescindable by only one party in the contract.

> ***Example***: John, a 15-year-old, enters into a contract with Steve, an adult, to purchase Steve's car. This contract is voidable by John only, as he is a minor at the time of execution.

Multiple Choice
> REG 2-Q22

j. Express and Implied Contracts
1) Express contracts are those contracts that are formed through the express written or verbal agreement of the parties. Express contracts are a more common form of contract.

> ***Example***: John and Steven enter into a contract whereby John agrees to purchase Steven's house. To formalize this agreement, John and Steven enter into a written contract.

2) Implied contracts are contracts that are formed, at least in part, by the parties conduct. An implied contract is one where the court creates a contractual agreement because to not do so would lead to the unjust enrichment of one of the parties.

> *Example*: John is hurt in a car accident and rendered unconscious. John is flown to a hospital where he is given life-saving surgery. Even though John did not enter into an agreement before he received the surgery (as he was unconscious) a contractual relationship whereby John has to pay a reasonable bill for services rendered is created because not to have a contract would unjustly enrich John.

k. Formal and informal contracts
   1) Formal contracts are contracts that require a special form of creation. These contracts are uncommon and include contracts made for negotiable instruments, contracts created under seal, and letters of credit.
   2) Informal contracts are all contracts that are not "formal contracts." These are much more common.

l. The Parole Evidence Rule states that any oral or written evidence that was discussed before the written contract is inadmissible in court to prove the content of a contract. This rule helps protect parties from having portions of a negotiation brought into a contract dispute. In the following, limited circumstances this evidence will be admissible:
   1) When the evidence proves Fraud or illegality by one of the parties;
   2) When the evidence is used to prove what occurred After the writing;
   3) When the evidence is used to prove a Mistake; or
   4) When the evidence is used to Explain the writing or to clear up other ambiguities.

Multiple Choice

REG 2-Q23

2. Performance

Explain the rules related to the fulfillment of performance obligations necessary for an executed contract.

Identify whether both parties to a contract have fulfilled their performance obligation given a specific scenario.

Contractual performance can be broken into several categories.

a. Complete Performance of a contract occurs when all aspects of the party's duties and responsibilities have been completed in perfect accordance with the terms of the contract.

> *Example*: John executes a contract with Billy to purchase Billy's car for $5,000 on or before June 1. On June 1st, John provides Billy with a check for $5,000, and Billy provides to John the car, keys, and title. The contract has been fully executed as both parties have fully performed.

b. Substantial Performance of a contract occurs when almost all of the terms and conditions of the agreement between the parties have been met. When substantial performance occurs, even though all of the terms of the contract have not been met, there is an honest effort to complete all of the terms of the contract.

> **Example**: John executes a contract with Billy to purchase Billy's car for $5,000 on or before June 1. John, who is not good with dates, honestly and mistakenly believes that June 1st is Saturday. On Saturday, June 2rd, John shows up to purchase the car. Even though John is one day late, his honest effort to complete the contract on time can be considered substantial performance on the contract.

c. Third party assignments
   1) Third party beneficiary contracts involve contracts that are made for the benefit of an individual not identified in the contract. In certain circumstances, the third party has actual rights in the contract, even though they are not identified in the contract, and in some cases, they have no actual rights in the contract. Some examples include:

      i. A donee beneficiary is a third party who receives a gift from one of the original parties of a contract. The beneficiary of the gift has the right to enforce the contract against the original promisor.

         > **Example**: Paul agrees to make a $1,000,000 donation to University X for the benefit of student scholarships. If Paul fails to make the payment, the recipient of the scholarship does have legal rights to sue to enforce the contract against Paul.

      ii. A creditor beneficiary is a thirty party who receives a benefit from a contract where one person agrees to pay the debt of another. In this case, the creditor has legal rights in the contract, as they are specifically stated in the contract. More specifically, the beneficiary could sue either of the parties in the contract to enforce the agreement.

         > **Example**: Paul agrees to pay the credit card debt of Amy and the two enter into a contract stating such agreement. Because the credit card is specifically outlined in the agreement, the credit card company could sue either, Paul or Amy, if the debt is not paid.

      iii. An incidental beneficiary are individuals who are unintentionally given benefits when two other parties reach an agreement. In this case, because the beneficiary is unintentional, and not referenced in the contract, they do not have rights to sue to enforce the agreement.

         > **Example**: Mark purchases a car that he plans on allowing his 16-year-old daughter, Betty, to drive. Betty's name is nowhere on the contract. If Mark stops making payments on the car, and the car is repossessed, Betty has no legal rights in or to the car.

d. Assignments and delegation of contracts
   When examining contracts involving third parties, it is important to determine if the contract is being assigned or delegated to that third party. Most contract rights can be either assigned or delegated to a third party. When a contract is assigned, the original party in the contract is replaced with the new party, the assignee. When this occurs, the original party is no longer responsible for, or liable for, any portion of the contract, and the assignee replaces the original party. Conversely, in a delegation of a contract, one of the original parties in the contract substitutes another party into the contract to do some, or all, of the items promised by the original party. The main difference between an assignment and delegation is seen in liability. As just discussed, in an assignment, the original party is no longer responsible for the contract; however, with a delegation, both the original party and new party who has accepted responsibility under the delegation will both be responsible for the contract.

> **Example of Assignment**: Ron agrees to paint Harry's house for $1000. Ron, realizing that he is very busy, assigns the contract to George. In this example, once the assignment is completed, Ron is no longer responsible for the work, and has no liability under the original contract.

> **Example of Delegation**: Ron agrees to paint Harry's house for $1000. Ron, realizing that he is very busy, hires George and agrees to pay George $800 to complete the work. In this example, Ron is not assigning the contract to George; he is simply delegating responsibilities set forth in the contract to George. If George fails to complete the work, both George and Ron could be liable for the contract.

In limited cases, parties to a contract are not permitted to either assign or delegate rights or responsibilities under a contract. These cases include:
1) Personal Service Contracts that call for specialized skills of one of the individuals in the contract.
2) In events where assigning or delegating the contract to a third party would materially increase risk or alter performance.
3) If the contract itself Prohibits assignment or delegation of the contract.
4) Insurance contracts.

e. Assuming and buying subject to a mortgage
   1) Assuming a Mortgage - buyer purchases land already encumbered by a mortgage
      Buyer agrees to take over the mortgage and the buyer is liable for the mortgage.
      Seller (original mortgagor) is still liable for mortgage.
   2) Buying Subject to a Mortgage - buyer purchases land encumbered by a mortgage.
      The buyer doesn't agree to take over the mortgage and is not liable.
      Seller (original mortgagor) is the only one liable for the mortgage.
      Buyer runs the risk of foreclosure if the seller doesn't pay.

Multiple Choice
REG 2-Q24 through REG 2-Q26

3. Discharge, breach, and remedies

Explain the different ways in which a contract can be discharged (e.g., performance, agreement, operation of the law, etc.)

Identify whether a contract has been discharged given a specific scenario.

Identify situations involving breach of a contract.

a. Discharge of contractual duties and breach
   The discharge of a contract looks at examples and situations where a contract has ended, and both party's rights and responsibilities under that contract end. Several situations can lead to a contract being discharged. These include:

   1) Discharge by novation is a situation where the parties agree to replace one party of a contract with a new party.

   > **Example**: John and Steven enter into a contract whereby John agrees to mow Steven's grass, and Steven agrees to pay John $100. John gets sick and can no longer complete the work. John introduces Steven to George, who is willing to perform the work agreed to by John. When John and Steven agree to substitute George for John in the contract, the contract, with regards to John is discharged.

2) Discharge by Breach
   i. Unintentional and minor breaches – these occur when a party fails to perform on a contract fully, but the failure was due to a reasonable mistake or unintentional act. These breaches typically are minor. While the aggrieved party can recover damages, but those damages have to be subtracted from the performance that did occur.

   > **Example**: John executes a contract with Billy to purchase Billy's car for $5,000 on or before June 1. John, who is not good with dates, honestly and mistakenly believes that June 1st is Saturday. On Saturday, June 2nd, John shows up to purchase the car. Even though John is one day late, his honest effort to complete the contract on time can be considered substantial performance on the contract. Billy can sue for breach, but his only damages are the damages associated with the 1-day delay in fulfilling the contract.

   ii. Material breach – a material breach is a major failure to perform one or more terms called for in the contract. When a material breach of the contract occurs where one side fails to perform fully, the breaching side discharges the other party from having to continue to perform on the contract. The non-breaching party also can sue for the material breach.

   > **Example**: Steven and Michael agree to a contract where Steven agrees to purchase Michaels car for $10,000. If Steven fails to pay Michael the money, Michael is discharged from his responsibility of having to give Steven the car and can sue Steven for the breach.

   Multiple Choice
   REG 2-Q27

   iii. Anticipatory repudiation of a contract is a situation whereby one party, before the time of performance repudiates the contract. In this case, the non-breaching party can sue immediately, or wait until the performance is set to occur and then sue for the breach.

   > **Example**: Steven and Michael agree to a contract where Steven agrees to purchase Michaels car for $10,000 with payment to come on July 1. If Steven repudiates the contract on June 29th, Michael can either sue immediately or wait until the official breach occurs on July 1st.

   iv. The doctrine of substantial performance involves an unintentional, but minor breach. The breaching party may still recover, but subtract damages for the minor breach.

   v. The impossibility of performance is when a contract will be discharged if it becomes objectively impossible to fulfill the terms of the contract. This discharge will relieve both parties from having to fulfill any of the terms of their contract. Situations, where impossibility occurs, include the death of one of the parties to the contract, or the destruction of the subject matter of the contract.

   vi. Accord and satisfaction will discharge a contract when the parties agree to change a contract by substituting one type of performance with another. In this scenario, an accord is the agreement to change performance, and the satisfaction is the completion of the accord.

> **Example:** John and Steven agree to a contract whereby John agrees to purchase Steven's car for $10,000. Before completing the transaction, John has the car inspected and learns that it needs $1,000 worth of work. If John and Steven subsequently agree to a new price, $9,000, and substitute that new price into the contract. Once the new price is agreed to the contract, concerning the old price, is discharged.

vii. The statute of limitations does not discharge the contract; it is merely a bar to judicial remedies.
   a) It is always measured from the date of the breach.
   b) For contracts, usually 6 years from breach, for sales its 4 years from breach.

Multiple Choice

REG 2-Q28

Summarize the different remedies available to a party for breach of a contract.

Identify the remedy available to a party for breach of a contract given a specific scenario.

b. Damages

Damages in a contract case are based on the underlying principle that the non-breaching party should be placed in as good a position as they would have been in, had the contract been fully performed. Different types of damages available to the parties in a contract case include:

1) *Compensatory damages* are damages that award money to compensate for any and all harm done to the non-breaching party. These are measured by looking at what was originally called for in the contract, and what was subsequently performed in the contract. The proper compensatory damage would be the difference between these two numbers. When looking at contract cases, it is important to note that rarely are punitive damages ever awarded in such breaches.

> **Example**: Bob and Steve agree to a contract valued at $10,000. Steven only pays $9,000, breaching the contract. Bob's recourse is to sue for $1,000.

2) *Specific performance* on a contract is a damage that is used when monetary damages alone would not be adequate to repay the party for the breach of a contract. This type of damage is only available in cases where the subject matter of the contract is unique. In this type of case, the non-breaching party sues the breaching party, seeking the court to enforce the terms of the contract. If the specific performance of a contract is awarded, the non-breaching party will not be entitled to receive compensatory damages also.

> **Example**: Bob contracts to buy a one of a kind car from Jeff for $1,000,000. The day before Bob is to pick up the car, Jeff sells the car to Jack for $1,500,000, in violation of the contract. Because the car is a one of a kind item, Bob can sue to enforce the terms of the original contract.

Multiple Choice

REG 2-Q29

3) *Injunction* is similar to specific performance; a party may seek an injunction as a means to obtain damages in a contract dispute. An injunction is a court order that requires one party to either do or refrain from doing a specific act. Injunctions are often awarded in situations where a temporary solution is needed to help resolve a broader problem.

> *Example*: Bob contracts to buy a one of a kind car from Jeff for $1,000,000. The day before Bob is to pick up the car, Jeff sells the car to Jack for $1,500,000, in violation of the contract. Because the car is a one of a kind item, Bob can sue to enforce the terms of the original contract. While involved in this litigation, a court may grant Bob an injunction, preventing Jeff from selling, driving, or otherwise damaging the car in question during the pendency of the litigation.

4) *Rescission* is a contract damage that is available to the parties that will restore the parties to their original positions. In this case, a court will typically determine that one or more portions of the contract are improper, and terminate the contract.

> *Example*: Bob agrees to buy Jeff's car for $1,000, with Bob giving Jeff a $500 deposit. Before completing the transaction, Bob learns that Jeff lied about the mileage on the car, and Jeff learns that Bob gave Jeff $250 instead of $500. Instead of drawn-out litigation, the court can unilaterally rescind the contract and order Jeff to return the money paid to Bob, thus returning the parties to their original position.

5) *Liquidating damages*
   i. The parties agree in advance their damages will be if there is a breach.
   ii. The damages must be reasonable to the damage done and not a penalty.

Multiple Choice

REG 2-Q30

4. Sales contracts
   a. Formation of sales contracts
      1) Sales contracts governed by Article 2 of the UCC must involve goods which are defined as moveable personal property. Article 2 Contracts do not involve personal services, real estate, or intangible personal property. In this respect, it is the item being sold, and not the goods themselves, that determines if the UCC will control the sale.

         The UCC differs from Common Law Contracts in several ways. One way is that the UCC allows for a "Firm Offer" to be made. A "Firm Offer," is an offer for the sale of goods that is irrevocable without consideration by the maker of the offeror. For a Firm Offer to be valid, three (3) elements must be met: A merchant must make the Offer, the offer must be in writing, and the writing must guarantee it will be held open. While a Firm Offer is considered to be irrevocable for a stated period of time (up to three (3) months). If no specific period of time is stated, the offer will be valid for a reasonable period of time.

         Additionally, The UCC is slightly different from Common Law Contracts when looking at the acceptance of those contracts. With UCC Contracts, Acceptance can be made by either accepting the contract verbally, or by sending the goods requested. With regards to the Mailbox Rule and the UCC, Acceptance is valid when it is sent with any reasonable means of communication (not necessarily by mail). Modification of contract under common law requires additional consideration, but not under UCC. Modifications on common law contracts require additional consideration, but not UCC contracts.

         Finally, UCC contracts differ from Common Law Contracts in that UCC Contracts allow for minor changes to be made between merchants while still having a valid acceptance. For example, if a Shoe Merchant orders 5,000 pairs of shoes that are black. The merchant, only having 2500 pairs of black shoes, sends 2500 black shoes and 2500 brown shoes, in the hopes that this fills the order. If both parties are agreeable to the brown shoes, the contract will be considered a valid contract. Conversely, the shoe Merchant may accept the 2500 black shoes, and return the 2500 brown shoes. A valid contract will exist as to the 2500 black shoes, with a breach existing for the outstanding 2500 shoes. Additionally, with a UCC Sales contract, one party may modify a contract without additional consideration. This requires that there be a writing if the modification results in a change in the contract of $500 or more, and the contract modification must be made in good faith. The term good faith means that the merchant must observe the reasonable commercial standards of fair dealing in the trade.

Multiple Choice

REG 2-Q31 through REG 2-Q32

b. Parties to a sales contract
The Seller in a Sales Contract has certain duties. Unless otherwise agreed to, the basic obligations of a seller are to hold conforming goods for the buyer and to give the buyer reasonable notification. The Seller in a UCC Contract must make a perfect tender, and if no place of delivery is stated, delivery will be at the seller's business (if practical).

A Buyer also has specific duties in a UCC transaction. In such a transaction, the buyer has the basic duty to accept conforming goods and pay for them at the time of delivery. The buyer has the right to inspect the goods before payment (except on COD Sales), and the buyer may reject goods when substantial defects occur. Finally, unless otherwise stated, the buyer can make payment by any reasonable means (including stock).

With regards to the Buyer of goods, it is important to remember that the buyer of goods has the ability to reject nonconforming goods for any nonconformity. With this rejection, the Buyer may reject all goods, or just those that are nonconforming. This rejection returns the ownership of those goods to the seller. It is important to remember that this notification must occur within a reasonable period of time and follow reasonable instructions. Finally, when looking at nonconforming goods, it is important to remember that the seller as a right to cure by notifying the buyer that the issue will be corrected prior to delivery.

Parties to a contract may anticipatorily breach a contract when one party states that they will not be performing prior to the time of performance. In these cases, the non-breaching party may either sue immediately or wait until performance should have occurred and then sue.

When a case arises where one party to a UCC Contract has concerns over another party's ability to perform on a contract, the concerned party may demand written assurances of performance. Either the buyer or the seller may demand written assurance when there are reasonable grounds to do so. If the written assurances are not received within a reasonable time, they are released from the contract.

c. The Statue of Frauds and the UCC
The Statute of Frauds requires that the sale of goods valued at over $500 must be in writing. The writing must include all aspects required of a writing in a common law contract, as well as, include the quantity ordered.

Exceptions to the Statute of Frauds in a UCC Contract include:
  i. Specially manufactured goods;
  ii. Payment of goods or receipt of goods;
  iii. Admissions in Court; and
  iv. Merchants confirming letters.

Multiple Choice

REG 2-Q33 through REG 2-Q34

d. Risk of Loss and Title for UCC Contracts
1) The concept of risk of loss and title in UCC Contracts looks at the point in time when the title (ownership) to the goods passes from the seller to the buyer, as well as when the risk of losing those same goods passes from one party to the other. While title and risk of loss often transfer at the same time, this is not always the case.

    The first step in determining who has a risk of loss and title to the goods, the goods must be identified. For example, if a buyer purchased 10,000 iPads from Apple before those iPads have to be identified in the Apple Warehouse as being "Buyers iPads." This is typically done by marking or otherwise tagging the good for a specific buyer. Once these goods have been identified to the contract, both the title and risk of loss transfers to the buyer.

e. Risk of loss and common carriers
A "Common Carrier" is a carrier of multiple types of goods (i.e., a boat or airplane). When looking at Risk of Loss and dealing with common carriers, the individual has to determine if the contract is a "Shipment Contract," or a "Destination Contract." A Shipment Contract is a contract that calls for the risk of loss of the goods, as well as title to those goods to pass to the buyer when the seller gets the goods in question to the carrier. For example, in this type of contract, once the seller placed the goods on the boat for shipping, title and risk of loss passes from the seller to the buyer. In contrast, a destination contract calls for title and risk of loss to pass from the seller to the buyer once the goods have gotten to their destination.

The concept of title and risk of loss, along with identifying who has title and risk of loss, it is important to understand that all goods can be insured. Therefore, it is important to know when the buyer and the seller have an insurable interest in the goods. Traditionally, and unless otherwise agreed, the buyer will have an insurable interest in the goods when those goods are identified. Furthermore, the seller has an insurable interest in the good when the seller has any risk of economic loss of their goods. As such, it is possible for both the buyer and the seller of goods to have an insurable interest in goods at the same time.

Finally, when looking at shipping and destination contracts, key terms include:
1) F.O.B. is the term for "Free on Board" and specifically fixes a time and place to where the risk of loss and title pass from the buyer to the seller. For example, the phrase "FOB seller's loading dock" means that the contract is a shipment contract and the buyer has title and risk of loss in the goods once the seller has placed them on their loading dock. In contrast, "FOB buyer's loading dock" defines a destination contract where the risk of loss goes from the seller to the buyer once the seller has placed the goods at the buyers loading dock.

Multiple Choice

REG 2-Q35 through REG 2-Q36

2) "CIF" means that the price of the sale includes the **cost** of the goods, **insurance** on the goods, and **freight** for shipping the goods.

3) "Sale on Approval" is where the buyer acquires goods and can determine whether they want to return them or keep them. During the period when the buyer is contemplating whether to return or keep the goods, the question is -- who has title or risk of loss during this time frame? During this period, the seller has title and risk of loss until the buyer approves. In contrast, with "Sale or Return," during the time that the buyer will decide whether to keep

the goods, or return the goods, again -- who has title or risk of loss during this time frame? During this period, the buyer gets the risk of loss and title, but the buyer may return the goods. A sale or return is generally a conditional sale, where the buyer is buying the goods for resale, which means that the buyer is a merchant. Merchant sellers are always held to a higher standard than non-merchant sellers. In a sale on approval, the buyer is purchasing the goods for his or her own use and is not a merchant. Therefore, the merchant seller has the title and risk of loss during the time frame when the buyer is deciding whether to return or keep the goods.

Multiple Choice

REG 2-Q37

f. Warranties and UCC contracts
Warranties in UCC Contracts fall into one of two categories, implied warranties and express warranties:

1) **Implied warranties** are warranties that require no words, either oral or written. These warranties can be disclaimed, but the disclaiming of the warranties must be specific and conspicuous. One example of an implied warranty is the implied warranty of merchantability. In this type of implied warranty, a merchant promises, without saying as such, that their goods are fit and safe for normal use.

2) **Implied warranties of title** are warranties given specifically to goods to help guarantee the owner of those goods. Title warranties include the promise of good title, which all sellers give, a warranty against encumbrances, where all sellers promise no unstated liens or attachments, and a warranty against infringements occur when a merchant seller promises that no patent or trademark violations occur.

   When looking at title, typically, the title the buyer of the goods gets cannot be a "better" title than the seller has to give. The only exception to this rule occurs when the rightful owner leaves goods with a merchant who sells them in error. In this case, the innocent buyer will receive "good" title from a seller who did not have title to the goods.

3) The **implied warranty of fitness** for a particular purpose. Buyer is relying on seller's expert opinion and the seller must know the purpose of the purchase.

4) Disclaimers of implied warranties:
   i. Merchantability – Goods are sold as is, or I disclaim the implied warranty of merchantability. It may be oral or written.
   ii. Title – Must state, I do not guarantee that I have title. It may be oral or written.
   iii. Fitness for a particular purpose - Goods are sold as is, or I disclaim the implied warranty of fitness for a particular purpose. It must be in writing.

5) **Express warranties** are warranties that a buyer receives from a seller, and typically include a material representation of a fact, or facts, regarding the goods being sold. A breach of these warranties is grounds for litigation. When looking at warranties, it is important to remember that opinions and statements of value are not considered an express warranty, unless an expert makes them. Finally, it is important to remember that when looking at express warranties, the warranty has to be part of the basis of the bargain.

Multiple Choice

REG 2-Q38 through REG 2-Q39

g. Breach of UCC Contracts
   1) Remedies of a Seller
      In a UCC Contract, the seller has several remedies if the buyer breaches a contract.
      i. The Seller may resell the goods and sue for damages, including charging the buyer for any loss, including expenses, lost profits and storage fees (but not punitive damages).
      ii. The Seller may rescind the contract and sue for damages; or
      iii. If the buyer becomes insolvent in a credit sale, the seller may stop delivery and demand a cash payment.

   2) Remedies of a Buyer
      i. In sales, a buyer can rescind (cancel) and sue for monetary damages. The buyer may recover from any loss, but may not collect punitive damages. When following this path, the buyer must give reasonable notice of cancellation.
      ii. The buyer may cover. In this scenario, the buyer obtains suitable goods elsewhere and charges seller for any loss.
      iii. The buyer may recover goods from the seller if the buyer has prepaid and the goods are identified.

Multiple Choice

REG 2-Q40 through REG 2-Q41

When considering specific performance in a UCC Contract, it is important to remember that specific performance may be used if the goods are unique or if the buyer cannot cover.

h. Statute of Limitations
   When looking to litigate a UCC Contract, it is vital to remember that a UCC suit must be brought within four (4) years of the breach. By agreement, this limitation can be lowered to 1 year, but cannot be extended beyond four (4) years.

i. Who can Sue Whom?
   1) Traditionally, only the original buyer can sue the original seller in contract. Under the UCC, not only can the original buyer and seller engage in litigation, users and those reasonable individuals affected by a product, may sue for damages if the product harms them. For example, if a car has a faulty part, hits and kills someone, the estate of the deceased individual (who is not a party to the ownership of the contract) can sue the manufacturer of the car.

   2) Individuals injured by negligent sellers may also sue. To prove negligence, four elements must be proven:

4 Elements of Negligence	
Duty of care	The seller owes the buyer a duty of due care
Breach	The seller failed to use reasonable care
Damages	The buyer suffered damages
Causality	The seller's breach caused the buyer's damages

3) Individuals harmed by a product can also sue makers of defective products under strict liability if they can show the following five (5) elements.

Defective products cause unreasonably dangerous business changes	
Defective products	Must show a Defective product
Cause	Must show the defect Caused injury
Unreasonably dangerous	Must show the defect was Unreasonably dangerous to users and consumers
Business	Must show seller was engaged in that Business
Changes	Must show it reached the user without substantial Changes

C. Debtor-Creditor Relationships
1. Rights, duties, and liabilities of debtors, creditors, and guarantors

> **Explain the rights, duties, and liabilities of debtors, creditors, and guarantors.**

> **Identify the rights, duties or liabilities of a debtors, creditors or guarantors given a specific scenario.**

a. <u>Surety relationships</u>

Surety relationships occur when one party, the Surety, promises to pay a creditor the amount owed by the debtor who defaults on a debt. Under the Statute of Frauds, the promise by the Surety must be in writing, signed by the Surety for the promise to be enforceable. When examining these relationships, it is important to know and understand whether additional consideration is to be paid to the Surety.

Certain bonds are an obligation of a Surety. An example would be an official bond. An official bond is where the surety (guarantor) guarantees that a public official will do their job. A surety does not guarantee that convertible bonds, debenture bonds and municipal bonds will be paid. Therefore, these bonds are not obligations of the Surety.

1) Consideration is found if the surety, creditor, and debtor are all created at the same time.

> ***Example***: Bill agrees to be a co-signer on a car loan for Betty at the time that Betty purchases the car from Lou's car dealership. As the surety relationship is created at the time of the original loan, consideration is present.

2) If the Surety comes in after the debtor/creditor relationship is created, additional consideration to the Surety is needed.

> ***Example***: Betty and Lou car dealership sign and contract whereby Betty purchases a car. Six months later, Betty got nervous and decided to ask Bill to guarantee the loan. To solidify this relationship, Betty pays Bill $500 to acts as a guarantor. This $500 represents the consideration needed to create this surety relationship.

3) Once created, Surety's have certain rights. These rights include:
   i. Right of Subrogation – this right ensures that after a Surety pays the debt to the creditor in full, the Surety obtains all of Creditor's rights.
   ii. Rights of Reimbursement – the Surety has the right to recover from the Debtor, all money that the Surety had to pay to the Creditor after the Debtor defaulted on the loan.
   iii. Right of Exoneration – prior to the Debtor defaulting on a debt, a Surety can obtain a court order that allows for the debtor to pay the debt. While the Surety will still be required to pay in the event of default, this court order helps establish that this is truly the debt of the debtor.

Multiple Choice

> **REG 2-Q42**

4) In addition to having situations where one surety exists, it is also possible to have "co-sureties". This occurs when two or more sureties of the same debt exist. In the case where co-suretors exist, there is a right of contribution from each co-suretor. This allows for each co-suretor to receive a pro rata share of the overall debt from each of their other co-suretors.

> **Example**: If there are three co-suretors acting as surety for a $10,000 debt, and co-surety 1 pays the entire debt, co-surety 1 has the right to go to each of the other co-suretors to seek a portion of the debt as repayment (i.e., each party would end up paying $3,333.33).

Multiple Choice
REG 2-Q43

Some exceptions to this general rule exist if a co-surety only agrees to act as a co-surety for a specific amount of the debt. For example, one surety could guarantee $9,000 of a $10,000 debt, while a second surety guarantees the remaining $1,000. In this example, the co-suretors are only liable for the amount they have specifically guaranteed. Finally, if a co-surety's obligation is discharged in a bankruptcy proceeding, their dollar amount should not be considered in determining the pro rate share of the other co-suretors.

b. Rights of creditors after a default
Creditors have specific rights once the original debtor has defaulted on a payment obligation. These include:
1) Immediately demanding payment of the debt from the Surety;
2) Immediately demanding payment of the debt from the Debtor; or
3) Immediately attempting to possess any collateral that exists that was used to help secure the loan.

One major exception to these rights exists. That is, when the surety is acting only as a guarantor of collection or a conditional guarantor. This is a circumstance where the surety has promised only to pay after the Creditor has exhausted all possible remedies against the Debtor. As such, a Creditor will have to turn to the Debtor first before attempting to collect the debt form the Surety.

Multiple Choice
REG 2-Q44

A Creditor can enforce the remedies identified above in a variety of ways. These include the Creditor using the following actions to collect a debt owed to them:

1) Creditor pre-judgment remedies
These are actions taken by a Creditor before receiving a judgment and include obtaining an attachment or a pre-judgment garnishment. Attachment is the process of attaching a lien to a Debtor's property so that it remains available to the Creditor if the Creditor obtains a judgment. In contrast, a Pre-Judgment Garnishment places specific property or money in the hands of a third party to hold if a judgment is obtained. Both of these methods involve going to court prior to receiving a judgment and having a judge agree to the prejudgment remedy.

2) Creditor post-judgment remedies
These remedies are available to the Creditor only after an original judgment is obtained, and include a Writ of Execution and a Garnishment. A Writ of Execution is a formal demand, served by a sheriff demanding payment of a judgment, and informing the Debtor that if the judgment is not paid, the Creditor may take the Debtor's property and force a public sale of the property to enforce the judgment. In contrast, a garnishment occurs when a Creditor can collect money from Debtor's wages or bank accounts as a way to satisfy the judgment.

3) Fraudulent conveyances
These are conveyances of property by the Debtor to a third party to attempt to keep the property from a Creditor. Because the property is conveyed for no purpose except to keep it

from the Creditor, it is considered by the court to be a "phony" transfer. In these events, the Creditor may still attach the property to the debt if they can show that the transfer was fraudulent and done to hide the property of the debtor. In determining if the conveyance was fraudulent, it is important to consider the following items:
  i. Does the Debtor remain in possession of the property? If so, the conveyance is likely fraudulent;
  ii. Does the Debtor retain an equitable interest in the property? If so, the conveyance is likely fraudulent; or
  iii. Was the transfer done in secret? If so, the conveyance is likely fraudulent.

c. Defenses of a Surety vs. a Creditor
If a Creditor attempts to sue a Surety for payment of a debt, the Surety has several options to defend themselves. These include:

1) Lack of a writing or consideration
In this case, the Surety argues that the relationship between the Creditor and the Surety is non-existent as it was never properly formed.

2) Payment or tender of performance by the Debtor
In this case, the Surety argues that the Creditor needs to seek the payment initially from the Debtor, or conversely, that the Debtor has paid the debt, making the Surety not liable for the debt.

3) Fraud by the Creditor
In this case, the Surety argues that the debt is invalid due to some type of fraud that the Creditor has committed upon either the Debtor or the Surety.

> *Hint*: When looking at possible defenses, it is important to remember that the Surety is not able to use defenses that are personal to the Debtor such as infancy, insanity, or bankruptcy. This is because these are defenses that are more appropriately used by the Debtor to attempt to remove/resolve the debt.

4) Actions by the Creditor that increase the risk of a Surety, release the Surety to the extent of the increased risk. As such, a Surety could defend themselves by arguing that they are not liable for an increased amount, as it was above what the Surety originally agreed to act for. Examples of when this would occur include:
  i. A binding extension of time by the Creditor will release the Surety, as they were not involved with this decision-making process. However, a simple delay by the Creditor will not release the Surety.
  ii. A release of one Co-surety by a Creditor without the consent of the other Co-sureties, increases the risk of other Co-sureties and is not permitted without the permission of the Co-sureties. For example, if Sam and Betty were "co-sureties" on a $1,000,000 loan. Technically the bank that holds the note cannot release Sam from the loan while keeping Betty solely liable without Sam's permission. If for some reason this was done, Sam's liability increases dramatically.
  iii. If a Creditor releases a Debtor without reserving rights against the Surety, the Surety will be released.

Multiple Choice

REG 2-Q45

d. Defenses/Debt Collection Relief for Debtors
A Debtor has several options available to them if they are subject to significant debts. These options include:

1) Composition of Creditors is a situation where Debtors and Creditors agree to discharge the debt of a Debtor in exchange for partial payment of the debt by the Debtor. These debts are only discharged when the Debtor completes all partial payments and is only enforceable against those Creditors who are parties to the agreement. This is often done as a way for both parties to limit risks and costs associated with potential litigation in these matters.

2) Assignment for the Benefit of Creditors
This type of debt collection relief transfers property to a third party for the sole purpose of using that property to pay creditors on a pro rata basis. This is done to help protect the property that has been assigned to the third party to help pay the debts from being attached by other creditors, as well as a way to easily resolve several outstanding debts at one time.

3) Fair Debt Collection Practices Act
This law forces a Creditor into collecting judgments against a Debtor in very specific manners. The law prohibits abusive, deceptive, and unfair debt collection practices by collection agencies including:
   i. Disclosing the debt to 3rd parties
   ii. Communicating with debtor at unreasonable times
   iii. Communicating with the debtor if (s)he has an attorney
   iv. Use of harassing, oppressive or abusive conduct or false representations.

A failure to abide by these laws will allow for a Debtor to sue for money damages, effectively lowering the amount of the debt owed to the Creditor.

4) Exempt Property
It is important for Debtors to remember that certain types of property are exempt from attachment or garnishment by a Creditor. These include:
   i. The Homestead Exemption which protects the equity that a Debtor has in their primary residence.
   ii. Social Security Benefits are exempt from attachment or garnishment.

Multiple Choice

REG 2-Q46

2. Bankruptcy and insolvency

CPA Exam
Blueprint
Representative Task

| Explain the rights of debtors and creditors in bankruptcy and insolvency. |

| Summarize the rules related to different types of bankruptcy. |

| Explain discharge of indebtedness in bankruptcy. |

| Identify the rights of the debtors and creditors in bankruptcy and insolvency given a specific scenario. |

| Identify the type of bankruptcy described in a specific scenario. |

a. Bankruptcy
Bankruptcy is governed almost exclusively by Federal law and is the process by which creditor's rights are protected, while at the same time providing relief to the debtor from their indebtedness. Bankruptcy laws are designed to provide the debtor with the ability to obtain a new start, and one that is free from prior debts. These laws provide the creditors with a process to be treated fairly and equitably in receiving repayment of their respective debts.

The process by which debts are paid in Bankruptcy law is by examining the "priority" of a particular debt as compared to other debts that the debtor may have:
1) Debts with a higher "priority" will be paid first.
2) This process ensures that debts are paid in an equitable manner.

The bankruptcy process typically occurs in one of two forms. A voluntary bankruptcy occurs when the debtor files for bankruptcy to seek relief from their debts. In contrast, Involuntary Bankruptcy occurs when one or more creditors of the debtor force the debtor into bankruptcy proceedings.

b. Chapter 7 Bankruptcy – Liquidation
1) General overview
A Chapter 7 Bankruptcy proceeding is the most common form of bankruptcy for companies. This form of bankruptcy is often referred to as "liquidation" or "straight bankruptcy", as it involves the process of turning a debtor's assets into cash to pay creditors. Once all assets have been liquidated, and either all debts have been paid, or the debtor has no additional assets to pay his creditors, the remaining debts are discharged. Virtually all debtors can file for Chapter 7 Bankruptcy, with the only exceptions being;
   i. Banking institutions;
   ii. Insurance companies;
   iii. Railroads;
   iv. Savings and loan associations;
   v. Credit Unions;
   vi. Health Maintenance Organizations (HMO's).

2) Filing for Chapter 7 Bankruptcy Protection
   i. Voluntary Petition
   The filing of a voluntary petition occurs when the debtor makes a formal request for relief. The debtor files a petition with the court identifying all assets and liabilities. Once this petition is filed, the debtor is provided with a "stay" (a court order halting all collection activity by the creditors) pending resolution of the bankruptcy proceedings. Finally, the court reviews the bankruptcy filing to ensure that the petitioner is not attempting to use bankruptcy laws to avoid paying debts that they can afford to pay. Once the case has been filed in court, the court will determine if the debtor meets state prescribed income limits for bankruptcy filings, along with circumstances, such as

medical issues, to determine if debtor meets income requirements for bankruptcy protection. If the debtor fails to meet the requirements for a Chapter 7 bankruptcy filing, the debtor may refile under Chapter 13. It is important to note that when individuals are filing for bankruptcy, the bankruptcy petition is filed jointly between spouses, and that no minimum number of creditors is required to file for voluntary bankruptcy protection.

ii. Involuntary Petition

The filing of an involuntary petition for a Chapter 7 bankruptcy is made by the creditors of a debtor requesting that the court intervene and provide relief. To file an involuntary petition, creditors must meet one of the following requirements:

- If less than twelve (12) creditors exist, any single creditor who is owed more than $15,325 in <u>unsecured debt</u> may file a petition. In contrast, if more than twelve (12) creditors exist, at least three of the unsecured creditors must join in the filing to meet the $15,325 amount needed to file an involuntary petition.

   > *Example*: Better Choices, Inc. (a company) is not paying its debts. Better Choices has three creditors. Creditor A is owed $25,000, Creditor B is owed $10,000, and Creditor C is owed $2,500. Creditor A can force Better Choices into bankruptcy; however, neither Creditors B nor C has the ability to do so, because B and C together are only owed $12,500 in unsecured claims. They would have to be owed $15,325 in unsecured claims to file a petition for involuntary bankruptcy.

   > *Example:* Bad Choices, Inc. is unable to meet its obligation due to making some inappropriate business decisions. They have 12 different creditors, which are owed a total of $30,000. Shady is one of the 12 creditors and is owed $20,000. Shady alone cannot force Bad Choices into Bankruptcy as there are 12 creditors. To force a bankruptcy, Shady will have to join with two other creditors to file a joint petition.

- There must be no dispute over the amount owed on the debt for the debt to qualify towards the $15,325 requirement.

   > *Example:* Bubba, Inc. is overdue on payments owed to its two creditors, Shrimp and Bait. Bubba is not paying his debts as they come due. Bubba is under the impression it owes Shrimp $13,000, but Shrimp insists that Bubba owes $19,000. Bubba agrees that the $5,000 is outstanding and overdue to Shrimp. Bubba agrees that the $13,000 is outstanding and overdue to Bait. The court will only look at the $5,000 and the $13,000 as the amounts toward the $15,325 requirement because those amounts are not in dispute. Shrimp is not able to force Bubba into bankruptcy alone, since the $5,000 overdue amount is below the $15,325 requirement. Therefore, to force Bubba into bankruptcy, both Shrimp and Bait must sign the petition, because both of the debts that were agreed owed to them by Bubba of $18,000 are greater than the $15,325 requirement.

Once filed, creditors who file for involuntary bankruptcy may need to indemnify the debtor for losses involving a frivolous filing. Furthermore, after the filing has been completed, the court will issue an order for relief as long as the requirements for filing are met, along with an order stating either of the following:
a) The petition is not being contested; or
b) In the case where the debtor is contesting the petition, a court hearing will occur, and where the creditors must show that the debtor is not paying its debts as they come due.

iii. Process after Filing

Upon filing either a voluntary petition or involuntary petition, a Court order of relief is granted; the Court will appoint an interim trustee. The trustee is the person appointed by the court who is responsible for collecting the debtor's available assets and liquidating all property into cash for distribution to the creditors. The interim trustee is responsible for beginning the process of organizing the debtor's assets, and arranging for the first meeting of all creditors. At this initial meeting:
- Debtor provides a list of all assets and creditors;
- Creditors have six (6) months from the initial creditors meeting to file a claim;
- Value of all claims are estimated; and
- Trustee is elected by the Creditors.

Once a permanent trustee has been appointed, the trustee has the following rights and responsibilities.
- to be compensated for work as trustee;
- to represent the debtor in the liquidation of debtor's assets;
- the authority to take legal action to carry out duties of the trustee;
- the authority to employ professionals, as reasonably necessary to carry out tasks;
- to timely notify debtor of actions taking place with the estate;
- to (within 60 days of the order for relief) assume or reject contracts, including leases, made by the debtor;
- the authority to set aside any transfers made within one year before the filing of the bankruptcy if the transfer was done to hinder, delay, or defraud a creditor, or the debtor received less than reasonable value for the transfer;
- the authority to set aside preferential transfers of property made within ninety (90) days of the filing for bankruptcy. These transfers include transfers made for preexisting debts, or debts that if paid, enable the creditor to receive more than they would have received under a Chapter 7 filing.

After the initial creditors meeting, the trustee begins the process of liquidating and distributing the estate to pay all debts of the debtor. Property that can be included in the sale to pay creditors includes:
- Property currently owned by the debtor;
- Property that is owned by one or more other parties that can be obtained by the trustee;
- Property obtained by the debtor after the filing date if the property is received by the debtor within 180 days of filing for Bankruptcy protection and is either an inheritance, life insurance, or a property settlement with a spouse, or income from property owned by the debtor that is obtained after the filing for bankruptcy protection.

While most properties can be liquidated in a bankruptcy proceeding, certain properties are exempt from the liquidation process. These properties include:
- Interest in property owned in joint tenancy (if those interests remain exempt under state law);
- Equity in the individual's principal residence (capped at $23,675);
- Equity in one motor vehicle (capped at $3,775);
- $2,375 in books and/or tools used in the debtor's trade;
- Up to $12,625 in personal family items;
- $1,600 in jewelry;
- Life insurance interest and dividends;
- Unmatured life insurance contracts;
- Social security benefits;
- Unemployment compensation;
- Disability, or unemployment benefits;
- Alimony and child support payments;
- Veteran's benefits;
- Prescribed health aide;
- Public Assistance;
- Pensions and retirement benefits;
- Payments for lost earnings;
- Wrongful death payments;
- 75% of the debtor's personal income;
- Crime victims' compensation; and
- Personal injury awards upon $23,675

iv. Property included in debtor's estate
   a) *Property as of filing date goes to trustee for creditors (includes proceeds gained after filing).*
      - Social security and disability benefits are exempt.
      - Things necessary to live are exempt (e.g., house, car, furniture, etc.).
   b) *Debtor keeps most property gained after filing – **3 exceptions**: property gained within 180 days after filing by **divorce, inheritance or by insurance** goes to trustee.*
   c) *With leases, the trustee can accept or reject (if no action in 60 days they are rejected).*

v. Avoiding Powers of Trustees
   Trustee can avoid or disaffirm payments on property transfers done by debtor prior to filing.

Preferential Transfers can be avoided (preferring 1 creditor over others). To disaffirm the prior payment, 5 tests must be met **(TANIM):**

T	Must have a **Transfer** of property that benefits a creditor
A	Transfer must have been for an **Antecedent debt** - an existing overdue debt • New debts are not antecedent debts (a contemporaneous exchange for new value) • Secured debts are not antecedent debts - can't prepay • Paying current bills in the ordinary course of business aren't antecedent debts - can't prepay • Consumer debts of $650 or less are not antecedent debts
N	Transfer must have been made within **Ninety days** of the filing date • May be up to 1 year prior to filing if creditor was an insider
I	Transfer must have been made while debtor was **Insolvent** • Insolvency is normally presumed if the transfer was made within 90
M	Creditor received **More** than (s)he would have received in bankruptcy

Fraudulent Conveyances are a phony transfer by Debtor to hide property from creditors.
   c) Trustee can disaffirm if within 1 year of filing.
   b) Done secretly, Debtor retains equitable title and usually remains in possession.

3) Types of claims
   If a creditor has a property right in a piece of property held by the debtor, the property is turned over to the creditor, as it is not considered part of the debtor's estate.

> **Example**: If Bob rents a moving truck for 1 week, and filed for bankruptcy protection during the 1-week period, the moving truck will be returned to the rental company and not considered part of Bob's estate.

A trust claim is made by a beneficiary for trust property, that property is not considered part of the debtor's estate.

> **Example**: For a trust that is part of a will, Tim is the trustee of a trust account of Madelyn. If Tim files for bankruptcy, Madelyn's trust account will not be considered part of Tim's estate, and Madelyn is allowed to subsequently claim the trust account as her own property.

Secured claims are claims that are held by a creditor who has an interest in a specific piece of property.

> **Example**: Bank X loans Steve money to purchase a car. Bank X will take a security interest in the car to ensure repayment of the loan.

Claims will be allowed if they are timely filed and are not objected to by the creditor. These claims may be objected to if:
   o The debt has not matured as of the date of filing for bankruptcy;
   o The claim is not enforceable by law;
   o A claim for unpaid property tax that is greater than the value of the property;
   o Attorney claims in excess of what is considered reasonable;

- Alimony or other support claims made for amounts that are not yet due;
- Employment tax claims;
- Landlord damages for lease terminations;
- Damages associated with the termination of an employment contract that exceed one (1) year's salary.

i. Priority of Claims for Payment
   a) Secured Creditors
   Secured creditors are creditors who have attached a specific piece of property held by the debtor in exchange for something of value (typically the money used to purchase that property). <u>Secured creditors' claims must be satisfied prior to liquidating assets for payment to other creditors.</u>

   If the value of the property held by the secured creditor is greater than the amount owed to the creditor, the money left over is used to satisfy other creditors.

   > **Example:** If Bank X has a secured interest in the car owned by Bob. The car loan has $1500 outstanding at the time that Bob files for bankruptcy. If Bank X sells the car for $5000, the Bank will keep $1500, and return the remaining $3500 to the estate to satisfy other creditors.

   If the property held by the secured creditor is valued at less than the amount owed to the creditor, the balance on the amount owed is treated as an unsecured debt.

   > **Example:** If Bank X has a secured interest in the car owned by Bob. The car loan has $1500 outstanding at the time that Bob files for bankruptcy. If Bank X sells the car for $500, the outstanding $1000 owed to the Bank will be treated as an unsecured debt.

   b) Unsecured Creditors
   Unsecured claims are paid in full at each level of priority before any claims at a lower level are paid. If funds are non-existent to pay all claims at a particular level of priority, then the payments are prorated to provide all creditors at that level with a portion of their debt owed, and claims at a lower level are not paid. Claims are paid in the following priority:
   - Support obligations such as child support and alimony.
   - Fees owed to accountants, attorneys, and other professionals involved in the administration of the bankruptcy.
   - Claims from the debtor's business after the bankruptcy petition is filed but before the order for relief is entered.
   - Wages, salaries, and commissions to debtor's employees that were earned within 90 days prior to the filing of the petition and the maximum amount per employee is $12,475.
   - Payments owed to employee benefit plans due and payable within 180 days prior to filing for bankruptcy, up to a maximum amount of $12,475 per employee.
   - Consumer deposits for undelivered goods or services.
   - Taxes.
   - Obligations owed to an insured bank.
   - Debts from motor vehicle accidents while under the influence of drugs or alcohol.
   - Miscellaneous unsecured creditors that were timely filed.

ii. Discharge
Discharge occurs when the debtor is released from paying any remaining unpaid debts during bankruptcy. This occurs when all assets have been liquidated, and payments to creditors have been made. All outstanding, remaining, debts (either fully or partially) are not paid since there are no funds left to pay them. In this process, creditors who do not receive payment cannot attempt to further collect the debt from a debtor who has had their debt discharged. Business organizations must have all assets liquidated before being discharged; however, once discharged, the individual can obtain a new financial start. This type of discharge can occur once every eight (8) years for consumer cases only.

iii. Debts that Cannot be Discharged
- Taxes within three years of filing for bankruptcy;
- Loans associated with the payment of federal taxes;
- Unscheduled debts;
- Alimony or child support;
- Liabilities associated with theft or embezzlement;
- Debts associated with fraud;
- Debts associated with intentional torts;
- Government guaranteed student loans;
- Government fines incurred within the previous three (3) years;
- Consumer debt associated with luxury goods
- Debt incurred from a violation of Sarbanes-Oxley Act laws, or other securities laws;
- Debts owed to pension plans; and
- Homeowners Association fees.

c. Chapter 11 Bankruptcy – Reorganization
1) General Overview
A Chapter 11 bankruptcy is a form of bankruptcy that permits the reorganization of debt, as opposed to the selling, or liquidation of assets to pay off the debts of the debtor. This form of bankruptcy allows for the creditors and the debtors to negotiate on discharging a portion of the debtor's debt, while the debtor agrees to a plan for paying the balance. This type of bankruptcy is most commonly used by Corporations, as they are allowed to stay in business while the Corporation resolves its debt issues, exceptions to corporations permitted to use this form of bankruptcy include:
i. Stockbrokers;
ii. Commodities brokers;
iii. Banks;
iv. Savings and loan companies.

This form of bankruptcy is seen as valuable as it permits the debtor to stay in business and pay off a smaller portion of their debt, while at the same time permitting the creditor to obtain greater value on the debt owned then would be gained through a liquidation process.

2) Filing for Chapter 11 Bankruptcy
i. Voluntary filings are filings initiated by individuals, partnerships, corporations, or other groups not eligible for filing under Chapter 7.
ii. Involuntary Filings are filings that are forced upon the debtor by the creditor. These filings are completed in the same manner as they are done in a Chapter 7 filing.

3) Process After Filing
The process for filing a Chapter 11 bankruptcy filing is similar to Chapter 7 bankruptcy proceedings, with the exception that the goal of a Chapter 11 bankruptcy is to reorganize

the debt of an entity to allow the company to continue operating, while paying off debts (no complete liquidation of assets). In a Chapter 11 bankruptcy filing, creditors form a committee to review the debtor's financial affairs. The committee determines if the debtor is able to continue operating, if new leadership is needed to run the business (if applicable), and create a reorganization plan to provide for payment of all or a part of the debtor's debts, while continuing to operate and eventually return to profitability. These plans typically involve creditors accepting reduced amounts on original debt, as well as, often requiring preferred shareholders to convert their stock to common stock, and have common shareholder reduce or forfeit their stock.

Final reorganizational plans need to be approved by a 51% majority of all the members who hold at least 2/3 of the total debt, and a 51% approval of all stockholders holding 2/3 of the stock in the company. Final approval rests with the court. Upon approval of the final plan, the debtor is discharged of all outstanding debts, except for those agreed to in the reorganization plan.

Filing under Chapter 7 or 11 acts as an **Automatic Stay** and **stops all collection efforts**.
- **Exception**: an automatic stay doesn't stop alimony and child support payments.

d. Chapter 13 Bankruptcy – Individual Repayment Plans (Wage Earner's Plan)
   1) General Overview
      Chapter 13 bankruptcies permit for the reorganization of debts by individuals. Corporations and Partnerships are *not* permitted to utilize Chapter 13 process. To be eligible for a Chapter 13 bankruptcy filing, individuals must have a regular income and have less than $383,175 in unsecured debt and $1,149,525 in secured debt. A Chapter 13 bankruptcy is a form of bankruptcy that creates a payment plan (typically between 36-60 months) for the repayment of debt. To this end, Chapter 13 is typically seen as a more cost-effective process for individuals, as opposed to Chapter 11.

   2) Voluntary vs. Involuntary Chapter 13 Bankruptcy Filings
      Chapter 13 filings are always voluntarily made by the debtor.

   3) Process After Filing
      After filing for bankruptcy protection, collection efforts are stayed, and the debtor has the exclusive right to create a plan for repayment of all debts. If the debtor fails to create a plan, creditors can move to force the debtor into a Chapter 7 Bankruptcy filing. Once agreed to by the creditors, the repayment plan must be approved by the court which appoints a trustee to oversee the execution of the approved plan.
      i. Any plan submitted by the debtor must allow unsecured creditors to obtain at least as much as they would have under a Chapter 7 filing.
      ii. If the plan provides for creditors not to be paid in full, the plan must account for payments to creditors for at least three (3) years.

      Once the plan is completed (i.e., all payments under the plan have been made), the debtor is discharged from outstanding debt.

      A family farmer, with regular annual income, may file a voluntary petition for bankruptcy under Chapter 7 (liquidation), 11 (business reorganization) and 13 (individual reorganization). Chapter 9 of the U.S. bankruptcy code is available exclusively to municipal governments, to assist them in the restructuring of their debts.

Multiple Choice

REG 2-Q47 through REG 2-Q51

3. Secured transactions

Explain how property can serve as collateral in secured transactions.

a. **Secured Transactions** are those transactions where the payment of a debt is guaranteed by the personal property owned by the debtor. Secured Transactions are often considered a "safer" transaction for the Creditor, as their investment has been protected, or secured, by some property, protecting the Creditor. Two key terms to consider when looking at secured transactions include Purchase Money Security Interests (PMSI) and After-Acquired Property Clauses.

1) Purchase Money Security Interest Creditors (PMSI) are Creditors who advance funds on the basis of credit to enable the debtor to buy the collateral used to secure the loan. The creditor immediately takes a security interest in the collateral that is purchased with the money. Often, the PMSI is sufficient to give the Creditor the highest priority in claiming the property in the event of a default.

> ***Example:*** Tom obtains a loan from Bank of Allegany to purchase a car. The Bank loans Tom the money to purchase the car, and in exchange takes a security interest in the car to secure the loan. Bank of Allegany has a PMSI in the car.

2) Non-Purchase Money Security Interest Creditor is a Creditor who takes collateral in exchange for advancing funds; however, the collateral taken is not the property for which the funds are used to purchase.

> ***Example:*** Claire wants to purchase a new car. To obtain a loan for the car, Claire goes to the Bank of Smithtown. To secure the loan, the Bank of Smithburg uses, as collateral, Claire's beach house. Since the loan is secured by property that Claire already owns, the Bank of Smithburg has a Non-Purchase Money security interest.

3) After-Acquired Property Clauses occur when Creditors has collateral property that is to be acquired by a debtor at a later date. It is used most often when the collateral is inventory and equipment.

> ***Example:*** Steven is the owner of a clothing store. To help Steven fund the business, Steven gets a loan from Bank of Cool to help purchase inventory. Over the next few months Steven purchases inventory for the store. Once the clothes are purchased, the Bank of Cool takes a security interest in the clothes.

Explain the requirements needed to create and perfect a security interest.

Identify whether a creditor has created and perfected a security interest given a specific scenario.

b. Attachment and Perfection of Security Interests
To fully protect a Creditor's security interest in property of a Debtor, the Creditor has to both attach the Creditors rights to the Debt and Perfect their interest in the collateral.

Attachment is the formal process of placing a claim on a piece of property owned by the Debtor, in exchange for credit. To formally attach, three elements must be met.

There must be an **Agreement** between the Creditor and Debtor. The agreement must be in writing and be signed by the debtor, but it can be oral if the creditor takes possession with debtor's agreement (pledge).

1) There must be **Value** placed on the property given by the Creditor; and
2) The **Debtor must have rights** in the collateral.

> *Example*: Claire wants to purchase a new car. To obtain a loan for the car, Claire goes to the Bank of Smithtown. To secure the loan, the Bank of Smithburg uses, as collateral, Claire's beach house. Claire and the Bank sign an agreement whereby the Bank loans Claire money and the Bank takes an interest in the beach house. Since there is an Agreement (the contract between the bank and Claire), Value (the Beach House has a value), and the debtor has rights in the collateral (Claire owns the Beach House). There is proper attachment of the debt.

Multiple Choice

REG 2-Q52 through REG 2-Q56

In addition to attaching property to the credit relationship, the Creditor also has to perfect their rights to be a fully secured party. This is an extremely important step, as a perfected security interest can have claims and rights to certain property that are ahead of unprotected or unperfected creditors. Perfection of a Security Interest can be accomplished in a variety of ways, such as:

1) Perfection by **Possession**
   This occurs when the Creditor takes the collateral used to secure the debt with debtor's agreement. This is the only way to perfect with negotiable instruments or stocks and bonds.

   > *Example*: Bob loans money to Steven to help Steven pay his bills. In exchange for making the loan, Steven uses his rare, Babe Ruth baseball as collateral. To help secure the debt, Bob takes possession of the baseball until Steven pays back the loan. Bob has perfected his security interest by holding onto the baseball until the loan is paid.

2) Perfection by **Filing** occurs when the Creditor files a Financing Statement with the appropriate state agency. This filing must contain names and addresses of parties, a description of the collateral and the signature of debtor, but does not require the amount of the obligation secured. The importance of this form of perfection is that it is a way to provide constructive notice to all 3RD parties of the security interest. It is important to note that filing is the only way to perfect an interest in accounts receivable.

   > *Example*: Steven is the owner of a clothing store. To help Steven fund the business, Steven gets a loan from Bank of Cool to help purchase inventory. Over the next few months Steven purchases inventory for the store. Once the clothes are purchased, the Bank of Cool files a financing statement putting other possible creditors on notice that they are taking a security interest in the clothes.

3) Perfection by **Attachment** is a form of perfecting a security interest to collateral automatically. This type of perfection is automatic but very limited to specific circumstances. Perfection by attachment can only occur with PMSI Creditors in consumer goods. This type of perfection is strategically important, as an individual who perfects by attachment has a higher priority over all other creditors. Finally, an individual who perfects by attachment loses collateral to any consumer purchaser from debtor without having notice of security interest, can protect against this by filing a financing statement.

   > *Example*: Bob wants to buy a new car. Bob goes to National Bank to get a loan to purchase the car. Once the bank extends money to purchase the car, they have a PMSI in the collateral (the car).

Multiple Choice

REG 2-Q57 through REG 2-Q58

Summarize the priority rules of security transactions.

Identify the prioritized ordering of perfected security interests given a specific scenario.

c. Secured Creditors, Unsecured Creditors, and the Priority of Claims
The concept of priority depends on where the Creditor is located on the list of the order of payments. The traditional school of thought is that the higher your priority, the more likely the Creditor is to getting paid should they have to make a claim against a Debtor. With respect to priority, typically a secured Creditor is paid prior to an unsecured Creditor. This is based on the concept that the secured creditor has attached a specific claim to a specific piece of collateral, whereas an unsecured creditor simply has a right to some assets of the debtor. Furthermore, the first creditor to file, or otherwise perfect their security interest in the property, will have the highest priority concerning that particular piece of collateral. While this is the common rule, there are some exceptions.

One major exception to the first to file rule involves PMSI Creditors. A PMSI creditor in non-inventory collateral has priority over other creditors (including those who perfect their security interest first) if they perfect their security interest within twenty (20) days of a debtor getting possession over the collateral. Additionally, a PMSI creditor in inventory collateral will have priority if the Creditor, before the Debtor gets possession of the collateral, the Creditor files and gives written notice to all Creditors ahead of them.

Collateral that is perfected in one state and is subsequently moved to another state, remains perfected for four (4) months after arrival in the new state.

1) Secured Creditors vs. Purchaser from Debtor
While we have looked at Secured Creditors, it is also important to consider how a purchaser from a Debtor plays into secured credit transactions. A purchaser from a debtor is one who purchases collateral from the debtor with no knowledge that it is being used as collateral. Typically, the rule is that the perfected creditor will have priority over a purchaser from a debtor, but like many items with the law, two exceptions to this rule are applicable.
   i. A purchaser from a debtor will have priority over a perfected PMSI Creditor, when that Creditor has perfected by attachment, if collateral is consumer goods.
   ii. A purchaser who buys from a merchant in the ordinary course of business will take the goods free of all security interest.

> *Example*: Jon goes into a clothing store and purchases a pair of jeans from Steve, the owner. Because Jon purchases those jeans from a merchant, he purchases those jeans free of any claim that a Creditor, who has attached Jon's inventory, may have on those same jeans.

2) Remedies for a Creditor
Even though a Creditor may have priority over other Creditors to a particular piece of property owned by the Debtor, the Creditor has to follow certain avenues to attempt to obtain the property.

i. **Repossess Property**
   The Creditor can move towards a peaceful repossession of the property in an attempt to pay the debt of the Debtor. When this occurs, the Creditor can sell the property at a public sale (which the Creditor can attend), or move to sell the property via a private sale. Once the property is sold, the money is used to initially repay the Creditor, with all remaining proceeds going to the Debtor. If the sale of the property fails to reimburse the Creditor fully, the Debtor will be liable for the difference. Before a sale of the property (via either a public or private sale), the Debtor has the right to redeem the property by paying the secured Creditors in full.

   > *Example*: Steve loans Bob money so that Bob can purchase a boat. As collateral, Steve takes a security interest in the boat. If Bob fails to pay Steve, Steve can repossess the boat, sell the boat at an auction, and use the proceeds of the sale to satisfy the debt.

ii. **Strict Foreclosure**
   If the Creditor decides to keep the collateral, thereby canceling the entire debt, he must send a written notification to the Debtor and the other Creditors. Upon receipt of the letter, the Debtor or the other Creditors have 21 days to object, thus forcing the Creditor to sell the collateral.

   Additionally, if the collateral is consumer goods, and the Debtor has paid 60% or more of the price of consumer goods, then the Creditor must sell the collateral.

   > *Example*: Steve loans Bob money so that Bob can purchase a boat. As collateral, Steve takes a security interest in the boat. If Bob fails to pay Steve, Steve has the option to take the boat and keep it for himself, canceling the debt.

iii. **Sue the Debtor**
   This type of collection action is the most common, and involves simply litigating the case in court. In these types of cases, if the Creditor wins, the debt is reduced to a judgment. This form of remedy is often used when collateral alone is not, or cannot pay the debt.

   > *Example*: Steven loans Bob $500,000 to purchase a boat, taking a security interest in the boat as collateral on the loan. Two days after the purchase, Bob crashes the boat, and after the accident, the boat is only worth $250,000. Bob decides that he is not going to continuing paying the loan, as the boat has lost so much value. Instead of taking the boat (which will not satisfy the debt), Steven has the option to sue the debtor, and obtain a judgment to help collect the full amount owed.

Under the Secured Transactions Article of the UCC, a secured party generally must comply with each of the following duties:
- Filing or sending the debtor a termination statement when the debt is paid.
- Confirming, at the debtor's request, the unpaid amount of the debt.
- Using reasonable care in preserving any collateral in the secured party's possession.

Multiple Choice

REG 2-Q59 through REG 2-Q61

D. Government Regulations of Business
1. Federal securities regulation

> **Summarize the various securities laws and regulations that affect corporate governance with respect to the Federal Securities Act of 1933 and the Federal Securities and Exchange Act of 1934.**

> **Identify violations of the various securities laws and regulations that affect corporate governance with respect to the Federal Securities Act of 1933 and the Federal Securities and Exchange Act of 1934.**

There are two federal securities laws in the US. They are the Securities Act of 1933 and the Securities Exchange Act of 1934. Also, there are various state laws also regulating securities legislation at the state and local level. These state laws are often called "blue sky laws". The Securities Act of 1933 focuses of providing investors with information needed to understand where the offering proceeds will be used. The Federal Securities and Exchange Act of 1934, created the Security and Exchange Commission, helps to oversee all publicly traded stocks within the country.

Under these laws, the term "Securities" has been broadly interpreted, and now includes almost any type of multistate investment contract. This allows for the SEC to regulate stocks, bonds, debentures, stock warrants, stock options, collateral trust certificates and limited partnership interests; however, it does not include general partnership interest or certificates of deposit.

While the two Acts differ in some ways, both Acts are administered by the Securities Exchange Commission (SEC), and allow for the SEC to suspend or revoke trading or registration for fraud or other illegality, conduct investigations, subpoena witnesses, books and records, and make recommendations on potential prosecutions. The SEC does NOT prosecute for criminal violations, the Justice Department does.

a. The Securities Act of 1933
As previously stated, the purpose of the Securities Act of 1933, is to provide investors with information to include the principal purposes for which the proceeds from the offering will be used. While this does not guarantee the accuracy of the information, and does not provide any assurances against loss, and there is no evaluation by the SEC, this Act provides a framework to help provide additional information to potential investors.

Under this Act, two major requirements for the public sale of securities are outlined; filing a registration statement with the SEC, and providing a prospectus to investors.

1) Filing a registration statement
Registration statements filed with the SEC under the '33 Act, are required to be filed by either issuers, underwriters, dealers of the security, or any individual with a significant say in the management of the company. These individuals are considered to be the most informed individuals on the securities being sold.

The Registration Statement itself needs to include four (4) key items (**PANS**): a **P**rospectus (a summary of the company), **A**udited financial statements of the company, **N**ames of the issuer(s) directors, and underwriters of the security, and the basic **S**ecurities information. Under the Act, this is determined to be enough information to provide the potential investor with an overview of the potential investment.

Once the registration statement is filed, issuers of stock have to wait twenty (20) days to start selling. This allows for issues to make oral offers to sell, while at the same time allowing investors to review the prospectus, and make inquiries into the information provided. During this 20-day period, issuers may only make limited written announcements to avoid providing inaccurate information to the public.

2) Prospectus
A prospectus is a formal legal document that provides details about an investment offering for sale. When looking at Prospectus', it is important to determine if the document being reviewed is the preliminary prospectus, or the final prospectus. The final prospectus contains important information such as a final price and information on the investment opportunity.

While a majority of all investment opportunities need to register under the '33 Act, there are some exceptions to the registration requirement (**I DANCE**)

3) **I**ntra-state Offerings are exempted from the formal registration process and include a transaction that takes place, in their entirety, in one state. In these cases, the issuer must be from the state where the transaction is going to take place, and the issuer must conduct 80% of their business within that state. Additionally, the issuance must only be sold to residents of that state, and the resale of the stock is restricted to residents of that state for nine (9) months. These transactions allow for smaller offerings to be completed less formally.

I

4) Regulation **D** of the '33 Act exempts the issuer from having to file a formal registration when the investment offering is made under Sections 504 and 506 of the '33 Act. In both circumstances, you must notify the SEC of the transaction within 15 days of the first sale.

D

	504	506**
Maximum Dollar Amount Exempt in 1	Up to $5,000,000 must be sold in a 12-month period	Private placement of unlimited $ amounts - may exceed 12 months
Solicitation	Permitted*	None permitted
Restrictions on Resale	NONE	Must hold for long-term investment - NOT resale (2 years or more)
Type & Number of Investors	Any type of investor Any number	Unlimited Accredited Investors 35 or less Unaccredited Investors
Disclosure	No Disclosure Required	Must disclose to include audited F/S if 1 or more Unaccredited Investors

*   As long as sold to accredited investors
** Rule 506 - (Under the JOBS Act), allows general solicitation and advertising, if all the purchasers are accredited investors.
Note: Rule 505 was removed and will no longer be tested on the CPA Exam (starting Q4 2017.)

5) **R**egulation **A** of the '33 Act includes simplified registrations for offerings under $5 Million dollars that plan on being sold within a 12-month period. While these offerings do not need a formal registration process, the offeror does need to provide an offering circular. **[A]**

6) **N**o Sale Transactions are transactions that do not require a formal registration process and include transactions where an issuer deals exclusively with existing stockbrokers and does not pay a commission. **[N]**

7) **C**asual Sales are transactions that do not require a formal registration process and include sales by an ordinary investor. **[C]**

8) **E**xempted Securities are exempted from the registration process and includes securities offered by banks, governments, common carriers and non-profit groups. Additionally, commercial paper that matures in 9 months or less is also exempted under this regulation. **[E]**

Generally, violations of the '33 Act can result in fines, imprisonment or both. Under Section 11 of the '33 Act, suits for money damages are permitted against the issuer, director, and experts involved in the violation. When attempting to prove such a violation, the party suing needs to show that they 1) acquired the stock, 2) suffered a loss, 3) that there was a material misrepresentation or omission of facts that lead to the stock acquisition, and 4) there was no scienter or reckless disregard for the truth, 5) no reliance, and the defendant is liable, unless (s)he can show due diligence. Typically, these suits also need to involve some type of mail or other interstate commerce.

Multiple Choice
REG 2-Q62 through REG 2-Q72

b. Securities Exchange Act of 1934
The purpose of the Securities Exchange Act of 1934 was to create the Securities and Exchange Commission. This commission regulates not only the stock offerings themselves, but the individuals working on stock offerings, as well as the stock exchanges themselves. Under the '34 Act, all national stock exchanges, brokers, and dealers must register with and be regulated by the SEC. Additionally, the Act requires that stock sold on a national exchange, or those companies with 500 or more shareholders and $10 million or more in assets register with the SEC. Reporting companies are required to file reports under the 1934 act.

For companies that are required to file reports under the '34 Act, a variety of reports are required to be filed. The reporting companies are required to file these reports as part of continuous disclosure under the 1934 act. Reporting companies are subject to continuous disclosure. Example of reporting companies are companies:
- That trade securities on all national stock exchanges, or
- If a company does not trade their securities on a national stock exchange, they have 500 or more shareholders and $10 million or more in assets registered with the SEC.

Some of the required reports include:
1) **10-K** Annual Reports are filed with SEC within 90 days of the end of fiscal year. The purpose of this report is to provide a comprehensive summary of a company's financial performance and must include audited financial statements.

2) **10-Q** Quarterly Reports filed with the SEC on a quarterly basis and is a comprehensive summary of a company's financial performance in that respective quarter. These reports include unaudited financial statements.

3) **8-K** Current Reports are reports that need to be filed with the SEC within four (4) business days of newly appointed officers or changes in auditors, or the filing of a report that changes the amount of issued stock and changes in corporate control

Multiple Choice

REG 2-Q73 through REG 2-Q74

In addition to these major reports, other reports include (**5% TIP**)

5%	**5% or more owners** - must file background information with the SEC and the issuer (information about the purchaser, source of their money and their purpose in buying).
T	**Tender offers** - offer to buy stock of a corporation at a specified price for a specified time.
I	**Insider trading** - all officers, directors, 10% or more owners, accountants and attorneys - must report all stock sales to SEC
P	**Proxy solicitation** - must file proxy statements with SEC and give to all stockholders.

Violations of the '34 Act can result in fines, imprisonment or both. Liability under the '34 Act is based under Section 10(b) and rule 10(b)(5). These Anti-Fraud Sections permit for suits for money damages against anyone who bought or sold any stock. Violations of Rule 10(b) apply even if securities are exempt from registration under '33 & '34. When attempting to prove such a violation, the party suing needs to show that the purchaser or seller of stock 1) suffered a loss, 2) that there was a material misrepresentation or omission of fact that lead to the stock acquisition, and 3) there were scienter, or reckless disregard for the truth, 4) and reliance on the misrepresentation. Typically, these suits also need to involve some type of mail or other interstate commerce.

If a publicly traded corporation pays a bride to a local zoning official, and the bride was recorded in the publicly traded corporation's financial statements as a consulting fee, the publicly traded corporation would have violated the securities acts of 1934.

Multiple Choice

REG 2-Q75 through REG 2-Q79

2. Other federal laws & regulations

Summarize Federal laws and regulations, for example, employment tax, qualified health plans, and work classification federal laws and regulations.

Identify violations of federal laws and regulations, for example, employment tax, qualified health plans, and work classification federal laws and regulations.

a. Federal Insurance Contribution Act (FICA)
FICA represents the federal payroll tax imposed on employees, employers, and independent contractors to fund Social Security and Medicare. These Social Security and Medicare programs provide benefits for retirees, disabled individuals, and children of deceased workers. Under FICA, wages are broadly interpreted to allow for virtually all types of income to be considered earned compensation, subject to the tax. Exceptions to this general rule are that annuities and CD's are not considered wages taxable under this act.

In practice, these taxes are withheld by the employer. A failure to withhold these payments will make the employer liable for both the employers and employees share of the payments. Should an employer voluntarily decide to pay the employee's portion of the FICA taxes, those amounts paid will be deductible on the employer's taxes. While FICA payments are typically equally split between the employer and employee, self-employed individuals pay a tax equal to the total contributions typically paid by the employer and employee.

With these payments, individual earn benefits during their old age, if they have a disability, or if they need hospital insurance. While the specific amount of each of these benefits varies depending on income and need, eighty-five percent (85%) of the benefits received from FICA are taxable.

b. Federal Unemployment Tax Act (FUTA)
FUTA provides for unemployment benefits to be collected by employees who have lost their jobs through no fault of their own, and are both willing, able, and looking for work. For example, if an individual gets fired for theft from the job, they are not eligible for unemployment benefits. While the specifics of the programs themselves are administered by each state individually, the program itself is governed by Federal law.

Unemployment taxes themselves are paid by the employer, based on each employee's salary. Currently, each employee is assessed a tax based on the first $7,000 in wages that they are paid on an annual basis. Employers are responsible for paying the tax when they have paid $1500 in wages during any calendar quarter or had one or more employees for a 20-week period during a calendar year. While the tax payments are deductible, they are only deductible by the employers. Finally, a credit is available for employees who paid a state unemployment tax in addition to a Federal unemployment tax.

c. Workers' Compensation
Workers' Compensation Insurance is designed to provide employees injured within the scope of employment, the help that they need to return to work. This includes both medical assistance and wage assistance while they recover. Since the program is designed to provide assistance to employees who have been injured, as long as the employee was working within their scope of employment, the employer is considered strictly liable, without regard to their actual fault. Benefits under this program are based on the actual injury sustained, as opposed to the employee's salary at the time of injury.

As previously stated, this program is designed to assist individuals who are injured within the scope of their employment. This means that an employee's negligence is not a limit or bar to recovery. The only exceptions to this policy include fighting, intoxication, or self-inflicted wounds incurred during the scope of employment.

Finally, employers have some rights under this program as well. As a result of accepting workers' compensation benefits, the employee is not eligible to sue the employer, unless the employer somehow intentionally injured the employee. Typically, in lawsuits surrounding workers' compensation benefits, recoveries are often obtained by insurance companies who initially funded the workers' compensation benefits.

Multiple Choice

REG 2-Q80 through REG 2-Q81

d. Occupational Safety and Health Act (OSHA)
OSHA is administered by the Occupational Safety and Health Administration and establishes safety and health standards to the workplace. While OSHA establishes these rules, it is important to understand that these regulations vary greatly based on the industry, as the safety needs to industries vary greatly. To help administer these rules and ensure a safe workplace, OSHA can inspect the workplace for violations either at the employee's request or upon their own decision. While OSHA is a federal agency, some states imposed additional safety rules and regulations concerning worker

safety. In these cases, it is important to remember that the state OSHA rules can provide for greater protections for workers, but not less.

Penalties for violating OSHA can range from citations to fines, depending greatly on the safety issues found at the location. If the safety issues are severe enough, temporary injunctions and criminal penalties can also be incurred. Circumstances like these are typically seen in cases where the violator has been continually violating an OSHA statute, or the violation is willful in nature.

e. Employment Discrimination
   1) <u>Title VII of the Civil Rights Act</u> prohibits discrimination in the workplace based on race, color, religion, sex, or national origin. This Act does NOT protect against age discrimination. This Act can enjoin the employer from engaging in unlawful behavior and allows individuals who have been wrongly fired or not hired to file a civil suit in federal court or intervene in suits by private individuals. Employees who are found guilty of violating this act can be forced to reinstatement of employee and award back pay. Finally, it is important to remember that this Act is civil in nature. There are no criminal penalties for violations of this Act, as virtually all penalties are civil in nature.

   2) <u>Age Discrimination Employment Act (ADEA)</u> prohibits discrimination in employment decisions based on age and protects workers age 40-70. This Act prohibits a mandatory retirement age below 70 years of work unless the age requirement is a reasonable business necessity. For example, police or fire personnel may have a reasonable age requirement. Penalties for violations of this Act include injunctive relief and back pay for violations.

   1) Discrimination of the Handicapped (Physical and Mental Handicaps). The <u>Rehabilitation Act of 1973</u> requires that employers with federal contracts of $2,500 or more take affirmative action to hire qualified disabled workers. Furthermore, the <u>Americans with Disabilities Act</u> provides protections for employees with handicaps to help ensure that employers cannot and do not discriminate against persons with disabilities, as long as the employee can do the basic job. Furthermore, this Act prohibits discrimination in public transportation and public accommodations. The Act requires that employers provide "reasonable accommodations" for employees with disabilities to be able to complete their jobs.

   2) <u>Equal Pay for Equal Work Act</u> prohibits discrimination based on sex. For violations of this act, it is important to remember that the result of the act would be raising the women's salary as opposed to lowering the man's salary. When looking at sex discrimination cases, it is important to remember some key defenses for alleged discrimination.

      These include:
      i. Bona Fide Occupational Qualification permits discrimination for a reasonable business necessity. For example, a woman who auditions for the role of Romeo in the play "Romeo and Juliet" cannot sue if she fails to get the role, as being a man is a reasonable business necessity for the role of Romeo.
      ii. National Security.
      iii. Professional developed ability testing.
      iv. Seniority or merit-based systems.

f. <u>Federal Labor Standards Act (FLSA)</u>
   FLSA provides protections for workers. Initially, the law was designed to prohibit employment of children under the age of 14. Children between the ages of 14-18 are permitted to work limited hours. The law does allow for exceptions to the age requirement for agricultural workers, newspaper carriers, child actors, and children employed by their parent.

In addition to providing an age limit for working, this law also addresses wage and hour restrictions. The FLSA creates a minimum wage and requires that all employees who work more than 40 hours for one company in any week are required to receive time and a half for additional hours worked. The minimum wage is determined based on an hourly, weekly, or monthly pay base. For example, if you are paid an "hourly rate," then that rate has to be at least the current minimum hourly wage. The FLSA also clarifies which employees are not entitled to overtime. Employees such as teachers, outside salesman, professional and supervisory workers, seasonal workers, and individuals working in the fishing industry do not receive overtime pay.

The FLSA is enforced by the Department of Labor who can initiate both civil and criminal actions for violations of these rules. The Department can investigate employers who are charged with violating these rules, as well as issue orders requiring employers to pay back wages if and when they are found to be due.

g. Employee Retirement Income Security Act (ERISA)
ERISA regulates pension plans but does not require that a company establish a pension plan. ERISA sets standards for funding and investment of pension plans to help ensure that there is no mismanagement of the investment funds. These rules and regulations apply to both pension funds contributed to employees as well as employers.

Under ERISA employers are prohibited from delaying an employee's participation in a pension program; however, ERISA does allow for employers to require that employees vest in a retirement program after five (5) years of contributions. Under this circumstance, while the employee can have access to their own contributions immediately, they typically have to wait five (5) years to gain access to their employer's contributions to the retirement program.

Finally, ERISA has built protections into the law to help protect pensions if they go bankrupt. The Pension Benefit Guarantee Corporation provides protections to help ensure that workers retirement savings are safe and only applies to defined benefit plans.

Multiple Choice

REG 2-Q82

h. Family Medical Leave Act (FMLA) entitles employees to take twelve (12) weeks of unpaid, job-protected leave in any one (1) year period to allow for the employee to deal with the birth of a newborn child, care for an adopted child, or a serious health condition for either themselves or someone in their immediate family. With FMLA, it is important to remember that the law allows the employee to take time off from work without fear of losing their job, this same law DOES NOT require that the employer pay the employee during that time off. Upon returning to work, the employee is permitted to return to their same job, or one of equal pay, benefits, and stature within the company. FMLA laws allow for private lawsuits for violations of this law, as well as investigations and lawsuits by the Department of Labor.

i. Environmental Regulation
   1) The Environmental Protection Agency (EPA) is considered to be the principal administrative agency for federal environmental laws. This agency may initiate both civil and criminal lawsuits through the Justice Department to help enforce Federal environmental laws.

   2) National Environmental Policy Act (NEPA) of 1969 requires that all branches of government consider the environmental effects of major federal actions before undertaking those actions. This act requires an environmental impact statement (EIS) to be drafted when major federal actions might significantly affect the quality of the human environment. The NEPA allows for private citizens to sue to force governmental compliance with NEPA. This often allows for

private parties to file EIS to be reviewed on all projects where there is major federal involvement.

3) The <u>Clean Air Act (CAA)</u> is the principal federal law for dealing with air pollution. This law allows for the EPA to establish national ambient air quality standards for major air pollutants. Additionally, the CAA requires each state to develop a plan, called a **State Implementation Plan** (SIP) for meeting air quality standards. The EPA must approve these plans, and once approved, the SIP becomes both federal and state law that can be enforced by both parties.

The CAA also establishes emission standards for motor vehicles, fuels, and fuel additives. The EPA must certify all new cars as meeting emission standards. Furthermore, if in actual use cars exceed emission standards, the EPA can order a recall.

Additionally, the CAA requires the EPA to set emission standards for hazardous air pollutants. The CAA requires that stationary sources of air pollution (e.g., factories and power plants) install the best available technology for reducing air pollution. To further help protect against pollution, the CAA addresses the problem of acid rain by placing a cap on overall emissions of nitrogen oxide and sulfur oxide and requiring that electric utilities must reduce emissions. While states have primary responsibility for enforcing air standards, the EPA may take action (usually through civil suit) when states fail to act. Additionally, private citizens may sue either state or federal officials to compel action.

4) The <u>Clean Water Act</u> (CWA) is the principal federal law for dealing with water pollution. The CWA requires industries discharging waste into our waters to install the best available water pollution control technology to help protect against continued pollution. To further help establish these standards, the CWA requires states to set water quality standards. The CWA permits the EPA to act if the state fails to set acceptable standards and requires an industry or municipality discharging into the water system to obtain a National Pollution Discharge Elimination System (NPDES) permit.

In addition to these protections, the CWA identifies the amount of designated pollutants permitted to be discharged and specifies the steps required to reduce present discharges. To remain in compliance, the permit holder must notify authorities if they will not meet permit requirement.

To continue efforts to help protect the environment, the CWA prohibits releasing oil or hazardous substances into the water, requires a permit for dredging or filling activities in wetlands areas, and regulates discharges into the water by nuclear power plants.

The CWA is enforced by both state and Federal government by allowing both civil and criminal penalties to apply for violating CWA. Additionally, private citizens can sue violators and sue EPA or state to compel action. In addition to paying fines to government agencies or individuals, violators can also be required to clean up the pollution or pay for doing so.

Multiple Choice

REG 2-Q83

j. The Comprehensive Environmental Response, Compensation and Liability Act (CERCLA) provides a federal Superfund to clean up controlled or abandoned hazardous waste sites. Parties liable for the cost of clean-up, including current owners and operators whether they caused it or not, past owners and operators of the site at the time of disposal, generators (i.e., the owner of the waste deposited at the site), and transporters of the hazardous waste to the site. While parties are typically responsible for the payments necessary to clean up these sites, if they cannot afford to pay for this cleanup, the EPA will pay the cleanup costs.

Multiple Choice

REG 2-Q84

k. The Resource Conservation and Recovery Act (RCRA) gives the EPA the power to control hazardous waste at current or future sites and to set standards for the disposal of nonhazardous solid waste. This law regulates facilities that generate, transport, treat, store or dispose of hazardous waste largely through a permit system. Additionally, the RCRA regulates underground product storage tanks and helps establish standards for nonhazardous solid waste. Violations of the RCRA has both civil and criminal penalties for violations.

l. The <u>Patient Protection and Affordable Care Act (PPACA)</u> provides a set of standards to ensure that all individuals in the country have access to affordable, quality health insurance and care. The PPACA prohibits insurers from denying coverage to individuals based on pre-existing conditions, as well as, requiring those insurers to provide the same premium price to all applicants of the same age and in the same geographic location. Additionally, this law provided a set of standards for all health insurance companies to use to ensure that all insurance policies provided basic, quality medical care. The law additionally imposes an individual mandate on all individuals not covered by an employer-sponsored health plan, Medicaid, or Medicare to obtain private-insurance, or pay a penalty. Finally, the law requires all employers who have employees that work more than 25 hours per week, be allowed to participate in an employer-sponsored health care plan.

m. <u>Same-Sex Marriage Laws</u>
While no federal statute legalizing or prohibiting same-sex marriage currently exists, the US Supreme Court in the case, <u>Obergefell v. Hodges</u>, ruled that there was a fundamental right to marry that is guaranteed to same-sex couples by both the Due Process Clause and the Equal Protection Clause of the US Constitution. This ruling has effectively legalized same-sex marriage in the United States, and affords all rights, protections, and privileges to same-sex couples who have been legally married, as are available to heterosexual couples.

n. <u>Presidential Executive Order Promoting Free Speech and Religious Liberty</u>
President Trump signed an executive order promoting free speech in May 2017. Among other things, this order directs the IRS not to enforce a provision in IRC Sec. 501(c)(3) that bars tax-exempt organizations from engaging in certain types of political activity.

o. <u>Foreign Account Tax Compliance Act (FATCA)</u>
This Act set up guidelines for individuals living outside U.S. to report specified foreign financial assets to IRS and Financial Crimes Enforcement Network (FinCEN).

p. <u>Adam Steele, et al. v. the United States of America</u>
This court case requires tax return preparers to have preparer tax identification number (PTIN), but the government can't charge for these numbers.

q. <u>James C. Sexton, Jr. and Esquire Group, LLC v. Karen L. Hawkins, Director of Office of Professional Responsibility, IRS</u>
In this case, court held that you can still prepare tax returns or offer tax advice if suspended from "practice before the IRS" since these activities don't meet that definition.

E. Business Structure
1. Selection and formation of business entity and related operation and termination

Summarize the processes for formation and termination of various business entities.

Summarize the nontax operation features for various business entities.

Identify the type of business entity that is best described by a given set of nontax-related characteristics.

   a. Sole proprietorships
      1) General
         A Sole Proprietorship is a business in which one person is in total control of the management and profits of the business. The sole proprietorship is often thought to be "one in the same" as the person who runs the business. Without the sole proprietor, the business would end. In this sense, there is no difference between the owner and the business. A Sole Proprietorships consist of one owner of the business where the owner has the sole ability to make all decisions concerning the business.

      2) The Sole Proprietorship is formed once the business starts to operate. No specific filings or registrations are needed to create a Sole Proprietorship initially. In this sense, these types of entities are considered to be the "easiest" to create.

         > ***Example***: Ryan decides that he wants to open a dog walking business called "Ryan's Dog Walking." By creating signs, obtaining new customers, and doing work he has created a sole proprietorship.

   b. General Partnerships
      1) General
         A partnership is defined as any voluntary association of two or more co-owners operating a business for profit. The key to creating a partnership is to show that the partnership has two or more parties. These parties can consist of individual persons, corporations, partnerships, or other business entities. The key to showing a partnership is to show that these two individuals are sharing both profits and the management of a business. As such, a partnership has to operate a business, not just co-own property.

      2) Formation
         A Partnership is formed by an agreement of all partners to conduct the business of the Partnership. This is often accomplished through a document called a partnership agreement. This agreement does not need to be in writing (unless otherwise required under contract law). In whatever form it comes, the partnership agreement is the document that will ultimately control how the partnership is operated.

      3) General partners
         i. Partners in a general partnership have unlimited liability,
            a) General partners are jointly and severally liable for all partnership debts and contract obligations
            b) They are jointly and severally liable for all partnership torts

         ii. General partners are agents of the partnership and agents of each other.
            a) Partners owe the same duties that all agents do
            b) When acting with authority, each can impose liability on partners and the partnership.

- c) Any partner committing a tort while acting on partnership business imposes tort liability on himself, the partnership and fellow partners (respondent superior)
- d) Each must give actual notice to old customers and publish a notice to new customers upon their termination from the partnership

4) Dissolution

A partnership ends, or is dissolved, when one, or more, of the partners ceases to be associated with the partnership. Dissolution can occur by either an act of one of the partners, or by operation of law. When a Partnership ends through an act of one of the partners, this typically occurs when one or more of the partners take an active step, such as withdrawing from the partnership. In contrast, a Partnership ends by operation of law when one of the partners dies, files for bankruptcy protection, or the partnership itself files for bankruptcy.

Upon dissolution of a Partnership, the business may be continued by one or more of the former partners and other individuals. When this occurs, the non-continuing partners are credited with their profits or charged with losses (where applicable). Additionally, creditors of the old business become creditors of the new business, as one or more of the partners are involved; however, new partners to the business will not be personally liable for debts incurred before their entry into the partnership. New partners are liable for the debts of the old partnership, only up to their capital contribution.

When the partnership is dissolved, three (3) steps need to occur to formally close the Partnership. The steps are as follows:

i. Dissolution. This is caused by any partner ceasing to be associated with the business.
ii. Winding up or liquidation. This is the process of the Partnership settling all affairs of the Partnership.
   - The first distribution is made to pay creditors with Partnership creditors having an initial claim on all Partnership assets and personal creditors having a claim on personal assets.
   - The second distribution is made to pay loans made by partners to the Partnership.
   - The third distribution is to pay capital contributions, or initial investments, made by the partners.
   - The final distribution is made to distribute all remaining profits to the Partners.

> **Example**: Bob and Steve decide they want to start a dog walking business. Instead of filing a tremendous amount of paperwork, they simply decide that they will each invest $1000, and run the company together. In this example, Bob and Steve have created a general partnership.

iii. Termination. The completion of the winding up process.

Dissolution occurs when a general partner ceases to be associated with the partnership.
- a) Changes in limited partners do not dissolve the partnership
- b) Any partner can dissolve the partnership by simply withdrawing, even if prohibited by the partnership agreement (if it breaches the agreement, the partner is liable)
- c) Dissolution may occur by operation of law (e.g., death of a partner, bankruptcy of a partner or bankruptcy of the partnership dissolves the partnership immediately.)

Exception – Under Revised Uniform Partnership Act, partners that own a majority of a partnership are permitted to continue the general partnership within 90 days of the partner's withdrawal, death, or bankruptcy.

Upon dissolution, the business may be continued by some of the former partners and others.
  a) Non-continuing partners are credited with their profits or charged with losses
  b) Liable to creditors even if continuing partners agree to hold them harmless
  c) Creditors of the old business are creditors of the new business
  d) A new partner has limited liability to creditors of the old partnership (liability is limited to his/her share of partnership property)

Multiple Choice

REG 2-Q85

Example: In the ABC partnership, A leaves and N takes A's place (ABC becomes NBC)

ABC Partnership	NBC Partnership
A is personally liable to creditors - even if other partners agree to hold A harmless	A is not personally liable unless there is a notice
N's liability is limited to N's capital contribution	N is personally liable N gets all the rights of a partner

iv. Distribution upon dissolution in a General Partnership
The order of distribution in a general partnership is as follows.
  a) Upon the distribution, the first order of distribution is to pay creditors
   - *Partnership creditors have first claim on partnership assets, but they may only sue a partner personally after all partnership assets are exhausted*
   - *Personal creditors have first claim on personal assets*
  b) The second order of distribution is to pay loans made by partners to the partnership
  c) The third order of distribution is to pay capital contributions made by the partners
  d) The last order of distribution is to distribute profits to the partners

c. Limited Partnerships
  1) The Limited Partnership is a Partnership that consists of two or more parties who have formed a Limited Partnership by filing documents with the State. A partnership that has at least one "general partner" and at least one "limited partner". In this type of partnership, the "general partners" assume all liability for the partnership debt and the "limited partner" is not liable for the partnership debt.

   i. "General Partners" are partners in a Limited Partnership that handle the day-to-day operation of the business.
   ii. "Limited Partners" are partners in a Limited Partnership that invest money into a Limited Partnership, but do not have a say in the day-to-day operation of the business.

Example: Bob and Steve decide they want to start a dog walking business. Bob is going to run the business and Steven is just going to invest money. Steve invests $5000, but Bob makes all the decisions regarding the business. In this example, a limited partnership has been created, with Bob being the "General Partner" and Steve being the "Limited Partner."

d. Limited Liability Partnership
   1) General
      A Limited Liability Partnership is a partnership that assumes the liability of any of its partner's professional malpractice, but only to the extent of the partnership assets. This type of partnership allows for professionals (such as lawyers, doctors, or accountants) to work together in a business environment, but not place their personal assets at risk. This liability only extends to the acts of the partners in furtherance of the LLP; a partner is still individually liable for their own misconduct. In a limited liability partnership, the partners are not personally liable for the debts of the partnership. The partners are not personally liable for the negligence of the other partners.

   2) Formation
      Similar to the formation of a Limited Partnership, an LLP is created by filing a certificate of partnership with the state, identifying who the partners are, as well as the type of business the LLP will be embarking upon.

   3) Dissolution
      When dissolving an LLP, the LLP will follow the same rules as those for dissolution of a General Partnership.

      > *Example*: Tim, Mike, and Steve are lawyers who decide they are going to create a new firm. To help avoid some liability issues, the partners create a Limited Liability Partnership. If any of them decide to leave the partnership, this will cause a dissolution of the Limited Liability Partnership

   4) Partners have an equal right to participate in management, except for limited partners.
      i. Most decisions require only a majority vote
      ii. Unless otherwise agreed, the following require the unanimous consent of all partners.
         a) To admit new general partners or new limited partners
         b) To transfer partnership property to others
         c) To change a written partnership agreement
         d) To admit liability in a lawsuit or submit a claim to an arbitrator
         e) Fundamental changes in partnership business to include selling the goodwill

   5) Each partner has an equal right to share in profits and distributions unless otherwise agreed.
      i. If a division of profits is specified but not losses, losses will follow profits
      ii. In a limited partnership, if it doesn't state how to divide up profits and losses, then they are divided up based on their capital contributions.

   6) Each partner has the right to be reimbursed for loans and advances made to the partnership.
      i. A partner is entitled to repayment only after all other creditors are paid.

   7) All partners and limited partners have the right to full information about the partnership.
      i. They have the right to inspect and copy books and records at reasonable times.

   8) Each partner is not a co-owner of partnership property.
      i. Each has an equal right to use partnership property for partnership purposes. But, the Partner has no right to use it for any other purpose without the consent of the other partners
      ii. A partner cannot transfer or assign his individual interest in partnership property to others.
      iii. Partnership property may not be attached by an individual partner's creditors.

Multiple Choice

REG 2-Q86

9) Assigning a partnership interest
   i. Any general or limited partner may assign or sell their partnership interest
      a) Assignment does not dissolve the partnership.
      b) Thus, the assignor remains a partner and is still liable for partnership debts.
   ii. The assignee does not become a partner without the consent of all other partners
      a) The only right an assignee has is the right to receive assignor's share of profits if any.
      b) The assignee is not liable for the assignor's share of losses.

e. Corporations
   1) General
   A corporation is a legal entity formed by issuing stock to individuals who are investing in the company. These investors become the owners of the corporation by becoming shareholders in the corporation. A corporation is considered a separate legal entity from its shareholders, meaning that it is possible to sue a corporation, as the corporation is considered to be separate from its shareholders. In this sense, shareholders are not personally liable for the debts of the corporation.

   From a tax perspective, a C Corporation is taxed on the profits they earn, and shareholders are taxed individually on the dividends that they receive from a corporation.

   2) Formation
   A corporation is initially formed by promoters who are primarily liable for all pre-incorporation activities of the corporation. Once the corporation is formed, if the corporation accepts a promoter's contract, then both the corporation and the promoter will be liable on the contract; however, the promoter will primarily be liable on a pre-incorporation activity unless the corporation agrees otherwise.

   A corporation is formed by filing Articles of Incorporation with the state. These Articles must provide, at a minimum the following information:
   i. Stock Provisions, including a number of authorized shares, voting stock, and a capital structure for the stock.
   ii. Names of the Corporation, its registered agent, and all incorporators.

   A Foreign Corporation is a Corporation doing business in any states other than the state of incorporation. When this occurs, the foreign corporation must obtain a certificate of authority from the state in which they are doing business, but not incorporated in.

Multiple Choice

REG 2-Q87

   3) Financing a Corporation
   A Corporation is financed by debt securities, equity securities, or retained earnings.

      i. Debt Securities are bonds which create a debtor-creditor relationship between the Corporation and the investor. These bonds are typically guaranteed payments at a defined rate, and at a defined time, in exchange for an initial investment in the Corporation. A bondholder is not considered a stockholder in the Corporation, even though they may be an important person or class of investor.

ii. Equity Securities are shares of stock evidence ownership in the Corporation. Common forms of stock include:
- *Common shares – shares with voting rights in a Corporation*
- *Preferred stock – a class of stock that has special rights over other forms of stock. This stock typically gets a preference when it comes to the payment of dividends.*
- *Cumulative preferred stock – dividend carryovers to future years.*
- *Authorized shares – the total amount of legally permitted shares to be issued by the Articles of Incorporation*
- *Issued shares – the total number of Authorized Shares distributed to investors*
- *Outstanding Shares – shares that are currently held by stockholders*
- *Treasury Stock – stock that has been issued but is not outstanding*

4) Mergers and consolidations
A legal merger occurs when A & B combine and one of them survives. A legal consolidation occurs when A & B combine and X emerges as a new company.

   i. Approval steps for merger or consolidation
      a) Submit a formal plan of merger or consolidation to both boards and get majority approval.
      b) Submit to all stockholders and get majority approval (give notice of time, date and place).
         o Right of appraisal – dissenting shareholders can buy out of corporation at FMV
      c) Submit a plan to the secretary of state who issues a certificate of the merger upon approval.
         o Short form merger – parent mergers with a 90%+ owned sub
            1. The only approval needed is from the board of the parent
            2. Only the stockholders of the sub get appraisal rights

Multiple Choice

REG 2-Q88

5) Dissolution
A Corporation typically has perpetual existence until the voluntary or involuntary dissolution. As a Corporation is greater than any individual stockholder, the Corporation will not dissolve automatically upon the death of a stockholder.

With a voluntary dissolution, initially, the stockholder will have to approve of the dissolution. Once this approval is agreed to, creditors are paid, and then shareholders receive a payment in proportion to the number of shares they own in the Corporation.

With an involuntary dissolution, a court typically dissolves that Corporation. This occurs when a state requests a court to dissolve a Corporation due to fraud, illegality, or lack of business activity. In addition to the state requesting that the court dissolve a Corporation, the stockholders can petition the court to dissolve a Corporation in the event that the Corporation is deadlocked, acting illegally, or wasting corporate assets. In the event of an involuntary dissolution, once the court approves the dissolution, creditors are paid, and then shareholders receive a payment in proportion to the number of shares they own in the Corporation.

> ***Example***: Bob and Steve want to create "Dangerous Dog Walkers," and plan to sell shares in the company over a period of 10 years to investors, as needed. The creation of Dangerous Dog Walkers, Inc., should be completed as a corporation so that stock can be sold over time to investors.

    f. Limited Liability Companies
       1) General
          Limited Liability Companies is a cross between a partnership and a corporation. The LLC is different from other entities in three major areas:
            i. The LLC members have no personal liability beyond their initial investment.
            ii. The LLC owner(s) may fully participate in management decisions similar to a Partnership.
            iii. An LLC can have the same federal tax advantages of a Partnership, or may elect to be taxed as a corporation (C or S Corporation).
            iv. An LLC does not have perpetual existence like a corporation.
            v. An LLC has an advantage over an S corporation in that appreciated property can be distributed, tax-free to an owner.

       2) Formation
          Limited Liability Companies are organized on a state by state basis. This includes filing Articles of Organization within the state. These Articles must include the name of the LLC, and identify the Company as an LLC, where its owners have limited liability. In addition to the Articles of Organization, the members of an LLC have to agree to an Operating Agreement. This is an agreement between the members of the LLC, outlining how the LLC will operate, and who will be responsible for the running of the LLC.

       3) Dissolution
          An LLC is dissolved in the same manner as a partnership. In this sense, when the decision is made to dissolve the LLC, creditors are paid, and then each member is paid a pro rata portion of the profits to coincide with their membership (ownership) interest in the LLC.

Multiple Choice
REG 2-Q89 through REG 2-Q90

2. Rights, duties, legal obligations, & authority of owners & managers

> **Summarize the rights, duties, legal obligations and authority of owners and management.**

> **Identify the rights, duties, legal obligations or authorities of owners or management given a specific scenario.**

    a. Sole Proprietorships
       1) Advantages to the Sole Proprietorship. The biggest advantage to a sole proprietorship is that it is the simplest type of business structure to have. As there are no specific formation documents needed, the sole authority and decision-making authority rests with one individual (the owner). As the sole owner of the business, this single individual has the sole decision-making authority, as well as the advantage of being able to keep all profits associated with the business.

       2) Disadvantages of Sole Proprietorships. While there are advantages to the Sole Proprietorship, there are disadvantages and significant legal obligations to the Sole Proprietorship as well. As the Sole Proprietorship is typically a single individual, the sole proprietor is personally liable for all losses and other liabilities associated with the Sole Proprietorship. This liability extends to both contracts entered into by the sole

proprietorship, as well as litigation and other expenses associated with running the business. This personal liability puts all assets of the owner (i.e., their house, car, furniture, personal bank accounts, etc.) at risk should there be a debt or other obligation incurred by the business that the business cannot pay.

This personal liability also extends to funding the business. Finding funding to help support a Sole Proprietorship is often difficult to locate, funding agencies do not see an easy ability to obtain ownership in the Sole Proprietorship to protect their investment adequately. This often leads the owner of the sole proprietorship to take on extreme amounts of financial risk to operate the business.

b. General Partnership
  1) Rights of Partners
     All partners in a Partnership have equal right to participate in the management of the Partnership. While all partners have the equal right to participate, most decisions in a Partnership only required a simple majority vote of the partners. The only decisions that require unanimous consent of all partners include the following:
     i. The admission of new partners;
     ii. The transfer of Partnership property to third parties;
     iii. The changing of the Partnership Agreement;
     iv. The admission of liability in a lawsuit or to submit a claim to an arbitrator; or
     v. any fundamental changes in the Partnership business to include selling goodwill.

     In addition to the rights of partners to participate in the management of the Partnership, partners also have the right to the following:
     i. Each partner has the right to share equally in the profits and distributions of the Partnership;
     ii. Each partner has the right to be reimbursed for loans and advances made to the partnership. However, a partner is entitled to repayment only after all other creditors have been paid;
     iii. Each partner has the right to full information about the partnership. This includes the right to inspect and copy all books and records of the Partnership, and
     iv. Each partner has an equal right to use Partnership property for Partnership purposes. This right to use the property does not include the right of the partner to assign their interest in any Partnership property without the consent of the other partners.
     v. Unless otherwise agreed upon, each partnership is considered to be an agent of the Partnership. This allows each partner to legally enter into a binding legal agreement on behalf of the Partnership.

  2) Liabilities in a Partnership. As each partner in a Partnership is considered to be an agent of the Partnership, each partner has unlimited personal liability for the Partnership debts. This allows for a creditor to sue both the Partnership and each partner individually, for the debts or other liabilities of the Partnership.

c. Limited Partnerships
  1) Rights of General Partners
     In a Limited Partnership, a general partner has all the rights of partners in a General Partnership.

  2) Rights of Limited Partners
     Limited partners have the right to inspect and copy partnership books and records to specifically include the right to receive copies of any partnership tax returns. While limited

partners have the right to inspect the records of the business, these limited partners have no right to manage the day to day operations of the business itself.

    3) Liabilities in a Limited Partnership
The key to a limited partnership is understanding who has personal liability for the debts of the entity. General partners in a Limited Partnership have unlimited personal liability. In contrast, limited partners in the partnership are only liable to the extent that of their investment. In this sense, the limited partner can protect their personal assets in the event of litigation.

d. Limited Liability Partnerships
General partners in an LLP have the same rights, obligations, and protections as they do in a traditional General Partnership. The major difference with this type of partnership relates the ability for the general partners to limit their liability. The partners have limited liability for the debts, contracts, and negligence of the other partners.

e. Corporations
    1) Rights and Liabilities of Stockholders
Stockholders of a Corporation have two management rights. These include electing a board of directors and voting on fundamental changes to the Corporation. These fundamental changes include:
      i. Amendments to the Articles of Incorporation;
      ii. Dissolution;
      iii. The sale of all or substantially all of the Corporate assets; and
      iv. Mergers and consolidations with another business.

Additional rights held by stockholders of a Corporation include the right to inspect the books and records of the Corporation, the rights to buy up a percentage of ownership in newly issues shares to maintain the same ownership percentage in the Corporation (otherwise known as "Pre-emptive rights"), and the right to bring a derivative suit. A derivative suit is a lawsuit brought by the shareholders of a Corporation, in the name of the Corporation, when the Corporation itself has decided not to move forward with litigation. In these cases, the stockholders must show how the inaction of the Corporation has led to a hardship to the Corporation and agree that any recovery will go directly to the Corporation.

When looking at the liability of shareholders of a Corporation, it is important to keep in mind that individual shareholders of a Corporation have no personal liability (beyond their investment). For example, if a Corporation were to lose a lawsuit and not be able to pay the debt, the prevailing party could not attempt to collect any money from the individual shareholders. The only exception to this rule occurs where there is fraud, intentional undercapitalization, or the commingling of personal and corporate funds. While rare, this process is called "piercing the corporate veil," as the protections provided to the individual through the Corporate shield has been pierced by the fraud and/or deceit of the individual.

    2) Rights and Liabilities of Directors and Officers
Directors and officers are those individuals elected by the shareholders to run the day to day operations of the Corporation. These individuals set policy, and manage the Corporation for the shareholders.

Directors and officers themselves owe a duty of loyalty to the Corporation and the stockholders. In this sense, these directors and officers must act in the best interest of the Corporation and stockholders when making decisions for the Corporation. These individuals are not permitted to make a decision that will lead to personal profit in lieu of profit for the Corporation, unless:

i. The director or officer makes a full disclosure of the conflict and does not participate in the decision-making process approving the conflict; or
ii. If approval is not obtained, the business deal leading to the conflict is fair and reasonable to the Corporation.

Directors and Officers of a Corporation are provided with broad latitude when it comes to making decisions for the Corporation and the effects that those decisions may have. Under the "Business Judgment Rule," as long as an officer or director is acting reasonably and in good faith, they will not be held personally liable for their decisions affecting the Corporation. This rule allows these individuals to work for and in the best interests of the Corporation, without having a fear of litigation resulting from a business decision that was "sound" when made, but later on, over time, turned out not looking so "sound" after all. The key to this rule is for the director or officer to act in good faith. If it can be shown that the individual acted negligently, then the business judgment rule will not apply, and the individual can be held personally liable.

In addition to the business judgment rule, in exchange for working for the Corporation as an officer or director, in addition to payment, these individuals are indemnified for decisions they made as officers and/or directors. This means that the Corporation will reimburse these individuals if they are sued for actions done while acting in their capacity as a director or officer.

3) Dividends
A dividend is a payment declared by the board of directors. There is no guarantee or right to any stockholder to obtain a dividend unless the Corporation approves one. These dividends represent payments directly to the stockholders of the Corporation, based on the amount of stock that they hold. When approved, all affected stockholders are provided with a public notice of the dividend. As this becomes a payment due to each of the affected stockholders, a dividend is considered a corporate debt, and the stockholder is considered an unsecured creditor until the dividend is paid. When obtaining dividends, it is important to remember that this is a payment by the Corporation to the stockholder, but it does not increase the value of the stock, nor does is increase the stockholder's percentage of ownership in the Corporation.

4) Limited Liability Company
   i. Rights and Liabilities of Members. Members of the LLC have a right to participate in the managing of the LLC and a right to profits from the LLC. Concerning management of the LLC, management is completed in accordance with the Operating Agreement. A member-managed LLC is one that is managed by the members. If the LLC members elect to have one member manage the LLC, that individual is given rights to make decisions similar to an officer of a corporation.

   ii. An LLC may be managed by managers who are elected by the members. LLC manager have the same limited liability as LLC members.

   With respect to profits, members have rights to the profits and/or losses of the LLC, as determined by the Operating Agreement. If the Operating Agreement does not specify how profits and losses are to be allocated, these are allocated in accordance with each member's ownership interest in the LLC.

   Members of the LLC are not personally liable for the debts of the LLC. In this sense, the LLC operates like a corporation, shielding the members from personal liability.

iii. A limited liability company can be treated as either a partnership or a corporation. To be treated like a corporation, the LLC must make an election. If an election is not made, the LLC is treated similar to a partnership.

Multiple Choice

REG 2-Q91

F. Property
1. Definition
   Real property is land, and all items attached to the land; including:
   a. Items under the land (e.g., mineral deposits)
   b. Items above the land (e.g., natural resource such as trees)

   Multiple Choice
   REG 2-Q92

2. Personal property vs. fixtures
   a. Tangible Personal Property includes property that can be physically held by an individual.
   b. Intangible Personal Property are an individual's interests or rights in property that cannot be held physically. These are often referred to as "intellectual property" and includes items such as copyrights, patents, and trademarks.

   Multiple Choice
   REG 2-Q93 through REG 2-Q94

   c. Fixtures are personal property that are attached to real estate in such a way that it becomes part of the real estate as a matter of law. (i.e., a bookshelf screwed into the wall of a rental apartment may be considered a permanent fixture of the apartment.) Factors to consider when looking at fixtures include:
      1) What was the intention of the person who attached it?
      2) How is the property attached to the real estate? The more permanent the attachment, the more likely the property will be considered a fixture.
      3) What is the damage that would occur as a result of the removal?
      4) Is the property a trade fixture? Trade Fixtures are items commonly used in a trade or business, which are always personal property.

   Multiple Choice
   REG 2-Q95

3. Acquisition of personal property
   a. Gift Acquisition. A method of voluntarily transferring property from one person to another without consideration. Gifts typically include three key elements:
      1) There must be intent to donate the gift;
      2) There must be actual delivery of the gift; and
      3) There must be acceptance of the gift.

   In this type of acquisition, a promise of a gift is not a gift in and of itself, because there is no actual delivery of the gift.

   When considering gifts, you may also want to consider *Inter vivos* gifts, or those gifts made while the gift giver is living. These are irrevocable, even upon death. In contrast, a Gift *causa Mortis* is a "deathbed" gift and is automatically revoked if the donor does not die.

   b. Inheritance Acquisition. This is a method of transferring property from one person to another either by will or by intestate succession.

   c. Found Property. This typically occurs with either lost property or abandoned property.
   When looking at lost property, the finder of the property has ownership over the property against all individuals but the true owner of the property. In contrast, with abandoned property, the finder gets good title against all individuals, including the true owner.

4. Real property deeds
   a. Types of Deeds
      1) Elements of a deed: An effective real property deed must be made in writing, **signed** by the grantor(seller), containing a **description of the property**, and be **delivered** to the grantee(buyer).

      2) A General Warranty Deed provides the best protection for the owner of a piece of property by guaranteeing that they have a good title, including the right to convey that title, that there are no unstated encumbrances on the property, and that the Buyer's title will be undisturbed by any adverse claims of ownership from others.

      3) A Special Warranty Deed is a deed that only guarantees ownership for the time in which the seller owns a piece of property.

      4) A Quitclaim Deed is a deed where the grantor gives whatever title or interest he's got but doesn't guarantee he has anything. This is commonly known as the deed with the least protection.

Multiple Choice
REG 2-Q96

The term **fee simple** represents absolute ownership of land, where the owner may do whatever they choose with the land. If the owner of a fee simple dies intestate, the land will go to their heirs.

An **easement** is a right-of-way that does not convey ownership of the real estate that is being used as a right-of-way. It only gives the user the right to use the property.

A **license** is granted by a governing body permitting the licensee to perform a task or operation. With property, examples include licensed real estate agents and contractors.

A **restrictive covenant** is a clause in a deed to real property that limits what the owner of the land can do with the property. Restrictive covenants allow surrounding property owners, who have similar covenants in their deeds, to enforce the terms of the covenants. For example, a land developer with a planned sub-division may impose certain limitations on the use of the lots in the development. These may include a provision restricting construction to a certain type of home (i.e., single-family vs. apartments).

Multiple Choice
REG 2-Q97

   b. Recording a Deed & Mortgage
      1) Recording of a Deed or mortgage gives notice to all 3rd parties of your interest in and to real property.

      2) Unrecorded mortgages may allow a subsequent party to obtain a superior interest in the property. Three different types of recording statutes are available:
         i. In a Notice Jurisdiction, failure to record a mortgage means you lose your rights to a subsequent party who does not have notice of your interest.
         ii. In a Race Jurisdiction, the first to record the mortgage will win, regardless of whether or not they had notice; and
         iii. In a Notice-Race or Race-Notice Jurisdiction, failure to record means you lose to subsequent recording parties without notice of your interest, and who ever records first.

5. Co-ownership of property
    a. Tenants in Common is a form of co-ownership where each co-owner has an undivided interest in the property. This interest can be inherited or transferred to another party without the permission of the co-owner.

    b. Joint Tenants ownership is when each co-owner has an undivided interest in the property. In this form of ownership, each co-owner must have an equal interest in the property, and each co-ownership has a right of survivorship in the property. This allows the property to be automatically transferred to the surviving ownership if one co-owner should die. Joint Tenancies have four (4) elements that create them (**Think PITT**):
        1) **Possession** – each person has an undivided right to use the whole property;
        2) **Interest** – each joint tenant's interest is of the same type and duration;
        3) **Time** – each joint tenant's interest arose at the same time;
        4) **Title** – each joint tenant acquired their title by the same instrument.

    c. Tenants by the Entirety is a form of joint tenancy exclusively permitted to be used by a husband and wife. In this form of co-ownership, neither party may transfer their interest without their co-owners' permission.

6. Mortgages & leases
    a. Mortgages
        1) A mortgage requires four elements to be effective. The Mortgage must be made in a **writing**, **signed** by the mortgagor, containing a **description of the property**, and be **delivered** to the mortgagee.
        2) The Lien theory of Mortgages (followed in most states), states that a mortgage is simply a lien on real estate to secure payment of a debt. The mortgagor retains legal title and right to possession of the land, and the mortgagee may assign the mortgage even if the contract prohibits it. Mortgages are regulated by the Real Estate Settlement Procedures Act.
        3) Upon foreclosure, all mortgage debts and expenses are paid in the order of their priority. This means that a 1st mortgage is paid in full before subsequent mortgagees are paid. If a foreclosure should occur, the mortgagor has a right to redeem the property after the default occurs, but before a judicial sale by paying all mortgages in full.
        4) Assuming a Mortgage occurs when one party agrees to be liable for the mortgage while at the same time the seller is still liable.
        5) When a Buyer assumes a mortgage of the Seller, the buyer becomes the principal debtor to the mortgage company, and the Seller is a guarantor of the debt. If the Seller asks the mortgage company to release them from being a guarantor on the mortgage, and this is done, this is called a Novation. A Novation is considered a general release of a part.
        6) Buyer subject to a Mortgage will not make a buyer liable on the original mortgage. The buyer just agrees to make the payments on the mortgage. The original Seller is the principal debtor on the mortgage.

    b. Leases
        1) A lease is an agreement whereby the tenant has the right to exclusive possession of a piece of property but does not have ownership of that property. Unlike mortgages, leases do not require a writing unless the lease is for more than one year. If the lease is in writing, it must include a description of the leased premises.
        2) Assignment vs. Subletting a Lease. In an assignment, the new tenant pays the landlord whereas, in a sublet, the new tenant pays the old tenant who then pays the landlord. Typically, unless otherwise prohibited in a lease, either assignments or sublets are permitted. In a sublet, the original tenant is still responsible for the rent, if not paid by the sublessor.

3) Constructive eviction deals with situations where the tenant can get out of the lease when the property is made unusable by the landlord.

Multiple Choice

REG 2-Q98 through REG 2-Q99

7. Bailments
   A bailment is the temporary transfer of possession, but not title, to personal Property.

   a. Three Requirements of Bailments
      1) Delivery of personal property by a bailor to a bailee;
      2) Transfer of possession of the personal property but not ownership; and
      3) Imposes an absolute duty on a bailee to return or send the item as bailor directs.

   b. Bailee Liability
      1) A Bailee is liable for negligence (lack of due care), as the Bailee is presumed to be negligent if the goods are lost or destroyed. If the bailee can prove that the goods were lost or damaged through no fault of the Bailee, then the Bailee is not liable.
      2) The Bailee has absolute liability without regard to fault in the following cases:
         i. The bailee is strictly liable for unauthorized use of the property; and
         ii. The bailee is strictly liable for misdelivery of the property.
      3) An extraordinary bailee (common carrier, airlines, trucking companies) have absolute liability, and their only defense to not being liable, is that the goods were destroyed by an act of God, or were improperly packed by the bailee.

This page is intentionally left blank.

Glossary: Business Law

A

Americans with Disabilities Act – provides protections for employees with handicaps to help ensure that employers cannot and do not discriminate against persons with disabilities, as long as the employee can do the basic job

Antecedent debt - an existing overdue debt

Attachment – formal process of placing a claim on a piece of property owned by the debtor, in exchange for credit

Agency – fiduciary relationship between two parties whereby one party (the agent) agrees to work for, represent, and/or act for the other party (the principal)

Agent – individual who has the authority to act on behalf of another (typically the principal)

Acceptance – offeree agrees to the terms and conditions presented by the offeror

Assignment of contract – original party in the contract is replaced with the new party, the assignee

Age Discrimination Employment Act (ADEA) – prohibits discrimination in employment decisions based on age, and protects workers age 40-70

B

Bankruptcy – governed almost exclusively by Federal law and is the process by which creditor's rights are protected while at the same time providing relief to the debtor from their indebtedness

Bilateral contract – contracts that call for a promise in exchange for a promise

Bailment – temporary transfer of possession, but not title, to personal property

C

Comprehensive Environmental Response, Compensation and Liability Act (CERCLA) – provides a federal Superfund to clean up controlled or abandoned hazardous waste sites

Clean Air Act (CAA) – principal federal law for dealing with air pollution

Chapter 7 bankruptcy – most common form of bankruptcy for companies, is often referred to as "liquidation" or "straight bankruptcy," and it involves the process of turning a debtor's assets into cash to pay creditors

Chapter 11 bankruptcy – reorganization of debt, as opposed to the selling, or liquidation of assets to pay off the debts of the debtor

Chapter 13 bankruptcy – reorganization of debts by individuals. Corporations and partnerships are not permitted to utilize the Chapter 13 process

Contract – any agreement between two or more parties where the parties make a set of promises, the breach of which the law provides a remedy

Consideration – giving up of a legal right that is either legally detrimental to the promisee, or legally beneficial to the promisor

Complete performance – occurs when all aspects of the party's duties and responsibilities have been completed in perfect accordance with the terms of the contract

Creditor beneficiary – thirty party who receives a benefit from a contract where one person agrees to pay the debt of another

Compensatory Damages – damages that aware money to compensate for any and all harm done to the non-breaching party

Common Carrier – carrier of multiple types of goods (i.e. cargo ship or airplane)

Clean Water Act (CWA) – principal federal law for dealing with water pollution

Corporation – legal entity formed by issuing stock to individuals who are investing in the company. These investors become the owners of the corporation by becoming shareholders in the corporation. A corporation is considered a separate legal entity from its shareholders

D

Discharge of debt – occurs when the debtor is released from paying their debts not paid in bankruptcy

Disclosed principal – principal whose identity is known to a third party at the time the agent makes a contract with the third party

Duress – forcing of an individual into a contract by force or threat of immediate force, violence, economic, or criminal action

Donee beneficiary contracts – where one party agrees to make a gift to another individual

Delegation of contract – original party in the contract substitutes another party into the contract to do some, or all, of the items promised by the original party

Destination contract – title and risk of loss pass from the seller to the buyer once the goods have gotten to their destination

E

Express contracts – contracts that at formed through the express written or verbal agreement of the parties.

Equal Pay for Equal Work Act – prohibits discrimination based on sex

Express warranty – buyer receives this from a seller and typically includes a material representation of a fact, or facts, regarding the goods being sold

Employee Retirement Income Security Act (ERISA) – regulates pension plans but does not require that a company establish a pension plan

Environmental Protection Agency (EPA) – principal administrative agency for federal environmental laws and may initiate both civil and criminal law suites through the Justice Department to help enforce federal environmental laws

Environmental impact statement (EIS) – must be drafted when major federal actions might significantly affect the quality of the human environment

Easement – right-of-way that does not convey ownership of the real estate that is being used as a right-of-way. It only gives the user the right to use the property

F

Federal Labor Standards Act (FLSA) – provides protection for workers that includes an age limit to work and also addresses wage and hour restrictons

Family Medical Leave Act (FMLA) – entitles employees to take twelve (12) weeks of unpaid, job-protected leave in any one (1) year period to allow for the employee to deal with the birth of a newborn child, care for an adopted child, or a serious health condition for either themselves or someone in their immediate family

Federal Unemployment Tax Act (FUTA) – provides for unemployment benefits to be collected by employees who have lost their jobs through no fault of their own, and are willing, able, and looking for work

Federal Insurance Contribution Act (FICA) – represents the federal payroll tax imposed on employees, employers, and independent contractors to fund Social Security and Medicare

Fair Debt Collection Practices Act – forces a creditor into collecting judgments against a debtor in very specifics manners

Fraudulent Conveyance – conveyances of property by the debtor to a third party to attempt to keep the property from a creditor

Fixtures – personal property that s attached to real estate in such a way that it becomes part of the real estate as a matter of law. (i.e. a bookshelf screwed into the wall of a rental apartment may be considered a permanent fixture of the apartment)

Free on board (FOB) – specifically fixes a time and place to where risk of loss and title pass from the buyer to the seller

Fraud – act of using deception to get another party to agree to the terms of a contract.

Fraud in the execution – occurs when the injured party enters into a contract not knowing that they have entered into a contract

Fraud in the inducement – occurs when the injured party knows that they have entered into a contract, but one or more terms of the contract have been misrepresented

Firm offer – offer for the sale of goods that is irrevocable without consideration by the maker of the offeror.

Federal Securities and Exchange Act of 1934 – created the Security and Exchange Commission (SEC) to help oversee all publicly traded stocks within the country

G

General Warranty Deed – provides the best protection for the owner of a piece of property by guaranteeing that they have good title, including the right to convey that title, that there are no unstated encumbrances on the property, and that the buyer's title will be undisturbed by any adverse claims of ownership from others

H

I

Implied contracts – contracts that are formed, at least in part, by the parties' conduct

Incidental beneficiaries – individuals who are unintentionally given benefits when two other parties reach an agreement

Injunction – court ordering one party to either do or refrain from doing a specific act

Implied warranty – require no words, either oral or written
Involuntary Petition – creditors of a debtor request that the court intervene and provide relief under bankruptcy
Intangible Personal Property – an individual's interests or rights in property that cannot be held physically and are often referred to as "intellectual property" (i.e., copyrights, patents, and trademarks)
J
K
L
Limited Liability Partnership – assumes the liability of any of its partner's professional malpractice, but only to the extent of the partnership assets
Limited Partnership – consists of two or more parties where there is at least one "general partner" and at least one "limited partner." In this type of partnership, the "general partners" assume all liability for the partnership debt and the "limited partner" is not liable for the partnership debt
Limited Liability Companies (LLC) – an organization where the LLC members have no personal liability beyond their initial investment, owners may fully participate in management (similar to a partnership) and can have the same tax advantages as a partnership
M
Material breach – major failure to perform one or more terms called for in the contract
Mailbox rule – acceptance of an offer will be valid when sent (not received) if the acceptance is properly addressed and the offeree uses the express means of communicating the acceptance, or a reasonable means of communication if no specific means are stated
Mutual mistakes – mistakes that both parties make as to a material fact involved in the contract
Minors – generally considered not competent to execute contracts, and contracts that they enter into can be disaffirmed by the minor at any time that the person is a minor, or for a reasonable time after that
N
Non-Purchase Money Security Interest Creditor – takes collateral in exchange for advancing funds; however, the collateral taken is not the property for which the funds are used to purchase
National Environmental Policy Act (NEPA) of 1969 – requires that all branches of government consider the environmental effects of major federal actions before undertaking those actions
O
Offer – presentation of terms and conditions made by one party (the offeror) to another party (the offeree).
Occupational Safety and Health Act (OSHA) – administered by the Occupational Safety and Health Administration and establishes safety and health standards to the workplace
Obergefell v. Hodges – court case that ruled there was a fundamental right to marry that is guaranteed to same-sex couples by both the Due Process Clause and the Equal Protection Clause of the U.S. Constitution
P
Perfected security interest - has claims and rights to certain property that are ahead of unprotected or unperfected creditors
Purchase Money Security Interest Creditors (PMSI) – have advance funds on the basis of credit to enable the debtor to buy the collateral used to secure the loan. The creditor immediately takes a security interest in the collateral that is purchased with the money
Preferential transfer – made within ninety (90) days of the filing for Chapter 7 bankruptcy and include transfers made for preexisting debts or debts that if paid, enable the creditor to receive more than they would have received under a Chapter 7 filing
Power of attorney – written authorization of agency
Principal – individual who authorizes agent(s) to act on their behalf
Parole Evidence Rule – evidence contradicting a written contract is inadmissible in court to prove the content of a contract
Patient Protection and Affordable Care Act (PPACA) – provides a set of standards to ensure that all individuals in the country have access to affordable, quality health insurance and care
Partnership – any voluntary associated of two or more co-owners operating a business for profit
Q
Quitclaim Deed – grantor gives whatever title or interest he's got, but doesn't guarantee that he has anything
R

Real property – land and all items attached to the land, including items above and below the land
Rehabilitation Act of 1973 – requires that employers with federal contracts of $2,500 or more take affirmative action to hire qualified disabled workers
Rescission – contract damage that is available to the parties that will restore the parties to their original positions
Resource Conservation and Recovery Act (RCRA) – provides the Environmental Protection Agency (EPA) the power to control hazardous waste at current or future sites and to set standards for the disposal of nonhazardous solid waste

S

Special Warranty Deed – only guarantees ownership for the time in which the seller owns a piece of property.
Sole Proprietorship – business in which one person is in total control of the management and profits
Securities and Exchange Commission (SEC) – created by the Federal Securities and Exchange Act of 1934 to regulate, not only the stock offerings themselves but the individuals working on stock offerings, as well as the stock exchanges themselves
Securities Act of 1933 – focuses on providing investors with information needed to understand where offering proceeds will be used
Secured claim – held by a creditor who has an interest in a specific piece of property
Secured creditor – have attached a specific piece of property held by the debtor in exchange for something of value (typically the money used to purchase that property). Secured creditors' claims must be satisfied prior to liquidating assets for payment to other creditors
Secured transaction – payment of a debt is guaranteed by the personal property owned by the debtor
Surety – party who promises to pay a creditor the amount owned if the debtor defaults on a debt
Statute of frauds – requires that certain contracts be in writing to be enforceable
Scienter – intent to deceive
Substantial performance – occurs when almost all of the terms and conditions of the agreement between the parties have been met
Specific performance – contract damage that is used when monetary damages alone would not be adequate to repay the party for the breach of a contract
Sales contract – governed by Article 2 of the UCC, it must involve goods which are defined as moveable personal property. Article 2 contracts do not involve personal services, real estate, or intangible personal property
Shipment Contract – risk of loss in the goods, as well as title to those goods, to pass to the buyer when the seller gets to goods in question to the carrier
Sale on approval – neither risk of loss nor title passes until the buyer approves the sale
Sale or return – buyer has the risk of loss and title on delivery, but may return the goods

T

Trust claim – made by a beneficiary for trust property, that property is not considered part of the debtor's estate.
Title VII of the Civil Rights Act – prohibits discrimination in the workplace based on race, color, religion, sex, or national origin. This Act does not protect against age discrimination
Third party beneficiary contracts – involve contracts that are made for the benefit of an individual not identified in the contract
Tangible Personal Property – includes property that can be physically held by an individual

U

Unsecured Creditor – where unsecured claims are paid in full at each level of priority before any claims at a lower level are paid
Undisclosed principal – principal whose identity is unknown by a third party, and the third party does not know that the agent is acting for a principal at the time the agent and the third party form a contract
Unilateral contract – contracts that are created when there is a promise for an act
Unilateral mistakes – mistakes that only one party made concerning a material fact in the contract
Under influence - occurs when a party uses their position of love, confidence, or affection to overcome the other party's free will and have that individual agree to the terms of a contract

V

Voluntary Petition – occurs when the debtor makes a formal request for relief for bankruptcyy
Void contracts – contracts that are unenforceable by either party
Voidable contracts – contracts that are rescindable by only one party in the contract

W
Workers compensation insurance – provides employees injured within the scope of employment the help that they need to return to work
X
Y
Z

This page is intentionally left blank.

Multiple Choice – Questions

REG 2-Q1 R41. Which of the following conditions must be met to form an agency?

A. An agency agreement must be in writing.
B. An agency agreement must be signed by both parties.
C. The principal must furnish legally adequate consideration for the agent's services.
D. The principal must possess contractual capacity.

REG 2-Q2 R209. Which of the following is a prerequisite for the creation of an agency relationship?

A. Consideration must be given.
B. The agent must have capacity.
C. The principal must have capacity.
D. The consideration must be in writing.

REG 2-Q3 R409. Lee repairs high-speed looms for Sew Corp., a clothing manufacturer. Which of the following circumstances best indicates that Lee is an employee of Sew and not an independent contractor?

A. Lee's work is not supervised by Sew personnel.
B. Lee's tools are owned by Lee.
C. Lee is paid weekly by Sew.
D. Lee's work requires a high degree of technical skill.

REG 2-Q4 R78. Under agency law, which of the following statements best describes ratification?

A. A principal's affirmation of an agent's authorized act.
B. A principal's affirmation of an agent's unauthorized act.
C. A principal's approval in advance of an agent's acts.
D. A principal's disapproval of an agent's unauthorized act.

REG 2-Q5 R310. Under the agent's duty to account, which of the following acts must a gratuitous agent perform?

	Commingle funds	Account for the principal's property
A.	Yes	Yes
B.	Yes	No
C.	No	Yes
D.	No	No

REG 2-Q6 R410. Blue, a used car dealer, appointed Gage as an agent to sell Blue's cars. Gage was authorized by Blue to appoint subagents to assist in the sale of the cars. Vond was appointed as a sub-agent. To whom does Vond owe a fiduciary duty?

A. Gage only.
B. Blue only.
C. Both Blue and Gage.
D. Neither Blue nor Gage.

REG 2-Q7 R290. Part agreed to act as Young's agent to sell Young's land. Part was instructed not to disclose that Part was acting as an agent of Young. Part contracted with Rice for Rice to purchase the land. After Rice discovered Young's identity, Young refused to fulfill the contract. Who does Rice have a cause of action against?

	Part	Young
A.	Yes	Yes
B.	Yes	No
C.	No	Yes
D.	No	No

REG 2-Q8 R328. Which of the following acts, if committed by an agent, will cause a principal to be liable to a third party?

A. A negligent act committed by an independent contractor, in performance of the contract, which results in injury to a third party.
B. An intentional tort committed by an employee outside the scope of employment, which results in injury to a third party.
C. An employee's failure to notify the employer of a dangerous condition that results in injury to a third party.
D. A negligent act committed by an employee outside the scope of employment that results in injury to a third party.

REG 2-Q9 R381. Under the Sales Article of the UCC, in an auction announced in explicit terms to be without reserve, when may an auctioneer withdraw the goods put up for sale?

I. At any time until the auctioneer announces completion of the sale.
II. If no bid is made within a reasonable time.

A. I only.
B. II only.
C. Either I or II.
D. Neither I nor II.

REG 2-Q10 R422. Patch, a frequent shopper at Soon-Shop Stores, received a rain check for an advertised sale item after Soon-Shop's supply of the product ran out. The rain check was in writing and stated that the item would be offered to the customer at the advertised sale price for an unspecified period of time. A Soon-Shop employee signed the rain check. When Patch returned to the store one month later to purchase the item, the store refused to honor the rain check. Under the Sales Article of the UCC, will Patch win a suit to enforce the rain check?

A. No, because one month is too long a period of time for a rain check to be effective.
B. No, because the rain check did not state the effective time period necessary to keep the offer open.
C. Yes, because Soon-Shop is required to have sufficient supplies of the sale item to satisfy all customers.
D. Yes, because the rain check met the requirements of a merchant's firm offer even though no effective time period was stated.

REG 2-Q11 R275. Which of the following types of mistake will generally make a contract unenforceable and allow it to be rescinded?

A. A unilateral mistake of fact.
B. A mutual mistake of fact.
C. A unilateral mistake of value.
D. A mutual mistake of value.

REG 2-Q12 R441. Which of the following types of conduct renders a contract void?

A. Mutual mistake as to facts forming the basis of the contract.
B. Undue influence by a dominant party in a confidential relationship.
C. Duress through physical compulsion.
D. Duress through improper threats.

REG 2-Q13 R428. If a person is induced to enter into a contract by another person because of the close relationship between the parties, the contract may be voidable under which of the following defenses?

A. Fraud in the inducement.
B. Unconscionability.
C. Undue influence.
D. Duress.

REG 2-Q14 R240. Which of the following promises is supported by legally sufficient consideration and will be enforceable?

A. A person's promise to pay a real estate agent $1,000 in return for the real estate agent's earlier act of not charging commission for selling the person's house.
B. A parent's promise to pay one child $500 because that child is not as wealthy as the child's sibling.
C. A promise to pay the police $250 to catch a thief.
D. A promise to pay a minor $500 to paint a garage.

REG 2-Q15 R423. A sheep rancher agreed, in writing, to sell all the wool shorn during the shearing season to a weaver. The contract failed to establish the price and a minimum quantity of wool. After the shearing season, the rancher refused to deliver the wool. The weaver sued the rancher for breach of contract. Under the Sales Article of the UCC, will the weaver win?

A. Yes, because this was an output contract.
B. Yes, because both price and quantity terms were omitted.
C. No, because quantity cannot be omitted for a contract to be enforceable.
D. No, because the omission of reasonable price and quantity terms prevents the formation of a contract.

REG 2-Q16 R38. To which of the following transactions does the common law Statute of Frauds not apply.

A. Contracts for the sale of real estate.
B. Agreements made in consideration of marriage.
C. Promises to pay the debt of another.
D. Contracts that can be performed within one year.

REG 2-Q17 R135. On December 1, 2015, Gem orally contracted with Mason for Mason to manage Gem's restaurant for one year starting the following January 1, 2016. They agreed that Gem would pay Mason $40,000 and that Mason would be allowed to continue to work for Gem if "everything worked out." On June 1, 2016, Mason quit to take a better paying job, alleging that the contract violated the statute of frauds. What will be the outcome of a suit by Gem for breach of contract?

A. Gem will win because the contract was executory.
B. Gem will win because the contract was for services not goods.
C. Gem will lose because the contract could not be performed within one year.
D. Gem will lose because the contract required payment of more than $500.

REG 2-Q18 R273. All of the following statements regarding compliance with the statute of frauds are correct except

A. Any necessary writing must be signed by all parties against whom enforcement is sought.
B. Contracts involving the sale of goods in an amount greater than $500 must be in writing.
C. Contract terms must be contained in only one document.
D. Contracts for which it is improbable to assume that performance will be completed within one year must be in writing.

REG 2-Q19 R311. Kram sent Fargo, a real estate broker, a signed offer to sell a specified parcel of land to Fargo for $250,000. Kram, an engineer, had inherited the land. On the same day that Kram's letter was received, Fargo telephoned Kram and accepted the offer. Which of the following statements is correct under the common law statute of frauds?

A. No contract could be formed because Fargo's acceptance was oral.
B. No contract could be formed because Kram's letter was signed only by Kram.
C. A contract was formed and would be enforceable against both Kram and Fargo.
D. A contract was formed but would be enforceable only against Kram.

REG 2-Q20 R320. On May 25, Fresno sold Bronson, a minor, a used computer. On June 1, Bronson reached the age of majority. On June 10, Fresno wanted to rescind the sale. Fresno offered to return Bronson's money and demanded that Bronson return the computer. Bronson refused, claiming that a binding contract existed. Bronson's refusal is

A. Not justified, because Fresno is not bound by the contract unless Bronson specifically ratifies the contract after reaching the age of majority.
B. Not justified, because Fresno does not have to perform under the contract if Bronson has a right to disaffirm the contract.
C. Justified, because Bronson and Fresno are bound by the contract as of the date Bronson reached the age of majority.
D. Justified, because Fresno must perform under the contract regardless of Bronson's minority.

REG 2-Q21 R416. Green was adjudicated incompetent by a court having proper jurisdiction. Which of the following statements is correct regarding contracts subsequently entered into by Green?

A. All contracts are voidable.
B. All contracts are valid.
C. All contracts are void.
D. All contracts are enforceable.

REG 2-Q22 R72. What type of conduct generally will make a contract voidable?

A. Fraud in the execution.
B. Fraud in the inducement.
C. Physical coercion.
D. Contracting with a person under guardianship.

REG 2-Q23 R679. In negotiations with Andrews for the lease of Kemp's warehouse, Kemp orally agreed to pay one-half of the cost of the utilities. The written lease, later prepared by Kemp's attorney, provided that Andrews pay all of the utilities. Andrews failed to carefully read the lease and signed it. When Kemp demanded that Andrews pay all of the utilities, Andrews refused, claiming that the lease did not accurately reflect the oral agreement. Andrews also learned that Kemp intentionally misrepresented the condition of the structure of the warehouse during the negotiations between the parties. Andrews sued to rescind the lease and intends to introduce evidence of the parties' oral agreement about sharing the utilities and the fraudulent statements made by Kemp. The parole evidence rule will prevent the admission of evidence concerning the

	Oral agreement regarding who pays the utilities	Fraudulent statements by Kemp
A.	Yes	Yes
B.	No	Yes
C.	Yes	No
D.	No	No

REG 2-Q24 R79. Pierce owed Duke $3,000. Pierce contracted with Lodge to paint Lodge's house and Lodge agreed to pay Duke $3,000 to satisfy Pierce's debt. Pierce painted Lodge's house but Lodge did not pay Duke the $3,000. In a lawsuit by Duke against Pierce and Lodge, who will be liable to Duke?

A. Pierce only.
B. Lodge only.
C. Both Pierce and Lodge.
D. Neither Pierce nor Lodge.

REG 2-Q25 R301. Which of the following contract rights can generally be assigned?

A. The right to receive personal services.
B. The right to receive a sum of money.
C. The right of an insured to coverage under a fire insurance policy.
D. A right whose assignment is prohibited by statute.

REG 2-Q26 R333. West, Inc. and Barton entered into a contract. After receiving valuable consideration from Egan, West assigned its rights under the Barton contract to Egan. In which of the following circumstances would West not be liable to Egan?

A. West released Barton.
B. West breached the contract.
C. Egan released Barton.
D. Barton paid West.

REG 2-Q27 R417. Which of the following actions if taken by one party to a contract generally will discharge the performance required of the other party to the contract?

A. Material breach of the contract.
B. Delay in performance.
C. Tender.
D. Assignment of rights.

REG 2-Q28 R329. When there has been no performance by either party, which of the following events generally will result in the discharge of a party's obligation to perform as required under the original contract?

	Accord and satisfaction	Mutual rescission
A.	Yes	Yes
B.	Yes	No
C.	No	Yes
D.	No	No

REG 2-Q29 R255. For which of the following contracts will a court generally grant the remedy of specific performance?

A. A contract for the sale of a patent.
B. A contract of employment.
C. A contract for the sale of fungible goods.
D. A contract for the sale of stock that is traded on a national stock exchange.

REG 2-Q30 R212. In June, Mullin, a general contractor, contracted with a town to renovate the town square. The town council wanted the project done quickly and the parties placed a clause in the contract that for each day the project extended beyond 90 working days, Mullin would forfeit $100 of the contract price. In August, Mullin took a three-week vacation. The project was completed in October, 120 working days after it was begun. What type of damages may the town recover from Mullin?

A. Punitive damages because taking a vacation in the middle of the project was irresponsible.
B. Compensatory damages because of the delay in completing the project.
C. Liquidated damages because of the clause in the contract.
D. No damages because Mullin completed performance.

REG 2-Q31 R59. On day 1, Jackson, a merchant, mailed Sands a signed letter that contained an offer to sell Sands 500 electric fans at $10 per fan. The letter was received by Sands on day 3. The letter contained a promise not to revoke the offer but no expiration date. On day 4, Jackson mailed Sands a revocation of the offer to sell the fans. Sands received the revocation on day 6. On day 7, Sands mailed Jackson an acceptance of the offer. Jackson received the acceptance on day 9. Under the Sales Article of the UCC, was a contract formed?

A. No contract was formed because the offer failed to state an expiration date.
B. No contract was formed because Sands received the revocation of the offer before Sands accepted the offer.
C. A contract was formed on the day Jackson received Sands' acceptance.
D. A contract was formed on the day Sands mailed the acceptance to Jackson.

REG 2-Q32 R379. Under the Sales Article of the UCC, which of the following statements is correct regarding a good faith requirement that must be met by a merchant?

A. The merchant must adhere to all written and oral terms of the sales contract.
B. The merchant must provide more extensive warranties than the minimum required by law.
C. The merchant must charge the lowest available price for the product in the geographic market.
D. The merchant must observe the reasonable commercial standards of fair dealing in the trade.

REG 2-Q33 R5. Under the Sales Article of the UCC, which of the following requirements must be met for a writing to be an enforceable contract for the sale of goods?

A. The writing must contain a term specifying the price of the goods.
B. The writing must contain a term specifying the quantity of the goods.
C. The writing must contain the signatures of all parties to the writing.
D. The writing must contain the signature of the party seeking to enforce the writing.

REG 2-Q34 R432. EG Door Co., a manufacturer of custom exterior doors, verbally contracted with Art Contractors to design and build a $2,000 custom door for a house that Art was restoring. After EG had completed substantial work on the door, Art advised EG that the house had been destroyed by fire and Art was cancelling the contract. EG finished the door and shipped it to Art. Art refused to accept delivery. Art contends that the contract cannot be enforced because it violated the Statute of Frauds by not being in writing. Under the Sales Article of the UCC, is Art's contention correct?

A. Yes, because the contract was not in writing.
B. Yes, because the contract cannot be fully performed due to the fire.
C. No, because the goods were specially manufactured for Art and cannot be resold in EG's regular course of business.
D. No, because the cancellation of the contract was not made in writing.

REG 2-Q35 R6. When do title and risk of loss for conforming goods pass to the buyer under a shipment contract covered by the Sales Article of the UCC?

A. When the goods are identified and designated for shipment.
B. When the goods are given to a common carrier.
C. When the goods arrive at their destination.
D. When the goods are tendered to the buyer at their destination.

REG 2-Q36 R380. Under the Sales Article of the UCC, which of the following statements is correct regarding a seller's obligation under a F.O.B. destination contract?

A. The seller is required to arrange for the buyer to pick up the conforming goods at a specified destination.
B. The seller is required to tender delivery of conforming goods at a specified destination.
C. The seller is required to tender delivery of conforming goods at the buyer's place of business.
D. The seller is required to tender delivery of conforming goods to a carrier who delivers to a destination specified by the buyer.

REG 2-Q37 R374. Under the Sales Article of the UCC, which of the following statements is correct regarding risk of loss and title to the goods under a sale or return contract?

A. Title and risk of loss are shared equally between the buyer and the seller.
B. Title remains with the seller until the buyer approves or accepts the goods, but risk of loss passes to the buyer immediately following delivery of the goods to the buyer.
C. Title and risk of loss remain with the seller until the buyer pays for the goods.
D. Title and risk of loss rest with the buyer until the goods are returned to the seller.

REG 2-Q38 R377. An appliance seller promised a restaurant owner that a home dishwasher would fulfill the dishwashing requirements of a large restaurant. The dishwasher was purchased but it was not powerful enough for the restaurant. Under the Sales Article of the UCC, what warranty was violated?

A. The implied warranty of marketability.
B. The implied warranty of merchantability.
C. The express warranty that the goods conform to the seller's promise.
D. The express warranty against infringement.

REG 2-Q39 R440. Under the Sales Article of the UCC, which of the following circumstances best describes how the implied warranty of fitness for a particular purpose arises in a sale of goods transaction?

A. The buyer is purchasing the goods for a particular purpose and is relying on the seller's skill or judgment to select suitable goods.
B. The buyer is purchasing the goods for a particular purpose and the seller is a merchant in such goods.
C. The seller knows the particular purpose for which the buyer will use the goods and knows the buyer is relying on the seller's skill or judgment to select suitable goods.
D. The seller knows the particular purpose for which the buyer will use the goods and the seller is a merchant in such goods.

REG 2-Q40 R118. Card communicated an offer to sell Card's stereo to Bend for $250. Which of the following statements is correct regarding the effect of the communication of the offer?

A. Bend should immediately accept or reject the offer to avoid liability to Card.
B. Card is not obligated to sell the stereo to Bend until Bend accepts the offer.
C. Card is required to mitigate any loss Card would sustain in the event Bend rejects the offer.
D. Bend may not reject the offer for a reasonable period of time.

REG 2-Q41 R378. Under the Sales Article of the UCC, which of the following circumstances will relieve a buyer from the obligation of accepting a tender or delivery of goods?

I. If the goods do not meet the buyer's needs at the time of the tender or delivery.
II. If the goods at the time of the tender or delivery do not exactly conform to the requirements of the contract.

A. I only.
B. II only.
C. Both I and II.
D. Neither I nor II.

REG 2-Q42 R136. Which of the following bonds are an obligation of a surety?

A. Convertible bonds.
B. Debenture bonds.
C. Municipal bonds.
D. Official bonds.

REG 2-Q43 R360. Teller, Kerr, and Ace are co-sureties on a $120,000 loan with maximum liabilities of $20,000, $40,000, and $60,000, respectively. The debtor defaulted on the loan when the loan balance was $60,000. Ace paid the lender $48,000 in full settlement of all claims against Teller, Kerr, and Ace. What amount may Ace collect from Kerr?

A. $0
B. $16,000
C. $20,000
D. $28,000

REG 2-Q44 R153. Camp orally guaranteed payment of a loan Camp's cousin Wilcox had obtained from Camp's friend Main. The loan was to be repaid in 10 monthly payments. After making six payments, Wilcox defaulted on the loan and Main demanded that Camp honor the guaranty. Regarding Camp's liability to Main, Camp is

A. Liable under the oral guaranty because the loan would be paid within one year.
B. Liable under the oral guaranty because Camp benefitted by maintaining a personal relationship with Main.
C. Not liable under the oral guaranty because Camp's guaranty must be in writing to be enforceable.
D. Not liable under the oral guaranty because of failure of consideration.

REG 2-Q45 R418. Which of the following events will release a non-compensated surety from liability to the creditor?

A. The principal debtor was involuntarily petitioned into bankruptcy.
B. The creditor failed to notify the surety of a partial surrender of the principal debtor's collateral.
C. The creditor was adjudicated incompetent after the debt arose.
D. The principal debtor exerted duress to obtain the surety agreement.

REG 2-Q46 R334. The federal Fair Debt Collection Practices Act prohibits a debt collector from engaging in unfair practices. Under the Act, a debt collector generally can be prevented from

A. Contacting a third party to ascertain a debtor's location.
B. Continuing to collect a debt.
C. Communicating with a debtor who is represented by an attorney.
D. Commencing a lawsuit to collect a debt.

REG 2-Q47 R359. Hall, CPA, is an unsecured creditor of Tree Company, who is owed $15,500. Tree has a total of 10 creditors, including Hall, all of whom are unsecured. Tree has not paid any of the creditors for three months. Under Chapter 7 of the federal Bankruptcy Code, which of the following statements is correct?

A. Hall and two other unsecured creditors must join in the involuntary petition in bankruptcy.
B. Hall may file an involuntary petition in bankruptcy against Tree.
C. Tree may not be petitioned involuntarily into bankruptcy under the provisions of Chapter 11 (reorganization).
D. Tree may not be petitioned involuntarily into bankruptcy because there are less than 12 unsecured creditors.

REG 2-Q48 R317. Under the federal Bankruptcy Code, which of the following rights or powers does a trustee in bankruptcy not have?

A. The power to prevail against a creditor with an unperfected security interest.
B. The power to require persons holding the debtor's property at the time the bankruptcy petition is filed to deliver the property to the trustee.
C. The right to use any grounds available to the debtor to obtain the return of the debtor's property.
D. The right to avoid any statutory liens against the debtor's property that were effective before the bankruptcy petition was filed.

REG 2-Q49 R429. Under the liquidation provisions of Chapter 7 of the federal Bankruptcy Code, certain property acquired by the debtor after the filing of the petition becomes part of the bankruptcy estate. An example of such property is

A. Inheritances received by the debtor within 180 days after the filing of the petition.
B. Child support payments received by the debtor within one year after the filing of the petition.
C. Social Security payments received by the debtor within 180 days after the filing of the petition.
D. Wages earned by the debtor within one year after the filing of the petition.

REG 2-Q50 R369. Under Chapter 7 of the federal Bankruptcy Code, what affect does a bankruptcy discharge have on a judgment creditor when there is no bankruptcy estate?

A. The judgment creditor's claim is nondischargeable.
B. The judgment creditor retains a statutory lien against the debtor.
C. The debtor is relieved of any personal liability to the judgment creditor.
D. The debtor is required to pay a liquidated amount to vacate the judgment.

REG 2-Q51 R370. A family farmer with regular annual income may file a voluntary petition for bankruptcy under any of the following Chapters of the federal Bankruptcy Code except

A. 7
B. 9
C. 11
D. 13

REG 2-Q52 R25. Under the Secured Transactions Article of the UCC, which of the following security agreements does not need to be in writing to be enforceable?

A. A security agreement collateralizing a debt of less than $500.
B. A security agreement where the collateral is highly perishable or subject to wide price fluctuations.
C. A security agreement where the collateral is in the possession of the secured party.
D. A security agreement involving a purchase money security interest.

REG 2-Q53 R8. Under the Secured Transactions article of the UCC, when does a security interest become enforceable?

A. A contract is executed between a debtor and a secured party under which the debtor gives the secured party rights in collateral if the debtor violates any of the terms contained in the contract.
B. The debtor and the secured party execute a security agreement describing the transfer of the collateral and, after doing so, the secured party files it with the requisite agency.
C. The debtor and the secured party execute a security agreement describing the transfer of collateral from seller to buyer and the secured party retains possession of the agreement.
D. The value has been given, the secured party receives a security agreement describing the collateral authenticated by the debtor, and the debtor has rights in the collateral.

REG 2-Q54 R160. Under the Secured Transactions Article of the UCC, what secured transaction document must be signed by the debtor?

A. Statement of Assignment.
B. Security Agreement.
C. Release of Collateral.
D. Termination Statement.

REG 2-Q55 R164. Under the Secured Transactions Article of the UCC, all of the following are needed to create an enforceable security interest, except

A. A security agreement must exist.
B. The secured party must give value.
C. The debtor must have rights in the collateral
D. A financing statement must be filed.

REG 2-Q56 R98. Under the Secured Transactions Article of the UCC, which of the following statements is correct regarding a security interest that has not attached?

A. It is effective against the debtor, but not against third parties.
B. It is effective against both the debtor and third parties.
C. It is effective against third parties with unsecured claims.
D. It is not effective against either the debtor or third parties.

REG 2-Q57 R26. Under the Secured Transactions Article of the UCC, which of the following items can usually be excluded from a filed original financing statement?

A. The name of the debtor.
B. The address of the debtor.
C. A description of the collateral.
D. The amount of the obligation secured.

REG 2-Q58 R159. Under the Secured Transactions Article of the UCC, for which of the following types of collateral must a financing statement be filed in order to perfect a purchase money security interest?

A. Stock certificates.
B. Promissory Notes.
C. Personal Jewelry.
D. Inventory.

REG 2-Q59 R313. Under the Secured Transactions Article of the UCC, a secured party generally must comply with each of the following duties except

A. Filing or sending the debtor a termination statement when the debt is paid.
B. Confirming, at the debtor's request, the unpaid amount of the debt.
C. Using reasonable care in preserving any collateral in the secured party's possession.
D. Assigning the security interest to another party at the debtor's request.

REG 2-Q60 R254. On April 1, Roe borrowed $100,000 from Jet to pay Roe's business expenses. On June 15, Roe gave Jet a signed security agreement and financing statement covering Roe's inventory. Jet immediately filed the financing statement. On July 1, Roe filed for bankruptcy. Under the federal Bankruptcy Code, can Roe's trustee in bankruptcy set aside Jet's security interest in Roe's inventory?

A. Yes, because a security agreement may only cover goods actually purchased with the borrowed funds.
B. Yes, because Roe giving the security interest to Jet created a voidable preference.
C. No, because the security interest was perfected before Roe filed for bankruptcy.
D. No, because the loan proceeds were used for Roe's business.

REG 2-Q61 R258. Under the Secured Transactions Article of the UCC, which of the following statements is(are) correct regarding the filing of a financing statement?

I. A financing statement must be filed before attachment of the security interest can occur.
II. Once filed, a financing statement is effective for an indefinite period of time provided continuation statements are timely filed.

A. I only.
B. II only.
C. Both I and II.
D. Neither I nor II.

REG 2-Q62 R228. The Securities Act of 1933 provides an exemption from registration for

Bonds issued by a municipality for governmental purposes	Securities issued by a not-for-profit charitable organization
A. Yes	Yes
B. Yes	No
C. No	Yes
D. No	No

REG 2-Q63 R100. Which of the following transactions is subject to registration requirements of the Securities Act of 1933?

A. The public sale of stock of a trucking company regulated by the Interstate Commerce Commission.
B. A public sale of municipal bonds issued by a city government.
C. The issuance of stock by a publicly-traded corporation to its existing shareholders because of a stock split.
D. The public sale by a corporation of its negotiable 10-year notes.

REG 2-Q64 R294. Which of the following securities is exempt from registration under the Securities Act of 1933?

A. Municipal bonds.
B. Securities sold by a discount broker.
C. Pre-incorporation stock subscriptions.
D. One-year notes issued to raise working capital.

REG 2-Q65 R137. According to the Securities Act of 1933, which of the following statements is correct regarding an issuer of securities?

A. All securities issuers must provide potential investors with a prospectus containing specified information.
B. An issuer is permitted to advertise an initial offering of securities only through distribution of the prospectus.
C. All securities issuers must register the securities offering with the Securities and Exchange Commission (SEC).
D. If an issuer sells a security and fails to meet certain disclosure requirements, the purchaser may sell it back to the issuer and recover the price paid.

REG 2-Q66 R312. Under the Securities Act of 1933, which of the following statements is(are) correct regarding the purpose of registration?

I. The purpose of registration is to allow for the detection of management fraud and prevent a public offering of securities when management fraud is suspected.
II. The purpose of registration is to adequately and accurately disclose financial and other information upon which investors may determine the merits of securities.

A. I only.
B. II only.
C. Both I and II.
D. Neither I nor II.

REG 2-Q67 R361. Under the Securities Act of 1933, which of the following acts by an accountant may subject the accountant to criminal penalties?

A. Negligently making a false entry in financial statements included in a registration statement.
B. Giving an unqualified opinion on negligently prepared financial statements in an audit report included in a registration statement.
C. Willfully including materially misstated financial statements in a registration statement.
D. Failing to use due diligence in the preparation of financial statements included in a registration statement.

REG 2-Q68 R372. The prospectus for the sale of securities of a not-for-profit corporation contained material misrepresentations due to the negligence of the person who prepared the financial statements. As a result of the misrepresentations, purchasers of the shares lost their investment. Do the anti-fraud provisions of the Securities Act of 1933 apply in this situation?

A. Yes, because the securities are required to be registered.
B. Yes, because the misrepresentations were material.
C. No, because the securities are exempt from registration.
D. No, because only the issuer was negligent.

REG 2-Q69 R181. Under Regulation D of the Securities Act of 1933, what is the maximum time period during which an exempt offering may be made?

A. Three months.
B. Six months.
C. Twelve months.
D. Twenty-four months.

REG 2-Q70 R363. Miner Corp. wants to make a $6 million public stock offering under the exempt transaction limited offering provisions of the Securities Act of 1933. What must Miner do to comply with the Act?

A. File a registration statement.
B. Advertise the offering.
C. Issue a "red herring" prospectus.
D. Limit sales of the offering to no more than 35 unaccredited investors.

REG 2-Q71 R371. Tork purchased restricted securities that were issued pursuant to Regulation D of the Securities Act of 1933. Which of the following statements is correct regarding Tork's ability to resell the securities?

A. Tork may resell the securities so long as the sale does involve interstate commerce.
B. Tork may resell the securities as part of another transaction exempt from registration.
C. Tork may not resell the securities if the certificates contain a legend indicating that they are unregistered securities.
D. Tork may not resell the securities unless Tork obtains a written SEC exemption.

REG 2-Q72 R202. Which of the following transactions is subject to registration requirements of the Securities Act of 1933?

A. The public sale by a corporation of its negotiable 10-year notes.
B. The public sale by a charitable organization of 10-year bearer bonds.
C. The sale across state lines of municipal bonds issued by a city.
D. Issuance of stock by a publicly-traded corporation to its shareholders because of a stock split.

REG 2-Q73 R259. Under Section 12 of the Securities Exchange Act of 1934, in addition to companies whose securities are traded on a national exchange, what class of companies is subject to the SEC's continuous disclosure system?

A. Companies with annual revenues in excess of $5 million and 300 or more shareholders.
B. Companies with annual revenues in excess of $10 million and 500 or more shareholders.
C. Companies with assets in excess of $5 million and 300 or more shareholders.
D. Companies with assets in excess of $10 million and 500 or more shareholders.

REG 2-Q74 R419. Dean, Inc., a publicly traded corporation, paid a $10,000 bribe to a local zoning official. The bribe was recorded in Dean's financial statements as a consulting fee. Dean's unaudited financial statements were submitted to the SEC as part of a quarterly filing. Which of the following federal statutes did Dean violate?

A. Federal Trade Commission Act.
B. Securities Act of 1933.
C. Securities Exchange Act of 1934.
D. North American Free Trade Act.

REG 2-Q75 R134. What defense must an accountant establish to be absolved from civil liability under Section 18 of the Securities Exchange Act of 1934 for false or misleading statements made in reports or documents filed under the Act?

A. Lack of gross negligence.
B. Exercise of Due Care.
C. Good faith and lack of knowledge of the statement's falsity.
D. Lack of privity with an injured party.

REG 2-Q76 R211. What is the standard that must be established to prove a violation of the anti-fraud provisions of Rule 10b-5 of the Securities Exchange Act of 1934?

A. Negligence.
B. Intentional misconduct.
C. Criminal intent.
D. Strict liability.

REG 2-Q77 R309. Under the liability provisions of Section 18 of the Securities Exchange Act of 1934, for which of the following actions would an accountant generally be liable?

A. Negligently approving a reporting corporation's incorrect internal financial forecasts.
B. Negligently filing a reporting corporation's tax return with the IRS.
C. Intentionally preparing and filing with the SEC a reporting corporation's incorrect quarterly report.
D. Intentionally failing to notify a reporting corporation's audit committee of defects in the verification of accounts receivable.

REG 2-Q78 R373. An original issue of transaction exempt securities was sold to the public based on a prospectus containing intentional omissions of material facts. Under which of the following federal securities laws would the issuer be liable to a purchaser of the securities?

I. The anti-fraud provisions of the Securities Act of 1933.
II. The anti-fraud provisions of the Securities Exchange Act of 1934.

A. I only.
B. II only.
C. Both I and II.
D. Neither I nor II.

REG 2-Q79 R414. Which of the following statements is(are) correct regarding the methods a target Corporation may use to ward off a takeover attempt?

I. The target corporation may make an offer ("self-tender") to acquire stock from its own shareholders.
II. The target corporation may seek an injunction against the acquiring corporation on the grounds that the attempted takeover violates federal antitrust law.

A. I only.
B. II only.
C. Both I and II.
D. Neither I nor II.

REG 2-Q80 R119. Worker's compensation benefits are available to which of the following parties?

A. Only those employees injured while working on workplace premises.
B. Only those employees injured while working within the scope of employment.
C. All agents injured while commuting to and from work.
D. All agents injured while using the employer's automobile for personal use.

REG 2-Q81 R420. Which of the following parties generally is ineligible to collect workers' compensation benefits?

A. Minors.
B. Truck drivers.
C. Union employees.
D. Temporary office workers.

REG 2-Q82 R267. Under the provisions of the Employee Retirement Income Security Act of 1974 (ERISA), which of the following statements is(are) correct regarding employee rights?

I. Employers are required to establish either a contributory or noncontributory employee pension plan.
II. Employers are required to include employees as pension-plan managers.

A. I only.
B. II only.
C. Both I and II.
D. Neither I nor II.

REG 2-Q83 R430. Under the federal statutes governing water pollution, which of the following areas is(are) regulated?

	Dredging of coastal or freshwater wetlands	Drinking water standards
A.	Yes	Yes
B.	Yes	No
C.	No	Yes
D.	No	No

REG 2-Q84 R330. Under the Comprehensive Environmental Response, Compensation, and Liability Act (CERCLA), if land is found to be contaminated, which of the following parties would be least likely to be liable for cleanup costs?

A. A bank that foreclosed a mortgage on the land and purchased the land at the foreclosure sale.
B. A parent corporation of the corporation that owned the land.
C. A minority stockholder of the public corporation that owned the land.
D. A trustee appointed by the owner of the land to manage the land.

REG 2-Q85 R411. Wind, who has been a partner in the PLW general partnership for four years, decides to withdraw from the partnership despite a written partnership agreement that states, "no partner may withdraw for a period of five years". Under the Uniform Partnership Act, what is the result of Wind's withdrawal?

A. Wind's withdrawal causes dissolution of the partnership by operation of law.
B. Wind's withdrawal has **no** bearing on the continued operation of the partnership by the remaining partners.
C. Wind's withdrawal is **not** effective until Wind obtains a court ordered decree of dissolution.
D. Wind's withdrawal causes dissolution of the partnership despite being in violation of the partnership agreement.

REG 2-Q86 R412. In a general partnership, which of the following acts must be approved by all the partners?

A. Dissolution of the partnership.
B. Admission of a partner.
C. Authorization of a partnership capital expenditure.
D. Hiring an employee.

REG 2-Q87 R413. Case Corp. is incorporated in State A. Under the Revised Model Business Corporation Act, which of the following activities engaged in by Case requires that Case obtain a certificate of authority to do business in State B?

A. Maintaining bank accounts in State B.
B. Collecting corporate debts in State B.
C. Hiring employees who are residents of state B.
D. Maintaining an office in State B to conduct intrastate business.

REG 2-Q88 R415. Acorn Corp. wants to acquire the entire business of Trend Corp. Which of the following methods of business combination will best satisfy Acorn's objectives without requiring the approval of the shareholders of either corporation?

A. A merger of Trend into Acorn, whereby Trend shareholders receive cash or Acorn shares.
B. A sale of all the assets of Trend, outside the regular course of business, to Acorn, for cash.
C. An acquisition of all the shares of Trend through a compulsory share exchange for Acorn shares.
D. A cash tender offer, whereby Acorn acquires at least 90% of Trend's shares, followed by a short-form merger of Trend into Acorn.

REG 2-Q89 R19. Which of the following statements is correct regarding a limited liability company's operating agreement?

A. It must be filed with a central state agency.
B. It must be in writing.
C. It is designed to forestall and resolve disputes among the owners.
D. It is necessary for a limited liability company to exist.

REG 2-Q90 R146. Which of the following can be an advantage of a limited liability company over an S corporation?

A. Double taxation of profits is avoided.
B. Owners receive limited liability protection.
C. Appreciated property can be distributed tax-free to an owner.
D. Incentive stock options can be used to compensate owners.

REG 2-Q91 R22. Able and Baker are equal members in Apple, an LLC. Apple has elected not to be treated as a corporation. Able contributes $7,000 cash and Baker contributes a machine with a basis of $5,000 and a fair market value of $10,000, subject to a liability of $3,000. What is Apple's basis for the machine?

A. $2,000
B. $5,000
C. $8,000
D. $10,000

REG 2-Q92 R295. Which of the following statements is the best definition of real property?

A. Real property is only land.
B. Real property is all tangible property including land.
C. Real property is land and intangible property in realized form.
D. Real property is land and everything permanently attached to it.

REG 2-Q93 R383. Which of the following actions would most likely be an infringement of the exclusive rights of the owner of a copyrighted work?

A. Preparing a foreign language translation of the copyrighted work.
B. Writing a book review of the copyrighted work that includes excerpts from the work.
C. Making multiple copies of extracts from the copyrighted work for classroom use.
D. Using the copyrighted work for research.

REG 2-Q94 R384. Kemp created and patented a new process to convert liquid gas to powder. Two years later, Mill independently, and without knowledge of the Kemp patent, developed the identical process. Mill only wanted to use the process for Mill's own business and did not attempt to patent the process. Kemp learned about Mill's process and sued for patent infringement. Will Kemp prevail?

A. Yes, because Kemp was the first to patent the process.
B. Yes, because Mill should have known about Kemp's patent.
C. No, because Mill came up with the process independently.
D. No, because Mill only used the process for Mill's own business.

REG 2-Q95 R331. Trees were cut down and made into lumber. The lumber was used to build a house. Which of the following statements best describes the property aspect of these events?

A. The trees were and remained tangible personal property.
B. The trees were and remained real property.
C. The trees were real property, then became and remained personal property.
D. The trees were real property, became personal property, then reverted to being real property.

REG 2-Q96 R230. Which of the following requirements must be met, by any type of deed, in order for title to real property to be transferred?

A. The deed must be delivered to the purchaser of the property.
B. The deed must be recorded by the seller of the property.
C. The deed must include a statement of the property's value.
D. The deed must include a general warranty of title.

REG 2-Q97 R99. Which of the following interests in real property gives the holder of that interest the greatest possessory interest in the property?

A. Easement
B. Restrictive Covenant
C. License
D. Fee Simple

REG 2-Q98 R138. Which of the following circumstances best describes a landlord's constructive eviction of a tenant who has a written lease for the property?

A. The landlord changes the lock and refuses to give the tenant a new key.
B. The landlord starts a legal proceeding against the tenant for failure to pay rent.
C. The landlord sues the tenant because the tenant complained to a government agency about the condition of the premises.
D. The landlord refuses to provide utilities to the tenant.

REG 2-Q99 R382. When the original tenant of real property subleases the property to a third party (sublessee), who is responsible for the payment of the rent to the owner of the property?

A. The sublessee only.
B. The original tenant only.
C. Either the original tenant or the sublessee.
D. Both the sublessee and the original tenant.

This page is intentionally left blank.

Multiple Choice – Solutions

REG 2-Q1 R41. The correct answer is D. With any contract; the parties must possess the capacity to enter into a contract.

Answer A is incorrect because not all agencies must be in writing. Agencies that must be in writing include situations where the agent buys or sells specific real estate and contracts that cannot be completed in one year.

Answer B is incorrect because generally the agency agreement must be signed by the principal only.

Answer C is incorrect because consideration is not required. This is called a gratuitous agency.

REG 2-Q2 R209. The correct answer is C. In an agency relationship, the parties to the contract are the principal, and the third party.

Answer A is incorrect because an agency does not require consideration to be given.

Answer B is incorrect because the agent does not have to have capacity to enter into a contract, only the principal and the third party must have capacity to enter into a contract.

Answer D is incorrect because an agency does not require consideration to be given.

REG 2-Q3 R409. The correct answer is C. An independent contractor controls his own results and is not paid a salary. Since Lee is paid a weekly salary, Lee is considered an employee.

Answer A is incorrect because an employee's work would be supervised by the employer's personal.

Answer B is incorrect because an independent contractor would own his own tools.

Answer D is incorrect because both an employee and independent contractor's work can require a high degree of technical skill.

REG 2-Q4 R78. The correct answer is B. Ratification is the principal's approval of an unauthorized act of an agent.

Answer A is incorrect because it is not a principal's approval of an authorized act as the agent is already authorized to act.

Answer C is incorrect because it is not a principal's approval in advance of an agent's unauthorized act. The approval of the unauthorized act of the agent by the principal occurs after the agent commits the unauthorized act.

Answer D is incorrect because ratification is not a disapproval of an unauthorized act of the agent; it is a principal's approval of an unauthorized act by the agent.

REG 2-Q5 R310. The correct answer is C. A gratuitous agent is an agent who is not paid by a principal for the work they do. A gratuitous agent, just like a non-gratuitous agent cannot commingle the agent's funds with the principal's funds. A gratuitous agent must account for any sales or purchases to the principal's property for which the agent is authorized to purchase or sell. If an agent is in possession of cash, the agent must account for all cash received and paid out for any authorized transactions.

REG 2-Q6 R410. The correct answer is C. Since Gage, Blue's agent, appointed Vond as the sub-agent, legally Vond is an agent of both Blue and Gage. Therefore, Vond has a fiduciary duty to both Blue and Gage making answers A, B and D all incorrect.

REG 2-Q7 R290. The correct answer is A. If an agent is instructed not to disclose that he is acting as an agent of a principal, then the principal is called an undisclosed principal. In an undisclosed principal relationship, both the principal and the agent are liable on the contract. If the agent discloses the identity of the principal to the third party, the agent and the principal remain liable on the contract. Therefore, Rice could bring a cause of action against both Part and Young because Young refused to fulfill the contract.

REG 2-Q8 R328. The correct answer is C. An employee (agent) must notify his employer (principal) of a dangerous condition that results in injury to a third party. If the agent does not notify the principal of the dangerous condition and a third party is injured, both the principal and the agent are liable for negligence.

Answer A is incorrect because where a negligent act is committed by an independent contractor (who is not considered an employee, nor an agent), in performance of the contract, which results in injury to a third party, the principal is not liable as the act was committed by an independent contractor who is not an agent of the principal. Only an employee is an agent of the principal.

Answer B is incorrect because the principal is only liable for the torts of his employee (agent) if they occur during the scope of the agent's employment. A tort is a civil wrong, brought by an individual or client against the principal. Examples of torts would include ordinary negligence and trespassing. A principal is generally not liable for the crimes of the agent, unless the principal was a participating party.

Answer D is incorrect because for the principal to be liable, the negligent act must be committed by the employee during the scope of employment.

REG 2-Q9 R381. The correct answer is B. In an auction without reserve, after the auctioneer calls for bids on the auction item, that item cannot be withdrawn unless no bid is made within a reasonable time.

Answer A is incorrect because this is the definition of an auction with reserve. In an auction with reserve the auctioneer may withdraw the goods at any time until he announces completion of the sale.

Answer C is incorrect because an auction without reserve is II.

Answer D is incorrect because it is not "neither", it is II.

REG 2-Q10 R422. The correct answer is D. When a merchant does not have the goods that the buyer wants to acquire, usually at a sale price, the merchant seller will give the buyer a rain check so that the buyer can take advantage of the sale for a certain number of days. A rain check is called a firm offer which under the UCC Sales Statute, states the offer will remain open for a period not to exceed 3 months, as long as the promise to keep it open is made by a merchant in writing and does require

additional consideration to be left open by the merchant.

Answer A is incorrect because the UCC specifies a 3-month period when not time is detailed.

Answer B is incorrect because when no time is stated, the UCC gives Patch 3 months to accept the offer.

Answer C is incorrect because there was not offer and acceptance when Patch first tried to purchase the advertised goods.

REG 2-Q11 R275. The correct answer is B because if there is a mutual mistake of fact in a contract, there is no meeting of the minds which makes the contract void and allows it to be rescinded.

Answers A, C and D are incorrect because these types of mistakes do not affect the enforceability of the contract.

REG 2-Q12 R441. The correct answer is C. The two types of duress are duress through physical compulsion and duress through improper threat. An example of duress through physical compulsion is where an individual is forced to enter into a contract because they were threatened with bodily harm. In these cases, the contract would be void. An example of duress through improper threats is where an individual is forced to enter into a contract because they felt there was no alternative due to the threats made to them. In these cases, the contract would be voidable.

Answer A is incorrect because mutual mistake as to facts forming the basis of the contract make the contract voidable.

Answer B is incorrect because undue influence by a dominant party in a confidential relationship to have another party enter into a contract as a result of unfair persuasion makes the contract voidable.

Answer D is incorrect because as previously stated above; duress by improper threats renders the contract voidable.

REG 2-Q13 R428. The correct answer is C. If a person is induced to enter into a contract by another person because of the close relationship between the parties, the contract may be voidable under the doctrine of undue influence. Undue influence is persuasion of an individual to enter into a contract because of the close relationship between the parties.

Answer A is incorrect because fraud in the inducement is fraud in the contract and the contract is voidable which means the injured party has the right to get out of the contract. Fraud in the inducement makes a contract voidable.

Answer B is incorrect. The word unconscionable as used in the courts, describes conduct that does not conform to the dictates of conscience. In addition, when something is judged unconscionable, a court will refuse to allow the perpetrator of the conduct to benefit. In contract law, an unconscionable contract is one that is unjust or extremely one-sided in favor of the person with the best bargaining power. An unconscionable contract is one that no person who is mentally capable would enter into and accept. Courts typically find unconscionable contracts stem from consumer exploitation due to being poor, under educated, or not able to find the best alternative competitive product or price. If the court determines the contract is one-sided, it could deem the contract voidable.

Answer D is incorrect. Duress is the unlawful pressure exerted on a person to coerce them into performing an act they would not normally perform. Duress can include the use of force or threats to compel someone to act contrary to their interests. If someone signs a contract under duress, a court could consider it null and void.

REG 2-Q14 R240. The correct answer is D. A promise to pay a minor $500 to paint a garage is new consideration and both parties are benefiting from the exchange of the promises. There is no pre-existing duty on either party. The exchange of promises, which is the consideration, is the promise by a party to pay a minor to paint their garage. The minor benefits by earning $500 and the other party benefits by having their garage painted.

Answer A is incorrect because it lacks consideration as there was a pre-existing duty by the real estate agent not to charge a commission.

Answer B is incorrect because there is not mutual consideration as the parent's promise to pay one child $500 because that child is not as wealthy as the child's sibling does not give any benefit to the person promising to pay the $500. Consideration must be such that both parties benefit from the agreement. The parents are not getting any benefit by paying the child $500 just because the child is not as wealthy as their sibling.

Answer C is incorrect because a police officer as a pre-existing duty to protect the public, so a promise to pay the police $250 to catch a thief lacks consideration. The office is not entitled the $250 because it is their duty to catch a thief and they are not entitled to any more money as they are already being paid to catch criminals (pre-existing duty).

REG 2-Q15 R423. The correct answer is A. An output contract is enforceable even though the actual quantity is not mentioned in the contract. The output contract is supported by consideration because the seller agreed not to sell that output to any other party.

Answer B is incorrect because when price is omitted, the UCC considers it as a reasonable price at the time of delivery.

Answer C is incorrect because the quantity may be omitted and is permitted to be determined by the output in UCC sales contracts.

Answer D is incorrect because the omission of price and quantity terms does not prevent the formation of a contract as UCC sales contracts allow them to be determined by output.

REG 2-Q16 R38. Per Statutes of Frauds, certain contracts have to be in writing to be enforceable. The correct answer is D. Only contracts that cannot be performed within one year must be in writing. Since D can be performed within one year, the Statutes of Frauds does not apply.

Answers A, B & C must be in writing under the Statutes of Frauds.

REG 2-Q17 R135. The correct answer is C because Gem will lose the lawsuit as contracts must be in writing if they cannot be completed within one year. The contract period was for 13 months, starting December 1, 2015 and ending on December 31, 2016.

Answers A, B and D are incorrect because they do not reflect contracts that have to be in writing under the Statute of Frauds.

REG 2-Q18 R273. The correct answer is C. The Statute of Frauds requires that certain contracts be in writing to be enforceable. The writing must be signed by the parties to be charged. In this question, we are looking for the incorrect statement. The incorrect statement is C because the Statute of Frauds does not stipulate the number of documents required as the contract terms may be contained in more than one document.

Answers A, B and D are incorrect because these items come under the Statute of Frauds and must in writing.

REG 2-Q19 R311. The correct answer is D. The statute of frauds states that certain contracts have to be in writing to be enforceable. The only party that the contract can be enforced against is the party who signed the agreement and is also the defendant in the dispute. A contract was formed when Fargo telephoned Kram and created an acceptance. If either of the parties breach the contract, the only party that the contract can be enforced against under the statute of frauds is the party who signed the agreement (Kram). The only one who signed the agreement is Kram, who sent a written offer. Since Kram sent a written offer, Fargo can enforce the contract against Kram if there is a breach.

Answer A is incorrect because a contract could be formed even if the acceptance was oral.

Answer B is incorrect because a contract could be formed even if only one party signed the contract. A contract can exist even if Kram (offeror) is the only one who signed the contract and Fargo (offeree) accepted orally. To have a valid contract, all that is needed is an offer and acceptance, whether it is in writing or oral. The statute of frauds does not state that a contract has to be in writing to be valid. The statute of frauds states that the contract can only be enforced if there is a breach or dispute against the party who signed the agreement.

Answer C is incorrect because the contract could not be enforced against Fargo, only Kram. Real estate contracts are within the Statute of Frauds and are generally enforceable against a party only if they signed it.

REG 2-Q20 R320. The correct answer is D. A minor may disaffirm a contract for personal property any time before the age of majority or a reasonable time after reaching the age of majority.

Answer A is incorrect because Fresno is bound by the contract even if Bronson ratifies (accepts) the contract after reaching the age of majority. Ratification is not binding on Bronson until Bronson reaches the age of majority.

Answer B is incorrect because Bronson is justified and Fresno still has to perform under the contract even though Bronson has the right to disaffirm the contract.

Answer C is incorrect because Bronson is bound not on the date Bronson reaches the age of majority but only when Bronson ratifies the contract after reaching the age of majority. Fresno is bound to the contract regardless of whether or not Bronson reaches the of majority at the time of the contract.

REG 2-Q21 R416. The correct answer is C. When an individual is adjudicated incompetent by a court having proper jurisdiction, all future contracts entered into by that individual are void.

REG 2-Q22 R72. The correct answer is B. Fraud in the inducement is defined as fraud in the contract. Both parties to the contract were aware of what they were entering into. However, one of the parties committed a misrepresentation of fact with deceit to induce the other party to enter into the contract. Fraud in the inducement makes a contract voidable.

Answer A is incorrect because fraud in the execution is where the parties are unaware of what they are entering into. A good example would be to ask an athlete for an autograph where the athlete is actually signing a promissory note payable to person requesting the autograph. Since the athlete did not know what he was signing, there is no meeting of the minds. This renders the contract to be null and void.

Answer C is incorrect because if someone is forced to enter into a contract, it is duress. Because this involves physical coercion, the contract is void.

Answer D is incorrect because a person under guardianship contracts are made by a person placed under guardianship by court order. These contracts are void.

REG 2-Q23 R679. The correct answer is C. The parol evidence rule prohibits the introduction at trial of oral or written evidence of prior or contemporaneous agreements which conflict with the terms of a written agreement. The courts assume that all negotiations and prior agreements are embodied in the written contract. In this case, the courts will not permit evidence with regard to the oral agreement concerning Kemp's obligation to pay one-half of the cost of the utilities. The written agreement is clear, and Andrews should have carefully read it. There are, however, exceptions to the parole evidence rule, as follows:

1. Oral evidence may be produced to show that the contract was void or voidable based upon fraud, misrepresentation, or mistake.
2. Oral evidence may be produced to show the meaning of terms when they are ambiguous.
3. Oral evidence will be permitted when a contract is incomplete, and lacks one or more essential terms.

In this case, the courts will permit oral evidence concerning the intentional misrepresentations by Kemp.

REG 2-Q24 R79. The correct answer is C. This question deals with an assignment of a payment from an assignor to an assignee. Pierce owed Duke $3,000 and Pierce entered into a contract with Lodge to paint Lodge's house. Pierce painted Lodge's house and Lodge agreed to pay Duke $3,000 instead of Pierce. Pierce, the assignor, assigned his right to receive the money to Duke, the assignee. Lodge is an original party to the contract. Duke is both an assignee and a third party creditor beneficiary. Duke can sue Pierce because in an assignment, the assignor (Pierce) is liable to the assignee (Duke) for any breach of contract. Duke can sue Lodge for breach of contract because Duke is a third party creditor beneficiary to Lodge. Since Duke was a third party creditor beneficiary, he can sue Lodge for payment because Duke is receiving a direct benefit from the contract between Pierce and Lodge.

REG 2-Q25 R301. The correct answer is B. The right to receive a sum of money is assignable even if the contract states that it is not.

Answer A is incorrect because the right to receive personal services is not assignable.

Answer C is incorrect because an insurance policy is not assignable.

Answer D is incorrect because a right whose assignment is prohibited by statute is not assignable.

REG 2-Q26 R333. The correct answer is C. West and Barton are the original parties to the contract. West is the assignor and Egan is the assignee of West's rights. In an assignment, when West assigned his rights to Egan, West guaranteed to Egan that Egan would be paid based on the assignment contract.

If an assignee releases one of the original parties to the contract then the assignee automatically releases the other parties to the contract. If Egan releases Barton (one of the original parties to the contract) from the contract, then West (the other original party to the contract and the assignor) is also released from the contract.

Answer A is incorrect because if West releases Barton, Egan is still the assignee of the West/Barton contract as West has no legal right to unilaterally release Barton and terminate the original contract. Therefore, the contract between West and Barton remains in effect and the assignment between West and Egan also remains in effect.

Answer B is incorrect because if West breached the contract with Barton, West (assignor) is still liable to Egan because a breach of contract between the original parties does not terminate the assignment between West and Egan.

Answer D is incorrect because if Barton paid West, West would still be liable to Egan as the assignment is another contract and Egan is entitled to payment from West.

REG 2-Q27 R417. The correct answer is A. A material breach of the contract by one party of the contract will discharge performance required of the other party to the contract.

Answers B, C and D are incorrect because they will not discharge performance required of the other party to the contract.

REG 2-Q28 R329. The correct answer is A. Accord and satisfaction is where the parties have decided to change some or all of the terms of the original contract. An example is where the offeree says to the offeror that he cannot pay the original amount of the contract. If the offeror agrees to accept a lesser amount, then that is the accord. Once the offeree pays the new amount, it represents the satisfaction of the accord. Accord and satisfaction generally will result in the discharge of a party's obligation to perform as required under the original contract.

Mutual rescission is where both parties to the contract agree to terminate the contract and restore themselves to their original positions before the contract was formed. If any money was exchanged, the money would be returned to the parties who paid it. Mutual rescission generally will result in the discharge of a party's obligation to perform as required under the original contract.

REG 2-Q29 R255. The correct answer is A. A patent is the exclusive right granted by a government to an inventor to manufacture, use, or sell an invention for a certain number of years and provides the patent holder the sole right to exclude others from making, using, or selling an invention which makes the patent unique. The remedy of specific performance is where the injured party wants the other party to perform because monetary damages will not be adequate. Specific performance is the only remedy where the contract is unique.

Answers B, C and D are incorrect because they are not contracts for a unique item or service.

REG 2-Q30 R212. The correct answer is C. Liquidated damages are damages defined in the construction contract and chargeable against funds due to the contractor for each day the contractor fails to complete the project beyond the contract completion date.

Answer A is incorrect because punitive damages are rarely awarded in contract disputes.

Answer B is incorrect because the clause in the contract is for liquidating damages and not for compensatory damages from a delay in completing the project.

Answer D is incorrect because there are damages due to the liquidating damages clause.

REG 2-Q31 R59. The correct answer is D because a contract was formed when Sands sent the acceptance per the "mailbox rule". The mailbox rule states that an offeree will make an immediate acceptance when the acceptance is sent by any reasonable means under the circumstances.

Answer A is incorrect because a contract can still be formed even if an expiration date is not stated. If no expiration date, it expires after a reasonable time.

Answer B is incorrect because a contract was formed when it was sent by Sands on day 7. An acceptance occurs immediately when the acceptance is made by Sands (the offeree), because an acceptance can be made by the offeree by any reasonable means under the circumstances. The offer cannot be revoked by the offeror because this is a firm offer. A firm offer is an option to keep an offer open without additional consideration under the UCC. A firm offer is valid if it is a promise made by a merchant in writing to keep an offer open for a period not exceeding 3 months. Therefore, the offer cannot be revoked.

Answer C is incorrect because acceptance occurred when sent not received.

REG 2-Q32 R379. The correct answer is D. The definition of good faith is that the merchant must observe the reasonable commercial standards of fair dealing in the trade.

REG 2-Q33 R5. Correct answer is B. At a minimum, a sales contract under the UCC must contain a writing containing a term specifying the quantity of the goods.

Answer A is incorrect because a writing that must contain a term specifying the price has to do with common law contracts. Common law contracts are contracts for services and real estate.

Answer C is incorrect because the writing must contain the signature of the party to be charged. The party to be charged is the defendant.

Answer D is incorrect because the writing does not contain the signature of the party seeking to enforce the contract, who is the plaintiff. It must contain the signature of the defendant (the party to be charged).

REG 2-Q34 R432. The correct answer is C. The UCC dealing with the sale of goods requires that contracts for goods that cost $500 or more, are only enforceable against a party who breaches a contract and the party who breached the contract must have signed the contract. If the party who breached the contract does not sign the contract for goods of $500 or more, the courts will not allow the plaintiff to enforce the contract against the party who breached it.

Answer A is incorrect because if there is a contract for $500 or more and the contract is for specially manufactured goods, then the oral contract for the specially manufactured goods can be enforced against the party who breached even if the party who breached did not sign the agreement.

Answer B is incorrect because the fire does not prevent the contract from being performed

Answer D is incorrect because the contract was fully enforceable because it dealt with specially manufactured goods which can be enforced against the party that is being sued even if that party did not sign the contract.

REG 2-Q35 R6. The correct answer is B. Under an FOB shipping contract, title and risk of loss pass when the goods are given to the common carrier. This is a shipping contract because it states in the question "under a shipping contract".

REG 2-Q36 R380. The correct answer is B. With an F.O.B. destination contract, risk of loss and title pass when the seller gets good to the destination and tenders delivery (notified the buyer that the goods have arrived).

Answer A is incorrect because the seller is not required to arrange for the buyer to pick up the conforming goods at a specified destination. Seller is only required to notify the buyer that the goods have arrived.

Answer C is incorrect because the seller is required to tender delivery of conforming goods but it doesn't have to be at the buyer's place of business. If the agreement is silent as to where the goods are to be delivered, it is the seller's place of business.

Answer D is incorrect because this relates to an FOB Shipping point contract. Under an FOB shipping point contract, the seller is required to tender delivery of conforming goods to a carrier who delivers to a destination specified by the buyer. In an FOB destination contract, the buyer will notify the carrier to pick up the goods from the seller, therefore not requiring the seller to arrange for the shipping from the seller to the buyer.

REG 2-Q37 R374. The correct answer is D. A sale or return contract gives the buyer the right to return the goods during a period of time until the buyer decides whether the buyer wants to keep the goods or return the goods. In a sale or return contract under the Sales Article of the UCC, the buyer is buying the goods for resale. This makes the buyer a merchant and a merchant/seller is held to a higher standard than a non-merchant/seller. Because a sale and return has the buyer being a merchant who is going to resell the goods, the higher standard issue states that during the period the buyer is deciding whether to keep the goods or not, the buyer has title and risk to the goods during the decision period.

REG 2-Q38 R377. The correct answer is C. When the merchant/seller promised the purchaser (restaurant owner) that the dishwasher would fulfill the dishwashing requirements of a large restaurant and subsequently was not powerful enough to fulfill the seller's promise, this is a breach of an expressed warranty that the goods conformed to the seller's promise.

Answer A is incorrect because when the seller makes a statement that is part of the basis of the bargain, it is not implied but expressed.

Answer B is incorrect because this is an expressed warranty, not implied.

Answer D is incorrect because a warranty against infringement refers to a warranty provided by a seller stating that goods being sold are not in violation of any patent, copyright or trademark. The seller is stating that the dishwasher would fulfill the dishwashing requirements of a large restaurant. The seller is not stating anything about a patent, copyright or trademark.

REG 2-Q39 R440. The correct answer is C. The implied warranty of fitness for a particular purpose is where the seller knows the particular purpose for which the buyer will use the goods and the seller knows that the buyer will rely on the seller's skill or judgment to select suitable goods.

Answer A is incorrect because the seller must know the particular purpose for which the buyer will use the goods.

Answers B and D are incorrect because the seller does not have to be a merchant.

REG 2-Q40 R118. The correct answer is B. Card is not obligated to sell the stereo to Bend until Bend accepts the offer.

Answer A is incorrect because Bend is not required to immediately accept or reject the offer to avoid liability to Card.

Answer C is incorrect because Card is required to mitigate any loss Card would sustain in the event Bend accepts, not rejects the offer.

Answer D is incorrect because Bend may reject the offer for a reasonable period of time.

REG 2-Q41 R378. The correct answer is B. If the goods at the time of the tender (good are made available by the seller to the buyer to pick up the goods) or delivery do not exactly conform to the requirements of the contract, then the buyer can get out of the contract as the seller has shipped nonconforming goods.

Answer A is incorrect because if the contract does not meet the buyer's needs at the time of the tender or delivery, does not allow the buyer to get out of the contract.

Answers C and D are incorrect because the buyer can only get out of the contract if there has been a shipment of nonconforming goods.

REG 2-Q42 R136. The correct answer is D. An official bond is where the surety (guarantor) guarantees that a public official will do their job.

Answers A, B and C are incorrect because they are bonds issued by corporations (convertible and debenture bonds) and municipalities (municipal bonds) to raise money. A surety does not guarantee that these bonds will be paid.

REG 2-Q43 R360. The correct answer is B. This question deals with the right of contribution when there are co-sureties guaranteeing the debt of the debtor. There are 3 co-sureties, Teller has a maximum liability of $20,000, Kerr with a maximum liability of $40,000 and Ace with a maximum liability of $60,000. When there are one or more co-sureties, who have different maximum liabilities and one of the co-sureties pays off the debt, look to the other co-sureties for their contribution compared to the co-surety who paid off the debt.

Add the maximum liabilities of all co-sureties. Teller's, maximum liability $20,000, Kerr's maximum liability $40,000, Ace's maximum liability $60,000. This will equal $120,000 ($20,000 + $40,000 + $60,000). Since Ace paid off the total liability of $48,000, to determine how much Teller and Kerr owe Ace, calculate a proration of Teller and Kerr's liability to the maximum liability of all the co-sureties.

Since Teller's maximum liability is $20,000, take the $20,000 and divide it by the maximum liabilities of all co-sureties, including Ace's maximum liability, which equals $120,000. Teller's contribution to Ace is $20,000 divided by $120,000 or, 1/6 of the debt Ace paid of $48,000, resulting in Teller owing Ace $8,000 (1/6 x $48,000).

Since Kerr's maximum liability is $40,000, take the $40,000 and divide it by the maximum liabilities of all co-sureties, including Ace's maximum liability, which equals $120,000. Kerr's contribution to Ace is $40,000 divided by $120,000 or, 1/3 of the debt Ace paid of $48,000, resulting in Kerr owing Ace $16,000 (1/3 x $48,000).

Since the question asks for Kerr's contribution to Ace, the correct answer is $16,000 or choice B.

REG 2-Q44 R153. The correct answer is C. The promise of a guarantor must be in writing per the statute of frauds, to enforce the guarantor's promise.

Answer A is incorrect because the time the loan has to be paid has nothing to do with the statute of frauds. Remember, the guarantor is liable only if the guarantee is in writing.

Answer B is incorrect because once again, the guarantee must be in writing.

Answer D is incorrect because lack of consideration is not relevant to the liability of the guarantor. What is important is that the promise of the guarantor must be in writing.

REG 2-Q45 R418. The correct answer is B. If the creditor fails to notify the surety of a partial surrender of the debtor's collateral, it increases the risk of the surety and the therefore will release the surety from liability to the creditor.

Answer A is incorrect because if the debtor is brought into bankruptcy, the surety is there to guarantee the debtor's debt to the creditor.

Answer C is incorrect because the surety will not be released from liability to the creditor if the creditor was adjudicated incompetent after the debt arose.

Answer D is incorrect because if the principal debtor exerted duress to obtain the surety to guarantee the debt of the debtor, the surety is not released.

REG 2-Q46 R334. The correct answer is C. The federal Fair Debt Collection Practices Act prohibits collection agencies from engaging in unfair practices. If the debtor engages the services of an attorney, the debt collector can no longer communicate with the debtor but, must communicate with the attorney. If a debt collector violates the act, they are liable for civil liability, not criminal liability.

Answer A is incorrect because the federal Fair Debt Collection Practices Act does not prevent a debt collector from contacting a third party to ascertain a debtor's location.

Answer B is incorrect because the federal Fair Debt Collection Practices Act does not prevent a debt collector from continuing to collect a debt.

Answer D is incorrect because a decision to commence a lawsuit to collect a debt is made by the company who has not been paid by the debtor and not the collection agency.

REG 2-Q47 R359. The correct answer is B. Under Chapter 7 involuntary bankruptcy, creditors file to force a liquidation and a trustee is appointed. With: Rule (a): 12 or more creditors (secured and unsecured): Need 3 or more unsecured creditors, who are owed in the aggregate, $15,325 in unsecured claims to file the petition.

Rule (b): With less than 12 creditors (secured and unsecured): Need 1 or more unsecured creditors to file the petition who are owed in the aggregate $15,325 in unsecured claims.

If a debtor has less than 12 creditors, one or more unsecured creditors who are owed at least $15,325 in unsecured claims, can file an involuntary petition in bankruptcy against the debtor. There are a total of 10 creditors. Hall, who is owed $15,500 can file the petition alone against the debtor per Rule (b) shown above.

Answer A is incorrect because when there are less than 12 creditors, only one unsecured creditors who is owed at least $15,325 need to sign the petition in involuntary bankruptcy.

Answer C is incorrect because Chapter 11 of the Federal Bankruptcy Act allows either the debtor (voluntary), or the creditor (involuntary) to file this petition in bankruptcy.

Answer D is incorrect because under Chapter 11 reorganization, no specific number of creditors is required to bring a debtor into Chapter 11 bankruptcy.

REG 2-Q48 R317. The correct answer is D. The trustee in bankruptcy has the powers stated in answers A, B and C, but cannot avoid (ignore) any lien that was placed on the debtor's property that was effective before the bankruptcy petition was filed. Any liens placed on the debtor's property before the petition was filed, belong to that individual or business that placed the lien on the property before the debtor went into bankruptcy.

In addition, answer A is incorrect because the trustee in bankruptcy will beat out a creditor with an unperfected security interest as the creditor with the unperfected security interest has not given constructive notice to other creditors and the trustee that the unperfected creditor has first rights to the collateral.

REG 2-Q49 R429. The correct answer is A. An inheritance by a debtor within 180 days of the filing of the petition, belongs to the trustee in bankruptcy.

Answer B is incorrect because child support payments received by the debtor always belong to the debtor and are considered exempt property, which means the trustee in bankruptcy can never take the child support payments away from the debtor.

Answer C is incorrect because social security payments received by the debtor always belong to the debtor and are considered exempt property, which means the trustee in bankruptcy can never take the social security payments away from the debtor.

Answer D is incorrect because wages earned by a debtor are relevant in determining who gets priority as far as the payments made to the different creditors.

REG 2-Q50 R369. The correct answer is C. Under Chapter 7 of the federal Bankruptcy Code, the debtor is relieved of any personal liability to the judgment creditor whether or not there is a bankruptcy estate from which to pay the debt. In a discharge in bankruptcy, most debts of a debtor are relieved, whether or not there is a bankruptcy estate from which to pay the debts.

Answer A is incorrect because the judgment creditor's claim is dischargeable.

Answer B is incorrect because the judgment creditor will not retain a statutory lien against the debtor.

Answer D is incorrect because the debtor is not required to pay a liquidated (definite) amount to vacate the judgment.

REG 2-Q51 R370. The correct answer is B. Farmers may file a voluntary petition for bankruptcy under Chapter 7 Liquidation, Chapter 11 – business reorganization and Chapter 13- individual reorganization. Chapter 9 of the United States Bankruptcy Code is available exclusively to municipalities to assist them in the restructuring of their debts.

REG 2-Q52 R25. The correct answer is C. A security agreement is an agreement that states the debtor is acknowledging to the creditor, that if the debtor defaults on the payments to the secured creditor, then that secured creditor has first rights to the collateral. This is one of the requirements of attachment. A security agreement can be in writing or oral. It can be oral if the secured creditor has possession of the collateral. Otherwise, if the secured creditor does not have possession of the collateral, then the security agreement must be in writing and signed by the debtor.

Answer A is incorrect because the UCC does not address anything about the dollar amount collateralizing the debt affecting whether writing is required or not.

Answer B is incorrect because whether the goods are highly perishable or subject to wide price fluctuations affects whether the agreement has to be in writing.

Answer D is incorrect because a security agreement whether if involves a purchase money secured creditor or a non-purchase money secured creditor does not affect whether there has to be a writing or not.

REG 2-Q53 R8. The correct answer is D. A secured transaction is merely a debt secured by personal property. The creation of the secured transaction is called attachment. Attachment occurs when three things happen:
1. Debtor has rights to the collateral (rights are where the debtor has possession of the collateral)
2. An agreement signed by the debtor must be entered into by the debtor and creditor. This agreement is called a security agreement. The security agreement must describe the collateral but not in a great amount of detail.
3. The creditor must give value. Value is given when the creditor extends credit to the debtor to but the collateral.

All three must occur in order to have attachment. Normally on the CPA exam, with questions on secured transactions, possession will be the last item to occur.

REG 2-Q54 R160. The correct answer is B. The security agreement is a document signed by the debtor where the debtor acknowledges that the secured creditor has first right to the collateral in the event the debtor defaults.

Answer A is incorrect because a statement of assignment is usually part of a contract, assigning something of value in exchange for a benefit and can take place by oral agreement.

Answer C is incorrect because to release collateral is where the secured party no longer claims an interest in the collateral. This is normally done as an amendment to the existing financing statement and does not have to be signed by the debtor.

Answer D is incorrect because a termination statement, which provides notice that the secured party has released its lien on the borrower's assets and therefore, the assets are free and clear, does not have to be signed by the debtor.

REG 2-Q55 R164. The correct answer is D. In order to create an enforceable security interest which is also known as attachment, 3 steps are required:

1) A security agreement must exist.
2) The secured party (creditor) must give value.
3) The debtor must have rights in the collateral.

However, a financing statement does not have to be filed to create attachment (an enforceable security interest).

REG 2-Q56 R98. The correct answer is D. Attachment is required to create a secured transaction. If there is no attachment, the secured transaction in not effective against the debtor of third parties because once attachment occurs, the secured transaction is created.

There are three requirements for attachment:
1. Debtor must have rights to the collateral.
2. There must be an agreement between the debtor and creditor called a security agreement which must be signed by the debtor. The security agreement signed by the debtor is an acknowledgement that if the debtor defaults, the creditor has the first rights to the collateral.
3. The creditor must give value. This means that the creditor gives money to the debtor to buy the collateral, or extends credit in order for the debtor to buy the collateral.

All three must occur to have attachment.

Answer A is incorrect because if there is no attachment, there is no security interest created between the debtor and the creditor.

Answer B is incorrect because it is not effective against either the debtor or third parties as there is no attachment.

Answer C is incorrect because there is no attachment.

REG 2-Q57 R26. The correct answer is D. The financing statement requires the name of the debtor, address of debtor, description of collateral, but does not require the amount of the obligation secured.

REG 2-Q58 R159. The correct answer is D. To secure protection against a third party claim to collateral, a secured party must perfect the security interest. It is perfected when a security interest in property is superior to other interests and claims to the property. This is accomplished by filing a financing statement at the proper governmental office, such as the state's secretary of state. When the collateral is inventory the secured creditor must file a financing statement to perfect. Inventory is personal property used in a trade or business. In order for a secured creditor to have first rights to the inventory in the event the debtor defaults is to file a financing statement.

Answer A and B are incorrect because when the collateral is negotiable instruments such as a promissory note and stocks, the only way to perfect is by taking possession of the collateral with the debtor's agreement.

Answer C is incorrect because personal jewelry is a consumer good and the creditor does not have to file a financing statement or take possession of the goods in order to perfect a purchase money security interest in the goods as this type of an interest is perfected at time of attachment.

REG 2-Q59 R313. The correct answer is D. The question is asking for the statement that the secured party does not have to comply with under the Secured Transactions Article of the UCC, or the statement which is false. The secured party must comply with choices A, B and C but not D as the assigning of the security interest to another party cannot be at the debtor's request, but only at the creditor's request.

REG 2-Q60 R254. The correct answer is B. A trustee in bankruptcy can set aside preferential transfers, such as a transfer of money, as long they were made by the debtor within the previous 90 days before the filing of the petition in bankruptcy while the debtor was insolvent. Another example of a preferential transfer is when the debtor makes an unsecured creditor a secured creditor within 90 days before the filing of the petition and the debtor was insolvent. Roe's trustee in bankruptcy can set aside Jet's security interest in Roe's inventory because when Roe borrowed money from Jet on April 1, Jet was an unsecured creditor. On June 15, when Roe gave Jet a signed security agreement and financing statement covering Roe's inventory, Jet went from being an unsecured creditor to a secured creditor which is considered a preferential transfer as long as it occurs within 90 days prior to the filing of the petition. Since this is a preferential transfer, the trustee in bankruptcy can set aside the transaction and get the collateral back from Jet, the secured creditor. The setting aside of the preference transfer by the trustee is called a voidable preference.

Answer A is incorrect because the laws regarding security agreements do not include that stated limitation.

Answers C and D are incorrect because, yes, it can be set aside. Putting the word "no" makes it incorrect.

REG 2-Q61 R258. The correct answer is B. Once a financing statement is filed, the financing statement is effective for an indefinite period of time provided continuation statements are timely filed.

Answer A is incorrect because a financing statement can be filed after attachment of the security interest.

Answer C is incorrect because statement II is correct.

Answer D is incorrect because statement II is correct.

REG 2-Q62 R228. The correct answer is A. Under the Securities Act of 1933 certain organizations are exempt from registration. Exempted securities are those issued by banks, governments, common carriers (i.e. UPS and Federal Express), and non-profit organizations. Exempted securities also include corporations who issue bonds with a maturity of nine months or less.

REG 2-Q63 R100. The correct answer is D. The public sale by a corporation of its negotiable notes which have a maturity of more than 9 months is considered a security under the SEC acts of 1933 and 1934.

Answers A, B and C are incorrect because certain securities issued by various organizations are exempt from registration under the 1933 act. They include:
1. Stock issued by a trucking company
2. Any public sale of municipal bonds issued by a city government
3. A publicly-traded corporation issuing stock to its existing shareholders such as a stock split and a stock dividend.

REG 2-Q64 R294. The correct answer is A. Securities of governments, banks, savings and loans, farmers, common carriers regulated by the ICC and also, commercial paper, notes (i.e., notes, drafts and checks) with a maturity of 9 months or less, are exempt for registration per the Securities Act of 1933. Therefore, answer A, municipal bonds would be exempt from registration per the Securities Act of 1933.

Answers B, C and D are incorrect because they would require registration per the Securities Act of 1933.

REG 2-Q65 R137. The correct answer is D. If an issuer sells a security and fails to meet certain disclosure requirements, the purchaser may sell it back to the issuer and recover the price paid.

Answer A is incorrect because certain issuers do not need to provide a prospectus.

Answer B is incorrect because an issuer is permitted to advertise an initial offering of securities only through distribution of the prospectus. They can also advertise initial public offerings in financial publications such as Barron's and the Wall Street Journal.

Answer C is incorrect because not all securities issuers must register the securities offering with the Securities and Exchange Commission (SEC). Those exempt include intrastate offerings, banks, non-for-profit and government agencies.

REG 2-Q66 R312. The correct answer is B. The purpose of registration Under the Securities Act of 1933 is to provide investors with information about the company so they can make informed decisions as to whether to invest or not invest in that company. Some of the information in the registration includes certified financial statements and what the company that is selling the stock intends to do with the proceeds from the issuance of the stock. Also, the registration statement, if approved by the SEC, does not guarantee the accuracy of the information in the registration, nor does it state that the SEC is stating the stock is a good investment.

REG 2-Q67 R361. The correct answer is C. Under the Securities Act of 1933, an accountant is subject to criminal penalties under Securities Act of 1933. Liability is based on willful violations in the sale of securities. Willful violations are may be considered fraud. The willful inclusion of materially misstated financial statements in a registration statement is willful fraud in the sale of securities in interstate commerce or through the use of mail and could subject an accountant to criminal penalties.

Answers A and B are incorrect because negligence will subject an accountant to civil liability rather than criminal penalties.

Answer D is incorrect because lack of due diligence is considered to be negligence and could result in civil liability instead of criminal penalties.

REG 2-Q68 R372. The correct answer is B. A not-for-profit organization is exempt from registration under the Securities Act of 1933. Even though the entity is exempt from registration under the Securities Act of 1933, the entity is still liable under the anti-fraud provisions dealing with material misrepresentations due to the negligence of the person who prepared the financial statements. The not-for-profit will be liable under the anti-fraud provisions of the Securities Act of 1933 if the investor suffered a material loss.

Answer A is incorrect because not-for-profits are not required to register under the Securities Act of 1933 but are still liable for the anti-fraud provisions of the Securities Act of 1933.

Answer C is incorrect because the anti-fraud provisions of the Securities Act of 1933 still apply even though the not-for-profit is exempt from registration under the Securities Act of 1933.

Answer D is incorrect because the anti-fraud provisions of the Securities Act of 1933 still apply even if the issuer is the only party negligent.

REG 2-Q69 R181. The correct answer is C. Regulation D of the Securities Act of 1933 provides an exemption from a full registration under Rules 504, 505 and 506. Under Regulation D, Rules 504, 505 and 506, the securities must be issued within a 12-month period.

REG 2-Q70 R363. The correct answer is D. Under Regulation D of the Securities Act of 1933, a corporation can apply for an exemption from filing a full registration. Regulation D has 2 exemptions, Rule 504 and Rule 506. Which rule applies depends on the amount the corporation is issuing to shareholders in a certain period. Because this public stock offering is $6,000,000, Rule 506 is the exemption for this question. Rule 506 limits the sales of the offering to no more than 35 unaccredited investors.

Answer A is incorrect because the purpose of Regulation D, Rule 506 is to seek exemption from filing a registration statement.

Answer B is incorrect because under Rule 506, a company cannot solicit or advertise the offering.

Answer C is incorrect because no preliminary prospectus also known as a red herring prospectus is issued.

REG 2-Q71 R371. The correct answer is B. Tork may resell the securities as part of another transaction exempt from registration under the SEC act of 1933.

Answer A is incorrect because Tork may not resell the securities within a two year period as long as the sale does involve interstate commerce.

Answer C is incorrect because Tork may resell the securities if the certificates contain a legend indicating that they are unregistered securities.

Answer D is incorrect because Tork may resell the securities as there is no written SEC exemption.

REG 2-Q72 R202. The correct answer is A. The public sale by a corporation of its negotiable 10-year notes is subject to a SEC registration under the Securities Act of 1933.

Answer B is incorrect because the public sale by a charitable organization of 10-year bearer bonds is exempt from registration under the Securities Act of 1933.

Answer C is incorrect because municipal and governmental bonds issued by state of local governments, as well as the federal government, are not subject to a registration under the Securities Act of 1933.

Answer D is incorrect because the issuance of stock to existing stockholders without paying commissions is exempt from registration under the Securities Act of 1933. Examples are stock splits and stock dividends.

REG 2-Q73 R259. The correct answer is D. Reporting companies are those companies that are required to report quarterly, annually and periodically to the SEC under the Securities Exchange Act of 1934. One example of a reporting company are companies with assets in excess of $10 million and 500 or more shareholders.

Answers A and B are incorrect because it should read as answer D states and also it has nothing to do with annual revenues.

Answer C is incorrect because it should state companies with assets in excess of $10 million and 500 or more shareholders.

REG 2-Q74 R419. The correct answer is C. If a client of a publicly traded corporation commits an illegal act such as paying a bribe to a local zoning official and the illegal act is recorded in the financial statements incorrectly, Dean would have violated the Securities Act of 1934.

Answer A is incorrect because the Federal Trade Commission does not apply to actions involving securities.

Answer B is incorrect because the Securities Act of 1933 deals with companies that are going through a public offering of their stock in interstate commerce.

Answer D is incorrect because the North American Free Trade Act is designed to promote free trade between the U.S, Canada and Mexico.

REG 2-Q75 R134. The correct answer is C. To resolve liability under Section 18, the accountant must show good faith and lack of knowledge of the statement's falsity.

Answers A, B and D are incorrect because they do not express adequate defenses under Section 18 of the Securities Exchange Act of 1934.

REG 2-Q76 R211. The correct answer is B. The plaintiff is suing a violator of the Securities Exchange Act of 1934, Rule 10b-5 and they must prove there was intentional misconduct. The term "intentional misconduct" means conduct by a person with knowledge that the conduct is harmful to the health or well-being of another person.

Answer A is incorrect because the plaintiff does not have to prove ordinary negligence.

Answer C is incorrect because the plaintiff does not have to prove criminal intent against the defendant.

Answer D is incorrect. Strict liability is defined as absolute legal responsibility for an injury that can be imposed on the wrongdoer without proof of carelessness or fault. Because the plaintiff has to prove fault, strict liability does not apply.

REG 2-Q77 R309. The correct answer is C. Liability under section 18 of the Securities Exchange Act of 1934 relates only to applications, reports, documents, and registration statements filed with the SEC. Section 18 applies only to buyers and sellers of securities. A buyer or seller filing a section 18 claim must demonstrate an auditor can be relieved of liability upon proof of good faith. This means that the minimum standard for auditor liability under section 18 is gross negligence. Intentionally preparing and filing with the SEC a reporting corporation's incorrect quarterly report would make an accountant generally liable to the SEC.

Answers A, B and D are incorrect because they do not mention anything about failure to report the information to the SEC.

REG 2-Q78 R373. The correct answer is C. Under the Securities Act of 1933 and 1934, the anti-fraud provisions of these acts would make the issuer liable to the purchaser of the securities if the prospectus contained intentional omissions of material facts.

REG 2-Q79 R414. The correct answer is C. To ward off a takeover attempt of one corporation by another, the targeted corporation may make an offer to acquire stock from its own shareholders. The target corporation may seek an injunction against the acquiring corporation on the grounds that the takeover would violate federal anti-trust laws.

REG 2-Q80 R119. The correct answer is B. Worker's compensation benefits are available to those employees injured while working within the scope of employment.

Answer A is incorrect because it states only those employees injured while working on workplace premises. Employees who drive a truck and are injured while driving a truck during their scope of employment would also be entitled to benefits.

Answer C is incorrect because it does not include agents injured while commuting to and from work.

Answer D is incorrect because it does not cover agents (employees) injured while using the employer's automobile for personal use. It must be for business use.

REG 2-Q81 R420. The correct answer is D. Temporary office workers are usually either independent contractors or employees of a separate employment agency not eligible to collect workers' compensation benefits.

Answers A, B and C are incorrect because they are all eligible to collect workers' compensation benefits.

REG 2-Q82 R267. The correct answer is D. The Employment Retirement Income Security Act (ERISA) does not require employers to have retirement plans. ERISA does not require that employers include employees as pension-plan managers.

REG 2-Q83 R430. The correct answer is A. Under the federal statutes governing water pollution, the dredging of coastal or freshwater wetlands and the drinking water standards are regulated by the Environmental Protection Agency (EPA) who establish minimum standards governing water pollution. Also, individual states can establish more rigorous standards governing water pollution.

REG 2-Q84 R330. The correct answer is C. CERCLA is the fund that the Environmental Protection Agency (EPA) uses to pay for environmental clean-ups. It is also known as the Super Fund. In an environmental catastrophe, generally anyone who is an owner, presently or previously, as well as, a party who manages the land would be liable for clean-up costs except a party who has virtually no control over the land. The minority stockholder of the public corporation that owned the land could not make the final decisions over the management of the land as the majority stockholders made final decisions.

Answer A is incorrect because the bank that foreclosed on the land and purchased the land at the foreclosure sale, is the owner of the land. Owners of the contaminated property would be liable for the clean-up costs.

Answer B is incorrect because the parent corporation owned the land and owners of the contaminated property would be liable for the clean-up costs.

Answer D is incorrect because the trustee appointed by the owner of the land to manage the land is liable as he is the manager of the contaminated land.

REG 2-Q85 R411. The correct answer is D. A withdrawal of a general partner causes dissolution (change in a legal relationship) between the partners and because Wind agreed not to withdraw for a period of 5 years and withdrew before the 5 years, which would be in violation of the partnership agreement.

Answer A is incorrect because a partner leaving a partnership causes dissolution by the act of the partner and not by operation of law.

Answer B is incorrect because Wind's withdrawal does have a bearing on the continued operation of the partnership by the remaining partners as the remaining partners must decide to continue or terminate the partnership.

Answer C is incorrect because the dissolution is effective once Wind withdraws from the partnership. A court ordered decree is not necessary.

REG 2-Q86 R412. The correct answer is B. In a general partnership, admission of a new general partner requires that all of the general partners approve the admission of the new partner.

Answer A is incorrect because if one of the general partners leaves the partnership, it causes dissolution.

Answer C is incorrect because each partner is an agent of the general partnership and my purchase items for the business of the firm.

Answer D is incorrect because any individual partner may hire an employee.

REG 2-Q87 R413. The correct answer is D.

Answer A is incorrect because maintaining bank accounts in a state that the company is not incorporated in, does not require a certificate of authority to do business.

Answer B is incorrect because collecting corporate debts in a state the company is not incorporated in, does not require a certificate of authority to do business.

Answer C is incorrect because hiring employees who are residents of a state that the company is not incorporated in, does not require a certificate of authority.

REG 2-Q88 R415. The correct answer is D. By acquiring 90% of Trend, Acorn has control of Trend and it can further its acquisition goals with a follow-up short-form merger, because it has a very larger percentage ownership of Trend.

Answers A, B and C are incorrect because they would require Acorn shareholder approval.

REG 2-Q89 R19. The correct answer is C. The operating agreement is established to resolve disputes among the owners. The operating agreement sets up the rules by which the business will be governed and provides a framework to follow in the event the rules are not followed.

Answer A is incorrect because an LLC is not required to file its operating agreement with any state agency.

Answer B is incorrect because there is no requirement that an LLC's operating agreement has to be in writing under the statute of frauds.

Answer D is incorrect because there is no requirement that an LLC have an operating agreement.

REG 2-Q90 R146. The correct answer is C. A limited liability company (LLC) is treated as a partnership. Partnerships are not subject to taxation for distributing appreciated property to its owners. LLC appreciated property can be distributed tax free to the owner. In an S corporation, if appreciated property is distributed to an owner, the amount of the gain will be reported on Schedule K-1 of Form 1120S and taxable to the owner (stockholder).

Answer A is incorrect because an LLC and an S corporation avoid double taxation of profits.

Answer B is incorrect because an LLC and S corporation owners have limited liability in the entities.

Answer D is incorrect because the question is asking for an advantage of an LLC over an S corporation. An S corporation has an advantage over an LLC as it can offer incentive stock options to compensate owners, but because an LLC does not issue stock, it cannot have stock options. In conclusion, D is incorrect because the only advantage in the question is the advantage of an S corporation over an LLC, not an advantage of an LLC over an S corporation.

REG 2-Q91 R22. Correct answer is B. Since the LLC has elected not to be treated like a corporation, they will be treated as a partnership. When a partner contributes property or cash to a partnership for interest in that partnership, there is no gain or loss to the partner or the partnership. Therefore, Apple (the partnership) would take on a transferred basis of $5,000 from Baker.

REG 2-Q92 R295. The correct answer is D. Real property is defined as land and everything permanently attached to it.

Answer A is incorrect because it says only. Answers with exclusive terms such as only, always and never are generally incorrect.

Answer B is incorrect because it states all tangible property which could include personal property.

Answer C is incorrect because real property is not intangible.

REG 2-Q93 R383. The correct answer is A. If preparing a foreign language translation of the copyrighted work, permission will be needed. You will need to seek permission to translate and republish the article as you would do if you were planning to reproduce an article in English. The translation shall not change the content, meaning, spirit or tone of the original material.

Answer B is incorrect because a reviewer may fairly cite from the original work, if the intention is to use the material for review and criticism, such as with a book review.

Answers C and D are incorrect because the fair use doctrine allows use for limited purposes without violating copy right laws. Examples include portions used for research or teaching.

REG 2-Q94 R384. The correct answer is A. Kemp was the first to patent the process and the fact that Mill wanted to use the patent for his own business and not attempt to patent the process is a violation of the intellectual property.

Answer B is incorrect because Kemp will not prevail because Mill should have known about Kemp's patent, Kemp will prevail as he was the first to patent the process.

Answers C and D are incorrect because Kemp will prevail as he was the first to patent the process.

REG 2-Q95 R331. The correct answer is D. Real property includes land and things attached to the land in a relatively permanent manner. Personal property is property not classified as real property. Trees when in the ground are considered real property. When they are cut down and become lumber, they become personal property. When the lumber is used to build a home, the lumber reverts back to being real property.

REG 2-Q96 R230. The correct answer is A. A valid deed must in writing, signed by the seller (grantor), contain a description of the property, and must be delivered.

Answer B is incorrect because a deed does not have to be recorded by the seller of the property.

Answer C is incorrect because there is no requirement that the deed must include a statement of the property's value.

Answer D is incorrect because the deed does not have to include a general warranty of title. A general warranty of title is where the seller guarantees to the buyer that there were no liens or encumbrances placed on the property before the seller acquired the property, or during any time the seller owned the property.

REG 2-Q97 R99. The correct answer is D. The term fee simple represents absolute ownership of land, where the owner may do whatever they choose with the land. If the owner of a fee simple dies intestate, the land will go to their heirs.

Answer A is incorrect because in an easement, the person who granted the easement has a right-of-way. For example, if I want to cross your property every day because it is the shortest way to get to the bus stop, I will fill out a document called an easement that gives me the right-of-way to cross your property to get to the bus stop. As the owner of the property, you would sign the easement giving me the right to cross the property. Easement does not give me ownership of the property I am crossing, just a right to cross.

Answer B is incorrect. A restrictive covenant is a clause in a deed to real property that limits what the owner of the land can do with the property. Restrictive covenants allow surrounding property owners, who have similar covenants in their deeds, to enforce the terms of the covenants. For example, a land developer with a planned sub-division may impose certain limitations on the use of the lots in the development. These may include a provision restricting construction to a certain type of home (i.e., single-family vs. apartments).

Answer C is incorrect. A license is granted by a governing body permitting the licensee to perform a task or operation. With property, examples include licensed real estate agents and contractors. Real estate agents represent buyers or sellers in a real estate transaction. Contractors who work on improving property with repairs and maintenance will likely hold a license that allows them to operate the business. The license does not give the licensee the right to own the property.

REG 2-Q98 R138. The correct answer is D. Constructive eviction deals with situations where the tenant can get out of the lease when the property is made unusable by the landlord.

Answer A is incorrect because if the landlord changes the lock and refuses to give the tenant a new key, the property is still useable by the tenant although the landlord is not allowing the tenant access.

Answer B is incorrect because the landlord starts a legal proceeding against the tenant for failure to pay rent. This is called eviction where the landlord is suing the tenant for failure to pay rent and it could lead to the possible removal of the tenant from the property.

Answer C is incorrect because the tenant can complain to a government agency about the conditions of the premises if the landlord makes the property inhabitable.

REG 2-Q99 R382. The correct answer is B. This question deals with a sublease. In a sublease, the sublessee pays the original tenant, and the original tenant pays the owner of the property. If there is not a sublease, one could have an assignment of a lease. In an assignment, the assignor assigns the lease to an assignee. The assignee makes the rent payments directly to the original owner of the property. In a lease of an apartment, subleasing and assigning are only permitted if they are agreed upon by the landlord and the original tenant.

REG 3 – Federal Taxation of Property Transactions

A. Acquisition and Disposition of Assets	**3A-1 – 3A-21**
1. Basis and holding period of assets	1
2. Taxable and nontaxable dispositions	5
3. Amount and character of gains and losses and netting process	11
4. Installment sales	15
5. Related party transactions (including imputed interest)	17
B. Cost Recovery including Depreciation, Depletion, and Amortization	**3B-1 – 3B-3**
1. Depreciation	1
2. Depletion	3
3. Amortization	3
C. Estate and Gift Taxation	**3C-1 – 3C-4**
1. Transfers subject to the gift tax	1
2. Gift tax annual exclusion and gift tax deductions	2
3. Determination of taxable estate	3
Glossary: Federal Taxation of Property Transactions	**Glossary 3-1 – 3-2**
Multiple Choice – Questions	**MCQ 3-1 – 3-8**
Multiple Choice – Solutions	**MCQ 3-9 – 3-18**

Federal Taxation of Property Transactions

Taxation of property transactions covers the life cycle of an asset. It starts with the acquisition, covers the holding of the asset, and addresses the final transfer of the asset. The transfer of the asset can be by sale, exchange, gift or bequest. Tax treatment will also depend upon the classification of the asset, which includes:

- Real property
  Legally, real property includes land and anything attached to the land that is immovable in nature. Consider as examples, real property, buildings, crops, and integrated equipment such as well pumps.
- Personal property
  This can be a definition by exclusion. If it is not real property, then it is personal property. Personal property, in contrast to real property, should always be moveable. Examples would be cars, jewelry, furniture, and stocks.
- Conversion
  Property can be real property, converted into personal property and then converted back into real property. An example would be trees. While a tree, it is real property. But if the tree is cut down, it becomes personal property. If the tree is cut into lumber and used in building a house, then the lumber becomes real property again as part of the house. The easiest way to define an item as either real or personal property is to look at the movable aspect of the property. If the property can be moved, even if not easily, then it is always personal property. If not, then it is real property.

Capital assets can be either real or personal property. The Internal Revenue Code (IRC) does not define a capital asset for tax purposes. It is a definition by exclusion. Meaning that certain items are specified as NOT being a capital asset. If not on the list, then the item is a capital asset. The items excluded are:

a. Inventory.
b. Personal property and real property, used in a trade or business and held for more then 12 months (Section 1231 assets)
c. Copyright, a literary, musical, or artistic composition, a letter or memorandum, or similar property if:
   1) The creator is still the owner
   2) The owner had the item produced
   3) The owner has a carryover basis
d. Accounts and notes receivable if developed within a business.
e. A covenant not to compete.

Multiple Choice
REG 3-Q1 through REG 3-Q6

A. Acquisition and Disposition of Assets
1. Basis and holding period of assets
   a. Calculate the tax basis of asset

Calculate the tax basis of an asset.

In most situations, the starting point for determining the basis of assets begins with the purchase price. Often, there may be other costs surrounding the purchase. The general rule is to capitalize all costs that are incurred to get the asset ready for its intended purpose. So, if a machine is purchased and a special concrete pad must be constructed, then the machine's cost is increased by the cost of the concrete pad. If installation or freight costs are required, then these costs will also be added to the capitalized cost. If real property is purchased, then all fees required as part of the purchase such as fees paid for a title search, sales tax, legal fees, or recording fees are also capitalized.

To this beginning cost, additions or improvements will be added in, and the depreciation or depletion will be subtracted. This final number is called adjusted basis and is key in determining the gain or loss upon disposition. However, not all assets are acquired through a direct purchase. There are other possible methods for determining an asset's basis.

1) Basket purchase
   Often, a group of assets can be acquired in a single transaction called a basket purchase. The acquisition cost must then be allocated among all of the assets acquired. The process involves determining a fair market value of each asset in the group, and then using the relative fair market values as a means to allocate the acquisition cost.

   > ***Example of a basket purchase***: Phyllis purchased land for $960,000. On the land Phyllis built four houses for resale. The fair market values (FMV) for the houses were $200,000 for house #1, $996,000 for house #2, $420,000 for house #3 and $275,000 for house #4. The allocation of the purchase price of the land to each house is calculated as follows:
   >
   > | | FMV | Relative FMV x Cost | Basis |
   > |---|---|---|---|
   > | House #1 | $200,000 | $200,000/$1,891,000 x $960,000 | $101,534 |
   > | House #2 | $996,000 | $996,000/$1,891,000 x $960,000 | $505,637 |
   > | House #3 | $420,000 | $420,000/$1,891,000 x $960,000 | $213,221 |
   > | House #4 | $275,000 | $275,000/$1,891,000 x $960,000 | $139,608 |
   > | | $1,891,000 | | $960,000 |

   To calculate: Determine the Relative FMV by taking the FMV of each house divided by the total FMV of all houses. Multiply this amount by the purchase price of the land to determine the amount of the purchase price of the land that is allocated to each house.

2) Inheritance
   The basis of the decedent's property is included in the estate at FMV at the date of the decedent's death. The executor of the estate may elect to use an alternate valuation date which is usually six months after death, if by selecting that election it will reduce both the estate tax liability and the gross estate.

   If the executor chooses the alternate valuation date and within six months of death, the property is sold or distributed, the basis of the property, to the beneficiary, is the FMV on the date of distribution, or sale. If the distribution of the assets is made to the beneficiary more than six months after the death of the decedent, the basis of the property, to the beneficiary, is the FMV of the property at six (6) months after death.

3) Gifts
   The basis of property received as a gift will be determined at the time the donee sells the gift. If the gift is sold at a gain, and the donee uses the donor's basis, the sale of the gift should result in a gain.
   i. If it does not result in a gain, determine if the transaction would result in a loss, by taking the lesser of the donor's basis or, the fair market value at the date of the gift.
   ii. If by taking the lesser of the donor's basis or, the fair market value at the date of the gift and it results in a gain, instead of a loss, then no gain or loss is recognized on the sale of the gift.

   > ***Hint***: If the donee uses the gain basis and the sale results in a loss or, the donee uses the loss basis and the sale results in a gain, then no gain or loss is recognized on the sale of the gift.

Examples of gifted property basis and the resulting gain or loss:

i. Donor's basis at date of gift $1,000
    Fair market value at date of gift $1,500
    Donee's sale price $1,200

The basis to donee for calculating gain will be $1,000, the donor's basis. By using the donor's basis, the sale results in a recognized gain of $200 ($1,200 - $1,000) to the donee.

ii. Donor's basis at date of gift $1,000
    Fair market value at date of gift $700
    Donee's sale price $600

When the donee uses the donor's basis of $1,000 for determining gain and compares it to the donee's selling price of $600, and it does not result in a gain, but it results in a loss of $400. Then determine if there is a loss by taking the lesser of the donor's basis of $1,000 or the fair market value at the gift date of $700, the basis of the gift for determining the loss is $700. If the asset is sold at $600, it does result in a loss of $100 ($600 - $700).

iii. Donor's basis $1,000
     Fair market value at date of gift $700
     Donee's sale price $800

If the donee sells the gift for $800 and uses the donor's basis of $1,000, which is the basis for determining gain, but the sale results in a loss of $200 and not a gain. Determine If the donee sold it at a loss, buy taking the lesser of the donor's basis of $1,000 or, the fair market value at the date of the gift of $700. Using a basis of $700 and comparing to the selling price of $800, results in a gain and does not result in a loss. Because the gain basis results in a loss, and loss basis result in a gain, no gain or loss is recognized to the donee on the sale of the asset.

4) Services rendered
Sometimes property can be received in exchange for services. If a service is performed and property vs cash is received as payment, then the taxpayer would have taxable income equal to the fair market value of the property received. The basis of the property to the taxpayer is equal to the fair market value of the property received.

5) Stock dividends
A stock dividend can be taxable or nontaxable.
i. Taxable stock dividend
If the stock dividend is a taxable stock dividend, the individual taxpayer will have taxable income equal to the number of shares distributed, times the fair market value per share at the date of distribution. This will equal the basis of the stock.

Example of taxable stock dividend: Bill Carter had 1,000 shares of common stock of Diamond Company and received 100 shares of Diamond Company preferred stock as a taxable stock dividend. The fair market value of the preferred stock at the date of distribution is $7.00 per share. The taxable stock dividend is the receipt of the 100 shares of preferred stock, times the $7.00 fair market value of the preferred stock at the date of distribution, which equals $700. The taxpayer will show a taxable stock dividend of $700, and the basis of the preferred stock is also $700.

ii. Nontaxable stock dividend
   If it is a nontaxable stock dividend, when the stock is received, the basis of the stockholder's original stock is allocated among the stock issued in the dividend and the original stock, in proportion to their relative fair market values. The holding period of the stock received as a stock dividend includes the holding period of the original stock.

   > *Example of nontaxable stock dividend:* In 2014, Bill Carter paid $180,000 for 1,000 shares of common stock of Diamond Company. In 2015, Carter received a nontaxable distribution of 100 preferred shares of Diamond Company. The fair market value of the 1,000 common shares at the date of distribution was $150,000, and the fair market value of the 100 preferred shares at the date of distribution was $50,000. The allocation of the $180,000 basis to the preferred and common shares is calculated as follows:
   >
   > Common shares: ($150,000/$200,000) x $180,000 = $135,000
   > Preferred shares: ($50,000/$200,000) x $180,000 = $45,000
   >
   > The holding period of the 100 preferred shares includes the holding period of the 1,000 shares of the common stock. Therefore, the holding period for the preferred stock begins in 2014, the same holding period as the common stock.

   > *Hint*: On the CPA exam, the question will indicate whether a stock dividend is non-taxable or taxable.

6) Stock split
   A stock split to an investor is not a taxable event. When a corporation declares a 2-for-1 stock split, the number of shares doubles and the cost basis per share is divided in half. For example, assume that Phil Yaeger purchased 100 shares of the ABC Corporation (an issuer) on January 2, 2013, for $10,000. ABC has a 2-for-1 stock split on January 2, 2015, when the fair market value per share was $120. With a 2-for-1 stock split, Phil would have 200 shares of ABC stock, and the cost of $10,000 would not change. The cost per share after the stock split would be $50 per share ($100/2). Phil sold 100 shares on June 1, 2015. The cost basis per share that Phil sold the stock at is $50 per share. The total basis of the stock sold is $5,000 ($50 x 100 shares).

   > *Hint*: When computing the basis per share after a 2-for-1 stock split, do not divide the fair market value per share by 2. The proper method is to divide the original cost basis per share by 2.

b. Determining the holding period of assets

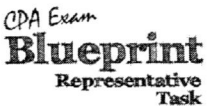

> Determine the holding period of a disposed asset for classification of tax gain or loss.

The holding period is a key component for separating out long term vs. short-term capital gains and losses. The holding period determination will follow the basis determination. If the basis is determined by fair market value such as in a purchase, then the holding period begins on the date of the purchase. However, if the basis is determined by reference to a previous holder, carryover basis, then the holding period begins on the date the previous holder acquired the property.

Capital sssets must be held longer than one year to receive any beneficial long-term capital gain treatment. If 12 months or less, it will be short-term capital gain and will receive ordinary tax treatment.

Contrary to this rule, any inherited property received by the beneficiary of an estate always has a holding period of more than 12 months (considered long-term). Gifted property will have a holding period determined by whether the taxpayer is using the gain basis, or the loss basis. If the donee sells the gift at a gain, they will use the gain basis (donor's basis), and the holding period to the donee will begin on the date when the donor purchased the gift. If the donee sells the gift at a loss, they will use the loss basis, which is the lesser of the donor's basis or, the fair market value at the date of the gift. If the fair market value at the date of gift is less than the donor's basis, the holding period for the gift sold is the date of the gift. If the donee uses the donor's basis instead of the fair market value at the date of gift, the holding period begins on the date the donor purchased the item to be gifted.

> *Hint*: Think about what is most beneficial for the IRS, if sold at a loss they want to limit you because that is a tax benefit. On the other hand, if sold at a gain they want the maximum money because that is a tax liability. Therefore, for tax benefits (losses) use the lower of basis or FMV and for tax liabilities (gains) use the donor's basis.

Multiple Choice

REG 3-Q7 through REG 3-Q12

2. Taxable and nontaxable dispositions

Analyze asset sale and exchange transactions to determine whether they are taxable or nontaxable.

The basis for the newly acquired replacement property in a like kind exchange is calculated as follows:

Starting point	Basis of property given up
Plus	Gain recognized
Plus	Boot basis paid
Reduce	Loss recognized
Reduce	Fair market value of boot received

1) Like-kind Exchange

Calculate the realized gain, recognized gain and deferred gain on like-kind property exchange transactions for federal income tax purposes.

A like-kind exchange is an exchange transaction where the business use or investment property is given up in exchange for a similar type of property. Similar type of property would be real property for real property and personal property for personal property.

Also, the property given up must match. If U.S. property, it must be exchanged for U.S. property. Similarly, if the property given up is foreign, then the property received must be foreign property as well.

As long as the above requirements are met, business use property can be exchanged for investment property or vice versa.

Specifically, the like-kind exchange rules will not apply to:
   i. Inventory
   ii. Investments in stocks, bonds, or notes
   iii. Interests in a partnership
   iv. Property held for personal use

Additionally, the property to be received must be identified within 45 days or less after the property being given up is transferred. The property being received must also be transferred within 180 days of the start of the transfer but no later than when the taxpayer files the tax return including extensions for the year of the transfer.

Boot will encompass any property given up or received that is not a like kind. The most common type of boot is cash. Cash is often needed as a way to equalize fair market values in the properties being exchanged.

Another common form of boot would be liabilities assumed or relieved. If the other party assumes the liability in the exchange, then the taxpayer has boot received equal to the liability relieved. If the taxpayer assumes a liability in the exchange, then the taxpayer is giving boot equal to the liability assumed.

CPA Exam
Blueprint
Representative Task

> Calculate the realized and recognized gain or loss on the disposition of assets for federal income tax purposes.

Example: Taxpayer A owns land, with an adjusted basis of $22,000 and a fair market value of $25,000. Taxpayer B owns land with an adjusted basis of $30,000, subject to a mortgage of $6,000, and a fair market value of $33,000. Taxpayers A and B exchanged real estate investments. Taxpayer B paid $3,000 cash to Taxpayer A. Taxpayer A is assuming taxpayer B's mortgage. The realized gain or loss, the recognized gain or loss, and the basis of the new property from Taxpayers A and B are calculated as follows:

Realized gain or loss:	Taxpayer A		Taxpayer B	
Proceeds: FMV of land received	$33,000		$25,000	
Boot received (paid)	3,000		6,000	
Amount realized on exchange		$36,000		$31,000
Less: Boot received (paid)			(3,000)	
Taxpayer B's mortgage assumed	(6,000)			
Adjusted basis	(22,000)		(30,000)	
Amount given-up on exchange		(28,000)		(33,000)
Gain (Loss) realized on exchange		$ 8,000		($ 2,000)

Gain (Loss) recognized on the exchange:
Though the $8,000 gain is calculated above as *realized*, for tax, the gain is only *recognized* to the extent of the lesser of the realized gain or the boot received. For Taxpayer A, gain recognized will be limited to the lesser of the $8,000 realized gain or the boot received of $3,000. Taxpayer A, assuming taxpayer B's liabilities, has no effect on the recognized gain of taxpayer A.

The loss by Taxpayer B is not recognized despite boot being received. The entire $2,000 loss is postponed and will impact the basis of the new asset received.

Basis of New Property:		Taxpayer A	Taxpayer B
	Basis of property given up	$22,000	$30,000
Plus	Gain recognized	3,000	--
Plus	Boot basis paid	6,000	3,000
Less	Loss recognized	--	--
Less	Boot received	(3,000)	(6,000)
	Basis in new property received	$28,000	$27,000

> *Hint*: A good way to remember how boot is treated when calculating the basis of the new property received is:
> - Boot received begins with an "R" and represents the **R**eduction in basis.
> - Boot paid begins with a "P" and Plus begins with "P" and represents the **P**lus, or an addition in the basis.

i. Liabilities assumed

In an exchange, if taxpayer A and taxpayer B assume each other's liabilities, the liabilities must be netted to determine if the exchange of the liabilities results in either boot paid or received. When the mortgages or debt are netted, and the result is net boot received, this is an addition to the gain recognized. If the taxpayer A nets the mortgages or debt and it results in net boot paid, it does not affect the gain or loss but will affect the basis of taxpayer A's new asset.

> *Hint* In a like kind exchange problem, if there is <u>cash received by one of the taxpayers</u>, and both taxpayers assume each other mortgages, the following steps apply in calculating the total boot received.
> 1) Each taxpayer nets the mortgage assumed by the other taxpayer and the new mortgage being taken on from the other taxpayer.
> 2) If the netting of the mortgages results in <u>net boot received</u>, add the net boot received from the mortgages to the cash received to arrive at the total net boot received.
>   a. The recognized gain is the lesser of the realized gain or, the total boot received.
> 3) If the netting of the mortgages results in <u>net boot paid</u>, ignore the net boot paid in the calculation of total net boot received. The net boot received will only be the cash received.
>   a. The recognized gain is the lesser of the realized gain or, the total net boot received, which is only the cash. However, do not forget, that the net boot paid from the netting of the mortgages will still affect the calculation of the basis of the new property.

Example: Taxpayer B assumes taxpayer A's mortgage of $8,000 in a like-kind exchange and taxpayer A takes on taxpayer B's mortgage of $6,000. Taxpayer B's adjusted basis of the old real estate transferred is $40,000 and a fair market value of $45,000. Taxpayer A's adjusted basis of the old real estate transferred is $30,000 and a fair market value of $60,000. Determine the realized gain, the recognized gain, in addition to the basis of the new property acquired taxpayer A.

Realized gain:	**Taxpayer A**		**Taxpayer B**	
Proceeds: FMV of land received	$45,000		$60,000	
Boot received (paid)	0		0	
"A" assumes "B" debt			6,000	
"B" assumes "A" debt	8,000			
Amount realized on exchange		$53,000		$66,000

Less: Cash received (paid) $0

"A" assumes "B" debt	(6,000)		
"B" assumes "A" debt			(8,000)
Adjusted basis	(30,000)		(40,000)
Amount given-up on exchange		(36,000)	(48,000)
Gain realized on exchange		$ 17,000	$ 18,000
Gain recognized		$2,000	$0

Gain recognized on the exchange:
Though the gain is calculated above as *realized*, for tax purposes, the gain is only *recognized* to the extent of the lesser of the realized gain or the net boot received from netting the mortgages.

For taxpayer A, taxpayer B assuming taxpayer A's mortgage of $8,000, which is boot received for taxpayer A. Taxpayer A assuming taxpayer B's mortgage of $6,000 is boot paid for taxpayer A. The netting of the mortgages results in a net boot received of $2,000 ($8,000 - $6,000). Since there is no other boot received mentioned in the facts of the example (such as cash), the gain recognized is the lesser of the realized gain of $17,000 or, the net boot received of $2,000 from the netting of the mortgages. Therefore, the recognized gain would be $2,000, the lesser of the two numbers.

For taxpayer B, there is no net boot received because taxpayer B did not receive any cash and when taxpayer B netted the mortgages, it was a net boot paid of $2,000 ($6,000 - $8,000). When there is net boot paid from the netting of the mortgages, it does enter into the calculation of the basis of the new property, but not the recognized gain.

Basis of New Property:

		Taxpayer A	Taxpayer B
	Basis of property given up	$30,000	$40,000
Plus	Gain recognized	2,000	0
Plus	"A" assumes "B" debt (Boot paid)	6,000	
Reduce	"B" assumes "A" debt (Boot received)	(8,000)	
Reduce	"A" assumes "B" debt (Boot received)		(6,000)
Plus	"B" assumes "A" debt (Boot paid)		8,000
	Basis in new property received	$30,000	$42,000

Multiple Choice

REG 3-Q13

2) **Involuntary Conversion**
Involuntary conversions cover theft, casualty or condemnation. Proceeds would typically be insurance proceeds, if any. Proceeds less the property's adjusted basis then equals the gain or loss upon the disposition.

   i. Gain transactions
   If the involuntary conversion results in a realized gain, the recognized gain is the lesser of the realized gain or, the amount the taxpayer does not spend of the insurance proceeds received. The taxpayer may elect to postpone the gain if the property is replaced with similar property. Otherwise, the gain is recognized in full.

a) If the gain is elected to be postponed, the replacement property must be acquired within two years after the close of the taxable year of the involuntary conversion.
b) If business or investment property is condemned, then the replacement period is three years versus two years.
c) The replacement property must be similar or related in service or use as the original property.
d) Any proceeds not reinvested into the replacement property will trigger gain recognition. The gain recognized will not exceed the original gain calculation or the amount not reinvested, whichever is less.
e) Basis of the reinvestment property equals the purchase price reduced by any gain postponed.

> **Example of involuntary conversion with a gain transaction:** Joe Dart has a building that was destroyed by fire. The insurance company paid $20,000 to Dart, whose property has a basis of $13,000. Dart replaced the building within the statutory limits and spent $12,000. The recognized gain and basis of the new building is calculated as follows:
>
> | | |
> |---|---|
> | Insurance proceeds | $20,000 |
> | Less: Basis of converted property | (13,000) |
> | Realized gain | $7,000 |
>
> | | |
> |---|---|
> | Insurance proceeds | $20,000 |
> | Less: Cost of new building | (12,000) |
> | Insurance proceeds not reinvested | $8,000 |
>
> Recognized gain is $7,000, which is the lesser of the $7,000 realized gain or, the $8,000 of insurance proceeds not reinvested. The basis of the new building is calculated as follows:
>
> | | |
> |---|---|
> | Cost of new building | $12,000 |
> | Less: Gain not recognized | (0) |
> | Basis of new building | $12,000 |

> **Hint:** Recognized gain is equal to the proceeds from conversion minus the greater of cost for new property or adjusted basis of converted property.

ii. Loss transactions
Loss on an involuntary conversion will be recognized in full, regardless if the replacement property is acquired or not.

Note that losses on personal use property, such as a home, generally are not deductible under federal tax law.

There is the potential to benefit from the loss as an itemized deduction for an individual taxpayer. This only applies to casualty or theft losses, and to condemnation. There is a $100 floor for each occurrence, and the loss must exceed 10% of the taxpayer's adjusted gross income.

> **Example of involuntary conversion with a loss transaction:** Jane Dart has a building that was destroyed by a hurricane. The insurance company paid $13,000 to Dart, whose property has a basis of $20,000. Dart has an adjusted gross income (AGI) of $10,000. Dart replaced the building within the statutory limits and spent $12,000.

> The recognized loss and basis of the new building in calculated as follows:
>
> | | |
> |---|---:|
> | Proceeds from Insurance Company | $13,000 |
> | Less: Basis | (20,000) |
> | Subtotal | ($7,000) |
> | Less: $100 loss | 100 |
> | Less: 10% of AGI | 1,000 |
> | Recognized loss | ($5,900) |
>
> The basis of the new building is the building's cost of $12,000.

3) **Wash Sales**

Wash sale rules apply to stocks or securities when sold at a loss, and substantially identical stocks or securities are acquired within 30 days either *before or after* the sale date.

If the wash sale rules are applicable, then the loss is postponed and will increase the basis of the newly acquired stocks or securities. Gains are not subject to the wash sale rules.

Dealers in stocks or securities are not subject to the wash sale rules.

> ***Wash sale example:*** Taxpayer owns 1,000 shares of Company A stock with a basis $2,000. Taxpayer sells 1,000 shares of Company A stock for $1,600 realizing a $400 loss. Taxpayer acquires 1,000 shares of Company A stock for $1,800, which is 20 days *before* selling the original 1,000 shares of Company A stock. Because the taxpayer acquired similar shares of company A's stock within 30 days before selling the original 1,000 shares of company A's stock, the $400 loss is not recognized but increases the basis of the new shares by $400. The new basis of the Company A's stock is $2,200 ($1,800 + $400).
>
> Suppose in the previous example that taxpayer acquired 500 additional shares of Company A stock, for $1,800, instead of 1,000 shares. The purchase of the 500 shares occurred 20 days *before* selling the original 1,000 shares of Company A stock. The taxpayer only acquired 50% of the original shares sold. Therefore, only 50% of the realized loss of $400, or $200 would be postponed, and the other $200 would be recognized for tax purposes. The loss postponed of $200 is added to the recent purchase of $1,800 to determine the new basis. The new basis of the Company A's stock is $2,000 ($1,800 + $200).
>
> Gains on wash sales are fully taxable.

4) **Sale or Exchange of Principal Residence**

An individual taxpayer is allowed to exclude $250,000 ($500,000 if married filing a joint return) of gain upon the sale of a home if certain requirements are met. If the gain exceeds the dollar limit for exclusion, then the balance of the gain is recognized. Postponement is not an option. Losses upon the sale of a principal residence are not allowed as a deduction or postponed.

   i. The home must have been owned *and* occupied as the primary residence for an aggregate of two of the prior five years.
   ii. The exclusion can only be used once every two years.
   iii. Married taxpayers are eligible for the exclusion as long as one of the spouses has met the ownership test, but both have to have met the occupancy test.
   iv. If one spouse has used the exclusion in the past two years, the other spouse may still use the exclusion up to $250,000 if all the requirements are met.
   v. If ownership and occupancy tests are not satisfied due to job location change, health reasons, or unforeseen circumstances, then the exclusion can be prorated based on the time owned and occupied out of the two-year requirement.

> ***Hint***: Loss from sale of a principal residence is not deductible.

5) Qualified Small Business Stock
   The <u>Protecting Americans from Tax Hikes Act of 2015</u> (PATH Act) includes permanent tax breaks, including exclusions on small business stock gains (Section 1202). The new law makes permanent the exclusion of 100 percent of the gain on the sale or exchange of qualified small business stock (QSBS) acquired after September 27, 2010, and held for more than five years. If the requirements are met to be a qualified small business stock, then 100% of any gain from the sale of the stock can be excluded up to the greater of $10 million or 10 times the stockholder's basis. The other requirements under the PATH Act, which makes the 100% exclusion of the gain permanent, are:
   i. The stock must have been held for more than five years.
   ii. The stock had to be acquired directly from the issuing corporation.
   iii. Only non-corporate taxpayers are eligible for the gain exclusion.
   iv. The qualifying corporation must be a C corporation and have not more than $50 million in gross assets.
   v. The qualifying corporation is in an active trade or business versus investments.

Section 1202 Stock	Capital Gain Exclusion
Acquired 8/11/1993 - 2/17/2009	50%
Acquired 2/18/2009 – 9/27/2010	75%
Acquired after 9/27/2010	100%

   Section 1202 relates to the date of acquisition of a small business corporation stock. The capital gain exclusion is the column that indicates how much of the gain is excludable for the various acquisition periods.

6) Section 1244 Stock
   Section 1244 allows a loss upon the sale of qualified small business stock to be treated as ordinary losses versus as capital losses up to $50,000 for an individual return or $100,000 for married filing jointly. The stock has to be acquired directly from the issuing corporation. The shareholder must be the original holder (individual or partner). The stock can be common stock or preferred stock and must be issued for money or property. In addition, the corporation must be a small business corporation as defined in the tax code. Basically, the corporation cannot have received more than $1 million in capital.

Multiple Choice

REG 3-Q14 through REG 3-Q23

3. Amount and character of gains and losses, and netting process
   a. Capital gains netting process
      All capital asset gains and losses must follow a specified netting process. Short-term capital gains (STCG) and losses (STCL) must be netted together separate from the long-term capital gains (LTCG) and losses (LTCL) netting process. Once a net short-term gain (NSTCG) or loss (NSTCL) and a separate net long-term capital gain (NLTCG) or loss (NLTCL) is determined, then the net short-term gain or loss and the net long-term gain or loss is netted together. The result will be the net capital gain (NCG) or net capital loss (NCL).

      STCG > STCL = NSTCG
      STCG < STCL = NSTCL
      LTCG > LTCL = NLTCG
      LTCG < LTCL = NLTCL

b. Individual capital gain/loss impact

Calculate the amount of capital gains and losses for federal income tax purposes.

1) Capital losses

    For taxpayers who file a joint return or, individual taxpayers who file single or head of household, they can take a net capital loss against ordinary income, up to a maximum of $3,000. Any amount not currently used may be carryforward indefinitely, either as short-term or long-term, based on the holding period.

2) Capital Gains

    All net capital gains are included in an individual's tax return. If the net capital gain is a net short-term capital gain, the net amount will be taxed at ordinary income rates.

    If an individual has a net short-term capital loss and a net long-term capital loss, when applying the $3,000 loss limit, always use up the net short-term capital loss first and then use the net long-term capital loss. Remember, no more than $3,000 of capital losses can be deducted against ordinary income in any one year. For married filing separately, the maximum capital loss that can be deducted against ordinary income is $1,500.

c. Corporate Capital Gains/Losses

Corporations receive no tax rate benefit from net long-term capital gains. The primary benefit of net long-term capital gains will be to offset any capital losses a corporation may have. Net long-term and net short-term capital gains will be taxed at the corporation's normal tax bracket.

Net capital losses cannot be used to offset ordinary income (taxable income). Capital losses may only be used to offset capital gains. Capital losses not used currently may be carried back three (3) years and forward five (5) years to offset capital gains in those years. Capital losses that are either carry back or carry forward are always treated as short term.

Review asset transactions to determine the character (capital vs. ordinary) of the gain or loss for federal income tax purposes.

Calculate the amount of ordinary income and loss for federal income tax purposes.

d. Section 1231 assets

The following assets qualify as Section 1231 property:
1) Depreciable personal property that is used in a trade or business or,
2) Real property used in a trade or business, and
3) Property must be held for more than one year

Once designated as a Section 1231 asset, all Section 1231 gains are netted against all net Section 1231 losses. If the net Section 1231 gain exceeds the net Section 1231 losses, the net gain is a Section 1231 gain, which is a long-term capital gain. If the net Section 1231 losses exceed the net Section 1231 gains, the net loss is a Section 1231 loss, which is an ordinary loss.

> **Example**: If an individual or a corporation sold personal property used in a trade or business, which was held for more than one year, if there is a gain on the sale, the amount of depreciation taken is recaptured as ordinary income under Section 1245, and any remaining balance of the gain is a Section 1231 gain, which is long-term capital gain.

> ***Example***: If an individual (or sole proprietor) sold real property used in a trade or business, which was held for more than one year, none of the gain is recaptured as ordinary income. The entire gain is Section 1231 gain, long-term capital gain.
>
> ***Example***: If a corporation sold real property used in a trade or business, which was held for more than one year, the corporation must recapture 20% of the depreciation taken under Section 291 as ordinary income, with any balance of gain treated as Section 1231 gain, long-term capital gain.

Personal property and real property used in a trade or business which are held for one year or less are not capital assets and are also not Section 1231 assets. If these assets are sold at a gain or loss, all gains or losses will be ordinary.

e. Non-recaptured IRC Section 1231 losses
When a business has IRC Section 1231 gains, it must look back five taxable years to determine if there have been IRC Section 1231 losses. If there are IRC Section 1231 losses in the prior years, then the losses will be "recaptured" against the current year IRC Section 1231 gains. The gains change character from capital to ordinary in the amount of the prior year IRC Section 1231 loss. The losses are recaptured in chronological order.

For example, Business A has current year IRC Section 1231 net gain of $40,000. Looking back to the five prior tax returns reveals IRC Section 1231 net non-recaptured losses of $45,000. The current year IRC Section 1231 net gain of $40,000 will be fully taxed as ordinary income by "recapturing" $40,000 of prior years' non-recaptured IRC Section 1231 losses. There will be a remaining $5,000 of non-recaptured IRC Section 1231 losses.

f. Section 1245 assets
These assets are generally depreciable personal property, used in a trade or business or, held for the production of income. These assets are held for one year or less. Examples include machinery equipment, trucks, and automobiles.

g. Section 1245 recapture
The gain from the sale or exchange of a Section 1231 asset will be recaptured as ordinary income to the extent of the lesser of all depreciation taken or, the recognized gain. This recaptured gain is Section 1245 gain. The excess gain will be taxed as (Section 1231 Gain), which is a long-term capital gain. If the asset is disposed of at a loss, then the loss will be treated as a Section 1231 loss, which is an ordinary loss.

h. Section 1250 assets
1) Section 1250 assets are real property subject to depreciation and used in a trade or business. If categorized as 1250 property, then IRC Section 1250 will override IRC Section 1231 for tax purposes.
2) Section 1250 assets must calculate additional depreciation to determine the amount of depreciation recapture. The additional depreciation is equal to the amount of total accelerated depreciation taken, minus depreciation as if the straight-line method had been used for real property, under the ACRS method. This additional depreciation is the amount to be recaptured as ordinary income upon a sale. Upon the sale or disposal of the asset, any gain over the additional depreciation will be taxed as a capital gain. Any loss on the sale or disposal will be an ordinary loss. The rule applies to any accelerated depreciation that was taken on post-1969 real estate using the ACRS depreciation method. Accelerated depreciation was allowed on real estate when the ACRS method was used for the depreciation of real property, used in a trade or business. After 1969, and before the Tax Reform Act of 1986, real estate could be depreciated using accelerated methods, under ACRS. Under the Tax Reform Act of 1986, real estate could no longer be depreciated on the accelerated basis and had to be depreciated on the straight-line

basis. The Tax Reform Act of 1986 created the MACRS depreciation method, which required that real property must be depreciated on a straight-line basis.

3) Since 1986, businesses are required to calculate depreciation using the straight-line method for real estate. Due to this change, additional depreciation recapture rules are no longer applicable.
4) However, if a depreciable business asset is held for one year or less, then all the depreciation taken is considered additional depreciation and is subject to recapture.
5) Since there is no longer any additional depreciation, tax law now addresses the unrecaptured Section 1250 gain. Basically, gain upon the sale of real property will be split into two pieces. The gain in excess of depreciation taken will be taxed at capital gain rates. The gain equal to the depreciation taken will be taxed at 25%. If the gain does not exceed the depreciation taken, then the entire gain is taxed at 25%. If there is a loss on the sale, the entire loss will be treated as an ordinary loss.

i. Section 1250 recapture
IRC Section 1250 recapture applies to all real property. If Section 1250 property was **held 12 months or less**, any gain on the disposition of the asset is recaptured as ordinary income, to the extent of all the depreciation taken. The depreciation taken includes the depreciation using the straight-line method.

If Section 1250 property was **held for more than 12 months**, the gain is recaptured as ordinary income, to the extent of the post-1969 additional depreciation. Additional depreciation is defined as accelerated depreciation, in excess of straight-line. After 1969, until January 2, 1987, the IRC allowed accelerated depreciation on real estate. Therefore, the taxpayer could take accelerated depreciation in excess of straight-line, which would cause a recapture of the gain, upon the sale of the real estate for post-1969 real property.

However, if a depreciable business asset is held for one year or less, then all the depreciation taken is still considered additional depreciation and still subject to recapture as ordinary income.

Since there is no longer any additional depreciation, tax law now addresses the unrecaptured Section 1250 gain which is all of the depreciation taken in the past. Gain upon the sale of an IRC Section 1250 asset will be split into two pieces. The gain in excess of depreciation taken will be taxed at capital gain rates under IRC Section 1231. The gain equal to the depreciation taken over the asset's life will be taxed at 25%. If the gain does not exceed the depreciation taken, then the entire gain is taxed at 25%.

For example, consider a sole proprietor who has sold real estate that was acquired after 12/31/1986, and was in service for more the one year.

Asset Information
Cost	$100,000
Depreciation taken	$ 55,000
Adjusted basis at sale date	$ 45,000
Sales price	$ 95,000
Adjusted basis at sale date	$ 45,000
Realized gain upon sale	$ 50,000

j. IRC Section 291

IRC Section 291 requires corporations that sell real estate used in a trade or business held in service for more than one year to take 20% of the depreciation taken, and recapture it as ordinary income (Section 291 recapture), not to the exceed the gain calculated. If any gain remains, treat it as Section 1231, long-term capital gain.

Using the information in the previous example directly above, assume that a corporation sold real estate used in a trade or business, with a holding period of more than one year, will treat the gain allocation changes under IRC Section 291 are as follows:

Gain Allocation

Gain taxed as ordinary income under IRC Section 291 (20% of $55,000)	$11,000
Section 1231 gain is taxed as long term capital gain	$39,000
Total gain	$50,000

4. Installment sales

Analyze an agreement of sale of an asset to determine whether it qualifies for installment sale treatment for federal income tax purposes.

An installment sale is a sale of property that results in a gain (not a loss) where a taxpayer receives at least one payment after the tax year of the sale. The character of the original gain (e.g., capital, ordinary, etc.) remains unchanged by this treatment. Installment sales rules apply automatically unless the taxpayer elects out of the installment sale treatment. Once made, the election can only be revoked with the IRS approval.

a. Transactions not covered:
1) Sale resulting in a loss.
2) Property held for sale in ordinary course of business.
   However, separate rules apply to the sales of time-share units, residential lots, property used or produced for farming.
3) Sale of stock or securities traded on an established securities market.

Calculate the amount of gain on an installment sale for federal income tax purposes.

Gains and losses are generally recognized in the year of the exchange, under the accrual basis. For tax purposes, installment sales are an exception for gain reporting only. Losses are always recognized in the exchange year. If the proceeds received are over more than one tax year, then the gain is recognized proportionately based upon the gross profit, divided by the total contract price (which is the gross profit %), and multiplied by the principal payment received in the tax year. If the installment sale has interest income to the seller, the interest income is recognized as income in full during the year and not multiplied by the gross profit percentage. The installment sales method cannot be used for the sale of inventory or the sale of stock or securities traded on a national stock exchange.

For each year of installment sales, the annual gain is:

$$\text{Annual gain recognized} = \frac{\text{Gross profit}}{\text{Total contract price}} \times \text{Amount received for the year}$$

If property is sold on an installment basis and there is income to be recaptured, the taxpayer must first recapture the ordinary income in the year of the sale, and the balance of the gain is shown as Section 1231 gain. The recaptured gain is the lesser of the depreciation taken or the gain.

Installment sale terms used in calculations for tax purposes:
- Contract price = Selling price – seller's liabilities assumed by the buyer, not in excess in the seller's basis in the property
- Gross profit on installment sales = Installment sales – Cost of installment sales
- Adjusted basis of property sold = Cost – Accumulated depreciation
- Realized gain = Selling price – Selling expenses – Adjusted basis
- Installment sale basis = Adjusted basis + Selling expenses + Depreciation recapture
- Gross profit percentage (GP%) = Gross profit / contract price
- Annual taxable profit = Annual payment x Gross profit percentage
- Selling expenses include legal fees and commissions

Calculation of gross profit:

Selling price for the property		$XX
Adjusted basis for the property	$XX	
Selling expenses	XX	
Adjusted basis for installment sales		(XX)
Gross profit		$XX

When there is no recapture on the asset sold, the recognized gain is the cash collections times the GP%. If the payment contains interest, all interest is recognized in full. Do not apply GP% to interest received.

What happens if the asset sold has recapture under Section 1245, or Section 291? Determine the gross profit from the sale, and treat the gross profit as ordinary income (for the recaptured amount) recognized in full in the first year, not to exceed the gross profit. Now, calculate a new gross profit percentage by taking the old basis and adding the amount recaptured to equal your new basis. Subtract the new basis from the selling price to arrive at a new gross profit percentage and multiply it by the cash collected in the first year. This will give the taxpayer the total amount of the recognized gain from the cash received. The total gain that is recognized in the first year is the recaptured amount (ordinary income) plus the recognized gain from the cash received (which would be a Section 1231 gain), if the asset sold is a Section 1231 asset.

Example: Assume that a corporation sells an apartment building placed in service in 1999 for $100,000 in cash and a $150,000 note, due in two years. The corporation's cost of the property was $180,000, and it had deducted depreciation of $130,000. Based on the numbers given, the basis in the property was $50,000 ($180,000 - $130,000), and the taxpayer recaptured $26,000 (20% of $130,000) as ordinary income, under Section 291. The taxpayer's recognized gain over the 2-year period is $200,000 ($250,000 - $50,000), and the $26,000 recapture must be recaptured in the year of sale. Of the $174,000 remaining under Section 1231, an additional $69,600 must be recognized in the year of sale. This is based on the cash received in the first year of $100,000 times the gross profit percentage of 69.6% which calculated below.

The original profit percentage would have been based on the following:

Selling price	$250,000
Less: Old basis	(50,000)
Gross profit	$200,000

The first step is to calculate a new gross profit percentage. Take the old basis of $50,000 and add the amount of ordinary income recaptured of $26,000, to arrive at the new basis of $76,000. Now, calculate new gross profit percentage:

Selling Price	$250,000
Less: New basis	(76,000)
Gross Profit	$174,000

New gross profit percentage = gross profit / selling price = $174,000 / $250,000 = 69.6%

The second step is to calculate the recognized gain from cash collected:
Cash collected × New gross profit % = Recognized gross profit from cash collected
$100,000 × 69.6% = $69,600

Gain recognized in the first year is:

Section 291 recapture	$26,000
Plus: Realized gain	$69,600
Total gain for the first year	$95,600

Cash collected in two years	$150,000
Gross profit %	x .696
Recognized gross profit in year 2	$104,400

Reconciliation of total profit from installment sale:

Selling price	$250,000
Less: Old basis	(50,000)
Gross profit from installment sale	$200,000

Total gain recognized in first year	$95,600
Recognized gross profit in second year	104,400
Gross profit from installment sale	$200,000

Multiple Choice

REG 3-Q24 through REG 3-Q35

5. Related party transactions (including imputed interest)

Recall related parties for federal income tax purposes.

Related party transactions are defined in IRC Section 267. If deemed to be related, then certain deductions or losses are denied currently.

If there is a sale between related parties and a loss results, then the loss is disallowed. If the purchaser sells the property later at a gain, then the disallowed loss can reduce the gain at that time.

For example, mom sells land to her son and generates a $10,000 loss. Years later the son sells the land and generates a $60,000 gain. The $60,000 gain will be reduced by the earlier $10,000 loss denied.

Related parties, if on different accounting methods (cash and accrual), will be forced to both be on the cash basis method for related party payments that straddle a year end. The idea is to match both sides of the transaction, which is the income and expense in the same tax year.

As an example, consider that dad hires his daughter to design a new website for his business. Dad is on the accrual basis, and the daughter is on the cash basis. Daughter performs the work in December 20X1 and dad pays her in January of 20X2. Dad cannot accrue the deduction in December. He must take the deduction in January when he makes the payment to the daughter. He gets the deduction at the same time she records the income.

a. Related Taxpayers

> Recall the impact of related party ownership percentages on acquisition and disposition transactions of property for federal income tax purposes.

Related taxpayers are defined as:
1) Members of a family including brothers and sisters, spouse, ancestors, and lineal descendants
2) A transaction between a corporation and an individual that owns more than 50 percent of the stock of the corporation, either directly or indirectly.
3) Two corporations, which are members of the same controlled group
4) A grantor, fiduciary or a beneficiary of any trust, if related
5) An individual and a charitable organization, which is controlled by the individual or by members of the individual's family
6) A corporation and a partnership if the same person owns more than 50 percent of the corporation and the partnership
7) **Two** S corporations, if owned by the same individual controlling more than 50 percent of each corporation
8) An S corporation and a C corporation, if the same person owns more than 50 percent of each corporation
9) An executor and a beneficiary of an estate.
10) A transaction between a partnership and a partner who owns directly or indirectly more than a 50% interest in the partnership.

b. Constructive Ownership of Stock

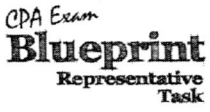

> Calculate the direct and indirect ownership percentages of corporation stock to determine whether there are related parties for federal income tax purposes.

IRC Section 267 also contains rules for determining if there are related taxpayers through various entities defined as:
1) Stock owned, directly or indirectly, by or for a corporation, partnership, estate, or trust, shall be considered as being owned proportionately by its owners
2) An individual shall be considered as owning the stock owned, directly or indirectly, by or for his family
3) An individual owning any stock in a corporation shall be considered as owning the stock owned, directly or indirectly, by or for his partner

Multiple Choice

REG 3-Q36 through REG 3-Q37

Calculate a taxpayer's basis in an asset that was disposed of at a loss to the taxpayer by a related party.

Example: Betty sells to Sean, her brother, a machine for $16,000 that has a basis to Betty of $22,000. Sean sold the machine to a non-related party for $19,000. The loss allowed to Betty and the gain allowed to Sean, are calculated as follows:

	Betty	Sean
Selling price	$16,000	$19,000
Basis	(22,000)	(16,000)
Loss	($6,000)	
Gain		$3,000
Disallowed loss	6,000	(3,000)
Gain or loss	$0	$0

Since Betty and Sean are brother and sister, the sale from Betty to Sean, results in a loss of $6,000, which is disallowed. Sean then sold the machine to a non-related party, resulting in a gain of $3,000. Sean can now use $3,000 of the $6,000 disallowed loss to bring Sean's gain to $0. The remaining $3,000 loss that was disallowed to Betty will be lost forever.

Calculate a taxpayer's gain or loss on a subsequent disposition of an asset to an unrelated third party that was previously disposed of at a loss to the taxpayer by a related party.

Example: Betty sells to Sean, her brother, a machine for $16,000 that has a basis to Betty of $22,000. Sean sold the machine to a non-related party for $14,000. The loss allowed to Betty and the loss allowed to Sean, are calculated as follows:

	Betty	Sean
Selling price	$16,000	$14,000
Basis	(22,000)	(16,000)
Loss	($6,000)	($2,000)
Loss allowed	$0	($2,000)

Since Betty and Sean are brother and sister, the sale from Betty to Sean, results in a loss of $6,000, which is disallowed. Sean then sold the machine to a non-related party, resulting in a loss of $2,000. Sean cannot use Betty's disallowed loss of $6,000 to increase Sean's loss from $2,000 to $8,000. Disallowed losses can only reduce gains, but never increase losses, to non-related parties.

Multiple Choice

REG 3-Q38

Calculate the impact of imputed interest on related party transactions for federal tax purposes.

In related party transactions involving a loan, the IRS requires a minimum amount of interest to be charged, because, without interest, the borrower has a benefit provided by the lender in the form of an interest-free loan. The applicable federal rate (AFR) is the minimum amount of interest that must be charged. The AFR is published each month by the IRS and represents the rate of interest that the Federal government pays on new borrowings. An interest rate for a loan to a related party that is less than the AFR must be treated as if the loan was set-up using the AFR. This is done to show the loan as an arms-length transaction. Because of the arms-length nature of the loan, using the AFR, the lender may have a bad debt deduction if the borrower defaults on the loan and the borrower may have discharge of indebtedness income.

The difference between the original interest stated in the loan and the AFR is called imputed interest. Imputed interest is considered a gift from the lender to the borrower and may be subject to gift tax. Examples of loans where imputed interest would apply include:
- Loans between family and friends, other than a spouse (gift loans).
- Loans from a corporation to one or more of its shareholders.
- Loans from an employer to an employee or independent contractor.

The interest payments made by the borrower to the lender is included in the lender's taxable interest income. Depending on what the loan will be used for, the interest paid by the borrower may or may not be deductible.
- A loan used for business purposes: The interest paid by the borrower is deductible as a business expense by the borrower.
- A loan used for investment purposes: The interest paid by the borrower is treated as investment interest expense, which is deductible up to the amount of investment income by the borrower.
- A loan used for personal reasons: The interest paid by the borrower is not deductible by the borrower.

> **Example**: Sarah is a recent college graduate and receives a $50,000, interest-free loan from Dan, her father, to start a business. The tax code requires interest to be charged on this loan. The AFR is 4%. Based on the AFR, the interest for the year is $2,000 ($50,000 x 4%). As a result:
> 1) Sarah has been gifted $2,000 by Dan. Assuming that this is Dan's only gift during the year to Sarah and it is less than the $14,000 annual gift tax exclusion, Dan does not have to file a gift tax return because it is not considered a taxable gift.
> 2) Sarah is considered to have paid $2,000 back to Dan as interest so; Dan will include the $2,000 as interest income.
> 3) Sarah will deduct the $2,000 interest payment because the loan was used to start a business.

Imputed interest rule exceptions:
- Imputed interest does not apply to loans of $10,000 or less, between individuals.
- A special rule applies for loans between individuals that do not exceed $100,000. Under this rule, the imputed interest on the loan will not exceed the borrower's net investment income during the year. Where the borrower's net investment income is less than $1,000, the borrower is treated as having no net investment income and will, therefore, have no imputed interest.

> **Example**: Sarah is a recent college graduate and receives a $5,000, interest-free loan from Dan, her father. The AFR is 4%. Since the loan is less than $10,000, it is not subject to the imputed interest rules
>
> **Example**: Sarah is a recent college graduate and receives a $50,000, interest-free loan from Dan, her father. The AFR is 4%. The imputed interest would be $2,000 for the year. Sarah has investment income of $1,500 for the year. The imputed interest is limited to Sarah's net investment income of $1,500 because the loan was less than $100,000.
>
> **Example**: Sarah is a recent college graduate and receives a $50,000, interest-free loan from Dan, her father. The AFR is 4%. The imputed interest would be $2,000 for the year. Sarah has investment income of $750 for the year. Imputed interest would not apply because the net investment income is less than $1,000 and the loan was less than $100,000.

> **Hint**:
> - Net investment income = Gross investment income – Investment Expenses.
> - If Net Investment Income < or = $1,000, then Imputed Interest = $0.
> - If Net Investment Income > $1,000, then Net Investment Income = (Lesser of the Imputed Interest or Actual Gross Investment Income) - Investment Expenses.

Sale of property in a deferred sales contract:
For the sale of property in a deferred sales contract that has a selling price of more than $3,000, imputed interest must be included if the contract does not contain a reasonable interest rate. If imputed interest is required, the result will be a restated selling price containing the discounted present value of the future payments. Interest income is then calculated as the difference between the present value of the future payments and the face amount of the payment.

> **Example**: A cash basis taxpayer sold 3 acres of land on 1/1/Year 1 for $100,000 in cash and a $7,000,000 note, due on 12/31/Year 2, with 3% interest payable on 12/31/Year 1 and 12/31/Year 2. The Federal rate at the time of sale was 6%.
>
> | Date | Interest Payment | PV Factor of $1 at 6% | Present Value | Imputed Interest |
> |---|---|---|---|---|
> | 12/31/Year 1 | $ 210,000 | 0.9434 | $ 198,114 | $ 11,886 |
> | 12/31/Year 2 | 7,210,000 | 0.8900 | 6,416,900 | 793,100 |
> | | $7,420,000 | | $6,615,014 | $804,986 |
>
> The restated selling price is $6,715,014 ($6,615,014 + $100,000), instead of the original selling price, prior to taking imputed interest into consideration of $7,100,000 ($7,000,000 + $100,000). Interest income for the seller (and interest expense for the buyer) is determined from the following amortization schedule as follows:
>
> | Year | Beginning Balance | 6 % Interest | Interest Received | Ending Balance |
> |---|---|---|---|---|
> | Year 1 | $6,615,014 | $396,901 | $ 210,000 | $6,801,915 |
> | Year 2 | 6,801,915 | 408,085 | 7,210,000 | 0 |

> **Hint**: The calculation of imputed interest is determined the same way for related parties and non-related parties.

Multiple Choice
REG 3-Q39 through REG 3-Q40

B. Cost Recovery including Depreciation, Depletion, and Amortization

Cost recovery is the simple act of allocating an asset's basis over the period of time benefited. Tax law has very specific rules regarding cost recovery. Depreciation applies to all tangible property, real or personal. Note that some tangible assets are not considered to be "used up" such as land. Therefore land is never depreciated. Depletion will apply to land that is being mined or harvested and has a natural resource such as gold, oil, gas, timber, etc. Amortization applies to intangible assets.

1. Depreciation

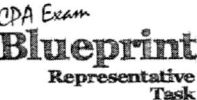

Calculate tax depreciation for tangible business property and tax amortization of intangible assets.

Reconcile the activity in the beginning and ending accumulated tax depreciation account.

For tangible property, real or personal, tax law requires the use of the Modified Accelerated Cost Recovery System (MACRS). MACRS is a simplified method of financial accounting depreciation and is an accelerated method compared to straight-line depreciation. Salvage value is ignored for all assets. The IRS has MACRS tables (see table A) for both personal and real property to facilitate all of the calculations. If the taxpayer prefers, a straight-line method can be elected for all assets.

   a. Personal Property Asset Guidelines
   The IRS has recovery life guidelines for all assets. Personal property assets can be 3, 5, 7, 10, 15, or 20 years. Most business assets will be either a 5 or 7-year life. Examples of 5-year assets are office machines, computers, and cars. An example of a 7-year asset would be office furniture and fixtures.

   A half-year convention is applied in the year placed into service. A half-year convention allows one-half year depreciation the year placed into service no matter when actually placed into service.

   An exception to the half-year convention applies if more than 40% of the business's asset acquisition occurs in the last three months of a tax year. If this happens, then the mid-quarter convention will apply. The mid-quarter convention will require the grouping of assets by the quarter placed in service, and the mid-point of that quarter will be used for the starting point of tax depreciation.

   For example, if the appropriate quarter was determined to be the first quarter, then there would be 10 ½ months of depreciation in the first year. If determined to be the second quarter, then 7 ½ months, the third quarter would be 4 ½ months and the last quarter would be 1 ½ months of depreciation.

   b. Real Property Asset Guidelines
   Real property is either classified as residential or non-residential real property. If determined to be residential, the recovery period is 27.5 years. If determined to be non-residential, the recovery period is 39 years. All real property is depreciated using a straight-line method.

   A mid-month convention is used for the date placed in service. As an example, if placed in service on May 30, the appropriate date for MACRS would be May 15.

   c. Dispositions and MACRS
   All MACRS property disposed of before being fully depreciated will record depreciation in the year of disposal using the same convention as when first placed into service. If the half-year convention was initially used, then no matter what month the asset is disposed of, the half-year convention will apply in the disposal year. The same applies to the mid-quarter and the mid-month convention.

d. IRC Section 179

> **Compare the tax benefits of the Section 179 expense deduction vs. the regular tax depreciation deduction.**

IRC Section 179 allows a taxpayer to directly expense in addition to depreciating under MACRS tangible personal property used in business. Section 179 requires that the property is purchased for use in a trade or business and is purchased from an unrelated party. There are limitations to this provision and can vary by the year. For 2017, the maximum limit that the taxpayer can take for Section 179 is $500,000. The limit is also reduced dollar for dollar for business assets purchased in excess of $2,010,000 for 2017. This means, if a taxpayer purchases total personal property assets in 2017 for $2,500,000, there is no available expensing option under Section 179.

Under Section 179, for tax years beginning in 2017, a taxpayer may expense the cost of new or used tangible personal property used in a trade or business subject to these limitations.

- The property must be purchased for use in the taxpayer's active trade or business.
- The property must be purchased from an unrelated party.
- There is a dollar limitation. The maximum deduction a taxpayer may elect to take for Section 179 is the lesser of $500,000, minus the amount that the total purchases exceed $2,010,000, or taxable income before Section 179.
- If more than $2,010,000 worth of Section 179 property is placed into service during a single taxable year, the deduction ($500,000) is reduced, dollar for dollar, by the amount exceeding the $2,010,000 threshold.

e. Bonus Depreciation (additional first-year depreciation)
Bonus depreciation is for property acquired and placed in service during 2015 through 2019. The bonus depreciation percentage is 50% for property placed in service during 2015, 2016 and 2017 and phases down, with 40% in 2018, and 30% in 2019. Bonus depreciation is calculated after the IRC Section 179 deduction and before the regular MACRS depreciation and is only available in the asset's first year of service.

f. Items to be used in the calculation of the first year's depreciation for tangible personal property, used in a trade or business.
   i. Cost of tangible personal property.
   ii. Apply Section 179 and deduct it from the cost.
   iii. Subtotal is the basis after Section 179.
   iv. Take bonus depreciation of 50% of "iii" and subtract it from "iii."
   v. This equals the remaining basis, which is used to calculate the averaging convention depreciation for the first year.

First year depreciation = "ii" + "iv" + "v"

g. Leasehold Improvements
A lessee's cost of leasehold improvements must be recovered over the recovery period of MACRS, apart from the lease term. Qualified leasehold improvement property, qualified restaurant property, and qualified retail improvement property, are recovered over 15 years under the straight-line method using the half-year convention, unless the mid-quarter convention applies to the assets placed in service during the year. Section 179 expense write-off is allowed for computer software and qualified real property (qualified leasehold improvement property, qualified restaurant property, and qualified retail improvement property).

CPA Exam Blueprint Representative Task

2. Depletion

   Calculate depletion for federal income tax purposes.

   Depletion is a cost recovery method applied to property with minerals or to standing timber. For mineral properties, the taxpayer can use either cost or percentage depletion. The decision as to which method can be made each year based on which will give the greater deduction. Standing timber is required to use the cost depletion method. Depletion will reduce a property's basis similar to depreciation.

   a. Percentage Depletion
      Percentage depletion is calculated by taking a predetermined percentage times the gross income from the producing property. The depletion deduction cannot exceed 50% of the taxable income from the property as calculated before the depletion deduction.

      Since the calculation is not based upon the original cost investment, it is possible for the amounts calculated under percentage depletion to exceed the original basis in the property. But the property's basis is never reduced below zero.

   b. Cost Depletion
      Cost depletion is calculated similarly to the units of production depreciation method. There are three numbers necessary to calculate the cost depletion deduction. These are property basis, estimated total quantity of mineral or timber, and the quantity sold during the tax year.

      Once determined, take the property's basis and divide it by the estimated total quantity, to determine a rate per unit number. Apply the rate per unit times the quantity sold during the year to arrive at the cost depletion deduction for the year.

      Unlike percentage depletion, the cost depletion calculated can never exceed the property's original basis.

3. Amortization
   Amortization is used to calculate the cost recovery deduction for intangible assets. The calculation only uses a straight-line rate, there is no salvage value, and it begins in the month acquired. Tax law specifies a 15-year life, beginning with the month in which the intangible is acquired. The intangibles are commonly referred to as Section 197 intangibles. Section 197 intangibles must be acquired by the taxpayer, and are held in connection with the taxpayer's trade or business. Intangibles specified in IRC Section 197 include:
   a. goodwill
   b. going concern value
   c. workforce in place
   d. business books and records, operating systems, or any other information base
   e. patent, copyright, formula, process, design, pattern, know-how, format, or other similar item
   f. any license, permit, or other right granted by a governmental unit or an agency or instrumentality thereof
   g. any covenant not to compete entered into in connection with an acquisition of an interest in a trade or business
   h. any franchise, trademark, or trade name

Multiple Choice

REG 3-Q41 through REG 3-Q50

C. Estate and Gift Taxation

Estate and gift taxation are part of a unified tax system. While gifts occur as the taxpayer is alive and estate transfers occur upon the death of the taxpayer, both involve the transfer of property and tax will be assessed. The government unified the system to provide cohesion between the two types of property transfers. But a higher tax base was also created by combining the two systems, which increases the possibility that the government will be able to assess more taxes. Generation-skipping tax was also added in to be part of the same unified system.

1. Transfers subject to the gift tax

> Recall transfers of property subject to federal gift tax.

    a. Gifts include all property transfers made for less than full and adequate consideration. Gifts can be to any individual or any entity. Taxable gifts are determined by calculating the gross amount of gifts made during the taxable year minus the deductions allowed. Certain gifts are exempt from the gift tax system as follow:
        1) Tuition or medical expenses paid on behalf of another individual *if* made directly to the receiving institution.
        2) Spousal gifts
        3) Political gifts
        4) Charitable gifts – completely non-taxable
        5) Gifts, less than the annual exclusion as defined in the tax code (annual exclusion for 2017 is $14,000) The exclusion is only for gifts of a present interest.

> Recall whether federal Form 709 — *United States Gift (and Generation-Skipping Transfer) Tax Return* is required to be filed.

    b. A gift tax return is required to be filed for each taxable year that total taxable gifts exceed the annual exclusion. The return, Form 709, is due on April 15 of the year following the calendar year of the gifts.

Gifts of a present interest are fully transferred gifts, without any restrictions. Gifts of future interests are gifts that have some kind of restriction attached to the gift that limits the full enjoyment of the gift, such as a remainder interest. Future interest gifts are still taxable in the year gifted but are not eligible for the annual exclusion. The gross taxable gifts, (gifts of present and futures interests), are calculated by taking the present value of the gifts. They are still taxed in the year gifted.

    c. Gift tax formula

> Calculate the amount and classification of a gift for federal gift tax purposes.

> Calculate the amount of a gift subject to federal gift tax.

	Gross gifts (cash + Property FMV at date of gift)
Plus:	One-half of spouse's gifts to third parties if gift-splitting is elected
Less:	Deductions allowed:
	One-half of gifts to third parties treated as given by spouse if gift-splitting is elected.
	Annual exclusion (up to $14,000 per donee for gifts of a present interest).
	Unlimited exclusion for tuition or medical expenses paid on behalf of the donee and the amounts are paid directly to the provider.
	Unlimited exclusion for gifts paid to political organizations.
	Unlimited exclusion for gifts for amounts paid to charitable organizations.
	<u>Unlimited exclusion for gifts to your spouse.</u>
Equals:	Taxable gifts for the current year

	Taxable gifts for the current year (continued from previous page)
Plus:	Taxable gifts from prior years
Equals:	Total taxable gifts
Calculate:	Transfer tax on total taxable gifts
Less:	Gift tax on taxable gifts from prior years
Equals:	Current year transfer tax
Less:	Applicable unified credit
Equals:	Net gift tax liability

2. Gift tax annual exclusion and gift tax deductions

Recall allowable gift tax deductions and exclusions for federal gift tax purposes.

Compute the amount of taxable gifts for federal gift tax purposes.

a. An annual exclusion is allowed to reduce what would normally be taxable gifts. If the gift is under the exclusion, no gift tax return is required. For 2017, the exclusion is $14,000.

b. Married couples are allowed to split gifts. If there is only one gift made, it is allowed to be considered to be made one-half by each spouse. This provision will maximize the annual exclusion for each spouse.

As an example, consider that a husband gives $5,000 to a niece. In the same tax year, the wife gives $20,000 to a nephew. The exclusion for this year is $14,000. If gift splitting were not allowed, then the husband would not have any taxable gifts and will not be required to file a gift tax return. The wife, though, would have a taxable gift of $6,000 and would file a gift tax return. Due to gift splitting, each spouse is considered to make one-half of the other spouse's gifts.

Recall situations involving the gift tax annual exclusion, gift-splitting and the impact on the use of the lifetime exclusion amount for federal gift tax purposes.

Under gift splitting, the husband would have total gifts of $12,500 ((1/2 x $5,000) + (1/2 x $20,000)). The wife would also have total gifts of $12,500 ((1/2 x $5,000) + (1/2 x $20,000)). Both spouses now fall under the annual exclusion and neither has a taxable gift, nor are they required to file a gift tax return.

c. Gift tax deductions include:
   1) Marital deduction
      An unlimited deduction is allowed for gifts to a spouse.

   2) Charitable deduction
      An unlimited deduction is allowed for gifts to charities where the gift is included in taxable gifts.

d. Applicable unified credit
   Under gift and estate transfer taxation, a credit is allowed to offset any tax liability calculated.

3. Determination of taxable estate

Recall assets includible in a decedent's estate for federal estate tax purposes.

The gross estate of an individual includes all property owned at the date of death located anywhere in the world. The property is valued at fair market value at the date of death unless the alternate valuation date is selected. The alternate date is six months after the date of death and may only be selected if the selection would lower the estate tax liability. If selected, the fair market value is determined at the alternate valuation date. Otherwise, date of death determines the fair market value for estate taxation.

The estate tax return, Form 706, is due within nine months after the date of death. The return only needs to be filed if the gross estate is greater than the applicable unified credit.

   a. Examples of properties included in the gross estate are:
      1) Concurrently held property:
         i. Tenants in common: If the decedent is the first one to die, put into the estate the FMV of the property at death, times the percentage owned by the decedent.
         ii. Joint tenants, not married: If the decedent is the first one to die, put into the estate the FMV of the property at death, times the percentage of the consideration paid by the decedent who died first.
         iii. Tenancy by the entirety: If property is held jointly by husband and wife, 50% of the FMV will go into the estate of the party who dies first.

      2) Property decedent had a general power of appointment.
      3) Value of life insurance proceeds, if payable to the estate or if decedent retained an incident of ownership.
      4) Income in respect of decedent or income earned by the decedent, but not paid by the date of death.
      5) Gifts of life insurance made within three years of decedent's death.
      6) Gift tax paid on all transfers made within three years of decedent's death.

Recall allowable estate tax deductions in a decedent's estate.

   b. Deductions allowed to reduce the gross estate are:
      1) Funeral and administrative expenses of the estate
      2) Debts of the decedent and mortgages on any estate property, which are unpaid
      3) Losses incurred during the administration of the estate, such as casualty or theft losses
      4) Unlimited marital deductions
      5) Unlimited charitable bequests specified by decedent
      6) State death taxes
      7) Medical expenses are allowed as a deduction if paid, however, if the executor makes an election, they can be deducted on Form 1040, schedule A, as long as they were paid within 12 months of death.
      8) Political contributions

   c. Applicable unified credit
     Under gift and estate transfer taxation, a credit is allowed to offset any tax liability calculated.

d. Estate tax formula

| Calculate the taxable estate for federal estate tax purposes. |

| Calculate the gross estate for federal estate tax purposes. |

| Calculate the allowable estate tax deductions for federal estate tax purposes. |

	Gross estate
Less:	Deductions
Equals:	Taxable estate
Plus:	Post 1976 taxable gifts
Equals:	Total taxable life and death transfers
Calculate	Unified transfer tax on total post 1976 transfers
Less:	Post 1976 gift taxes
Less:	Foreign death taxes
Less:	Applicable unified credit
Equals:	Net estate tax liability

1) Generation-skipping tax
Generation-skipping tax is an addition to the gift and estate taxation system. A tax planning technique used involves making gifts or bequests to a skipped generation. A skipped generation is defined as two or more generations younger than the transferor. By skipping a generation on property transfers, the transferor has omitted one level of property transfer taxation. To ensure that the property transfer tax is calculated and addressed for each generation, the generation-skipping tax was created.

The generation-skipping tax is reported on either the estate or the gift tax return, Form 706 or 709, whichever is appropriate. The tax is calculated at a flat 40% rate. There is a lifetime exemption available to each transferor to minimize the impact of this tax. This exemption is distinct from the exclusion amount or the applicable unified credit available for estate or gift taxes. Generation-skipping transfers are also eligible for gift splitting, thereby enabling a married couple to effectively double the exemption amount. The exemption will be $5,345,000 for 2017.

Hint: The exemption amount changes each year. It is unlikely to be tested unless the examiner provides the amount to use. Be sure to understand the concept rather than memorize the numbers.

2) Unified credit
The unified credit is an amount available to offset both gift and estate tax liability. As the gift and estate tax systems are unified, the credit is a lifetime amount utilized as needed to offset either of these liabilities.

Multiple Choice

REG 3-Q51 through REG 3-Q54

This page is intentionally left blank.

Glossary: Federal Taxation of Property Transactions

A

Adjusted basis – initial basis (i.e., purchase price plus costs to ready the asset) plus improvements, less depreciation or depletion

Amortization – cost recovery applicable to intangible assets

Applicable federal rate (AFR) – minimum amount of interest that must be charged to a related party transactions involving a loan for IRS purposes, published each month by the IRS

B

Basis – see initial basis or adjusted basis

Basket purchase – group of assets can be acquired in a single transaction

Boot – any property given up or received that is not alike in a like-kind exchange (e.g., cash)

C

Capital asset – asset not classified as inventory, personal property or real property used in a trade or business and held for greater than 12 months, copyright, business account receivable, or covenant not to compete

Carryover basis – the basis is determined by reference to a previous holder

Cost depletion – a method of calculating depletion calculated by applying a rate per unit (property's basis divided by the estimated total quantity) multiplied by the quantity sold during the year

Cost recovery – act of allocating an asset's basis over the period of time benefited

D

Depletion – cost recovery applicable to land that is being mined or harvested and has a natural resource such as gold, oil, gas, timber, etc.

Depreciation – cost recovery applicable to all tangible property, real or personal

E

F

Form 706 – estate tax return due nine months following a taxpayer's date of death

Form 709 – form required for annual gifts exceeding the yearly gift tax exclusion

G

Generation-skipping – a tax planning technique that involves making gifts or bequests to a younger taxpayer, skipping a generation (two or more generations younger than the transferor)

Gift – property transfers made for less than full and adequate consideration made prior to death of taxpayer

Gross estate – all property owned by an individual at the date of death

H

Half-year convention – practice of recognizing one-half year depreciation the year an asset is placed into service no matter when actually placed into service

Holding period – duration asset held from date of purchase or, if carryover is applicable, date the previous holder acquired the property

I

Imputed interest – difference between the original interest stated in a related-party loan and the applicable federal rate (AFR)

Inheritance basis – FMV at the date of the decedent's death or FMV on alternative valuation date elected by executor, which is usually six months after death

Initial basis – purchase price plus costs to ready the asset for its intended purpose

Installment sale – a sale of property that results in a gain (not a loss) where taxpayer receives at least one payment after the tax year of the sale

Involuntary conversions – proceeds, typically insurance proceeds, that are the result of theft, casualty, or condemnation of property

J

K

L

Like-kind exchange – an exchange transaction where business use or investment property is given up in exchange for similar type of property

Long-term capital assets – capital assets held longer than one year that have the potential to receive beneficial tax treatment

M

Modified Accelerated Cost Recovery System (MACRS) – a simplified method of financial accounting depreciation; accelerated depreciation method compared to straight-line depreciation

N

O

P

Percentage depletion – a method of calculating depletion using a predetermined percentage multiplied by the gross income from the producing property

Personal property – moveable property; opposite of real property (e.g., cars, jewelry, furniture, and stocks)

Principal residence – home owned *and* occupied as the primary residence for an aggregate of two of the prior five years

Q

Qualified small business stock – stock that meets the requirements for classification including being held for more than five years, acquired directly from the issuing corporation, non-corporate shareholder, issuing company must be a C Corp with less than $50 million in gross assets, and an active trade or business

R

Real property – land and anything attached to the land that is immovable in nature (e.g., buildings, crops, and integrated equipment)

Related party transactions – transactions between parties defined in IRC Section 267 (includes transactions between members of a family and transactions between a corporation and an individual that owns more than 50 percent of the stock of the corporation, either directly or indirectly)

S

Section 1231 assets – assets that include depreciable personal or real property that is used in a trade or business and held for more than one year

Section 1244 stock – loss upon the sale of qualified small business stock that is treated as ordinary loss versus as capital loss up to $50,000 for an individual return ($100,000 for married filing jointly)

Section 1245 capital asset – depreciable personal property, used in a trade or business or, held for the production of income (e.g., machinery equipment, trucks, and automobiles)

Section 1245 recapture – the gain from the sale or exchange of Section 1245 property that is recaptured as ordinary income to the extent of the lesser of all depreciation taken or the recognized gain

Section 1250 assets – real property subject to depreciation and used in a trade or business

Section 1250 recapture – for real property held for more than 12 months, any gain on disposition of the asset is recaptured as ordinary income, to the extent of all depreciation

Section 179 – for tangible personal property used in a trade or business, subject to limitations, a taxpayer is permitted to directly expense the asset rather than depreciating under MACRS

Short-term capital assets – capital assets held less than one year

T

U

Unified credit – an amount available to offset both gift and estate tax liability

V

W

Wash sale – transaction where stocks or securities sold at a loss and substantially identical stocks or securities are acquired within 30 days either before or after the sale date

X

Y

Z

Multiple Choice – Questions

REG 3-Q1 R47. For an individual business owner, which of the following would typically be classified as a capital asset for federal income tax purposes?

A. Accounts receivable.
B. Marketable securities.
C. Machinery and equipment used in a business.
D. Inventory.

REG 3-Q2 R183. Which of the following is a capital asset?

A. Inventory held primarily for sale to customers.
B. Accounts receivable.
C. A computer system used by the taxpayer in a personal accounting business.
D. Land held as an investment.

REG 3-Q3 R203. Which of the following items is a capital asset?

A. An automobile for personal use.
B. Depreciable business property.
C. Accounts receivable for inventory sold.
D. Real property used in a trade or business.

REG 3-Q4 R278. Which of the following sales should be reported as a capital gain?

A. Sale of equipment.
B. Real property subdivided and sold by a dealer.
C. Sale of inventory.
D. Government bonds sold by an individual investor.

REG 3-Q5 R295. Which of the following statements is the best definition of real property?

A. Real property is only land.
B. Real property is all tangible property including land.
C. Real property is land and intangible property in realized form.
D. Real property is land and everything permanently attached to it.

REG 3-Q6 R331. Trees were cut down and made into lumber. The lumber was used to build a house. Which of the following statements best describes the property aspect of these events?

A. The trees were and remained tangible personal property.
B. The trees were and remained real property.
C. The trees were real property, then became and remained personal property.
D. The trees were real property, became personal property, then reverted to being real property.

REG 3-Q7 R197. Dunn received 100 shares of stock as a gift from Dunn's grandparent. The stock cost Dunn's grandparent $32,000 and it was worth $27,000 at the time of the transfer to Dunn. Dunn sold the stock for $29,000. What amount of gain or loss should Dunn report from the sale of the stock?

A. $0
B. $2,000 gain.
C. $3,000 gain.
D. $3,000 loss.

REG 3-Q8 R234. Taylor owns 1,000 shares of Media Corporation common stock with a basis of $22,000 and a fair market value of $33,000. Media paid a nontaxable 10% common stock dividend. What is the basis for each share of Media common stock owned by Taylor after receipt of the dividend?

A. $20
B. $22
C. $30
D. $33

REG 3-Q9 R293. Starr, a self-employed individual, purchased a piece of equipment for use in Starr's business. The costs associated with the acquisition of the equipment were:

Purchase price	$55,000
Delivery charges	725
Installation fees	300
Sales tax	3,400

What is the depreciable basis of the equipment?
A. $55,000
B. $58,400
C. $59,125
D. $59,425

REG 3-Q10 R321. Greller owns 100 shares of Arden Corp., a publicly-traded company, which Greller purchased on January 1, 2001, for $10,000. On January 1, 2003, Arden declared a 2-for-1 stock split when the fair market value (FMV) of the stock was $120 per share. Immediately following the split, the FMV of Arden stock was $62 per share. On February 1, 2003, Greller had his broker specifically sell the 100 shares of Arden stock received in the split when the FMV of the stock was $65 per share. What is the basis of the 100 shares of Arden sold?

A. $5,000
B. $6,000
C. $6,200
D. $6,500

REG 3-Q11 R337. Allen owns 100 shares of Prime Corp., a publicly-traded company, which Allen purchased on January 1, 2008, for $10,000. On January 1, 2010, Prime declared a 2-for-1 stock split when the fair market value (FMV) of the stock was $120 per share. Immediately following the split, the FMV of Prime stock was $62 per share. On February 1, 2013, Allen had his broker specifically sell the 100 shares of Prime stock received in the split when the FMV of the stock was $65 per share. What amount should Allen recognize as long-term capital gain income on his Form 1040, *U.S. Individual Income Tax Return*, for 2013?

A. $300
B. $750
C. $1,500
D. $2,000

REG 3-Q12 R391. Smith made a gift of property to Thompson. Smith's basis in the property was $1,200. The fair market value at the time of the gift was $1,400. Thompson sold the property for $2,500. What was the amount of Thompson's gain on the disposition?

A. $0
B. $1,100
C. $1,300
D. $2,500

REG 3-Q13 R774. Robert Efron owned an apartment house that he bought in 2002. Depreciation was taken on a straight-line basis. In 2014, when Efron's adjusted basis for this property was $100,000, he traded it for an office building having a fair market value of $300,000. The apartment house has 100 dwelling units, while the office building has 50 units rented to business enterprises. The properties are not located in the same city. What is Efron's reportable gain on this exchange in 2014?

A. $0
B. $200,000 long-term capital gain.
C. $200,000 Section 1231 gain.
D. $200,000 Section 1250 gain.

REG 3-Q14 R23. In the current year, Fitz, a single taxpayer, sustained a $48,000 loss on Code Sec. 1244 stock in JJJ Corp., a qualifying small business corporation, and a $20,000 loss on Code Sec. 1244 stock in MMM Corp., another qualifying small business corporation. What is the maximum amount of loss that Fitz can deduct for the current year?

A. $50,000 capital loss.
B. $68,000 capital loss.
C. $18,000 ordinary loss and $50,000 capital loss.
D. $50,000 ordinary loss and $18,000 capital loss.

REG 3-Q15 R56. An individual entered into several exchanges during the current tax year. Which of the following exchanges is classified as like-kind?

A. Partnership interest for partnership interest.
B. Common stock for common stock.
C. Apartment building for unimproved land.
D. Manufacturing equipment for factory building.

REG 3-Q16 R58. Summer, a single individual, had a net operating loss of $20,000 three years ago. A Code Sec. 1244 stock loss made up three-fourths of that loss. Summer had no taxable income from that year until the current year. In the current year, Summer has gross income of $80,000 and sustains another loss of $50,000 on Code Sec. 1244 stock. Assuming that Summer can carry the entire $20,000 net operating loss to the current year, what is the amount and character of the Code Sec. 1244 loss that Summer can deduct for the current year?

A. $35,000 ordinary loss.
B. $35,000 capital loss.
C. $50,000 ordinary loss.
D. $50,000 capital loss.

REG 3-Q17 R84. Hogan exchanged a business-use machine having an original cost of $100,000 and accumulated depreciation of $30,000 for business-use equipment owned by Baker having a fair market value of $80,000 plus $1,000 cash. Baker assumed a $2,000 outstanding debt on the machine. What taxable gain should Hogan recognize?

A. $0
B. $3,000
C. $10,000
D. $11,000

REG 3-Q18 R85. A married couple purchased their principal residence for $300,000. They spent $40,000 on improvements. After living in it for 10 years, the couple sold the home for $650,000 and paid $36,000 in real estate commissions. What gain should the couple recognize on their joint return?

A. $0
B. $60,000
C. $274,000
D. $310,000

REG 3-Q19 R141. In the current year Tatum exchanged farmland for an office building. The farmland had a basis of $250,000, a fair market value (FMV) of $400,000, and was encumbered by a $120,000 mortgage. The office building had an FMV of $350,000 and was encumbered by a $70,000 mortgage. Each party assumed the other's mortgage. What is the amount of Tatum's recognized gain?

A. $0
B. $ 50,000
C. $100,000
D. $150,000

REG 3-Q20 R142. Danielson invested $2,000,000 in DEC, a qualified small business corporation on October 1, 1995. Six years later, Danielson sold all of the DEC stock for $16,000,000, and purchased an office building with the proceeds. Danielson had not previously excluded any gain on the sale of small business stock. What is Danielson's taxable gain after the exclusion?

A. $0
B. $6,000,000
C. $7,000,000
D. $9,000,000

REG 3-Q21 R155. Wynn, a single individual age 60, sold Wynn's personal residence for $450,000. Wynn had owned Wynn's residence, which had a basis of $250,000, for six years. Within eight months of the sale, Wynn purchased a new residence for $400,000. What is Wynn's recognized gain from the sale of Wynn's personal residence?

A. $0
B. $50,000
C. $75,000
D. $200,000

REG 3-Q22 R179. Sands purchased 100 shares of Eastern Corp. stock for $18,000 on April 1 of the prior year. On February 1 of the current year, Sands sold 50 shares of Eastern for $7,000. Fifteen days later, Sands purchased 25 shares of Eastern for $3,750. What is the amount of Sand's recognized gain or loss?

A. $0
B. $500
C. $1,000
D. $2,000

REG 3-Q23 R188. A heavy equipment dealer would like to trade some business assets in a nontaxable exchange. Which of the following exchanges would qualify as nontaxable?

A. The company jet for a large truck to be used in the corporation.
B. Investment securities for antiques to be held as investments.
C. A road grader held in inventory for another road grader.
D. A corporate office building for a vacant lot.

REG 3-Q24 R1125. Vivian sells property with a basis of $100,000 to her friend for $200,000, in the form of a note payable with equal payments over five years. In addition, the friend assumes an existing $50,000 mortgage on the property. How much gain on sale should Vivian recognize each year?

A. $10,000
B. $12,000
C. $18,000
D. $30,000

REG 3-Q25 R1126. Vivian sells property with a basis of $20,000 to her friend for $200,000. Her friend agrees to assume $50,000 mortgage and pay the remainder, together with the applicable interest, in five equal installments. How much gain on sale should Vivian recognize each year after the property is sold?

A. $20,100
B. $20,000
C. $30,000
D. $10,000

REG 3-Q26 R16. In year 1, a taxpayer sold real property for $200,000, receiving $100,000 at closing and $50,000 plus accrued interest at the prime rate in the next year. The buyer also assumed a $50,000 mortgage on the property. The taxpayer's adjusted basis was $75,000, and the taxpayer incurred $10,000 of selling expenses. If this transaction qualifies for installment sale treatment, what is the gross profit on the sale?

A. $115,000
B. $125,000
C. $165,000
D. $175,000

REG 3-Q27 R67. Individual Lark's year 2 brokerage account statement listed the following capital gains and losses from the sale of stock investments:

Short-term capital gain	$6,000
Long-term capital gain	14,000
Short-term capital loss	4,000
Long-term capital loss	8,000

In addition, two stock investments became worthless in year 2. Public Company X stock was purchased in December, year 1, for $5,000, and formal notification was received by Lark on July, year 2, that it was worthless. Private company Section 1244 stock was issued to Lark for $10,000 in January, year 1, and was determined to be worthless in December, year 2. What is Lark's year 2 net capital gain or loss before any capital loss limitation?

A. $2,000 net capital loss
B. $3,000 net capital gain
C. $7,000 net capital loss
D. $8,000 net capital gain

REG 3-Q28 R64. The sale of which of the following types of business property should be reported as Section 1231 (Property Used in the Trade or Business and Involuntary Conversions) property?

A. Inventory held for resale.
B. Machinery held for six months.
C. Cattle held for 6 months.
D. Land held for 18 months.

REG 3-Q29 R104. Decker sold equipment for $200,000. The equipment was purchased for $160,000 and had accumulated depreciation of $60,000. What amount is reported as ordinary income under Code Sec. 1245?

A. $0
B. $ 40,000
C. $ 60,000
D. $100,000

REG 3-Q30 R105. Lobster, Inc. incurs the following losses on disposition of business assets during the year:

Loss on the abandonment of office equipment	$ 25,000
Loss on the sale of a building (straight-line depreciation taken in prior years of $200,000)	250,000
Loss on the sale of delivery trucks	15,000

The assets were held in service more than one year. What is the amount and character of the losses to be reported on Lobster's tax return?

A. $40,000 Section 1231 loss only.
B. $40,000 Section 1231 loss, $50,000 long-term capital loss.
C. $40,000 Section 1231 loss, $250,000 long-term capital loss.
D. $290,000 Section 1231 loss.

REG 3-Q31 R101. In the current year, Essex sold land with a basis of $80,000 to Yarrow for $100,000. Yarrow paid $25,000 down and agreed to pay $15,000 per year, plus interest, for the next five years, beginning in the second year. Under the installment method, what gain should Essex include in gross income for the year of sale?

A. $25,000
B. $20,000
C. $15,000
D. $ 5,000

REG 3-Q32 R184. Aviary Corp. sold a building for $600,000. Aviary received a down payment of $120,000 as well as annual principal payments of $120,000 for each of the subsequent four years. Aviary purchased the building for $500,000 and claimed depreciation of $80,000. What amount of gain should Aviary report in the year of sale using the installment method?

A. $180,000
B. $120,000
C. $54,000
D. $36,000

REG 3-Q33 R225. A taxpayer sold for $200,000 equipment that had an adjusted basis of $180,000. Through the date of the sale, the taxpayer had deducted $30,000 of depreciation. Of this amount, $17,000 was in excess of straight-line depreciation. What amount of gain would be recaptured under Section 1245 (Gain from Dispositions of Certain Depreciable Property)?

A. $13,000
B. $17,000
C. $20,000
D. $30,000

REG 3-Q34 R226. Four years ago, a self-employed taxpayer purchased office furniture for $30,000. During the current tax year, the taxpayer sold the furniture for $37,000. At the time of the sale, the taxpayer's depreciation deductions totaled $20,700. What part of the gain is taxed as long-term capital gain?

A. $0
B. $7,000
C. $20,700
D. $27,700

REG 3-Q35 R347. In 2014, Bach sold a painting for $50,000 purchased for his personal use in 2011 at a cost of $20,000. In Bach's 2014 income tax return, the sale of the painting should be treated as a transaction resulting in

A. No taxable gain.
B. Section 1231 (capital gain–ordinary loss rule) gain.
C. Long-term capital gain.
D. Ordinary income.

REG 3-Q36 R123. Terry, a taxpayer, purchased stock for $12,000. Later, Terry sold the stock to a relative for $8,000. What amount is the relative's gain or loss?

A. $2,000 loss.
B. $0
C. $2,000 gain.
D. $4,000 gain.

REG 3-Q37 R236. Gibson purchased stock with a fair market value of $14,000 from Gibson's adult child for $12,000. The child's cost basis in the stock at the date of sale was $16,000. Gibson sold the same stock to an unrelated party for $18,000. What is Gibson's recognized gain from the sale?

A. $ 0
B. $ 2,000
C. $ 4,000
D. $ 6,000

REG 3-Q38 R1078. Aki Corp., which was organized on January 2, 2012, had a book income of $500,000 for the year ended December 31, 2015. The following information was recorded in Aki's books and records during 2015:

Sale of treasury stock to unrelated broker:
Proceeds received	$100,000
Cost	70,000
Par value	5,000

Dividends received from unaffiliated taxable domestic corporations — 3,000

Long-term capital gains on sale of stock of unrelated corporations — 12,000

Short-term capital losses on sale of stock of unrelated corporations — 30,000

Sale of land (used in business) to Max Carr, who owns 55% of Aki's outstanding stock, but is neither an officer nor a director of Aki:
Sales price to Carr	40,000
Adjusted basis to Aki	44,000

Insurance premiums paid on policy insuring the life of Luke Ross, Aki's president (Aki is beneficiary of policy) — 9,000

Cash dividends paid on outstanding 10% cumulative preferred stock — 20,000

Interest paid to Ira Farb, who owns 1% of Aki's outstanding stock and is one of Aki's directors (Aki has a note payable to Farb for $60,000 borrowed from Farb in 2014 at 10% interest) — 6,000

What is the allowable loss that Aki can claim in its 2015 return for the sale of land to Max Carr?

A. $4,000 Section 1231 loss.
B. $4,000 Section 1245 loss.
C. $4,000 Section 1250 loss.
D. $0

REG 3-Q39 R1145. For related party loans between individuals, imputed interest would not apply to which of the following loan amounts:

A. $8,000
B. $15,000
C. $25,000
D. $100,000

REG 3-Q40 R1146. Steve's mother gave him an interest free loan of $60,000 on January 1, 2016. As of December 31, 2016, Steve had net investment income of $2,300. The applicable federal rate in 2016 is 5%. What would be the imputed interest for 2016?

A. $0
B. $1,500
C. $2,300
D. $3,000

REG 3-Q41 R83. During 2017, a taxpayer purchased five acres of land for $20,000 and placed in service other tangible business assets that cost $100,000. Disregarding business income limitations and assuming that the annual Section 179 (Election to Expense Certain Depreciable Business Assets) limit is $108,000, what maximum amount of cost recovery can the taxpayer claim for 2017?

A. $120,000
B. $108,000
C. $100,000
D. $20,000

REG 3-Q42 R103. On January 1, Fast, Inc. entered into a covenant not to compete with Swift, Inc. for a period of five years, with an option by Swift to extend it to seven years. What is the amortization period of the covenant for tax purposes?

A. 5 years.
B. 7 years.
C. 15 years.
D. 17 years.

REG 3-Q43 R350. During 2017, a taxpayer purchased and placed in service during 2017, a $2,014,000 piece of equipment. The equipment is 7-year property. The first-year depreciation for 7-year property is 14.29%. The taxpayer took the maximum Section 179 depreciation for 2017 but, did not elect to take bonus depreciation. What amount is the maximum allowable depreciation for 2017?

A. $496,000
B. $215,493
C. $710,493
D. $500,000

REG 3-Q44 R397. For 2017, which of the following conditions must be satisfied for a taxpayer to expense, in the year of purchase, under Internal Revenue Code Section 179, the cost of new or used tangible depreciable personal property?

I. The property must be purchased for use in the taxpayer's active trade or business.
II. The property must be purchased from an unrelated party.

A. I only.
B. II only.
C. Both I and II.
D. Neither I nor II.

REG 3-Q45 R434. Bent Corp., a calendar-year C corporation, purchased and placed into service residential real property during February 1998. No other property was placed into service during 1998. What convention must Bent use to determine the depreciation deduction for the alternative minimum tax?

A. Full-year.
B. Half-year.
C. Mid-quarter.
D. Mid-month.

REG 3-Q46 R451. During 2017, Ted Cook purchased $180,000 worth of equipment for use in his business. Ted has taxable income of $140,000 and elected the maximum Section 179 expense deduction. What is Ted's deduction for 2017?

A. $90,000
B. $180,000
C. $140,000
D. $25,000

REG 3-Q47 R452. Fred Rubble owns a heavy construction company. In 2017, he decided to spend a portion of his total purchases of equipment of $3,000,000 on a heavy duty bulldozer that cost $300,000 for the business that was placed in service in November, 2017. Fred elected to take the maximum Section 179 deduction on the bulldozer, plus the MACRS depreciation deduction for 5-year property. The first year factor per the IRS MACRS depreciation tables for 5-year property is 5%. Heavy construction equipment is considered to be 5-year property. No other fixed assets were purchased during 2017. Fred had taxable income in 2017 of $5,000,000 before Section 179 and did not elect to take bonus depreciation. What is the total deduction for depreciation for the bulldozer in 2017?

A. $25,000
B. $150,000
C. $300,000
D. $500,000

REG 3-Q48 R453. During 2017, a taxpayer purchased 8 acres of land for $40,000 for their business and placed into service other tangible personal property that is used in a trade or business for a cost of $50,000. What is the maximum Section 179 deduction that the taxpayer can claim for 2017?

A. $50,000
B. $25,000
C. $90.000
D. $40,000

REG 3-Q49 R454. On January 1, 2017, Jane Davis purchased a $150,000 machine (5-year property) for use in her business. She expensed $25,000 under Section 179 in addition to the regular MACRS depreciation (per IRS tax tables) factor is 20% for the first year of 2017. Jane's total deduction for 2017 on the machine is:

A. $0
B. $30,000
C. $50,000
D. $25,000

REG 3-Q50 R455. During 2017, George Hoffman placed into service for his business, machinery and equipment that cost $500,000 and furniture and fixtures that cost $1,600,000. What is the maximum Section 179 deduction that Hoffman can take in 2014?

A. $400,000
B. $0
C. $25,000
D. $500,000

REG 3-Q51 R21. Upon her grandfather's death, Jordan inherited 10 shares of Universal Corp. stock that had a fair market value of $5,000. The estate is valued at FMV date of death. Her grandfather acquired the shares in 1995 for $2,500. Four months after her grandfather's death, Jordan sold all her shares of Universal for $7,500. What was Jordan's recognized gain in the year of sale?

A. $2,500 long-term capital gain.
B. $2,500 short-term capital gain.
C. $5,000 long-term capital gain.
D. $5,000 short-term capital gain.

REG 3-Q52 R49. What is the due date of a federal estate tax return (Form 706), for a taxpayer who died on May 15, year 2, assuming that a request for an extension of time is **not** filed?

A. September 15, year 2.
B. December 31, year 2.
C. January 31, year 3.
D. February 15, year 3.

REG 3-Q53 R277. Carter purchased 100 shares of stock for $50 per share. Ten years later, Carter died on February 1 and bequeathed the 100 shares of stock to a relative, Boone, when the stock had a market price of $100 per share. One year later, on April 1, the stock split 2 for 1. Boone gave 100 shares of the stock to another of Carter's relatives, Dixon, on June 1 that same year, when the market value of the stock was $150 per share. What was Dixon's basis in the 100 shares of stock when acquired on June 1, if property of the estate was valued at FMV date of death.

A. $5,000
B. $5,100
C. $10,000
D. $15,000

REG 3-Q54 R356. Daven inherited property from a parent. The property had an adjusted basis to the parent of $1,600,000. It was valued at $2,000,000 at the date of death and valued at $1,800,000 six months after the date of death. The executor elected the alternative valuation date. What is Daven's basis in the property?

A. $ 0
B. $1,600,000
C. $1,800,000
D. $2,000,000

Multiple Choice – Solutions

REG 3-Q1 R47. The correct answer is B. Marketable securities are a capital asset. The Internal Revenue Code lists what items are not capital assets, and therefore if not listed, it is a capital asset. The following are listed examples of non-capital assets:
- Accounts receivable and notes receivable from a trade or business
- Tangible personal property and real property used in a trade or business
- Inventory and items held for resale in ordinary course of business
- Covenants not to compete

REG 3-Q2 R183. The correct answer is D. Land held as investment property is a capital asset. Business property is generally not a capital asset. Examples of business property which are not capital assets are inventory, accounts receivable and notes receivable in a trade or business and personal property used in a trade or business such as a computer system used in a trade or business. Therefore, answers A, B and C are not capital assets.

REG 3-Q3 R203. The correct answer is A. The internal revenue code states what assets are not capital assets and those assets not stated are capital assets.

Assets that are non-capital assets include:
- Depreciable business property (personal property used in a trade or business)
- Accounts receivable and notes receivable in a trade or business
- Real property used in a trade or business
- Covenant not to compete
- Inventory or goods held for resale

Assets that are capital assets include anything not on the list above.

REG 3-Q4 R278. The correct answer is D. The internal revenue code does not list what is a capital asset but, has a list of what is not a capital asset. Those items which are not capital assets include, personal property used in a trade or business, real property used in a trade or business, inventory and covenants not to compete. Therefore, government bonds sold by an individual investor are not on the list and would give rise to a capital gain or loss.

Answer A is incorrect because sales of personal property used in a trade or business is not a capital asset.

Answer B is incorrect because real property subdivided and sold by a dealer is inventory and is not a capital asset.

Answer C is incorrect because inventory is not a capital asset.

REG 3-Q5 R295. The correct answer is D. Real property is defined as land and everything permanently attached to it.

Answer A is incorrect because it says **only**. Answers with exclusive terms such as only are generally incorrect.

Answer B is incorrect because it states all tangible property which could include personal property.

Answer C is incorrect because real property is not intangible.

REG 3-Q6 R331. The correct answer is D. Real property includes land and things permanently attached to the land. Personal property is property that does not have a real property classification. Trees when in the ground are considered real property. When they are cut down and become lumber, they become personal property. When the lumber is used to build a home, the lumber reverts back to being real property.

REG 3-Q7 R197. The correct answer is A. This question deals with the gain or loss to the donee, when the donee receives a gift from the donor and the donee sells the gift. In a question where the donee receives the gift, the question will give the candidate the donor's basis and fair market value (FMV) at date of gift. If a donee sells the gift at a gain, the donee's basis is the donor's basis. To determine the gain, take the selling price of the gift ($29,000) and subtract the donee's basis which is the donor's basis ($32,000). This results is a loss of $3,000 ($29,000 - $32,000). To determine loss on the sale of the asset by the donee, the donee's basis for loss is the lesser of the donor's basis or the FMV at date of gift. To compute this, take the selling price ($29,000) and subtract the lesser of the donor's basis ($32,000) or the FMV ($27,000). The lesser amount is the FMV of $27,000. Take the selling price of $29,000 minus $27,000 (donee's basis) and instead of it resulting in a loss, it results in a gain. In conclusion, if we use the donee's basis for gain and it results in a loss and then we use the donee's basis for a loss and it results in a gain, there is no gain or loss on the sale of the gift.

REG 3-Q8 R234. The correct answer is A. If the taxpayer has common stock and receives a stock dividend of common stock, it is non-taxable. To calculate the basis per share, take the 1,000 shares and add 100 shares (10% stock dividend). The taxpayer would now have 1,100 shares and a basis, which has not changed, of $22,000. To calculate the basis per share, take the $22,000 and divide it by 1,100 shares, which results in a new basis per share of $20.

REG 3-Q9 R293. The correct answer is D. All the costs: the purchase price, delivery charges, installation fees and sales tax are included in the calculation of depreciable basis of the equipment which results in $59,425 ($55,000 + $725 + $300 + $3,400).

REG 3-Q10 R321. The correct answer is A. When a corporation declares a 2-for-1 stock split, the number of shares doubles and the cost basis per share is divided in half. Greller owns 100 shares of Arden Corp with a basis of $10,000. After the 2-for-1 stock split, Greller owns 200 shares with a basis of $10,000. The cost per share was $100 per share, and with the 2-for-1 stock split, the cost per share is half of the $100 or $50 per share. The basis of 100 shares at $50 per share is $5,000.

Note: When computing the basis per share after a 2-for-1 split, **do not** divide the fair market value per share ($120 in the question) by 2. The proper method is to divide the original cost basis per share of $100 by 2.

REG 3-Q11 R337. The correct answer is C. Allen purchased 100 shares of Prime Corp on January 1, 2008 for $10,000 giving Allen a basis of $100 per share. On January 1, 2010, Allen received a 2-for-1 stock split giving Allen an additional 100 share of Prime resulting in Allen having 200 shares of stock with a cost of $10,000 or a basis of $50 per share. The holding period for the new shares is the date Allen bought the original 100 shares which is January 1, 2008. On February 1, 2013, Allen sold 100 shares of Prime stock with a basis of $50 per share for a total of $5,000 and a selling price of $6,500 ($65 x 100), resulting in a long-term capital gain of $1,500.

The reason the gain is long-term is because the holding period begins on January 1, 2008 and ends on the date of sale, February 1, 2013, which is long term (held more than 12 months).

REG 3-Q12 R391. The correct answer is C. When a donee receives a gift, which has appreciated in value, the donee basis is the donor's basis. The donor, Smith, had a basis in the gift of $1,200. Since Thompson sold the gift for $2,500, the gift sold would result in a gain. When a gift sold results in a gain, the donee will take on the donor's basis which in this question is $1,200. To determine the gain, take the selling price of $2,500 minus the donee's basis of $1,200, which gives Thompson a $1,300 gain on the disposition.

REG 3-Q13 R774. The correct answer is A. The fact that both buildings are considered to be used as business ventures by Efron results in their being classified as like-kind properties for federal tax purposes. Generally, a like-kind exchange does not result in taxable income when Section 1245 or Section 1250 property is disposed of, except when boot is received. Since there was no boot received in this exchange, there is no reportable gain on this exchange.

REG 3-Q14 R23. The correct answer is D. Sec. 1244 stocks allows a small business corporation to treat some of the loss to the taxpayer as an ordinary loss. This loss can occur from the sale of the stock or if the stock becomes worthless. The amount of the loss that is ordinary for a single taxpayer is $50,000, with the balance of the loss as capital loss. A taxpayer filing a joint return can treat up to $100,000 as ordinary and the balance as capital loss. In this question, this has a loss of $48,000 from JJJ Corp. stock and a $20,000 loss from MMM Corp.; both are Sec. 1244 stocks. Since Fitz filed as a single taxpayer, he can treat $50,000 of the $68,000 ($48,000 + $20,000) total loss as ordinary and the balance of $18,000 ($68,000 - $$50,000) as capital loss.

REG 3-Q15 R56. The correct answer is C. This question deals with like-kind exchanges. In a like-kind exchange, there is no gain or loss generally recognized. Like-kind exchanges only deal with business or investment property but not exchanges of property of a non-business nature. A like-kind exchange also occurs when business personal property is exchanged for business personal property. In turn, it also occurs when business real property is exchanged for business real property. There is no like-kind exchange if business personal property is exchanged for business real property. In answer C, an exchange of an apartment building for unimproved land is considered an exchange of business real estate.

There are exceptions when like-kind exchanges do not apply:

Answer A is incorrect because they do not apply to exchange of a partnership interest for another partnership interest.

Answer B is incorrect because like-kind exchanges do not apply for investments in common stock for investments in common stock of another corporation. It also does not apply to exchanges of investments in preferred stock for investments in preferred stock in another corporation. It does not apply to investments in bonds. It also does not apply to exchanges of inventory.

Answer D is incorrect because business personal property is exchanged for business real property.

REG 3-Q16 R58. The correct answer is C. Section 1244 stock permits an individual shareholder to deduct ordinary loss on stock sales or if the stock becomes worthless. Summer, who has Section 1244 stock and is a single taxpayer can deduct up to $50,000 of loss each year as an ordinary loss. Summer has no taxable income for the year in which he has a Section 1244 loss made up of ¾ of the net operating loss of $20,000. ¾ of $20,000 net operating loss is the Section 1244 loss as stated in the question. Since Summer has no taxable income that year (ordinary income), he cannot deduct any of the Section 1244 loss (ordinary loss).
In the current year, Summer has ordinary income of $80,000 and a current year Section 1244 loss (ordinary loss) of $50,000. Summer can deduct the ordinary loss of $50,000 against the ordinary income of $80,000.

REG 3-Q17 R84. The correct answer is B. This question deals with like-kind exchanges. A like-kind exchange is an exchange of business use property for business use property. Also, it is like-kind because it is a personal property used in a trade or business for personal property used in a trade or business. To calculate:

Items received by Hogan	
Fair market value of equipment	$80,000
Cash received	1,000
Baker assumed Hogan mortgage	2,000
Total received	$83,000

Items given up by Hogan	
Basis of property given up:	
(cost $100,000 - $30,000 depr.)	(70,000)
Realized gain	$13,000

Recognized gain is lesser of realized gain of $13,000 or boot received (cash received of $1,000 plus assumption of mortgage by Baker of $2,000) of $3,000. The recognized gain is $3,000, which is answer B.

REG 3-Q18 R85. The correct answer is A. This question deals with the sale of a personal residence. For a taxpayer who files a joint return, they can exclude up to $500,000 of the realized gain. In order to exclude up to $500,000, at least one of the parties had to occupy the principal residence for at least 2 of the last 5 years prior to the sale and only one of the taxpayers has to own the property for 5 years prior to the sale.

Selling price	$650,000
Commissions	(36,000)
Adjusted selling price	$614,000
Basis of residence	$300,000
Improvements	40,000
New basis	(340,000)
Realized gain	$274,000
Exclusions	(274,000)
Recognized gain	$0

REG 3-Q19 R141. The correct answer is B. This question deals with like-kind exchange, which is an exchange of business real estate for business real estate. First, calculate the realized gain and then the recognized gain.

Received by Tatum	
Fair market value (FMV) of office building	$350,000
Assumption of Tatum's mortgage (boot received)	120,000
Total received by Tatum	470,000
Surrendered by Tatum	
Old basis of property transferred	(250,000)
Tatum takes on new mortgage (boot paid)	(70,000)
Total surrendered by Tatum	(320,000)
Realized gain	$150,000

Gain is recognized to the extent of the lesser of the realized gain or the boot received. To get the boot received or boot paid, net the mortgages. Now, take the mortgage which was boot received of $120,000 and net it against the new mortgage of Tatum which was $70,000 to arrive at a net boot received from the mortgages of $50,000. The recognized gain is the lesser of the realized gain ($150,000) or the boot received ($50,000). The recognized gain is $50,000. If you net the mortgages and they give you net boot paid, ignore that in the computation of recognized gain.

REG 3-Q20 R142. The correct answer is C. This question deals with the taxable gain after an exclusion on the sale of qualified small business stock held for six years. For acquired qualified small business stock between 8/11/1993 - 2/17/2009, the capital gain exclusion is 50%. An individual taxpayer can exclude 50% of the capital gain resulting from the sale of qualified small business corporation stock held for more than 5 years. The amount of gain that is excludable is limited to the greater of $10,000,000 or 10 times the investor's stock basis. Here, the sale of the stock was $16,000,000 and the basis was $2,000,000 resulting in a gain of $14,000,000. Since 50% of the gain can be excluded, Danielson's taxable gain is $7,000,000 ($14,000,000 x 50%).

REG 3-Q21 R155. The correct answer is A. A single taxpayer can exclude up to $250,000 of the gain from the sale of a principal residence. To be eligible, the taxpayer must own and occupy the principal residence for at least two out of the prior five years before the sale of the principal residence. In this question, the selling price is $450,000 and the basis is $250,000, giving the taxpayer a realized gain of $200,000. Since the property was his personal residence for least 2 out of the past 5 years prior to the sale, the taxpayer can exclude the full $200,000 of the realized gain resulting in a recognized gain of $0.

REG 3-Q22 R179. The correct answer is C. This questions deals with a wash sale. Sands purchased 100 shares of Eastern for $18,000. He sold 50 of the 100 shares for $7,000. Sands' basis of the 50 shares sold is one half of $18,000, or $9,000. If the selling price is $7,000 and the basis is $9,000, there is a realized loss of $2,000. If a taxpayer buys back the same identical stock in the same corporation within 30 days before or after the sale of the old shares, the loss is disallowed. In this question, Sands purchased 25 shares of the 50 shares of Eastern within 30 days, so a proration of the loss is disallowed for the number of shares purchased divided by the number of shares sold in the identical corporations. Sands purchased 25 of the 50 shares within 15 days after selling the old shares, which results in one half (25 shares / 50 shares) of the $2,000 realized loss, or $1,000 being disallowed. The remaining $1,000 loss is recognized and the remaining stocks basis is increased by $1,000.

REG 3-Q23 R188. The correct answer is D. Real estate used in a trade or business may be exchanged with other real estate used in a trade or business. A corporate office building exchanged for a vacant lot is an example of real estate used in a trade or business exchanged with other real estate used in a trade or business.

Answer A is incorrect because when inventory (large truck) is exchanged for another asset (company jet); inventory is not subject to like-kind exchange rules and it would be a taxable exchange.

Answer B is incorrect because exchange of investment securities for another asset is not subject to like-kind exchange rules and would be a taxable exchange.

Answer C is incorrect because once again, it deals with inventory creating a taxable exchange.

REG 3-Q24 R1125. The correct answer is D.

The total gain on the installment sale is the selling price, reduced by the selling expenses and the adjusted basis of property. The selling price is the total consideration received by seller which includes seller's liabilities assumed by buyer. The contract price is the consideration received by the seller minus the seller's liabilities that are assumed by buyer. The installment sales formula is the total gain (gross profit) divided by the contract price multiplied by the amount received for the year (do not include the mortgage assumed by the buyer because the payments of the mortgage go directly to the lender/mortgagee).

Calculation:
Gross profit = (Sales price + Liability assumed by buyer from seller) – Property basis = $200,000 + $50,000 - $100,000 = $150,000

Selling price = Consideration received by the seller + Liabilities assumed = $200,000 + $50,000 = $250,000

Contract price = (Consideration received by seller - Liability assumed by buyer from seller) = $250,000 - $50,000 = $200,000

Amount to be received each year = Contract price/Years of payment = $200,000/5 years = $40,000 per year

Total gain = Consideration received by seller – Basis = $250,000 - $100,000 = $150,000

Gross profit percentage = (Gross profit/Total contract price) = ($150,000/$200,000) = 0.75 or 75%

Amount of gain to be recognized each year = Amount to be received each year x GP percentage= $40,000 * 75% = $30,000

To check: $30,000 per year * 5 years = $150,000 total gain or the gross profit on the sale

REG 3-Q25 R1126. The correct answer is C. Note that sales price is reduced by the amount of any liabilities assumed by the buyer. However, this reduction in liabilities should not exceed the seller's basis in the property. Therefore, in this case, liability assumed is $20,000 (basis in the property) and not $50,000 (actual amount of liability assumed by the buyer).

Contract Price= (Sales price – Liability assumed, not to exceed the basis) = $200,000-20,000 = **$180,000**

Gross Profit = (Sales Price - Basis) = $200,000 - $20,000 = **$180,000**

Amount to be received each year = Contract Price/Years of payment = $150,000/5 = **$30,000**

Gross Profit Percentage=Gross Profit/Contract Price x100%= $180,000/$180,000=**100%**

Amount of gain to be recognized each year = Amount to be received each year x GP Percentage = $30,000 x 100% = $30,000

REG 3-Q26 R16. The correct answer is C. To calculate the gross profit, take the selling price plus the buyer's assumption of the mortgage and subtract the seller's adjusted basis and selling expenses.

Amount realized from sale	$250,000
Adjusted basis of property sold	(75,000)
Selling expenses	(10,000)
Gross profit on sale	$165,000

REG 3-Q27 R67. The correct answer is B. First calculate the net short-term transactions. Then, calculate the long-term transactions.

Short term capital gain	$6,000
Short-term capital loss	(4,000)
Net short-term capital gain	$2,000
Long-term capital gain	$14,000
Long-term capital loss	(8,000)
Net long-term capital gain	6,000
Public company X stock short term loss	(5,000)
Net capital gain	$3,000

REG 3-Q28 R64. The correct answer is D. Section 1231 assets are personal property and real property used in a trade or business and must be held for more than 12 months.

Answer A is incorrect because inventory held for resale is not considered personal property.

Answer B is incorrect because the machinery must be held for more than 12 months to be a Section 1231 asset.

Answer C is incorrect because even though cattle are personal property used in a trade or business, they still must be held for more than 12 months to be a Section 1231 asset.

REG 3-Q29 R104. The correct answer is C. Equipment used in a trade or business held for more than one year is considered a Section 1231 asset. When the equipment is sold, first calculate the total gain by taking the selling price minus the basis. In this question, the selling price is $200,000 and the basis is the purchase price of $160,000 minus the accumulated depreciation of $60,000, which equals $100,000. The gain is the selling price of $200,000 minus the basis of $100,000 for a gain of $100,000. Whatever depreciation the taxpayer took is recaptured as ordinary income. The depreciation taken was $60,000, so $60,000 of the $100,000 gain is ordinary income (Section 1245 gain) and the remaining gain of $40,000 is Section 1231 gain (long-term capital gain).

REG 3-Q30 R105. The correct answer is D. Personal property and real property used in a trade or business placed in service for more than one year is called a Section 1231 asset. Determine what type and amount of loss there is with each asset.
- Loss on the abandonment of office equipment of $25,000 is a Section 1231 loss because the office equipment is a Section 1231 asset.
- Loss on the sale of a building (straight-line depreciation taken in prior years of $200,000) of $250,000 which is a Section 1231 loss because the building is a Section 1231 asset.
- Loss on the sale of delivery trucks of $15,000 is a Section 1231 loss because delivery trucks are a Section 1231 asset.

To arrive at the answer, add all the Section 1231 losses ($25,000 + $250,000 + $15,000) to get a net Section 1231 loss of $290,000.

Do not forget a Section 1231 asset is either real estate used in a trade or business or personal property used in a trade or business. Each of the three losses mentioned in the question are either personal property or real property used in a trade or business. The last step is to net Section 1231 gains against Section 1231 losses. If you come up with a net Section 1231 loss, it is shown on the tax return as an ordinary loss, but do not choose the answer ordinary loss. You must call these Section 1231 losses unless they ask you where you classify these on the tax return, then you would show it as ordinary loss. If you net the Section 1231 gains and losses, and the gains exceed the losses, they are a Section 1231 gain (a net long-term capital gain).

REG 3-Q31 R101. The correct answer is D. This question involves the installment sales method in taxation. To determine the amount of gross income to be included in the year of the sale, you must know the installment sale formula. The numerator is the gross profit divided by the denominator which is the contract price (selling price – debt assumed by buyer). Multiply this fraction by the amount received for the year which only includes the principal, not the interest income. The interest income is recognized in full.

Gross profit (sales – basis)
$100,000 - $80,000 = $20,000
$100,000 - $0 = $100,000
Contract price (Selling price – debt assumed by buyer)

$20,000 / $100,000 = gross profit percentage of 20%

Cash received $25,000 (year 1) X 20% = $5,000 (gross income recognized)

REG 3-Q32 R184. The correct answer is D. This question deals with installment accounting in taxation. To determine the amount of the gain recognized in the year of the sale, use the installment sales formula times the cash payment received. The formula's numerator is the gross profit (sales – cost of item, net of depreciation) or $600,000 – ($500,000 - $80,000) = $180,000. The denominator is the contract price, which is the selling price less any debt assumed by the buyer. This amount is the selling price of $600,000 minus zero (no debt assumed by the buyer).

$180,000 / $600,000 x $120,000 = $36,000

REG 3-Q33 R225. The correct answer is C. When a business, whether a corporation or a sole proprietor, sells personal property used in a trade or business held for more than one year, the asset sold is a Section 1231 asset. The portion of the gain that is under Section 1231 is the long-term capital gain portion of the total gain. However, before a Section 1231 gain is recognized, determine the actual gain by taking the selling price minus the basis. The selling price is $200,000 and the basis is $180,000 resulting in a gain of $20,000 ($200,000 - $180,000). The next step is to determine how much of the gain is recaptured as ordinary income under Section 1245. The recaptured gain is the lesser of the depreciation taken or the gain. The depreciation taken was $30,000 and the gain on the sale was $20,000, so the recaptured ordinary income is $20,000. Since all of the gain is recaptured as ordinary income under Section 1245, there is no remaining gain to be taxed under Section 1231 (long-term capital gain).

REG 3-Q34 R226. The correct answer is B. This question is dealing with what portion of the gain is long-term capital gain under Section 1231. A 1231 asset is either personal property or real property used in a trade or business, held for more than one year. The office furniture is a Section 1231 asset because it is used in a trade or business and it was held for more than one year.

To calculate the Section 1231 gain (long-term capital gain), take the selling price minus the basis to determine the gain. The basis is calculated by taking the cost minus the depreciation taken. The basis of the asset is the cost of $30,000 minus the depreciation taken of $20,700, resulting in a basis of $9,300. Therefore, the gain is $37,000 - $9,300 = $27,700. First, determine the recapture portion of the gain. The recaptured portion of the gain, which is the ordinary income portion under Section 1245 is the lesser of the depreciation taken or the gain. The depreciation taken was $20,700 and the gain is $27,700, so the portion of the gain that is ordinary income under Section 1245 is $20,700. Take the total gain of $27,700 and subtract the ordinary income portion of $20,700 to arrive at a long-term capital gain under Section 1231 of $7,000.

REG 3-Q35 R347. The correct answer is C. If an individual taxpayer owns a painting for his personal use, it is considered a capital asset. Only capital gains and not losses are recognized on assets for personal use. The painting sold for $50,000 with a basis of $20,000 resulting in a capital gain of $30,000. Because the capital asset was held for more than 12 months, the capital gain is long-term capital gain.

Answer A is incorrect because there is a taxable long-term capital gain.

Answer B is incorrect because Section 1231 assets are personal property and real property used in a trade or business that are held for more than one year. The painting is not trade or business property.

Answer D is incorrect because the gain is long-term capital gain.

REG 3-Q36 R123. The correct answer is B. Losses are disallowed between sales and purchases of related parties. If Terry's relative later sells the stock to a non-related party, then depending on what it's sold for there may be a gain or loss. For instance, if the stock is later sold to a non-related party for $7,500 then Terry's relative would report a $500 loss and that loss would be classified as a long-term capital loss because Terry's relative retains the holding period which we will assume is greater than 1 year unless otherwise specified. Calculated as follows:

$7,500 - $8,000 = $500

If instead it was sold for $13,000, then Terry's relative would have a long-term capital gain of $1,000 because the disallowed loss is allowed to reduce the gain calculated as follows:

$13,000 - $8,000 = $5,000 - $4,000 disallowed loss = $1,000

Lastly, if it was sold for $10,000 then there would be no gain or loss recognized because the Terry's disallowed loss is greater than his relative's gain calculated as follows:

$10,000 - $8,000 = $2,000 but since the $4,000 disallowed loss is greater, the gain is reduced but not below zero.

REG 3-Q37 R236. The correct answer is B. This question deals with sales between related parties. If a related party sells an asset which would normally generate a taxable loss, the loss is disallowed. When the related party resells the asset to a non-related party for a gain, the disallowed loss can reduce the gain. Gibson bought stock from Gibson's child (related party) and paid $12,000 to Gibson's child, the child's basis in the stock was $16,000. This would result in a loss to Gibson's child of $4,000, which is disallowed to Gibson's child. Then, Gibson sold the same stock to an unrelated party for $18,000 and Gibson's basis in the stock was $12,000, resulting in a gain to the non-related party of $6,000. The disallowed loss between the related parties can be used to reduce the gain of $6,000. The disallowed loss was $4,000, which will reduce the gain of $6,000 to a recognized gain to Gibson of $2,000.

REG 3-Q38 R1078. The correct answer is D. No deduction for a loss is allowed if a sale is made, either directly or indirectly between a corporation and any individual who owns more than 50% of the outstanding stock of the corporation. In this situation, Carr owns 55% of the outstanding stock of Aki; therefore, the loss of $4,000 on the sale of the land to Carr (adjusted basis of $44,000 less sales price to Carr of $40,000) is not deductible by Aki.

REG 3-Q39 R1145. The correct answer is A. Imputed interest does not apply to loans of $10,000 or less, between individuals.

REG 3-Q40 R1146. The correct answer is C. In related party transactions involving a loan between individuals of more than $10,000, the IRS requires a minimum amount of interest to be charged and the applicable federal rate (AFR) is the minimum amount of interest that must be charged. For loans that are not greater than $100,000, imputed interest reported on the loan is limited to the amount of the borrower's net investment income during the year.

Steve's imputed interest is $3,000 (5% x $60,000) however, because the loan was less than $100,000, imputed interest is limited to the amount of net investment income for the year, which is $2,300.

REG 3-Q41 R83. The correct answer is C. This question deals with Section 179 expense write-off for tax year 2017. Effective for tax year 2017, the maximum Section 179 expense write-off is $500,000 and the phase-out of the $500,000 begins when the total purchases for the year exceed $2,010,000.

Section 179 expense write-off only applies to tangible personal property used in a trade or business, but not real estate. So, in the question above, the five acres of land would not be subject to the Section 179 write-off. The Section 179 deduction would be $100,000, which would not exceed the assumed phase-out of $108,000. Although the phase-out for 2017 starts at $2,010,000, the assumption was made in this question that the phase-out limitation began at $108,000. The total cost of $100,000 did not exceed $108,000.

Therefore, the entire $100,000 of purchases of tangible business assets is deductible as Section 179.

Additional example: If the purchases for 2017 were $2,110,000, for every dollar in excess of $2,010,000, $1 of the $500,000 maximum write-off is phased out. Since we are over the $2,010,000 by $100,000, the maximum Section 179 write-off would be $400,000.

REG 3-Q42 R103. The correct answer is C. Covenants not to compete are considered Internal Revenue Code Section 197 Intangibles. Section 197 Intangibles are amortized over a 15 year straight-line basis beginning with the period in which the covenant not to compete is purchased. Do not use the actual period stated in the covenant not to compete to amortize the covenant for tax purposes (always use 15 years for tax purposes).
Other examples of Section 197 Intangibles include goodwill, franchises, and trademarks. These intangibles must be acquired to be used in a trade or business.

REG 3-Q43 R350. The correct answer is C. For 2017, the Section 179 expensing limits is $500,000, with a $2,010,000 phase-out. The phase-out begins when more than $2,010,000 in assets are purchased, which reduces the $500,000 deduction dollar-for-dollar, for each dollar over $2,010,000.

To calculate the depreciation for 2017, take the total cost of $2,014,000 and subtract the allowable Section 179 expensing limit which is $496,000. The $496,000 is arrived at by taking the maximum Section 179 of $500,000 and subtracting the amount that exceeds the phase-out of $4,000 ($2,014,000 - $2,010,000). Take the cost of $2,014,000 and subtract the allowable Section 179 of $496,000. The remaining basis of $1,518,000 ($2,014,000 - $496,000) is then multiplied by the first year's depreciation factor for seven- year property of 14.29%, resulting in $215,493 (14.29% x $1,518,000). The total depreciation for the first year is Section 179 of $496,000 plus the MACRS depreciation for the first year of $214,922 which equals $710,493. The 14.29% contains the averaging convention percentage for the first year's depreciation. Bonus depreciation was not elected by the taxpayer as stated in the question.

REG 3-Q44 R397. The correct answer is C. Under Section 179, which allows for tax years beginning in 2017, a taxpayer to expense up to $500,000 of the cost of new or used tangible personal property used in a trade or business, but the $500,000 starts being phased out when the total purchases exceed $2,010,000, which reduces the $500,000 deduction dollar-for-dollar, for each dollar over $2,010,000. In addition, two other requirements must be met to take Section 179:

I. The property must be purchased for use in the taxpayer's active trade or business.
II. The property must be purchased from an unrelated party.

REG 3-Q45 R434. The correct answer is D. The averaging convention methods are used to determine allowable deductions that can be taken in the first year on either tangible personal property used in a trade or business or real estate used in a trade or business. Because this asset is real estate, the averaging convention method is the mid-month method. For the first year, the mid-month method assumes that the real estate is placed in service in the middle of that month.

Answer A is incorrect because the taxpayer will never take a full year depreciation in the first year.

Answers B and C are incorrect because they are the averaging convention methods for personal property used in a trade or business for the first year and are either the half year or mid-quarter method.

For example, if the taxpayer placed the real estate in service April 28th for the first year, take the depreciation from April 15th of that first year to December 31st of that first year.

REG 3-Q46 R451. The correct answer is C. Under Section 179, for tax years beginning in 2017, a taxpayer may expense the cost of new or used tangible personal property used in a trade or business subject to these limitations.
- The property must be purchased for use in the taxpayer's active trade or business.
- The property must be purchased from an unrelated party.
- There is a dollar limitation. The maximum deduction a taxpayer may elect to take for Section 179 is the lesser of $500,000, less the amount that total purchases exceeding $2,010,000, or taxable income before Section 179.
- If more than $2,000, 000 worth of Section 179 property is placed into service during a single taxable year, the deduction ($500,000) is reduced, dollar for dollar, by the amount exceeding the $2, 010,000 threshold.

One of these limitations states that Section 179 expense write-off cannot exceed taxable income before the Section 179 deduction. Cook's purchases were $180,000 and his taxable income was $140,000 before the Section 179 expense deduction. The Section 179 expense deduction is $140,000, (limited to taxable income of $140,000 before the Section 179 write-off). Since the $140,000 is less than the $180,000, the Section 179 expense write-off for 2017 is $140,000. The remaining unused 179 expense is carried forward into the next tax year(s).

REG 3-Q47 R452. The correct answer is B. Since the maximum Section 179 deduction is $500,000 for tax year 2014 and the phase out begins at $2,010,000, there is no Section 179 because the cost of the Section 179 property was $300,000 and the total purchases of equipment was $3,000,000, which was $1,000,000 in excess of the $2,000,000. This eliminates any Section 179 deduction. However, the construction company can take regular MACRS depreciation on the total $3,000,000 purchases of equipment by multiplying the amount from the IRS depreciation tables for 5-year property of 5% for the first year, which results in MACRS depreciation for the first year of $150,000 ($3,000,000 x 5%).

REG 3-Q48 R453. The correct answer is A. Section 179 expense write-off allows a business to write-off immediately up to $500,000 of tangible personal property used in a trade or business rather than having to depreciate it. Section 179 expense deduction is phased out when the total purchases of Section 179 assets exceed $2,000,000. For every dollar that exceeds $2,000,000, the business losses $1 of Section 179 write-off.

In this question, the taxpayer can write-off $50,000 of the $50,000 purchases of tangible personal property used in a trade or business and there is no phase-out as the purchases do not exceed $2,000,000.

Section 179 cannot be taken on real estate used in a trade or business. When calculating the total expense deduction (including applicable depreciation) for 2017, a business would first deduct Section 179 from the asset's cost basis and the remaining balance would be subject to the 50% bonus depreciation and the remaining cost basis would be subject to the first year's averaging depreciation convention.

REG 3-Q49 R454. The correct answer is C. Jane Davis can write-off in 2017 up to $500,000 of Section 179 expense deduction. Since Jane's purchases do not exceed $2,010,000, Jane can take Section 179 expense write-off of up to $150,000. In addition to Section 179, Jane can take regular MACRS depreciation on the remaining basis after subtracting the Section 179 expense write-off of $25,000 from the original cost of $150,000, which would be $125,000. The additional expense write-off is the depreciation on the remaining basis of $125,000. Multiple the $125,000 by the 20% factor, resulting in MACRS depreciation of $25,000. Therefore, the total deduction for 2017 is the Section 179 of $25,000 and the MACRS depreciation of $25,000 or $50,000.

REG 3-Q50 R455. The correct answer is A. The maximum Section 179 deduction for tax year 2017 that a taxpayer can take is $500,000. Since the total purchases exceeded $2,010,000, for every dollar that Hoffman spent over the $2,010,000, it reduces the $500,000 Section 179 by $1. The total purchases during 2017 were $2,110,000, which will reduce the Section 179 expense deduction from $500,000 to $400,000.

Under Section 179, for tax years beginning in 2017, a taxpayer may expense the cost of new or used tangible personal property used in a trade or business subject to these limitations:
- The property must be purchased for use in the taxpayer's active trade or business.
- The property must be purchased from an unrelated party.
- There is a dollar limitation. The maximum Section 179 deduction a taxpayer may elect to take is $500,000 for tax years beginning in 2017.
- If more than $2,010,000 worth of Section 179 property is placed into service during a single taxable year, the deduction is reduced, dollar for dollar, by the amount exceeding the $2,010,000 threshold.

REG 3-Q51 R21. Correct answer is A. Since the question did not state that the estate elected the alternate valuation method to value the estate, it must be assumed that they are valuing the assets of the estate at fair market value (FMV). Jordan's basis in the shares is the FMV of $5,000. If Jordan sells the shares for $7,500, Jordan would have a capital gain on the sale of the securities of $2,500. The $2,500 capital gain would be long-term because any property acquired by a beneficiary as a result of death automatically results in a holding period of long-term.

REG 3-Q52 R49. Correct answer is D. The federal estate tax Form 706 must be filed within 9 months of decedent's death unless an extension of time has been granted. An automatic 6-month extension can be granted by filing Form 4768.

REG 3-Q53 R277. The correct answer is A. This question deals with gifting away stock that has appreciated in value and the donor has received the stock as a beneficiary of the estate. Carter died bequeathing 100 shares of stock to Boone, having a fair market value (FMV) at date of death of $100 per share. One year later the stock split 2 for 1, giving Boone 200 shares with basis of $50 per share. Boone now gifts 100 shares of the stock received in the inheritance to Dixon when the FMV of the stock increased to $150 per share. If a donor (Boone) gifts 100 appreciated shares to the donee (Dixon), the basis of the stock to Dixon is a transferred basis from the donor (Boone) or $5,000 (100 shares x $50).

REG 3-Q54 R356. The correct answer is C. Daven's basis of property received from a decedent is valued at fair market value (FMV) at date of death, or the estate can use the alternative valuation, which is FMV up to 6 months after death. Since they used the alternate valuation and elected to value the property 6 months after death, Deven's basis in the property is $1,800,000.

REG 4 – Federal Taxation for Individuals

A. Gross Income   4A-1 – 4A-28

     1. Accounting periods (year-end and taxable year)   1
     2. Tax accounting methods   2
     3. Summary of taxable year and accounting method requirements   5
     4. Installment Sale Income Recognition   6
     5. Long-Term Construction Contracts   7
     6. Uniform capitalization rules (UNICAP)   8
     7. Gross Income (inclusions and exclusions)   10

B. Reporting of Items from Pass-Through Entities   4B-1 – 4B-7

C. Adjustments & Deductions to Arrive at Adjusted Gross Income & Taxable Income   4C-1 – 4C-21

D. Passive Activity Losses (Excluding Foreign Tax Credit Implications)   4D-1 – 4D-2

E. Loss Limitations   4E-1 – 4E-4

F. Filing Status and Exemptions   4F-1 – 4F-11

G. Computation of Tax and Credits   4G-1 – 4G-15

H. Alternative Minimum Tax   4H-1 – 4H-3

Glossary: Federal Taxation for Individuals   Glossary 4-1 – 4-2

Multiple Choice – Questions   MCQ 4-1 – 4-14

Multiple Choice – Solutions   MCQ 4-15 – 4-27

Tax Forms   Form 4-1 – 4-26

     Form 1040: U.S. Individual Income Tax Return   1
     Form 1040, Schedule A: Itemized Deductions   2
     Form 1040, Schedule B: Interest and Ordinary Dividends   3
     Form 1040, Schedule C: Profit and Loss From Business   4
     Form 1040, Schedule D: Capital Gains and Losses   5
     Form 1040, Schedule E: Supplemental Income and Loss   6
     Form 1040, Schedule SE: Self-Employment Tax   7
     Form 1040, Schedule EIC: Earned Income Credit   8
     Form 1065, Schedule K-1   9
     Form 8867, Paid Preparer's Due Diligence Checklist (formerly Earned Income Credit Checklist)   10

Form 8815, Tax for Certain Children Who Have Unearned Income	11
Form 8582, Passive Activity Loss Limitations	12
Form 4797, Sales of Business Property	14
Form 4562, Depreciation and Amortization	15
Form 4684, Casualties and Thefts	16
Form 2441, Child and Dependent Care Expenses	17
Form 6251, Alternative Minimum Tax – Individuals	18
Form 1099-C, Cancellation of Debt	19
Form 1099-INT, Interest Income	19
Form 1099-MISC, Miscellaneous Income	20
Form W-2, Wages and Tax Statement	21
Form 1099-R, Distributions from Pensions, Annuities, Profit-Sharing Plans, IRAs, Insurance Contracts, etc.	22
Form 1099-DIV, Dividends and Distributions	23
Form 1099-B, Proceeds from Broker and Barter Exchange Transactions	24
Form 1099-G, Certain Government Payments	25
Form 1098-T, Tuition Statement	25
Form 1099-SSA, Social Security Benefit Statement	26

Federal Taxation of Individuals

A. Gross Income

Hint: This chapter includes some introductory information prior to discussing the AICPA Blueprint representative tasks. While these topics are not overtly mentioned in the AICPA blueprints, understanding this information is necessary to succeed on the CPA Exam and in the profession.

1. Accounting periods (year-end and taxable year)
   A tax year is an annual accounting period for keeping records and reporting taxable income. A taxpayer's accounting period is established upon filing their first tax return. If a taxpayer does not keep books, then the taxpayer uses a calendar year.

   Unless a particular taxable year is required, there are numerous different taxable years an entity may choose, including:
   - Calendar year
   - Fiscal year (ends on the last day of a month OTHER THAN December)
   - 52-53-week year: An annual period always ending on the same day of the week (e.g., last Saturday of a month, or the Saturday nearest month's end).
   - Natural tax year: The year in which 25% or more of gross receipts occur in the last two months of the year. This test must be passed for three consecutive years to be considered a natural business year.

   a. Which taxable year? While some entities can choose their taxable year, other entities must use the taxable year dictated by the IRS.

Taxpayer	Taxable Year
Individual	• An Individual is one who is an employee (for salary or wages), must use a calendar taxable year.
Sole Proprietor	• Personal and business returns are required to have the same taxable year.
Personal Service Corporation	• Always uses a calendar taxable year.
C Corporation	• There are no restrictions as to the taxable year, but it does not include personal service corporations.
Partnership	• Same tax year as the tax year used by partners with greater than 50% of total partnership capital and income. • For a substantial business purposes where a different taxable year is preferable, a different taxable year may be used. • Partnerships are pass-through entities.
S Corporation	• Usually files on a calendar taxable year. • For a substantial business purposes where a different taxable year is preferable, a different taxable year may be used. • S corporations are pass-through entities.
Estates (Form 1041)	• There are no restrictions as to the taxable year.
Trusts (Form 1041)	• Always uses a calendar taxable year. • Does not include tax-exempt trusts and charitable trusts.

Multiple Choice

REG 4-Q1

b. Modifying a tax year
In some cases, no approval is required to change tax years. For example:
- Newlyweds: May adopt the taxable year of their new spouse without approval
- Corporations (not an S corporation) may change its year if:
    - It has not done so within the past 10 years ending with the calendar year of change
    - It does not result in a Net Operating Loss for the resulting short period
    - The annualized taxable income for the short period is 90% or more of the previous year's taxable income
- A newly acquired subsidiary that will be included in a consolidated return MUST adopt the taxable year used by its parent

In all other cases, substantial business purpose and IRS approval are required.

The request is filed with the IRS using Form 1128, Application for Change in Accounting Period and must be filed by the 15th day of the second month after the close of the short period.
- If the request is to change to a natural business year, the substantial business purpose requirement may be satisfied.
- The substantial business purpose requirement will be deemed to be satisfied if,
    - The last two months of the selected year represent at least 25% of gross receipts, and
    - 25% of gross receipts in the last two months of the selected year has occurred for three consecutive years.
- Before approving a request for change, the IRS may require taxpayer to meet certain conditions (e.g., partners might be required to adopt the same tax year that the partnership is requesting)

2. Tax accounting methods
To calculate an individual or entity's income tax liability, it is important first to take a look at when the entity or individual will recognize revenue and expenses (i.e., its tax accounting method) and when the individual's or entity's tax year will begin and end.

An individual or entity's method of tax accounting will not affect how an item is classified. It may, however, affect the timing of recognition of income or deduction items when computing taxes.
The selection of an accounting method for tax purposes by a taxpayer or new entity is made simply by using the chosen method on the taxpayer or entity's initial tax return.

Common tax accounting methods include:
- Accrual Method
- Cash Method
- Hybrid Method

a. Accrual method
The accrual method for tax purposes is very similar to the financial accounting accrual method. Where exceptions exist, they usually serve to increase taxable income.

1) "All events" test
In the accrual method, income and expenses are recognized when the "all events" test has been met.

Under the "all events" test, income is recognized when:
- All events have occurred that determine the taxpayer's right to receive the income
- The amount of income can be determined with reasonable accuracy

> *Hint:* For tax purposes, unearned (prepaid) income is recognized in the year the income received, not necessarily in the year it is earned, even if the taxpayer uses the accrual method.

Expenses are recognized when:
- All events have occurred that determine the fact of the liability
- The amount of the liability can be determined with reasonable accuracy
- Economic performance has occurred, meaning that the property or service to which the accrual relates is actually provided or used
  There are a few exceptions to this rule where expenses are concerned. For example, a taxpayer can treat property or services as provided when he pays for them, but only if he can reasonably expect the property or services to be provided within 3.5 months after payment is made.
  Certain recurring expenditures may be treated as incurred in the year the all events test is otherwise met if:
    - An expenditure is recurring and economic performance occurs within 8.5 months after the close of the tax year (or when return is filed, if earlier) the expenditure can generally be deducted in year incurred
    - The item is not material or accruing the expense now results in better matching of income and expenses

Multiple Choice

REG 4-Q2

Under the accrual method, it is sometimes not clear when economic performance has occurred. Here are some guidelines to help make that determination:
- If there is an obligation to perform in the future (i.e., provide goods and/or services), the associated expense should not be deducted until the goods or services are provided
- If there is an obligation to pay for future goods or services, that expense should not be deducted until the goods or services are received
- Certain expenses can only be deducted when they are actually paid, including:
  - Refunds
  - Rebates
  - Awards
  - Prizes
  - Provision of warranty work/service contracts
  - Taxes
  - Insurance premiums
- Vacation pay and bonuses can only be deducted as expenses for a particular tax year if they are paid within 2.5 months after the close of that tax year.

2) Estimates
If income is accrued based on a reasonable estimate and the exact amount will be determined later, any difference between the estimate and exact amount should be included in income or deducted in the year when the exact amount becomes known.

b. Cash method
Under the cash method, income is recognized when it is received (or constructively received) and expenses are recognized when they are paid. Income can be received in the form of cash or property. A cash basis taxpayer does NOT need to reduce property to cash to trigger income recognition.

> *Hint*:
> - Not all property and cash received are income, such as loan proceeds.
> - Not all payments are deductible, such as payments representing expenses, which will benefit future years.

Multiple Choice

REG 4-Q3

The concept of **constructive receipt** requires a cash basis taxpayer to include the value of property in income in the period in which the cash or property is available to the taxpayer without restriction. Income is not constructively received if substantial restrictions exist on the taxpayer's use of the funds.

> *Hint*:
> - Expenses paid by check should be deducted when the bank honors the check.
> - Payments by credit card are deducted at the time of the charge (not when the credit card bill is paid).

Multiple Choice

REG 4-Q4

1) Prepaid expenses
   Prepaid expenses should be prorated for cash basis if the taxpayer's recognition of the entire expense in the current tax year would distort taxable income or if the benefit of the prepayment extends substantially beyond the tax year.

   Capitalizing payments are NOT REQUIRED if:
   - The benefit does not exceed 12 months after the date when the benefit is first received
   - The benefit does not extend beyond the end of the taxable year following the taxable year when the payment was made

   > *Hint:* Prepaid interest must ALWAYS be amortized over the life of the loan

   > *Example:* In January 2015, a taxpayer signed a 2-year lease and pre-paid the rent for all 24 months. Even though the rent was paid for both 2015 and 2016, the taxpayer can only deduct the rent for 2015 on his 2015 tax return. The rent payments that correspond to 2016 can be deducted on the taxpayer's 2016 return.

2) Accounts receivable and loans
   Remember that in cash basis accounting, a taxpayer has no Accounts Receivable because no accounting entry is made for sales on account (i.e., no property has been received). Consequently, cash basis taxpayers can NOT write off Accounts Receivable. (Bad Debts)

However, cash basis taxpayers can write off a bad loan. While no accounting entry is made for sales on account, a loan does require an entry (i.e., DR Loan Receivable CR Cash).

The cash method cannot be used by:
- Any company that has inventory
- C corporations, generally not having more than an average of 5 million dollars in the past three years, and having inventory
- Partnerships that have a C corporation as a partner
- Tax shelters
- Certain tax-exempt trusts

The cash method can be used by:
- Qualified personal service corporations
- An entity other than a tax-shelter
- Entities that for the prior three years, had average annual growth receipts of $5,000,000 or less and does not have inventory
- Small business taxpayer that for the prior three years, have gross average annual growth receipts of $1,000,000 or less and did have inventory
- A business that has average annual growth receipts of more than $1,000,000 and less than $10,000,000 and the business meets one of the following requirements:
    1) Principal business activity is not retailing, wholesaling, manufacturing or mining
    2) Principal business activity is the provision of services or custom manufacturing
    3) No matter what the principal business activity is, the taxpayer may use the cash method with respect to any separate business that separates #1 or # 2 above.

Multiple Choice

REG 4-Q5 through REG 4-Q6

c. Hybrid method
In general, businesses with inventories must use accrual method to report purchases (COGS) and sales. This is known as the hybrid method of accounting if other accounts are kept using cash basis.

Taxpayers with annual gross receipts less than $1M can use the cash method for their purchase and sales accounts. The test satisfied for prior year if average gross receipts for the previous three-year period are less than $1M. Once the test is failed, the entity must use accrual forever.

Taxpayers with average annual gross receipts between $1M and $10M for the past 3 years, can use the cash method for purchase and sales accounts if their primary business is delivering services (not manufacturing, wholesale, retail).

1) Changes in tax accounting methods
Once a taxpayer selects a certain accounting method, the method cannot be changed without IRS consent.

2) Special rules regarding methods of accounting
Whether a business is on the cash or accrual basis, any income received in advance is taxable as income when the income is received. When a business pays an expense in advance, treat the prepaid expense as though the business is on the accrual basis. For example, if a business prepays three years of rent, write off the expense on the tax return as a deductible expense, as the expense expires.

3. Summary of taxable year and accounting method requirements

Entities and Taxable Year and Accounting Method Requirements		
Entity Type	**Taxable Year**	**Accounting Method**
Individual Taxpayer (i.e., not an entity) who does not keep books	Must adopt a calendar year	Cash method
Regular C Corporations (not personal service corps) with annual gross receipts over $5M and inventory	No restriction on taxable year	Must use accrual method
Regular C Corporations (not personal service corps) with annual gross receipts UNDER $5M and NO inventory	No restriction on taxable year	Can use accrual or cash method
Personal Service Corporations	Must adopt a calendar year Different taxable year might be used if a substantial business purpose exists	Can use cash method (if qualified – i.e., corporation performing services in health. Law, engineering, accounting, actuarial science, performing arts, or consulting) if at least 95% of stock is owned by specified shareholders including employees
Sole Proprietor	Must use same taxable year for both business and personal returns	Must use the same accounting method for business and personal returns
Partnership (no C corp. as partner)	Must use the same tax year as the one used by partners who own over 50% of the income and capital of the partnership Different taxable year might be used if a substantial business purpose exists	Can use accrual or cash method
Partnership (WITH C corp. as partner)	Must use the same tax year as the one used by partners who own over 50% of the income and capital of the partnership Different taxable year might be used if a substantial business purpose exists	Can use accrual or cash method
S Corporations	Generally, must adopt a calendar year unless a substantial business purpose exists	Can use accrual method or cash method as long as no shareholder is a tax shelter
Estate	No restriction on taxable year	Can use accrual or cash method
Tax Shelters	Follows the reporting for the entity (i.e., limited partnership)	Must use accrual basis; No cash method
Trust (other than charitable and tax-exempt trusts)	Must use a calendar year	Can use accrual or cash method
Trust (tax-exempt trusts)	Must use a calendar year	No cash method (accrual only)

4. Installment Sale Income Recognition

Under the installment method, a gain on a sale (not a loss) is reported as payments are received instead of reporting all the gain in the year of the sale. The installment method must be used regardless of cash or accrual method if at least one payment is to be received after the close of the tax year in which the sale is made, unless:

- The taxpayer actively opts out – OR –
- The transaction is one for which the installment method cannot be used
  - Cannot be used by dealers of real or personal property
  - Cannot be used for sales of stock or securities traded on an established securities market

Use of the installment method does not change the character of the gain (capital, ordinary, etc.).

The formula for calculating gain recognized under installment method:

$$\text{Gain Recognized} = \frac{\text{Total Gain}}{\text{Contract Price}} \times \text{Payment received}$$

Where:

Total contract price = Selling price less debt assumed by buyer

---

Example: Jane sells property for $80,000. The property had an adjusted basis to Jane of $45,000. As part of the purchase price, the buyer assumes a $20,000 mortgage and pays the remaining $60,000 to Jane in 4 annual installments of $15,000, starting this year.
- Jane's gross profit is $35,000 ($80,000 – $45,000).
- The total contract price is $60,000 ($80,000 – $20,000).
- Jane's gross profit percentage is $35,000/$60,000, or 58.34%
- Each year, Jane must report $8,750 (58.34% x $15,000) as a gain on the sale.
- The remainder of each payment of $6,250 ($15,000 - $8,750) is the tax-free return of Jane's adjusted basis.

Multiple Choice

REG 4-Q7 through REG 4-Q9

5. Long-Term Construction Contracts

Special rules apply to recognizing income for production projects that take more than one year to complete (e.g., aircraft, ships).

The percentage of completion method usually must be used to recognize income, so that gross profit is recognized over a period of time to complete the project.

Percentage-of-Completion method should be used for contracts that are not completed within the year they were started, and income is recognized each year based on the percentage of the contract that is completed.
- If less than 10% of the estimate of total contract costs were incurred as of the end of the year, an election may be made not to recognize the income or, account for the costs from the contract in that tax year.

Another method, the completed contract method, may be used in certain circumstances. This method allows the gross profit from a project to be deferred until the year production process is complete. This method may be used by:
- Companies with $10M or less in average gross receipts during proceeding three years if project will last 2+ years
- Home construction contractors
- Contract where less than 10% of total costs relates to actual construction of property on land

    a. Definition of gross income and inventory methods for taxation
Gross income for a business is defined as sales minus cost of goods sold, plus other income. Inventory for taxation can be valued at cost or market, whichever is lower. The cost methods that can be used are FIFO, LIFO, and specific identification. If LIFO is used for taxes, it must also be used for financial accounting purposes. The lower of cost or market method must be used with LIFO, for tax purposes. The other cost methods, value inventory at the lower of cost or net realizable value.

6. Uniform capitalization rules (UNICAP)
Uniform capitalization rules require businesses to capitalize certain costs that benefit or are incurred because of the *production* or *resale* activities of the business. These costs are not allowed to be immediately expensed as operating expenses. Instead, they are required to be added to the basis of property or inventory and are later recovered through depreciation, amortization, or COGS when the property is sold or disposed of.

    a. Applicable entities
Applicable entities include entities that:
        1) *Produce and use tangible personal property in a trade or business.*
        2) *Produce and sell tangible personal property to customers.*

However, if the average annual gross receipts for the past three years do not exceed $10 million, the entity is called a small retailer. Small retailers are not subject to the uniform capitalization rules.

Multiple Choice

REG 4-Q10

        1) Capitalized costs
- *Direct costs*
Capitalized direct costs include direct materials and direct labor.

- *Indirect Costs*
Capitalized indirect costs can include warehousing costs, storage, repair and maintenance, utilities, rent, indirect labor (wages of supervisors and quality control specialists; employee pension and benefit plans) indirect materials and supplies, taxes, depreciation and amortization, depletion, insurance, licensing and franchising costs, engineering and design, repackaging, spoilage and scrap, environmental remediation expense and etc.

        2) Do not capitalize
            i. Marketing, selling, distribution costs.
            ii. General and administrative expenses.
            iii. Research and experimental costs.

3) Methods for Farming Businesses
   - Income from farming business is reported on Schedule F
   - Inventories can be measured using cost, farm-price market, LCM, unit-livestock-price method.
   - After a farmer calculates net earnings from self-employment on Schedule F, they must file Schedule SE to determine self-employment tax.
   - Preparing Schedule F is similar to preparing Schedule C.
   - The rules for preparing Schedule C for non-farm sole proprietorship, are used for preparing Schedule F.
   - A cash basis farmer, who received insurance proceeds from crop damage, can include the proceeds in income in the year after the damage, but the farmer must show that the damaged crop income would have typically been reported in the following year.
   - If a farmer borrows money and pledges the crops as security, the loan proceeds are reported as income in the year received, rather than in the year the crop is sold.
   - A farmer can generally deduct soil and water conservation expenditures. The deduction is limited each year to 25% of the farmer's income from farming. Any excess expenses over the 25% limit can be carried over for an indefinite number of years, subject to the 25% limitation in each carryover year. Land clearing expenses are capitalized and added to the farmer's basis in the land.
   - A cash basis farmer can deduct prepaid livestock feed costs in the year of payment if: (1) the payment isn't a deposit, (2) the farm isn't trying to avoid taxes and the purchase has a business purpose, and (3) the deduction doesn't materially distort the farm's income. In general, the deduction for prepaid farm supplies (e.g., feed, seed, and fertilizer) not used or consumed during the year is limited to 50% of total deductible farm expenses.
   - Concerning tangible personal property used in farming, a farmer must use MACRS 150% declining balance, over 5 years.

7. Gross Income (Inclusions and Exclusions)

CPA Exam Blueprint Representative Task

> Calculate the amounts that should be included in or excluded from an individual's gross income as reported on federal Form 1040 – *U.S. Individual Income Tax Return*.

> Analyze projected income for use in tax planning in future years.

> Analyze client-provided documentation to determine the appropriate amount of gross income to be reported on federal Form 1040 – *U.S. Individual Income Tax Return*.

a. Overall summary of the steps to compute taxable income and individual income tax
Each of the steps required to compute an individual's income tax liability is described in great detail throughout this section. However, as it is sometimes helpful to start with the big picture before getting into the weeds, a summary of the individual income tax calculation process is provided here.

To Compute Taxable Income:
Step 1: Compute gross income by determining what is included and what can be excluded.
Step 2: Subtract deductions (above the line) to arrive at Adjusted Gross Income (AGI)
Step 3: Subtract "itemized" deductions or the standard deduction (whichever is greater)
Step 4: Subtract personal exemptions
Result: Taxable Income

To Compute Individual Income Tax Liability:
Step 1: Compute annual income tax liability
Step 2: Decrease this tax liability by any available tax credits
Step 3: Add to tax liability any other applicable taxes (for example, self-employment tax or the Alternative Minimum Tax)
Step 4: Deduct payments that were made to the IRS during the tax year, including:
- Taxes that were withheld during the year by an employer
- Estimated tax payments made during the year

Result: Taxes due to IRS or **tax refund due** to taxpayer

b. Gross income defined
The Internal Revenue Code defines gross income as "all income from whatever source derived." In other words, all income should be assumed to be included in gross income and reported unless the Internal Revenue Code specifically excludes it.
There are a few important points to keep in mind when trying to determine what the IRS defines as income:

- Income must be **realized**; that is, there must be some event or transaction which gives rise to income that can be valued.

> *Example*: Peter purchases a ring today and finds out tomorrow that is has doubled in value. At this point, has he **realized** any income as a result of the purchase? No, because no transaction has taken place. Alternatively, if he sells the ring on day two for twice the purchase amount, he has indeed **realized** income.

- The transaction or event that gave rise to the income must be recognized by the Internal Revenue Code as a **taxable event**.

> *Hint*: A transaction does not have to only involve the exchange of cash. Transactions can be represented by the creation of a receivable or a payable or the exchange of property.

> *Example*: Jane purchases a ring today and gives it to her friend Jack. Even though an event has taken place (i.e., transfer of ownership), Jack does not have to include this ring in his income because receiving a gift is not a taxable event.

- For property received by the taxpayer to realized and/or recognized, it must be able to be valued.

  > *Hint*: Keep in mind that income may be realized, but not taxable. In order to be included in income, the income must be both realized AND recognized by the IRS as a taxable event.

- References to income in this section refer to taxable income unless otherwise specified.

  Several special rules exist to address income recognition in unusual circumstances. These concepts include the tax benefit rule, the claim of right doctrine, and the assignment of income doctrine.

c. Tax benefit rule
The tax benefit rule requires taxpayers to include expense reimbursements in income if the reimbursement relates to an expense that was deducted in the prior period and the deduction provided a tax benefit to the taxpayer. In other words, if the expense reduced the taxpayer's taxable income for a particular period and then that expense was later reimbursed, the taxpayer has to include the reimbursement as income.

A common example of this is the receipt of a tax refund. If taxes are paid by the taxpayer and deducted from gross income in a previous year, and then are later refunded, that refund must be reported as income by the taxpayer in the year of recovery.

> *Hint*: The reimbursement must only be included if it provided a tax benefit in the year of the deduction. For taxpayers that take the standard deduction (i.e. they do not itemize their deductions), no adjustment would be necessary because they received no tax benefit.

Examples of reimbursements subject to the tax benefit rule are:
- Employment-related expenses that were deducted, but later reimbursed
- Certain tax refunds, including:
    - State income taxes
    - Personal property taxes
    - Real property taxes
    - Federal excise taxes
    - Farmland preservation expenses
    - State sales and use taxes
    - State corporate franchise taxes
    - Stamp taxes
    - Customs duties

d. Assignment of Income Doctrine
Income is taxed to the individual who earned the income even if the taxpayer directs the funds to be paid directly to someone else, even if the taxpayer never takes possession of the income. In other words, income can NOT be assigned for tax purposes to someone other than the one who earned it.

e. "In" or "out" of gross income? **These Items Are Always IN!**
Many gray areas crop up when deciding what to include and exclude in gross income. An important rule of thumb to keep in mind is that income is always included unless the tax code specifically excludes it. When in doubt, unless a particular reason for excluding it can be identified, it should be included.

This section will explain what is always included, followed by sections that explain what is always excluded and some items that are a bit more complicated.

These items are **always included** when computing gross income:
- Any income that is realized and recognized by the IRS as resulting from a taxable event unless specifically excluded by the IRS
- Income received by the taxpayer even if it is assigned to another individual
- Compensation for services (salaries, bonuses, fees, commissions, and similar items)
    - For example:
        - Independent contractor earnings (1099 earnings)
        - Jury duty pay
            - If jury pay is remitted to employer in exchange for receiving regular wages, a deduction FOR AGI (above the line) is received to offset this income, but still, must be included in gross income
        - Election board duty pay
        - Tip income
            - All tip income (regardless of amount) is included in gross income in the month earned
            - Tip income $20 or more per month must be reported to the employer by the 10th day of the next month;
            - Daily tip record should be kept
    - Compensation can be received in cash, property, or services
        - If property is received as compensation, the property is included income at the FMV, on the date of receipt.

Multiple Choice
REG 4-Q11

- Gross Income from a business or profession, calculated as:

Sales - Cost of Goods Sold + Other Income

In determining the cost of goods sold for tax purposes:
- LIFO, FIFO and Specific identification are allowed.
- If LIFO is used for tax purposes, it must also be used for book purposes.
- Except for LIFO, Inventory is typically valued at the lower of cost or net realizable value.
- Lower of cost or market is used with LIFO

Accounting for inventory for tax purposes generally follows the same rules as the rules for financial accounting.

> *Hint:* This formula always holds, even if the income is generated by a drug trafficking business, or any other type of illegal business.

- Unemployment Benefits, employer supplemental unemployment benefits, strike benefits from union funds

Multiple Choice
REG 4-Q12

- Gifts from an employer

> *Hint:* Does NOT INCLUDE non-cash holiday gifts.

- Distributive share of S corporation income (loss) or partnership income (loss)
- Dividend income

- Gain from sale or exchange of real estate, securities, property
- Rents and Royalties
    - Rent income included when received, even if in advance
    - Lease cancellation payments are also treated as rental income

> **Example:** A landlord receives a non-refundable $500 security deposit plus $3,000 rent for each of the first and last months of the tenant's 3-year lease, for a total of $6,500.
>
> How much of the rent should the cash-basis landlord include in this year's gross income? All $6,500 should be included in this year's gross income.

Multiple Choice
REG 4-Q13 through REG 4-Q14

- Income in respect of a decedent
    - Income(money) that was owed to the decedent, that had been earned before death, and not recognized as income at death. The beneficiary will include this income on the form 1040, in the year it is received.
    - Some common examples are accrued income, accrued interest in US savings bonds/accounts, dividend for which the record date was before taxpayer's death
- Gambling winnings
- Embezzled or illegal income
- Employee death benefits paid by employer to family upon employee's death

> **Hint:** This is NOT life insurance proceeds, which are treated differently

f. "In" or "Out" of Gross Income? **These Items Are Always OUT!**
Because the Internal Revenue Code (IRC) defines income in such a broad manner, it is sometimes simpler to describe what is NOT included in reportable income. Because these items are completely excluded from gross income, they are referred to as **exclusions**.

The IRC includes a full list of exclusions, but this text will focus on only the most common items.

> **Hint:** EXCLUDED in gross income means that is exempt from income tax, but may be taxed due to other tax rules (i.e. gift tax).

These items are **always excluded** when computing gross income:
- Income that is not yet realized (stock went up in value but hasn't been sold) or recognized by the IRS as resulting from a taxable event
- Return of capital
- Property transferred to former spouse under divorce decree

> **Hint:** The transferor's basis in the property moves to the transferee

- Proceeds to a beneficiary from a life insurance policy as the result of the death of a decedent
- Workers compensation payments related to occupation-related injury or sickness
- Reimbursement from employer-provided accident and health plan for medical expenses paid for and NOT deducted by employee
- Accident and health insurance benefits paid to an employee from an employee-purchased policy

> *Hint:* These benefits are excluded even if payments are a substitute for lost wages.

- Qualified foster care payments
- Welfare payments received from government entities
- Payments received for support of minor children.

g. "In" or "out" of gross income? **It Depends...**
As mentioned earlier, some items are sometimes included and sometimes excluded from gross income, depending on specific circumstances. This section addresses the most important (and most commonly tested) items that can be included or excluded based on the situation.

1) **Interest Income**
   i. When is interest income INCLUDED?
      - Interest income is generally included in gross income when received in cash or, when constructively received (for cash basis) or when accrued (accrual basis).
      - Prepaid interest is always taxed when received, regardless of whether or not it has been earned.
      - Common sources of interest income that are included:
        - Bank deposits
        - US debt (e.g., T-notes and US savings bonds)
        - Interest on federal and state tax refunds
        - Imputed interest from interest-free and low-interest loans
        - Mortgage interest received
        - Private activity or arbitrage bonds that are not used to fund regular government activities
        - Corporate bonds

        > *Hint:* Interest on these bonds is included even though they may be issued by state or local governments (see exception for certain private activity bonds).

      - For interest-free or below-market loans, special rules may apply
        - In general, treat as if the borrower paid market interest rate (based on rates published monthly by the IRS) to the lender
        - The borrower will have interest expense and lender will have interest income for the hypothetical payment
        - This "income" received by the lender is treated for tax purposes as:
          - Compensation income if borrower is an employee
          - Dividend income if borrower is shareholder
      - Investment in bonds purchased at a premium. The premium must be amortized over the constant yield to maturity method, similar to the straight-line method, over the number of periods until the bonds mature. The amortization of the premium is a reduction of interest income and a reduction of the basis of the investment

   ii. When is interest income EXCLUDED?
       In the instances listed in this section, interest income is excluded from gross income.

       > *Hint:* Even though these interest income items are excluded from gross income, they can sometimes be used in other tax calculations (such as, for example, computation of AMT or exclusion of Social Security benefits).

- Interest income from state and local bonds (i.e., municipal bonds) that are used to fund traditional government functions
    - "State and local" includes US Territories such as Puerto Rico, Guam, and the Virgin Islands.
    - Interest on District of Columbia bonds
    - Mutual funds that invest in tax-exempt bonds can pass the exemption on bond interest to its shareholders when the tax-exempt interest is distributed in the form of dividends. To qualify, the mutual fund has to have at least 50% of its total asset value invested in tax-exempt municipal bonds at the close of each quarter of the taxable year.

Multiple Choice

REG 4-Q15

- Interest income from U. S. Series EE bonds are excludable If certain conditions are met:
    - All bond proceeds (including both principal and interest) must be used to pay qualified higher education expenses or fees for the taxpayer or the taxpayer's spouse or dependents
        - If total qualified higher education expenses are less than total bond proceeds, making it impossible to use all proceeds toward expenses, the taxpayer can exclude a pro rata share of the bond interest
    - The taxpayer must be the sole owner (or joint owner with spouse), i.e. the bond cannot be in the child's name
    - Taxpayer must be at least 24 years old at time of purchase
    - The bond must have been issued on or after 1/1/1990
    - Married taxpayers must file jointly to use the exclusion

- The interest exclusion on U.S. Series EE bonds is phased out for taxpayers over a certain MAGI range based on filing status.
    - MFS: cannot claim the exemption
    - MFJ: $116,300-$146,300
    - S/HOH: $77,500-$92,500
    - No exclusion is available if the taxpayer's MAGI is over the high end of the phase-out range.
    - The exclusion is phased out proportionately over a $15,000 range for Single and Head of Household filers, and over a $30,000 range for Married Filing Jointly filers.

> **Example:** A married filing separate taxpayer, redeems Series EE bonds and wants to use the proceeds to pay for his qualified education expenses. Will the interest be tax-free?
>
> No, because taxpayers who file Married, Filing Separate, cannot take the exclusion.

> **Example:** A married, filing jointly taxpayer redeemed $5,000 of Series EE bonds, which was comprised of $4,000 of principal and $1,000 of interest. He had $4,500 of qualified higher education expenses. How much of the bond interest can be excluded from his gross income?
>
> He can exclude ($4,500/$5,000) x ($1,000) or $900 from his gross income.

2) **Dividend Income**
    i. When is dividend income INCLUDED?
        - Dividends received in the form of cash or property are generally taxed as dividend income if the distribution is made from Retained Earnings (called Earnings & Profits or, E&P for tax purposes) from a corporation.
            - To determine the taxability of dividends, follow a 3-step process:
                - Dividend income to the extent of E&P
                - Then a decrease of stock basis
                - Once basis is exhausted, excess is capital gain
        - In what period should dividend income be recognized?
            - Dividends received should be included in income on whichever date comes first – actual receipt or constructive receipt. In other words, when the cash or property is freely available to the shareholder. Dividends delivered via mail should be included when actually received.
            - Generally, stock dividends on COMMON STOCK are NOT TAXABLE. Usually what happens is you simply adjust your basis in the stock. If you paid $100 for 100 shares (basis = $1/share) and you receive 5 more shares as a stock dividend, this is not a taxable event. Your basis per share, however, has to be adjusted to $100/105 or $0.952/share.
            - However, some special situations will affect whether or not the stock dividend is treated as income:
                - If you or any other shareholder is given the option to receive cash/other property instead of the stock, then you have to report it as income. It doesn't matter if they actually take it as cash or not – if the option is there, it's treated as income.
                - If the corporation gives cash/property to some shareholders and stock to other shareholders, it has to be reported as income
                - If not, all common shareholders receive the dividend in the form of common stock (CS); for example, if a corporation gives preferred stock (PS) to some CS holders and CS to other CS holders, then not all CS holders were treated the same, and it must be treated as income.
            - Stock dividends on PREFERRED STOCK are taxable.

> *Example*: So, to go through each possible scenario:
> 1. **Common stockholder gets more common stock as a dividend** – If all CSholders are given CS only and no one receives anything else or even has the option to receive anything else, then it is EXCLUDED from gross income; basis must be adjusted as mentioned above.
> 2. **Common stockholder gets preferred stock as a dividend** – If some CSholders get a CS dividend and others get a PS dividend, then all recipients must treat the stock dividend as taxable.

> 3. **Preferred stockholder gets more preferred stock as a dividend** – This is TAXABLE since any stock dividend on preferred stock is taxable
> 4. **Preferred stockholder gets common stock as a dividend** – This is TAXABLE since any stock dividend on preferred stock is taxable.

- Distributions from mutual funds
  - Usually characterized as either ordinary dividends or capital gain distributions
    - All ordinary dividends are treated as dividend income and mutual fund will indicate if these are qualified dividends taxed at 20% or lower rates
    - All capital gain distributions are treated as long-term capital gains

ii. When is dividend income EXCLUDED?
- Dividends paid in the form of shares of stock or as a stock split to Common Shareholders
  - The receipt of stock dividends on common stock are NOT taxable events so long as dividend is proportionate (i.e., the same dividend percentage is paid to all shareholders)
  - Requires the taxpayer to adjust basis of the stock based on the new number of shares owned
  - The stock dividend can be paid in the form of Preferred Stock or Common Stock

    > *Hint*: If the taxpayer is given the option to receive cash in lieu of stock, dividend income must be recognized.

Multiple Choice

REG 4-Q16

- Dividends on life insurance policies:
  - Treated as a return of premiums, and are not taxable. unless policy specifically states they're interest payments

3) **Income Received As a Result of Divorce, Separation, Child Support**
   i. This type of income is INCLUDED when it is considered to be **alimony**.
   Alimony is taxable to the one receiving the money and deductible for AGI (above the line) by the one making the payments. Therefore, the payment is only taxed once to the ultimate recipient.

To be treated as alimony, certain conditions must be met:
- The payments must be required by decree or written agreement and not characterized as something other than alimony
- The payments must be made in cash
- The payments must be paid to or on behalf of former spouse
- The payments must terminate upon death of recipient
- Payer and payee cannot be members of the same household or file a joint return

> *Hint*: To be considered alimony, payments must end before the recipient's death, but not after.

> *Hint*: If the amount of required alimony changes based on some condition involving the child (i.e. recipient's payment is reduced by $400 per month when the child reaches 18 years of age), that portion of the payment has to be pulled out and treated as child support.

The rental value for parsonages, or a residence provided by a church parish for its pastor, is not taxable income to the pastor and EXCLUDED from gross income.

Multiple Choice

REG 4-Q17 through REG 4-Q19

ii. This type of income is EXCLUDED when it is considered to be **child support**.
A divorce decree or separate maintenance agreement must specify what portion of each payment is child support and what portion is alimony to ensure that the payment is not treated as alimony (and therefore included in the recipient's gross income). Payments made must be for the payer's child.

Child support payments are not taxable to one receiving the money and not deductible by the one making the payments. If the required amount of child support and alimony is not received, payments are first assumed to be child support.

iii. This type of income is EXCLUDED when it is considered to be **a division of property** upon divorce or separation.

Payments to a former spouse that do not qualify as alimony or child support, are treated as a division of property and are NOT a taxable event. In this event, the transferor's basis carries to the recipient.

Multiple Choice

REG 4-Q20 through REG 4-Q21

4) **Income Received as a Result of Damages**
   i. Income awarded for damages is INCLUDED in gross income when it:
      o Is awarded as punitive damages, even if related to sickness/injury
   ii. Income awarded for damages is EXCLUDED from gross income when it:
      o Represents non-punitive damages that are awarded to compensate for physical sickness/injury, even if the injured party is reimbursed for lost wages
      o Represents damages awarded for emotional distress if cause is underlying physical illness/injury

5) **Income Received as Gifts, Bequests, Inheritances**
Income subsequently derived from a gift is INCLUDED in gross income. If a taxpayer receives property as a gift, the gift itself is NOT included in gross income, but any income generated by that property (rental receipts, interest, etc.) must be included in gross income. The basis of property received as a result of death is the FMV at the date of death or, an alternative valuation, which is generally not more than FMV, six months after death. The holding period is always long-term.

Multiple Choice

REG 4-Q22 through REG 4-Q23

6) **Income Received as Scholarships & Fellowships**
Scholarship and fellowship income is INCLUDED in gross income when it is:
- Received in the form of grants or tuition reductions that represent payment for services, such as teaching and/or research.
- Granted to non-degree seeking students.
- Used for room and board even if going for a degree.

Scholarship and fellowship income is EXCLUDED from gross income when it is:
- Used by a degree-seeking candidate for eligible tuition and related expenses

Hint: Amounts used for other purposes (including housing) must be INCLUDED in gross income.

7) **Political Contribution Income**
Political contributions that are received are INCLUDED in gross income when used for personal purposes. These contributions are EXCLUDED from gross income when received by the candidate's campaign (rather than the candidate personally) and used for election-related purposes.

8) **Discharge of Debt**
Under most circumstances, the discharge of debt is INCLUDED in gross income.
Debt discharge can be EXCLUDED from gross income under the following circumstances:
- Discharge of student loan debt occurs after fulfilling length of service requirement
- Discharge is of corporate debt by a shareholder, in which case the discharge is treated as contribution of additional capital
- Discharge is a gift
- Discharge is purchase money debt reduction
- Debt is canceled that relates to real property used in a trade or business
    - In this case, this income is EXCLUDED from gross income even if the taxpayer is not bankrupt nor insolvent
    - The taxpayer must decrease the basis of property by the amount of debt forgiven.
- Debt is canceled as a result of a bankruptcy proceeding

9) **Leasehold Improvements Made To Rented Property by Renter**
Any increase in property value that results from improvements made by a renter are INCLUDED in gross income if the improvements are made instead of rent. In this case, the amount of income recognized is equal to the reduction in rental payments granted in return for the property improvements.

If the renter makes property improvements that are NOT instead of rent, but that result in a property value increase, that increase is EXCLUDED from income.

10) **Prizes and Awards**
Under most circumstances, income received as the result of a prize or award is INCLUDED in gross income.

> *Hint:* Cash awards must be INCLUDED in gross income.

- o   Awards received in recognition of accomplishments in religious, charitable, scientific, artistic, educational, literary, or civic fields EXCLUDED if the taxpayer:
  - Was selected without taking any action to receive the award
  - Is not required to perform substantial future services as a condition of receipt
  - Directs the payer to transfer the award directly to a governmental unit or tax-exempt charitable organization. Note that in this case, no charitable deduction will be allowed for the amount transferred, since the amount was never included in gross income.

Multiple Choice
REG 4-Q24

11) **Life Insurance Policy Proceeds**
    i. Life insurance proceeds received as a result of death are generally nontaxable.
    ii. Life insurance proceeds received NOT as a result of death, or accelerated benefits must be INCLUDED in gross income. The exchange or sale of a life insurance policy for cash is treated as a sale, and any proceeds received in excess of cost are included in income.

> *Example:* John purchases from David an existing life insurance policy for $10,000. Shortly after that, David dies and John, now the named beneficiary, receives $15,000 in cash. The first $10,000 is excluded from gross income as a return of capital. The remaining $5,000 is included in gross income.

Multiple Choice
REG 4-Q25

    iii. Life insurance benefits that are received in installment payments must be prorated. The payment is made up of the proceeds of the life insurance policy, plus interest income.

> *Example:* Jim has a $100,000 life insurance policy, of which the beneficiary is Jim's wife, Jane. Jim died in Year 1 when Jane's life expectancy is 20 years. In year 1, Jane receives $6,200 from the insurance company. Each year's payment is made up the principal and interest. The proceeds are $5,000 ($100,000/20 years) per year, which is not taxable. Jane received in year 1, $6,200, which is made up of $5,000 non-taxable proceeds and $1,200 taxable interest income.

    iv. Life insurance proceeds are EXCLUDED from gross income when:
      - o   Benefits are paid upon the death of the insured

> *Hint:* These proceeds are usually still subject to the estate tax.

12) **Tax Refunds**
Tax refunds received are INCLUDED in gross income to the extent the refunded amount was deducted in a prior year and the deduction provided a benefit. To determine the amount of a state income tax refund that is included in the following year's individual tax return as taxable, do the following:
- First, determine if the taxpayer itemized in the prior year tax return.
- If the taxpayer did itemize in the prior year tax return, then the state income tax refund will be taxable in next year's individual tax return.
- If the taxpayer did not itemize the prior year, the state income tax refund would not be taxable in next year's individual tax return.
- If the taxpayer did itemize in the prior year's tax return and the only itemized deduction on that prior year's tax return was state income taxes paid; the amount of state income tax refund to be reported on the next year's Form 1040 is the excess of the itemized state income taxes paid, over the standard deduction for the prior year's individual tax return.

Multiple Choice

REG 4-Q26 through REG 4-Q27

Hint:
- If a taxpayer only takes the standard deduction (does not itemize), the taxpayer does not have to include the state income tax refund in taxable income.
- If the taxpayer itemizes in the prior year, the state income tax refund may be taxable.

13) **Qualified moving expense reimbursement**
If an employee is reimbursed by his or her employer for a qualified move, the reimbursement is not taxable. A qualified move is where the employee generally moves more than 50 miles from this old job location and remains at that location for at least 39 weeks during the year.

Qualified moving expenses include the cost of moving the family, including pets, household goods, insurance on the household goods during the move. It also includes the cost of driving an automobile from the old to the new location, the cost of lodging from the old to the new job, but does not include meals while driving from the old job to the new job.

Qualified moving expense do not include pre-move house hunting trips, temporary housing after arriving at the new location, closing costs for the sale of the old residence, the cost of purchasing the new residence, and the cost of breaking a lease. If the employee is reimbursed for non-qualified moving expenses, the reimbursement is taxable to the employee.

14) **Incentive stock options (qualified stock options)**
An incentive stock option plan that is generally offered to all employees so that the company is not discriminating against who the options are offered to is called a qualified stock option plan. There are situations where the company could discriminate and still be an incentive stock option plan. An example of nondiscrimination is where the employee must be with the company for one year before they have the right to receive stock options, or a company can offer it to a specific class of employees, such as officers.

Employees who have incentive stock options generally receive favorable tax treatment. The favorable treatment includes:
- No taxable income to the employee at the time the option is granted or exercised,
- If the employee holds the stock acquired through exercising the options for at least two years from the date the option was granted and holds the stock itself for at least one year, the sale of the stock from the exercise of the option will get long-term capital gain treatment, which could result in lower taxes.

A non-qualified stock option plan, (which is not an incentive stock option plan), is one where the company discriminates and would offer options only to certain employees. For example, if the president of the company is the only employee who can receive stock options, then that stock option plan is non-qualified. In a non-qualified stock option plan, ordinary income is recognized by the employee when the options are exercised. The amount of income recognized when the date the options are exercised, is the excess of the FMV of the stock, at the date of exercise, over option price at the date of exercise. The rest of the gain could be short-term or long-term capital gain, when the shares are sold. The employer will receive a deduction for the amount ordinary income reported by the employee.

15) **Pensions and Annuities**
Pension and annuities are excluded to the extent that they represent a return of capital. The formula to determine the amount excluded from income is the employee's cost (contributions), divided by the total expected return (benefits), multiplied by the total payments received for that year. After calculating this exclusion ratio, it stays the same until the recovery of the cost of the annuity.

Multiple Choice

REG 4-Q28

16) **Social Security Benefits**
The amount of Social Security benefits that should be included in gross income is based on a taxpayer's provisional income. The calculations can be rather complicated, but the following guidelines provide a good overview and should be enough to answer exam questions correctly:
- For higher-income taxpayers, between 50% and 85% of Social Security benefits are INCLUDED in gross income; specifically,
    - If taxpayer provisional income > **$32,000K (MFJ), $0 (MFS), $25,000K (all others)**
        - Up to 50% of Social Security benefits can be included
    - If taxpayer provisional income > **$44,000 (MFJ), $0 (MFS), $34,000 (all others)**
        - Up to 85% of Social Security benefits can be included
- For low-income taxpayers, all Social Security benefits are generally EXCLUDED from gross income; specifically, those taxpayers with provisional income under $25,000

Provisional income = AGI + tax-exempt income + 50% of Social Security benefits

17) **Self-Employment Income**
   i. The following items are considered self-employment income and subject to self-employment tax:
       - Income from sole proprietorships.
       - Distributive share of income for general partners.
       - Guaranteed payment to general partners.
       - Consulting fees
       - Board of director fees

ii. Other taxable items, which are **not** considered self-employment income and therefore not subject to self-employment tax, include:
- Distributive share of ordinary income for limited partners.
- Distributive share of ordinary income from S Corporations.
- Fees received for serving as an executor

Multiple Choice

REG 4-Q29

18) **Employee Benefits Provided by Employer**

Employee benefits provided by an employer include items such as employee life-insurance, accident & health benefits, meals or lodging, qualified moving expense reimbursement, workers compensation, and employee discounts. These benefits are generally not taxable to the employee. Also, an employer can contribute to a health savings account or, a medical savings account for an employee and the employer contributions for the employees is not taxable.

An employer can give to an employee, as a tax-free employee benefit, the premiums paid by the employer for the first $50,000 of group term life insurance.

One important factor that determines whether the benefit is included in gross income or not included, is if the plan is offered to all employees and does not discriminate. A plan discriminates when it is only offered to a select group of employees. A plan that does not discriminate is a qualified plan. A plan that does discriminate is called a nonqualified plan.

i. **Employee Expense Reimbursements Provided by Employer**

When employees are reimbursed for expenses, determination of whether or not the reimbursement is INCLUDED in gross income depends on whether the reimbursements were made under an "accountable plan." For a plan to be considered accountable, the employee is required to substantiate all expenses for reimbursement, and any excess reimbursements must be returned to the employer.

If employee expenses are reimbursed **under an accountable plan**, reimbursements are EXCLUDED from gross income (for FICA or income tax).

Hint: If employee expense reimbursements are EXCLUDED from gross income, the related expenses cannot then be treated as itemized deductions. Both the expense itself and the resulting reimbursement are simply ignored for tax purposes.

If expenses are reimbursed **under a non-accountable plan**, the reimbursement must be INCLUDED in income (for FICA and income tax). Under non-accountable plans, all expense reimbursements paid to the employee are included in gross income, even if the employee returns some of the money.

ii. **Insurance Benefits Provided by Employer**

With regard to insurance benefits provided by an employer, the following **general rule** applies:
- If the accident & health insurance premiums are paid by the employer:
  - The premiums paid are EXCLUDED from the employee's gross income
  - Any benefits received by the employee from the policy are INCLUDED in the employee's gross income

- If the accident & health insurance premiums are paid by the taxpayer:
  - The premiums paid are not deductible from the employee's gross income
  - Any benefits received by the employee from the policy are EXCLUDED from the employee's gross income

Here are a few examples that illustrate this general rule, along with some notable exceptions.

These benefits are INCLUDED in gross income:
- Group Term Life insurance premiums paid by the employer that relate to the amount of coverage over $50,000
- Employer-paid premiums on whole life insurance policy for an employee
- Employer-paid premiums for wage continuation insurance
- Benefits received from employer-purchased disability policies (with a notable exception addressed below)

These benefits are EXCLUDED from gross income:
- Employer-paid premiums on Group Term Life Insurance policy for coverage up to $50,000
- Premiums paid by employer for accident, disability, long-term care, health insurance plans
- In some cases, members of armed forces injured during combat duty can exclude disability payments from income

Multiple Choice

REG 4-Q30

19) **"Cafeteria Plan" Benefits**
Cafeteria plans are referred to as such because they include a "menu" of benefits. The employee can choose between cash and certain "qualified benefits" offered.

A few important notes about the inclusion or exclusion of these benefits in gross income:
- If the employee opts to receive cash instead of a particular benefit, that cash is INCLUDED in gross income as wages.
- Qualified benefits are EXCLUDED from gross income if they would have been tax-free if not offered through a cafeteria plan
  - Qualified benefits include:
    - Accident and health benefits
    - Adoption assistance
    - Dependent care assistance
    - Group-term life insurance coverage (including costs that cannot be excluded from wages)
    - Health savings accounts (HSAs). Distributions from an HSA may be used to pay eligible long-term care insurance premiums or qualified long-term care service
    - Section 401(k) plans (profit sharing plans)

20) **Retirement Plans – Contributions and Withdrawals**
   i. Contributions to Employer-Sponsored Plans
   To be considered a qualified plan, it must meet non-discriminatory, funding, vesting, and participation/coverage requirements.

Two annual limits apply to contributions made to an employer-sponsored qualified plan:
- A limit on employee elective contributions; and
- An overall limit on contributions to a participant's plan account (including the total of all employer contributions, employee elective deferrals, and any forfeiture allocations).

ii. **Contributions Made by Employers**
Contributions made by an employer to an employee's qualified retirement plan are EXCLUDED from the employee's gross income until those contributions are withdrawn from the plan.

iii. **Contributions Made by Employees**
Employees can make elective deferrals from certain qualified plans. Whether or not the employee contributions can be excluded from gross income depends on whether the plan is traditional, Roth, or educational.

iv. **Contributions to Traditional Employer-Sponsored Plans**
Regular contributions can be made annually to a traditional IRA until the year the taxpayer reaches 70½. Contributions to these plans can be deductible from gross income if the taxpayer is not eligible to participate in a pension plan at work. Income generated by these contributions is EXCLUDED from gross income until the employee withdraws funds from the plan.
The most common traditional employer-sponsored plan is a 401(k), but there are other plans as well, which include the following:
- 403(b) plan: This plan is similar to a 401(k) plan but offered by an educational institution. Contributions are subject to the same limits as 401(k) plans
- Simplified Employee Pension (SEP-IRA): This is a plan where employers may contribute to an IRA for each employee. SEP plans allow an employer to make contributions to its employee retirement accounts subject to higher limits than those applicable to IRA contributions without having to deal with complex compliance and reporting rules that apply to qualified retirement plans
- SIMPLE IRA plan: A plan that is established by an employer who then makes either matching or non-elective contributions.
- SIMPLE IRA plans are available to any small business (generally those with fewer than 100 employees) that offers no other retirement plan.

v. **Contributions to Non-Employer-Sponsored Plans**
Additionally, or alternatively, taxpayers may choose to contribute to a separate traditional or Roth IRA (not offered through an employer) whether or not they participate in another retirement plan through their employer or business.

For 2016, total allowable contributions to all traditional and Roth IRAs (not counting contributions to an employer-sponsored plan) cannot exceed:
- $5,500 ($6,500 for taxpayers age 50 or older), or
- The taxpayer's taxable compensation for the year, if that compensation was less than the specified dollar limit.

Hint: Amounts rolled over into these plans do not count toward this limit.

If a taxpayer is not eligible to participate in a qualified pension plan (401(K)), then any contributions to a traditional IRA are deductible. Distributions from a traditional IRA, where the contributions are deductible, are generally taxable (and subject to a penalty if taken out too early).

Contributions to a **Roth IRA** are never deductible and are fully INCLUDED in gross income if they are not a qualified distribution. A Roth IRA can be made regardless of the contributor's age. The allowable contribution amounts ($5,500 or $6,500 for older taxpayers) are phased out proportionally if a taxpayer's MAGI exceeds a specified limit (S/HOH: $117,000; MFS: $10,000; MFJ: $184,000). Taxpayers with a MAGI over the top threshold (S/HOH: $132,000; MFS: $10,000; MFJ: $194,000) may not make any Roth IRA contributions.

Qualified distributions from a Roth IRA are not taxable. Qualified distributions include:
1) Money must be in the plan for five years, and the individual reached the age of 59 ½.
2) Money must be in the plan for five years, and the payments are made to a beneficiary after the death of the owner of the Roth IRA.
3) Money has to be in the plan for five years, and the owner of the policy becomes disabled.
4) Money can be paid for first time home buyer expenses of the owner of the policy, the owner's spouse, the owner's children and grandchildren, subject to a $10,000-lifetime cap.

A traditional IRA can be converted to a Roth IRA (and vice versa). Any such conversion results in a taxable event in which the taxpayer must recognize a gain upon conversion to the extent that conversion amount exceeds tax basis in the IRA.
For a traditional IRA, if a taxpayer withdraws money before the age of 59 ½, except for certain exceptions, they will have to pay a 10% early withdrawal penalty plus the amount withdrawn times the taxpayer's marginal tax rate. DO NOT multiply the amount withdrawn times the effective tax rate.

Contributions to **educational IRA plans,** called Coverdell Education Savings Accounts are not deductible. Distributions may not be subject to tax if the account was established and the proceeds are used exclusively to pay higher education costs (tuition, fees, books, room/board – reduced by tax-free scholarships and similar payments, including elementary and secondary school expenses for a beneficiary under 18 years old). Contributions are limited to $2,000 per beneficiary per year. This limit is phased out proportionally if the taxpayer's MAGI is between $95,000 and $110,000 (between $190,000 and $220,000 for MFJ filers).

21) **Retirement Plan – Distributions**
   i. Distributions from Traditional IRAs and Employer-Sponsored Traditional Plans
   Most taxpayer contributions to qualified retirement plans, such as 401(k) plans, are EXCLUDED from the employee's gross income when those contributions were made. Additionally, any employer contributions to qualified employer-sponsored plans are likewise excluded from gross income. Therefore, taxpayers generally do not have basis in traditional retirement plans. Therefore, withdrawals from **traditional** plans are generally fully taxable as part of gross income in year of withdrawal.

   If the taxpayer made non-deductible contributions to the IRA, that means that the taxpayer does have basis for those contributions. As a result, the withdrawals are prorated between total non-deductible contributions and remaining balance in account. The portion of the withdrawals that represent a return of capital to the taxpayer are not subject to tax.

Withdrawals from traditional IRAs may be subject to 10% penalty levied by the IRS. However, no penalty is applied if:
- The taxpayer is aged 59 ½ or older
- The taxpayer is disabled
- The proceeds are used for death or disability benefits
- The proceeds are made in form of certain periodic payments
- The proceeds are used to pay medical expenses in excess of allowable % of AGI
- The proceeds are used to purchase health insurance of individual who is unemployed for at least 12 weeks
- The proceeds are used for first time home buyer expenses
- The proceeds are distributed for qualified higher education expenses
- The withdrawal is made by individuals called or ordered to active military duty

ii. Tax on excess accumulations
Withdrawals from traditional IRA plans **MUST** begin when taxpayer reaches 70 ½. Distributions must begin by a "required beginning date" and must equal the required minimum distribution.
- "Required beginning date" is on or after April 1st of either year the taxpayer reaches 70 ½ or the year the employee retires
- If the required distribution not made, a penalty is assessed equal to 50% of the required distribution

Up to $100,000 of IRA distributions are tax-free if they are contributed to a charitable organization by an individual aged 70 ½ or more.

Multiple Choice

REG 4-Q31

iii. Distributions from Roth IRAs and Employer-Sponsored Roth Plans
Withdrawals from Roth plans are not taxed as income if:
- The withdrawal is 5 or more years after date of the first contribution, and the individual is at least 59 ½ years old
- The proceeds are used for death, or disability benefits and the contributions were in the plan for 5 or more years
- The proceeds are used for first time home buyer expenses (5-year rule does not apply)
- The proceeds are paid to a beneficiary after the individual's death, and the distribution is made after a 5-year period

iv. Distributions from Education Savings Plans
- Withdrawals from Coverdell Savings Account are NOT subject to tax if used to pay higher education expenses or rolled into another Coverdell for a member of beneficiary's family. Taxpayers may waive the exclusion for withdrawals from Coverdell if they prefer to claim the American Opportunity Tax Credit or Lifetime Learning Credit for qualified education expenses.
- If the withdrawal (or portion thereof) from Coverdell is not used for education expenses, any earnings of the education IRA that are distributed, but not used to pay for the beneficiary's educational expenses, must be included in the gross income of the party the money is distributed to and is subject to a 10% penalty tax.

v. Health Savings Account (HSA) Contributions and Distributions
Health Savings Accounts (HSAs) allow certain taxpayers to save for medical expenses while receiving a tax benefit.

Individuals who are covered by a high-deductible health plan can make annual contributions to a health savings account of up to $3,350 for self-only coverage and $6,750 for family coverage. Typically, any adult who is covered by a high-deductible health plan (and has no other first-dollar coverage) may establish an HSA.

A **"high deductible health plan"** is a type of HSA, where:
- The annual deductible is equal to at least $1,300 for individual coverage ($2,600 for family coverage), and
- The annual out-of-pocket expenses (deductibles, co-payments, and other amounts, but not premiums) do not exceed $6,550 for individual coverage ($13,100 for family coverage)

Taxpayer contributions to an HSA up to the allowable limit are treated as deductions for AGI.

Amounts withdrawn from a health savings account that are used for qualified medical expenses are EXCLUDED from gross income. Distributions that are used for non-qualified expenses are INCLUDED in gross income and subject to a 20% penalty.

vi. Section 529 Plan Contributions and Distributions
Section 529 plans are used to save for the higher education expenses of a specified beneficiary.

Contributions to 529 plans are not deductible for federal tax purposes.

Earnings from the plan are EXCLUDED from gross income if used for higher education expenses, including tuition, fees, books, and reasonable room and board. Non-qualified distributions are subject to income tax plus a 10% penalty.

B. Reporting of Items from Pass-Through Entities

> Prepare federal Form 1040 – *U.S. Individual Income Tax Return* based on the information provided on Schedule K-1.

Certain types of entities use pass-through taxation, which shifts the income tax liability from the entity earning the income to those who have a beneficial interest in it. Pass-through entities include partnerships, S corporations, trusts, and estates.

Each pass-through entity must prepare a Schedule K-1 to report the amounts that are passed through to each partner. Even though the Schedule K-1 will vary slightly depending on whether it comes from a trust, partnership, or S corporation, all K-1s provide detailed information about the type of income, deduction or loss, so the recipient can accurately report the information on a tax return.

The taxpayer must then include items from any Schedule K-1s when preparing his or her individual tax return.

1. Schedule K-1, Parts I and II – Information about the Partnership and the Partner
   Parts I and II of the Schedule K-1 include information about the partnership and the partner. These parts of the form provide information to the taxpayer about whether or not the partnership is publicly traded, the type of partnership, the partner's share of profit and loss and the partner's basis in the partnership. Additionally, Part II lists the taxpayer's share of partnership liabilities. These amounts are used to determine the taxpayer's at-risk amount.

   The form to prepare a partnership return is Form 1065, which calculates the three types of partnership income.
   1) Ordinary income (loss)
   2) Passive income (loss)
   3) Portfolio income items

4B-1
Regulation (REG)
Copyright © 2018 Yaeger CPA Review. All rights reserved.

2. Schedule K-1, Part III – Partner's Share of Current Year Income, Deductions, Credits, & Other Items
   Part III of the Schedule K-1 contains all of the income, deductions, credits and other items that pass through from the entity to the taxpayer and therefore must be included in the taxpayer's individual return.

   > **Hint:** Most of the items reported on the K-1 are placed into the **Form 1040 and the associated schedules.** Take a moment to look over the schedules at the end of the Individual Taxation section to get a **general** idea of what type of schedules there are and where items should be placed. With a good sense of what schedules exist and how the tax items are organized, there is no need to memorize all of these items and their placement for the exam.

   > **Hint:** Since items pass through from the entity to the individual, knowing the treatment of each item for an individual taxpayer will inform where the K-1 items should be placed.

   1) Loss Limitations
      There are potential limitations on partnership losses that a taxpayer can deduct. Certain deductions may have specific limits. These limits are generally applied first.
      Once the deduction-specific limits are applied, these general limitations must be taken into consideration in this order:
      - Limitations based on taxpayer's basis in the entity
      - At-risk limitations

   2) Basis Rules
      Generally, a taxpayer may only claim his or her share of a partnership loss (including a capital loss) to the extent that it is less than or equal to the taxpayer's adjusted basis in the partnership interest at the end of the partnership's tax year.

      Any losses and deductions not allowed in a particular tax year because of the basis limit, can be carried forward indefinitely and deducted in a later year subject to the basis limit for that year.

      The taxpayer's adjusted basis in a partnership interest is computed by adding items that increase basis and then subtracting items that decrease basis.

   3) At-Risk Limitations
      The at-risk rules generally limit the amount of loss and other deductions that a taxpayer can claim to the amount the taxpayer has contributed to the entity (in the form of cash and property) plus any debt assumed by the taxpayer for which he is directly liable (the amount the taxpayer has at-risk).

      Losses are deductible only up to the at-risk basis. Any losses in excess of the basis are suspended, carried forward indefinitely and are deductible against income in future years from that activity, when they have additional basis.

      The partnership should identify on a statement attached to Schedule K-1 any losses that are not subject to the at-risk limitations.
      Generally, a taxpayer is not **at risk** for amounts such as the following.
      - Nonrecourse debt to the partnership that is not secured by property owned by the taxpayer
      - Borrowed amounts used in the activity that are protected against loss, for example by a guarantee

4) Passive Activity Limitations
Losses from passive activities can only be deducted to the extent of passive income.

Item 1: Ordinary business income (loss)
The amount reported in box 1 is the taxpayer's share of the entity's ordinary business-related income or loss. Where this amount ends up on the taxpayer's Form 1040 depends on whether the activity that generated the income was passive or non-passive to the taxpayer.

Non-passive income, non-passive losses, and passive income are **fully** reported as Supplemental Income or Loss on Form 1040, Schedule E.

For **passive losses**, Form 8582-Passive Activity Loss Limitations must be used to determine the portion of the loss that can be reported. Once determined, the **allowable portion** is also reported as Supplemental Income or Loss on Form 1040, Schedule E.

Item 2: Net rental real estate income (loss)
Generally, amounts reported in box 2 are treated as passive activity income (loss) for all partners. However, the income (loss) in box 2 is not considered to be from a passive activity if the taxpayer was a real estate professional who materially participated in the activity. If the partnership had more than one rental real estate activity, a statement identifying the income or loss from each activity will be attached to the K-1.
Net rental real estate income (loss) from box 2 is reported as Supplemental Income or Loss on Form 1040, Schedule E.

Item 3: Other net rental income (loss)
Amounts reported by the entity for other net rental income (loss) are considered to be passive to all partners. If the partnership had more than one rental activity, a statement identifying the income or loss from each activity will be attached to the K-1.
Other net rental income (loss) is reported as Supplemental Income or Loss on Form 1040, Schedule E.

Item 4: Guaranteed payments
>Guaranteed payments are payments to partners which are guaranteed to be paid, whether there is income or loss in the partnership. Guaranteed payments are considered net earnings from self-employment. If the partnership pays for any fringe benefits of a partner, such as health insurance, they are considered guaranteed payments to partner. These amounts should be reported by the taxpayer as Supplemental Income or Loss on <u>Form 1040, Schedule E</u>.
>
>Portfolio Income (Loss) Items
>Portfolio income or loss (shown in boxes 5 through 9b and in box 11, code A) is not subject to passive activity limitations. Portfolio income includes income (not derived in the ordinary course of a trade or business) from interest, ordinary dividends, annuities or royalties, as well as, short-term and long-term capital gains and losses on the sale of property that produces such income or is held for investment.

Item 5: Interest income
>Interest income should be reported by the taxpayer on <u>Form 1040</u>, schedule B. Interest on municipal bonds are reported to the partner on the K-1 and then flows through to the front of Form 1040 as tax exempt interest income.

Item 6: Ordinary and Qualified Dividends
>Ordinary and qualified dividend income should be reported by the taxpayer on <u>Form 1040</u>.

Item 7: Royalties
>Royalty income should be reported by the taxpayer as Supplemental Income and Loss on <u>Form 1040, Schedule E</u>.

Item 8: Net short-term capital gain (loss)
>Net short-term capital gain (loss) should be reported by the taxpayer on <u>Form 1040, Schedule D Capital Gains and Losses</u>.

Item 9a: Net long-term capital gain (loss)
>Net long-term capital gain (loss) should be reported by the taxpayer on <u>Form 1040, Schedule D Capital Gains and Losses</u>.

Item 9b: Collectibles (28%) gain (loss)
>Gain (loss) from collectibles should be reported on the 28% Rate Gain Worksheet that is contained in the instructions to <u>Form 1040, Schedule D Capital Gains and Losses</u>.

Item 9c: Unrecaptured section 1250 gain
>Unrecaptured section 1250 gain should be reported on the Unrecaptured Section 1250 Gain Worksheet which is contained in the instructions to <u>Form 1040, Schedule D Capital Gains and Losses</u>.

Item 10: Net section 1231 gain (loss)
>Net section 1231 gain (loss) is reported by the taxpayer on <u>Form 4797, Sales of Business Property</u>.
>
>Whether or not the gain (loss) resulted from a passive activity will determine the exact treatment of the gain (loss) on Form 4797.

Item 11: Other income (loss)
>Box 11 may contain numerous other items of income or loss that the partnership may pass through to the taxpayer. The more common items are addressed here in detail. In each case, the

partnership will provide a description of the item so that the taxpayer can properly report the income (loss).

Portfolio income (loss), other than interest, ordinary dividend, royalty, and capital gain (loss) income is indicated in this item. The partnership attaches a statement describing what type portfolio income is reported. This income (loss) should be reported by the taxpayer as Supplemental Income and Loss on Form 1040, Schedule E.

Involuntary conversions display the taxpayer's net gain (loss) resulting from any involuntary conversions due to casualty or theft. This gain (loss) should be reported on Form 4684, Casualties and Thefts.

Cancellation of debt is generally reported by the taxpayer on Form 1040 as an increase in gross income.

Item 12: Section 179 deduction
The Section 179 deduction indicated in box 12 should be added to the total cost of section 179 property placed in service during the year from other sources, to complete Part I of Form 4562, Depreciation and Amortization. The maximum section 179 that the partnership can take is $500,000 and there is a phase-out beginning at $2,010,000. For every dollar of purchases that go over $2,010,000, there is a dollar reduction of the $500,000.

Item 13: Other deductions
Similar to the other income (loss) items, box 13 lists various other deductions that partnership is passing through to the taxpayer. The more common items are addressed here in detail. Other items that could be included here relate to Section 59(e)(2) expenditures, pre-productive period expenses, the commercial revitalization deduction, reforestation expenses, domestic production activities and QPAI information, and numerous other deductions.

Several items listed here pertain to the entity's **charitable contributions**. The partnership will provide a statement that indicates which charitable contributions subject to the 50%, 30%, and 20% adjusted gross income limitations. All charitable contributions listed should be reported by the taxpayer on Form 1040, Schedule A, Itemized Deductions.

Investment interest expense reported here should be combined with the taxpayer's investment income and expenses from other sources to figure how much total investment interest is deductible. This information is also required to compute the taxpayer's investment interest expense deduction. For additional detail regarding investment interest income and expenses, refer to the Itemized Deductions section.

Deductions related to **royalty income** should be reported by the taxpayer on Form 1040, Schedule E.
Deductions clearly and directly allocable to **portfolio** income (other than investment interest expense and section 212 expenses from a REMIC) are generally reported as an itemized deduction on the taxpayer's Form 1040, Schedule A.

Amounts paid for **medical insurance** by the partnership during the tax year for insurance that constitutes medical care the taxpayer, spouse, dependents, and children under age 27 who are not dependents. These amounts can generally be deducted on Form 1040 whether or not the taxpayer itemizes deductions. If the taxpayer does itemize deductions, any amounts not deducted on Form 1040 should be reported on Schedule A, Itemized Deductions.

Education assistance benefits should be deducted on Schedule E (Form 1040) up to the $5,250 limitation. For more information on the exclusion of education assistance benefits, see the section on Gross Income.

Dependent care benefits received by the taxpayer from the entity may or may not be included in gross income. To determine what portion of the benefit can be excluded from gross income, complete Form 2441, Child and Dependent Care Expenses.

Pension and IRA payments made the taxpayer's behalf (including payments to an IRA, a qualified plan, a simplified employee pension (SEP), or a SIMPLE IRA plan) should be reported by the taxpayer on Form 1040. For payments made to a defined benefit plan, the entity should provide a statement showing the amount of the benefit accrued for the current tax year. For further information regarding the tax treatment of retirement plan contributions and withdrawals, see Deductions for AGI.

Item 14: Self-employment earnings (loss)

The taxpayer's partnership net earnings from self-employment income should be reported on Form 1040, Schedule SE.

General partners must reduce this amount before entering it on Schedule SE (Form 1040) by any section 179 expense deduction claimed, unreimbursed partnership expenses claimed, and depletion claimed on oil and gas properties.

Net earnings from self-employment should not be reduced by any separately stated deduction for health insurance expenses.

If a partnership self-employment loss is reported, only the deductible amount on should be reported Schedule SE (Form 1040).

Item 15: Credits

There are numerous credits that can be passed on to the taxpayer from the entity. They are listed in box 15 of the K-1 and should be reported by the taxpayer on the appropriate tax form. The entity provides a statement which identifies the type of credit and any other information the taxpayer might need to properly take the credit.

For example, a Work Opportunity Credit that is passed on to the taxpayer should be reported on Form 5884, Work Opportunity Credit.

Item 16: Foreign transactions

Information about foreign transactions, including the foreign country in which the transaction took place and any gain (loss) that resulted from the transaction is reported to the taxpayer in item 16.

Item 17: Alternative minimum tax (AMT) items

The information reported related to AMT items should be used by the taxpayer in conjunction with information from other sources (including the taxpayer's AMT adjustments and tax preference items) to prepare Form 6251, Alternative Minimum Tax – Individuals.

Item 18: Tax-exempt income and nondeductible expenses

The taxpayer's share of **tax-exempt interest** received or accrued by the partnership during the year is reported by the taxpayer on Form 1040 as an item of information. The taxpayer's adjusted basis in the entity is increased by this amount.

Income indicated here as **other** tax-exempt income increases the taxpayer's adjusted basis in the partnership, but should not be reported on Form 1040.

Nondeductible expenses paid or incurred by the partnership that are indicated in box 18 are not deductible on the taxpayer's individual return. The taxpayer's adjusted basis in the partnership should be decreased by this amount.

Item 19: Distributions

This item shows distributions made to the taxpayer by the entity. Distributions can be made in the form of cash, marketable securities, property, etc.

If distributions to the taxpayer exceed the taxpayer's adjusted basis in the entity immediately before the distribution, the excess is treated as gain from the sale or exchange of the partnership interest.

Item 20: Other information

Numerous other miscellaneous items such as section 179 deduction recapture and unrelated business taxable income are included in item 20.

C. Adjustments & Deductions to Arrive at Adjusted Gross Income & Taxable Income

> Calculate the amount of adjustments and deductions to arrive at adjusted gross income and taxable income on federal Form 1040 – U.S. Individual Income Tax Return.

> Analyze client-provided documentation to determine the validity of the deductions taken to arrive at adjusted gross income or taxable income on federal Form 1040 – U.S. Individual Income Tax Return.

Once gross income is determined, adjustments and deductions (if available) are applied to reduce taxable income.

Deductibility of expenses follows a similar rule as "includability" of income in a taxpayer's gross income. Income is generally included for tax purposes unless there is a specific IRS rule that excludes it. Conversely, expenses should be considered NOT deductible unless a specific IRS rule exists that allows it to be deducted.

Expenses benefitting more than one period must be capitalized rather than expensed.
There are two broad categories of deductions:
- The first category includes a group of deductions that are subtracted from gross income to arrive at Adjusted Gross Income or AGI. These are deductions FOR AGI, also known as "above the line" deductions.
- The second category of deductions includes deductions that are subtracted FROM AGI, also known as "below the line" deductions. Taxpayers who itemize deductions reduce AGI by individual allowable deductions. Taxpayers who choose not to itemize deductions reduce AGI by the standard deduction.

These deductions, plus personal exemptions, are subtracted to arrive at taxable income.

Taxpayer expenses can be divided into three mutually exclusive categories:
1) Trade/Business
   Expenses related to business operations are deductible from income if they **are ordinary, necessary, and** (in the case of compensation payments) **reasonable.**

   An expense is considered "**ordinary**" if it is customary or usual in the taxpayer's business. An unusual expense can be considered ordinary if it is reasonably consistent with the business operations.

   An expense is considered to be "**necessary**" if the taxpayer deems the expense appropriate and useful for maintaining and/or developing the business operations. The expense does not have to be essential to be considered necessary.

   Compensation must be "**reasonable**" to be deductible as a trade or business expense. Issues surrounding whether or not compensation expenses are reasonable most often arise when compensation is paid to a related party (for example, a family member or company stockholders)

> *Hint:* Ordinary, necessary and reasonable expenses of operating illegal businesses (**other than illegal drug businesses**) are deductible as business expenses as long as the expense itself is not against public policy.

2) Investment
Expenses related to taxpayer investments, including those related to management or maintenance of property, are deductible if they are ordinary and necessary.

3) Personal
Personal expenses can NOT be deducted unless specifically provided for in the IRC. Examples of deductible personal expenses include charitable contributions, mortgage interest, and tax planning services.

> *Hint*: Expenses incurred in connection with the determination of any tax are deductible.

a. Disallowed Deductions
Certain items are simply never deductible or are only deductible under very specific circumstances as indicated in the IRC.
- No expenses can be deducted if they are against public policy
    - Payments in violation of public policy are not necessary and therefore not deductible (e.g., bribes, fines, penalties)
    - Expenses of operating an illegal **drug** business are NOT deductible

> *Hint:* Although operating expenses related to the operation of an illegal drug business are not deductible, COGS can still be deducted when calculating the illegal business's gross income.

Multiple Choice
REG 4-Q32

- No expenses can be deducted if the expense was used to generate tax-exempt income.

> ***Example***: Following this rule, the taxpayer may not deduct premiums for life insurance in which the taxpayer is directly or indirectly the beneficiary, since life insurance proceeds when paid upon death are excluded from gross income. Similarly, an employer may deduct the group term life insurance premiums paid when the insured employee or other named beneficiary would receive the proceeds.

- Business expenses related to lobbying at the state and federal level are NOT deductible.

> *Hint:* These expenses ARE permitted when related to lobbying at the city and county

- For publicly traded companies, executive compensation for the CEO and the four other most highly paid officers that exceed $1M per person are NOT deductible unless the income is based on a performance-based compensation plan
- Other specifically disallowed deductions include:
    - Personal life insurance premiums
    - Funeral and burial expenses
    - Disability insurance premiums
    - Fees and licenses (for autos, marriage, dog tags)
    - Illegal bribes or kickbacks
    - Fines and tax penalties
    - Campaign expenses of a candidate for any office
    - Political contributions

b. Deductions FOR AGI ("above the line")

Generally speaking, deductions that can be taken FOR AGI ("above the line") are subject to fewer limits than itemized deductions. They are often claimed on separate schedules of the Form 1040 where the deductions serve to directly offset the income generated by a specific activity. For example, trade expenses directly offset trade income on Schedule C; rental expenses directly offset rental income on Schedule E.

These are the most common **deductions for AGI (above the line)**:
- Business expenses associated with a trade or self-employment
- Expenses arising from rents and royalties
- One half of self-employment tax
- Alimony and separate maintenance payments
- Unreimbursed, qualified moving expenses
- IRA and self-employed retirement plan contributions
- Student loan interest
- Jury duty pay remitted to employer
- Contributions to Health Savings Accounts
- Attorney's fees and court costs for discrimination suits and whistleblower awards
- Forfeited interest or penalties paid on premature withdrawals from a time-savings account
- Domestic production activities deduction
- Losses from the sale or exchange of property
- Expenses of elementary and secondary teachers

1) Business expenses associated with a "trade" or self-employment

Business expenses that are deductible for AGI are expenses incurred by a taxpayer who is self-employed or who operates a trade or business.

> *Hint:* A **"trade"** is defined as an activity with a continuous level of profit seeking; i.e. self-employed taxpayer who depends on this activity for his livelihood or a taxpayer who operates a business "on the side."

Deductible taxpayer business expenses are reported on Schedule C and netted against the business' gross income if self-employed. If not self-employed, the business expenses are reported by an employee on for 2106, and then they flow through to schedule A, miscellaneous 2% itemized deductions.

i. **Details regarding the deductibility of business expenses**
- Dues paid to professional organizations are deductible as business expenses. For example, dues paid to join accounting, medical, legal associations; chambers of commerce, public service organizations (such as Kiwanis, Rotary, etc.)

> *Hint:* Dues paid for recreation clubs are treated differently by the IRS and are NOT deductible. See below for more detail on this topic.

- Expenses related to the first telephone line to a taxpayer's residence cannot be deducted and is instead treated as a non-deductible personal expense. Other expenses related to the line ARE deductible, however, if they represent legitimate business expenses (for example, long distance charges, equipment rental, etc.)
- Certain meal and entertainment expenses that are directly related to active conduct of the taxpayer's trade can be deducted up to certain limits
    o To be deductible, the taxpayer must be in attendance

- NO DEDUCTION is allowed for:
  - Dues paid to membership clubs (such as golf, country, airline, hotel, etc.)
- The deductible cost of tickets to entertainment events (concerts, etc.) is limited to its face value even if the actual cost was more.
- The deduction is limited to 50% of the allowable total meals and entertainment cost. This 50% limit can be waived if:
  - The recipient of the meal or entertainment includes the full amount in income as a fringe benefit
  - The cost is for a traditional company event paid for by the employer (e.g., annual Christmas party)
  - The expenses relate to a qualified charitable fund-raiser
  - The meals and entertainment that were purchased, are then sold at full cost
- Required recordkeeping:
  - Records must be kept for meals and entertainment that substantiate amount, who, when, where, and why
  - Receipts must be maintained for any expense over $75

- Expenses related to business travel (other than meals and entertainment) are deductible if they are incurred in the active conduct of trade or business when "away from home."
  - Business travel expenses are 100% deductible and include transportation between two business locations, but DO NOT include commuting expenses from home to job.
  - NO deduction is allowed for expenses related to attending a convention, seminar, investment meeting, or when traveling for educational purposes.

- Business Gifts
  - The total deduction allowed is limited to $25 per recipient per year.
  - Deductions for advertising or promotional gifts of $4 or less are not limited.

- Taxpayers can deduct awards OF TANGIBLE PERSONAL PROPERTY to employees for safety or length of service costing up to:
  - $400 under a non-qualified plan.
  - $1,600 under a written, non-discriminatory qualified plan. The average cost of all items awarded during the year must be $400 or less.

- Expenses related to the business use of the taxpayer's home (i.e., home office) are deductible on Schedule C, if self-employed and a miscellaneous 2% itemized deduction, if the taxpayer is an employee.
  - Home office expenses can be deducted for the portion of residence that is used as an office if one of the following requirements are met:
    - The home office is used exclusively and on a regular basis as the taxpayer's principal place of business
    - The home office is used as an ordinary meeting place for clients
    - The home office is used for business management or administration if there is no other fixed location used for this purpose
    - The home office is the location where the primary income-generating functions of the trade/business are conducted. In this case, the "primary function" can NOT include childcare or storage.

- Expenses related to the home office must be allocated between the portion of the dwelling used as residence and the portion used as an office
- Deductions for the use of a home office are limited to income after non-office expenses. To determine that limit, the activity's income is first reduced by:
  - All other allowable deductible expenses
  - All business deductions that cannot be allocated to the use of the home (e.g., supplies, travel expenses, etc.)
- Allowable home-office-related expenses are applied toward income in a specific order:
  1. Mortgage interest and real estate taxes are applied first.
  2. Cash expenses are applied next.
  3. Depreciation is applied last.
- Excess deductions that cannot be taken in the current year due to business income limitations can be carried forward to future years, but will be subject to the same rules.
- IRS provides a simplified method: multiply allowable square footage by $5 with a max allowable square footage of 300, limiting the deduction to $1,500.

- Bad debts arising from a taxpayer's involvement in a trade or business can be deducted when deemed totally or partially worthless.
  - An item cannot be deductible as both a bad debt and a loss. If it is eligible for either treatment, it must be treated as bad debt.
  - Bad debts can only be deducted using the direct write off method (no allowance for bad debt can be deducted). The taxpayer must be on accrual basis.

  > *Hint:* Non-business bad debts are deductible as short-term capital losses (as computed on Schedule D) and may ONLY be deducted when they become totally worthless.

  - Non-business bad debt is any bonafide loan not made in a trade capacity.
  - Whether loan is bona fide or a disguised gift depends on facts such as whether interest is charged and collateral required
  - Non-business bad debts are deductible FOR AGI as short-term capital losses in the year of complete worthlessness (no partial worthlessness allowed) and are subject to the overall loss limitation for individual capital losses of $3,000

- Certain expenses related to taxpayer self-employment are deductible to arrive at AGI as follows:
  - 50% of self-employment tax
  - 100% of self-employed medical insurance premiums including insurance for spouse, dependents, and any child of the taxpayer under age 27 as of tax year end.
    - This deduction is only allowed if the taxpayer or spouse is NOT eligible to participate in an employer-subsidized health plan.
    - The deduction cannot exceed self-employment income

- - Any premiums not deductible under these rules are treated as an itemized medical expense deduction FROM AGI.
  - Contributions to tax-favored retirement plans for the self-employed (sometimes called a Keogh plan) are deductible for AGI.
    - A taxpayer can make contributions for the taxable year up until the due date of the return (including extensions).

Multiple Choice

REG 4-Q33

- Costs related to the acquisition of trade-related property and inventory must generally be capitalized under the Uniform Capitalization Rules (UNICAP) of Code Sec. 263A Uniform capitalization rules require businesses to capitalize certain costs that benefit or are incurred because of the *production* or *resale* activities of the business. These costs are not allowed to be immediately expensed as operating expenses. Instead, they are required to be added to the basis of property or inventory and are later recovered through depreciation, amortization, or COGS when the property is sold or disposed of.

Applicable entities include entities that
a. Produce and use tangible personal property in a trade or business.
b. Produce and sell tangible personal property to customers.

However, if the average annual gross receipts for the past three years do not exceed $10 million, the entity is called a small retailer. Small retailers are not subject to the uniform capitalization rules.

Uniform capitalization rules (UNICAP) requires that all direct and indirect costs be capitalized as part of the cost of the property for:
- Manufacturing or constructing real or personal property, or
- In purchasing or holding property for resale.

Capitalized costs:
a) Direct costs – Capitalized direct costs include direct materials and direct labor.
b) Indirect Costs – Capitalized indirect costs can include warehousing costs, off-site storage, repair and maintenance, utilities, rent, indirect labor (wages of supervisors and quality control specialists; employee pension and benefit plans) indirect materials and supplies, taxes (excluding income taxes), depreciation and amortization, depletion, insurance, licensing and franchising costs, engineering and design, repackaging, spoilage and scrap, environmental remediation expense and etc. Handling costs, such as expenses attributable to handling, processing, assembling, repackaging, and other similar activities, including transporting property acquired for resale, are capitalized to inventory.

- These expenditures then become part of property's basis and are recovered through depreciation expenses, which then ARE deductible.

- What does NOT need to be capitalized? The UNICAP rules do not apply to the following expenses:
  - Advertising and marketing
  - Selling
  - Research and experimentation expenditures
  - Mine development and exploration costs
  - Property held for personal use
  - Freelance authors, photographers, and artists whose personal efforts create the product.

Multiple Choice
REG 4-Q34 through REG 4-Q39

ii. **Expenses associated with rental and royalty activities**
   For vacation homes that are rented:
   - Expenses associated with the rental of a vacation home are subject to certain conditions and limitations
     - If there is any personal use of the property (it is used by the taxpayer or anyone else to whom a fair rent is not charged), the deductible amount on Schedule E is calculated as:

   $$\frac{\text{# of days rented}}{\text{total days used}} * \text{total expenses} = \text{Amount deductible}$$

   For residences that are rented:
   - If the residence is rented for less than 15 days in a year, it is treated as a personal residence, and the rental income is not reported and rental expense deductions NOT allowed. The mortgage interest and property taxes related to the property are deductible on Schedule A, Itemized Deductions
   - If the residence is rented for more than 15 days in a year **and IS NOT used** for personal purposes for more than the greater of **fourteen days or, 10% of number of days rented**, the residence is considered to be a rental property. In this case, all expenses such as utilities, maintenance expenses, and property taxes on the property must be allocated between the personal use and rental use. For the property taxes, the amount allocated to personal use can be deducted as an itemized deduction. Any mortgage interest allocated to personal use cannot be deducted as an itemized deduction, because the property is not considered a qualified residence.
   - If the residence is rented for more than 15 days in a year **and IS used** for personal purposes for more than the greater of **fourteen days or, 10% of number of days rented**, the residence is considered personal/rental use residence. In this case, all expenses must be allocated between the personal use and rental use. The prorated real estate taxes and mortgage interest must be deducted first from gross rental income. If the result is positive net rental income, expenses other than depreciation that are deductible are

maintenance, utilities and insurance are deducted next. Then, depreciation is allowed as a deduction on any positive net rental income remaining. Any disallowed rental expenses will be carried forward to be used in future years and will be subject to the same limitations.

Multiple Choice

REG 4-Q40 through REG 4-41

iii. **Alimony and separate maintenance payments**
Alimony and separate maintenance payments are deductible to arrive at AGI. Child support payments are not deductible to arrive at AGI.

iv. **Moving expenses**
Unreimbursed qualified moving expenses that are associated with a job change or with a taxpayer's first job are deductible for AGI if several conditions are met.
- The new job location must add 50 miles to the taxpayer's old commute or, for a new job, the place of employment must be at least 50 miles from the taxpayer's former residence
- To deduct the expenses, the taxpayer must be active in the new job for a substantial period of time after the move.
    - 39 weeks during 12 months following move if working for an employer
    - If self-employed, 39 weeks during 12 months following move plus 78 weeks during next 24 months
- Qualified expenses for the move are limited to reasonable amounts paid for the following:
    - To move household goods
    - Transportation costs (NOT MEALS) for taxpayers and others who live with the taxpayer
    - If the taxpayer's personal auto is used for the move, the taxpayer can deduct actual auto expenses or use the standard rate (23 cents/mile)
    - Costs of storing and insuring possessions while moving are deductible but are limited to any consecutive 30-day period after the possessions are moved from the former residence and before delivered to new residence

Hint: This deduction is reported on Form 1040, FOR AGI.

Multiple Choice

REG 4-Q42

v. **IRA and Self-Employed Retirement Plan Contributions**
- As discussed in the gross income section, regardless of deductibility, total IRA contributions are limited to the lesser of:
    - $5,500 or 100% of compensation including alimony (up to $6,500 for taxpayers 50 years and over, at tax year end)
    - For married filing jointly taxpayers, each taxpayer can contribute up to $5,500 so long as the combined earned income of both spouses is at least equal to the amounts contributed to the IRA
- Employees and self-employed taxpayers who are NOT active participants in an employer-sponsored retirement plan can deduct up to the total allowed IRA contribution limit.

Taxpayers who are active participants in an employer retirement plan or a Keogh plan can still contribute up to the $5,500 limit.
- Reporting requirements:
    - If a traditional IRA includes nondeductible contributions and a distribution was received in 2017, Form 8606 must be used to determine the amount of the 2017 IRA distribution that is tax-free.

vi. **Student loan interest**
- A student loan is one where the proceeds are used to pay for the "qualified education expenses" of the taxpayer, spouse, and individuals who qualify as dependents at the time of the expenditure.
- **Qualified education expenses** include tuition, fees, and room and board expenditures reduced by educational exclusions (scholarships, education IRAs, education savings bonds, etc.).
- There is no time limit on the number of years the deduction can be taken so long as the loan exists.
- The student must be enrolled on at least a half-time basis.
- Deduction not available if the student is claimed as a dependent on another taxpayer's return
- Deduction limited to $2,500 of interest. The $2,500 is phased out if AGI exceeds certain limits. Because the phase-out changes every year, the candidate will not be required to know the phase-outs.

> *New Exam Content:* Tax years that begin after 6/29/15 as a condition of receiving the American Opportunity Tax Credit and Lifetime Learning Credit taxpayer must receive a Form 1098-T containing all the information required by that form.

> *New Exam Content:* This credit was retroactively extended as part of the Protecting Americans from Tax Hikes Bill of 2015 (PATH Act).

Multiple Choice

REG 4-Q43 through REG 4-Q45

vii. **Jury Duty pay remitted to an employer**
- Regular compensation and jury duty pay are included in gross income. The employee then deducts the amount of jury duty pay that was turned over to the employer in return for compensation received during the period of jury duty service.

viii. **Contributions to Health Savings Accounts (HSAs)**
- Taxpayers who are covered under a high deductible health plan (HDHP) and are not covered under any other health plan that is not an HDHP can deduct contributions to an HSA up to the maximum annual limit of $3,350 for self-only coverage and $6,700 for family coverage.
- The maximum HSA contribution (and allowable above the line deduction) is increased by an additional catch up contribution amount of $1,000 per year for

individuals 55 and older as of the last day of the calendar year who are not enrolled in Medicare.
- There is no requirement that the individual has earnings.
- Contributions can be made until the account holder's tax return due date without extensions.

ix. **Attorney's fees and court costs for civil rights suits and whistleblower awards**
- The allowable above the line deduction is limited to the amount of the settlement that is included in the taxpayer's gross income for the tax year.

x. **Forfeited interest or penalties on premature withdrawals**
- In the case of forfeited interest, gross income includes the full amount of interest received. The forfeited interest amount is then subtracted as an above the line deduction.

xi. **Elementary and Secondary Teacher Expenses**
Eligible teachers are allowed to take a $250 deduction ($500 for joint filers) for unreimbursed expenses related to the purchase of classroom materials, including books, supplies, software, and computer equipment.

> *New Exam Content:* This credit was permanently extended as part of the Protecting Americans from Tax Hikes Bill of 2015 (PATH Act).

xii. **A domestic production activities deduction** (DPAD) was enacted to change a variety of tax provisions so that U.S. corporations would produce more in the United States than in foreign countries. Congress created DPAD to give a deduction based on the amount of income from manufacturing certain qualifying products in the U.S. The DPAD is shown as a deduction to arrive at AGI.

xiii. **Repayments of supplemental unemployment compensation**

c. Deductions FROM AGI ("below the line")
Once Adjusted Gross Income is determined by applying available above the line deductions, the next step is to apply **either** itemized deductions or a standard deduction, along with personal exemptions, to arrive at taxable income.

1) Determination of the total available "below the line" deductions
All taxpayers are allowed to take either a standard deduction or to itemize deductions. To choose which will provide the greatest reduction in taxable income, the taxpayer should:
- Evaluate the standard deduction
- Calculate the total of all itemized deductions after applying the limits specific to each specific type of deduction
- Claim whichever is larger, thereby reducing taxable income as much as possible.

> *Hint:* Spouses filing separately must either both itemize or both take the standard deduction.

d. Standard deduction
The standard deduction is a deduction from AGI (below the line) that can be claimed by most taxpayers instead of itemized deductions. Standard deduction amounts are indexed for inflation and vary according to the taxpayer's filing status, age, whether the taxpayer is a dependent, and whether the taxpayer is blind.

- Basic standard deduction (2017):
  - Married filing jointly or surviving spouse $12,700
  - Married filing separately $6,350
  - Head of Household $9,350
  - Single $6,350
- An additional amount is added for each applicable item:
  - Unmarried/HOH and age 65+ $1,550
  - Unmarried/HOH and blind $1,550
  - Married/Surviving Spouse and age 65+ $1,250
  - Married/Surviving Spouse and blind $1,250

Certain taxpayers are not entitled to the standard deduction. These taxpayers include:
- A married individual filing "married filing separately" whose spouse itemizes deductions. Married individuals who file separately must either both take the standard deduction or both itemize deductions.
- An individual who was a nonresident alien or dual status alien during any part of the year (see below for certain exceptions)
- An individual who files a return for a period of fewer than 12 months due to a change in his or her annual accounting period
- An estate or trust, common trust fund, or partnership

e. Itemized deductions

Itemized deductions are reported on <u>Form 1040, Schedule A</u> and consist primarily of non-trade business expenses and a few personal expenses that are specifically allowed by the IRS.

Most personal expenses that can be itemized fit into these broad categories:
- Medical expenses
- Taxes
- Interest
- Charitable contributions
- Casualty and theft losses
- Gambling losses
- Miscellaneous deductions

> **Hint:** Some of the itemized expenses listed here, when related to a taxpayer's self-employment or trade or when incurred in the production of rents and royalties, would be **above the line** deductions as described above. However, when they are **unrelated** to the taxpayer's trade or business, they are itemized deductions.

1) Medical expenses

   Medical expenses include any qualified expenditure for the care, prevention, cure or treatment of a disease or bodily function.

   i. Examples of deductible items include:
   - Dental, medical, or hospital care
   - Equipment (e.g., crutches, artificial limbs)
   - Medical and hospital insurance premiums, except disability and accident premiums.
   - Prescribed medicines plus insulin (insulin is the only drug that can be reimbursed without a prescription)
   - Qualifying long-term care expenses and insurance
   - Alcohol and drug rehabilitation expenses
   - Weight loss programs if part of medical treatment for obesity or another disease
   - Stop-smoking programs and prescriptions for nicotine withdrawal
   - Nursing home expenses if primary reason for being there is medical

- Cosmetic surgery ONLY IF necessary to treat a congenital or accident-related deformity or disfiguring disease
- A procedure to promote proper body function or prevent or treat illness or disease
- Expenses incurred by physically handicapped individuals for removal of structural barriers in their residences to accommodate their condition (for example – entrance or exit ramps, widening doorways, railing installation, etc.)
- Medical related capital expenditures can be deducted if all of these conditions are met:
    - The expense was incurred based on doctor's advice
    - Family facility primarily used by patient alone
    - The expenditure is reasonable

> *Hint:* The deduction for medical related capital expenditures is limited to the extent it exceeds resulting increase in property value.

Multiple Choice

REG 4-Q46

- Qualified auto expenditures (actual expenses or 23 cents per mile plus parking and tolls)
- Meals and lodging provided by a hospital during medical treatment or by rehabilitation facility during addiction treatment, up to a certain limit:
    - Lodging is deductible up to $50/night. The deduction is also available to the person required to travel with the patient.

Multiple Choice

REG 4-Q47 through REG 4-Q48

ii. Examples of NON-DEDUCTIBLE items:
- Funeral, burial, cremation expenses
- Non-prescription drugs (except insulin)
- Bottled water, toiletries, etc.
- Unnecessary cosmetic surgery simply for improvement of appearance. Examples include teeth whitening, liposuction, etc.
- Meals while traveling for medical reasons unless those meals are part of the treatment
- Costs of diet foods are not deductible if they replace food the taxpayer would normally consume

iii. Medical Expense Deduction Computation and Limitations
Qualified expenses paid by the taxpayer for the taxpayer, taxpayer's spouse, and any dependents that exceed a defined limit based on AGI are deductible.

> *Hint:* Relationship, support, and citizenship tests must be met to deduct a dependent's medical expenses. However, unlike other deductions, gross income and joint return tests do not apply for this purpose.

> *Hint:* The child of separated or divorced parents is considered a dependent of both parents for qualified medical expenses.

Only the portion of qualified medical expenses that exceed 7.5% of the taxpayer's AGI are deductible.

Deductible Medical Expenses = **Qualified Medical Expenses** − **Any Medical Expense Reimbursements** − **7.5% of AGI**

Multiple Choice

REG 4-Q49

If deductions are itemized and an expense deducted in an earlier year is reimbursed, the reimbursement must be included in gross income in the year received.

Multiple Choice

REG 4-Q50

2) Taxes

Certain taxes are deductible by the person on whom the taxes are imposed. They can be deducted in year paid or withheld (even if they relate to a different tax year).

i. What taxes ARE deductible:
   - **Income** taxes imposed by state, local, or foreign governments (NOT FEDERAL TAXES)
     - Includes any withholdings from salary, estimated payments made, and payments made for prior year taxes during the tax year
   - Personal proper**ty taxes based on property value (ad valorem)**
   - **Real estate** taxes (state/local/foreign) on personal use property
     - When real property is sold, the deduction is apportioned between buyer and seller on a daily basis (regardless of whether the costs are actually apportioned at the sale); the buyer is allocated the date of sale itself;
     - Special assessments for **property repairs or maintenance** ARE NOT deductible as taxes but, are added to the property's basis.

Hint: Property taxes on property used for a business can be deducted as a business expense (i.e. an above the line deduction).

ii. What taxes are NOT deductible:
   - Federal income taxes
   - State and local fees
   - Federal/state/local death, estate, or gift taxes are generally not deductible
   - Special assessments for **improvements** are generally NOT deductible. These assessments are instead added to the taxpayer's basis in the property.
   - Fees and Licenses are not deductible
   - Social security and other employment taxes:
     - Paid by employee (including self-employment taxes)
     - Paid by employer on wages of domestic employee (e.g., maid, nanny)

Hint: All taxes that are allowed as itemized deductions are reported on Schedule A.

Multiple Choice

REG 4-Q51

3) Interest
   There are a few general rules on the deductibility of interest:
   - Any interest that is related to the production of tax-exempt income is NOT deductible
   - Prepaid interest must be allocated to years to which payments relate, regardless of whether the taxpayer uses the cash or accrual method. Taxpayers must allocate and deduct prepaid interest ratably over the life of the loan.
   - Personal interest is, generally speaking, NOT deductible:
     - Personal interest includes any form of interest incurred when purchasing an asset for personal use, interest on income tax underpayments
     - There are certain types of personal interest that ARE deductible, including:
       - **Qualified Residence Interest:** Mortgage interest paid on debt secured by a taxpayer's personal residence can be deducted as an itemized deduction on Schedule A
         - This deduction applies to interest on debt related to the taxpayer's principal home plus a second home
         - Interest on a maximum of $1M of acquisition indebtedness can be deducted if the debt is used to purchase, construct or improve the residence
         - Interest on home equity loan is based on the lesser of $100,000 (or $50,000 if filing MFS) on loans secured by the residence, regardless of how the proceeds from the loan are used **OR**, the equity in the home (FMV less other mortgages).
         - Points are deductible if paid by the taxpayer in the year of purchase or when funds are obtained for improvement of the residence. Otherwise, points are considered prepaid interest that must be amortized over the life of the loan.
           - Fees paid for services (i.e., loan processing fees) do NOT qualify as points and are not deductible.
         - Mortgage prepayment penalties **are deductible** as interest

   > *New Exam Content:* Additional Information is now required on returns related to mortgage interest. For returns and statements due after 12/31/16, statements are now required to report:
   > - The outstanding principal on the mortgage at the beginning of the year
   > - The address of the property securing the mortgage
   > - The mortgage origination date.

   - Investment Interest Expense
     - The allowable deduction for investment interest expenses is limited to net investment income for non-corporate taxpayers
   - Investment expenses are interest paid or accrual on indebtedness, properly allocated to property held for investments, and includes:
     - Interest expense attributed to loans received to buy investments which generate portfolio income.
   - Investment income includes:
     - Interest
     - Dividends (other than qualified dividends)
     - Rents
     - Royalties and annuities if NOT derived from trade/business
     - Net short-term capital gains

- Net long-term capital gains, only if the taxpayer pays their regular individual income tax rate, instead of the lower rates for net long-term capital gains.

$$\text{Net Investment Income} = \text{Investment Income} - \text{Non-Interest Investment Expenses in Excess of AGI Limitations}$$

- Disallowed investment interest can be carried over indefinitely to future years, but the same limits apply. That is, it will be allowed only to the extent of net investment income in subsequent years

> *Example:* For 20X5, a taxpayer had $28,000 of investment interest expense and net investment income of $25,000. The deductible interest expense for 20X5 is limited to the net investment income of $25,000. The remaining $3,000 of the investment interest expense can be carried forward in future years as long as there is net investment income.

Multiple Choice

REG 4-Q52 through REG 4-Q53

4) **Charitable Contributions**
An itemized deduction is allowed for contributions of cash or property to qualified charities, subject to certain limits and reporting requirements.
Allowed charitable contributions are deductible in the year actually paid or donated, regardless of whether the taxpayer uses the cash or accrual method. Credit card charges are deductible, regardless of whether or not the actual cash has been paid.

> *Hint:* A pledge is not deductible – the donation must have actually been made to be deductible.

Qualified organizations include:
- Public charities operating for religious, scientific, educational or other charitable purposes; includes government subdivisions, hospitals, churches, schools, war veterans' organizations, fraternal orders, etc. so long as the donor or organization makes NO attempt to influence legislation or any political campaign
- A US state, possession or District of Columbia, if the contribution is used exclusively for public purposes
- Nonprofit cemetery companies, if the funds are dedicated to the care of the cemetery as a whole and not for the benefit of a particular lot or crypt

> *Hint:* Political organizations are not included in the definition of qualified charitable organizations.

i. What types of contributions **can** be deducted?
- Contributions of cash or property – NOT SERVICES – to a qualified organization, reduced by the FMV of any value or benefit received by the contributing taxpayer
- Dues, fees, assessments paid to qualified organizations (less any benefits received)

- Unreimbursed expenses incurred while providing free services to a qualified organization (including either actual auto expenses or standard rate of 14 cents/mile).

> *Hint:* The FMV of the services themselves is NOT DEDUCTIBLE.

ii. What types of contributions CANNOT be deducted?
- Dues, fees, assessments paid to veterans' or fraternal organizations, lodges, or country clubs

To take a deduction for charitable contributions, specific written records are required:
- Cash, check or other monetary contributions are ONLY DEDUCTIBLE if there is a canceled check, credit card statement or written proof from the charity.
- Contributions of $250 or more are only deductible with a written record from donee organization: The letter does not have to be attached to the Form 1040.
    - Record must be received by earlier of tax return due date including extensions, or date return is actually filed
    - Must state the amount of contribution
    - Must provide a good faith estimate of any goods/services provided to donor in exchange for contribution

> *Hint:* A cancelled check is NOT sufficient record.

- Contributions of property valued at > $5,000 are subject to these additional records are required when the contribution is non-cash:
    - The approximate date and manner in which the taxpayer originally acquired the donated property
    - The cost or basis of the property if it was held under 12 months
    - A description of the donated property
- For contributions of property valued at > $5,000, in addition to all reporting requirements above, the taxpayer must also obtain a qualified appraisal and attach a summary of the appraisal to the tax return.
- For contributions of property valued at > $500,000 in addition to all reporting requirements above, the taxpayer must also obtain a qualified appraisal and attach the qualified appraisal to the tax return.

iii. **Calculating the Charitable Contribution Deduction**

The maximum charitable contribution deduction under any circumstances is limited to **50% of AGI for aggregate contributions of cash and property**. In some cases, the deduction can be further limited:
- Deduction for contributions of long-term capital gain property to **public charities** is FMV, limited to 30% of AGI. If short-term capital gain property it is adjusted basis, limited to 50% of AGI
- Deductions for contributions of long-term capital gain property to **private charities** is FMV, limited to 20% of AGI (ignoring cash contributions)

Typically, public charities obtain funding from the general public, governmental grants, and private foundations. A private foundation typically receives its funding from a single source, such as a company, an individual or, a family. Private foundations do not solicit funds from the public.

> *Hint:* The 50% limit is applied before the 30% limits. The 30% limits are applied before 20% limits. All contributions are limited to 50% of AGI!

Any non-deductible excess can be carried forward for 5 years in all cases; the carryforwards remain subject to the 50%, 30%, and 20% limitations
- For LTCG property (Includes securities that are appreciated and held for more than 12 months). Securities are intangible assets
    - The deduction is the lesser of fair market value (FMV) or 30% of adjusted gross income (AGI); this limit will increase to 50% of AGI if the taxpayer elects to deduct only the basis.

Multiple Choice

REG 4-Q54

    - If tangible appreciated personal property held for more than one year, and is given to a charity, where the property is related to its tax-exempt purpose, deduction is the lesser of FMV, or 30% of AGI. Not related to its purpose, the deduction is lesser of adjusted basis or 50% of AGI.

Multiple Choice

REG 4-Q55

- For contributions of clothing and household goods (HHG), FMV value can be deducted only if items are in good condition or better; deduction may be disallowed for contributions of clothing or HHG of minimal value; the rule of minimal value, doesn't apply if value of a single item is greater than $500 and qualified appraisal is attached
- For donations of a car, boat, plane worth more than $500 and donee sells vehicle without significant use; donation limited to gross sales proceeds; donee must substantiate amount for donor to attach to donor's tax return. Donee must sell to take deduction.
- Reporting – noncash contributions are reported on Form 8283.

5) Personal Casualty Losses
A casualty is defined for tax purposes as a sudden unexpected event that damages or destroys an asset. Theft of an asset qualifies as a casualty event. Losses that result from a casualty are deductible subject to certain limitations.
Any type of asset can generate a deductible casualty loss, but the type of deduction depends on whether the asset was used for business or personal purposes.
- Casualty losses involving personal assets are eligible for treatment as an itemized deduction

- Losses of business assets are deductible as business losses, not itemized deductions, and are not subject to the same limits as personal casualty losses. The total destruction of a business asset due to a casualty is fully deductible for the adjusted basis less insurance proceeds. A partial business casualty loss is the lesser of the decrease in FMV or basis, less the insurance proceeds if any

Examples of deductible personal casualty losses include damage from a fire or storm, damage to property from vandalism, and damage to trees if it lowers the total real estate value.

Examples of losses that are NOT deductible include regular wear and tear, incidental expenses due to a casualty (such as temporary lodging), breakage of property resulting from regular use or by a family pet, or loss of future profits due to a casualty event.

> **Hint:** Casualty insurance premiums cannot be deducted.

> **Hint:** Appraisal fees, even if properly incurred to determine casualty losses, are deductible as 2% miscellaneous itemized deductions. They are not considered part of the casualty loss.

i. Calculating the casualty loss deduction
- For personal casualty losses, the **allowable deduction amount** is computed as:
  LESSER of:

  Asset's Adjusted Basis OR Decline in Asset FMV − Any Insurance Reimbursement − $100 Per Casualty − 10% of AGI*

- If a GAIN results from a casualty, all casualty gains and losses are netted. This netting is done **before** 10% of AGI reduction. A net casualty gain is usually treated as a capital gain.

When to apply the casualty loss deduction?
- Allowable casualty losses are deducted in the year the casualty occurs or when the theft is discovered.
- In the case of a federally declared disaster area, the loss is deductible in the year the loss occurs or in the previous year.

Multiple Choice

REG 4-Q56 through REG 4-Q57

There are two types of miscellaneous itemized deductions. One group which must exceed 2% of AGI and the second group is deductible in full. The group that is deductible in full includes these deductions:

1) Gambling losses to the extent of winnings
   - All gambling winnings, regardless of gambling losses, are reported as other income on Form 1040. Gambling losses are deductible only to the extent of gambling winnings.

Multiple Choice

REG 4-Q58

2) Amortizable bond premium
3) Impairment-related work expenses of handicapped taxpayers
4) Estate taxes related to income in respect of a decedent

Miscellaneous itemized deductions THAT EXCEED (2%) of AGI are usually referred to as "2% miscellaneous deductions." These deductions are allowed, but are subject to a "2% of AGI floor" limitation.

Multiple Choice

REG 4-Q59 through REG 4-Q60

i. Calculating the Deductible Amount of 2% Miscellaneous Deductions
For 2% itemized deductions that are subject to individual limits, those limits are applied first, before the 2% limitation is applied. The 2% floor is applied by totaling all of the itemized deductions that are subject to the floor and then subtracting 2% of AGI from that total. Any deduction amount that remains after 2% of taxpayer AGI is subtracted is then included with other itemized deductions.

> For example, only 50% of meal expenses are deductible. That limitation is applied first. The meal expenses are then combined with other allowable 2% miscellaneous deductions. The 2% total limit is then applied.

Miscellaneous itemized deductions up to the 2% floor are lost. No carryover is allowed. These are the major types of itemized deductions that are subject to the 2% floor limitation:

a) **Employee Business Expenses**
Employee business expenses that are not reimbursed at all or that are reimbursed under a **nonaccountable** plan are INCLUDED in gross income (for both FICA and income tax) and deductible as 2% miscellaneous expenses.

> *Hint:* Recall from the section about gross income, that reimbursement of employee expenses **under an accountable plan** are EXCLUDED from gross income (for FICA or income tax) and the corresponding expenses cannot then be taken as itemized deductions. Both the expense itself and the resulting reimbursement are simply ignored for tax purposes.

The total allowable employee business expenses are computed on Form 2106 and transferred to Schedule A as a 2% miscellaneous itemized deduction.

Allowable employee expenses include necessary expenses related to the taxpayer's role as an employee, including:
- Job hunting in the same trade or business
- The purchase of specialized clothing
- Job-related education expenses if they are incurred to improve or maintain skills required in the taxpayer's current business or employment

> *Hint:* Educational expenses incurred to meet minimum entry level education requirements at the taxpayer's place of employment are NOT deductible.

- Employee Travel Expenses
  - Deductions for employee travel costs are only allowed when related to trips that have a business purpose or when they relate to allowable

travel between two employer locations. Examples of allowable trips include:
- Travel from one work area to another
- Travel from home to a "temporary work location" is deductible if the assignment is short-term

> *Hint:* Regular commuting expenses between residence and work are NEVER deductible.

> *Hint:* If the taxpayer is assigned to a new location for an indefinite period of time or for more than one year, no expenses can be claimed for travel from the taxpayer's residence to this new location as it is now considered a regular commuting expense for tax purposes.

- The amount and purpose of all business-related travel as an employee must be substantiated
- Allowable business-related travel expenses include:
    - Transportation costs, including:
        - Amounts paid for airfare, train travel, rental car, parking, tolls, etc.
        - If a personal automobile is used, includes either gas, depreciation, insurance, etc. or a standard mileage rate
    - All lodging expenses and 50% of meal expenses when the taxpayer is away from home overnight.
- Business-related travel expenses that are NOT DEDUCTIBLE include:
    - Travel for educational purposes

- Entertainment Expenses Incurred by Employee
    - Deductions for employee expenditures on entertainment are closely regulated and are limited to 50% of total expenditures
        - Deduction for tickets to events are limited to 50% of face value, regardless of the amount actually paid
        - Business gifts are limited to $25 per recipient per year

    > *Hint:* The 50% limit does not apply to meals and entertainment which is a means of advertising or marketing or which is provided to employees as compensation.

    - The entertainment must:
        - Be directly related to business operations or have a legitimate business person
        - Involve person with a business relationship (for example, a client, customer, employee, or partner) and substantial business discussions must occur before, during and after event on the same business day
    - Contemporaneous written records which establish cost, time, activity, relationship, and business purpose must be maintained
    - No deductions are allowed for facility/club dues, EXCEPT for dues paid to public service clubs, professional organizations, and trade association dues which ARE deductible
- Home office expenses of employee

- b) **Investment expenses (investment counseling expenses and tax advice)**
- c) **Tax return preparation expenses**
- d) **Hobby expenses**
  According to the IRS, a **hobby** is any activity that is not primarily profit-oriented, but is primarily undertaken for personal enjoyment.

  Hobby expenses may be deducted only to the extent that the hobby generates revenue. No hobby losses are deductible and expenses that are not allowed due to insufficient income do NOT carry over.

  The limitation imposed by deducting hobby expenses in this order, which mimics the application of expenses related to a home office:
  1. Mortgage interest and real estate taxes are applied first.
  2. Cash expenses are applied next.
  3. Depreciation is applied last.

  To avoid the hobby designation, the taxpayer must provide evidence of a real profit motive. The burden of proof of profit motive can be shifted to IRS when activity generates profit in 3 of 5 consecutive years. However, if there are losses in at least 3 of the previous 5 years, the taxpayer has the burden of proof that activity is a business, not a hobby.

  > **Example:** Martha makes cakes as a hobby and, every once in a while, decides to sell one of her cakes. During 2015, she incurred expenses of $10,000 related to making cakes and generated $4,000 in revenue from cake sales. Martha earned a salary of $50,000 from her employer as a teacher. Martha should include the full $4,000 of revenue in her gross income. Since Martha itemizes her deductions, with no other miscellaneous itemized deductions, the deduction for the hobby expenses would be $3,000 [$4,000 − (2% * $50,000)].

Multiple Choice

REG 4-Q61

- e) **Other 2% Miscellaneous Deductions**
  Other miscellaneous itemized deductions which are subject to the 2% floor include:
  - Appraisal fees to determine personal casualty losses and charitable contributions of property
  - Legal fees to procure alimony
  - Custodial fees for an IRA (must be paid by a separate check)

- f) **Limits on Itemized Deductions**
  Itemized deductions are subject to limits individually and in the aggregate. Itemized deductions NOT subject to phase-out based on income exceeding certain limits are:
  - Medical expenses
  - Investment interest expenses
  - Personal casualty and theft losses
  - Gambling losses

D. Passive Activity Losses (Excluding Foreign Tax Credit Implications)

- Recall passive activities for federal income tax purposes.
- Calculate net passive activity gains and losses for federal income tax purposes.
- Prepare a loss carryforward schedule for passive activities for federal income tax purposes.
- Calculate utilization of suspended losses on the disposition of a passive activity for federal income tax purposes.

1. Passive activities
   A **passive activity** is a profit-seeking activity where the taxpayer does not "materially participate" in its management. For income tax purposes, rental activities and all limited partnership interests are treated as passive activities.

   Material participation occurs when a taxpayer is involved in an activity's operations in a regular, continuous, and substantial way. This requirement can be met in one of two ways:
   a. By working more than 500 hours on the activity during the tax year
   b. By working more than 100 hours on the activity if no other individual works more than 100 hours

   A trust materially participates in an activity if a fiduciary materially participates (in his role as fiduciary). A closely held C Corporation or personal service corporation materially participate, generally speaking, only if one or more of its shareholders, who own more than 50% of the value of its stock, themselves materially participate.

   All limited partners and **rental activities** are considered passive without regard to the taxpayer's participation.

   Special passive activity rules apply to real estate professionals, who must perform 50% of their personal services in trades/business involving real property and more than 750 hours of services in real estate trades/business to meet the material participation standard. These professionals will file schedule C or Form 1120, if a corporation.

2. Passive activity losses
   Passive activity loss limits dictate that if the taxpayer does not materially participate in the entity's management, any loss from the activity is limited to the revenue produced by the activity. Passive losses cannot be used to offset active income or portfolio income.

   Passive activity loss limitations apply to individuals, estates, trusts, personal service corporations, and closely held C corporations.

   To calculate allowable passive activity losses, expenses and revenue from passive activities are netted and expenses in excess of revenue (that is, the passive losses) are suspended.

   a. **Suspended losses** become deductible in later years if passive income is generated or the passive activity is sold. In the year a passive activity is sold, the suspended passive losses are released and can offset all types of income.

If the activity becomes active, suspended losses are allowed against income from the now active business.

b. **Rental real estate**
An exception to the passive activity loss limitation exists for taxpayers who actively manage rental realty. In this case, **active participation** is assumed when a taxpayer owns 10% or more of the property and participates significantly in decision making.

An active manager of the rental real estate can deduct a maximum loss of $25,000/year. This exception is phased out for taxpayers with modified AGI over $100,000. For every dollar over $100,000, the taxpayer loses 50 cents of the $25,000 write-off against non-passive income. The write-off is fully phased out when a taxpayer's AGI is greater than $150,000. For this purpose, AGI is computed before including:
- Taxable social security income
- IRA contribution deductions
- The exclusion of interest from Series EE bonds used for higher education

Multiple Choice

REG 4-Q62

Reporting rental income or losses depends on whether you are in the rental business on a full-time basis, or you are in a profession other than rental properties, and you have a rental property as an investment. If a taxpayer is in the business of renting properties on a full-time basis, the rental income could be reported on Schedules C, if self-employed, or in a corporate or partnership return. In these cases, the rental income is ordinary, not passive.

If you just have a property that just is an investment, the rental income(loss) is passive. In this case, the rental income(loss) will be reported on Form 1040, Schedule E, and is passive.

Multiple Choice

REG 4-Q63 through REG 4-Q66

E. Loss Limitations

Calculate loss limitations for federal income tax purposes for an individual taxpayer.

Analyze projections to effectively minimize loss limitations for federal income tax purposes for an individual taxpayer.

Determine the basis and the potential application of at-risk rules that can apply to activities for federal income tax purposes.

When taxpayer property is transferred, stolen, destroyed, confiscated or becomes worthless and the taxpayer is not adequately compensated, a loss is sustained. This loss may or may not be deductible based on the circumstances.

A loss is deductible in the year that it is evidenced by a completed transaction (such as a sale or exchange). Remember that mere fluctuations in an asset's value do not result in deductible losses.

When a taxpayer **disposes of trade or business property** and incurs a loss, the **deductible loss** is calculated as:

Adjusted Basis of Property	–	Cash or FMV of Property/Services Received	–	Any Reimbursement or Compensation for the Loss	–	Property's Salvage Value (if any)

a. Losses on Trade or Business Activities
Losses incurred by individual taxpayers are deductible if the losses are from a **trade or business** or if the transaction is entered into **for a profit**.

A trade or business is an activity that is carried out with a profit motive, whether or not a profit actually results. An activity is presumed to be engaged in for profit if it shows a profit in any 3 years out of the previous 5 consecutive years.

Losses on the disposition of capital assets for an individual, and assets used in a trade or business held for more than one year. These trade assets are known as Section 1231 assets (these include tangible personal property, and real property), and the Section 1231 gains are netted against the 1231 losses.

- Losses on capital assets can occur if the net capital losses exceed net capital gains for an individual. The deduction for net capital losses that is deducted against ordinary income for individuals is limited to $3000, or $1500 for married filing separately. If net capital gains exceed net capital losses, they are taxable in full. Investment assets subject to netting rules for capital assets (i.e., if an individual taxpayer has net capital gains and net capital losses, they must net them.)

The netting rules for Section 1231 assets are as such: If 1231 assets, gains and losses are netted, and there is a loss, the loss is Section 1231 loss, which is an ordinary loss. If 1231 assets gains and losses are netted, and there is a gain, it is known as a Section 1231 gain (long-term capital gain).

1) **Limitation on Deductions for Business-Use of Home**
Recall that deductions for the use of a home office are limited to gross income from the business, and cannot create a loss. The home expenses, first deducts the portions of mortgage interest and real estates that are allocated to the home office. An excess mortgage interest, and real estate taxes not deducted as home office expenses are then deducted as

itemized deductions. Then the remaining allocated home office expenses are deducted. The home office expenses of an employee are a miscellaneous itemized deduction that exceeds 2% of AGI. If the home office expenses pertain to a self-employed individual, deduct them on Schedule C.

2) **At-Risk Loss Limitation**
When trade or business loss is incurred, the deductible loss is limited to the amount the taxpayer has "at risk."

This loss limitation applies to all the activities of individuals and closely held regular corporations, except for the leasing of personal property by a closely held corporation. The amount that a taxpayer has "at risk" is defined as:

The sum of any cash and the adjusted basis of other property contributed plus the amounts borrowed for the activity for which the taxpayer is personally liable for.

Losses are deducted up to the at-risk basis.

If the taxpayer has excess losses, those losses can be carried into the future indefinitely and deducted when taxpayer's "at risk" amount allows.

Multiple Choice

REG 4-Q67

3) **Net Operating Losses (NOLs)**
A net operating loss (NOL) is the excess of allowable business deductions over the gross income of the business activity for a particular tax year, with a few modifications.

> *Hint:* An NOL usually arises from a business loss, but may be incurred by an individual in the case of a personal casualty loss. An individual's NOL is loss from SCH C and casualty.

NOL deductions are allowed to individuals, corporations, estates, and trusts. NOL deductions are not allowed to partnerships, but the deduction IS allowed to the partners themselves. Similarly, NOLs are not allowed to S corporations, but the losses are passed through to shareholders.

  i. **NOL Computation**
  To compute NOL for non-corporate taxpayers:
  ```
      Gross Income from Business Activity
   −  Allowable Business Deductions
   =  Business Activity Loss
   +  Any NOL carrybacks or carryforwards from other years
   +  Personal and dependency exemptions
   +  Exclusion of gain from qualified small business stock
   +  Domestic production activities deduction (DPAD)
   +  Excess of non-business deductions over non-business income
   +  Excess of capital losses over capital gains (up to $3,000)
   =  Non-Corporate Net Operating Loss
  ```

  To compute NOL for corporate taxpayers:
  ```
      Gross Income
   −  Allowable Business Deductions
   =  Business Activity Loss
  ```

- Any deduction for dividends received that was disallowed due to corporation's taxable income
- Any deduction for dividends paid on certain preferred stock of public utilities without limiting it to the year's taxable income
- Exclusion of gain from qualified small business stock
+ <u>Domestic production activities deduction (DPAD)</u>
= Corporate Net Operating Loss

   ii. **NOL Carryback and Carryforward**
   The NOL can be taken in the form of a two-year carryback and/or a 20-year carryforward. A taxpayer may elect to only carry the NOL forward, but once that election is made it is irrevocable for that year. That is, the two-year carryback is lost for that year's NOL.

   iii. **NOL Deduction- NOL Carryforward**
   In the year to which NOL is applied, the NOL carryforward is a deduction for AGI (above the line) for individuals and a regular business deduction for a corporation.

Multiple Choice

REG 4-Q68 through REG 4-Q69

b. Losses from Hobbies(Not-For-Profit Activities)
When "not for profit" activities result in a loss (for example, hobbies), those losses are only deductible up to the income generated by the activity.

c. Losses on Worthless Stock or Securities
In general, a stock or security must be totally worthless (with no residual value) to be deductible. No deduction is allowed for partial worthlessness, or for a mere decline in value, unless the taxpayer is a dealer with an inventory of securities).

The taxpayer must show that the security had value at the end of the preceding year and that an identifiable event occurred that caused a loss in the year of the deduction.
A worthless asset is treated as sold for $0 on the last day of the year.

Special rules apply if section 1244 qualified small corporation stock is sold at a loss or becomes worthless. Losses are deductible up to $100,000 as ordinary losses for married filing joint, and $50,000 for other than joint filing. The remaining loss is treated as capital loss. To qualify for this loss treatment, the individual selling the stock must be the original holder.

To qualify as section 1244 stock, the total capitalization of the corporation must be less than or equal to $1M at the time of stock issuance.

d. Gambling Losses
As discussed earlier in the book, all gross gambling income (regardless of gambling losses) must be included in gross income. Gambling losses are then deductible as an itemized deduction from AGI (below the line), but only to the extent of gambling winnings, which is a miscellaneous itemized deduction, not subject to the 2% limitation.

e. Losses Resulting from Personal Transactions
Losses on the **personal transactions** of an individual, estate or trust are deductible **only** if they qualify as a casualty or theft. Property that is held by the taxpayer for both personal use and business use is treated as two properties, one business property, and one personal property, and the property's value is apportioned (based on relative FMV) between the two properties. Loss on the personal

portion (except by casualty or theft) is not deductible. For example, a loss on a personal residence is not deductible, but a gain on a personal residence is taxable.

f. Capital Losses
If capital losses are greater than capital gains, this is a "net capital loss" and is subject to a $3,000 deduction limit for individuals. No deduction allowed for net capital losses for corporations. Corporations can only deduct capital losses against capital gains, not ordinary income.

F. Filing Status and Exemptions

CPA Exam Blueprint *Representative Task*

> Recall taxpayer filing status for federal income tax purposes.

> Recall relationships qualifying for personal exemptions reported on federal Form 1040 – U.S. Individual Income Tax Return.

> Identify taxpayer filing status for federal income tax purposes given a specific scenario.

> Identify the number of personal exemptions reported on federal Form 1040 – U.S. Individual Income Tax Return given a specific scenario.

a. Filing Status Definition and Options

A taxpayer's filing status is a classification that is used to determine filing requirements, tax rates, the standard deduction amount, and a taxpayer's eligibility for certain deductions and tax credits.

The filing status for which a taxpayer might be eligible is generally based on marital status (married, single, etc.) and/or whether or not the taxpayer has dependents, although other considerations are involved. The filing status is based on the taxpayer's status either on the last day of the tax year or the last day the taxpayer is alive.

There are five different filing statuses. Although a taxpayer may qualify for one or two statuses in a given year, only one status per year can be selected. The status, however, can vary from year to year based on which offers the greatest tax advantage.

1) Married Filing Jointly (MFJ)

Taxpayers who are married at year-end or at time of spouse's death must choose to file either a joint return or separate returns, based on which produces the lower tax liability. Taxpayers who file jointly must have the same tax year. Married taxpayers filing jointly can have different accounting methods. Married filing jointly can file with a non-resident alien, as long as both taxpayers sign the election to file jointly.

Married taxpayers who file jointly (MFJ) are treated to wider tax brackets.

Taxpayers who were married but lived apart during the year are still considered to be married on the last day of the taxable year. Therefore, they are allowed to file a joint return.

i. Non-Resident Spouses

An election can be made to treat a non-resident alien spouse as a U.S. citizen for income tax and wage withholding purposes. Therefore, a taxpayer who is married to a non-resident alien can still elect to file married filing jointly, as long as both taxpayers agree to the election.

ii. Impact on Liability for Payment

The election to file jointly generally means that any tax liability is joint and several. A spouse can avoid joint liability when income is omitted from a joint return if that spouse qualifies as **innocent**, meaning that spouse had no reason to know of the income omission and error can be fully attributed to the other spouse.

Multiple Choice
> REG 4-Q70

2) Married Filing Separate (MFS)

Married taxpayers who do not file a joint return must choose the married filing separate status. This status requires that spouses divide their income and expenses according to ownership.

Special rules exist to prevent taxpayers from receiving additional unintended benefits from filing separately:
- Both spouses must either elect to itemize deductions or elect to take the standard deduction.
- Neither spouse can claim the earned income credit (EIC)
- Neither spouse can claim child and dependent care credit
- Neither spouse can claim the American Opportunity Tax Credit (AOTC)
- Neither spouse can claim the adoption credit
- Deduction for net capital losses are limited to $1500

3) **Qualifying Widower with Dependent Child (aka Surviving Spouse)**
When a spouse dies during the tax year, the surviving spouse may still choose the **married filing jointly status for that tax year**. For the **two years after** the year of death, if the spouse has a dependent child, he or she may choose the **qualifying widower with dependent child** status. This status is sometimes referred to as **surviving spouse**.

To qualify for this status, the taxpayer must provide more than 50% of the cost of maintaining the household **for a dependent child/stepchild/adoptee.** The child's principal place of abcde must be with the taxpayer.

In determining if child/relative is dependent, the regular dependency rules apply **except for**:
- Joint return test
- Gross income test for qualifying relatives
- Rule that dependent cannot also have dependents

> **Example**: A taxpayer is married, and he provides more than 50% of the household costs for his children, who are qualified dependents. The taxpayer's spouse passes away in August of 20X6. When filing his 20X6 return, he may still choose a filing status of married filing jointly. For his 20X7 and 20X8 returns, he may choose the qualifying widower with dependent child status. After that point, if he still has a qualifying dependent, he can choose the Head of Household status.

The **cost of maintaining a household** includes items such as rent, mortgage interest, taxes, insurance, repairs, food, utilities, etc. It **does not include** expenses, such as clothing, education, vacations, transportation, value of taxpayer services, rental value of the residence, medical expenses, etc.

Multiple Choice

REG 4-Q71 through REG 4-Q72

4) **Head of Household**
To claim head of household status, a taxpayer must be unmarried and have a qualifying dependent. That is, the taxpayer must provide more than 50% of the cost of maintaining a household for a:
- Qualifying child of the taxpayer (i.e., taxpayer's children, siblings, step-siblings and their dependents under age 19, or under age 24 if a student) who lives with the taxpayer for more than 50% of the year and is:
  - A dependent, if the qualifying child is married. If a qualifying child is unmarried, the child need not qualify as a dependent for the taxpayer to be eligible for head of household status.
  - A citizen, resident or US national or a resident of Canada or Mexico
- A relative (closer than cousin) for whom the taxpayer can take a dependency exemption

- A parent whose household is maintained by the taxpayer (for example, a parent who lives in a nursing home) and who qualify as the taxpayer's dependents.

> *Hint*: A taxpayer cannot qualify for head of household status through a multiple support agreement.

> *Hint*: A taxpayer who was a nonresident alien at any time during the tax year cannot qualify for head of household status.

> *Hint*: A non-relative of any age living at home, even if for whole tax year, does NOT qualify (for example, a boyfriend, girlfriend, etc.)

An **abandoned spouse** can also choose the head of household status. A married taxpayer is considered abandoned and allowed to file as though unmarried when:
- The taxpayer's spouse has not lived in the home for the last 6 months of calendar year **AND**
- The taxpayer provides more than 50% of the cost for maintaining a home for himself and a dependent child (who is a descendant of taxpayer, i.e., son/daughter; grandchild; adopted/foster/stepchild).

5) Single
Single is the default filing status for taxpayers who are not eligible to use any of the other filing statuses. An individual who is unmarried and who has no dependent child should use this filing status. Taxpayers who were married but who lived under a legal separation agreement at the end of the year are considered single on the last day of the taxable year.

> *Hint:* A taxpayer who resides with a dependent child will most likely be eligible for some special tax treatment (e.g. head of household or surviving spouse status).

Multiple Choice

REG 4-Q73

b. Filing Status Examples and Illustrations
Example Set #1: Select the appropriate filing status for each situation:

	Scenario	Filing Status
1.	Andrew and Fiona were divorced on December 31.	Each should choose the Single filing status.
2.	Eleanor and Garrett were married on December 31.	Married Filing Jointly
3.	Susan's husband died on July 12 of this year. Susan has not remarried.	Married Filing Jointly
4.	Samuel's wife died on October 10, 2014. Samuel has no children and has not remarried. What would his 2014 and 2015 filing status be?	2014: Married Filing Jointly 2015: Single
5.	Between Single, Married Filing Jointly, Head of Household and Qualifying Widower with dependent child, which filing status has lower tax rates?	The lowest tax rates apply to two filing statuses: Married Filing Jointly and Qualifying Widow(er) with Dependent Child.
6.	A taxpayer has dependent children. The taxpayer's spouse died in 2015. Before the death of the spouse, the taxpayer was eligible to use the Married Filing Jointly filing status. Which filing status will the taxpayer probably use in 2016?	The taxpayer will probably use the Qualifying Widow(er) with Dependent Child filing status because it has the lowest tax rates. The taxpayer probably qualifies for the Head of Household filing status but will not use it because the tax rates are higher than those for the Qualifying Widow(er) with Dependent Child filing status.
7.	Peter and Anne are married and live together, but they are experiencing difficulties caused by Anne's financial problems. Peter wants to be responsible for his own taxes, but he does not want to be financially responsible for Anne's tax issues. Which filing status should Peter and Anne use?	A married taxpayer who does not want to be responsible for his or her spouse's tax liability should use the married filing separately filing status.

c. Personal and Dependency Exemptions
Personal and dependency exemptions are amounts deducted from AGI.

1) Personal exemptions
Most taxpayers can claim an exemption for themselves and their spouse in computing taxable income on their own return. The personal exemption amount for 2017 is $4,050.

No personal exemption can be claimed for a taxpayer or spouse who is claimed as a dependent by another taxpayer. A personal exemption can be claimed on a taxpayer's final return even if the taxpayer or her spouse dies during the tax year.

If spouses file separately (i.e. MFS), each spouse typically claims a personal exemption on his/her return.

> *Hint:* If one spouse has no gross income and no one else has claimed him as a dependent, the other spouse can claim him as an exemption on his **married filing separately** return.

2) Dependency exemptions
Dependency exemptions are flat deductions allowed for individuals other than the taxpayer who satisfy several specific tests that are applied on last day of the tax year or the last day the dependent was alive. All tests must be met to claim an individual as a dependent.

   i. Qualifying Child
   To claim a dependency exemption for a **qualifying child**, the child must pass the following tests:
   - Relationship test:
     - The dependent must be the taxpayer's natural child, stepchild, legally adopted child, foster child, sibling, step-sibling, or a descendant of any of these (includes brothers, sisters, nieces, nephews)
   - Residence test:
     - The dependent must have the same principal place of abode as the taxpayer for more than half of the tax year. One individual could live with several taxpayers who could potentially qualify to claim the individual as a dependent (mother, aunt, grandfather) at the same time.
   - Age test:
     - At the end of the tax year, the dependent must be under age 19 (or under age 24, if the individual is a full-time student for at least 5 months of tax year).
     - The qualifying child must be younger than the taxpayer claiming the qualifying child as a dependent.

     > *Hint*: An individual who is totally and permanently disabled automatically meets the age test.

   - Joint Return test:
     - A qualifying child can file jointly only to obtain a refund (dependent not required to file according to gross income level). Otherwise a married filing jointly taxpayer will not qualify as a dependent, despite passing all other tests.
   - Citizenship/residency test:
     - A qualifying child must be a citizen or resident of the U.S. or resident of Canada or Mexico.
   - Non self-supporting test:
     - The qualifying child must not have provided more than 50% of his own support.
     - **Support** includes all necessary living expenses including food, clothes, housing and other necessities. Support does NOT include services provided by the taxpayer.
   - Other Requirements:
     - Also, if a parent is eligible to claim a qualifying child but declines, no other individual can claim the qualifying child unless that individual's AGI is greater than the AGI of any parent.

       Tie Breaker Rules apply if more than one individual qualifies to claim the potential dependent, the following rules apply:
       a) If one individual is the parent, the parent claims the exemption; if the parent is eligible to claim the qualifying child, the parent cannot allow another eligible individual to claim the qualifying child unless the other individual has a higher AGI for tax year than AGI of the parent eligible to claim the child.

b) If both individuals are parents and do not file jointly, the parent with whom the child resided most during tax year claims the exemption.
c) If both individuals are parents and do not file jointly and the child lives with both equally, the parent with the highest AGI claims the exemption.
d) If none of the individuals is a parent, the taxpayer with the highest AGI claims the exemption.

> **Example:** Patty is a single, 18-year-old, Canadian citizen, who lives in Vancouver with her mother the entire year. In 2014, Patty earned $2,450. Patty's mother provided 60 percent of Patty's total support. Patty's mother is not the dependent of anyone else. Can Patty's mother claim a dependency exemption as a "qualifying child" for her?
> - The dependent taxpayer test is met—Patty's mother is not the dependent of anyone else
> - The joint return test is met— Patty is single
> - The citizen or resident test is met— Patty is a Canadian citizen
> - The relationship test is met— Patty is the child of the taxpayer
> - The age test is met— Patty is under 19
> - The residency test is met— Patty lived with her mother the entire year
> - The support test is met— Patty did not provide more than half of her own support
>
> Patty's mother can, therefore, claim a dependency exemption for Patty, as a qualifying child.

ii. Qualifying **Relative**

A **qualifying relative** is defined very broadly and includes any **relative** (except cousins, see below) who lived with the taxpayer all year. An individual can be temporarily absent from the taxpayer's home for the purpose of vacation, schooling, nursing home stays, or illness and still qualify as a qualifying relative.

A qualifying child cannot also be claimed as a qualifying relative. To claim a dependency exemption for a **qualifying relative**, the individual must pass the following tests in addition to the relationship test:

- Relationship test:
    - All relatives **except cousins** are included in the definition of a relative. This definition includes siblings, aunts and uncles, step-relatives, in-laws, ancestors, and nephews and nieces. For the qualifying relative definition, if a relationship was established by marriage, it is not ended by death or divorce.
- Support test:
    - The qualifying relative must not have provided more than 50% of his own support.
    - The multiple support agreement provision still applies
    - A child less than 19 years old can receive significant amounts of income and not violate support test so long as it's not used to pay for necessities (i.e., goes to savings)
    - Scholarships DO NOT equal support

> **Example:** An 18-year-old child of a taxpayer earned $6,000 and received a scholarship that paid tuition of $7,500. If the child uses his wages for necessities, the child will still satisfy the support test if the taxpayer provides $6,001 or more of the child's necessities.

- Gross Income Test:
    - The dependent's gross income must be less than the exemption amount for the year ($4,050 in 2016).
    - Children who are under 19 (or under 24 and a full-time student) at the end of the tax year are **exempt from the gross income test**.
- Joint Return Test
- Citizen/Residency Test
- Other Dependency Rules deal with situations where individuals may be supported but not meet all tests for the dependency exemption:
    - In the case of multiple support agreements and divorced parents, the law provides for a dependency exemption despite technical violation of 1+ tests
        - Multiple support agreements
            - An agreement between a group of taxpayers who together support an individual more than 50%
            - Except for support test, each individual in group would otherwise be eligible to claim the individual as a dependent
            - Written agreement allocates dependency exemption to a member of the group who provides between 10% and 50% of the qualifying relative's support
            - All members providing >10% of the qualifying relative's support must sign the agreement
        - Divorced Parents
            - An exception applies for children supported by parents who are divorced or legally separated for the last 6 months of the year
            - The parent with custody (> 50% of year) is entitled to the dependent exemption in the absence of any written agreement
            - The custodial parent can waive the exemption to the other parent by signing Form 8332. The non-custodial parent must attach this form to claim the exemption.

> *Hint:* In order for an individual to be a qualifying relative and to be considered a dependent, an individual must meet all of the following "CRAIS" test criteria, to be a dependent: first the qualifying relative cannot be a qualifying child
>
> **"C"** Person must be a <u>citizen</u> or resident of the U.S., Canada, or Mexico.
>
> **"R"** Person must be <u>related</u> (closer than cousin) if they do not live with the taxpayer for the entire year.
>
> **"A"** <u>Absence</u> of joint return (means they cannot file a join return with another individual).
>
> **"I"** Cannot have more gross taxable <u>income</u> than the exemption amount ($4,050).
>
> **"S"** Must furnish more than one-half of <u>support</u>.
>
> Remember, the "CRAIS" test is only used to determine if a qualifying relative is a

> **Example**: Ms. Sofia is 74 years old and lives in an apartment. In 2016, Ms. Sofia received $3,000 in nontaxable Social Security benefits and $400 in taxable interest income, all of which was used for her support. Ms. Sofia's taxable income of $400 was less than the exemption amount of $4,050. Ms. Sofia's daughter, Jane, paid $4,800 during the year toward her mother's support.
> Can Jane claim a dependency exemption for Ms. Sofia?
> To answer this question, first, determine if Ms. Sofia is a qualifying relative of Jane. The tests to determine if an individual is a qualifying relative are the following:
> Ms. Sofia is not a qualifying child, and the CRAIS test must be met:
> **"C"** Ms. Sofia is a resident of the U.S.
> **"R"** Ms. Sofia is related to Jane because Jane is her daughter.
> **"A"** Ms. Sofia did not file a joint return.
> **"I"** Ms. Sofia's gross taxable <u>income</u> of $400 was less than the exemption amount ($4,050).
> **"S"** Jane furnished more than one-half of Ms. Sofia's <u>support</u>. Total support includes taxable and nontaxable income. Ms. Sofia's total support is $8,200 ($3,000 + $400 + $4,800). Jane paid more than half of her mother's support ($4,800/$8,200 = 59%).
> Ms. Sofia meets the tests as a qualifying relative of Jane, and therefore give Jane an additional exemption deduction

3) Phaseout of Exemptions
Personal and dependency exemptions are phased out for high AGI taxpayers. 2% of the total exemption is lost for each $2,500 increment of AGI (or portion thereof) above the trigger AGI.

Phaseout amounts are based on filing status and are as follows:
- Single - $259,400
- MFJ - $311,300
- MFS - $155,650
- HOH - $285,350

As a shortcut, note that all exemptions are phased out when a taxpayer's AGI is $122,501 over the trigger AGI.

4) Comprehensive Examples of Personal and Dependency Exemptions

Example 1:

1.	Two individuals – both with gross income - are married and file a joint return. Neither can be claimed as a dependent on any other tax return. How many personal exemptions can this married couple claim on their tax return?	Because they cannot be claimed dependents on any other tax return, the couple can claim two personal exemptions - one for each taxpayer (husband and wife).
2.	Wendy is 16 years old and earned $3,200 during the summer. She is also a full-time student. She can be claimed as a dependent on her parents' tax return. How many personal exemptions can Wendy claim on her own tax return?	Because she can be claimed as a dependent on her parents' tax return, Wendy cannot claim a personal exemption for herself on her tax return.
3.	Jenny and Ryan are married. Both use the married filing separately status. Neither can be claimed as a dependent on any other tax return. How many personal exemptions can Jenny claim on her tax return?	Jenny can claim one personal exemption for herself on her tax return. She cannot claim a personal exemption for her husband, Ryan, because Ryan is not a dependent.
4.	A married couple filed a joint return in 2014. The husband died in 2015 and the wife did not remarry. How many personal exemptions can the wife claim on her 2015 tax return?	Because she did not remarry, the wife can claim two personal exemptions on her 2015 joint tax return-one for herself and one for her deceased husband.

Example 2:

Theodore and Olivia Stone are a married couple who live in the United States and file a joint return. They are not claimed as dependents on anyone else's return. Their two children, Elijah 10 and Sam 12, lived with them for the entire year and received 100% of their support from their parents. Neither child had any income during the year. In addition, a cousin, who is a U.S. citizen and earned $400 as a carpenter, lived with the Stone family for the entire year and received more than half of his support from Theodore and Olivia. Their cousin did not file a joint return with anyone else and cannot be claimed as a dependent of anyone else. When Theodore and Olivia file their joint return, how many exemptions can they claim?

The Stones can claim five exemptions:
- two personal exemptions (one each for Theodore and Olivia)
- three dependency exemptions (one each for their children and their cousin)

Dependency Tests for the Stone Family

After determining the personal exemptions for each adult, next determine if the children qualify for an exemption. Remember that a dependent is a **qualifying child** or **qualifying relative** who meets certain tests. To determine if the Stone children are qualifying children, they must pass the following tests:

Qualifying Child Tests	Do the children qualify?
1. Relationship test: The child must be the taxpayer's son, daughter, stepchild, eligible foster child, brother, sister, half-brother, half-sister, stepbrother, stepsister, or a descendant of any of them.	Yes.
2. Age test: The child must be (a) under age 19 at the end of the year and younger than the taxpayer (or taxpayer's spouse if filing jointly), (b) a full-time student under age 24 at the end of the year and younger than taxpayer (or taxpayer's spouse if filing jointly), (c) any age if permanently and totally disabled.	Yes – the children are under 19.
3. Residency test: The child must have lived with the taxpayer for more than half of the year.	Yes – the children lived with their parents the entire tax year.
4. Support test: The child must not have provided more than half of his or her own support for the year.	Yes – the children did not provide any of their own support.

In conclusion, the children cannot be claimed by any other taxpayer as a dependent because Theodore and Olivia will report the children as qualifying children and they will take the children as dependents.

Special rules for qualifying children, who satisfy the requirement of being a qualifying child for more than one taxpayer:
- If the child meets the rules to be a qualifying child of more than one person, the child cannot be claimed as a dependent on more than one return, even though the child is qualifying child for two or more taxpayers.
- If none of the taxpayers is the child's parent, the child is a qualifying child for the taxpayer with the highest AGI.
- If only one of the taxpayers is the child's parent, the child is a qualifying child for that parent. If two of the taxpayers are the child's parents and they do not file a joint return together, the child is a dependent of the parent with whom the child resided for the longest time period during the year.

Next, determine if the cousin that is living with the Stone family qualifies for an exemption. Remember that in order for an individual to be a qualifying relative and to be considered a dependent, he or she must meet all of the following "CRAIS" test criteria:

Qualifying Relative Test	Does the cousin qualify?
Not a qualifying child test: The person cannot be the taxpayer's qualifying child or the qualifying child of anyone else.	Yes - He is a cousin, so he is not a qualifying child.
"C" test: The person must be a <u>citizen</u> or resident of the U.S., Canada, or Mexico.	Yes - The cousin is a U.S. citizen.
"R" test: Person must be <u>related</u> (closer than a cousin) if they do not live with the taxpayer for the entire year.	Yes - He lived with the Stone family for the entire year.
"A" test: <u>Absensee</u> of joint return (means they cannot file a joint return with another individual).	Yes – He does not file a joint return with any other individual.
"I" test: Cannot have more gross taxable <u>income</u> than the exemption amount ($4,050).	Yes - He earned only $400.
"S" test: Must furnish more than one-half of <u>support.</u>	Yes - They provided more than half of the cousin's support.

G. Computation of Tax and Credits

Representative Task:

Calculate the impact of tax deductions and tax credits and their effect on federal Form 1040 – *U.S. Individual Income Tax Return*.

Recall and define the minimum requirements for individual federal estimated tax payments to avoid penalties.

Calculate the tax liability based on an individual's taxable income for federal income tax purposes.

1. Tax credits
   Tax credits directly reduce tax liability and therefore are much more powerful/desirable than deductions or exemptions, which reduce taxable income.

   Tax credits can generally be grouped into personal credits (refundable and non-refundable) and business credits.

   a. Refundable Personal Credits
      1) Earned Income Credit (EIC)
         The earned income credit (EIC) can be applied to eligible low-income workers who have "earned income."

         The most common sources of earned income that qualify for credit are:
         - Wages
         - Tips
         - Self-employment earnings
         - Combat Pay
         - Taxable disability payments (until taxpayer reaches retirement age)

         Eligible taxpayers include those individuals who:
         - Have earned income
         - Have been US citizen/resident alien for whole tax year
         - Are filing a return that covers a 12-month period
         - Maintain a household for more than half the year for a qualifying child in the US
         - Must have a child under the age of 19 or, is a full-time student under the age of 24 or, is permanently and totally disabled.
         - ARE NOT filing MFS
         - ARE NOT the qualifying child of another taxpayer
         - ARE NOT claiming the foreign earned income exclusion
         - DO NOT have disqualified income > $3400
           - **Disqualified income** includes dividends, net capital gain income, net passive income, net rental and royalty income and both taxable and tax-exempt interest

Multiple Choice
REG 4-Q74

The credit is calculated by applying a percentage to the taxpayer's earned income. The allowable percentage is based on number of dependents that can be claimed by the taxpayer:
- **Qualifying dependent** definition for the EIC is the same as the definition used for dependent exemption rules

- Qualifying child must have lived in taxpayer's home in the United States for more than 50% of the tax year
- Qualifying child can only be used by one taxpayer to claim the EIC
  - If more than one taxpayer qualifies to claim child, tiebreaker rules similar to dependent exemption rules are applied
  - The individual who claims the qualifying child as a dependent must be the same person who claims the EIC

- For taxpayers with no qualifying dependents:
  - The maximum credit is 7.65% of first $6,580 of earned income. For taxpayers with earned income over $8,240 ($13,750 MFJ), the credit is reduced by 7.65% of earned income over the threshold.
  - To qualify, the taxpayer must:
    - Be between ages 25 and 64
    - Not be claimed as a dependent on another's return
    - Have lived in the U.S. for more than ½ the tax year

- For taxpayers with qualifying dependents:
  - 1 qualifying child:
    - Credit is 34% of first $9,880 of earned income
    - Maximum credit is reduced by 15.98% of the amount by which earned income exceeds $18,110 ($23,630 for MFJ)
  - 2 qualifying children:
    - Credit is 40% of first $13,870 of earned income
    - Maximum credit is reduced by 21.06% of the amount by which earned income exceeds $18,110 ($23,630 for MFJ)
  - 3+ qualifying children:
    - Credit is 45% of first $13,870 of earned income
    - Maximum credit is reduced by 21.06% of the amount by which earned income exceeds $18,110 ($23,630 for MFJ)

- Reporting Requirements:
  - Information on qualifying dependents is reported on Form 1040, Schedule EIC
  - Amount of credit taken is reported on Form 1040
  - A paid preparer must complete Form 8867, a checklist to ensure due diligence is met. A $500 penalty is imposed for each failure to meet requirements.

> **New Exam Content**: This credit was permanently extended as part of the Protecting Americans from Tax Hikes Bill of 2015 (PATH Act).

> **Example:** Assuming all other rules are met, which of the following taxpayers cannot claim the earned income tax credit?
> - Helen is a waitress who receives most of her income through tips
> - Mary is a Mexican citizen but was a resident of the U.S for the entire tax year
> - All of Peter's income is comprised of dividends and interest
> - John is married and files a joint return with his spouse, Stacy
>
> Peter cannot claim the earned income tax credit because interest and dividends do not qualify as earned income.

2) **Health Coverage Tax Credit (HCTC)**
   Eligible individuals can elect a credit equal to 72.5% of the amount paid by the taxpayer for "qualified health insurance" coverage for the taxpayer and qualifying family members (spouse and dependents).

   Qualified health insurance includes:
   - Individual health insurance
     - After 1/1/2016, this EXCLUDES coverage obtained through an Affordable Care Act Exchange; expenses related to exchange-obtained insurance is addressed by the Premium Assistance Credit (see below)
   - COBRA continuation coverage
   - VEBA (voluntary employees' beneficiary association) coverage, that was established through the bankruptcy of your former employer;
   - Certain state-qualified health plans established before January 1, 2014

   Qualifying family members can claim the HCTC for up to 24 months after the eligible individual enrolls in Medicare, divorces, or dies.

   Married taxpayers filing separate returns CAN claim the credit.

   An individual can NOT claim the HCTC if he can be claimed as a dependent on another taxpayer's return.

3) **Child Tax Credit**
   Taxpayers with AGI under a certain threshold are allowed to take a credit of $1,000 for each qualifying child (as defined under dependency rules) UNDER AGE 17.
   To take the credit, the qualifying child must be:
   - A US citizen or resident
   - The taxpayer's dependent, adopted or eligible foster child, stepchild, step-sibling or any descendant of these
   - UNDER AGE 17 as of the end of the calendar year
   - Listed on return with name and social security number

   > **Example**: Dave and Liz have an adopted daughter who lives with them all year and is a U.S. resident. Their daughter, Janna, turns 14 during the tax year and receives 100% of her support from her adoptive parents.
   >
   > Is Janna a qualifying child for the child tax credit?
   > Yes, because she:
   > - Is under 17
   > - Is a resident of the U.S.
   > - Lives for the whole tax year with those who will claim the credit (her adoptive parents)
   > - Does not provide more than half of her own support
   > - Is the adopted child of those who are claiming the credit

   > **Example:** Jeffrey, a U.S. citizen and the son of a taxpayer, turned 17 on October 15, 2015. He lives with the taxpayer and is fully supported by him. Is Jeffrey a qualifying child for the purposes of the child tax credit?

No, because although he meets all other tests, he fails the age test (under the age of 17). Jeff turned 17 during the tax year.

> **Example**: Graham's foster son Bennett is a citizen of the U.S. and turned 12 on August 15, 2015. He lives with Graham, who provides 100% of his financial support. Is Bennett a qualifying child for the purposes of the child tax credit?
>
> Yes, because he:
> - Is under 17
> - Is a citizen/resident of the U.S.
> - Lives for the whole tax year with those who will claim the credit (his foster parent)
> - Does not provide more than half of his own support
> - Is the foster child of those who are claiming the credit

The child tax credit is phased out for married taxpayers with AGI > $110,000 ($55,000 for MFS, $75,000 for S/HOH)
- Credit reduced $50 for each $1,000 or portion thereof over the trigger AGI
- These thresholds are not indexed for inflation

The credit is refundable to extent of 15% of the taxpayer's earned income in excess of $3,000, up to the per child credit amount of $1,000. Combat pay is treated as earned income for the purposes of computing this credit, even though combat pay is not included in gross income.

> **New Exam Content:** This credit was permanently extended as part of the Protecting Americans from Tax Hikes Bill of 2015 (PATH Act).

> **Example:** A married couple files a joint return and has two dependent children under age 17 who qualify for the child tax credit. Their modified adjusted gross income is $67,500, and their tax liability is $3,250.
>
> Their modified adjusted gross income ($67,500) is less than the maximum amount for their filing status ($110,000). Therefore their initial child tax credit is $2,000.
>
> Because their tax liability ($3,250) is more than their initial child tax credit ($2,000), they are allowed to take the full $2,000 child tax credit.

> **Example:** Peter and Pamela are married with three dependent children who are qualifying children for the purposes of the child tax credit. Peter and Pamela will file jointly this year. Peter and Pamela's modified adjusted gross income is $113,100, and their tax liability is $3,575.
>
> Because Peter and Pamela's modified adjusted gross income is over the maximum of $110,000, they are not eligible to claim a full child tax credit. Their modified AGI is $3,100 over the limit. Since they lose $50 of the credit for every $1000 or portion thereof over the limit, they lose $200 ($50 x 4) of the credit, for a total maximum credit of $1,800.

> **Example:** Joanne and Chris are married and will file jointly this year. They have two children who qualify for the child tax credit. Their modified adjusted gross income is $92,500, and their tax liability is $600. Even though their adjusted gross income is less than the maximum of $110,000, and therefore would otherwise qualify to claim the full $2,000, they cannot claim more than their tax liability. Therefore, they can only claim $600, reducing their tax to zero.

4) **American Opportunity Tax Credit (AOTC)**
   The AOTC is allowed a **max of $2500/year** for each eligible student, computed as:
   - 100% of first $2,000 of qualified educational expenses
   - 25% of next $2,000 of qualified educational expenses

   Qualified educational expenses are non-deductible tuition, fees, course materials (reduced by tax-free benefits, like scholarships) incurred during student's **first four years of post-secondary education**. The expenses must relate to the academic period beginning in the current tax year or first three months of next tax year.

   A **qualified student** is any taxpayer, spouse or dependent enrolled at least half-time in a **degree program** at an institution of higher education.

   The credit is phased out ratably for single taxpayers with AGI > $80,000 ($160,000 MFJ) over a $10,000 range ($20,000 MFJ). Therefore, the credit is totally lost when the taxpayer's AGI is greater than or equal to $90,000 ($180,000 MFJ).

   Married taxpayers MUST file jointly to receive the credit.

   > *Hint:* This credit is only partly-refundable. 40% of credit is refundable. The non-refundable portion of the credit can be claimed against the taxpayer's AMT as well as regular tax liability.

   > *Hint:* For a particular student, a taxpayer must select either the AOTC OR the Lifetime Learning Credit, but cannot utilize both.

   > *New Exam Content:* Tax years that begin after 6/29/15 as a condition of receiving the American Opportunity Tax Credit and the Lifetime Learning Credit, the taxpayer must receive a Form 1098-T containing all the information required by that form.

   > *New Exam Content:* This credit was permanently extended as part of the Protecting Americans From Tax Hikes Bill of 2015 (PATH Act).

b. Non-Refundable Personal Credits
   Non-refundable personal credits are subject to an overall limit. The sum of these non-refundable credits cannot exceed the regular tax liability for the tax year reduced by the foreign tax credit plus the applicable AMT. In other words, all of the otherwise allowable nonrefundable credits can be used to reduce AMT as well as regular tax.

   1) **Elderly Credit**
      The elderly credit is available to taxpayers and their spouse age 65 or permanently and totally disabled.

The credit is equal to 15% of the difference between an initial flat amount ($5,000 for single taxpayers; $7,500 for taxpayer and spouse) and income.

"Income" for this purpose includes certain types of retirement pay plus 50% of any AGI over $7500 ($10,000 if MFJ).

2) **Child and Dependent Care Credit**
A credit can be taken for a portion of the expenses paid for caregiving while the taxpayer is employed or seeking employment.

   i. Rules and Qualifying Expenditures
   The qualified individual needing care must live with the taxpayer for more than half the year
   Qualified individual:
   - A child or dependent under 13 (includes taxpayer's child, stepchild, sibling, stepsibling, or descendant of any of these)
   - Other dependents or spouse if incapable of self-care

   Qualifying expenditures
   Include those required for the care of a qualifying individual so that the taxpayer can work or look for work, such as:
   - Expenses for child below kindergarten
   - Before and after school expenses for child in kindergarten or higher (may qualify)
   - Full amount paid for day camp, even if program is specialized
   - Sick child centers may qualify for this credit or as a medical expense (but cannot qualify for both)
   - Cost to provide room/board for caregiver may qualify if expenses are in addition to normal HH expenses

   > *Hint:* Summer school or tutoring are considered education and do not qualify.

   > *Hint:* For boarding school, amounts paid for food, lodging, clothing, and education must be separated from other amounts paid for other goods/services

   > *Hint:* Payments to taxpayer's child under age 19 or to a dependent relative do NOT qualify

   > *Example*: Liz and Eric are a married couple (joint filers) and both are employed outside of their home. Their 8-year-old son is cared for by their 17-year-old daughter every day after school, and they pay her for this service. Because the expenses are paid to their child who is under age 19, Liz and Eric cannot claim the credit for child and dependent care expenses.
   >
   > *Example*: Samuel and Orla are married (joint filers) and have lived together for the entire tax year. Samuel is a full-time student, and Joan works as an accountant. Their three-year-old daughter spends 20 hours a week in daycare. Samuel and Orla can claim a credit for child and dependent care expenses.
   >
   > *Example*: Tracy earned $29,000, and her husband earned $4,400. Daycare expenses for their two children were $5,000. The amount of expenses which qualify for the child and dependent care credit are $4,400.

ii. Income requirements and other rules
The taxpayer must earn at least as much as the amount of expenditures.
Income of $250/month for one qualifying individual requiring care ($500/month for 2+) is imputed to a full-time student (at least 5 months/year) or a spouse who is incapable of self-care.

If married, the taxpayer must file MFJ (unless abandoned) and spouse must also be employed to claim the credit.

iii. Credit calculation
(qualified expenditure) * (appropriate %)
Credit % begins at 35% if AGI < $15,000; reduced 1% for each $2,000 increment or portion in AGI > $15,000; minimum % is 20%; i.e. taxpayers w/AGI > $43,000 use 20%)

Maximum eligible credit = $3,000 ($6,000 if more than one individual qualifies for care)

Multiple Choice

REG 4-Q75

3) **Adoption Credit**
A credit is allowed for qualified adoption expenses up to $13,460 for each eligible child. Typical expenses include adoption fees, court costs, attorney fees and other expenses directly related to the legal adoption of an eligible child.

> *Hint:* Expenses incurred in surrogate parenting or adopting the child of a spouse do not qualify.

A $13,460 credit is available for expenses related to the adoption of children with special needs regardless of actual expenses incurred.

The adoption credit is partially phased out for taxpayers with AGI > $201,920, and is completely phased out if the taxpayer's modified AGI exceeds $241,920.

The credit that can be taken is limited to the taxpayer's regular tax liability, but any excess can be carried forward 5 years.

Married taxpayers must file jointly to receive the credit, unless they are legally separated or living apart.

When can the credit be claimed?
- If expenses are incurred before the adoption is finalized, the credit can be claimed for the year after when they're paid or incurred
- For expenses incurred during or after the tax year the adoption becomes final, the credit is allowed for the year they are incurred

4) **Lifetime Learning Credit (LLC)**
A credit can be taken for a portion of the qualified education expenses incurred for the taxpayer, spouse, or dependent. The credit is computed as 20% of education expenses up to $10,000, for a maximum credit of $2,000.

Qualified education expenses include non-deductible tuition and academic fees (reduced by tax-free benefits). Materials and books only qualify if they are required to be purchased from the university.

> *Hint:* This is a difference between the AOTC and the LLC.

Expenses must be for post-secondary education but need NOT relate to a degree program. Student need NOT be half-time to qualify.

The credit is phased out ratably for single taxpayers with AGI > $55,000 ($111,000 MFJ) over a $10,000 range ($20,000 MFJ).

> *New Exam Content:* Tax years that begin after 6/29/15 as a condition of taking the American Opportunity Tax Credit and the Lifetime Learning Credit the taxpayer must receive a Form 1098-T containing all the information required by that form.

   i. Lifetime Learning Credit and AOTC Differences and Notable Items
   AOTC and LLC and distributions from education IRAs are mutually exclusive. That is, a single education expenditure can never qualify for more than one benefit (no double dipping).

   AOTC and LLC Summary:
   - Different % applied to expenses to calculate the credit
     - AOTC = 100% and 25%
     - LLC = 20%
     - Total expenses eligible
       - AOTC = $4,000/year
       - LLC = $10,000/year
     - Timeframe
       - AOTC = first 4 years of post-secondary education
       - LLC = any post-secondary education
     - Availability
       - AOTC = available for the qualifying expenses of each qualifying student
       - LLC = available only once per taxpayer, regardless of how many students in the family might qualify
     - Degree Program
       - AOTC = student must be in a degree-seeking program
       - LLC = student, need NOT be enrolled in a degree-seeking program, it can be for any vocational school, or other postsecondary education.
     - Half-time Requirement
       - AOTC = Student must be enrolled at least half-time
       - LLC = No half-time enrollment requirement
     - Refundable
       - AOTC = 40% is refundable
       - LLC = NOT REFUNDABLE

5) **Foreign Tax Credit**
The United States taxes income from all sources (including income earned in foreign countries). This credit is one of a few provisions in the tax code to prevent double taxation of income that is earned abroad.

The credit is limited to the lower of foreign taxes paid or the proportion of US tax allocable to foreign sourced income (also known as the **foreign tax credit limit**)

> *Hint:* In lieu of taking this credit, taxpayers can elect to mitigate taxes in 2 other ways:
> - Taxpayers can claim foreign tax as itemized deduction, not subject to any limitation
> - Taxpayers can elect to exclude income earned (in excess of housing costs) while a bona fide resident in a foreign country
>   - Exclusion max = $99,200 if the taxpayer is physically located outside of the United States at least 330 days in any consecutive 12 months

Multiple Choice

REG 4-Q76

c. Business Tax Credits
1) **General Business Credit (GBC)**
   The general business credit is available to businesses and is comprised of a combination of credits, such as:
   a) Rehabilitation Credit
   b) Business Energy Credit
   c) Work Opportunity Credit
   d) Alcohol fuels credit
   e) Research credit
   f) Employer-Provided Child Care Credit
   g) Small Employer Health Insurance Credit

   While each is calculated independently, the combination of all of these credits is subject to an overall limit, equal to:
   - **Net income tax** LESS the greater of:
     - 25% of **net regular tax liability** over $25,000
     - Tentative minimum tax
   - **Net income tax** is equal to regular income tax, plus AMT, less non-refundable tax credits (except the alternative minimum tax credit)
   - **Net regular tax liability** is equal to the regular tax liability less non-refundable tax credits (except the alternative minimum tax credit)

   The upshot of the credit limitation is that the credit cannot offset all of the regular tax if liability exceeds $25,000.

   Additionally, the total of all GBCs cannot decrease the regular liability below the "tentative" tax required under AMT

   > **Example**: A taxpayer has a regular tax liability of $135,000. The total of GBCs = $80,000 and no other credits are available.
   > - What amount of general business tax credit can the taxpayer claim? The maximum credit is $107,500, calculated as:
   >   135,000 – ((135,000 – 25,000)*.25)
   >   Since the total GBCs are less than that limit, the taxpayer can take the full total ($80,000).
   > - If the taxpayer had tentative minimum tax liability of $110,000 he could only reduce regular tax liability to the tentative tax. In this case, the maximum GBC credit he can take is $25,000 because the credit cannot reduce regular tax liability below the tentative minimum tax for AMT purposes.

Unused credits can be carried back 1 year and carried forward 20 years.

a) Rehabilitation Credit

The rehabilitation credit is an investment credit for qualified expenditures incurred to rehabilitate old buildings.

The allowable percentage applied to calculate the credit depends on type of expenditure:
- Expenditures to rehab nonresidential buildings placed in service before 1936 (other than certified historic structures) get a 10% credit
- Expenditures to rehab residential or non-residential certified historic structures get a 20% credit

Qualified expenditures are often used to adjust the taxpayer's basis in the property and may be subject to recapture.
- The taxpayer's adjusted basis in the property is decreased by credit amount
- Rehabilitation credits will be recaptured if the building held for less than 5 years (recapture rate = 20%/year)

b) Business Energy Credit

The business energy credit is granted for certain solar and geothermal property constructed or first used by the taxpayer. Credit is also allowed for facilities using marine and hydrokinetic renewable energy or wind.

The credit allowed is equal to 10-30% of qualified expenditures.

The recoverable basis of the property must be reduced by 50% of the amount of the credit.

c) Work Opportunity Credit

A credit given for each qualified new employee who meets certain requirements.

Qualified new employees include, qualified veterans, qualified ex-felons, designated community residents, vocational rehabilitation referrals, qualified summer youth employees, qualified food stamp recipients, qualified SSI recipients, long-term family assistance recipients, unemployed veterans, and disconnected youths.

The credit is generally equal to:
- 40% of the first $6000 of qualified first-year wages paid to each new qualified employee
- 40% of the first $3000 of wages for qualified summer youth employees for services performed during any 90-day period between May and September 15

The employer's deduction for wages paid is reduced by the credit amount. Therefore, the employer may choose not to claim the credit to maintain the full wage deduction amount.

> ***New Exam Content:*** This credit was retroactively extended as part of the Protecting Americans From Tax Hikes Bill of 2015 (PATH Act).

d) Alcohol Fuels Credit

A credit allowed for the production for a certain amount of ethanol by an eligible small ethanol producer.

e) **Research Credit**
A credit is allowed for expenses paid for qualified research.
The taxpayer can elect to calculate the credit using an alternative simplified credit computation or can be calculated as the sum of:
- 20% of the excess of qualified research expenses for the current year over a base period amount
- 20% of the basic research payments made to a qualified organization
- 20% of amounts paid to an energy research consortium for qualified energy research

> ***New Exam Content:*** This credit was permanently extended as part of the Protecting Americans From Tax Hikes Bill of 2015 (PATH Act).

f) **Employer-Provided Child Care Credit**
The cost of operating employee child care facilities generates a 25% credit for employers of up to $150,000/year.

g) **Small Employer Health Insurance Credit**
Eligible small employers (ESEs) can claim a credit equal to 35% of their non-elective contributions for health insurance for employees.
To be eligible, the ESE has to contribute 50% or more of the employees' costs for premiums.
The full credit is available only to ESEs with 10 or less full-time equivalent employees whose average annual full-time equivalent wages are less than or equal to $50,000.

For purposes of the credit, the owner of the business and specified relatives are not treated as employees and therefore no credit is allowed for employer contributions for health insurance for those employees.

d. Calculation of Individual Income Tax Liability
1) **Tax Tables**
Taxpayers whose taxable income is less than $100,000 must use tax tables created by the IRS to calculate income tax liability. The tax tables indicate the taxpayer's tax liability based on taxable income and filing status.

2) **Tax Rate Schedules**
For individual taxpayers with taxable income greater than or equal to $100,000, the tax rate schedules (2015 tax rate schedules are included below) must be utilized.
The federal income tax has 7 tax brackets: 10%, 15%, 25%, 28%, 33%, 35%, and 39.6%. The amount of federal income tax due depends on the taxpayer's filing status and income level. When a taxpayer's income level causes a jump to the next tax bracket, it does not mean that all of the taxpayer's income is taxed at the higher rate. Instead, only taxable income within a particular tax bracket is subject to the tax rate.

> ***Hint:*** When preparing for the CPA exam, do not waste time memorizing these tables. It is important, however when given a particular taxable income, a filing status, and the tables, that you can correctly calculate the income taxes due.

Single Filing Status (2017):

Taxable Income	Tax Rate
$0 to $9,325	10%
$9,326 to $37,950	$932.50 plus 15% of the amount over $9,325
$37,951 to $91,900	$5,226.25 plus 25% of the amount over $37,950
$91,901 to $191,650	$18,713.75 plus 28% of the amount over $91,900
$191,651 to $416,700	$46,643.75 plus 33% of the amount over $191,650
$416,701 to $413,200	$120,910.25 plus 35% of the amount over $416,700
$418,401 or more	$121,505.25 plus 39.6% of the amount over $418,401

Married Filing Jointly or Qualifying Widow(er) (2017):

Taxable Income	Tax Rate
$0 to $18,650	10%
$18,651 to $75,900	$1,865 plus 15% of the excess over $18,650
$75,901 to $153,100	$10,452.50 plus 25% of the excess over $75,900
$153,101 to $233,350	$29,752.50 plus 28% of the excess over $153,100
$233,351 to $416,700	$52,222.50 plus 33% of the excess over $233,350
$416,701 to $470,700	$112,728 plus 35% of the excess over $416,700
$470,701 or more	$131,628 plus 39.6% of the excess over $470,700

Married Filing Separately (2017):

Taxable Income	Tax Rate
$0 to $9,325	10%
$9,326 to $37,950	$932.50 plus 15% of the amount over $9,325
$37,951 to $76,550	$5,226.25 plus 25% of the amount over $37,950
$76,551 to $116,675	$14,876.25 plus 28% of the amount over $76,550
$116,676 to $208,350	$26,111.25 plus 33% of the amount over $116,675
$208,351 to $232,425	$56,364 plus 35% of the amount over $208,350
$235,351 or more	$65,814 plus 39.6% of the amount over $235,350

Head of Household (2017):

Taxable Income	Tax Rate
$0 to $13,350	10%
$13,351 to $50,800	$1,335 plus 15% of the excess over $13,350
$50,801 to $131,200	$6,952.50 plus 25% of the excess over $50,800
$131,201 to $212,500	$27,052.50 plus 28% of the excess over $131,200
$212,501 to $416,700	$49,816.50 plus 33% of the excess over $212,500
$416,701 to $444,500	$117,202.50 plus 35% of the excess over $416,701
$444,551 or more	$126,950 plus 39.6% of the excess over $444,550

e. Other Applicable Taxes
   1) **The "Kiddie" Tax**
      The kiddie tax was designed to discourage taxpayers from giving income-generating property to their children, who would be charged at a lower tax rate than the parent, thereby reducing the income tax liability of the parent.

      Keep in mind that the **earned income of a child of any age** and the **unearned income of a child over 24 years old** as of the end of the tax year is taxed at the **child's own marginal rate**.

The kiddie tax (generally speaking) applies to **unearned income exceeding $2,100** of a child under age 18 (or aged 19-23 if the child is a full-time student).

Specifically, the kiddie tax applies if ALL of the following apply:
1. The child is either
   - Under 18 at the end of the tax year
   - Age 18, or age 19 to 23 if a full-time student, AND whose earned income is less than or equal to 50% of total support received for the year
2. Either parent is alive at the end of the tax year
3. The child does not file a joint return for the tax year
4. The child's **unearned income** is more than $2,100

How is the kiddie tax calculated?
- The child's taxable income is divided into **net unearned** and **other** income
- To compute **net unearned income**:
  - Subtract $2,100 from the child's unearned income (for taxpayers **who do not itemize** deductions)
  - Subtract $1,050 plus itemized deductions allocated to unearned income from unearned income (for taxpayers **who itemize** deductions)
- Net unearned income is taxed at the parent's rate (if parents are divorced, tax rate of custodial parent is used). All other income taxed at child's rate.

Parents can elect to report child's income on their tax return and pay tax if:
- Child is < 19 (or < 24 if a full-time student)
- Child's income is only from interest, dividends, and capital gain distributions
- Child's gross income is < $10,000
- Child does not file a joint return
- No estimated payments, backup withholding, or prior year refunds can be applied

The kiddie tax is reported on <u>Form 8615</u>.

2) **Self-Employment Tax**
Self-employment tax is imposed on income from self-employment.
To understand how self-employment taxes work, it is important to understand payroll taxes. When an employee receives wages from an employer, both the employer and the employee are responsible for paying certain payroll taxes.

- Social Security (FICA):
  - This tax is imposed on **both employers and employees**
  - It is comprised of as at least two components:
    - OASDI: 6.2% (only applied to first $118,500 of wages)
    - Medicare hospital insurance (HI): 1.45% (not capped; applied to all wages)
    - Total combined rate: 7.65% for both employers and employees
  - Additional third component of 0.9% is levied on wages over $200,000 (S/HOH), $250,000 (MFJ), $125,000 (MFS)

- Federal Unemployment (FUTA):
  - This tax is imposed only on **employers**
  - It is calculated as 6.2% of the first $7,000 wages paid to each employee
  - A credit of up to 5.4% for unemployment taxes paid to a state, resulting in a net federal unemployment tax of 0.8%

When taxpayers are self-employed, they essentially play the role of both employer and employee and are therefore responsible for paying both the employer and employee portion of payroll taxes related to their self-employment income.

There are several steps required to calculate self-employment tax:

1. Calculate **self-employment income**:

   Self-Employment Income = Gross Income from Self-Employment − Deductions Associated with the Activity (including director's fees)

2. Use self-employment income to calculate **net earnings from self-employment**:

   Net Earnings from Self-Employment = Self-Employment Income * 92.35%

   > *Hint:* To understand where the 92.35% comes from, remember that an employee is only required to pay one side of payroll taxes, but a self-employed individual must pay "both halves," or 15.3%. So, the law equalizes the tax burden by reducing the income subject to tax by 7.65% (that is, multiplying the taxpayer's self-employment income by 92.35%).

   > *Hint:* The taxpayer does not need to pay any self-employment tax if net earnings from self-employment are less than $400.

   > *Hint:* 50% of the self-employment tax is deductible FOR AGI.

3. Calculate Part 1 - Social Security portion:

   Social Security Taxes = Net Earnings from Self-Employment (up to $118,500) * 12.4%

4. Calculate Part 2 – Medicare portion:

   Medicare Taxes = Net Earnings from Self-Employment (no ceiling) * 2.9%

5. Calculate Part 3 – Additional 0.9% Medicare tax portion (if necessary):
   If net earnings from self-employment **exceed certain limits** (S: $200,000; MFJ: $250,000; MFS: $125,000) an additional 0.9% Medicare tax is imposed

   Additional Medicare Tax = Ceiling Based on Filing Status − Net Earnings from Self-Employment * 0.9%

6. **The total self-employment tax is the sum** the 12.4% Social Security, the 2.9% Medicare, and the .9% Additional Medicare tax portions.

Self-employment taxes are reported on Form 1040, Schedule SE

> *Hint:* There is a long and short form of Schedule SE. Most taxpayers can use the short form unless wages plus self-employment income exceed annual wage base limit for Social Security taxes and/or the taxpayer works as a minister, pastor, etc.

f. Estimated Tax Payments
Taxpayers who either do not have any taxes withheld from their earnings or whose withholdings do not sufficiently cover their regular and Alternative Minimum Tax liability must make quarterly estimated tax payments to the IRS. If these payments are not made, a penalty will be assessed. There are two methods that can be used to calculate the required annual payment of estimated taxes, which are the annualized income method and the seasonal method.
   1) The annualized income installment method annualizes tax at the end of each period based on a reasonable estimate of income, deductions, and other items relating to events that occurred from the beginning of the tax year through the end of the period.
   2) The seasonal method is only used by a limited number of companies that earn most of their income in certain months based on the items they sell. Examples of businesses using the seasonal method include: an outdoor amusement park in Chicago and a lawn furniture company in Maine.

The estimated tax payment that is required to avoid a penalty depends on whether or not the taxpayer meets a certain AGI threshold ($150,000 for joint returns and single filers; $75,000 for married filing separately).

For taxpayers with an AGI **at or below** the threshold in the prior year, estimated tax payments plus withholdings must equal the lesser of:
- 90% of the current year's tax
- 90% of the tax determined using the annualized income method
- 100% of the prior year's tax, even if there was no tax liability in the prior year.

For taxpayers with an AGI **above** the threshold ($150,000 for joint returns and single filers; $75,000 for married filing separately) in the prior year, estimated tax payments plus withholdings must equal the lesser of:
- 90% of the current year's tax
- 90% of the tax determined using the annualized income method
- **110% of the prior year's tax**

Quarterly estimated tax payments are due by the 15th day of the 4th, 6th, 9th and 1st month. For calendar-year taxpayers, the due dates are April 15th, June 15th, and September 15th of the current year and January 15th of the following year.

The penalty is determined based on the difference between the amount required and the amount actually paid. No penalty is assessed if:
- The total tax due was less than $1,000
- The taxpayer had no tax liability for the prior year (which was a 12-month period), and the taxpayer was a US citizen or resident for the whole year

Additionally, the IRS may waive the penalty if the failure to pay was due to reasonable cause (not willful neglect) or due to a casualty, disaster or other unusual circumstances.

Multiple Choice

REG 4-Q77

H. Alternative Minimum Tax

Recall income and expense items includible in the computation of an individual taxpayer's alternative minimum taxable income (AMTI).

Calculate alternative minimum tax (AMT) for an individual taxpayer.

The Alternative Minimum Tax (AMT) was designed to prevent a taxpayer from avoiding all tax liability by applying exclusions, deductions, and credits. It is a separate tax system that calculates income tax on a broader tax base by modifying taxable income. A two-tiered rate schedule (26% or 28%) is then applied to that modified tax base. If this tentative minimum tax exceeds the taxpayer's regular tax liability, an alternative minimum tax is due to the IRS.

Modifications on income imposed by the AMT rules serve to increase taxable income by adding income items not recognized by the regular tax system and disallowing deductions that do not necessarily represent economic outlays.

Taxpayers who are subject to the regular tax are generally also subject to the AMT. Therefore, partnerships and S corporations are not subject to AMT, but their partners and shareholders are subject to AMT. Foreign corporations are only subject to AMT as it relates to taxable income connected with their conduct of a US trade or business.

a. **Computation of Alternative Minimum Tax (AMT)**
   The Alternative Minimum Tax is computed using Form 6251, Alternative Minimum Tax.
   The formula for computing AMT is:
   Regular Taxable Income
   - + or -   Adjustments
   - +   Preferences
   - =   AMT Income ("AMTI")
   - -   (Exemption)
   - =   AMT Base
   - x   Rate (26% or 28%; reduced rates for qualified dividends and NCG)
   - =   Tentative Min Tax before Foreign Tax Credit
   - -   (Certain Tax Credits including AMT Foreign Tax Credit)
   - =   Tentative Minimum Tax
   - -   (Regular Tax Liability)
   - =   AMT (if Positive)

b. **Adjustments**
   Adjustments and preferences are applied to regular taxable income to determine a taxpayer's Alternative Minimum Taxable Income (AMTI).
   The first step in calculating the AMT is to apply adjustments that either increase or decrease taxable income. Adjustments involve **substituting** AMT treatment of an item for the regular tax treatment. Therefore, AMT adjustments usually increase, but can in some cases decrease taxable income. These adjustments often represent income or deductions that were used to defer the taxation of economic income. As a result, many (not all) adjustments are merely timing differences that will reverse in future periods.

   Some examples of adjustments include:
   o Personal exemptions and standard deduction (if used) are added back

Multiple Choice

REG 4-Q78

- Adjustments related to itemized deductions
  - Itemized deductions for AMT purposes are computed the same as for regular tax purposes, except for certain specific cases, including:
    - Any deduction taken for **personal, state, or local taxes** must be **added back**
    - **2% miscellaneous deductions** are not allowed and must be **added back**
    - **Home mortgage interest** must be **added back** if loan proceeds were used for anything other than to acquire, build or improve the home
    - Personal exemptions and standard deductions are added back
    - For real estate placed in service after 1986 and before 1999, depreciation must be over straight line 40 years. For any property placed in service after 1/1/1999, the depreciation methods are the same for regular tax and alternative minimum tax.
    - For personal property used in a trade or business that is placed in service after 1986, the depreciation is 150% declining balance for AMT, versus the 200% declining balance for regular taxes.
    - The excess of the stock's FMV over the amount paid upon exercise of incentive stock options.
    - For construction accounting, the percentage completion must be used instead of completed contract for AMT

Multiple Choice

REG 4-Q79 through REG 4-Q81

- For **real property placed into service after 1986 and before 1999**, straight-line depreciation must be used and the life must be 40 years.
  - For **real property purchased after 1999, there is no difference** between AMT cost recovery and regular cost recovery.

- For **personal property placed into service after 1986**, an adjustment must be made for the amount of the regular tax depreciation using the 200% declining balance method, less the 150% the amount under the declining balance method. Therefore, you must use 150% declining balance for AMT instead of 200% for regular taxes.

c. **Preferences**

After adjustments are made to regular taxable income, AMT preferences are applied, resulting in Alternative Minimum Taxable Income (AMTI). Preferences involve adding the difference between the AMT treatment of an item and the regular tax treatment of an item. Therefore, preferences **always increase** taxable income.

The most common AMT preference items are:
- Tax-exempt interest on certain private activity bonds.
  - Exception:
    - This preference item does not apply to any private activity bonds issued in 2009 or 2010
- Excess intangible drilling costs (IDCs)
- Mine exploration and development costs are adjusted.
- Accelerated depreciation of real estate, before 1/1/1987 vs. straight-line, under ACRS.

d. **AMT Exemption**

AMTI is reduced by an exemption that is phased out at a rate of 25% of AMTI over a certain threshold and ultimately completely phased out once AMTI exceeds the upper end of the phase-out range.

e. **AMT Tax Rates and Tentative Minimum Tax Computation**
Once adjustments, preferences and the AMT exemption is applied, the result is the taxpayer's **AMT base**. At this point, a tax rate is applied to the AMT base to calculate the taxpayer's **tentative minimum tax**.

To calculate the tentative minimum tax:
- Multiply the first $186,300 ($93,150 for MFS filers) of the AMT base by 26%
- Any amounts over $186,300 ($93,150 for MFS filers) should be multiplied by 28%
- Tentative minimum tax on net capital gains and qualified dividend income is computed using the long-term capital gain rates that apply for regular tax purposes.

f. **Tax Credits**
Tax credits reduce an individual's regular tax liability to the extent that the regular tax liability exceeds the tentative minimum tax liability. The alternative min tax can be a credit against regular tax liability but against alternative min tax liability.
The tentative alternative minimum tax is reduced by; is also reduced by several other:
- The AMT foreign tax credit

g. **AMT Due and Minimum Tax Credit (MTC)**
If AMT exceeds the regular tax liability, the taxpayer will owe the difference.
The amount of AMT paid (net of exclusion preferences) can be taken in future years as a credit against regular tax liability, known as the minimum tax credit (MTC).

The credit cannot be carried back but CAN be carried forward indefinitely and can ONLY be used to reduce future REGULAR tax liability, NOT future AMT liability. The minimum tax credit (MTC) is non-refundable as it relates to the current year.

This page is intentionally left blank.

Glossary: Federal Taxation for Individuals

A

Accountable plan – for a plan to be considered accountable, the employee must be required to substantiate all expenses for reimbursement, and any excess reimbursements must be returned to the employer

Active income – includes income from wages, salaries, professional fees, etc. Represents income from an activity in which the taxpayer has material participation. This is contrasted with passive activities in which the taxpayer does not materially participate

"Above the line" deductions – deductions which are applied to a taxpayer's gross income to arrive at AGI

Adjusted Gross Income (AGI) – represents an individual taxpayer's income after applying "above the line" deductions

Alimony – payments made from one party to another as the result of a divorce

Alternative minimum tax (AMT) – tax designed to prevent a taxpayer from avoiding all tax liability by applying exclusions, deductions, and credits

Alternative minimum tax income (AMTI) – results from applying AMT adjustments and preferences to a taxpayer's regular taxable income

At Risk limitation – the amount of loss and other deductions that a taxpayer can claim; the initial at-risk amount is equal to the amount the taxpayer has contributed in cash plus the adjusted basis of any property contributed plus any debt assumed by the taxpayer for which he is directly liable

B

Basis – the amount that a taxpayer has contributed toward the purchase of an asset or an interest in an entity

C

Casualty – a sudden unexpected event that damages or destroys an asset. Theft of an asset qualifies as a casualty event. Losses that result from a casualty are deductible subject to certain limitations

Child Support – payments between two divorced parties that are not considered alimony and that are intended for the support of a minor child. Child support payments are not taxable to the one receiving the money and not deductible by the one making the payments

Closely-held C corporation – a corporation with five or fewer shareholders owning more than 50% of corporation stock

Community property – property that was acquired during marriage (unless by gift/inheritance). Personal service income is usually community property

Credit – a tax credit is an amount that directly reduces a taxpayer's tax liability

D

De minimis fringe benefit – benefits that are of such a small value that accounting for them would be impractical or impossible

Deduction – a tax deduction reduces a taxpayer's taxable income.

Discriminatory benefit plan – a benefit plan where certain benefits are extended only to highly-compensated employees

E

Earned Income - income generated by personal services as opposed to income generated by property

Exclusion – amount that is not included in gross income because it pertains to a specific IRC rule that allows it to be ignored in the calculation of gross income.

Exemption – an amount that is deducted from AGI along with either the standard deduction or itemized deductions to arrive at taxable income. Taxpayers can usually claim an exemption for themselves and for their spouse in addition to an exemption for each dependent

F

Filing Status – a classification that is used to determine filing requirements, tax rates, the standard deduction amount, and a taxpayer's eligibility for certain deductions and tax credits. There are five filing status options: Single, Head of Household, Married Filing Jointly, Married Filing Separately, Qualifying Widower with Dependent Child (sometimes referred to as Surviving Spouse).

Fringe benefit – a benefit provided to an employee by his or her employer in addition to cash compensation.

G

Gross income - amount of realized income after eliminating deferred and excluded income.

H
High deductible health plan (HDHP) – a health insurance plan where the annual deductible is equal to at least $1,300 for individual coverage ($2,600 for family coverage), and the annual out-of-pocket expenses (deductibles, co-payments, and other amounts, but not premiums) do not exceed $6,550 for individual coverage ($13,100 for family coverage).

I
Income in Respect of a Decedent (IRD) – income that a taxpayer had earned before death, but had not yet recognized as income.
Itemized deductions – deductions applied to a taxpayer's AGI to arrive at taxable income. Note that a taxpayer can choose to itemize deductions or to apply the standard deduction, but cannot apply both.

M
Material Participation – a threshold of participation in an activity defined by the IRC that determines whether any resulting gain or loss from the activity is considered passive or non-passive.
Modified Adjusted Gross Income (MAGI) – an adjusted version of a taxpayer's AGI that is used in certain tax calculations

P
Pass-through entity – an entity that is not directly taxed, but instead passes all income and loss items through to its members or shareholders for taxation. Pass-through entities include partnerships, S corporations, trusts, and estates.
Passive Loss – a loss generated by a passive activity. Passive losses can only be offset by passive income.
Personal service corporation – an incorporated service business with more than 10% of stock owned by shareholder-employees
Portfolio income – Income from interest, dividends annuities, royalties, etc.
Provisional Income – Calculated to determine what portion of Social Security Benefits can be excluded from gross income. Provisional income is equal to a taxpayer's AGI + tax-exempt income + 50% of Social Security benefits

Q
Qualified Education Expenses – includes the Series EE bond interest exclusion, student loan interest deductibility, American opportunity tax credit, and lifetime learning credit
Qualifying child – an individual for whom the taxpayer can claim a dependency exemption because the child meets numerous tests defined by the IRC, including the relationship test, age test, support test, residence test, joint return test, and citizenship/residency test
Qualifying relative – an individual other than a qualifying child for whom the taxpayer can claim a dependency exemption because the relative meets numerous tests defined by the IRC, including the relationship test, support test, gross income test, joint return test, and citizenship/residency test.

S
Separate Property – property that was owned before marriage or acquired by gift or inheritance while married
Standard deduction – a deduction subtracted from a taxpayer's AGI to arrive at taxable income. A taxpayer must decide either to apply the standard deduction or to itemize deductions, but cannot do both

T
Taxable Event – an event recognized by the IRS as having tax implications
Trade – an activity with a continuous level of profit-seeking; i.e., an activity that a self-employed taxpayer engages in for-profit as his livelihood or in addition to his regular employment
Uniform Capitalization Rules (UNICAP) – uniform capitalization rules require businesses to capitalize certain costs that benefit or are incurred because of the *production* or *resale* activities of the business

Multiple Choice – Questions

REG 4-Q1 R227. One of the elections a new corporation must make is its choice of an accounting period. Which of the following entities has the most flexibility in choosing an accounting period?

A. C corporation.
B. S corporation.
C. Partnership.
D. Personal service corporation.

REG 4-Q2 R284. Which one of the following will result in an accruable expense for an accrual-basis taxpayer?

A. An invoice dated prior to year end but the repair completed after year end.
B. A repair completed prior to year-end but **not** invoiced.
C. A repair completed prior to year-end and not paid until the next year.
D. A signed contract for repair work to be done and the work is to be completed at a later date.

REG 4-Q3 R338. Mosh, a sole proprietor, uses the cash basis of accounting. At the beginning of the current year, accounts receivable were $25,000. During the year, Mosh collected $100,000 from customers. At the end of the year, accounts receivable were $15,000. What was Mosh's gross taxable income for the current year?

A. $ 75,000
B. $ 90,000
C. $100,000
D. $110,000

REG 4-Q4 R349. Chrisp, a freelance photographer, uses the cash method for business. The tax year ends on December 31. Which of the following should **not** be included in the determination of Chrisp's gross income for the following year?

A. Chrisp owns controlling shares of a closely-held corporation and is planning to delay the bonus payment from the corporation until January of the next year. Bonus was authorized on December 15, of the current year and may be drawn at any time.
B. Chrisp received a check from a client on December 28 of the current year for a family portrait produced on December 22 of the current year. The check was dated December 23 of the current year but was **not** deposited until January 4 of the following year.
C. A client notified Chrisp on December 27 of the current year that a check was ready. The check was **not** picked up until January 4 of the following year.
D. Chrisp received a dividend check on January 4 of the following year. The dividends were declared payable on December 30 of the current year.

REG 4-Q5 R176. Dart, a C corporation, distributes software over the Internet and has had average revenues in excess of $20 million dollars per year for the past three years. To purchase software, customers key-in their credit card number to a secure web site and receive a password that allows the customer to immediately download the software. As a result, Dart doesn't record accounts receivable or inventory on its books. Which of the following statements is correct?

A. Dart may use either the cash or accrual method of accounting as long as Dart elects a calendar year end.
B. Dart may utilize any method of accounting Dart chooses as long as Dart consistently applies the method it chooses.
C. Dart must use the accrual method of accounting.
D. Dart may utilize the cash basis method of accounting until it incurs an additional $10 million to develop additional software.

REG 4-Q6 R403. Which of the following taxpayers may use the cash method of accounting?

A. A tax shelter
B. A qualified personal service corporation
C. A C corporation with annual gross receipts of $50,000,000
D. A manufacturer

REG 4-Q7 R16. In year 1, a taxpayer sold real property for $200,000, receiving $100,000 at closing and $100,000 plus accrued interest at the prime rate in the next year. The buyer also assumed a $50,000 existing mortgage on the property. The taxpayer's adjusted basis was $75,000, and the taxpayer incurred $10,000 of selling expenses. If this transaction qualifies for installment sale treatment, what is the gross profit on the sale?

A. $115,000
B. $125,000
C. $165,000
D. $175,000

REG 4-Q8 R101. In the current year, Essex sold land with a basis of $80,000 to Yarrow for $100,000. Yarrow paid $25,000 down and agreed to pay $15,000 per year, plus interest, for the next five years, beginning in the second year. Under the installment method, what gain should Essex include in gross income for the year of sale?

A. $25,000
B. $20,000
C. $15,000
D. $ 5,000

REG 4-Q9 R184. Aviary Corp. sold a building for $600,000. Aviary received a down payment of $120,000 as well as annual principal payments of $120,000 for each of the subsequent four years. Aviary purchased the building for $500,000 and claimed depreciation of $80,000. What amount of gain should Aviary report in the year of sale using the installment method?

A. $180,000
B. $120,000
C. $54,000
D. $36,000

REG 4-Q10 R1147. The uniform capitalization method must be used by

I. Retailers of personal property who have average annual gross receipts of $4,000,000 for the three preceding years.
II. Tangible personal property manufacturers.

A. I only
B. II only
C. Both I and II
D. Neither I nor II

REG 4-Q11 R124. Winkler, a CPA, provided accounting services to a client, Thompson. On December 15 of the same year, Thompson gave Winkler 100 shares of Foster Corp. as compensation for services. The adjusted basis of the stock was $4,000, and its fair market value at the time of transfer was $5,000. Two months later, Winkler sold the stock on February 15 for $7,500. What is the amount that Winkler should recognize as gain on the sale of stock?

A. $0
B. $1,000
C. $2,500
D. $5,000

REG 4-Q12 R270. Jones was unemployed for part of the year. Jones received $35,000 of wages, $4,000 from a state unemployment compensation plan, and $2,000 from his former employer's company-paid supplemental unemployment benefit plan. What is the amount of Jones' gross income?

A. $35,000
B. $37,000
C. $39,000
D. $41,000

REG 4-Q13 R157. Kant, a cash-basis individual, owns and operates an office building. Kant received the following payments during the current year:

Current rents	$30,000
Advance rents for the next year	10,000
Refundable security deposits held in a segregated account	5,000
Lease cancellation payments	15,000

What amount is included in gross income?

A. $30,000
B. $40,000
C. $55,000
D. $60,000

REG 4-Q14 R192. Nare, an accrual-basis, calendar-year taxpayer, owns a building that was rented to Mott under a 10-year lease expiring August 31, year 3. On January 2, year 1, Mott paid $30,000 as consideration for canceling the lease. On November 1, year 1, Nare leased the building to Pine under a five-year lease. Pine paid Nare $5,000 rent for each of the two months of November and December, and an additional $5,000 for the last month's rent. What amount of rental income should Nare report in its year 1 income tax return?

A. $10,000
B. $15,000
C. $40,000
D. $45,000

REG 4-Q15 R307. During 2001, Adler had the following cash receipts:

Wages	$18,000
Interest income from investments in municipal bonds	$400
Unemployment compensation	$1,500

What is the total amount must be included in gross income on Adler's 2001 income tax return?

A. $18,000
B. $18,400
C. $19,500
D. $19,900

REG 4-Q16 R321. Greller owns 100 shares of Arden Corp., a publicly-traded company, which Greller purchased on January 1, 2001, for $10,000. On January 1, 2003, Arden declared a 2-for-1 stock split when the fair market value (FMV) of the stock was $120 per share. Immediately following the split, the FMV of Arden stock was $62 per share. On February 1, 2003, Greller had his broker specifically sell the 100 shares of Arden stock received in the split when the FMV of the stock was $65 per share. What is the basis of the 100 shares of Arden sold?

A. $5,000
B. $6,000
C. $6,200
D. $6,500

REG 4-Q17 R125. Which of the following should be included when determining adjusted gross income?

A. Alimony received.
B. Compensation for injuries or sickness.
C. Rental value of parsonages.
D. Tuition scholarship.

REG 4-Q18 R401. Which of the following conditions must be present in a post-1984 divorce agreement for a payment to qualify as deductible alimony?
I. Payments must be in cash.
II. The payments must end at the recipient's death.

A. I only.
B. II only.
C. Both I and II.
D. Neither I nor II.

REG 4-Q19 R251. In the current year Jensen had the following items:

Salary	$50,000
Inheritance	25,000
Alimony from ex-spouse	12,000
Child support from ex-spouse	9,000
Capital loss on investment stock sale	(6,000)

What is Jensen's AGI for the current year?

A. $44,000
B. $59,000
C. $62,000
D. $84,000

REG 4-Q20 R165. An individual received $50,000 during the current year pursuant to a divorce decree. A check for $25,000 was identified as annual alimony, checks totaling $10,000 as annual child support, and a check for $15,000 as a property settlement. What amount should be included in the individual's gross income?

A. $50,000
B. $40,000
C. $25,000
D. $0

REG 4-Q21 R291. Tana's divorce decree requires Tana to make the following transfers to Tana's former spouse during the current year:
 Alimony payments of $3,000.
 Child support of $2,000.
 Property division of stock with a basis of $4,000 and a fair market value of $6,500.

What is the amount of Tana's alimony deduction?

A. $ 3,000
B. $ 7,000
C. $ 9,500
D. $11,500

REG 4-Q22 R1150 Which of the following statements is true about damages?

A. Compensatory damages are taxable.
B. Damages for physical illness/injury.
C. Punitive damages are taxable.
D. No damages received by a taxpayer are taxable.

REG 4-Q23 R233. Cassidy, an individual, reported the following items of income and expense during the current year:

Salary	$50,000
Alimony paid to a former spouse	10,000
Inheritance from a grandparent	25,000
Proceeds of a lawsuit for physical injuries	50,000

What is the amount of Cassidy's adjusted gross income?

A. $ 40,000
B. $ 50,000
C. $115,000
D. $125,000

REG 4-Q24 R327. DAC Foundation awarded Kent $75,000 in recognition of lifelong literary achievement. Kent was not required to render future services as a condition to receive the $75,000. What condition(s) must have been met for the award to be excluded from Kent's gross income?

I. Kent was selected for the award by DAC without any action on Kent's part.
II. Pursuant to Kent's designation, DAC paid the amount of the award either to a governmental unit or to a charitable organization.

A. I only.
B. II only.
C. Both I and II.
D. Neither I nor II.

REG 4-Q25 R387. Fuller was the owner and beneficiary of a $200,000 life insurance policy on a parent. Fuller sold the policy to Decker, for $25,000. Decker paid a total of $40,000 in premiums. Upon the death of the parent, what amount must Decker include in gross income?

A. $0
B. $135,000
C. $160,000
D. $200,000

REG 4-Q26 R143. Robbe, a cash basis single taxpayer, reported $50,000 of adjusted gross income last year and claimed itemized deductions of $5,500, consisting solely of $5,500 of state income taxes paid last year. Robbe's itemized deduction amount, which exceeded the standard deduction available to single taxpayers for last year by $1,150, was fully deductible and it was not subject to any limitations or phase-outs. In the current year, Robbe received a $1,500 state tax refund relating to the prior year. What is the proper treatment of the state tax refund?

A. Include none of the refund in income in the current year.
B. Include $1,150 in income in the current year.
C. Include $1,500 in income in the current year.
D. Amend the prior-year's return and reduce the claimed itemized deductions for that year.

REG 4-Q27 R40. Randolph is a single individual who always claims the standard deduction. Randolph received the following in the current year:

Wages	$22,000
Unemployment compensation	6,000
Pension distribution (100% taxable)	4,000
A state tax refund from the previous year (did not itemize in previous year)	425

What is Randolph's gross income?

A. $22,000
B. $28,425
C. $32,000
D. $32,425

REG 4-Q28 R1148. Wallace Green retired on May 31, 2015. He is entitled to receive a monthly pension benefit of $350 for life. At his retirement date, his life expectancy is five years. Green's received his first pension check on June 15, 2015. Green contributed $6,000 into his company's pension plan during his years of employment. How much can Green exclude from taxable income for the pension amounts received for the 2015, 2016, and 2017?

	2015	2016	2017
A.	$700	$1,200	$1,200
B.	$1,200	$1,200	$1,200
C.	$700	$700	$700
D.	$0	$0	$0

REG 4-Q29 R400. Freeman, a single individual, reported he following income in the current year:
- Guaranteed payment from services rendered to a partnership $50,000
- Ordinary income from a S corporation $20,000

What amount of Freeman's income is subject to self-employment tax?

A. $0
B. $20,000
C. $50,000
D. $70,000

REG 4-Q30 R42. Johnson worked for ABC Co. and earned a salary of $100,000. Johnson also received, as a fringe benefit, group term-life insurance at twice Johnson's salary. The annual IRS-established uniform cost of insurance is $2.76 per $1,000. What amount must Johnson include in gross income?

A. $100,000
B. $100,276
C. $100,414
D. $100,552

REG 4-Q31 R187. A 33-year-old taxpayer withdrew $30,000 (pretax) from a traditional IRA. The taxpayer has a 33% effective tax rate and a 35% marginal tax rate. What is the total tax liability associated with the withdrawal?

A. $10,000
B. $10,500
C. $13,000
D. $13,500

REG 4-Q32 R398. Mock operates a retail business selling illegal narcotic substances. Which of the following item(s) may Mock deduct in calculating business income?

I. Cost of merchandise.
II. Business expenses other than the cost of merchandise.

A. I only
B. II only
C. Both I and II
D. Neither I nor II

REG 4-Q33 R208. A self-employed taxpayer had gross income of $57,000. The taxpayer paid self-employment tax of $8,000, health insurance of $6,000, and $5,000 of alimony. The taxpayer also contributed $2,000 to a traditional IRA. The taxpayer is not eligible to participate in another company's pension plan. What is the taxpayer's adjusted gross income?

A. $55,000
B. $50,000
C. $46,000
D. $40,000

REG 4-Q34 R35. The Uniform Capitalization Rules of Code Sec. 263A apply to retailers whose average gross receipts for the preceding three years exceed what amount?

A. $ 1,000,000
B. $ 2,500,000
C. $ 5,000,000
D. $10,000,000

REG 4-Q35 R348. Which of the following costs is includible in inventory under the uniform capitalization rules for merchandise manufactured by a company for sale to its customers?

A. Advertising.
B. General legal fees.
C. Engineering.
D. Selling expenses.

REG 4-Q36 R82. Which of the following costs are subject to the Uniform Capitalization Rules of Code Sec. 263A for manufactured tangible personal property?

A. Off-site storage.
B. Advertising.
C. Research.
D. Marketing.

REG 4-Q37 R262. Which of the following is subject to the Uniform Capitalization Rules of Code Sec. 263A?

A. Editorial costs incurred by a freelance writer.
B. Research and experimental expenditures.
C. Mine development and exploration costs.
D. Warehousing costs incurred by a manufacturing company with $12 million in annual gross receipts.

REG 4-Q38 R265. Under the uniform capitalization rules applicable to taxpayers with property acquired for resale, which of the following costs should be capitalized with respect to inventory if **no** exceptions have been met?

	Repackaging costs	Off-site storage costs
A.	Yes	Yes
B.	Yes	No
C.	No	Yes
D.	No	No

REG 4-Q39 R402. Which of the following costs is not included in inventory under the Uniform Capitalization rules for goods manufactured by the taxpayer?

A. Research
B. Warehousing costs
C. Quality control
D. Taxes excluding income taxes

REG 4-Q40 R298. Barkley owns a vacation cabin that was rented to unrelated parties for 10 days during the year for $2,500. The cabin was used personally by Barkley for three months and left vacant for the rest of the year. Expenses for the cabin were as follows:

Real estate taxes $1,000
Mainenance and utlities $2,000

How much rental income(loss) is included in Barkley's adjusted gross income?

A. $ 0
B. $ 500
C. $ (500)
D. $(1,500)

REG 4-Q41 R396. Adams owns a second residence that is used for both personal and rental purposes. During 2013, Adams used the second residence for 50 days and rented the residence for 200 days. Which of the following statements is correct?

A. Depreciation may not be deducted on the property under any circumstances.
B. A rental loss may be deducted if rental-related expenses exceed rental income.
C. Utilities and maintenance on the property must be divided between personal and rental use.
D. All mortgage interest and taxes on the property will be deducted to determine the property's net income or loss.

REG 4-Q42 R7. Davidson was transferred from Chicago to Atlanta. In connection with the transfer, Davidson incurred the following moving expenses:

Moving the household goods	$2,000
Temporary living expenses in Atlanta	400
Lodging on the way to Atlanta	100
Meals	40

What amount may Davidson deduct if the employer reimbursed Davidson $2,000 (not included in Form W-2) for moving expenses?

A. $100
B. $120
C. $500
D. $520

REG 4-Q43 R87. Cole earned $3,000 in wages, incurred $1,000 in unreimbursed employee business expenses, paid $400 as interest on a student loan, and contributed $100 to a charity. What is Cole's adjusted gross income?

A. $3,000
B. $2,600
C. $2,500
D. $1,600

REG 4-Q44 R126. An individual starts paying student loan interest in the current year. How many years may the individual deduct a portion of the student loan interest?

A. Current year only.
B. Five years.
C. Ten years.
D. Duration of time that interest is paid.

REG 4-Q45 R288. In the current year, an unmarried individual with modified adjusted gross income of $25,000 paid $1,000 interest on a qualified education loan entered into on July 1. How may the individual treat the interest for income tax purposes?

A. As a $500 deduction to arrive at AGI for the year.
B. As a $1,000 deduction to arrive at AGI for the year.
C. As a $1,000 itemized deduction.
D. As a nondeductible item of personal interest.

REG 4-Q46 R308. In the current year, Drake, a disabled taxpayer, made the following home improvements:

	Cost
Pool installation, which qualified as a medical expense and increased the value of the home by $25,000	$100,000
Widening doorways to accommodate Drake's wheelchair. The improvement did not increase the value of his home	10,000

For regular income tax purposes and without regard to the adjusted gross income percentage threshold limitation, what maximum amount would be allowable as a medical expense deduction in the current year?

A. $110,000
B. $ 85,000
C. $ 75,000
D. $ 10,000

REG 4-Q47 R335. Smith paid the following unreimbursed medical expenses:

Dentist and eye doctor fees	$ 5,000
Contact lenses	500
Facial cosmetic surgery to improve Smith's personal appearance (surgery is unrelated to personal injury or congenital deformity)	10,000
Premium on disability insurance policy to pay him if he is injured and Unable to work	2,000

What is the total amount of Smith's tax-deductible medical expenses before the adjusted gross income limitation?

A. $17,500
B. $15,500
C. $7,500
D. $5,500

REG 4-Q48 R450. Sally Burke is a 45 year old individual taxpayer and had adjusted gross income (AGI) of $60,000 on her 2017 tax return. She incurred the following medical expenses in 2017:

Prescription medicine and drugs	$3,000
Doctor fees for illnesses	5,000
Medical insurance premiums	3,000
Over the counter vitamins and cold remedies	500

She received insurance reimbursements of $3,000 in 2017. What is the net medical expense deduction that Sally can take as an itemized deduction for 2017?

A. $11,000
B. $3,500
C. $11,500
D. $2,000

REG 4-Q49 R395. Carroll, age 66, is an unmarried taxpayer with an adjusted gross income (AGI) of $100,000, incurred and paid in 2017 the following unreimbursed medical expenses for the year:

Doctor bills resulting from a serious fall	$5,000
Cosmetic surgery that was necessary to correct a congenital deformity	15,000

Carroll had no medical insurance. For regular income tax purposes, what was Carroll's maximum allowable medical expense deduction, after the applicable threshold limitation, for the year?

A. $0
B. $12,500
C. $15,000
D. $20,000

REG 4-Q50 R17. Which of the following statements is correct regarding the deductibility of an individual's medical expenses?

A. A medical expense paid by credit card is deductible in the year the credit card bill is paid.
B. A medical expense deduction is allowed for payments made in the current year for medical services received in earlier years.
C. Medical expenses, net of insurance reimbursements, are disregarded in the alternative minimum tax calculation.
D. A medical expense deduction is not allowed for Medicare insurance premiums.

REG 4-Q51 R268. The Smiths are married, file a joint income tax return, and qualify to itemize their deductions in the current ear. Their adjusted gross income for the year was $55,000, and during the year they paid the following taxes:

Real estate tax on personal residence $2,000
Ad valorem tax on personal automobile $500
Current-year state and city income taxes withheld from paycheck $1,000

What total amount of the expense should the Smiths claim as an itemized deduction on their current-year joint income tax return?

A. $1,000
B. $2,500
C. $3,000
D. $3,500

REG 4-Q52 R20. An individual taxpayer earned $10,000 in investment income, $8,000 in noninterest investment expenses, and $5,000 in investment interest expense. How much is the taxpayer allowed to deduct on the current-year's tax return for investment interest expenses?

A. $0
B. $2,000
C. $3,000
D. $5,000

REG 4-Q53 R229. Wilson, CPA, uses a commercial tax software package to prepare clients' individual income tax returns. Upon reviewing a client's computer-generated year 1 itemized deductions, Wilson discovers that the schedule's deductible investment interest expense is less than the amount paid by the taxpayer and the amount that Wilson entered into the computer. After analyzing the entire tax return, Wilson determines that the computer-generated investment interest expense deduction is correct. Why is the computer-generated investment interest expense deduction correct?

I. The client's investment interest expense exceeds net investment income.
II. The client's qualified residence interest expense reduces the deductible amount of investment interest expense.

A. I only.
B. II only.
C. Both I and II.
D. Neither I nor II.

REG 4-Q54 R190. Taylor, an unmarried taxpayer, had $90,000 in adjusted gross income for year 13. During year 13, Taylor donated land to a church and made no other contributions. Taylor purchased the land in year 1 as an investment for $14,000. The land's fair market value was $25,000 on the day of the donation. What is the maximum amount of charitable contribution that Taylor may deduct as an itemized deduction for the land donation for year 13?

A. $25,000
B. $14,000
C. $11,000
D. $0

REG 4-Q55 R386. Smith, a single individual, made the following charitable contributions during the current year. Smith's adjusted gross income is $60,000.

- Donation TO Smith's church $5,000
- Art work donated to the local art museum. Smith purchased it for $2,000 four months ago. A local art dealer appraised it for   3,000
- Contribution to a needy family.   1,000

What amount should Smith deduct as a charitable contribution?

A. $5,000
B. $7,000
C. $8,000
D. $9,000

REG 4-Q56 R1105. Glen Blake, aged 67 and single, had an adjusted gross income of $50,000 in 2016. During 2016 Gene paid the following unreimbursed medical and dental expenses:

Medical insurance premiums $ 300
Dental surgery   5,000

Also in 2016, Gene suffered a $4,000 loss due to vandalism, for which Gene had no insurance. Gene itemized his deductions for 2016.

How much was deductible in Gene's 2016 return as a casualty loss?

A. $0
B. $ 100
C. $3,900
D. $4,000

REG 4-Q57 R1051. Eric Ross, who is single, age 68 and has no dependents, had an adjusted gross income (AGI) of $40,000 in 20X5, comprised of the following:

Salary	$34,000
Net investment income	6,000

During 20X5, uninsured art objects owned by Eric, with a basis of $50,000 and a fair market value of $70,000, sustained casualty fire damage reducing the fair market value to $0. Also during 20X5, Eric made the following payments:

Interest on margin account at stockbroker	$18,000
Real estate taxes on condominium owned by Eric's mother, in which Eric resides	3,000
State and City gasoline taxes	180
Medical insurance premiums	300
Unreimbursed dental expenses	4,500
Contribution to political committee of elected public official	500

Eric elected to itemize his deductions for 20X5.

How much can Eric claim in his itemized deductions for the casualty loss on his 20X5 return?

A. $0
B. $65,900
C. $45,900
D. $66,000

REG 4-Q58 R88. Doyle has gambling losses totaling $7,000 during the current year. Doyle's adjusted gross income is $60,000, including $3,000 in gambling winnings. Doyle can itemize the deductions. What amount of gambling losses is deductible?

A. $0
B. $3,000
C. $5,800
D. $7,000

REG 4-Q59 R86. Carter incurred the following expenses in the current year: $500 for the preparation of a personal income tax return, $100 for custodial fees on an IRA which is paid by a separate check, $150 for professional publications, and $2,000 for union dues. Carter's current year adjusted gross income is $75,000. Carter, who is not self-employed, itemizes deductions. What will Carter's deduction be for miscellaneous itemized deductions after any limitations in the current year?

A. $0
B. $ 750
C. $1,250
D. $2,750

REG 4-Q60 R201. Which of the following is a miscellaneous itemized deduction subject to the 2% of adjusted gross income floor?

A. Gambling losses up to the amount of gambling winnings.
B. Medical expenses.
C. Real estate tax.
D. Employee business expenses.

REG 4-Q61 R31. Brenda, employed full time, makes beaded jewelry as a hobby. In year 2, Brenda's hobby generated $2,000 of sales, and she incurred $3,000 of travel expenses. What is the proper reporting of the income and expenses related to the activity?

A. Sales of $2,000 are reported in gross income, and $2,000 of expenses are reported as an itemized deduction subject to the 2% limitation.
B. Sales of $2,000 are reported in gross income, and $3,000 of expenses are reported as an itemized deduction subject to the 2% limitation.
C. Sales and expenses are netted, and the net loss of $1,000 is reported as an itemized deduction not subject to the 2% limitation.
D. Sales and expenses are netted and deducted for AGI.

REG 4-Q62 R65. Smith has an adjusted gross income (AGI) of $120,000 without taking into consideration $40,000 of losses from rental real estate activities. Smith actively participates in the rental real estate activities. What amount of the rental losses may Smith deduct in determining taxable income?

A. $0
B. $15,000
C. $20,000
D. $40,000

REG 4-Q63 R11. An individual taxpayer reports the following items for the current year:

Ordinary income from partnership A, operating a movie theater in which the taxpayer materially participates	$70,000
Net loss from partnership B, operating an equipment rental business in which the taxpayer does not materially participate	(9,000)
Rental income from building rented to a third party	7,000
Short-term capital gain from sale of stock	4,000

What is the taxpayer's adjusted gross income for the year?

A. $70,000
B. $72,000
C. $74,000
D. $77,000

REG 4-Q64 R69. A review of Bearing's year 2 records disclosed the following tax information:

Wages		$18,000
Taxable interest and qualifying dividends		4,000
Schedule C trucking business net income		32,000
Rental (loss)	(35,000)	
Limited partnership (loss)		(5,000)

Bearing actively participated in the rental property and was a limited partner in the partnership. Bearing had sufficient amounts at risk for the rental property and the partnership. What is Bearing's year 2 adjusted gross income?

A. $14,000
B. $19,000
C. $29,000
D. $54,000

REG 4-Q65 R144. Lane, a single taxpayer, received $160,000 in salary, $15,000 in income from an S Corporation in which Lane does not materially participate, and a $35,000 passive loss from a real estate rental activity in which Lane materially participated. Lane's modified adjusted gross income was $165,000. What amount of the real estate rental activity loss was deductible?

A. $0
B. $15,000
C. $25,000
D. $35,000

REG 4-Q66 R106. In the current year, a taxpayer reports the following items:

Salary	$50,000
Income from partnership A, in which the taxpayer materially participates	20,000
Passive activity loss from partnership B	(40,000)

During the year, the taxpayer disposed of the interest in partnership B, which had a suspended loss carryover of $10,000 from prior years. What is the taxpayer's adjusted gross income for the current year?

A. $20,000
B. $30,000
C. $60,000
D. $70,000

REG 4-Q67 R71. What is the tax treatment of net losses in excess of the at-risk amount for an activity?

A. Any loss in excess of the at-risk amount is suspended and is deductible in the year in which the activity is disposed of in full.
B. Any losses in excess of the at-risk amount are suspended and carried forward without expiration and are deductible against income in future years from that activity.
C. Any losses in excess of the at-risk amount are deducted currently against income from other activities (trade or business), and the remaining loss, if any, is carried forward without expiration.
D. Any losses in excess of the at-risk amount are carried back two years against activities with income and then carried forward for 20 years.

REG 4-Q68 R1127. Sam Cook, age 68, is a single taxpayer and had reported the following income and deductions for 2016:

Salary and wages	$18,000
Savings account interest income	500
Net rental income	5,000
Net short-term capital loss from stock sale	1,000
Net loss from business	35,000

Cook's personal exemptions amount is $4,050 and his standard deduction is $6,300. Cook's carryback or carryforward from his net operating loss (NOL) for 2016 is

A. $5,700
B. $30,700
C. $12,000
D. $35,000

REG 4-Q69 R1128. Sarah Miller is a 45 year old single taxpayer, had the following income and deductions for 2016:

Salary	$75,000
Long-term capital gain from sale of securities	4,000
Personal casualty loss (fire destroyed her home)	88,000
Standard deduction	6,300
Personal exemption	4,050

For 2016, Miller should report a net operating loss carryover of

A. $9,000
B. $13,000
C. $15,300
D. $19,350

REG 4-Q70 R283. In which of the following situations may taxpayers file as married filing jointly?

A. Taxpayers who were married but lived apart during the year.
B. Taxpayers who were married but lived under a legal separation agreement at the end of the year.
C. Taxpayers who were divorced during the year.
D. Taxpayers who were legally separated but lived together for the entire year.

REG 4-Q71 R127. A taxpayer's spouse dies in August of the current year. Which of the following is the taxpayer's filing status for the current year?

A. Single.
B. Qualified widow(er).
C. Head of household.
D. Married filing jointly.

REG 4-Q72 R346. Parker, whose spouse died during the preceding year, has not remarried. Parker maintains a home for a dependent child. What is Parker's most advantageous filing status?

A. Single.
B. Head of household.
C. Married filing separately.
D. Qualifying widow(er) with dependent child.

REG 4-Q73 R217. A couple filed a joint return in prior tax years. During the current tax year, one spouse died. The couple has no dependent children. What is the filing status available to the surviving spouse for the first subsequent tax year?

A. Surviving spouse.
B. Married filing separately.
C. Single.
D. Head of household.

REG 4-Q74 R145. Which of the following disqualifies an individual from the earned income credit?

A. The taxpayer's qualifying child is a 17-year-old grandchild.
B. The taxpayer has earned income under the earned income limit..
C. The taxpayer's five-year-old child lived in the taxpayer's home for only eight months.
D. The taxpayer has a filing status of married filing separately.

REG 4-Q75 R449. Which of the following statements about the child and dependent care credit is correct?

A. The credit is nonrefundable and refundable.
B. The child must be under the age of 18 years.
C. The child must be a direct descendant of the taxpayer.
D. The maximum credit is $600.

REG 4-Q76 R242. How may taxes paid by an individual to a foreign country be treated?

A. As an itemized deduction subject to the 2% floor.
B. As a credit against federal income taxes due.
C. As an adjustment to gross income.
D. As a nondeductible.

REG 4-Q77 R319. A CPA's adjusted gross income (AGI) for the preceding 12-month tax year exceeds $150,000. Which of the following methods is(are) available to the CPA to compute the required annual payment of estimated tax for the current year in order to make timely estimated tax payments and avoid the underpayment of estimated tax penalty?

I. The annualization method.
II. The seasonal method

A. I only.
B. II only.
C. Both I and II.
D. Neither I nor II.

REG 4-Q78 R63. Which of the following may **not** be deducted in the computation of alternative minimum taxable income of an individual?

A. Traditional IRA account contribution.
B. One-half of the self-employment tax deduction.
C. Personal exemptions.
D. Charitable contributions.

REG 4-Q79 R33. On their 2017 joint tax return, Sam and Joann, both 66 years of age, had adjusted gross income (AGI) of $150,000 and claimed the following itemized deductions:
- Interest of $15,000 on a $100,000 home equity loan to purchase a motor home
- Real estate tax and state income taxes of $18,000
- Unreimbursed medical expenses of $15,000 (prior to AGI limitation)
- Miscellaneous itemized deductions of $5,000 (prior to AGI limitation).

Based on these deductions, what would be the amount of AMT add-back adjustment in computing alternative minimum taxable income?

A. $21,750
B. $23,750
C. $35,375
D. $38,750

REG 4-Q80 R108. Farr, an unmarried taxpayer, had $70,000 of adjusted gross income and the following deductions for regular income tax purposes:

Home mortgage interest on a loan to
  acquire a principal residence $11,000
Miscellaneous itemized deductions
  above the threshold limitation 2% $ 2,000

What are Farr's total allowable itemized deductions for computing alternative minimum taxable income?

A. $0
B. $ 2,000
C. $11,000
D. $13,000

REG 4-Q81 R250. Robert had current-year adjusted gross income (AGI) of $100,000 and potential itemized deductions as follows:

Medical expenses (before any excess over AGI limitation)	$12,000
State income taxes	4,000
Real estate taxes	3,500
Qualified housing and residence mortgage interest	10,000
Home equity mortgage interest (used to consolidate personal debts)	4,500
Charitable contributions (cash)	5,000

What are Robert's itemized deductions for alternative minimum tax?

A. $17,000
B. $19,500
C. $21,500
D. $25,500

Multiple Choice – Solutions

REG 4-Q1 R227. The correct answer is A. Usually, C corporations have the same flexibility in choosing accounting periods as individuals do.

Answer B is incorrect because unless a valid purpose for a different tax year is provided, an S corporation must adopt the calendar year.

Answer C is incorrect because there are limitations in choosing an accounting period (taxable year) for partnerships. Usually, a calendar year is required unless the partnership provides a valid purpose for a different taxable year. For example:

If Partner's Taxable Year is...	Then Partnership's Taxable Year Must be...
One or more of the majority interest partners have the same taxable year.	Partnership must have that same taxable year.
One or more of the majority interest partners do not have the same taxable year.	Partnership must have the same taxable year as all of its "principal" partners.

If neither of the above rules applies, the partnership has to elect the taxable year which results in the least aggregate deferral of income to the partners.

Answer D is incorrect because, a personal service corporation typically must use a calendar year unless a valid purpose for a different taxable year is provided.

REG 4-Q2 R284. The correct answer is B. In order to accrue an expense at the end of the year, the repair would have been completed prior to the year end and not invoiced. Even if it was invoiced at year end, the taxpayer could still accrue the expense as long as the work was completed prior to year end.

Answer A is incorrect because the repair was not completed before year end.

Answer C is incorrect because it was paid before year end.

Answer D is incorrect because the work was not completed before year end.

REG 4-Q3 R338. The correct answer is C. The cash basis of taxation states that a taxpayer will recognize income in the year that they collect the cash, even if it is cash from prior year sales. During the current year, the taxpayer, Mosh, collected $100,000 from customers. The accounts receivable went down from the beginning of the year of $25,000 to the end of the year of $15,000, which indicates that the $100,000 contains collections during the current year of prior year sales (decrease in the accounts receivable) of $10,000. **Do not** let the examination division try to trick you because cash basis states that income is recognized when collected even if it contains collections of prior year's sales. Total cash collected by Mosh $100,000, correct answer is C.

REG 4-Q4 R349. The correct answer is D. This question deals with the concept of constructive receipt, which states that income must be recognized when it is available and not when the taxpayer decides to deposit the funds. In answer D, dividends declared by a corporation are available to the stockholders when the stockholder receives the dividend check and not the date the dividends were declared. On date of declaration, the funds are not available to the stockholders because the stockholders cannot go to the board of directors and demand the funds, even though they were declared. The income is recognized by Chrisp on January 4th of the following year.

Answer A is incorrect because an employee cannot delay a bonus check until the next year. Since the bonus was authorized during the current year and could be drawn by the employee at any time, the funds were available in the current year.

Answer B is incorrect because the check received by Chrisp was dated during the current year and could have been deposited in the current year and recorded as income in the current year. The fact that Chrisp did not deposit until the next year was a decision made by Chrisp so that Chrisp believed the income would be taxable in year 2 and not in year 1. Chrisp is not allowed to determine what year the income is taxable if the money is available to Chrisp.

Answer C is incorrect because the check was ready for pick-up during the current year in which the funds were available and therefore it is taxable in the current year.

REG 4-Q5 R176. The correct answer is C. Dart is a C corporation. Generally, C corporations must use the accrual method of accounting. An exception to this is where a C corporation, for every year it has annual gross receipts of $5,000,000 or less, and does not have inventory, can use the cash basis. Since Dart had revenues in excess of $20,000,000 for the past three years and has inventory, they cannot be on the cash basis.

Answer A is incorrect because whether Dart uses a calendar year end or not, does not affect the accounting method (cash or accrual) to be used.

Answer B is incorrect because even though Dart consistently applies the method it chooses, does not affect the accounting method (cash or accrual) to be used.

Answer D is incorrect because it has nothing to do with the amount of money used to develop software that determines the accounting method but rather, it is determined by the amount of revenue.

REG 4-Q6 R403. The correct answer is B. Qualified personal service corporations which provide a service such as accounting firms, legal firms and physician's offices, may use the cash method of accounting for tax purposes.

The following entities must use the accrual basis for tax purposes:
1) Tax shelters
2) C corporations
3) Manufacturers (company that manufactures goods for resale)

REG 4-Q7 R16. Correct answer is C. To calculate the gross profit, take the selling price plus the buyer's assumption of the mortgage and subtract the seller's adjusted basis and selling expenses.

Real property sold	$200,000
Buyer's assumption of mortgage	50,000
Amount realized from sale	$250,000
Basis of property sold	(75,000)
Selling expenses	(10,000)
Gross profit on sale	$165,000

REG 4-Q8 R101. The correct answer is D. This question involves the installment sales method in taxation. To determine the amount of gross income to be included in the year of the sale, you must know the installment sale formula. The numerator is the gross profit divided by the denominator which is the contract price (selling price – debt assumed by buyer). Multiple this fraction by the amount received for the year which only includes the principal, not the interest income. The interest income is recognized in full.

Gross profit (sales – basis)
$100,000 - $80,000 = $20,000
Contract price (Selling price – debt assumed by buyer) $100,000 - $0 = $100,000

$20,000 / $100,000 = gross profit percentage of 20%

Cash received $25,000 (year 1) X 20% = $5,000 (gross income recognized)

REG 4-Q9 R184. The correct answer is D. This question deals with installment accounting in taxation. To determine the amount of the gain recognized in the year of the sale, use the installment sales formula times the cash payment received. The formula's numerator is the gross profit (sales – cost of item, net of depreciation) or $600,000 – ($500,000 - $80,000) = $180,000. The denominator is the contract price, which is the selling price less any debt assumed by the buyer. This amount is the selling price of $600,000 minus zero (no debt assumed by the buyer).

$180,000 / $600,000 x $120,000 = $36,000, answer D.

REG 4-Q10 R1147. The correct answer is B. Uniform capitalization rules require businesses to capitalize certain costs that benefit or are incurred because of the *production* or *resale* activities of the business. Applicable entities include entities that:
- Produce and use tangible personal property in a trade or business
- Produce and sell tangible personal property to customers.

However, if the average annual gross receipts for the past three years do not exceed $10 million, the entity is called a small retailer. Small retailers are not subject to the uniform capitalization rules.

REG 4-Q11 R124. The correct answer is C. Stock of property received as compensation has a basis to the party performing the services at fair market value (FMV). Here, Winkler received stock for services rendered to Thompson having a FMV of $5,000. Two months later, Winkler sold the stock for $7,500. This gives a gain to Winkler of $2,500 ($7,500 - $5,000).

REG 4-Q12 R270. The correct answer is D. Jones is taxed on his wages ($35,000), state unemployment compensation ($4,000) and the former employer's company-paid supplemental unemployment benefit plan ($2,000), which equals $41,000.

REG 4-Q13 R157. The correct answer is C. Current rents ($30,000) are taxable. Any rents received in advance ($10,000) are taxable when received. Security deposits ($5,000) are not taxable income because they are not earned and the landlord has to return it to the tenant. Lease cancellation payments ($15,000) are earned income and therefore taxable income to the landlord. The total amount of gross income which is taxable is $30,000 + $10,000 + $15,000 = $55,000.

REG 4-Q14 R192. The correct answer is D. When a lessor receives income in advance even though they are on the accrual basis, they are taxed on income paid in advance in the year they receive the income. In year one, Nare received $30,000 from Mott for cancelling the lease which is considered rental income and taxable. Nare received $5,000 rent from Pine for each of the two months of November and December which totals $10,000 and is taxable. In addition, Nare received an additional $5,000 for the last month's rent. Therefore, the total rental income received in year one equals $45,000 ($30,000 + $10,000 + $5,000).

REG 4-Q15 R307. The correct answer is C. Wages of $18,000 are taxable income. Unemployment compensation of $1,500 is taxable income, however interest income from investments in municipal bonds are tax exempt. The total taxable income is $19,500 ($18,000 + $1,500).

REG 4-Q16 R321. The correct answer is A. When a corporation declares a 2-for-1 stock split, the number of shares doubles and the cost basis per share is divided in half. Greller owns 100 shares of Arden Corp with a basis of $10,000. After the 2-for-1 stock split, Greller owns 200 shares with a basis of $10,000. The cost per share was $100 per share and with the 2-for-1 stock split, the cost per share is half of the $100 or $50 per share. The basis of 100 shares at $50 per share is $5,000.

Note: When computing the basis per share after a 2-for-1 split, **do not** divide the fair market value per share ($120 in the question) by 2. The proper method is to divide the original cost basis per share of $100 by 2.

REG 4-Q17 R125. The correct answer is A. Alimony received is taxable income to determine adjusted gross income.

Answers B, C and D are excluded from income.

REG 4-Q18 R401. The correct answer is C. In a post-1984 divorce agreement, some of the requirements to be considered alimony are:
2) Payments must be payable in cash
3) Payments must end at the recipient's death

Other requirements include:
1) A taxpayer cannot file a joint return with their former spouse
2) The taxpayers cannot live together
3) The taxpayers must be unmarried at the end of their taxable year
4) The payments must be pursuant to a decree of divorce or written separation instrument.

Therefore, I and II are both requirements to be considered deductible alimony. Alimony is taxable income to the recipient. Child support is not deductible by the payer or taxable to the recipient.

REG 4-Q19 R251. The correct answer is B. To calculate Jensen's AGI for the current year, start with the salary ($50,000), add the alimony ($12,000), then, subtract the maximum capital loss that can be deducted per year on Form 1040 of $3,000. This will give Jensen an AGI of $59,000 ($50,000 + $12,000 - $3,000).

An inheritance is never taxable. Child support received by a taxpayer is never taxable and Jensen, who had a capital loss of $6,000, is limited to a deduction of $3,000 per taxpayer, per year. The unused loss of $3,000 can be carried forward against capital gains for an indefinite period and takes on the character of whatever loss it was. For example, if the loss was a long-term capital loss, the carry forward would be long-term. If the loss was a short-term capital loss, the carry forward would be short term.

REG 4-Q20 R165. The correct answer is C. When a person goes through a divorce proceeding, alimony is taxable as long as the alimony payments meet certain requirements. In this question, we not going to worry about the alimony requirements because they are telling us the check for $25,000 was identified as alimony. So, we can conclude the $25,000 is alimony. Child support received is never taxable, so the $10,000 for child support is not taxable. Lastly, any money that an individual receives as a property settlement in a divorce is not taxable. In conclusion, only the alimony of $25,000 is includable in the individual's gross income.

REG 4-Q21 R291. The correct answer is A. Child support and division of property in a divorce dispute are not alimony and therefore, not taxable to the recipient or deductible by the payer. The only item deductible on the Tana's tax return is the alimony payments of $3,000. Alimony payments are deductible to arrive at adjusted gross income (AGI).

REG 4-Q22 R21. The correct answer is C. Punitive damages are included in gross income for tax purposes.

Answers A, B are incorrect because they are not taxable income.

Answer D is incorrect because punitive damages are taxable income.

REG 4-Q23 R233. The correct answer is A. To get the adjusted gross income (AGI) of the taxpayer, take the gross income items which are taxable of which the salary is the only one provided in the question. Then, subtract alimony paid which is a deduction to arrive at AGI. Inheritance from a grandparent and proceeds of a lawsuit for physical injuries are non taxable.

Salary	$50,000
Alimony paid to a former spouse	(10,000)
AGI	$40,000

REG 4-Q24 R327. The correct answer is C. If an individual receives an award for literary achievement, the taxpayer will not be taxed on the award if the following requirements are met:

1) Taxpayer was selected without any action on their part (they did not enter the contest).
2) No future services are required of the taxpayer to receive the award.
3) The award must be given away to a governmental unit or a charitable organization. If given to a charitable organization, the taxpayer cannot deduct the amount given to the charitable organization as an itemized deduction.

REG 4-Q25 R387. The correct answer is B. Decker purchased the insurance policy from another person in an arm's length transaction. Normally, if a life insurance policy is purchased from an insurance company and the insured dies, the proceeds are not taxable to the beneficiary. Since this policy was acquired by Decker from Fuller and not from an insurance company, Decker, becomes the beneficiary and owner. Upon the death of the parent, Decker, the beneficiary, must recognize income of $135,000. This is arrived at by taking the amount received by Decker of $200,000 minus Decker's basis in the policy consisting of $25,000 paid for the policy and $40,000 in premiums paid by Decker or $65,000, which equals $135,000 ($200,000 - $65,000).

REG 4-Q26 R143. The correct answer is B. This question deals with how much of the state income tax refund is included in the following year's individual tax return as taxable. To calculate this, first determine if the taxpayer itemized in the prior year tax return. If the taxpayer did itemize in the prior year tax return, then some of the state income tax refund will be taxable on next year's individual tax return. Take the standard deduction in excess of the state income tax paid for the prior year. In this question, the itemized deduction for state income taxes paid exceeded the standard deduction by $1,150 which was fully deductible on last year's return. The amount taxable of the state income tax refund on next year's return is the lesser of the $1,150 or the actual state income tax refund of $1,500. The correct answer is $1,150, selection B.

REG 4-Q27 R40. The correct answer is C.
The total gross income of Randolph includes the following:

Wages $22,000
Unemployment compensation 6,000
Pension distribution (100% taxable) 4,000
Total $32,000

Since the taxpayer only takes the standard deduction, the taxpayer does not have to include the state income tax refund in taxable income. If the taxpayer itemizes in the prior year, the state income tax refund would be taxable.

REG 4-Q28 R1148. The correct answer is A. The formula to determine the amount excluded from income is the employee's cost (contributions), divided by the total expected return (benefits), multiplied by the total payments received for that year. The amount Green can exclude from taxable income is calculated as follows:

For 2015: $6,000/(60 months x $350) x ($350 x 7 months) = $6,000/$21,000 x $2,450 = $700
For 2016 & 2017: $6,000/(60 months x $350) x ($350 x 12 months) = $6,000/$21,000 x $4,200 = $1,200

REG 4-Q29 R400. The correct answer is C. The question asks which of the following income items are subject to self-employment tax or which of the following items is self-employment income. Guaranteed payments to a partner from a partnership are self-employment income which is $50,000. Ordinary income from an S corporation is not self-employment income because it comes from a corporation. If the ordinary income came from a partnership it would be considered self-employment income. Therefore, the only self-employment income is the guaranteed payments from services rendered to a partnership of $50,000.

REG 4-Q30 R42. The correct answer is C. Premiums on the first $50,000 of group term life insurance premiums paid by the employer are a tax-free fringe benefit. The premiums on the coverage in excess of $50,000 are taxable to the employee.

Since the employee received $200,000 of group term life insurance and the premiums on the first $50,000 are tax-free, the premiums on the $150,000 are taxable.

$200,000 - $50,000 = $150,000
$150,000 / $1,000 = 150
150 x $2.76 = $414 (taxable premiums to employee)
The taxable premiums are added to the salary to arrive at gross income:
$100,000 + $414 = $100,414

REG 4-Q31 R187. The correct answer is D. If a taxpayer withdraws money before the age of 59 ½, except for certain exceptions, will have to pay a 10% early withdrawal penalty plus the amount withdrawn times the taxpayer's marginal tax rate. To calculate, multiple 10% time $30,000 which is $3,000 (early withdrawal penalty) and $30,000 times the marginal tax rate of 35% which is $10,500. Add the $3,000 to the $10,500 which is $13,500, the amount the taxpayer owes the government. Do not multiply the amount withdrawn times the effective tax rate.

REG 4-Q32 R398. The correct answer is A. Business expenses incurred in an illegal activity are deductible if they are ordinary and necessary and reasonable in amount. However, there is a special exception in which no deduction is allowed for any amount in a trade or business of expenses, which have to do with trafficking of controlled substances. As a result, in arriving at gross income from the business, Mock can reduce total sales by the cost of goods sold and thus is allowed to deduct the cost of merchandise in determining business income.

REG 4-Q33 R208. The correct answer is D. In calculating adjusted gross income (AGI) for a taxpayer who is self-employed, start with self-employed gross income of $57,000 and subtract 50% of the self-employment tax of $4,000 ($8,000 x 50%), self-employed health insurance of $6,000, $5,000 of alimony and the $2,000 contribution to a traditional IRA. Because the question did not state that the taxpayer was in a qualified pension plan, the taxpayer can deduct the full amount of the IRA contribution. Since the taxpayer is not eligible to participate in another company's pension plan, they can deduct the full amount of the IRA contribution. Therefore, the taxpayer's adjusted gross income is:
$57,000 - $4,000 - $6,000 - $5,000 - $2,000 = $40,000, answer D.

REG 4-Q34 R35. The correct answer is D. The Uniform Capitalization (UNICAP) Rules determines what costs the business capitalizes to tangible or intangible property acquired for resale rather than expensed. The UNICAP Rules of Code Sec. 263A apply to retailers whose average gross receipts for the preceding three years exceed $10,000,000.

REG 4-Q35 R348. The correct answer is C. Engineering costs incurred to manufacture a product are part of getting the asset ready for its intended use (selling to customers). Uniform capitalization rules (UNICAP) generally requires that all costs, both direct and indirect, in manufacturing or constructing real or personal property, or in purchasing or holding property for resale, must be capitalized as part of the cost of the property. The UNICAP rules do not apply to advertising, selling, research and experimentation expenditures, as well as, mine development and exploration costs.

Answers A and D are incorrect because advertising and selling expenses are not includable.

Answer B is incorrect because the word "general" is too vague and must be more specific.

REG 4-Q36 R82. The correct answer is A. The Uniform Capitalization Rules determine what costs are capitalized rather than expensed, for manufactured tangible personal property and inventory. Advertising, research and marketing costs are expensed and are not subject to the Uniform Capitalization Rules. Off-site storage costs are capitalized under the Uniform Capitalization Rules.

REG 4-Q37 R262. The correct answer is D. The Uniform Capitalization Rules (UNICAP) of Code Sec. 263A do not apply to advertising, selling, research and experimentation expenditures, mine development and exploration costs, property held for personal use, and to freelance authors, photographers, and artists whose personal efforts create the product. Warehousing costs incurred by a manufacturing company, regardless of annual gross receipts are capitalized to inventory.

Answers A, B and C are incorrect because they do not apply under Uniform Capitalization Rules (UNICAP) of Code Sec. 263A.

REG 4-Q38 R265. The correct answer is A. The uniform capitalization (UNICAP) rules generally require that all costs incurred in acquiring property for resale must be capitalized as part of the cost of inventory. The costs that must be capitalized include the costs of purchasing, handling, processing, repackaging and assembly, and off-site storage. An off-site storage facility cannot be physically attached to the facility that sells the inventory. Therefore, repackaging costs and off-site storage costs are capitalized under the UNICAP rules.

REG 4-Q39 R402. The correct answer is A. The Uniform Capitalization rules for goods manufactured by the taxpayer determine what costs are capitalized to the goods manufactured and what goods are expensed.

Research costs are not included in the cost of the inventory but are expensed. Answers B, C & D are all capitalized to the inventory cost and not separately expensed.

REG 4-Q40 R298. The correct answer is A. If a vacation home is used as a residence and rented for less than 15 days per year, the income is not reported and rental expense deductions are not allowed. In this question, the vacation home was rented for 10 days which is less than 15 days and no rental income or loss is allowed.

REG 4-Q41 R396. The correct answer is C. If a second residence is used for both personal use and rental use, the taxpayer can only use it for personal use for the greater of 14 days or 10% of the number of days rented. The greater of 14 days or 20 days (10% of 200 days) is 20 days. The taxpayer can use it for personal use for no more than 20 days. Adams used it for 50 days which exceeds 20 days (number of days it can be used for personal use), so all utilities and maintenance expenses on the property must be divided between personal and rental use.

Answer A is incorrect because since depreciation could be deducted if Adams gross rental income exceeds the allocated out of pocket rental expenses.

Answer B is incorrect because Adams personal use exceeded the greater of 10% of the number of days rented or 14 days. In this case, Adams exceeded the limit for personal use, so no rental loss is allowed as the allocable rental deductions are limited to rental income.

Answer D is incorrect because only the mortgage interest and taxes are allocable to rental use would be deducted in determining net rental income or loss.

REG 4-Q42 R7. The correct answer is A. Normally, household moving expenses are deductible by the taxpayer as long as they are not reimbursed by the employer. Since the moving of the household goods was reimbursed, Davidson cannot deduct them. The only other moving expense that is a qualified unreimbursed moving expense that is deductible is the lodging on the way to Atlanta of $100.
Meals and temporary living expenses are not qualified moving expenses and therefore not deductible.

Make sure you look at the questions on moving expenses because you must move at least 50 miles from your old job to be a qualified.

REG 4-Q43 R87. The correct answer is B. To arrive at the adjusted gross income (AGI), we take the wages of $3,000 and subtract deductions to arrive at AGI. The only deduction to arrive at AGI is student loan interest of $400, giving us AGI of $2,600. The unreimbursed employee business expenses and the contributions to a charity are itemized deductions or are deductions from AGI to arrive a taxable income.

REG 4-Q44 R126. The correct answer is D. The individual can deduct a portion of student loan interest for the duration of time that interest is paid.

REG 4-Q45 R288. The correct answer is B. Interest on a qualified education loan is a deduction to arrive at adjusted gross income (AGI). A qualified education loan is any debt incurred to pay the qualified higher education expenses of the taxpayer, taxpayer's spouse or any dependent that existed at the time the debt was incurred. The student must be enrolled on at least a half time basis. The interest can be deductible for an unlimited number of years as long as the loan exists. The maximum amount a taxpayer can deduct is $2,500. The $2,500 is phased out if AGI exceeds certain limits. Because the phase-out changes every year, the candidate will not be required to know the phase-outs.

REG 4-Q46 R308. The correct answer is B. The maximum amount of medical expense deduction in the current year, ignoring the adjusted gross income (AGI) percentage threshold limitation, is calculated as follows. Capital expenditures which qualify as medical expenses, such as the swimming pool are deductible to the extent the cost of $100,000 exceeds the increase in the value of the home which is $25,000, which equals a medical expense of $75,000.

The widening of the doorways to accommodate the taxpayer's wheelchair equals $10,000. Since there is no increase in the value of the home due to this improvement, then the medical expense is $10,000. The total medical expenses before the AGI threshold limitation is $75,000 + $10,000 which equals $85,000.

REG 4-Q47 R335. The correct answer is D. Unreimbursed medical expenses that are deductible before the adjusted gross income (AGI) limitation include dentist and eye doctor fees ($5,000) and contact lenses ($500) which equal $5,500. The facial cosmetic surgery is not deductible because the surgery is unrelated to personal injury or congenital deformity and is considered elective surgery. Medical insurance premiums are deductible if paid for a dental insurance plan, hospital and surgical procedures, and medical insurance premiums for a plan to reimburse the taxpayer for prescriptions. Medical insurance premiums paid for disabilities and accidents are not considered medical insurance premiums.

REG 4-Q48 R450. The correct answer is B.

Prescription medicine and drugs	$3,000
Doctor fees for illnesses	5,000
Medical insurance premiums	3,000
Total Medical	$11,000
Less: Reimbursements	3,000
Unreimbursed medical	$8,000
Less: 7.5% AGI limit (7.5% x $60,000)	4,500
Net medical expense itemized deduction	$3,500

REG 4-Q49 R395. The correct answer is B. To calculate Carroll's maximum allowable medical expense deduction, after the applicable threshold limitation for the year, add the unreimbursed doctor's bills and the cosmetic surgery which equals $20,000. Cosmetic surgery is a deductible medical expense as long as it is not an elective surgery, such as a nose job. Cosmetic surgery that was necessary to correct a congenital deformity is not elective surgery and therefore is a deductible medical expense. The deductible medical expenses are the total medical expenses in excess of 7.5% of AGI. To calculate the deduction, take the $20,000 total medical and subtract 7.5% of AGI ($100,000 x 7.5%) or $7,500, leaving a medical expense deduction of $12,500 ($20,000 - $7,500).

REG 4-Q50 R17. The correct answer is B.

A is incorrect because medical expenses paid by credit card are deductible in the year the credit card is charged.

C is incorrect because medical expenses less insurance reimbursements are unreimbursed medical expenses which are includable as deduction in determining alternative minimum tax (AMT).

D is incorrect because Medicare insurance premiums are a medical expense deduction.

REG 4-Q51 R268. The correct answer is D. Real estate taxes on a personal residence, personal property taxes and state and city income taxes withheld are itemized deductions.

Real estate tax on personal residence	$2,000
Ad valorem tax on personal automobile	500
Current-year state and city income taxes withheld	1,000
Total itemized deduction	$3,500

REG 4-Q52 R20. Correct answer is B. Investment interest expense for an individual taxpayer can only be deducted up to net investment income. The investment expense is $5,000. The net investment income is the $10,000 (gross investment income) less the $8,000 (noninterest investment expenses) which equals $2,000. The investment expense of $5,000 is limited to $2,000. So, the most the taxpayer can deduct is $2,000. The remaining $3,000 of investment interest expense can be carried forward against net investment income in future years.

REG 4-Q53 R229. The correct answer is A. Computer-generated investment interest expense deduction is limited to net investment income of the taxpayer. Any excess amount is carried forward indefinitely. For example, assume the taxpayer had $8,000 of investment interest for a year but, had investment income of only $6,000. The tax preparer would enter the $8,000 paid as investment interest and the computer would then allow only a $6,000 deduction for investment interest in the year. The remaining $2,000 of expense would be carried forward indefinitely to be applied to investment income in future years. Qualified residence interest is NOT investment interest expense and would not affect investment interest income.

Answers B, C and D are incorrect because of the information stated in the explanation for the correct answer A.

REG 4-Q54 R190. The correct answer is A. When an individual contributes appreciated long term capital gain property, the deduction is the lesser of fair market value (FMV) or 30% of adjusted gross income (AGI). The FMV is $25,000 and 30% of AGI ($90,000) is $27,000. Select the lesser of FMV or 30% of AGI which would result in the correct answer of $25,000.

REG 4-Q55 R386. The correct answer is B. The charitable contribution includes the donation to Smith's church of $5,000. When an individual contributes tangible personal property to a charity and the tangible personal property is held for more than 12 months and is related to the donee's function, the deduction would be the property's fair market value (FMV) limited to 30% of AGI. Smith donated artwork to a museum. This is tangible personal property related to the museum's function. However, if the artwork was not held by the taxpayer for more than 12 months, the deduction is the basis of $2,000 limited to 50% of AGI. A contribution to a needy family is not a contribution to a charity.

In conclusion, the contributions that are deductible by Smith are cash of $5,000 plus the artwork donated to the local museum of $2,000, which equals $7,000. The $7,000 is limited to 50% of AGI of $60,000, which is $30,000. The contribution deduction is $7,000.

REG 4-Q56 R1105. The correct answer is A. The amount of allowable deduction for a personal casualty loss is the actual loss sustained reduced by any insurance recovery, 10% of adjusted gross income and $100. That is, we deduct from the sustained loss the actual recovery, if any, from insurance, and in addition, the loss is only deductible to the extent that it exceeds 10% of adjusted gross income and a further nondeductible amount of $100. In this case, since Gene's adjusted gross income for 1984 was $50,000, a loss of $4,000 would not be deductible at all since it does not exceed 10% of adjusted gross income ($5,000).

REG 4-Q57 R1051. The correct answer is C. The starting point to calculate the casualty loss is to take the lower of the basis versus the decrease in the fair market value of the objects that were stolen. The lesser of the $50,000 basis or the decrease in the fair market value, which is $70,000 ($70,000 - $0), is $50,000. Subtract any insurance proceeds, which in this question, there are none because the property was uninsured. The next step is to subtract $100 from the $50,000 and then subtract 10% of AGI. The total deduction is $50,000 minus $100, minus 10% of AGI, which equals $45,900 ($50,000 - $100 - (10% x $40,000)).

REG 4-Q58 R88. The correct answer is B. Gambling losses are deductible up to gambling winnings. They are a miscellaneous itemized deduction not subject to the 2% phase out. In this question, Doyle has gambling losses of $7,000 but winnings of only $3,000. The maximum gambling losses that are deductible is $3,000.

REG 4-Q59 R86. The correct answer is C. Miscellaneous itemized deductions subject to the 2% limit:

Preparation of a personal income tax return	$500
Custodial fees on an IRA	100
Professional publications	150
Union dues	2,000
Total	$2,750
Less: 2% of AGI ($75,000 x 2%)	(1,500)
Deduction of miscellaneous itemized deductions	$1,250

REG 4-Q60 R201. The correct answer is D. Unreimbursed employee business expenses are a miscellaneous itemized deduction subject to the 2% of adjusted gross income (AGI) floor.

Answer A is incorrect because gambling losses up to the amount of gambling winnings are a miscellaneous itemized deduction not subject to the 2% of adjusted gross income (AGI) floor.

Answer B is incorrect because medical expenses are an itemized deduction called unreimbursed medical expenses.

Answer C is incorrect because real estate taxes is one of the itemized deductions called taxes and is not subject to the 2% of adjusted gross income (AGI) floor.

REG 4-Q61 R31. The correct answer is A because sales of $2,000 are reported in gross income, and $2,000 of expenses are reported as an itemized deduction subject to the 2% limitation. This is how you would handle a business which is deemed by the IRS as a hobby.

REG 4-Q62 R65. The correct answer is B. Rental losses are passive losses. However, an individual can deduct up to $25,000 of rental losses against non-passive income. The $25,000 deduction against non-passive income starts phasing out beginning when adjusted gross income (AGI) exceeds $100,000. For every dollar over $100,000, 50 cents of the $25,000 write-off against non-passive income is lost.

The taxpayer's AGI is $120,000. The taxpayer went over the AGI by $20,000. Multiple $20,000 by 50% which equals $10,000 which is the amount of the $25,000 what will not be deducted against non-passive income.

If we take the $25,000 and deduct the $10,000 (the amount not deductible against non-passive income), we are left with $15,000, the amount that will be deductible against non-passive income.

REG 4-Q63 R11. The correct answer is C. Ordinary income from partnership A, in which the partner materially participates, is active income. Therefore, the $70,000 is taxable.

The net loss from partnership B operating an equipment rental business in which the tax payer does not materially participate in is a passive loss. Please note, when reading this, do not assume it is a passive loss because they are renting equipment. Renting equipment is not a rental property. Renting equipment is a business, but it is passive because the taxpayer does not materially participate in it. The passive loss of $9,000 from renting equipment, which is a passive activity, can offset the passive income from the rental property of $7,000.

Therefore, none of the rental income from the rental property is taxable.

The short-term capital gain of $4,000 is taxable because it is portfolio income.
To summarize: The amount of adjusted taxable income is:

Ordinary income from partnership A, operating a movie theater in which the taxpayer materially participates	$70,000
Short-term capital gain from sale of stock	4,000
Total Adjusted taxable income	$74,000

REG 4-Q64 R69. The correct answer is C. The taxpayer has gross taxable income consisting of:

Wages	$18,000
Taxable interest and qualifying dividends	4,000
Schedule C trucking business net income	32,000
Total gross taxable income	$54,000
Rental (loss) from residential property	(25,000)
Adjusted gross income (AGI)	$29,000

A taxpayer can take up to $25,000 of rental loss against non-passive income, as long as the AGI does not exceed $100,000 before the rental loss deduction. The AGI before rental loss deduction is $54,000. To take the $25,000 loss, the taxpayer must actively participate in the property.

The limited partnership loss is passive loss, which can only offset passive income. Since there is no passive income, none of the loss from the limited partnership can be deducted, but may be carried forward indefinitely or used against non-passive income when the entire limited partnership interest if sold.

REG 4-Q65 R144. The correct answer is B. This question deals with how much passive loss can be deducted on Lane's individual tax return. Passive losses can only reduce passive income. In the question, there is a passive loss of $35,000 from real estate rental activity in which Lane materially participated and there is passive income of $15,000 from an S corporation in which Lane does not materially participate. Lane can take $35,000 of the rental loss which is passive and net it against the passive income from the S corporation of $15,000. This gives the taxpayer a net rental loss of $20,000 in which Lane materially participates in. A special rule would allow the remaining $20,000 of rental loss to be deductible against non-passive income sources. However, if the taxpayer's adjusted gross income (AGI) exceeds $100,000, for every dollar you go over the $100,000, you will lose 50% of those dollars from being deductible against non-passive sources. The taxpayer's AGI of $165,000 exceeds the $100,000 by $65,000. If you multiply 50% of the $65,000, you cannot deduct up to $32,500 of the rental loss against non-passive income. Since the rental loss was $20,000, it cannot be deductible against non-passive income. In conclusion, the only amount that was deductible on the tax return was $15,000 of the passive loss against the passive income from the S corporation of $15,000. The correct answer is B. The remaining $20,000 rental loss (passive loss) can be forward indefinitely against future passive income. If there is no future passive income, then the $20,000 can be deducted against non-passive income when you dispose of the passive activity in a taxable transaction.

REG 4-Q66 R106. The correct answer is A. This question deals with identifying whether the items above are included in the computation of adjusted gross income (AGI). The first item, the salary of $50,000 is ordinary income which is includable in AGI. Income from partnership A, in which the taxpayer materially participates, is ordinary income because the tax payer materially participates in the partnership. The passive activity loss from partnership B can only be deducted against passive income, not ordinary income. Since there is no passive income in the current year, any passive losses cannot be deducted against ordinary income and can be carried forward indefinitely until there is passive income or the passive loss carry forward can be deducted against non-passive income in the year the tax payer disposes against the entire passive activity. During the current year, the passive loss from partnership B of $40,000 and the passive loss carryover from prior years can be deducted against non-passive income because the tax payer is disposing of the entire interest in partnership B (the passive activity).

To arrive at AGI for the current year, add the salary of $50,000 to the income from partnership A in which the taxpayer materially participates of $20,000 and subtract the current passive loss of $40,000 and the prior year's passive loss of $10,000.

You can deduct the passive loss of $50,000 against the non-passive income of $70,000 because we are disposing of the entire partnership B (the passive activity). The resulting answer is: $50,000 + $20,000 - $40,000 - $10,000 = $20,000 AGI.

REG 4-Q67 R71. The correct answer is B. The at-risk basis is the sum of the cash and adjusted basis of property contributed, plus the amount borrowed for the use of the activity for which the taxpayer is personally liable for. Losses are deductible only up to the at-risk basis. Any losses in excess of the basis are suspended, carried forward indefinitely and are deductible against income in future years from that activity.

Answer A is incorrect because there is no such requirement that the activity has to be disposed of in full to deduct the loss.

Answer C is incorrect because it states that any losses in excess of the at-risk amount are deducted currently against income from other activities. The correct statement would state that losses in excess of the at-risk amount are deducted currently against income only from that activity.

Answer D is incorrect because it is not carried back 2 years and carried forward 20 years. It is carried forward indefinitely.

REG 4-Q68 R1127. The correct answer is C. Cooks total income is 23,500 ($18,000 + $500 + $5,000) and total deductions are $46,350 ($35,000 + $1,000 + $4,050 + $6,300). Total deductions exceeded total income by $22,850. In calculating an NOL, capital losses are not allowed. Also, an individual's dependency exemptions, personal exemptions and any excess of nonbusiness deductions (such as standard deductions) over nonbusiness income (such as saving account interest) are not subtracted to determine the NOL.

Items not allowed in determining NOL:
Net short-term capital loss
 from stock sale $1,000
Nonbusiness deductions ($6,300 standard
 deduction - $500 interest income) 5,800
Personal exemption deduction 4,050
Total items not allowed in determining NOL $10,850

Cook's 2016 NOL:
Total income $23,500
Less:
 Total initial deductions $46,350
 Less: Net rental income (10,850) (35,500)
Net operating loss ($12,000)

REG 4-Q69 R1128. The correct answer is B. In calculating an individual taxpayer's net operating loss (NOL), the taxpayer's salary is included in income. The long-term capital gain from sale of securities is not included in income in determining an NOL. Dependency exemptions, personal exemptions and standard deductions are not allowed in determining NOL. The casualty loss deduction is allowed in determining the NOL.

Miller's net operating loss for 2016:
Salary $75,000
Less: Personal casualty loss (fire
destroyed her home) (88,000)
Miller's net operating loss for 2016 ($13,000)

REG 4-Q70 R283. The correct answer is A. Taxpayers who were married but lived apart during the year are still married on the last day of the taxable year. Therefore, they are allowed to file a joint return.

Answer B is incorrect because taxpayers who were married but lived under a legal separation agreement at the end of the year are considered single on the last day of the taxable year. Having a legal separation agreement from the courts is treated as though the taxpayers are divorced and not married on the last day of the taxable year.

Answer C is incorrect because taxpayers who were divorced during the year cannot file a joint return as they are not married on the last day of the taxable year.

Answer D is incorrect because taxpayers who were legally separated but lived together for the entire year are considered divorced on the last day of the taxable year. Not all states grant a legal separation agreement. If a state does not grant a legal separation agreement, then the taxpayers are considered married.

REG 4-Q71 R127. The correct answer is D. The taxpayer's best filing status for the year in which the taxpayer's spouse dies is married filing jointly with the deceased taxpayer as long as the taxpayer does not remarry.

REG 4-Q72 R346. The correct answer is D. A taxpayer whose spouse died during the preceding year and has not remarried and maintains a home for a dependent child, can file a as a qualifying widow(er) with dependent child for two years after the year of death of the spouse. In this question, Parker's spouse died during the prior year. Normally, in the year of death, the taxpayers would file jointly. For the next two years, as long as Parker has not remarried and maintains the home for a dependent child, the filing status for Parker will qualifying widow(er) with dependent child.

REG 4-Q73 R217. The correct answer is C. This question deals with the appropriate filing status for the first subsequent year after the year of death. In the year of death, the couple files a joint return and in the second and third years, the surviving spouse can elect the filing status of unmarried widow or widower (surviving spouse) as long as the surviving spouse has a dependent child living with them. In this example, the surviving spouse has no dependent children living with them so, the filing status of unmarried widow or widower is not allowed. The next best filing status is head of household but, this taxpayer is not the head of a household. The next best filing status is single which this taxpayer qualifies for. This person cannot file married filing separately because they are not married on the last day of the taxable year.

REG 4-Q74 R145. The correct answer is D. To qualify for the earned income credit the taxpayer must have a filing status other than married a separate return.

Answer A is incorrect because the child must be under the age of 19 or, is a full time student under the age of 24 or, is permanently and totally disabled. . The child in this question is 17 years old which would qualify the child to calculate the earned income credit.

Answer B is incorrect because earned income under the earned income limit would qualify for the calculation of the earned income credit.

Answer C is incorrect because the taxpayer does qualify for the earned income credit as the child must live with the taxpayer for more than one half of the year.

REG 4-Q75 R449. The correct answer is A. The child and dependent care credit is both non-refundable, and refundable.

Answer B is incorrect because the child must be under the age of 13 years old.

Answer C is incorrect because the child does not have to be a direct descendant of the taxpayer a descendant of a taxpayer's child, step child, sibling or step sibling will still qualify the taxpayer for the credit.

Answer D is incorrect because the credit can far exceed $600.

REG 4-Q76 R242. The correct answer is B. An individual taxpayer who pays foreign income taxes can elect to deduct them as an itemized deduction under taxes or can compute a foreign tax credit by filing Form 1116.

Answer A is incorrect because it is an itemized deduction but not subject to the 2% floor.

Answer C is incorrect because it is not an adjustment to income.

Answer D is incorrect because it is deductible as an itemized deduction under taxes or can be taken as a tax credit by filing Form 1116.

REG 4-Q77 R319. The correct answer is A. The annualized income installment method annualizes tax at the end of each period based on a reasonable estimate of income, deductions, and other items relating to events that occurred from the beginning of the tax year through the end of the period. The question did not state that the CPA's business was a seasonal business. The seasonal method is only used by a limited number of companies that earn most of their income in certain months based on the items they sell. Examples of businesses using the seasonal method include: an outdoor amusement park in Chicago and a lawn furniture company in Maine.

REG 4-Q78 R63. The correct answer is C. The calculation of alternative minimum tax (AMT) for individuals begins with taxable income from Form 1040 and includes adjustments to arrive at alternative minimum taxable income. One of the adjustments is the personal exemptions that the taxpayer deducted on the Form 1040. Since the computation of AMT had its own exemptions, the personal exemptions on Form 1040 are added back to taxable income, as they are disallowed in the calculation of AMT.

Answers A, B and D are incorrect because they are allowed in the calculation of AMT and therefore deductible to arrive at AMT.

REG 4-Q79 R33. The correct answer is C. Interest on a mortgage is only deductible for AMT if the money was to buy, build or improve a qualified residence. A motor home is not qualified residence. Therefore, the $15,000 interest would not be deductible for AMT and added back as an adjustment. The real estate taxes and state income taxes are not deductible for AMT. Therefore, the $18,000 of real estate taxes and state income taxes must be added back as an adjustment. The medical deduction for AMT is 10% of AGI, and regular taxes is 7.5% of AGI. Finally, the miscellaneous 2% itemized deductions are not deductible for AMT and therefore must added back as an adjustment to compute AMT tax.

Interest on $100,000 home equity loan		$15,000
Real estate tax and state income taxes 18,000		$18,000
Miscellaneous 2% itemized deductions	$5,000	0
2% of AGI	(3,000)	0
Miscellaneous itemized after 2%		$2,000
Excess medical of 2.5% of $15,000		$375
Total adjustment for AMT		$35,375

REG 4-Q80 R108. The correct answer is C. This question deals with, which of the two deductions above are also used to compute alternative minimum taxable income. Home mortgage interest is only deductible to compute alternative minimum tax (AMT) on loans to buy, build or improve the principal residence. The $11,000 is exactly that. The miscellaneous itemized deduction is not allowable as a deduction to compute AMT. So, the $2,000 is not deductible for AMT.

REG 4-Q81 R250. The correct answer is A. The itemized deductions that are deductible for the calculation of alternative minimum tax (AMT) are:

Medical expenses in excess of 10% of AGI $12,000 – $10,000 (10% of $100,000 AGI) =	$2,000
Qualified housing and residence mortgage interest	10,000
Charitable contributions (cash or credit card)	5,000
Total itemized deductions for AMT	$17,000

State income taxes and real estate taxes are not deductible for AMT because they are considered state and local income taxes which are not deductible itemized deductions for AMT. Home equity mortgage interest (used to consolidate personal debts) is not deductible for AMT because a taxpayer can only deduct mortgage interest if the proceeds borrowed were used to buy, build or improve the principal residence. The home equity loan proceeds were used to pay off personal debt, therefore preventing the interest from being deductible to calculate AMT. The qualified housing and residence mortgage interest was deductible for AMT because this interest is paid on a loan to acquire real estate.

This page is intentionally left blank.

Tax Forms

Form 1040: U.S. Individual Income Tax Return

Form 1040 — Department of the Treasury—Internal Revenue Service — U.S. Individual Income Tax Return — 2016

OMB No. 1545-0074 — IRS Use Only—Do not write or staple in this space.

For the year Jan. 1–Dec. 31, 2016, or other tax year beginning _____, 2016, ending _____, 20 ___ See separate instructions.

Your first name and initial | Last name | Your social security number

If a joint return, spouse's first name and initial | Last name | Spouse's social security number

Home address (number and street). If you have a P.O. box, see instructions. | Apt. no. | ▲ Make sure the SSN(s) above and on line 6c are correct.

City, town or post office, state, and ZIP code. If you have a foreign address, also complete spaces below (see instructions).

Presidential Election Campaign — Check here if you, or your spouse if filing jointly, want $3 to go to this fund. Checking a box below will not change your tax or refund. ☐ You ☐ Spouse

Foreign country name | Foreign province/state/county | Foreign postal code

Filing Status — Check only one box.
1. ☐ Single
2. ☐ Married filing jointly (even if only one had income)
3. ☐ Married filing separately. Enter spouse's SSN above and full name here. ▶
4. ☐ Head of household (with qualifying person). (See instructions.) If the qualifying person is a child but not your dependent, enter this child's name here. ▶
5. ☐ Qualifying widow(er) with dependent child

Exemptions
- 6a ☐ Yourself. If someone can claim you as a dependent, do not check box 6a .
- b ☐ Spouse
- c Dependents:
  - (1) First name Last name
  - (2) Dependent's social security number
  - (3) Dependent's relationship to you
  - (4) ✓ if child under age 17 qualifying for child tax credit (see instructions)

If more than four dependents, see instructions and check here ▶ ☐

Boxes checked on 6a and 6b ____
No. of children on 6c who:
• lived with you ____
• did not live with you due to divorce or separation (see instructions) ____
Dependents on 6c not entered above ____
Add numbers on lines above ▶ ____

- d Total number of exemptions claimed . . .

Income
Attach Form(s) W-2 here. Also attach Forms W-2G and 1099-R if tax was withheld.

If you did not get a W-2, see instructions.

- 7 Wages, salaries, tips, etc. Attach Form(s) W-2 7
- 8a Taxable interest. Attach Schedule B if required . . . 8a
- b Tax-exempt interest. Do not include on line 8a . . . 8b
- 9a Ordinary dividends. Attach Schedule B if required . . 9a
- b Qualified dividends . . . 9b
- 10 Taxable refunds, credits, or offsets of state and local income taxes . . . 10
- 11 Alimony received . . . 11
- 12 Business income or (loss). Attach Schedule C or C-EZ . . . 12
- 13 Capital gain or (loss). Attach Schedule D if required. If not required, check here ▶ ☐ 13
- 14 Other gains or (losses). Attach Form 4797 . . . 14
- 15a IRA distributions . 15a b Taxable amount . . . 15b
- 16a Pensions and annuities 16a b Taxable amount . . . 16b
- 17 Rental real estate, royalties, partnerships, S corporations, trusts, etc. Attach Schedule E . 17
- 18 Farm income or (loss). Attach Schedule F . . . 18
- 19 Unemployment compensation . . . 19
- 20a Social security benefits 20a b Taxable amount . . . 20b
- 21 Other income. List type and amount . . . 21
- 22 Combine the amounts in the far right column for lines 7 through 21. This is your total income ▶ 22

Adjusted Gross Income
- 23 Educator expenses . . . 23
- 24 Certain business expenses of reservists, performing artists, and fee-basis government officials. Attach Form 2106 or 2106-EZ . 24
- 25 Health savings account deduction. Attach Form 8889 . 25
- 26 Moving expenses. Attach Form 3903 . . . 26
- 27 Deductible part of self-employment tax. Attach Schedule SE . 27
- 28 Self-employed SEP, SIMPLE, and qualified plans . . 28
- 29 Self-employed health insurance deduction . . . 29
- 30 Penalty on early withdrawal of savings . . . 30
- 31a Alimony paid b Recipient's SSN ▶ _____ 31a
- 32 IRA deduction . . . 32
- 33 Student loan interest deduction . . . 33
- 34 Tuition and fees. Attach Form 8917 . . . 34
- 35 Domestic production activities deduction. Attach Form 8903 . 35
- 36 Add lines 23 through 35 . . . 36
- 37 Subtract line 36 from line 22. This is your adjusted gross income ▶ 37

For Disclosure, Privacy Act, and Paperwork Reduction Act Notice, see separate instructions. Cat. No. 11320B Form **1040** (2016)

Form 1040, Schedule A: Itemized Deductions

SCHEDULE A (Form 1040)	Itemized Deductions	OMB No. 1545-0074
Department of the Treasury Internal Revenue Service (99)	▶ Information about Schedule A and its separate instructions is at www.irs.gov/schedulea. ▶ Attach to Form 1040.	2016 Attachment Sequence No. 07

Name(s) shown on Form 1040 | Your social security number

Medical and Dental Expenses

Caution: Do not include expenses reimbursed or paid by others.
1. Medical and dental expenses (see instructions) 1
2. Enter amount from Form 1040, line 38 | 2 |
3. Multiply line 2 by 10% (0.10). But if either you or your spouse was born before January 2, 1952, multiply line 2 by 7.5% (0.075) instead 3
4. Subtract line 3 from line 1. If line 3 is more than line 1, enter -0- 4

Taxes You Paid

5. State and local (check only one box):
   a. ☐ Income taxes, or
   b. ☐ General sales taxes 5
6. Real estate taxes (see instructions) 6
7. Personal property taxes 7
8. Other taxes. List type and amount ▶ _____ 8
9. Add lines 5 through 8 9

Interest You Paid

Note: Your mortgage interest deduction may be limited (see instructions).

10. Home mortgage interest and points reported to you on Form 1098 10
11. Home mortgage interest not reported to you on Form 1098. If paid to the person from whom you bought the home, see instructions and show that person's name, identifying no., and address ▶ _____ 11
12. Points not reported to you on Form 1098. See instructions for special rules 12
13. Mortgage insurance premiums (see instructions) 13
14. Investment interest. Attach Form 4952 if required. (See instructions.) 14
15. Add lines 10 through 14 15

Gifts to Charity

If you made a gift and got a benefit for it, see instructions.

16. Gifts by cash or check. If you made any gift of $250 or more, see instructions 16
17. Other than by cash or check. If any gift of $250 or more, see instructions. You must attach Form 8283 if over $500 17
18. Carryover from prior year 18
19. Add lines 16 through 18 19

Casualty and Theft Losses

20. Casualty or theft loss(es). Attach Form 4684. (See instructions.) 20

Job Expenses and Certain Miscellaneous Deductions

21. Unreimbursed employee expenses—job travel, union dues, job education, etc. Attach Form 2106 or 2106-EZ if required. (See instructions.) ▶ 21
22. Tax preparation fees 22
23. Other expenses—investment, safe deposit box, etc. List type and amount ▶ _____ 23
24. Add lines 21 through 23 24
25. Enter amount from Form 1040, line 38 | 25 |
26. Multiply line 25 by 2% (0.02) 26
27. Subtract line 26 from line 24. If line 26 is more than line 24, enter -0- 27

Other Miscellaneous Deductions

28. Other—from list in instructions. List type and amount ▶ _____ 28

Total Itemized Deductions

29. Is Form 1040, line 38, over $155,650?
   ☐ No. Your deduction is not limited. Add the amounts in the far right column for lines 4 through 28. Also, enter this amount on Form 1040, line 40.
   ☐ Yes. Your deduction may be limited. See the Itemized Deductions Worksheet in the instructions to figure the amount to enter. 29
30. If you elect to itemize deductions even though they are less than your standard deduction, check here ..... ☐

For Paperwork Reduction Act Notice, see Form 1040 Instructions. | Cat. No. 17145C | Schedule A (Form 1040) 2016

Form 1040, Schedule B: Interest and Ordinary Dividends

SCHEDULE B
(Form 1040A or 1040)
(Rev. January 2017)
Department of the Treasury
Internal Revenue Service (99)

Interest and Ordinary Dividends

▶ Attach to Form 1040A or 1040.
▶ Information about Schedule B and its Instructions is at www.irs.gov/scheduleb.

OMB No. 1545-0074

2016
Attachment
Sequence No. 08

Name(s) shown on return | Your social security number

Part I — Interest

(See instructions on back and the Instructions for Form 1040A, or Form 1040, line 8a.)

Note: If you received a Form 1099-INT, Form 1099-OID, or substitute statement from a brokerage firm, list the firm's name as the payer and enter the total interest shown on that form.

		Amount
1	List name of payer. If any interest is from a seller-financed mortgage and the buyer used the property as a personal residence, see instructions on back and list this interest first. Also, show that buyer's social security number and address ▶	
2	Add the amounts on line 1	
3	Excludable interest on series EE and I U.S. savings bonds issued after 1989. Attach Form 8815	
4	Subtract line 3 from line 2. Enter the result here and on Form 1040A, or Form 1040, line 8a ▶	

Note: If line 4 is over $1,500, you must complete Part III.

Part II — Ordinary Dividends

(See instructions on back and the Instructions for Form 1040A, or Form 1040, line 9a.)

Note: If you received a Form 1099-DIV or substitute statement from a brokerage firm, list the firm's name as the payer and enter the ordinary dividends shown on that form.

		Amount
5	List name of payer ▶	
6	Add the amounts on line 5. Enter the total here and on Form 1040A, or Form 1040, line 9a ▶	

Note: If line 6 is over $1,500, you must complete Part III.

Part III — Foreign Accounts and Trusts

(See instructions on back.)

You must complete this part if you (a) had over $1,500 of taxable interest or ordinary dividends; (b) had a foreign account; or (c) received a distribution from, or were a grantor of, or a transferor to, a foreign trust.

		Yes	No
7a	At any time during 2016, did you have a financial interest in or signature authority over a financial account (such as a bank account, securities account, or brokerage account) located in a foreign country? See instructions		
	If "Yes," are you required to file FinCEN Form 114, Report of Foreign Bank and Financial Accounts (FBAR), to report that financial interest or signature authority? See FinCEN Form 114 and its instructions for filing requirements and exceptions to those requirements		
b	If you are required to file FinCEN Form 114, enter the name of the foreign country where the financial account is located ▶		
8	During 2016, did you receive a distribution from, or were you the grantor of, or transferor to, a foreign trust? If "Yes," you may have to file Form 3520. See instructions on back		

For Paperwork Reduction Act Notice, see your tax return instructions. Cat. No. 17146N Schedule B (Form 1040A or 1040) 2016

Form 1040, Schedule C: Profit and Loss From Business

Form 1040, Schedule D: Capital Gains and Losses

SCHEDULE D (Form 1040)

Department of the Treasury
Internal Revenue Service (99)

Capital Gains and Losses

► Attach to Form 1040 or Form 1040NR.
► Information about Schedule D and its separate instructions is at www.irs.gov/scheduled.
► Use Form 8949 to list your transactions for lines 1b, 2, 3, 8b, 9, and 10.

OMB No. 1545-0074

2016

Attachment Sequence No. 12

Name(s) shown on return

Your social security number

Part I — Short-Term Capital Gains and Losses—Assets Held One Year or Less

See instructions for how to figure the amounts to enter on the lines below.
This form may be easier to complete if you round off cents to whole dollars.

	(d) Proceeds (sales price)	(e) Cost (or other basis)	(g) Adjustments to gain or loss from Form(s) 8949, Part I, line 2, column (g)	(h) Gain or (loss) Subtract column (e) from column (d) and combine the result with column (g)
1a Totals for all short-term transactions reported on Form 1099-B for which basis was reported to the IRS and for which you have no adjustments (see instructions). However, if you choose to report all these transactions on Form 8949, leave this line blank and go to line 1b				
1b Totals for all transactions reported on Form(s) 8949 with **Box A** checked				
2 Totals for all transactions reported on Form(s) 8949 with **Box B** checked				
3 Totals for all transactions reported on Form(s) 8949 with **Box C** checked				

4 Short-term gain from Form 6252 and short-term gain or (loss) from Forms 4684, 6781, and 8824	**4**	
5 Net short-term gain or (loss) from partnerships, S corporations, estates, and trusts from Schedule(s) K-1	**5**	
6 Short-term capital loss carryover. Enter the amount, if any, from line 8 of your **Capital Loss Carryover Worksheet** in the instructions	**6** (	)
7 **Net short-term capital gain or (loss).** Combine lines 1a through 6 in column (h). If you have any long-term capital gains or losses, go to Part II below. Otherwise, go to Part III on the back	**7**	

Part II — Long-Term Capital Gains and Losses—Assets Held More Than One Year

See instructions for how to figure the amounts to enter on the lines below.
This form may be easier to complete if you round off cents to whole dollars.

	(d) Proceeds (sales price)	(e) Cost (or other basis)	(g) Adjustments to gain or loss from Form(s) 8949, Part II, line 2, column (g)	(h) Gain or (loss) Subtract column (e) from column (d) and combine the result with column (g)
8a Totals for all long-term transactions reported on Form 1099-B for which basis was reported to the IRS and for which you have no adjustments (see instructions). However, if you choose to report all these transactions on Form 8949, leave this line blank and go to line 8b				
8b Totals for all transactions reported on Form(s) 8949 with **Box D** checked				
9 Totals for all transactions reported on Form(s) 8949 with **Box E** checked				
10 Totals for all transactions reported on Form(s) 8949 with **Box F** checked				

11 Gain from Form 4797, Part I; long-term gain from Forms 2439 and 6252; and long-term gain or (loss) from Forms 4684, 6781, and 8824	**11**	
12 Net long-term gain or (loss) from partnerships, S corporations, estates, and trusts from Schedule(s) K-1	**12**	
13 Capital gain distributions. See the instructions	**13**	
14 Long-term capital loss carryover. Enter the amount, if any, from line 13 of your **Capital Loss Carryover Worksheet** in the instructions	**14** (	)
15 **Net long-term capital gain or (loss).** Combine lines 8a through 14 in column (h). Then go to Part III on the back	**15**	

For Paperwork Reduction Act Notice, see your tax return instructions.
Cat. No. 11338H
Schedule D (Form 1040) 2016

Form 1040, Schedule E: Supplemental Income and Loss

SCHEDULE E (Form 1040)
Department of the Treasury
Internal Revenue Service (99)

Supplemental Income and Loss
(From rental real estate, royalties, partnerships, S corporations, estates, trusts, REMICs, etc.)
▶ Attach to Form 1040, 1040NR, or Form 1041.
▶ Go to www.irs.gov/ScheduleE for instructions and the latest information.

OMB No. 1545-0074

2017

Attachment Sequence No. **13**

Name(s) shown on return | Your social security number

Part I — Income or Loss From Rental Real Estate and Royalties
Note: If you are in the business of renting personal property, use Schedule C or C-EZ (see instructions). If you are an individual, report farm rental income or loss from Form 4835 on page 2, line 40.

A Did you make any payments in 2017 that would require you to file Form(s) 1099? (see instructions) ☐ Yes ☐ No
B If "Yes," did you or will you file required Forms 1099? ☐ Yes ☐ No

1a Physical address of each property (street, city, state, ZIP code)
A
B
C

1b Type of Property (from list below)	2 For each rental real estate property listed above, report the number of fair rental and personal use days. Check the QJV box only if you meet the requirements to file as a qualified joint venture. See instructions.		Fair Rental Days	Personal Use Days	QJV
A		A			☐
B		B			☐
C		C			☐

Type of Property:
1 Single Family Residence 3 Vacation/Short-Term Rental 5 Land 7 Self-Rental
2 Multi-Family Residence   4 Commercial   6 Royalties 8 Other (describe)

Income:	Properties:		A	B	C
3 Rents received		3			
4 Royalties received		4			
Expenses:					
5 Advertising		5			
6 Auto and travel (see instructions)		6			
7 Cleaning and maintenance		7			
8 Commissions		8			
9 Insurance		9			
10 Legal and other professional fees		10			
11 Management fees		11			
12 Mortgage interest paid to banks, etc. (see instructions)		12			
13 Other interest		13			
14 Repairs		14			
15 Supplies		15			
16 Taxes		16			
17 Utilities		17			
18 Depreciation expense or depletion		18			
19 Other (list) ▶		19			
20 Total expenses. Add lines 5 through 19		20			
21 Subtract line 20 from line 3 (rents) and/or 4 (royalties). If result is a (loss), see instructions to find out if you must file **Form 6198**		21			
22 Deductible rental real estate loss after limitation, if any, on **Form 8582** (see instructions)		22	( )	( )	( )

23a	Total of all amounts reported on line 3 for all rental properties	23a	
b	Total of all amounts reported on line 4 for all royalty properties	23b	
c	Total of all amounts reported on line 12 for all properties	23c	
d	Total of all amounts reported on line 18 for all properties	23d	
e	Total of all amounts reported on line 20 for all properties	23e	
24	**Income.** Add positive amounts shown on line 21. **Do not include any losses**	24	
25	**Losses.** Add royalty losses from line 21 and rental real estate losses from line 22. Enter total losses here	25	( )
26	**Total rental real estate and royalty income or (loss).** Combine lines 24 and 25. Enter the result here. If Parts II, III, IV, and line 40 on page 2 do not apply to you, also enter this amount on Form 1040, line 17, or Form 1040NR, line 18. Otherwise, include this amount in the total on line 41 on page 2	26	

For Paperwork Reduction Act Notice, see the separate instructions. Cat. No. 11344L Schedule E (Form 1040) 2017

Form 1040, Schedule SE: Self-Employment Tax

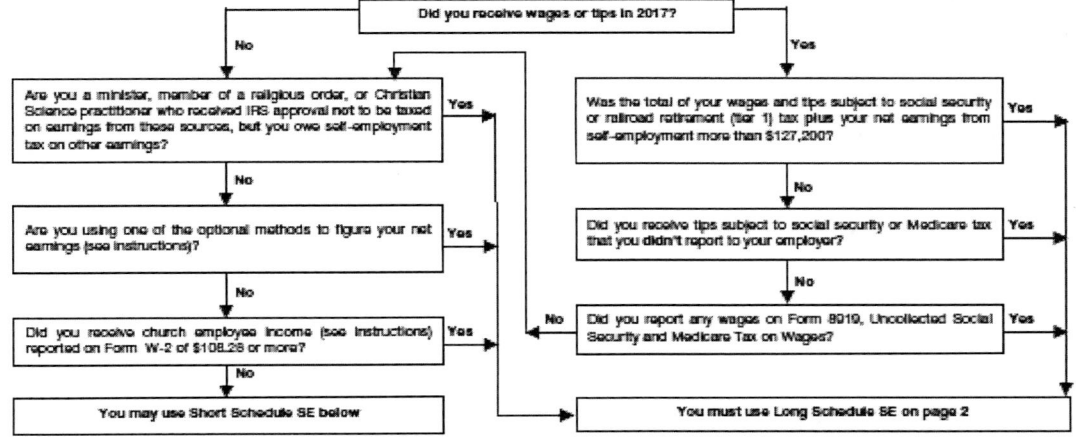

Form 1040, Schedule EIC: Earned Income Credit

Form 1065, Schedule K-1

Form 8867, Paid Preparer's Due Diligence Checklist (formerly Earned Income Credit Checklist)

Form 8867
Department of the Treasury
Internal Revenue Service

Paid Preparer's Due Diligence Checklist
Earned Income Credit (EIC), Child Tax Credit (CTC), and American Opportunity Tax Credit (AOTC)
▶ To be completed by preparer and filed with Form 1040, 1040A, 1040EZ, 1040NR, 1040SS, or 1040PR.
▶ Information about Form 8867 and its separate instructions is at www.irs.gov/form8867.

OMB No. 1545-1629
2016
Attachment Sequence No. 70

Taxpayer name(s) shown on return

Taxpayer identification number

Enter preparer's name and PTIN

Due Diligence Requirements

	Please complete the appropriate column for all credits claimed on this return (check all that apply).	EIC	CTC/ACTC	AOTC
1	Did you complete the return based on information for tax year 2016 provided by the taxpayer or reasonably obtained by you?	☐ Yes ☐ No	☐ Yes ☐ No	☐ Yes ☐ No
2	Did you complete the applicable EIC and/or CTC/ACTC worksheets found in the Form 1040, 1040A, 1040EZ, or 1040NR instructions, and/or the AOTC worksheet found in the Form 8863 instructions, or your own worksheet(s) that provides the same information, and all related forms and schedules for each credit claimed?	☐ Yes ☐ No	☐ Yes ☐ No	☐ Yes ☐ No
3	Did you satisfy the knowledge requirement? Answer "Yes" only if you can answer "Yes" to both 3a and 3b. To meet the knowledge requirement, did you:	☐ Yes ☐ No	☐ Yes ☐ No	☐ Yes ☐ No
a	Interview the taxpayer, ask adequate questions, and document the taxpayer's responses to determine that the taxpayer is eligible to claim the credit(s)?	☐ Yes ☐ No	☐ Yes ☐ No	☐ Yes ☐ No
b	Review adequate information to determine that the taxpayer is eligible to claim the credit(s) and in what amount?	☐ Yes ☐ No	☐ Yes ☐ No	☐ Yes ☐ No
4	Did any information provided by the taxpayer, a third party, or reasonably known to you in connection with preparing the return appear to be incorrect, incomplete, or inconsistent? (If "Yes," answer questions 4a and 4b. If "No," go to question 5.)	☐ Yes ☐ No	☐ Yes ☐ No	☐ Yes ☐ No
a	Did you make reasonable inquiries to determine the correct or complete information?	☐ Yes ☐ No	☐ Yes ☐ No	☐ Yes ☐ No
b	Did you document your inquiries? (Documentation should include the questions you asked, whom you asked, when you asked, the information that was provided, and the impact the information had on your preparation of the return.)	☐ Yes ☐ No	☐ Yes ☐ No	☐ Yes ☐ No
5	Did you satisfy the record retention requirement? To meet the record retention requirement, did you keep a copy of any document(s) provided by the taxpayer that you relied on to determine eligibility or to compute the amount for the credit(s)?	☐ Yes ☐ No	☐ Yes ☐ No	☐ Yes ☐ No
	In addition to your notes from the interview with the taxpayer, list those documents, if any, that you relied on. _____ _____ _____ _____			
6	Did you ask the taxpayer whether he/she could provide documentation to substantiate eligibility for and the amount of the credit(s) claimed on the return?	☐ Yes ☐ No	☐ Yes ☐ No	☐ Yes ☐ No
7	Did you ask the taxpayer if any of these credits were disallowed or reduced in a previous year? (If credits were disallowed or reduced, go to question 7a; if not, go to question 8.)	☐ Yes ☐ No	☐ Yes ☐ No	☐ Yes ☐ No
a	Did you complete the required recertification form(s)?	☐ Yes ☐ No	☐ Yes ☐ No	☐ Yes ☐ No
8	If the taxpayer is reporting self-employment income, did you ask adequate questions to prepare a complete and correct Form 1040, Schedule C?	☐ Yes ☐ No	☐ Yes ☐ No	☐ Yes ☐ No

For Paperwork Reduction Act Notice, see separate instructions.   Cat. No. 26142H   Form **8867** (2016)

Form 8815, Tax for Certain Children Who Have Unearned Income

Form **8615**	**Tax for Certain Children Who Have Unearned Income**	OMB No. 1545-0074
Department of the Treasury Internal Revenue Service (99)	▶ Attach only to the child's Form 1040, Form 1040A, or Form 1040NR. ▶ Information about Form 8615 and its separate instructions is at www.irs.gov/form8615.	**2016** Attachment Sequence No. 33

Child's name shown on return | Child's social security number

Before you begin: If the child, the parent, or any of the parent's other children for whom Form 8615 must be filed must use the Schedule D Tax Worksheet or has income from farming or fishing, see **Pub. 929**, Tax Rules for Children and Dependents. It explains how to figure the child's tax using the **Schedule D Tax Worksheet** or **Schedule J (Form 1040)**.

A Parent's name (first, initial, and last). Caution: See instructions before completing. | **B** Parent's social security number

C Parent's filing status (check one):
☐ Single ☐ Married filing jointly ☐ Married filing separately ☐ Head of household ☐ Qualifying widow(er)

Part I Child's Net Unearned Income

1. Enter the child's unearned income (see instructions) **1**
2. If the child **did not** itemize deductions on **Schedule A** (Form 1040 or Form 1040NR), enter $2,100. Otherwise, see instructions **2**
3. Subtract line 2 from line 1. If zero or less, **stop;** do not complete the rest of this form but **do** attach it to the child's return **3**
4. Enter the child's **taxable income** from Form 1040, line 43; Form 1040A, line 27; or Form 1040NR, line 41. If the child files Form 2555 or 2555-EZ, see the instructions **4**
5. Enter the **smaller** of line 3 or line 4. If zero, **stop;** do not complete the rest of this form but **do** attach it to the child's return **5**

Part II Tentative Tax Based on the Tax Rate of the Parent

6. Enter the parent's **taxable income** from Form 1040, line 43; Form 1040A, line 27; Form 1040EZ, line 6; Form 1040NR, line 41; or Form 1040NR-EZ, line 14. If zero or less, enter -0-. If the parent files Form 2555 or 2555-EZ, see the instructions **6**
7. Enter the total, if any, from Forms 8615, line 5, of **all other** children of the parent named above. **Do not** include the amount from line 5 above **7**
8. Add lines 5, 6, and 7 (see instructions) **8**
9. Enter the tax on the amount on line 8 based on the **parent's** filing status above (see instructions). If the Qualified Dividends and Capital Gain Tax Worksheet, Schedule D Tax Worksheet, or Schedule J (Form 1040) is used to figure the tax, check here . . . . ▶ ☐ **9**
10. Enter the parent's tax from Form 1040, line 44; Form 1040A, line 28, minus any alternative minimum tax; Form 1040EZ, line 10; Form 1040NR, line 42; or Form 1040NR-EZ, line 15. **Do not** include any tax from **Form 4972, 8814,** or **8885** or any tax from recapture of an education credit. If the parent files Form 2555 or 2555-EZ, see the instructions. If the Qualified Dividends and Capital Gain Tax Worksheet, Schedule D Tax Worksheet, or Schedule J (Form 1040) was used to figure the tax, check here . . . . ▶ ☐ **10**
11. Subtract line 10 from line 9 and enter the result. If line 7 is blank, also enter this amount on line 13 and go to **Part III** **11**
12a. Add lines 5 and 7 . . . . **12a**
  b. Divide line 5 by line 12a. Enter the result as a decimal (rounded to at least three places) . . . **12b**   × .
13. Multiply line 11 by line 12b **13**

Part III Child's Tax—If lines 4 and 5 above are the same, enter -0- on line 15 and go to line 16.

14. Subtract line 5 from line 4 . . . . **14**
15. Enter the tax on the amount on line 14 based on the **child's** filing status (see instructions). If the Qualified Dividends and Capital Gain Tax Worksheet, Schedule D Tax Worksheet, or Schedule J (Form 1040) is used to figure the tax, check here . . . . ▶ ☐ **15**
16. Add lines 13 and 15 . . . . **16**
17. Enter the tax on the amount on line 4 based on the **child's** filing status (see instructions). If the Qualified Dividends and Capital Gain Tax Worksheet, Schedule D Tax Worksheet, or Schedule J (Form 1040) is used to figure the tax, check here . . . . ▶ ☐ **17**
18. Enter the **larger** of line 16 or line 17 here and on the **child's** Form 1040, line 44; Form 1040A, line 28; or Form 1040NR, line 42. If the child files Form 2555 or 2555-EZ, see the instructions . . **18**

For Paperwork Reduction Act Notice, see your tax return instructions. | Cat. No. 64113U | Form **8615** (2016)

Form 8582, Passive Activity Loss Limitations

Form 8582
Department of the Treasury
Internal Revenue Service (99)

Passive Activity Loss Limitations
► See separate instructions.
► Attach to Form 1040 or Form 1041.
► Go to www.irs.gov/Form8582 for instructions and the latest information.

OMB No. 1545-1008
2017
Attachment Sequence No. 88

Name(s) shown on return

Identifying number

Part I 2017 Passive Activity Loss
Caution: Complete Worksheets 1, 2, and 3 before completing Part I.

Rental Real Estate Activities With Active Participation (For the definition of active participation, see Special Allowance for Rental Real Estate Activities in the instructions.)

- 1a Activities with net income (enter the amount from Worksheet 1, column (a)) 1a
- b Activities with net loss (enter the amount from Worksheet 1, column (b)) 1b
- c Prior years' unallowed losses (enter the amount from Worksheet 1, column (c)) 1c
- d Combine lines 1a, 1b, and 1c 1d

Commercial Revitalization Deductions From Rental Real Estate Activities

- 2a Commercial revitalization deductions from Worksheet 2, column (a) . 2a
- b Prior year unallowed commercial revitalization deductions from Worksheet 2, column (b) 2b
- c Add lines 2a and 2b 2c

All Other Passive Activities

- 3a Activities with net income (enter the amount from Worksheet 3, column (a)) 3a
- b Activities with net loss (enter the amount from Worksheet 3, column (b)) 3b
- c Prior years' unallowed losses (enter the amount from Worksheet 3, column (c)) 3c
- d Combine lines 3a, 3b, and 3c 3d

4 Combine lines 1d, 2c, and 3d. If this line is zero or more, stop here and include this form with your return; all losses are allowed, including any prior year unallowed losses entered on line 1c, 2b, or 3c. Report the losses on the forms and schedules normally used 4

If line 4 is a loss and:
- Line 1d is a loss, go to Part II.
- Line 2c is a loss (and line 1d is zero or more), skip Part II and go to Part III.
- Line 3d is a loss (and lines 1d and 2c are zero or more), skip Parts II and III and go to line 15.

Caution: If your filing status is married filing separately and you lived with your spouse at any time during the year, **do not** complete Part II or Part III. Instead, go to line 15.

Part II Special Allowance for Rental Real Estate Activities With Active Participation
Note: Enter all numbers in Part II as positive amounts. See instructions for an example.

- 5 Enter the **smaller** of the loss on line 1d or the loss on line 4 5
- 6 Enter $150,000. If married filing separately, see instructions . . 6
- 7 Enter modified adjusted gross income, but not less than zero (see instructions) 7

Note: If line 7 is greater than or equal to line 6, skip lines 8 and 9, enter -0- on line 10. Otherwise, go to line 8.

- 8 Subtract line 7 from line 6 8
- 9 Multiply line 8 by 50% (0.50). Do not enter more than $25,000. If married filing separately, see instructions 9
- 10 Enter the **smaller** of line 5 or line 9 10

If line 2c is a loss, go to Part III. Otherwise, go to line 15.

Part III Special Allowance for Commercial Revitalization Deductions From Rental Real Estate Activities
Note: Enter all numbers in Part III as positive amounts. See the example for Part II in the instructions.

- 11 Enter $25,000 reduced by the amount, if any, on line 10. If married filing separately, see instructions 11
- 12 Enter the loss from line 4 12
- 13 Reduce line 12 by the amount on line 10 13
- 14 Enter the **smallest** of line 2c (treated as a positive amount), line 11, or line 13 . . . 14

Part IV Total Losses Allowed

- 15 Add the income, if any, on lines 1a and 3a and enter the total 15
- 16 Total losses allowed from all passive activities for 2017. Add lines 10, 14, and 15. See instructions to find out how to report the losses on your tax return 16

For Paperwork Reduction Act Notice, see instructions.   Cat. No. 63704F   Form **8582** (2017)

This page is intentionally left blank.

Form 4797, Sales of Business Property

Form 4797
Department of the Treasury
Internal Revenue Service

Sales of Business Property
(Also Involuntary Conversions and Recapture Amounts Under Sections 179 and 280F(b)(2))
► Attach to your tax return.
► Information about Form 4797 and its separate instructions is at www.irs.gov/form4797.

OMB No. 1545-0184
2016
Attachment Sequence No. **27**

Name(s) shown on return | Identifying number

1. Enter the gross proceeds from sales or exchanges reported to you for 2016 on Form(s) 1099-B or 1099-S (or substitute statement) that you are including on line 2, 10, or 20. See instructions **1**

Part I — Sales or Exchanges of Property Used in a Trade or Business and Involuntary Conversions From Other Than Casualty or Theft—Most Property Held More Than 1 Year (see instructions)

2	(a) Description of property	(b) Date acquired (mo., day, yr.)	(c) Date sold (mo., day, yr.)	(d) Gross sales price	(e) Depreciation allowed or allowable since acquisition	(f) Cost or other basis, plus improvements and expense of sale	(g) Gain or (loss) Subtract (f) from the sum of (d) and (e)

3. Gain, if any, from Form 4684, line 39 . . . . **3**
4. Section 1231 gain from installment sales from Form 6252, line 26 or 37 . . . . . **4**
5. Section 1231 gain or (loss) from like-kind exchanges from Form 8824 . . . . . . **5**
6. Gain, if any, from line 32, from other than casualty or theft **6**
7. Combine lines 2 through 6. Enter the gain or (loss) here and on the appropriate line as follows: **7**

   Partnerships (except electing large partnerships) and S corporations. Report the gain or (loss) following the instructions for Form 1065, Schedule K, line 10, or Form 1120S, Schedule K, line 9. Skip lines 8, 9, 11, and 12 below.
   Individuals, partners, S corporation shareholders, and all others. If line 7 is zero or a loss, enter the amount from line 7 on line 11 below and skip lines 8 and 9. If line 7 is a gain and you didn't have any prior year section 1231 losses, or they were recaptured in an earlier year, enter the gain from line 7 as a long-term capital gain on the Schedule D filed with your return and skip lines 8, 9, 11, and 12 below.

8. Nonrecaptured net section 1231 losses from prior years. See instructions **8**
9. Subtract line 8 from line 7. If zero or less, enter -0-. If line 9 is zero, enter the gain from line 7 on line 12 below. If line 9 is more than zero, enter the amount from line 8 on line 12 below and enter the gain from line 9 as a long-term capital gain on the Schedule D filed with your return. See instructions **9**

Part II — Ordinary Gains and Losses (see instructions)

10. Ordinary gains and losses not included on lines 11 through 16 (include property held 1 year or less):

11. Loss, if any, from line 7 . . . . **11** (   )
12. Gain, if any, from line 7 or amount from line 8, if applicable **12**
13. Gain, if any, from line 31 . . . . **13**
14. Net gain or (loss) from Form 4684, lines 31 and 38a **14**
15. Ordinary gain from installment sales from Form 6252, line 25 or 36 . . . . . . **15**
16. Ordinary gain or (loss) from like-kind exchanges from Form 8824 . . . . **16**
17. Combine lines 10 through 16 . . . . **17**
18. For all except individual returns, enter the amount from line 17 on the appropriate line of your return and skip lines a and b below. For individual returns, complete lines a and b below:

    a. If the loss on line 11 includes a loss from Form 4684, line 35, column (b)(ii), enter that part of the loss here. Enter the part of the loss from income-producing property on Schedule A (Form 1040), line 28, and the part of the loss from property used as an employee on Schedule A (Form 1040), line 23. Identify as from "Form 4797, line 18a." See instructions . . **18a**

    b. Redetermine the gain or (loss) on line 17 excluding the loss, if any, on line 18a. Enter here and on Form 1040, line 14 **18b**

For Paperwork Reduction Act Notice, see separate instructions.   Cat. No. 13086I   Form **4797** (2016)

Form 4562, Depreciation and Amortization

Form 4562 — Depreciation and Amortization
(Including Information on Listed Property)
▶ Attach to your tax return.
▶ Information about Form 4562 and its separate instructions is at www.irs.gov/form4562.

Department of the Treasury
Internal Revenue Service (99)

OMB No. 1545-0172
2016
Attachment Sequence No. 179

Name(s) shown on return | Business or activity to which this form relates | Identifying number

Part I — Election To Expense Certain Property Under Section 179
Note: If you have any listed property, complete Part V before you complete Part I.

1. Maximum amount (see instructions) 1
2. Total cost of section 179 property placed in service (see instructions) 2
3. Threshold cost of section 179 property before reduction in limitation (see instructions) . . . 3
4. Reduction in limitation. Subtract line 3 from line 2. If zero or less, enter -0- 4
5. Dollar limitation for tax year. Subtract line 4 from line 1. If zero or less, enter -0-. If married filing separately, see instructions 5

6	(a) Description of property	(b) Cost (business use only)	(c) Elected cost

7. Listed property. Enter the amount from line 29 7
8. Total elected cost of section 179 property. Add amounts in column (c), lines 6 and 7 . . . 8
9. Tentative deduction. Enter the **smaller** of line 5 or line 8 9
10. Carryover of disallowed deduction from line 13 of your 2015 Form 4562 10
11. Business income limitation. Enter the smaller of business income (not less than zero) or line 5 (see instructions) . . 11
12. Section 179 expense deduction. Add lines 9 and 10, but don't enter more than line 11 . . . 12
13. Carryover of disallowed deduction to 2017. Add lines 9 and 10, less line 12 ▶ | 13 |

Note: Don't use Part II or Part III below for listed property. Instead, use Part V.

Part II — Special Depreciation Allowance and Other Depreciation (Don't include listed property.) (See instructions.)

14. Special depreciation allowance for qualified property (other than listed property) placed in service during the tax year (see instructions) 14
15. Property subject to section 168(f)(1) election 15
16. Other depreciation (including ACRS) 16

Part III — MACRS Depreciation (Don't include listed property.) (See instructions.)

Section A

17. MACRS deductions for assets placed in service in tax years beginning before 2016 17
18. If you are electing to group any assets placed in service during the tax year into one or more general asset accounts, check here . . . . ▶ ☐

Section B—Assets Placed in Service During 2016 Tax Year Using the General Depreciation System

(a) Classification of property	(b) Month and year placed in service	(c) Basis for depreciation (business/investment use only—see instructions)	(d) Recovery period	(e) Convention	(f) Method	(g) Depreciation deduction
19a 3-year property						
b 5-year property						
c 7-year property						
d 10-year property						
e 15-year property						
f 20-year property						
g 25-year property						
h Residential rental property						
i Nonresidential real property						

Section C—Assets Placed in Service During 2016 Tax Year Using the Alternative Depreciation System

20a Class life						
b 12-year						
c 40-year						

Part IV — Summary (See instructions.)

21. Listed property. Enter amount from line 28 21
22. **Total.** Add amounts from line 12, lines 14 through 17, lines 19 and 20 in column (g), and line 21. Enter here and on the appropriate lines of your return. Partnerships and S corporations—see instructions . 22
23. For assets shown above and placed in service during the current year, enter the portion of the basis attributable to section 263A costs . . . . | 23 |

For Paperwork Reduction Act Notice, see separate instructions.   Cat. No. 12906N   Form **4562** (2016)

Form 4684, Casualties and Thefts

Form **4684**	**Casualties and Thefts**	OMB No. 1545-0177
Department of the Treasury Internal Revenue Service	▶ Information about Form 4684 and its separate instructions is at www.irs.gov/form4684. ▶ Attach to your tax return. ▶ Use a separate Form 4684 for each casualty or theft.	**2016** Attachment Sequence No. 26
Name(s) shown on tax return		Identifying number

SECTION A—Personal Use Property (Use this section to report casualties and thefts of property **not** used in a trade or business or for income-producing purposes.)

1. Description of properties (show type, location, and date acquired for each property). Use a separate line for each property lost or damaged from the same casualty or theft.

   Property A _____
   Property B _____
   Property C _____
   Property D _____

	Properties			
	A	B	C	D
2 Cost or other basis of each property				
3 Insurance or other reimbursement (whether or not you filed a claim) (see instructions)				
Note: *If line 2 is more than line 3, skip line 4.*				
4 Gain from casualty or theft. If line 3 is more than line 2, enter the difference here and skip lines 5 through 9 for that column. See instructions if line 3 includes insurance or other reimbursement you did not claim, or you received payment for your loss in a later tax year				
5 Fair market value **before** casualty or theft				
6 Fair market value **after** casualty or theft				
7 Subtract line 6 from line 5				
8 Enter the **smaller** of line 2 or line 7				
9 Subtract line 3 from line 8. If zero or less, enter -0-				

10. Casualty or theft loss. Add the amounts on line 9 in columns A through D **10**
11. Enter the smaller of line 10 or $100 . . . . **11**
12. Subtract line 11 from line 10 . . . . **12**
    Caution: *Use only one Form 4684 for lines 13 through 18.*
13. Add the amounts on line 12 of all Forms 4684 . . . . **13**
14. Add the amounts on line 4 of all Forms 4684 . . . . **14**
15. • If line 14 is **more** than line 13, enter the difference here and on Schedule D. **Do not complete the rest of this section** (see instructions).
    • If line 14 is **less** than line 13, enter -0- here and go to line 16.
    • If line 14 is **equal** to line 13, enter -0- here. **Do not complete the rest of this section.** **15**
16. If line 14 is **less** than line 13, enter the difference **16**
17. Enter 10% of your adjusted gross income from Form 1040, line 38, or Form 1040NR, line 37. Estates and trusts, see instructions **17**
18. Subtract line 17 from line 16. If zero or less, enter -0-. Also enter the result on Schedule A (Form 1040), line 20, or Form 1040NR, Schedule A, line 6. Estates and trusts, enter the result on the "Other deductions" line of your tax return **18**

For Paperwork Reduction Act Notice, see instructions. Cat. No. 12997O Form **4684** (2016)

Form 2441, Child and Dependent Care Expenses

Form 2441 — Child and Dependent Care Expenses

► Attach to Form 1040, Form 1040A, or Form 1040NR.
► Information about Form 2441 and its separate instructions is at www.irs.gov/form2441.

Department of the Treasury
Internal Revenue Service (99)

OMB No. 1545-0074
2016
Attachment Sequence No. 21

Name(s) shown on return | Your social security number

Part I — Persons or Organizations Who Provided the Care—You must complete this part.
(If you have more than two care providers, see the instructions.)

1	(a) Care provider's name	(b) Address (number, street, apt. no., city, state, and ZIP code)	(c) Identifying number (SSN or EIN)	(d) Amount paid (see instructions)

Did you receive dependent care benefits?
— No → Complete only Part II below.
— Yes → Complete Part III on the back next.

Caution: If the care was provided in your home, you may owe employment taxes. If you do, you cannot file Form 1040A. For details, see the instructions for Form 1040, line 60a, or Form 1040NR, line 59a.

Part II — Credit for Child and Dependent Care Expenses

2 Information about your **qualifying person(s)**. If you have more than two qualifying persons, see the instructions.

(a) Qualifying person's name First / Last	(b) Qualifying person's social security number	(c) Qualified expenses you incurred and paid in 2016 for the person listed in column (a)

3 Add the amounts in column (c) of line 2. **Do not** enter more than $3,000 for one qualifying person or $6,000 for two or more persons. If you completed Part III, enter the amount from line 31 . . . . **3**

4 Enter your **earned income**. See instructions **4**

5 If married filing jointly, enter your spouse's earned income (if you or your spouse was a student or was disabled, see the instructions); **all others**, enter the amount from line 4 . **5**

6 Enter the **smallest** of line 3, 4, or 5 . . . . **6**

7 Enter the amount from Form 1040, line 38; Form 1040A, line 22; or Form 1040NR, line 37 . . . . . **7**

8 Enter on line 8 the decimal amount shown below that applies to the amount on line 7

If line 7 is:		Decimal	If line 7 is:		Decimal
Over	But not over	amount is	Over	But not over	amount is
$0	15,000	.35	$29,000	31,000	.27
15,000	17,000	.34	31,000	33,000	.26
17,000	19,000	.33	33,000	35,000	.25
19,000	21,000	.32	35,000	37,000	.24
21,000	23,000	.31	37,000	39,000	.23
23,000	25,000	.30	39,000	41,000	.22
25,000	27,000	.29	41,000	43,000	.21
27,000	29,000	.28	43,000	No limit	.20

8 X.

9 Multiply line 6 by the decimal amount on line 8. If you paid 2015 expenses in 2016, see the instructions **9**

10 Tax liability limit. Enter the amount from the Credit Limit Worksheet in the instructions **10**

11 **Credit for child and dependent care expenses**. Enter the **smaller** of line 9 or line 10 here and on Form 1040, line 49; Form 1040A, line 31; or Form 1040NR, line 47 . . . . **11**

For Paperwork Reduction Act Notice, see your tax return instructions.   Cat. No. 11862M   Form **2441** (2016)

Form 6251, Alternative Minimum Tax – Individuals

Form **6251**	**Alternative Minimum Tax—Individuals**	OMB No. 1545-0074
Department of the Treasury Internal Revenue Service (99)	► Information about Form 6251 and its separate instructions is at www.irs.gov/form6251. ► Attach to Form 1040 or Form 1040NR.	**2016** Attachment Sequence No. 32
Name(s) shown on Form 1040 or Form 1040NR		Your social security number

Part I Alternative Minimum Taxable Income (See instructions for how to complete each line.)

1. If filing Schedule A (Form 1040), enter the amount from Form 1040, line 41, and go to line 2. Otherwise, enter the amount from Form 1040, line 38, and go to line 7. (If less than zero, enter as a negative amount.) **1**
2. Medical and dental. If you or your spouse was 65 or older, enter the **smaller** of Schedule A (Form 1040), line 4, or 2.5% (0.025) of Form 1040, line 38. If zero or less, enter -0- **2**
3. Taxes from Schedule A (Form 1040), line 9 .... **3**
4. Enter the home mortgage interest adjustment, if any, from line 6 of the worksheet in the instructions for this line **4**
5. Miscellaneous deductions from Schedule A (Form 1040), line 27 .... **5**
6. If Form 1040, line 38, is $155,650 or less, enter -0-. Otherwise, see instructions .... **6** ( )
7. Tax refund from Form 1040, line 10 or line 21 .... **7** ( )
8. Investment interest expense (difference between regular tax and AMT) **8**
9. Depletion (difference between regular tax and AMT) **9**
10. Net operating loss deduction from Form 1040, line 21. Enter as a positive amount **10**
11. Alternative tax net operating loss deduction .... **11** ( )
12. Interest from specified private activity bonds exempt from the regular tax **12**
13. Qualified small business stock, see instructions **13**
14. Exercise of incentive stock options (excess of AMT income over regular tax income) **14**
15. Estates and trusts (amount from Schedule K-1 (Form 1041), box 12, code A) **15**
16. Electing large partnerships (amount from Schedule K-1 (Form 1065-B), box 6) **16**
17. Disposition of property (difference between AMT and regular tax gain or loss) **17**
18. Depreciation on assets placed in service after 1986 (difference between regular tax and AMT) **18**
19. Passive activities (difference between AMT and regular tax income or loss) **19**
20. Loss limitations (difference between AMT and regular tax income or loss) **20**
21. Circulation costs (difference between regular tax and AMT) **21**
22. Long-term contracts (difference between AMT and regular tax income) **22**
23. Mining costs (difference between regular tax and AMT) **23**
24. Research and experimental costs (difference between regular tax and AMT) **24**
25. Income from certain installment sales before January 1, 1987 .... **25** ( )
26. Intangible drilling costs preference **26**
27. Other adjustments, including income-based related adjustments **27**
28. Alternative minimum taxable income. Combine lines 1 through 27. (If married filing separately and line 28 is more than $247,450, see instructions.) **28**

Part II Alternative Minimum Tax (AMT)

29. Exemption. (If you were under age 24 at the end of 2016, see instructions.)

IF your filing status is ...	AND line 28 is not over ...	THEN enter on line 29 ...
Single or head of household	$119,700	$53,900
Married filing jointly or qualifying widow(er)	159,700	83,800
Married filing separately	79,850	41,900

If line 28 is **over** the amount shown above for your filing status, see instructions. **29**

30. Subtract line 29 from line 28. If more than zero, go to line 31. If zero or less, enter -0- here and on lines 31, 33, and 35, and go to line 34 .... **30**
31. • If you are filing Form 2555 or 2555-EZ, see instructions for the amount to enter.
    • If you reported capital gain distributions directly on Form 1040, line 13; you reported qualified dividends on Form 1040, line 9b; or you had a gain on both lines 15 and 16 of Schedule D (Form 1040) (as refigured for the AMT, if necessary), complete Part III on the back and enter the amount from line 64 here.
    • **All others:** If line 30 is $186,300 or less ($93,150 or less if married filing separately), multiply line 30 by 26% (0.26). Otherwise, multiply line 30 by 28% (0.28) and subtract $3,726 ($1,863 if married filing separately) from the result. **31**
32. Alternative minimum tax foreign tax credit (see instructions) **32**
33. Tentative minimum tax. Subtract line 32 from line 31 .... **33**
34. Add Form 1040, line 44 (minus any tax from Form 4972), and Form 1040, line 46. Subtract from the result any foreign tax credit from Form 1040, line 48. If you used Schedule J to figure your tax on Form 1040, line 44, refigure that tax without using Schedule J before completing this line (see instructions) **34**
35. **AMT.** Subtract line 34 from line 33. If zero or less, enter -0-. Enter here and on Form 1040, line 45 .... **35**

For Paperwork Reduction Act Notice, see your tax return instructions.   Cat. No. 13600G   Form **6251** (2016)

Form 1099-C, Cancellation of Debt
Form 1099-C is sent to individual taxpayers by creditors when debts are canceled for more than $600 in a single tax year. Canceled debt is typically treated like any other amount of ordinary income. Examples of when Form 1099-C is used include canceled credit card debt and home short sales or, foreclosures, in which a home is sold below the amount due on the mortgage. However, not all canceled debt is reported as income. For example, debt discharged in bankruptcy is not considered income and some student loan debt that is forgiven may not be considered income (Publication 4861 is used to describe student loan debt that may be forgiven in this circumstance). The amount in box 2 (amount to be discharged) is reported on line 21 (other income) of Form 1040.

Form 1099-INT, Interest Income
Form 1099-INT is sent to an individual taxpayer who earned more than $10 of interest from a financial institution in the tax year. The amount in box 2 (early withdrawal penalty) is reported on line 30 (penalty on early withdrawals) of Form 1040.

Form 1099-MISC, Miscellaneous Income
Form 1099-MISC is sent to an individual taxpayer to show compensation as an independent contractor (shown in box 7). The criteria that must be met in order to be an independent contractor (worker) and be eligible to receive a 1099-MISC (instead of a W-2) include:
- Worker determines the work schedule.
- Worker can accept (or choose not to accept) assignments on a project-by-project basis.
- Typically, the worker provides their own training.

Note, alimony is reported in box 3, other income.

Form W-2, Wages and Tax Statement

Form W-2 is sent to individual taxpayers by their employers, who are required by the IRS to report wage and salary information, in addition to federal, state and other taxes that are withheld from an employee's paycheck. The criteria that must be met in order to be considered an employee and eligible to receive a W-2 include:

- Worker hours are set by the company (employer).
- The work flow and process are established by the company
- Worker training and necessary tools to perform the job are provided by the company.
- Workers report to a supervisor and must meet performance goals and standards.

Form 1099-R, Distributions from Pensions, Annuities, Profit-Sharing Plans, IRAs, Insurance Contracts, etc.

Form 1099-R is sent to individual taxpayers and shows all distributions from pensions, annuities, profit sharing, insurance contracts and IRAs for the tax year, except transfers of one IRA to another IRA and early withdrawal fess and penalties. For IRA distributions, the amount in box 1 (gross distribution) is reported on line 15a (gross distribution) and the amount of the gross distribution that is taxable is shown on line 15b of Form 1040. For gross distributions from pensions and annuities, the amount in box 1 (gross distribution) is reported on line 16a (gross distribution) of Form 1040 and the amount of the gross distribution from the pensions and annuities that is taxable is shown on line 16b of Form 1040.

Form 1099-DIV, Dividends and Distributions

Form 1099-DIV is sent to individual taxpayers and shows the amount of dividends paid by an entity if it paid $10 or more in dividends or, if the company was liquidated and paid a liquidating distribution.

Form 1099-B, Proceeds from Broker and Barter Exchange Transactions
A broker or barter exchange must file this form for each person:
- For whom, they sold stocks, commodities, regulated futures contracts, foreign currency contracts, forward contracts, debt instruments, options, securities futures contracts, etc., for cash,
- Who received cash, stock, or other property from a corporation that the broker knows or has reason to know has had its stock acquired in an acquisition of control or had a substantial change in capital structure reportable on Form 8806, or
- Who exchanged property or services through a barter exchange.

Form 1099-G, Certain Government Payments

Form 1099-G is sent to individual taxpayers for **certain government payments including:**
- Box 1: Unemployment compensation (goes to Form 1040, line 19)
- Box 2: State or local income tax refunds (goes to Form 1040, line 10) and the taxpayer must calculate the amount of the state income tax refund that is taxable.

Form 1098-T, Tuition Statement

Form 1098-T is sent to individual taxpayers for payments of qualified tuition and related expenses. It also reports any scholarships or grants received by the individual taxpayer. The amount reported as qualified tuition payments comes from box 1 (payments received for qualified tuition and related expenses), minus box 5 (scholarships or grants), to arrive at net qualified tuition and related expenses. This amount can be reported on line 34 of Form 1040, or can be only used once to calculate the American Opportunity Tax Credit, or the Lifetime Learning Credit.

Form 1099-SSA, Social Security Benefit Statement

Form 1099-SSA is sent to individual taxpayers who receive social security, but not Medicare. The gross amount of the benefits paid is reported in box 3 (benefits paid in 20XX). The amount in box 5 (net benefits for 20XX) is reported on Form 1040, line 20a (social security benefits). The amount of the social security benefits that are taxable are reported on line 20b (taxable amount). The amount of line 20b is calculated by the taxpayer.

FORM SSA-1099 – SOCIAL SECURITY BENEFIT STATEMENT

2016
- PART OF YOUR SOCIAL SECURITY BENEFITS SHOWN IN BOX 5 MAY BE TAXABLE INCOME.
- SEE THE REVERSE FOR MORE INFORMATION.

Box 1. Name	Box 2. Beneficiary's Social Security Number
Box 3. Benefits Paid in 2016	Box 4. Benefits Repaid to SSA in 2016	Box 5. Net Benefits for 2016 *(Box 3 minus Box 4)*

DESCRIPTION OF AMOUNT IN BOX 3	DESCRIPTION OF AMOUNT IN BOX 4
	Box 6. Voluntary Federal Income Tax Withheld
	Box 7. Address
	Box 8. Claim Number *(Use this number if you need to contact SSA.)*

Form SSA-1099-SM (1-2017)   DO NOT RETURN THIS FORM TO SSA OR IRS

REG 5 – Federal Taxation for Entities

A.	Tax Treatment of Formation and Liquidation of Business Entities	5A-1 – 5A-8
B.	Differences between Book and Tax Income (Loss)	5B-1 – 5B-6
C.	C Corporations	5C-1 – 5C-41
	1. Computations of taxable income (including alternative minimum taxable income), tax liability and allowable credits	2
	2. Net operating losses and capital loss limitations	14
	3. Entity/owner transactions, including contributions, loans and distributions	16
	4. Consolidated tax returns	30
	5. Multijurisdictional tax issues (including consideration of local, state and international tax issues)	32
D.	S Corporations	5D-1 – 5D-15
	1. Eligibility and elections	1
	2. Determination of ordinary business income (loss) and separately stated items	3
	3. Basis of shareholder's interest	6
	4. Entity/owner transactions (including contributions, loans and distributions)	7
	5. Built-in gains tax	11
	6. Corporate reorganizations	12
E.	Partnerships	5E-1 – 5E-20
	1. Determination of ordinary business income (loss) and separately stated items	2
	2. Basis of partner's interest and basis of assets contributed to the partnership	4
	3. Partnership and partner elections	9
	4. Transactions between a partner and the partnership (including services performed by a partner and loans)	11
	5. Impact of partnership liabilities on a partner's interest in a partnership	12
	6. Distribution of partnership assets	13
	7. Ownership changes	15
F.	Limited Liability Companies	5F-1
G.	Trusts and Estates	5G-1 – 5G-4
	1. Types of trusts	1
	2. Income and deductions	1
	3. Determination of beneficiary's share of taxable income	4
H.	Tax-Exempt Organizations	5H-1 – 5H-5
	1. Types of organizations	1

	2. Obtaining and maintaining tax-exempt status	2
	3. Unrelated business income	5

Glossary: Federal Taxation for Entities — Glossary 5-1 – 5-3

Multiple Choice – Questions — MCQ 5-1 – 5-20

Multiple Choice – Solutions — MCQ 5-21 – 5-43

Forms — Forms 5-1 – 5-26

Form	Page
Form 1120 – U.S. Corporation Income Tax Return	1
Form 1120X – Amended U.S. Corporation Income Tax Return	2
Form 1120 Schedule PH – U.S. Personal Holding Company (PHC) Tax	3
Form 1139 – Corporation Application for Tentative Refund	4
Form 8938 – Statement of Specified Foreign Financial Assets	5
Form 1120F Schedules M-1 and M-2 – Reconciliation of Income (Loss) and Analysis of Unappropriated Retained Earnings per Books	6
Form 1120 Schedule M-3 – Net Income (Loss) Reconciliation for Corporations with Total Assets of $10 Million or More	7
Form 1120S – U.S Income Tax Return for an S Corporation	8
Form 1120 Schedule K-1 – Shareholder's Share of Income, Deductions, Credits, etc.	9
Form 1065 – U.S. Return of Partnership Income	10
Form 1065 Schedule K – Partners' Distributive Share Items	11
Form 1065 Schedule K-1 – Partner's Share of Income, Deductions, Credits, etc.	12
Form 8832 – Entity Classification Election	13
Form 1041 – U.S Income Tax Return for Estates and Trusts	15
Form 1041 Schedule K-1 – Beneficiary's Share of Income, Deductions, Credits, etc.	16
Form 1023 – Application for Recognition of Exemption	17
Form 1023-EZ – Streamlined Application for Recognition of Exemption under Section 501(c)(3) of the Internal Revenue Code	18
Form 1024 – Application for Recognition of Exemption under Section 501(a)	19
Form 990 – Return of Organization Exempt From Income Tax	20
Form 990 Schedule PF – Return of Private Foundation	21
Form 990T – Exempt Organization Business Income Tax Return	22
Form 5471 – Information Return of U.S. Persons with respect to Certain Foreign Investments	23
Form 5472 – Information Return of a 25% Foreign-Owned U.S. Corporation or a Foreign Corporation Engaged in a U.S. Trade or Business	24
Form 8938 – Statement of Specified Foreign Financial Assets	25
Form 926 – Return by a U.S. Transferor of Property to a Foreign Corporation	26

Federal Taxation of Entities

A. **Tax Treatment of Formation and Liquidation of Business Entities**

> Calculate the realized and recognized gain for the owner and entity upon the formation and liquidation of business entities for federal income tax purposes.

> Compare the tax implications of liquidating distributions from different business entities.

a. Gain(Loss) Issues during Entity Formation
   1) Corporations (including S corporations)
      Corporations do not recognize gain or loss on the issuance of stock or on the issuance of corporate debt.

      Under Section 351, **Shareholders** recognize no gain or loss when they contribute property to a corporation in exchange for corporate stock, so long as they are part of the control club (owning 80% or more of the stock) immediately after the transaction and no boot is received. Instead, the shareholder's basis in the corporation is increased by the shareholder's basis in the contributed property. In the case where boot (cash or property other than stock) is received, a gain (but no loss) may be recognized by the shareholder. The gain recognized is the lesser of the gain realized, or the boot received. For example, the amount of cash and the fair market value of the other property received. If the shareholder assumes any corporate debt, it is considered boot received.

      When shareholders contribute property in exchange for corporate stock but are not part of the control club (acquire 80% or more of the stock) immediately after the transaction, the transaction is treated as a regular sale of property, and the shareholder would recognize the appropriate gain or loss, which is the difference between the FMV and BASIS of the property.

   2) Partnerships (Including LLCs)
      Contributions to a partnership in exchange for a partnership interest usually are not taxable events for either the partnership or the partners. No gain or loss is recognized by any party on contributions to a partnership, but the partners and the partnership are required to calculate a basis for their partnership interest.

      No distinction is made between initial contributions to a partnership and later additional contributions. No deferral is available for contributions to a partnership that are made in exchange for any consideration other than an interest in the partnership. Deferral is only available when property is exchanged for a partnership interest.

      Unlike C and S corporations, the 80% control test is not a factor with contributions to a partnership.

b. Gain (Loss) Issues during Entity Liquidation
   1) C Corporations (Including S corporations)
      In a **non-liquidating distribution** of appreciated property, a C or S corporation can **recognize gains, but not losses**, as if the property had been sold for its FMV. **Appreciated property** is property with a FMV that is greater than its adjusted basis. If the property is subject to a liability that exceeds the property's basis, the corporation's gain is equal to the excess of the liability over the property's adjusted basis.

In a **liquidating distribution,** a C or S corporation can generally recognize both gain and loss on distributions of property to shareholders.

Non-liquidating distributions to shareholders of a **C corporation** are generally taxable to the shareholders as dividends to the extent of current and accumulated E&P. Any distributions in excess of this amount are considered a return of stock basis and are not taxable events. Additional distributions past E&P and stock basis are treated as capital gains.

In the case of a **non-liquidating distribution** from an **S corporation to a shareholder**, the distribution is first treated as a distribution out of the Accumulated Adjustment Account, which is non-taxable, and reduces the shareholder's basis in stock. Next it a return of stock basis and is a non-taxable event (up to the shareholder's stock basis). Any distribution in excess of the S corporation shareholder's stock basis is treated as a capital gain. There are generally no dividends paid by S corporations because there are no earnings and profits. If an S corporation was previously a C corporation, and there are undistributed earnings and profits from the C corporation, then the distribution would be dividends to the extent of those earnings and profits. The dividend would come after the distributions from the Accumulated Adjustment Account, then a return of stock basis, which is not taxable, and next, if there are any distributions remaining, balance is capital gain.

Liquidating distributions to a shareholder of a C Corp or S Corp, can generally result in capital gain or loss for the shareholder of C or S corporation stock, as it is generally treated as received in exchange for corporate stock.

2) Partnerships (Including LLCs) LLCs are taxed as partnerships by default. LLCs can elect to be taxed like a corporation.
Partnerships generally do not recognize gain or loss on distributions, regardless of whether they are liquidating or non-liquidating, pro rata or non-pro rata.

Partners **can only recognize gain on non-liquidating distributions of cash** and then only if cash exceeds the partner's basis in the partnership.

Partners can only recognize a gain on **liquidating distributions** if the cash received by the partner exceeds the partner's basis in the partnership. Similar to non-liquidating distributions, if a partner is relieved of a liability, it is treated as a cash distribution.

A partner can also recognize losses on **liquidating distributions** if two conditions are met:
1. The distribution consists only of cash and hot assets (inventory and unrealized accounts receivable).
2. The basis of the partner's interest must be greater than the sum of cash plus the basis of the distributed hot assets (inventory and unrealized accounts receivable).

Multiple Choice

REG 5-Q1

c. Formation of a new business entity
When starting a business venture, the decision regarding which business structure to choose is of critical importance. Each business structure has advantages and disadvantages that must be considered, both from a tax perspective and from an operational perspective.

> **Analyze the tax advantages and disadvantages in the formation of a new business entity.**

1) Sole Proprietorships
   In a sole proprietorship, the business and its owner are essentially one in the same from a taxation and legal perspective.

   i. Advantages of forming a sole proprietorship include:
      - The owner receives all profits and has complete decision-making authority.
      - Start-up is simpler and costs less because there are no filing fees and very few filing requirements.
      - The owner is responsible only for personal income taxes. There is no additional level of taxation as there is, for example, in a C corporation.

   ii. Disadvantages
      - The owner has full liability for any business debts. If the business cannot repay loans, creditors can take possession of the owner's personal assets to meet business obligations.
      - Raising capital is much more difficult, as there is no pool of potential shareholders to invest in the business. Capital is limited to the owner's personal funds or loans that the owner is able to secure from other individuals or institutions.
      - The life of the business is tied to the life of the owner and, usually, comes to an end with the owner's death.

   iii. Tax-advantages and disadvantages of sole-proprietorships
      - Advantages are:
        1. Simple Tax Returns
        2. Pass-through entities
        3. All profits and losses from the business pass directly to the business owners.
        4. A separate tax return does not have to be filed.

      - Disadvantages are:
        1. Owner must pay self-employment taxes
        2. Some tax benefits may not be deductible to arrive at net self-employment income, such as health insurance premiums for the self-employed, spouse, and dependents. This will cause the net-earnings from self-employed to be higher, and the self-employment tax will be higher.

2) General Partnerships
In a general partnership, two or more partners share ownership, profits/losses, and management responsibilities in a manner that is determined among the partners.

   i. Advantages of forming a partnership include:
      - All profits and losses flow through to the partners, who report business profits and losses on their personal income tax returns. The entity itself does not pay taxes on its income.
      - Partnerships are relatively easy to establish.
      - Partnerships have great flexibility in how ownership, profits, losses, and voting rights are allocated.
      - Contributions to a partnership can generally be made tax-free without consideration of ownership percentage after the transfer.
      - With more than one owner, raising capital can be a bit easier.
      - Partnerships can be voluntary dissolved and terminated, without filing a dissolution document with the state of organization.

   ii. Disadvantages of forming a partnership include:
      - In a general partnership, all partners are jointly and severally liable for all partnership debts, liabilities, and misconduct.
      - Potential instability in the case of dissolution due to the death or withdrawal of a partner.

   iv. Tax-advantages and disadvantages a general partnership

      - Tax advantages of general partnership
         1. Minimal tax filings as form 1065 is not a complicated filing
         2. Flow-through entity which avoids double taxation
         3. General partnerships do not pay taxes
         4. Partners can deduct the cost of health insurance, dental insurance, and long-term health care insurance on their personal tax return.

      - Tax disadvantages of general partnership
         1. A partner's share of ordinary income and guaranteed payments are subject to the self-employment tax. This is the combined employer and employee rate on social security and Medicare.

3) Limited Partnerships
   A limited partnership consists of at least one general partner, who assumes the responsibility for the management of the business, and at least one limited partner who contributes assets but who has no role in the entity's management.

   i. Advantages of forming a limited partnership include:
      - Limited liability for the limited partner, whose losses are limited to the amount of capital contributed to the partnership. The limited partner cannot be held liable for entity debts or misconduct.
      - Capital is even easier to attract with the option of a limited partner who can share in partnership profits without being personally liable for entity debts.
      - All profits and losses flow through to the partners, who report business profits and losses on their personal income tax returns. The entity itself does not pay taxes on its income.
      - Partnerships have great flexibility in how ownership, profits, losses, and voting rights are allocated.
      - Contributions to a partnership can generally be made tax-free without consideration of ownership percentage after the transfer.

   ii. Disadvantages of forming a limited partnership include:
      - The general partner or partners are still jointly and severally liable for all partnership debts, liabilities and misconduct.
      - The limited partner can lose her "limited liability" if she becomes active in the business
      - Potential instability in the case of dissolution due to the death or withdrawal of a general partner.
      - Limited partnerships require a bit more documentation to set up and generally require state filing fees.

Withdrawal of the only general partner in a limited partnership will cause a dissolution of the limited partnership. Withdrawal of a limited partner in a limited partnership will NOT cause a dissolution of the limited partnership, because they are investors in the entity.

Tax Advantages of a Limited Partnership
1. Flow through entity, and no double taxation
2. The ordinary income of a limited partner is passive, and is not subject to self-employment tax
3. Because the ordinary income of the limited partner is passive income, it can offset other passive losses
4. The limited partnership does not pay taxes

Tax Disadvantages of a Limited Partnership
1. Because the ordinary income(loss) of a limited partner is passive, it cannot offset non-passive income and losses of the limited partner.
2. The general partner in a limited partnership will pay self-employment taxes on the share of ordinary income, and guaranteed payments to partners.

Multiple Choice

REG 4-Q2 through REG 4-Q10

4) Limited Liability Companies (LLCs)

A Limited Liability Company is a hybrid of sorts in that it offers the limited liability of a corporation but the pass-through taxation of a partnership. In an LLC, members can retain their limited liability while still actively participating in the management of the entity. An LLC is generally considered a partnership. Because the members are not personally liable for the debts of the LLC, the members are effectively limited partners. The LLC can elect to be taxed as a Corporation, and if it qualifies, can elect to be an S corporation.

i. Advantages of forming an LLC include:
- LLC members enjoy limited liability and cannot be held liable for entity debts or misconduct.
- All profits and losses flow through to the members, who report business profits and losses on their personal income tax returns. The entity itself does not pay taxes on its income.
- Partnerships have great flexibility in how ownership, profits, losses, management responsibilities and voting rights are allocated.
- LLCs can have an unlimited number of members, unlike an S corporation which is limited to 100. Also, unlike a partnership, an LLC can have just one member.
- Contributions to an LLC can generally be made tax-free without consideration of ownership percentage after the transfer.
- Unlike S corporations, LLCs are not limited to one class of ownership, but instead can have different membership classes.
- LLCs do not face the annual reporting or formal meeting requirements imposed on C corporations and S corporations.

ii. Disadvantages of forming an LLC include:
- LLCs are a bit more complex to form in that there is not a separate tax classification for LLCs; a LLC may be classified as a sole-proprietorship, a partnership, or a corporation for tax purposes.
- Unless an LLC opts to be taxed as a corporation, LLCs are usually subject to self-employment taxes, if they file a partnership return.
- In many jurisdictions, an LLC ceases to exist if a member departs the entity, and therefore does not have the unlimited life that an S or C corporation enjoys
- The stock of an LLC is not easily transferable.
- The LLC does not have perpetual existence.

iii. Tax advantages of an LLC
1. Because an LLC by default is taxed like a partnership, it is a flow through entity, and it is not subject to taxes.
2. It can elect to be taxed like an S Corporation, which is a flow through entity, and is not subject to double taxation like a C Corporation.
3. The ordinary income of the S Corporation is not self-employment income, and is not subject to self-employment tax.

iv. Tax disadvantages of an LLC
1. Because it could elect to be a C Corporation it is subject to double taxation
2. If it elects S Corporation status, subject to requirements, such as no more than 100 Members, no non-resident alien shareholders, and only one class of members.

Multiple Choice

REG 4-Q11 through REG 4-Q15

5) **S Corporation**
   An S corporation is a hybrid of sorts in that it follows many of the C corporation rules, but is treated like a partnership for taxation purposes. To elect "S" status, all shareholders must agree to the election, cannot have more 100 shareholders (husband and wife count as one), no non-resident alien shareholders are allowed, can only issue one class of stock, can only have individuals, estates and trusts as shareholders, and must be a domestic corporation. To terminate an S corporation, more than 50% of the shareholders must agree. Once an S corporation is terminated, the corporation must wait for 5 years before an S corporation election can be made again. An S corporation must have a calendar year-end.

   i. Advantages of forming an S corporation include:
      - Much like a partnership, profits and losses flow through to the shareholders. The entity itself does not pay taxes on its income.
      - Shareholders enjoy limited liability and cannot be held liable for the debts or misconduct of the entity.
      - Ownership of S corporation shares can be freely transferred (unlike ownership of a partnership or a sole proprietorship)
      - S corporation shareholders can be both owners of the corporation as well as compensated employees, so long as the compensation is reasonable
      - Shareholders of an S corporation can contribute property to the S corporation without being taxed.
      - The ordinary income is not subject to self-employment taxes. The ordinary income(loss) is not passive.

   ii. Disadvantages of forming an S corporation include:
      - S corporation set up is a bit more complicated. Articles of Incorporation must be filed in the corporation's home state, and the entity must have a registered agent in the state.
      - Annual filings are also more complicated for S corporations, including annual report fees and franchise taxes imposed by most states.
      - An S corporation can only have 100 shareholders and can only issue one class of stock. A husband and wife count as one shareholder. Additionally, there are many restrictions on who is eligible to be an S corporation shareholder. Shareholders can only be individuals, estates, and trusts. A 501(c)(3) exempt organization can be a shareholder. Non-resident aliens cannot be shareholders.
      - Because profit and loss allocation is based on stock ownership, S corporations do not have the flexibility that partnerships have in allocating income
      - An S corporation must pay taxes on built-in gains and excess passive investment income.
      - If S status is revoked, a company must wait for five years to become an S Corp. again.

Multiple Choice

REG 4-Q16 through REG 4-Q23

6) C Corporations
   i. Advantages of forming a C corporation include:
      - Shareholders enjoy limited liability and cannot be held liable for the debts or misconduct of the entity
      - Unlike S corporations, C corporations can have an unlimited number of shareholders.
      - Ownership can be easily transferred through the sale of stock.
      - A C corporation has an unlimited life, which is not tied to the life of its owner(s)
      - Like S corporations, C corporation shareholders can be both owners of the corporation as well as compensated employees, so long as the compensation is reasonable
      - Unlike with pass-through entities (S corporations, partnerships, LLCs), C corporation earnings are not automatically taxed to the owners. Shareholders only pay taxes on corporate earnings if they are distributed as dividends.
      - Capital can be raised simply by selling stock.
      - Shareholders of a C corporation can contribute property to the S corporation without being taxed.

   ii. Disadvantages of forming a C corporation include:
      - Corporate profits are subject to double taxation. The corporate entity itself is taxed on its profits, and the shareholders are also taxed on corporate income distributed as dividends.
      - C corporation set up is more complicated. Articles of Incorporation must be filed in the corporation's home state, and the entity must have a registered agent in the state.
      - Annual filings are also more complicated for C corporations, including annual report fees and franchise taxes imposed by most states
      - Stockholders who have a majority (or significant) amount of the voting stock in a corporation have a greater say in what management is doing than stockholders who do not have that amount of stock ownership in the corporation.
      - A more complicated tax return (Form 1120)

Multiple Choice

REG 5-Q24

7) Tax advantages of an LLP (Limited liability Partnership)
   - It is a flow through entity, and is not subject to double taxation
   - The filing is done on form 1065, which is relatively easy
   - The partnership does not pay taxes
   - The partners are liable for filing their own personal returns
   - The partners are liable for their own social security and Medicare by paying self-employment taxes
   - The partners can deduct one-half of self-employment taxes on their personal returns
   - Can increase their basis, by their share of at risk debt (recourse debt) for deducting losses on their individual return.

   Tax disadvantages of a LLP
   - The partners have to pay self-employment taxes on their own guaranteed payments and share of ordinary income.
   - The partners can only deduct losses on their personal returns, if there is basis.

B. **Differences between Book and Tax Income (Loss)**

Identify permanent vs. temporary differences to be reported on Schedule M-1 and/or M-3.

Calculate the book/tax differences to be reported on a Schedule M-1 or M-3.

Prepare a Schedule M-1 or M-3 for a business entity.

a. Book Income vs. Taxable Income
As a refresher, **book income** is the income that is computed by applying GAAP to the corporations accounting records (i.e., its **books**) and communicated to the shareholders in the financial statements. **Taxable income** is the income that is used to compute a taxpayer's income tax liability.

In many, even most, cases, the rules that govern income and expense recognition when calculating book income are quite similar to the rules applicable to the calculation of taxable income. However, in some cases, income will be recognized in the financial statements, but not for tax purposes, such as municipal bond interest or a portion of dividends received by a corporation.

Conversely, some items that are not yet included as income or expense on the financial statements must be included in taxable income. For example, rental income will not appear in the financial statements until it is earned but is always taxable when received, whether earned or not.

When these, and other, situations occur a difference arises between book income and taxable income.

b. Permanent vs. Temporary Differences
Some differences between the book and taxable income are merely temporary differences that will reverse in future periods. Other differences are permanent and will never reverse.

1) Permanent Differences
Permanent differences can arise from income items that are never taxable or expense items that are never deductible. These items are either on the books or the tax return but never reverse themselves.

Examples of permanent income difference items that are never taxable include:
- Municipal bond interest income
- Life insurance proceeds on key man policies received by a corporation
- The portion of dividends received from other corporations that qualify for the dividends received deduction

Hint: These items will cause book income to be greater than taxable income and therefore must be subtracted from book income when calculating taxable income.

Examples of permanent expense items that are never deductible include:
- 50% of meal and entertainment expenses
- Expenses related to the generation of tax-exempt income (e.g., interest on a loan to buy municipal bond)
- Lobbying and other political contribution expenses
- Life insurance premiums paid on key employee are deductible if the beneficiary is not the corporation. If the corporation is the beneficiary, then it is not deductible.

Hint: These items will cause book income to be less than taxable income and therefore must be added back to book income when calculating taxable income.

2) Temporary Differences
Temporary differences arise when GAAP rules dictate that income and expense to be recognized in one period, but tax accounting rules dictate that they are recognized in another period. Temporary differences will smooth out over time.

Examples of temporary differences include:
- Use of straight-line vs. accelerated depreciation
- Prepaid income recognized for taxes but not earned under GAAP
- Excess of capital losses over capital gains
- Charitable contributions in excess of the 10% limitation
- For construction accounting, using completed contract for taxes, and percentage of completion for financial accounting

c. Reconciling Book to Tax Income (Schedule M-1)
When filing a corporate tax return, entities must reconcile their book income to their taxable income, before dividend received deduction (DRD), on either Schedule M-1 or Schedule M-3. Schedule M-1 should be completed by entities with less than $10 million of total assets (although these smaller corporations can elect to complete Schedule M-3 if desired).

For corporations with more than $10 million in total assets, Schedule M-3 (and NOT Schedule M-1) must be completed.

Schedule M-1 starts with book income (loss), Line 1, and then adjusts up or down based on permanent or temporary differences. The result is the taxable income amount (before the NOL deduction and the DRD) that is reported on the current year's tax return, Line 10.

Schedule M-1 Reconciliation of Income (Loss) per Books With Income per Return
Note: The corporation may be required to file Schedule M-3 (see instructions).

1	Net income (loss) per books		7	Income recorded on books this year not included on this return (itemize):
2	Federal income tax per books			
3	Excess of capital losses over capital gains		a	Tax-exempt interest $
4	Income subject to tax not recorded on books this year (itemize):		b	Other (itemize):
			8	Deductions on this return not charged against book income this year (itemize):
5	Expenses recorded on books this year not deducted on this return (itemize):			
a	Depreciation . . . . $		a	Depreciation . . $
b	Charitable contributions $		b	Charitable contributions $
c	Travel and entertainment $		c	Other (itemize):
d	Other (itemize):			
			9	Add lines 7 and 8 . . . .
6	Add lines 1 through 5		10	Income—line 6 less line 9 . . . .

d. Reconciling Book to Tax Income (Schedule M-3)

Schedule M-3 is divided into three parts:
1) Part I contains financial information and reconciles the corporation's worldwide consolidated net income on the corporation's financial statements to book income for the entities included on the corporation's income tax return.

SCHEDULE M-3 (Form 1120)
Department of the Treasury
Internal Revenue Service

Net Income (Loss) Reconciliation for Corporations With Total Assets of $10 Million or More

▶ Attach to Form 1120 or 1120-C. ▶ Information about Schedule M-3 (Form 1120) and its separate instructions is available at *www.irs.gov/form1120*.

OMB No. 1545-0123

2016

Name of corporation (common parent, if consolidated return) | Employer identification number

Check applicable box(es): (1) ☐ Non-consolidated return (2) ☐ Consolidated return (Form 1120 only)
(3) ☐ Mixed 1120/L/PC group (4) ☐ Dormant subsidiaries schedule attached

Part I Financial Information and Net Income (Loss) Reconciliation (see instructions)

1a Did the corporation file SEC Form 10-K for its income statement period ending with or within this tax year?
  ☐ Yes. Skip lines 1b and 1c and complete lines 2a through 11 with respect to that SEC Form 10-K.
  ☐ No. Go to line 1b. See instructions if multiple non-tax-basis income statements are prepared.
 b Did the corporation prepare a certified audited non-tax-basis income statement for that period?
  ☐ Yes. Skip line 1c and complete lines 2a through 11 with respect to that income statement.
  ☐ No. Go to line 1c.
 c Did the corporation prepare a non-tax-basis income statement for that period?
  ☐ Yes. Complete lines 2a through 11 with respect to that income statement.
  ☐ No. Skip lines 2a through 3c and enter the corporation's net income (loss) per its books and records on line 4a.
2a Enter the income statement period: Beginning MM/DD/YYYY Ending MM/DD/YYYY
 b Has the corporation's income statement been restated for the income statement period on line 2a?
  ☐ Yes. (If "Yes," attach an explanation and the amount of each item restated.)
  ☐ No.
 c Has the corporation's income statement been restated for any of the five income statement periods immediately preceding the period on line 2a?
  ☐ Yes. (If "Yes," attach an explanation and the amount of each item restated.)
  ☐ No.
3a Is any of the corporation's voting common stock publicly traded?
  ☐ Yes.
  ☐ No. If "No," go to line 4a.
 b Enter the symbol of the corporation's primary U.S. publicly traded voting common stock . . . .
 c Enter the nine-digit CUSIP number of the corporation's primary publicly traded voting common stock . . . .
4a Worldwide consolidated net income (loss) from income statement source identified in Part I, line 1 | 4a
 b Indicate accounting standard used for line 4a (see instructions):
  (1) ☐ GAAP (2) ☐ IFRS (3) ☐ Statutory (4) ☐ Tax-basis (5) ☐ Other (specify) _____
5a Net income from nonincludible foreign entities (attach statement) . . . . | 5a (   )
 b Net loss from nonincludible foreign entities (attach statement and enter as a positive amount) . . . | 5b
6a Net income from nonincludible U.S. entities (attach statement) . . . . | 6a (   )
 b Net loss from nonincludible U.S. entities (attach statement and enter as a positive amount) . . . . | 6b
7a Net income (loss) of other includible foreign disregarded entities (attach statement) . . . . | 7a
 b Net income (loss) of other includible U.S. disregarded entities (attach statement) . . . . . | 7b
 c Net income (loss) of other includible entities (attach statement) . . . . | 7c
8 Adjustment to eliminations of transactions between includible entities and nonincludible entities (attach statement) . . . . | 8
9 Adjustment to reconcile income statement period to tax year (attach statement) . . . . . | 9
10a Intercompany dividend adjustments to reconcile to line 11 (attach statement) . . . . . | 10a
 b Other statutory accounting adjustments to reconcile to line 11 (attach statement) . . . . | 10b
 c Other adjustments to reconcile to amount on line 11 (attach statement) . . . . . . | 10c
11 **Net income (loss) per income statement of includible corporations.** Combine lines 4 through 10 . | 11
  Note: Part I, line 11, must equal Part II, line 30, column (a) or Schedule M-1, line 1 (see instructions).
12 Enter the total amount (not just the corporation's share) of the assets and liabilities of all entities included or removed on the following lines.

	Total Assets	Total Liabilities
a Included on Part I, line 4 . . . . ▶		
b Removed on Part I, line 5 . . . . ▶		
c Removed on Part I, line 6 . . . . ▶		
d Included on Part I, line 7 . . . . ▶		

For Paperwork Reduction Act Notice, see the Instructions for Form 1120. Cat. No. 37961C Schedule M-3 (Form 1120) 2016

2) Part II reconciles book income from Part I to the taxable income amount shown on Form 1120. For each reconciliation item, the effect due to permanent differences and temporary differences must be shown.

Schedule M-3 (Form 1120) 2016 — Page 2

Name of corporation (common parent, if consolidated return) | Employer identification number

Check applicable box(es): (1) ☐ Consolidated group (2) ☐ Parent corp (3) ☐ Consolidated eliminations (4) ☐ Subsidiary corp (5) ☐ Mixed 1120/L/PC group
Check if a sub-consolidated: (6) ☐ 1120 group (7) ☐ 1120 eliminations

Name of subsidiary (if consolidated return) | Employer identification number

Part II Reconciliation of Net Income (Loss) per Income Statement of Includible Corporations With Taxable Income per Return (see instructions)

Income (Loss) Items (Attach statements for lines 1 through 12)	(a) Income (Loss) per Income Statement	(b) Temporary Difference	(c) Permanent Difference	(d) Income (Loss) per Tax Return
1 Income (loss) from equity method foreign corporations				
2 Gross foreign dividends not previously taxed				
3 Subpart F, QEF, and similar income inclusions				
4 Section 78 gross-up				
5 Gross foreign distributions previously taxed				
6 Income (loss) from equity method U.S. corporations				
7 U.S. dividends not eliminated in tax consolidation				
8 Minority interest for includible corporations				
9 Income (loss) from U.S. partnerships				
10 Income (loss) from foreign partnerships				
11 Income (loss) from other pass-through entities				
12 Items relating to reportable transactions				
13 Interest income (see instructions)				
14 Total accrual to cash adjustment				
15 Hedging transactions				
16 Mark-to-market income (loss)				
17 Cost of goods sold (see instructions)	( )			( )
18 Sale versus lease (for sellers and/or lessors)				
19 Section 481(a) adjustments				
20 Unearned/deferred revenue				
21 Income recognition from long-term contracts				
22 Original issue discount and other imputed interest				
23a Income statement gain/loss on sale, exchange, abandonment, worthlessness, or other disposition of assets other than inventory and pass-through entities				
b Gross capital gains from Schedule D, excluding amounts from pass-through entities				
c Gross capital losses from Schedule D, excluding amounts from pass-through entities, abandonment losses, and worthless stock losses				
d Net gain/loss reported on Form 4797, line 17, excluding amounts from pass-through entities, abandonment losses, and worthless stock losses				
e Abandonment losses				
f Worthless stock losses (attach statement)				
g Other gain/loss on disposition of assets other than inventory				
24 Capital loss limitation and carryforward used				
25 Other income (loss) items with differences (attach statement)				
26 **Total income (loss) items.** Combine lines 1 through 25				
27 **Total expense/deduction items** (from Part III, line 36)				
28 Other items with no differences				
29a Mixed groups, see instructions. All others, combine lines 26 through 28				
b PC insurance subgroup reconciliation totals				
c Life insurance subgroup reconciliation totals				
30 **Reconciliation totals.** Combine lines 29a through 29c				

Note: Line 30, column (a), must equal Part I, line 11, and column (d) must equal Form 1120, page 1, line 28.

Schedule M-3 (Form 1120) 2016

3) Part III breaks down the expense and deduction items that affect the reconciliation of book income to taxable income in Part II. The total is carried back to Part II and combined with income items listed in Part II.

e. **Schedule M-2 – Analysis of Unappropriated Retained Earnings per Books**
As its title suggests, Schedule M-2 analyzes the entities unappropriated retained earnings. The calculation begins with the unappropriated retained earnings balance at the beginning of the year and adds net book income and other increases and subtracts dividends and other decreases to arrive at the ending unappropriated retained earnings balance.

Schedule M-2 Analysis of Unappropriated Retained Earnings per Books

1	Balance at beginning of year		5	Distributions: a Cash
2	Net income (loss) per books			b Stock
3	Other increases (itemize):			c Property
			6	Other decreases (itemize):
			7	Add lines 5 and 6
4	Add lines 1, 2, and 3		8	Balance at end of year (line 4 less line 7)

Multiple Choice
REG 5-Q25

Reconcile the differences between book and taxable income (loss) of a business entity.

To calculate taxable income, the following items are **added** to book income:
- **Non-deductible expenses**, including federal taxes, net capital losses, expenses that exceed deductible limits, certain fines, and penalties, etc.
- **Income that is taxable** but not included in book income. For example, rents received in advance.

To calculate taxable income, the following items are **deducted** from book income:
- **Non-taxable income** that is included in book income, such as municipal interest and life insurance proceeds, etc.
- **Deductions that are not expensed** in book income, including the dividends received deduction, the election to take the Section 179 expense, depreciation on the tax return in excess of book depreciation.

Example: Find taxable income (TI) in each of the following scenarios (Reconciliation of Schedule M-1):

Scenario 1:
Book income	$150,000
Federal Tax	$12,000
Municipal Bond Interest	$19,000

What is TI?
$150,000
$12,000
($19,000)
$143,000

Scenario 2:
Book income	$275,000
Meals Expense	$40,000
Federal Tax	$49,000

What is TI?
$275,000
$20,000
$49,000
$344,000

Scenario 3:
Book income	$190,000
Provision for Federal Tax	$36,000
Net Capital Loss	$6,000
Insurance Premiums-Corp is beneficiary	$5,000

What is TI?
$190,000
$36,000
$6,000
$5,000
$237,000

Scenario 4:
Book income	$180,000
Municipal Interest	$60,000
Federal Tax	$75,000
Interest on debt related to Muni Bonds	$4,000

What is TI?
$180,000
($60,000)
$75,000
$4,000
$199,000

Multiple Choice
REG 5-Q26 through REG 5-Q27

C. C Corporations

"C corporations" are so called because the rules governing corporate taxes are contained in Subchapter C of the IRC. Unlike partnerships, S corporations, or sole proprietorships, C corporations are subject to corporate income tax at the entity level.

As a refresher, corporations are artificial legal entities in which the owners, referred to as shareholders, typically enjoy limited liability. This "corporate veil" shields corporate shareholders from personal liability and generally limits a shareholder's losses to the amount invested in the corporate stock. Also, corporations can exist into perpetuity, unlike other business entities which cease to exist once the owners die or leave the entity.

In exchange for limited liability and unlimited lifespan, corporate earnings are subject to "double taxation." This means that not only is the corporation itself taxed on earnings, but shareholders too are taxed on earnings (dividends) distributed by the corporation.

Multiple Choice
REG 5-Q28 through REG 5-Q29

Corporations are subject to several specific accounting and tax requirements:

a. Fiscal Year
Corporations (other than S corporations or personal service corporations) can choose their own fiscal year.

Multiple Choice
REG 5-Q30

b. Accounting Method
The accrual basis must generally be used by C corporations that have inventory, and have average annual gross sales over $5 million for the previous three-year period that are not personal service corporations.

A corporation (other than a tax shelter) that has average gross receipts under $5 million for any prior three-year period, and does not have inventory, can be on a cash basis. Tax shelters must be on the accrual basis.

A C corporation selects its accounting method by using the chosen method on its initial tax return.

C corporations that have average sales for the past three years of less than $1 million can use the cash method, even if it has inventory which was purchased and is sold.

A small business taxpayer is eligible to use the cash method with average sales for the last three years of over $1 million and less than $10,000,000, and the small business taxpayer satisfies either of the following requirements:
1) The principal business activity is not manufacturing, retailing, or wholesaling and they do not have inventory.
2) The principal business activity is the provision of services or custom manufacturing.

A business that is a personal service corporation (PSC) with an average of $5 million or less in sales over the past 3 years is **not** required to use the accrual method. If gross receipts exceed $15 million over a rolling three-year period, then they are required to use the accrual method even if they are a personal service corporation. Qualified personal service corporation can use the cash method if their average annual gross receipts for a three-year period are between $1 million and $10 million, and their primary business is a service-oriented business.

Multiple Choice
REG 5-Q31 through REG 5-Q33

Corporate capital gains are taxed at regular corporate tax rates. Multiple tax brackets are not available for members of a "controlled group" or for personal service corporations. Instead, a straight 35% tax rate is used.

c. Tax Return Filing and Due Dates (due dates are not tested after 4/1/2017)
Corporations must file Form 1120 annually, regardless of whether or not it has taxable income.

> *New Exam Content:* Effective for tax years beginning after 12/31/2015, C corporations with a fiscal year other than 6/30 must file their returns by **the 15th day of the 4th month** after the end of the tax year.
>
> Effective for tax years beginning after 12/31/2015, C corporations will be allowed a 6-month extension, except that calendar-year corps get a 5-month extension until 2026 and corporations with a June 30 year-end get a 7-month extension until 2026.

d. Estimated Tax Payments
Estimated corporate tax payments are required if the corporation's tax liability is expected to exceed $500. The estimated required payment must be the lesser of:
- 100% of the current tax liability, or
- 100% of the prior year's tax and if in the prior year, the corporation had a tax liability. The prior year must be 12-month period.

1. Computations of taxable income (including alternative minimum taxable income), tax liability and allowable credits

| Calculate taxable income and tax liability for a C corporation. |

The corporate income tax calculation is very similar to the formula used to calculate individual income taxes. Use the following calculation for a C corporation:

	Gross profit on sales
+	Gross dividends
+	Interest income
+	Gross rents and royalties
+	Capital gains
+	Other income
=	**Gross Income**
-	Deductions
=	Taxable Income before net operating loss deduction and special deductions
-	Special deductions (i.e. charitable contributions and DRD)
=	**Taxable Income**
*	Tax Rate
=	Gross Tax Liability
-	Credits
-	Payments (includes estimated tax payments)
+	Other Taxes (includes AMT)
=	**Net Tax Liability**

Generally speaking, the income and deduction rules for corporations are the same as those rules applied to individual taxpayers. Some tax rules, however, are applied to corporations differently.

Remember that issuance of corporate stock, issuance of corporate debt and contributions of capital are all EXCLUDED from gross income of a corporation.

a. Short year tax returns
If a corporation is formed or dissolved in the middle of a tax year, the tax computation requires no special adjustment and the year is treated as a full tax year.

However, if the short year results from a change of the taxpayer's annual accounting period, the short period's taxable income must be annualized.

To annualize, taxable income for the short period is multiplied by 12 months and then divided by the number of months in the short period. The result is the annualized taxable income that should be used to compute the tentative tax due. The amount of computed tax is multiplied by the number of months in the short period and then divided by 12 to derive the corporation's tax for the short period.

> **Example:** On January 1, 20X6, a corporation switched to a calendar tax year (January-December) from a fiscal year that started on October 1, 20X5, and ended on September 30, 20X6. As a result, the company has a short tax year of October 1, 20X5, through December 31, 20X5. During this period the company had taxable income of $50,000 and a tax rate of 15%. What taxes are due for the short tax year?
>
> $\dfrac{\$50,000 * 12}{3}$ = $200,000 * 15\%$ = $\dfrac{\$30,000 * 3}{12}$ = $7,500
>
> (taxable income * 12) / months in short year   Ann. income * Tax rate =   Ann. tax due * # of months in short year / 12   Tax due

Multiple Choice
REG 5-Q34

b. Corporate deductions
Most of the rules around corporate deductions are quite similar to the manner in which individual deductions are calculated. There are, however, several important differences between corporate tax deductions and individual deductions.
- Business-related expenses are generally allowable as business deductions and are subject to the same requirement that they be reasonable and ordinary.

  > *Hint:* Although C corporations must use the accrual method to keep their books, for tax purposes, corporations can only deduct expenses related to certain related taxpayers (e.g. cash basis shareholders) when paid. Also, recurring expenses must be paid within 8 ½ months of year end to be deductible for tax purposes when on the accrual basis. Examples of recurring expenses include insurance, prizes/awards, or warranty costs.

- Depreciation, depletion and amortization expense is calculated just as they are for individual taxpayers.
- Research and development expenditures follow the same treatment as for individuals (that is, they can be expensed in the year incurred, depreciated over their useful life, or depreciated over 60 months if useful life is not determinable).
- Business gifts are limited to $25 per recipient.

Multiple Choice
REG 5-Q35 through REG 5-Q36

c. Special corporate deductions

> **Hint:** Corporate deductions must be applied in a very specific order, which is discussed in more detail below.

1) Organization and Start-Up Expenditures

   Organization expenses are those incurred in connection with the formation and organization of a corporation. Any costs having to do with the issuance of the stock are not organization costs and are not amortizable. Typical organization expenses include legal and accounting services, expenses related to organizing meetings of shareholders and directors, and fees paid to incorporate the entity. To be considered organization costs (and receive the corresponding tax treatment), these expenses must be incurred before the end of the tax year in which the business begins.

   Up to $5,000 of these types of expenditures may be deducted in the year of the corporation's organization if the total of such expenditures is less than or equal to $50,000. This deduction is lost dollar for dollar for each dollar spent over $50,000 and therefore is totally lost when organization expenditures exceed $55,000.

   > **Hint:** The expenses must be incurred by the end of the formation year, but do not have to be paid by year end, to qualify for this deduction. This is true even for entities which file on a cash basis.

   Organization expenditures that are in excess of $5000 must be capitalized and amortized over 180 months, beginning with the month the corporation begins its business operation.

   Amortization of organization expenditures must be made in the initial year of the formation of the corporation. If the corporation does not amortize the organization cost in the year of formation, they have made an election not to amortize the organization costs at all.

   Similar rules apply for start-up costs. If a taxpayer investigates an acquisition that is not in a similar line of business as the taxpayer now owns, these investigation expenses are capitalized and amortized the same way as organizational costs. These costs include, engineering fees, surveys, marketing reports, and accounting and legal expenses. If these investigation expenses are to acquire a business in a similar line as your present business, the investigations costs are expensed.

2) Syndication Expenses

   Syndication expenses include costs associated with the issuance and sale of corporate stock. These costs must be capitalized and cannot be amortized.

   > **Hint:** In the case of a complete dissolution, filing fees, professional fees, and other expenditures incurred in connection with the liquidation and dissolution are a deductible in full by the dissolved corporation.

Multiple Choice

REG 5-Q37 through REG 5-Q38

3) Charitable contributions
The limit on the corporate charitable contribution deduction is calculated as:

Charitable Contribution Deduction Limit = 10% of the corporation's taxable income **before**:
- The deduction for charitable contributions
- The dividends-received deduction
- Any loss carrybacks (e.g., NOL carryback, capital loss carryback)

> *Hint:* The 10% limit is calculated **before loss carrybacks, not carryforwards.** Loss carryforwards are applied to taxable income to calculate the 10% limitation.

Any excess charitable contribution amount above the 10% limit can be carried forward for up to 5 years, but there is **no carryback**.

An accrual basis corporation, where the board of directors authorizes a contribution to be paid in the next year, can accrue the contribution in the current year and deduct it, as long as it is paid by the 15th day of the third month of the next year.

Multiple Choice

REG 5-Q39 through REG 5-Q40

4) Dividends received deduction (DRD)
The dividends received deduction (DRD) represents a deduction for a percentage of domestic dividends received by the corporation.

To be eligible, the dividend must be received from ownership of stock of a domestic corporation that has been held for more than 45-days (90 days for preferred stock).

The DRD cannot be claimed by S corporations, personal service corporations or personal holding companies.

The allowable amount of the DRD deduction depends on the percentage ownership of stock held by the corporation. If the corporation's stock holdings represent:

Less than 20% ownership,	deduction = **70%** of dividends received
20% to 79% ownership,	deduction = **80%** of dividends received
80% ownership or more,	deduction = **100%** of dividends received

If a corporation has a profit from operations, the dividend received deduction is always the DRD percentage times the gross dividends.

If a corporation has a loss from operations, the dividend received deduction is the DRD percentage times the gross dividends only when the result of this amount, when subtracted from taxable income before the DRD, creates a loss.

If it doesn't create a loss, the DRD is the DRD percentage times the taxable income before the DRD (taxable income limitation).

> **Example #1 – profit from operations (general rule):** A corporation received $100 in dividends from a domestic corporation of which it owns 19%. The corporation has:
> - Profit from operations of $400
> - Taxable income before the dividends received deduction of $200
>
> What is the allowable DRD?
>
> In this example, take the full DRD of $70 (70% x $100 gross dividends) because the corporation had a profit from operations and therefore would apply the general rule. The corporation's taxable income after the DRD is $130 ($200 - $70).
>
> **Example #2 – loss from operations, DRD creates a loss (no taxable income limitation):** A corporation received $100 in dividends from a domestic corporation of which it owns 19%. The corporation has:
> - Losses from operations of $35 plus the gross dividends $100 = $65
> - Taxable income before the dividends received deduction of $65
>
> What is the allowable DRD?
>
> In this example, if the corporation deducts the full DRD of $70 (70% x $100 gross dividends) since the DRD creates a loss ($65 - $70 = $5 loss). The taxable income limitation is not applicable. Therefore, the DRD is $70 (70% x gross dividends). The taxable loss is $5.
>
> **Example #3 – loss from operations, DRD does not create loss (taxable income limitation):** A corporation received $100 in dividends from a domestic corporation of which it owns 19%. The corporation has:
> - Losses from operations of $20 plus gross dividends $100 = $80
> - Taxable income before the dividends received deduction of $80
>
> What is the allowable DRD?
>
> In this example, taking the full DRD of $70 (70% x $100 gross dividends) would not create an NOL, because the taxable income before the dividend received deduction of $80 minus $70 (70% x $100) equals a taxable income of $10. The DRD is limited to the appropriate DRD percentage of the taxable income of $80. Therefore, the DRD is limited to $56 (70% x $80). The taxable income after the DRD is $24 ($80 - $56 DRD).

What happens if we take the 70% of dividends received and it does not add to or create a loss? Then, the dividends received deduction would be 70% of the taxable income before the dividends received deduction.

Additional limits are imposed on the DRD if debt is used to finance the stock investment that generates the deduction.

> *Hint:* When an exam question does not specify the company's ownership percentage, assume that it is less than 20% and therefore the DRD percentage would be 70%.

A few important notes about what dividend income cannot be included in the DRD calculation:
- No DRD if the dividend is on common stock held for < 46 days.
- No DRD if the dividend is on preferred stock held for < 91 days.
- No DRD for dividend received from a Real Estate Investment Trust (REIT) because REITs are pass-through entities with taxes paid only at the shareholder level.
- No DRD for capital gains dividends, which pass through as capital gains.
- No DRD for money market or mutual fund dividends where all income is derived from investments in "interest-paying securities" as opposed to dividend-paying stocks.

Multiple Choice

REG 5-Q41 through REG 5-Q43

5) Transactions with related taxpayers
Losses are disallowed when they result from the sale or exchange of property between a corporation and:
- A more than 50% shareholder in the corporation, directly or indirectly.
- An S corporation if the same person owns a controlling share of each (more than 50%)
- A Partnership if the same person owns a controlling share of each (more than 50% of the capital and profits interest in the partnership, either directly or indirectly)
- Another corporation when both are members of a controlled group. These losses are deferred until the property is sold to a taxpayer outside the controlled group.

When determining ownership, constructive ownership rules apply. If you have parties who are related, for example, a brother owns 50% interest in a partnership with his sister, and his sister owns 50% interest in the partnership, then if the brother sells an asset to the partnership at a loss, the loss is disallowed because if the brother owns more than 50% interest in the partnership both directly and indirectly this creates a related party transaction. The partner (the brother) owns 50% directly(himself), or 50% indirectly, (through his sister), which gives the brother a 100% interest in the partnership. Adding the sister's 50% interest to the brother's 50% interest gives the brother an ownership in the partnership of 100%, which is known as constructive receipt.

6) Capital Losses
Deductible capital losses offset recognized capital gains, just as they are with individual taxpayers. However, corporations are **not allowed to deduct any net capital losses against ordinary income**, while individual taxpayers are allowed to deduct up to $3,000 of net capital losses per year against ordinary income and portfolio income (except married filing separately) which has a limit of $1500 in net capital losses. Any capital losses that are disallowed for an individual can be carried forward indefinitely, retaining their original identity as short term or long term. If you have a total of $3,000, coming from both short-term and long-term losses, always use the short term up first.

Corporations instead are allowed to carry net capital losses back three years and forward five years to offset net capital gains in other years. When carried back or forward, they are treated as short-term capital losses.

7) Passive losses
   Passive loss rules apply to:
   - Individuals,
   - Estates,
   - Trusts (other than grantor trusts),
   - Personal service corporations, and
   - Closely held corporations.

   > **Hint:** A corporation is closely held if at any time during the last half of the taxable year more than 50% of the value of the corporation's outstanding shares is owned either directly or indirectly by five or fewer individuals.

8) Casualty Losses
   The computation of corporate casualty losses is very similar to the computation for individual taxpayer casualty losses, except that there is no $100 floor or any AGI limitation, and in the case of complete destruction of business property, the loss is equal to the adjusted basis of the destroyed property less any insurance proceeds. To compute a partial business casualty loss, use the same method as for individuals, which is taking the lesser of the decrease in FMV or, adjusted basis less any insurance proceeds.

d. Ordering rules for C corporation deductions
   The deductions allowed to corporations should be applied in a very specific order:

	Gross income
	All deductions EXCEPT:
LESS:	• Charitable
	• DRD
	• NOL Carryback
	• Capital Loss Carryback
=	**Taxable Income for Charitable Limitation**
LESS:	Charitable contributions (limited to 10% of TI above)
=	**Taxable Income for DRD** (Note that NOL carryforwards are NOT allowed for computing the DRD limit)
LESS:	DRD
=	**Taxable Income after the contribution and DRD**

e. Alternative minimum tax (AMT) for C corporations

   Calculate alternative minimum taxable income and alternative minimum tax for a C corporation.

   The corporate AMT is similar to the individual AMT formula in that taxable income is increased or decreased by adjustments and increased by preferences in an alternative tax liability calculation. Note: ACE stands for adjusted current earnings.

	Regular Taxable Income before NOL Deduction
+/-	AMT Adjustments (not ACE or NOL)
+	AMT Preferences
=	AMTI before ACE Adjustment and NOL
+/-	ACE Adjustment
-	NOL Deduction
=	AMTI after ACE Adjustment and NOL Deduction

=	*AMTI after ACE Adjustment and NOL Deduction*
-	AMT Exemption (maximum amount $40,000)
=	AMT base
*	20% AMT rate
=	Tentative Minimum Tax before credits
-	AMT Foreign Tax Credit
=	Tentative Minimum Tax after AMT foreign tax credit
-	Regular Tax Liability
=	AMT Due (if positive)

1) Adjustments and Preferences
   Similar to the individual AMT formula, adjustments and preferences should be applied to taxable income before NOL carryovers.

   i. AMT Adjustments
      AMT adjustments either increase or decrease taxable income when computing pre-ACE AMTI. These adjustments often represent income or deductions that are used to defer taxation of economic income.
      - For personal property placed into service after 1986 which was depreciated using the 200%-declining balance method. For AMT purposes, the 150%-declining balance method must be used over the property's life.
      - For real property placed into service before January 1, 1999, AMT requires straight-line depreciation over 40 years. Beginning in 1999, AMT and regular taxes use the same lives and methods of depreciation.
      - Difference in percentage-of-completion method of income recognition over the completed-contract method of income recognition for long-term contracts
      - Adjustments are necessary related to use of the installment sales method, which is not allowed when calculating AMT.

   ii. AMT Preferences
       AMT preferences always increase taxable income. These items often represent economic income that is excluded from regular taxable income or deductions that are allowed when computing regular taxable income but which are not allowed when computing AMTI.
       - Tax-exempt interest, net of related expenses. Tax-exempt interest includes interest from private activity bonds. Tax-exempt interest on private activity bonds, issued in 2009 and 2010, are not a tax preference items.

         > *Hint:* Interest from general obligation bonds is not added back because it was not exempt from tax in the first place. That is, it was already included when calculating taxable income. These are not tax exempt.

       - Excess of accelerated over straight-line depreciation for pre-1987 acquired real estate and leased personal property under ACRS
       - Excess of percentage depletion deduction over the property's adjusted basis
       - Excess amortization of intangible drilling and development costs

2) **Adjusted Current Earnings (ACE) Adjustments**
   Adjusted current earnings (ACE) adjustments are required based on the recognition that the list of adjustments and preferences contained in the AMT formula is not all-inclusive. A positive ACE represents high pretax economic earnings. Therefore, a positive ACE increases AMTI and therefore can increase the company's AMT.

   To calculate the ACE adjustment, modify AMTI by adding economic income and adjusting for timing differences.

   Common adjustments include:
   - Increases for life insurance proceeds less policy-related expenses
   - Increases for tax-exempt general obligation bond income less related expenses
   - Increases for the **70%** DRD which is not allowed in ACE (Note that no adjustment is required for the 80% and 100% DRD)
   - Adjustments for the amortization of intangible drilling costs
   - Adjustments for the amortization of organization expenses

   When computing ACE, no adjustment is required for the following items:
   - Excess charitable contributions
   - Net capital losses
   - Penalties paid
   - Federal Income tax payments
   - 80% and 100% dividends received deduction

   To calculate the ACE adjustment:

   $$[(ACE) - (Pre\text{-}ACE\ AMTI)] * 75\% = ACE\ adjustment$$

   Because of timing differences, ACE can be a positive or negative adjustment. Any negative adjustment, however, is limited to the cumulative amount of positive adjustments in prior years.

3) **AMT Exemption**
   The AMT exemption for corporations is calculated as:

   $40,000 (the maximum amount) less 25% of the AMTI amount over $150,000

   The exemption is totally phased out when AMTI equals $310,000.

4) **Corporate AMT Due**
   Corporations must pay the greater of the AMT tentative tax or the regular tax.

5) **Small Corporation Exemption**
   The corporate AMT does not apply to small corporations who meet a gross receipts test. A corporation's tentative minimum tax (TMT) will automatically equal $0 for any corporation with average gross receipts over the past 3 years less than or equal to $7.5M.

   For brand new corporations, the corporation will be automatically exempt for the first year. The average gross receipts threshold for year 2 is lowered to $5M.

Example: A corporation was started in 2015. What are the average gross receipts tests that must be passed each year for the corporation to be exempt from the corporate AMT?

Year 1:	Automatically exempt from AMT
Year 2:	The testing period is Year 1. Year 1 gross receipts must be less than or equal to $5M to be exempt from the AMT.
Year 3:	The testing period is Years 1 and 2. The average gross receipts for years 1 and 2 must be less than or equal to $7.5M to be exempt from the AMT.
Year 4:	The testing period is Years 1, 2 and 3. The average gross receipts for years 1, 2, and 3 must be less than or equal to $7.5M to be exempt from the AMT.
Year 5:	The testing period is Years 2, 3 and 4. The average gross receipts for years 2, 3 and 4 must be less than or equal to $7.5M to be exempt from the AMT.

If the average gross receipt for year 2 through Year 5 exceed 7.5 million, they will have to compute alternative minimum tax for all years after year 5.

6) Depreciation averaging convention methods for AMT
The averaging convention methods are used to determine allowable deductions that can be taken in the first year on either tangible personal property used in a trade or business or real estate used in a trade or business.

For an asset that is real estate, used in a trade or business, the averaging convention method is the mid-month method. For the first year, the mid-month method assumes that the real estate is placed in service in the middle of that month. A taxpayer can never take a full year depreciation in the first year. From 1999 and thereafter, MACRS and AMT use the same depreciation methods and lives.

For an asset that is personal property, used in a trade or business, the averaging convention methods are the mid-quarter method and the half-year convention. The mid-quarter method must be used if 40% or more of the purchases occurred in the last quarter of the year. If the 40% test is not met, then take half-year depreciation.

Multiple Choice

REG 5-Q44

f. Penalty Taxes for Corporations
Certain penalty taxes are imposed on corporations.

1) Accumulated Earnings Tax
Remember that when income is distributed to shareholders, it is also taxed to the shareholders as dividend income. The accumulated earnings tax is imposed by the IRS if it determines that the corporation is trying to avoid these taxes by accumulating income in excess of reasonable business needs. Corporations can avoid this tax by either distributing income as dividends or by documenting the business reasons for accumulating income. For the accumulated earnings tax, dividends include consent dividends and dividends paid within 2 ½ months of the end of the tax year.

A consent dividend is one that is not actually paid to shareholders. Instead, shareholders consent to be taxed as though a dividend were paid. The purpose is to allow shareholders to avoid the penalty tax by distributing dividends after year end.

Accumulated taxable income is computed by adjusting taxable income to reflect retained economic income. An accumulated earnings credit is subtracted from any accumulated earnings to represent the "reasonable" accumulation of earnings for business purposes.

The accumulated earnings tax is equal to 20% of undistributed accumulated taxable income.
The Accumulated Earnings Tax formula is:

Taxable Income
+/- Adjustments such as:
(corporate income tax which includes federal and foreign)
(charitable contributions over 10% limit)
(net capital loss)
(net long-term capital gains in excess of short-term capital losses)
dividends received deduction
consent dividends
(dividends paid within last 9.5 months of tax year and 2.5 months after the close)
(accumulated earnings credit)

= **Accumulated Taxable Income**
* 20%

= **Accumulated Earnings Tax**

As indicated in the formula above, there are several modifications made to taxable income to reflect economic income accumulations:
- Taxable income is **reduced** by deducting:
    1. Accrued income taxes
    2. Excess charitable contributions
    3. Either net capital losses or net after-tax capital gains (only one can occur in a given year)
    4. Dividends paid or deemed paid
- Taxable income is **increased** by adding back:
    4. Any dividends received deduction that was taken in the current year
    5. Any NOL or capital loss carryovers

2) Accumulated Earnings Credit
The accumulated earnings credit is calculated as the greater of two numbers, both related to Earnings and Profits (E&P).
1. The amount of current E&P required for the "reasonable needs" of the business
The reasonable needs of the business are a question of fact, but usually include any cash necessary to finance business expansion, to fund working capital requirements, and to retire liabilities. They generally do not include amounts retained for unrealistic needs or for loans to shareholders.
2. If a corporation cannot establish a reason to keep earnings, then a flat $250,000 ($150,000 for personal service corporations) less the accumulated E&P as of the close of the preceding year. This is called the minimum credit.

There is no limit to the Accumulated Earnings Credit. It is based on the amount warranted by business needs.

g. Personal Holding Company (PHC) tax
PHC tax is a penalty tax that is triggered by relatively high levels of investment income in a corporation. Like the Accumulated Earnings Tax, it imposes a penalty on undistributed income. The PHC tax can be avoided by paying out dividends to the shareholder. PHC tax is only imposed on corporations which qualify as a PHC. Exempt entities include banks, insurance companies, and finance companies because their business purpose is to manage investments.

A corporation qualifies as a PHC if **two** tests are met: An income test and a stock ownership test

1. The **income test** is met if passive income and portfolio income represent 60% or more of the entity's adjusted ordinary gross income (AOGI).

> *Hint:* For PHC tests, interest earned on tax-exempt obligations is excluded from PHC income.

PHC income includes income from:
- Dividends
- Annuities
- Mineral, Oil, Gas Royalties
- Produced Film Rents
- Amounts received under personal service contracts
- Interest (non-tax-exempt)
- Rents
- Copyright and Patent Royalties
- Amounts received from estates and trusts
- Compensation for > 25% use of corporate property by shareholders

2. The **ownership test** is met if more than 50% of the value of the corporation's stock is owned, directly or indirectly, by 5 or fewer individuals at any point during the last half of the tax year. A corporation with 10 or more equal and unrelated shareholders would not be a PHC because it would not pass the ownership test, because 5 or fewer stockholders, will own 50%(5 equal stockholders who each own 10%). 5 or fewer must own more than 50% to meet the stock ownership test.

The Personal Holding Company Tax formula is:
Taxable Income
   +/- Adjustments such as:
   (federal and foreign income tax)
   (charitable contributions in excess of 10% limit)
   (net long-term capital gains over net short-term capital loss, net of tax)
   dividends received deduction
   (net capital losses)
= Adjusted Taxable Income
   (dividends paid during the year)
   (dividends paid within 2.5 months of the close of the year) limited to 20% of dividends paid during the year
   (consent dividends)
= Undistributed PHC Income

The undistributed PHC income is multiplied by 20% to arrive at the PHC tax.

Consent dividends are hypothetical dividends that are treated as if they were paid on the last day of the taxable year.

The PHC tax is imposed on undistributed income and, like the Accumulated Earnings tax, the PHC tax can be avoided by paying dividends. To decrease PHC income, dividends must be paid on a pro-rata basis. Dividends cannot be distributed disproportionately among shareholders.

For PHC tax, dividends include dividends paid during the year and within 2 ½ months of the tax year end, consent dividend.

Unlike the accumulated earnings tax, the PHC tax is self-assessing. It is computed on Schedule PH and submitted with Form 1120. The PHC tax has a stock ownership and income test, the accumulated earning tax does not. A PHC could be subject to AMT.

Multiple Choice

REG 5-Q45

Calculate credits allowable as a reduction to regular and alternative minimum tax for a C corporation.

h. AMT Credit
In years in which a corporation pays AMT, a credit is generated that can be used in future tax years to reduce corporate tax liability. This credit for a C Corporation is not limited to the amount of AMT generated from timing differences like individuals. The entire alternative minimum tax of a C Corporation is available to the corporation for a credit to reduce regular corporation tax liability in future years. Any amount not used as a credit next year against regular tax liability, can be carried forward indefinitely.

2. Net operating losses and capital loss limitations

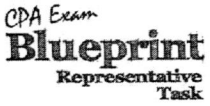

Calculate the current-year net operating or capital loss of a C corporation.

Prepare a net operating and/or capital loss carryforward schedule for a C corporation.

Analyze the impact of potentially expiring net operating and/or capital losses during tax planning for a C corporation.

Analyze the impact of the charitable contribution and/or dividends received deductions on the net operating loss calculation of a C corporation.

a. Net Operating Loss (NOL)
A corporation's net operating loss is the excess of an entity's business deductions over its gross income during a particular tax year. A deduction is then allowed for this loss in other tax years when the entity's gross income exceeds its allowable business deductions.

NOL is calculated similarly to taxable income with a few modifications.
- The dividends received deduction can be taken without limitation. In other words, once the proper DRD percentage is determined based on ownership, the full amount can be subtracted without regard to taxable income when calculating the company's NOL.
- Charitable contributions are deductible in calculating the NOL, subject to the 10% limitation.

In the determination of NOL, the following are not included:
- Any NOL carryover from previous or subsequent years should not be included in calculating the current year's NOL (no net operating loss carryovers or carryforwards are allowed for NOL).
- Excess of capital losses over capital gains are not included.

b. NOL Carryovers
A NOL can be carried back two years and forward 20 years and therefore used to offset corporate taxable income in those years.

Small businesses can carry NOLs back for three years instead of two. A small business corporation is one with average annual gross receipts of $5 million or less for the prior three tax years.
If a company so chooses, it can elect to only carry the NOL forward, not backward. Once this election is made, it cannot be rescinded.

c. NOL Reporting
NOLs are reported by filing an amended return (Form 1120X) or Form 1139 can be filed by the end of the tax year following the year of the loss.

d. Capital losses
Capital losses are deductible only against capital gains. They are not deductible against ordinary income on a corporate return. Unused capital losses can be carried back three years and carried forward five years, to offset capital gains. All capital loss carrybacks and carryforwards are shown as short-term.

e. Tax planning for expiring NOL or capital losses
For tax planning, always accelerate deductions and try to postpone the recognition of income. For NOL, consider whether to carryback the NOL, or do take the carryback and carry the NOL forward. A taxpayer might want to carry the NOL forward, if the taxpayer anticipates being in a higher tax bracket in future years.

For capital losses, to determine if the capital loss carryover is to be carried back or not taken and carried forward, consideration must be given to the amount of capital gains to net the loss against. If there is more capital gains in the past three years and it is anticipated that there will be no capital gains in future years, the NOL carryback should be taken. If there is no capital gains in the prior three years and it is expected that there will be capital gains in future years, the NOL carryforward should be taken.

3. Entity/owner transactions, including contributions, loans and distributions

> **Calculate the tax gain (loss) realized and recognized by both the shareholders and the corporation on a contribution.**

a. Contributions to a corporation
   1) Gain or loss issues when acquiring corporate stock
      i. From the shareholder's perspective
         When acquiring corporate stock in exchange for property, the determination of whether or not the purchaser should recognize a gain or loss depends on how much of the corporation he/she owns immediately after the transfer.

         a) Purchaser is part of control club immediately post-transfer (Section 351 Transfer)
            No gain (loss) can be recognized by the taxpayer if **both conditions** are met:
            - Property is transferred to a corporation **solely in exchange for corporate stock**
            - The taxpayer(s) who contributed the property and acquires at least 80% of the corporation's stock, and immediately after the transfer they have control. Control is defined as owning at least 80% of the voting and non-voting stock of the corporation.

            Generally speaking, to be eligible to defer gain or loss recognition, only property must be contributed in exchange for only stock (**not boot**). Property does not include services. Stock in this context is any equity interest in the corporation except "non-qualified" preferred stock, which is treated as **boot**. Non-qualified preferred stock is preferred stock is expected to be redeemed within 20 years.

            Boot is property received other than stock. Examples include cash and non-qualified preferred stock, short-term notes, and securities in another corporation. When boot is received, it will result in the recognition of gain, but not a loss, even if the shareholder has control. A shareholder will recognize a gain if the property transferred by a shareholder includes a liability, which is assumed by the corporation and this liability exceeds the total basis of the property that the shareholder transferred in.

            If stock is exchanged for **services**, the transferor has wage income and basis in the corporation's stock equal to the FMV of the stock received from the corporation. The corporation gets a salary expense deduction, unless the value of the services rendered would be classified as organization expenditures.

            When a taxpayer **contributes property, and receives boot** in addition to corporate stock in return, and is part of the control club immediately after the transfer, **gain (but not loss) should be recognized**.

            If boot is received, gain recognized to the shareholder is the lower of:
            - Realized gain (FMV less property's adjusted basis)
            - The FMV of boot received

> **Example:** A taxpayer contributes land with a FMV of $50,000 and an adjusted basis of $30,000. In exchange, he receives 100% of the corporation's stock and $10,000 in cash. What is the taxpayer's basis in the corporation immediately after the transfer?
>
> | | $30,000 | Basis of property transferred |
> |---|---|---|
> | + | $10,000 | Gain recognized* |
> | − | $10,000 | Boot received (assumption of liabilities is always treated as boot to arrive at stock basis) |
> | = | $30,000 | **Shareholder Basis in Corporate Stock** |
>
> * Taxpayer's recognized gain = the lower of:
> - Taxpayer's realized gain ($50,000 - $30,000) = $20,000
> - **Boot received by the taxpayer = $10,000**

b) Corporation's basis of property
The corporation's basis of the property is the transferor's adjusted basis, plus the gain recognized by the transferor.

c) Debt Assumption
When debt is assumed by a corporation as part of the shareholder's acquisition of stock for property, it is not considered boot when determining the shareholder's gain or loss so long as the liability is less than the property's adjusted basis. However, assumption of a liability by the corporation is always considered boot received for calculating the shareholder basis in the stock,

> **Hint:** Although an assumed liability that is less than the property's adjusted basis is not considered boot for the purposes of gain recognition, it IS factored into the calculation of the shareholder's basis in the corporation's stock after the transfer

> **Example:** A taxpayer contributes a building worth $200,000 to a corporation in exchange for 100% of the corporation's stock. The taxpayer's adjusted basis in the building is $100,000. The property is subject to a $25,000 mortgage, which is assumed by the corporation. What gain does the taxpayer recognize on the transaction?
>
> Because the liability is less than the adjusted basis of the property, no gain will be recognized on the transaction. The assumption of liability by a corporation is always boot received for shareholder's basis in the stock calculation, but not for gain recognition.

Gain may be recognized in **two circumstances** if a corporation assumes shareholder's debt.

Circumstance 1: If the **total liability assumed exceeds the total adjusted basis** of property from the shareholder, gain must be recognized by the shareholder as follows:

Recognized Gain = Liability Assumed − Basis of Transferred Property

> **Example:** A taxpayer contributes property to a corporation with a FMV of $150,000 and an adjusted basis to the taxpayer of $75,000. A liability of $90,000 is attached to the property and assumed by the corporation. The taxpayer owns 90% of the corporation's stock immediately after the transfer. What is the taxpayer's recognized gain.
>
> Because the liability assumed by the corporation exceeds the shareholder's adjusted basis, the taxpayer recognizes a gain equal to the excess of debt over her adjusted basis in the transferred property, calculated as $90,000 - $75,000 = $15,000.

> **Example:** Taxpayer M contributes machinery with an adjusted basis of $45,000, a FMV of $65,000 and associated debt of $55,000. The corporation assumes the debt as part of the transfer. What gain must M recognize?
>
> Because the liability assumed by the corporation exceeds the shareholder's adjusted basis, M recognizes a gain equal to the excess of debt over her adjusted basis in the transferred property, calculated as $55,000 - $45,000 = $10,000.

Circumstance 2: If the debt was not incurred by the shareholder for valid business reasons, the corporate assumption causes ALL debt relief to be treated as boot received for calculation of stockholder's basis in stock. Gain will be recognized by the shareholder for the lesser of realized gain or boot received (assumption of liability).

> **Example:** A taxpayer contributes property to a corporation with a FMV of $100,000, an adjusted basis of $60,000, and an attached liability of $50,000 which is assumed by the corporation not for valid business purpose. What is the shareholder's recognized gain?
>
> If a corporation has no business purpose, an assumption of a liability is still boot received for shareholder basis. As a result, the full $50,000 of liability assumption is treated as boot received, whether or not the liability exceeds the shareholder's adjusted basis.
>
> Gain is recognized because there is not a valid business purpose. The gain is the lesser of the realized gain (FMV $100,000 minus Basis $6,000) $40,000, or debt assumed of $50,000. Recognized gain is $40,000.

Multiple Choice

REG 5-Q46

b. Basis issues related to acquisition of corporate stock

Calculate an entity owner's basis in C corporation stock for federal income tax purposes.

Reconcile an owner's beginning and ending basis in C corporation stock for federal income tax purposes.

1) Shareholder basis in corporate stock
   The shareholder's basis in the corporate stock is equal to:

       Basis of all property transferred to the corporation
   + Gain recognized by the shareholder
   − Boot received by the shareholder (including liabilities assumed by the corporation)
   = Shareholder Basis in Corporate Stock

   i. Debt assumption
      Although an assumed liability that is less than the property's adjusted basis is not a gain to the shareholder, it is considered boot received for calculation of shareholder's basis in the stock.

      Example: A taxpayer contributes a building worth $200,000 to a corporation in exchange for 100% of the corporation's stock. The taxpayer's adjusted basis in the building is $100,000. The property is subject to a $25,000 mortgage, which is assumed by the corporation. What is the taxpayer's basis in the stock immediately after the transfer?

      Remember that because the liability is less than the adjusted basis of the property, it is not treated as a gain to the shareholder. Assumed liabilities are always treated as boot received when calculating the shareholder's basis in the corporate stock.

            $100,000   Basis of property transferred
      + $0   Gain recognized*
      − $25,000   Boot received
      = $75,000   **Shareholder Basis in Corporate Stock**

      Example: A taxpayer contributes property to a corporation with a FMV of $150,000 and an adjusted basis to the taxpayer of $75,000. A liability of $90,000 is attached to the property and assumed by the corporation. The taxpayer owns 90% of the corporation's stock immediately after the transfer. What is the taxpayer's recognized gain and what is the taxpayer's basis in the stock after the transfer?

      Because the liability assumed by the corporation exceeds the shareholder's adjusted basis, the taxpayer recognizes a gain equal to the excess of debt over her adjusted basis in the transferred property, calculated as $90,000 - $75,000 = $15,000. The liability assumed by corporation is considered boot received for the calculation of basis.
      The taxpayer's basis in the stock is:

              $75,000   Basis of property transferred
      + $15,000   Gain recognized*
      − $90,000   Boot received
      = $0   **Shareholder Basis in Corporate Stock**

Example: Taxpayer M contributes machinery with an adjusted basis of $45,000, a FMV of $65,000 and associated debt of $55,000. The corporation assumes the debt as part of the transfer. What gain must M recognize and what is M's basis in the corporate stock received?

Because the liability assumed by the corporation exceeds the shareholder's adjusted basis, M recognizes a gain equal to the excess of debt over her adjusted basis in the transferred property, calculated as $55,000 - $45,000 = $10,000. The assumption of the liability ($55,000) by the corporation is boot received, and reduces basis.
M's basis in the corporate stock is calculated as:

	$45,000	Basis of property transferred
+	$10,000	Gain recognized*
−	$55,000	Boot received
=	$0	**Shareholder Basis in Corporate Stock**

Example: A taxpayer contributes property to a corporation with a FMV of $100,000, an adjusted basis of $60,000, and an attached liability of $50,000, which is not incurred for a valid business reason, is assumed by the corporation. What is the shareholder's recognized gain and what is the shareholder's resulting basis in the corporation?

Since the liability assumed by a corporation that does not have a valid business reason, the full $50,000 of liability assumption is still treated as boot received. Since there is not a valid business purpose gain is recognized for the lesser of the excess of the FMV over the property's basis or the boot received, which is the liability assumed the corporation. If this corporation had a valid business purpose, gain would only be recognized to the shareholder if the liability assumed by the corporation is greater basis of the property contributed to the corporation.

	$60,000	Basis of property transferred
+	$40,000	Gain recognized*
−	$50,000	Boot received
=	$50,000	**Shareholder Basis in Corporate Stock**

* Taxpayer's recognized gain = the lower of:
- **Taxpayer's realized gain ($100,000 - $60,000) = $40,000**
- Boot received by the taxpayer = $50,000

2) Corporation basis in acquired property
   When property is transferred to a corporation in exchange for corporate stock, the adjusted basis for qualifying property is a carryover basis.

Corporation's adjusted basis in property	=	Transferor's basis in property	+	Any gain recognized by the transferor

> **Example:** Taxpayer B contributes a building with a FMV of $85,000 and an adjusted basis of $50,000. The taxpayer received $25,000 in cash and 60% of the corporation's stock. Taxpayer A received the other 40%, so the 80% control test was met. What is the corporation's basis in the building immediately after the transfer?
>
> The corporation's basis in the building is equal to:
>
> | $50,000 | + | $25,000* | = | $75,000 |
> |---|---|---|---|---|
> | B's Basis | | B's recognized gain | | Corporation's Basis in the property |
>
> * B's recognized gain = the lower of:
>   - B's realized gain ($85,000 - $50,000) = $35,000
>   - **Boot received by the taxpayer = $25,000**

> **Example:** A taxpayer contributes a building worth $200,000 to a corporation in exchange for 100% of the corporation's stock. The taxpayer's adjusted basis in the building is $100,000, and the property is subject to a $25,000 mortgage, which is assumed by the corporation. What is the corporation's basis in the building immediately after the transfer?
>
> | $100,000 | + | $0* | = | $100,000 |
> |---|---|---|---|---|
> | B's Basis | | B's recognized gain | | Corporation's Basis in the property |
>
> *B's recognized gain = $0 because an assumed liability only triggers gain recognition if it exceeds the adjusted basis of the property.

Multiple Choice
REG 5-Q47 through REG 5-Q48

3) Holding period
   i. Shareholder holding period in corporate stock
      The shareholder's holding period of the stock may or may not include the amount of time the shareholder held the property just given to the corporation.
      When a capital asset or Section 1231 asset is transferred to the corporation, the transferor's property holding period is tacked on to the stock holding period. For all other property transferred, the transferor's stock holding period begins on the date of the transfer and does not include the holding period of the property transferred.

   ii. Corporation holding period in acquired property
      The corporation's holding period always tacks onto the period the shareholder held the property before the exchange.

Example – reconciliation of beginning owner's equity to ending owner's equity in a C Corporation:

Assume that a stockholder has a beginning basis in the stockowner's equity of $50,000. The ending balance for the stock basis (owner's equity) is $95,000.

Reconcile the beginning basis to the ending basis for the period. Changes in basis are due to the following transactions:
1. The stockholder contributed additional assets of property to the corporation. The basis of the property is $35,000, and the FMV is $65,000. There is a mortgage on the property of $55,000, which is assumed by the corporation. The stockholder received an additional 10% of the stock for the property contributed.
2. There is a non-liquidating distribution of property of $65,000, when the earnings and profits are $10,000, and stockholder's basis at the time is $35,000.
3. There is a stock redemption of $20,000 by the corporation.

Reconciliation

Beginning Basis	$50,000
Contribution of property for stock	65,000
Boot Received (assumption of debt)	(55,000) (b)
Gain Recognized (liability assumed exceeds basis of property transferred)	20,000 (c)
Non-Liquidating Distribution return of basis	(35,000) (d)
Stock Redemption	(20,000)
Ending Basis	**$25,000**

(a) Because the stockholder did receive stock for property contributed Section 351 applies. The stockholder only received 10% of stock, not 80%, and the contribution of property is a taxable event to the corporation and the stockholder, and increase the stockholder's basis by the FMV of the property transferred.
(b) The assumption of debt is boot received.
(c) If the corporation assumes a debt in excess of property basis, there is a gain to the stockholder.
(d) In a non-liquidating distribution which is a dividend distribution, any distribution in excess of earnings and profits is a return of basis. The distribution is $65,000, the earnings and profits are $10,000. Therefore the $35,000 is a return of stock basis.

Comprehensive Example: Taxpayer F contributes equipment with an adjusted basis of $35,000, a FMV of $65,000 and associated loan of $25,000 in exchange for 50% of corporate stock. The corporation assumes the debt as part of the transfer. The equipment had been used for 3 years and was transferred to the corporation on April 1, 2015. Taxpayer G contributes printers that were purchased on November 1, 2014, and had an adjusted basis of $15,000, a FMV of $65,000 and no associated liabilities, in exchange for 20% of corporate stock. Taxpayer H contributes services valued at $35,000 in exchange for 20% of the corporation's stock. The business began on 6/1/2015.

Shareholder Gain Calculation:
  Shareholder F: No gain recognized because no boot received (liability is less than the adjusted basis of the property)
  Shareholder G: No gain recognized because no boot received.
  Shareholder H: Because he is receiving stock in exchange for services, he must recognize a gain equal to the FMV of stock received, or $35,000.

Shareholder Basis Calculation:

		F	G	H
	Basis of all property transferred to the corporation	$35,000	$15,000	$0
+	Gain recognized by the shareholder	$0	$0	$35,000
−	Boot received by the shareholder	$0	$0	$0
−	Any liability assumed by the corporation	($25,000)	$0	$0
	Shareholder's basis in the corporate stock	**$10,000**	**$15,000**	**$35,000**

Shareholder Holding Period Calculation
  Shareholder F: Remember that if a capital asset or a Section 1231 asset (i.e., an asset used in trade or business and owned more than one year) is transferred, the shareholder adds the property holding period to the stock holding period. Since the equipment meets this definition, Taxpayer F's holding period begins when the equipment was purchased, which is 3 years ago.
  Shareholder G: The printers are used for a trade or business but have been held less than one year, so the holding period does not tack on. The holding period for the stock would begin when G had become a stockholder.
  Shareholder H: Holding period is not applicable to services. Therefore, the holding period of the stock for Taxpayer H starts the day completed the services for the stock.

Corporation Basis and Holding Period Calculation:
  Equipment:

  $35,000   + $0*   = $35,000
  F's Basis   F's recognized gain   Corporation's Basis in the
                             (calculated below)   Transferred Property

  * F's recognized gain = the lower of:
    - F's realized gain ($35,000 − $25,000) = $10,000
    - **Boot received by the taxpayer = $0**
  Holding Period = Taxpayer's holding period, which begins 3 years ago.

  Printers:
  $15,000   + $0**   = $15,000
  G's Basis   G's recognized gain   Corporation's Basis in the
                             (calculated below)   Transferred Property

  ** G's recognized gain = the lower of:
    - G's realized gain ($15,000 − $0) = $5,000
    - **Boot received by the taxpayer = $0**

  Holding Period of the printers to the corporation began when G became a stockholder.

4) Debt vs. equity
Corporate debt can be reclassified as equity depending on certain factors such as the characteristics of the debt (for example, the type of instrument, collateral, interest, etc.) and whether or not the corporation is thinly capitalized (i.e., the debt to equity ratio is too high).

c. Distributions from a corporation

> **Calculate the tax gain (loss) realized and recognized by both the shareholders and the corporation on a distribution in complete liquidation of a C corporation for federal income tax purposes.**

> **Calculate the tax gain (loss) realized and recognized on a nonliquidating distribution by both a C corporation and its shareholders for federal income tax purposes.**

> **Calculate the amount of the cash distributions to shareholders of a C corporation that represents a dividend, return of capital or capital gain for federal income tax purposes.**

Distributions to shareholders are calculated as:

$$\text{Amount Distributed} = \text{Cash} + \text{FMV at distribution date of property received} - \text{Liabilities assumed by the shareholder}$$

If the liability on the property exceeds the property's FMV, the FMV is treated as equal to the amount of the liability.

$$\text{Amount Distributed} = \text{Cash} + \text{Liability assumed by shareholder (when liability > FMV)}$$

The shareholder's basis for property received in a corporate distribution is equal to:

$$\text{Cash} + \text{FMV at distribution date of property received}$$

> *Hint:* While the valuation of the distribution includes liabilities assumed by the shareholder, the basis calculation does not.

Multiple Choice

REG 5-Q49

1) Ordinary (non-liquidating) distributions
   i. Corporation gain or loss recognition
   The distribution of appreciated property causes a corporation to **recognize gains, but not losses**, as if the property had been sold for its FMV. **Appreciated property** is property with a FMV that is greater than its adjusted basis. If the property is subject to a liability that exceeds the property's adjusted basis, the corporation's gain is equal to the difference between the liability and the property's adjusted basis.

   > **Example:** Salt Corporation distributes property with a FMV of $50,000 and an adjusted basis of $30,000 to shareholder Pepper. A gain of $20,000 will be recognized by the corporation on the distribution.
   >
   > Assuming the same facts, but that there is also a liability on the property of $55,000. A gain of $25,000 will be recognized by the corporation on the distribution.

> **Example:** Salt Corporation distributes property with a FMV of $50,000 and an adjusted basis of $60,000 to shareholder Pepper. No loss will be recognized by the corporation on the distribution (only gains can be recognized). This is for non-liquidating distributions only.

    ii. Earnings and Profits (E&P)
To properly classify corporate distributions, the corporation's E&P must be known. The candidate does not have to calculate the earnings and profits. The candidate has to know how current and accumulated earnings have to do with corporate distributions. Only C Corporations have earnings and profits, not S Corporations. But if an S corporation was a previous C Corporation, and there were some previous Earnings & Profits in the C corporation that were never distributed, the S Corporation would have dividends paid to their shareholders. The CPA candidate does not have to know how to compute earnings and profits.

> *Hint:* On the CPA exam, you do not need to know how to calculate E&P, just know what to do with current E&P and accumulated E&P.

    iii. Shareholder gain or loss recognition
The taxation of corporate distributions to shareholders depends on the Earnings & Profits (E&P) accumulated in the corporation before the distribution.

        1. Distributions are taxable as dividend income to the shareholder if the corporation has positive current and accumulated Earnings and Profits.
            • First go to the current earnings and profits and next go to the accumulated earnings and profits

> **Example:** A corporation has a CEP balance of $25,000 and an accumulated earnings and profits (AEP) balance of $0. During the year, it makes a $20,000 distribution to its preferred shareholders and a $20,000 distribution to its common shareholders. What portion of the distribution is considered a dividend?
>
> $20,000 of the CEP balance is allocated first to preferred shareholders, who will treat the entire distribution as a taxable dividend.
> The remaining $5,000 of CEP will be allocated to the common shareholders and treated as a taxable dividend. The remaining $15,000 distribution could be treated as a tax-free return of stock basis or as a capital gain, depending on the shareholders' stock basis in the corporation.

            • When there is a distribution of cash and, or property at FMV, this amount of the distribution t is dividends to the extent of the earnings and profits. First go to current E&P, if positive. This amount represents dividends to shareholders,
            • Once CEP is exhausted, then look to AEP. If the AEP is positive, this amount represents additional dividends to the shareholders. Once all Earnings and Profits are exhausted, then go to next step.

        2. If any further distribution remains, the excess is tax-free to the extent of the shareholder's basis in the stock because it reduces that basis. It is treated as a return of the shareholder's initial investment.

        3. If there is Any additional distribution, it is taxed to the shareholder as a capital gain.

Both current and accumulated E&P are used to determine whether a distribution is a dividend.
- Current E&P is equal to the E&P generated during the year.
- Accumulated E&P is the amount on day one of the current tax year.

Distributions generally reduce E&P. However, distributions cannot create a deficit in E&P. Only actual losses can create an E&P deficit.

Once all current year earnings and distributions have been accounted for, the current year's activities are used to adjust the Accumulated E&P account balance up or down to then start the next fiscal year.

Four possible E&P scenarios determine whether a distribution is a dividend:
1. If current E&P and accumulated E&P are **negative**:
   Distributions are considered a return of capital and are tax free up to the shareholder's adjusted basis. Any excess is treated as a capital gain.
2. If current E&P and accumulated E&P are **positive**:
   The distribution is taxed as a dividend that is deducted first from current E&P. Once current E&P is depleted, distributions reduce accumulated E&P

   > **Example:** A corporation has current earnings and profits (CEP) of $20,000 and accumulated earnings and profits (AEP) of $15,000. In the current year, it makes a distribution of $50,000 to shareholder Q, who owns 90% of the corporation and who has basis in the corporation of $13,000.
   >
   > The portion of CEP and AEP that shareholder Q is entitled to is 90% of $20,000 and 90% of $15,000, for a total of $31,500. Therefore, the shareholder should treat the distribution as follows:
   > - $31,500 is considered taxable as dividend income.
   > - $13,000 is considered a non-taxable return of stock basis, reducing Q's basis in the corporation stock to $0.
   > - The remaining $5,500 is treated as a capital gain.

3. If **current E&P are positive** and **accumulated E&P are negative**:
   The distribution is a dividend only to the extent of current E&P.

   > **Example:** A corporation has current earnings and profits (CEP) of $20,000 and a deficit in the accumulated earnings and profits (AEP) account of $7,500. In the current year, it makes a distribution of $27,000 to shareholder Q, who owns 100% of the corporation and has basis in corporate stock of $5,000.
   >
   > The CEP account has a positive balance of $20,000, causing the first $20,000 to be treated as dividend income to the shareholder. Next go to the accum. E&P which is negative. If negative, the accum. E&P are not dividends, The next $5,000 is treated as a return of capital to the shareholder, reducing the shareholder's basis to $0.
   > - The remaining $2,000 is treated as a capital gain to the shareholder.

4. If **current E&P are negative** and **accumulated E&P are positive**: First net the current E&P if negative against the positive Accumulated E&P, if the net is positive, then that represents the portion of the distribution which is a dividend. If negative, then go on to step 2: which is the portion of the distribution which is a return of the stock basis, and not taxable. If there is still additional distribution, this amount is a capital gain to the stockholder.

2) Stock Distributions
   If a corporation distributes stock, it is not taxable to the shareholder if there was **no option to receive property** in lieu of stock and there is **no change in the proportionate interests** of shareholders.

   A stock bailout is treated as a dividend to shareholders to the extent of E&P at the time of the sale or redemption. A **stock bailout** is the distribution of non-voting stock followed by the sale or redemption of that stock by the corporation.

Multiple Choice

REG 5-Q50 through REG 5-Q57

i. Constructive Dividends
Constructive dividends are treated as distributions. **Constructive dividends** are payments to shareholders that are not formally declared as dividends. Property distributions to shareholders are often treated as constructive dividends.

> **Example:** A taxpayer is the sole shareholder of Tree Corp. Tree Corp. paid the taxpayer a salary of $155,000 when reasonable compensation would have been $75,000. The excess $80,000 is unreasonable compensation and is therefore not deductible by Tree Corp. It is instead treated as a constructive dividend payment to the taxpayer.

ii. Corporate Stock Redemptions
The total redemption of stock occurs when a corporation repurchases stock from shareholders. It is generally treated by the shareholder as a sale of stock that will trigger recognition of a capital gain or loss by the shareholder.

Multiple Choice
REG 5-Q58

3) Corporate Liquidations
Complete liquidations occur when a corporation completely dissolves and distributes all of its remaining assets. This is similar to a stock redemption in that shareholders receive assets in exchange for canceling their shares of stock.

   i. Shareholder Gain/Loss Recognition and Basis
   Shareholders may recognize a gain or a loss on the liquidating distribution. This gain or loss is calculated as:

   $$\left(\text{FMV of distribution} - \text{Any liabilities associated with the distributed property} \right) - \text{Stockholder's Basis}$$

   The basis to the shareholder of property received in complete liquidation will equal the FMV of the property received.

   > **Example:** A taxpayer received property worth $100,000 in the complete liquidation of Paper Corp. The taxpayer's basis in Paper Corp stock was equal to $25,000. The property had an associated mortgage of $45,000.
   >
   > The taxpayer will recognize a gain of ($100,000 − $45,000 − $25,000) = $30,000. The taxpayer's adjusted basis in the property is equal to its FMV of $100,000.

   ii. Corporation Gain/Loss Recognition
   A corporation may recognize a gain or a loss when it makes a liquidating distribution. This gain or loss is calculated as the FMV less the adjusted basis of the distributed property. The nature of the gain or loss depends on the nature of the distributed asset (e.g. ordinary, capital, Section 1231).

   > **Example:** In the complete liquidation of a corporation, inventory and other similar assets worth $300,000 with an adjusted basis of $120,000 were distributed to shareholders. The corporation recognized ordinary income of $180,000 on the liquidation.

If the distributed property is subject to a liability, the FMV of the property cannot be less than the associated liabilities.

> **Example:** As part of a complete liquidation, Noodle Corp distributed a factory building with a FMV of $150,000, an adjusted basis of $70,000 and associated debt of $165,000. The corporation's gain on the distribution is equal to ($165,000 – $70,000), or $95,000. The FMV cannot be less than the debt.

Expenses incurred in the liquidation are deducted on the corporation's final tax return.

> **Hint:** If a corporation distributes appreciated property, with debt, in a complete liquidation, the gain to the corporation is the excess of the any debt assumed by the stockholder, in excess of its basis of the property transferred to the stockholder.

iii. Subsidiary Liquidation Gain/Loss Recognition
When a controlled subsidiary is liquidated, no real disposition of assets has occurred. The assets are merely transferred from one corporation to a related corporation.

Parent companies do not recognize any gain or loss on the liquidation of a subsidiary if two conditions are present:
- Parent must own 80% of all the total value of the stock of the subsidiary
- Subsidiary must distribute the assets within the tax year (or within three years of the close of the tax year in which the first distribution takes place.
- The subsidiary must be solvent.

The parent company inherits the adjusted basis of property transferred by the subsidiary.

The subsidiary corporation, which is 80% owned by the parent, does not recognize any gain or loss on the distribution of property to its parent corporation, even if the property is transferred to satisfy a debt that is owed by the subsidiary to the parent company.

This non-recognition rule applies only to majority shareholders. The distribution of the property to the minority shareholders are treated like a non-liquidating distribution which means the minority stockholders must recognize gain but not loss on the distributed property.

The difference between the FMV of the asset received, and minority shareholder's basis in the stock generally results in a capital gain or (loss) to the minority shareholder.

Multiple Choice

REG 5-Q59

4. Consolidated tax returns

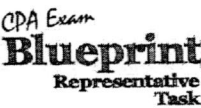

> Recall the requirements for filing a consolidated federal Form 1120 – U.S. Corporation Income Tax Return.

> Prepare a consolidated federal Form 1120 – U.S. Corporation Income Tax Return

> Calculate federal taxable income for a consolidated federal Form 1120 – U.S. Corporation Income Tax Return.

a. Taxation of Related Corporations
   1) Election to file consolidated returns
   An eligible group of affiliated corporations can elect to file a consolidated tax return. Consolidation has certain advantages, including allowing corporations to eliminate intercompany (I/C) profits and losses, allowing profitable corporations to offset its income against an affiliated company's losses, and allowing net capital losses of one corporation to offset the capital gains of another.

   Gains and losses on intercompany (I/C) sales are deferred until the assets are disposed outside of the group of affiliated companies. The gain or loss will be recognized at the time of the eventual disposition outside the consolidated firm, but the nature of the gain or loss is determined by the use of the property at the time of the I/C sale. I/C dividends are not taxable.

   Foreign corporations, exempt corporations, S corporations, and insurance companies are not eligible to consolidate.

   The election to consolidate must be unanimous, and once an affiliated group chooses to consolidate, it must do so in all future years. The election creates a joint and several tax liability among the consolidating entities.

   The members of the group must conform their tax years to the tax year utilized by the parent company. The parent adjusts the basis of the stock of the consolidated subsidiary for the allocable portion of income, losses, and dividends.

   Multiple Choice

   REG 5-Q60

   2) Affiliated Groups
   An affiliated group may elect to file a consolidated return.

   An affiliated group exists when one corporation owns 80% or more of the voting power of another corporation **and** holds shares representing at least 80% of the owned corporation's value. This test must be met on **every single day** of the tax year.

   Ownership is determined by examining the amount of voting stock as well as other classes of stock. To qualify as a parent corporation, a corporation must own 80% or more of each class of stock. Once a parent-subsidiary relationship exists, related corporations can be included in the affiliated group if the total ownership (including all corporations within the group) rises to 80% or more.

> **Example:**
> Pie Corp owns 85% of Square Corp
> Pie Corp owns 25% of Circle Corp
> Square Corp owns 75% of Circle Corp
> All other shares held by unrelated individuals.
> Pie and Square form an affiliated group. Therefore, Circle is also part of the group because in the aggregate, Pie and Square also own 80% or more of Circle stock.

3) Controlled Groups
   Controlled groups include parent-subsidiary corporations, brother-sister groups, and certain insurance companies.

   A controlled group of corporations is entitled to one $250,000 accumulated earnings tax credit and is limited to taxable income in each of the first two tax brackets as though the group were one corporation.

   A controlled group receives only one Section 179 expense deduction and one AMT exemption.

   The following tests are applied on the last day of the tax year to determine controlled group eligibility:
   i. Parent-Subsidiary
      Note that under GAAP, if a parent owns more 50% of the stock of a subsidiary, they must file consolidated financial statements. However, for tax purposes, a parent corporation may only elect to file consolidated returns if they own at least 80%-controlled subsidiaries.

      For the parent-subsidiary test, the focus is on corporate ownership. A parent-subsidiary controlled group exists if the parent company owns both 80% of the combined voting power and 80% of the total value of the corporate stock's total value.

   ii. Brother-Sister (two or more corporations where 5 or less people own more than 50% of the total ownership test, and 50% of the common stock ownership.

      Note that brother-sister controlled groups do not own stock in each other and therefore cannot elect to file a consolidated return.

      A brother-sister controlled group exists if two or more corporations are **owned by five or fewer individuals/estates/trusts** who own:
      - More than 50% of the total combined voting power of corporate stock
        And:
      - More than 50% of the total value of all shares of stock of each corporation (when looking at only the stock ownership of each person that is identical with respect to each corporation)

Multiple Choice

REG 5-Q61 through REG 5-Q63

5. Multijurisdictional tax issues (including consideration of local, state and international tax issues)

Define the general concept and rationale of nexus with respect to multijurisdictional transactions.

Identify situations that would create nexus for multijurisdictional transactions.

a. Jurisdiction to Tax
   1) Domestic vs. Foreign Corporations
   A domestic corporation is an entity that is incorporated in a particular state. A foreign corporation is an entity that was incorporated in another state.

   > **Example**: A Virginia-based corporation is a domestic corporation with respect to the state of Virginia. It is a foreign corporation with respect to other states, such as Maryland or Pennsylvania.

   The Supreme Court developed several tests to determine an entity's tax jurisdiction:
   1. The business activity must have substantial nexus in a state.
   2. The tax must be fairly apportioned.
   3. The tax cannot discriminate against interstate commerce.
   4. The tax must be fairly related to the services provided by the state.

   Nexus is the degree of the relationship that must exist between a state and a foreign corporation for the state to have the right to impose a tax. Nexus is determined on a year by year basis. It applies to the sale of tangible personal property. It does not apply to the sale of services or to the leasing or renting of property.

   The following activities are usually sufficient to establish nexus in a state if they occur within the state:
   - Approving and rejecting orders
   - Hiring and/or supervising employees other than sales staff
   - Installation that must be conducted and supervised
   - Maintenance of an office or a warehouse; if maintained by an independent contractor, this does not establish nexus
   - Providing maintenance or engineering services
   - Making repairs
   - Investigating creditworthiness or collecting delinquent accounts
   - Providing training for employees other than sales staff

   Nexus for taxing a corporation's income does not exist if the business's activity in a particular state is limited to:
   - Soliciting sales of tangible personal property that are approved and shipped outside the state
   - Advertising
   - Determining the reordering or resupply needs of customers
   - Furnishing automobiles to sales staff
   - To carry samples for display
   - Providing shipping information to the home office.

   > **Hint:** The rules defining what constitutes nexus vary greatly from state to state and are always changing. For the purposes of preparing for the exam, focus on understanding the concept of nexus, not necessarily the peculiarities of how each state determines whether or not a particular entity has nexus in that state.

Example: In its first year of business, all of the employees of a Virginia-based company are physically located in Virginia, and all of the company's sales are to Virginia customers. The company is a domestic company with respect to Virginia. Because of its physical presence in Virginia and because all of its operations and sales occur only in Virginia, the company has nexus only in Virginia. This means that the company only has to register to do business in Virginia and is only required to pay state taxes to the Commonwealth of VA.

In year two, the company decides to try to expand its sales to Maryland and DC customers by advertising in those states, but at the end of year two, all of the company's operations and sales were still all concentrated in Virginia. The company still only has nexus in Virginia.

In year three, in addition to advertising in MD and DC, the company registered to do business in MD and DC and hired three employees to be physically located and work in those states. The company generated 1/3 of its sales in those states. The company is now a foreign corporation with respect to MD and DC and a domestic corporation with respect to Virginia. The company also now has nexus in all three states – VA, MD, and DC.

Define the general concept and rationale of apportionment and allocation with respect to state and local taxation.

Calculate the apportionment percentage used in determining state taxable income.

    b. Multijurisdictional Tax Issues
        1) State and Local Taxation (SALT)
           States determine the taxation of taxpayers within their jurisdiction. There are numerous types of state and local taxes that can be applied, including sales, property, unemployment, incorporation, and excise taxes just to name a few.

          i. State Income Tax Computation
              To calculate a particular corporation's state income tax, the starting point is usually federal taxable income, which is then **increased** by certain adjustments (depending on the particular state);
- Dividends received deduction
- Expenses related to interest earned on US bonds
- State income taxes
- Depreciation that exceeds what is allowed by the state
- Municipal interest that is taxed for state purposes

The following adjustments are then applied which **decrease** federal taxable income (depending on the particular state);
- Federal income taxes paid
- Expenses related to municipal interest income
- Interest on US bonds
- Depreciation that is allowed by the state but not the federal government

        2) Uniform Division of Income for Tax Purposes (UDITPA)
           A model law known as the Uniform Division of Income for Tax Purposes (UDITPA) helps minimize differences among state income tax laws. The act was adopted by the National Conference of Commissioners on Uniform State Laws and the American Bar Association to promote uniformity in state allocation and apportionment rules.

The act provides that if the income-producing activity occurs in more than one state, the receipts should be assigned to the state where the greatest cost of performance occurred. Not all states have adopted the model act.

i. Apportioning Multi-State Business Income
UDITPA provides guidelines for apportioning income among states and foreign countries. For businesses, which operate in more than one state or country, the business categorizes income as either **business** or **non-business** and then apportions that income accordingly.

Non-business income generally includes:
- **Interest and dividend income**, which is allocated to the taxpayer's home state
- **Net rent and royalty income from real property** and **capital gains and losses on real property that is sold**, which is attributable to the state in which the property is in.
- **Net rent and royalty income from tangible personal property** are apportioned based on the extent to which the property was used within that state, if the company has nexus within the state. If the company does not have nexus within the state, net rent and royalty income from tangible personal property are allocated to the taxpayer's home state
- **Royalties from patents and copyrights** are apportioned based on the extent to which the property was used within that state. Otherwise, the royalties are allocated to the taxpayer's home state
- **Capital gains and losses on tangible personal property** that is sold are attributable to the state in which the property was in when the property was sold. Otherwise, gains and losses from the sale of tangible personal property are attributable to the taxpayer's home state.
- **Capital gains and losses on intangible personal property that is sold** is attributable to the taxpayer's home state.

> *Hint:* If investment income is generated by the regular operations of the company, this income is treated as business income and must be allocated appropriately among the states in which it was earned.

Business income is apportioned among all states where the corporation does business. Business income generally includes income which is generated by the regular operations of the business (referred to as the transaction test) or from the sale of property that is an integral part of the business (referred to as the functional test).

If more than one state has nexus to tax a business, the business's income must be apportioned among the states.

Business income must be apportioned among the states in which it was earned. This apportionment is usually based on **three factors: sales, payroll, and property**. To determine the amount of business income that is apportioned to a particular state, the company would calculate the sales, payroll and property factors and perform the following calculation:

$$\text{Business income for State M} = \frac{\text{Sales Factor} + \text{Payroll Factor} + \text{Property Factor}}{3}$$

In general, states have the discretion to apply different tax rules to different types of income. Some states use only one factor. Other states vary how the individual factors are weighted. Despite the many different method or factors used to apportion income among various states, the idea behind all of them is divide income logically among the states in which it was earned.

ii. Sales Factor
A business's sales income is apportioned based on the state which is the point of delivery of the sale. If the business doesn't have nexus in the state, the sale is apportioned to the state where the sale originated.

$$\text{Sales Factor} = \frac{\text{Total Sales to In-State Customers}}{\text{Total Sales (net of discounts and returns)}}$$

iii. Property Factor
The value of a business's property is apportioned based on the state in which the property is located. Property is only included in the apportionment if it is used in the production of business income.

Property for this purpose does not include cash. It does include real property and tangible personal property, which for this purpose is valued at cost or book value, depending on the state. Property also includes leased property, which is usually valued at the annual lease amount multiplied by 8. Intangible assets are usually excluded from the property factor under the standard formula, but some states specifically include intangible property.

$$\text{Property Factor} = \frac{\text{Avg. Cost of Real \& Tangible Pers. Prop Owned/Rented \& Located In-State}}{\text{Total Average Cost of All Such Property}}$$

iv. Payroll Factor
A business's compensation expenses are included in the payroll apportionment calculation only if they relate to the production of business income. Compensation for this purpose includes fringe benefits as well if they are taxable under federal law. Payments to independent contractors and amounts paid into 401(k) plans are usually not included in this calculation.

$$\text{Payroll Factor} = \frac{\text{Compensation Paid or Accrued to In-State Employees}}{\text{Total Compensation Paid or Accrued}}$$

> **Example:** During 2017, a Maryland corporation had $300,000 of business income generated from providing consulting services. $200,000 of those sales occurred in Maryland to Maryland customers. The remainder represented sales that occurred in Virginia to Virginia customers. It also had $15,000 of non-business income, comprised of interest income. The company had $50,000 in assets that were physically located in Maryland as of 12/31/2015. Three employees worked for the company. Two were located full-time in Maryland and had a total payroll of $60,000. The third employee was located full-time in Virginia and received $20,000 in payroll.

Assuming that both Maryland and Virginia use the standard three factors to apportion an entity's business income, how much of the company's total income, property and payroll expenses must be apportioned, and therefore reported, to each state for the 2017 tax year?

To determine how to apportion the business income, determine the apportionment based on the sales, property and payroll factors and then apply those factors to the company's total business income.

Maryland Apportionment:

MD Sales Factor	=	Total Sales to In-State Customers / Total Sales (net of discounts and returns)
	=	$200,000 / $300,000
	=	0.667
MD Property Factor	=	Avg. Cost of Real & Tangible Pers. Prop Owned/Rented & Located In-State / Total Average Cost of All Such Property
	=	$50,000 / $50,000
	=	1.00
MD Payroll Factor	=	Compensation Paid or Accrued to In-State Employees / Total Compensation Paid or Accrued
	=	$60,000 / $80,000
	=	0.75

Therefore, the apportionment factor for Maryland would be:
(0.667 + 1.00 + 0.75) / 3 = 83.33%

As a result, (83.33%)($300,000) = $250,000 of the company's business income would be taxed in the state of Maryland.

Since the corporation is based in Maryland, all $15,000 of the non-business income will be allocated to Maryland.

Therefore, the total income that should be reported to and taxed in Maryland for 2017 is $250,000 + $15,000 = $265,000

The remainder, $300,000-$250,000 = $50,000 should be reported to and taxed in Virginia.

Multiple Choice

REG 5-Q64 through REG 5-Q66

Explain the difference between a foreign branch and foreign subsidiary with respect to federal income taxation to a U.S. company.

A foreign branch gets a current U.S. deduction for foreign losses. A foreign subsidiary does not get a deduction for operating losses. A foreign branch can qualify for a foreign tax credit, if taxes are paid to other jurisdictions. A foreign subsidiary can get an indirect foreign tax credit when any profits from offshore businesses are sent back to the United States.

Explain how different types of foreign income are sourced in calculating the foreign tax credit for federal income tax purposes.

Recall payment sources to determine federal tax withholding requirements.

c. Taxation of Foreign Income
Treaties between the United States and other countries generally override domestic United States tax provisions and the specific tax provisions of the foreign country involved in the transaction. In other words, if a transaction takes place between a United States corporation and a foreign corporation, any applicable treaties between the US and that country will determine the tax treatment of the transaction, even if that treatment contradicts US tax law.

Foreign taxpayers are only taxed on income that is from a U.S. source. United States taxpayers are taxed on all worldwide income, regardless of the source. However, several deductions and credits are available (depending on the specific situation) that help to minimize double taxation of income by the U.S. and the foreign government.

1) Sourcing of Income and Deductions
Determining the source of income is critical for computing U.S. federal income tax. The IRS has the authority to change the allocation of income or deductions if it determines that the taxpayer's methods do not appropriately reflect the source of the income or deductions.

Earned income is sourced where it is earned, including any employee benefits that may be associated with that income.

Unearned income is considered to be from a foreign source if it is received from a foreign resident or if it is related to property used in a foreign country. Otherwise, it is considered to be U.S. sourced.

The source of income from the sale of (personal property) is determined based on the residence of the seller. A U.S. resident who sells personal property (regardless of where the sale takes place) should treat any resulting income as U.S. sourced.

There are two exceptions to this rule for income from the sale of:
- Inventory, which should be sourced where the title transfers.
- Depreciable property. Any recapture should be sourced where the depreciation was claimed. Any remaining gain should be sourced where the title transfers.

Income from the sale of **intangible property** should be sourced wherever the amortization expenses were claimed. Income that comes from the use of **tangible property** should be sourced where the property was used.

Income from the use, sale or exchange of **real property** should be sourced based on the location of the property.

Interest income is considered to be from a U.S. source if it received from the U.S. government, non-corporate U.S. residents, or a domestic corporation. However, if a U.S. corporation receives 80% or more of its active business income from foreign sources over the previous three years, any interest received from that corporation is considered to be from a foreign source.

Dividends from U.S. corporations are U.S. source. Dividends from a foreign corporation are foreign source. However, if the foreign corporation receives 25% or more of its gross income from a U.S business for the three preceding tax years, any dividends received from that corporation are considered to be from a U.S. source.

Deductions must also be allocated or apportioned based on their source.

2) Potential Double Taxation of Worldwide Income
As mentioned earlier, United States taxpayers are taxed on all worldwide income, regardless of the source. There are three provisions in place to mitigate the potential double taxation of income:
- Foreign taxes paid are allowable as itemized deductions for individual taxpayers and are deductible by C Corporations
- In lieu of the itemized deduction, taxpayers can claim a credit for foreign taxes paid

   i. Foreign Tax Credit
   The foreign tax credit is a credit allowed for foreign taxes paid. It is limited if the U.S. effective tax rate exceeds the foreign effective tax rate. In other words, the taxpayer cannot end up paying fewer taxes to a foreign government than he would have paid on that same income had the tax been levied by the U.S.

$$\text{Foreign tax credit limitation} = \text{U.S. tax on worldwide income} * \frac{\text{Foreign source taxable income}}{\text{Worldwide taxable income}}$$

Individuals must add any personal exemptions to their worldwide taxable income. Any excess foreign tax credits can be carried back one year and carried forward 10 years.

Individuals who have only passive income of $300 or less ($600 or less for joint returns) can elect to be exempt from the foreign tax credit limitation.

> **Example:** Virginia Corp earned $135,000 of U.S. source income and $95,000 of foreign source income. It paid $40,000 in foreign taxes and had a tax liability of $72,250 before the foreign tax credit. What amount of foreign tax credit can the company claim?
>
> The company can claim the lower of the $40,000 in foreign taxes paid or
>
> $$\text{Foreign tax credit limitation} = \text{U.S. tax on worldwide income} * \frac{\text{Foreign source taxable income}}{\text{Worldwide taxable income}}$$
>
> $$= \$72,250 * \frac{\$95,000}{\$135,000 + \$95,000}$$
>
> $$= \$29,842$$
>
> Therefore, the company can claim a foreign tax credit of $29,842.

ii. **Foreign Earned Income Exclusion**
To qualify for the foreign earned income exclusion, an individual must meet one of two tests. Only applies to Earned Income.
   1. During a continuous period that includes an entire tax year, an individual must be a bona fide resident of at least one foreign country.
   2. The individual must have a tax home in the foreign country and have been present in one or more foreign countries for at least 330 days during any 12 consecutive months.

If the taxpayer was present in a foreign country for at least 330 days, but less than the whole year, the exclusion is prorated based on the number of days the taxpayer was present in a foreign country.

Taxpayers must file an election to take the exclusion, which is binding for future tax years until it is revoked.

> **Example**: A U.S. taxpayer is a resident of Germany. In 2015, she received a salary of $130,000 and interest income of $35,000. She paid German income tax of $27,000 on the salary and $9,000 on the interest income. The interest income was from a German savings account. Her total U.S.-source earned income was $85,000, and U.S. tax liability on all worldwide income is $80,000
>
> If she elects to take the foreign tax credit, how much credit could she claim?
>
> Her maximum credit would be limited to the lower of the total taxes paid to Germany ($27,000 + $9,000 = $36,000) or the credit limit as calculated:
>
> $$= \$80,000 * \frac{(\$130,000 + \$35,000)}{(\$130,000 + \$35,000 + \$85,000)} = \$52,800$$
>
> Therefore, the maximum credit that can be taken is $36,000.
>
> If she elects to use the foreign earned income exclusion, how much of her income could she exclude if, after qualifying for the credit in a previous tax year, she lived in Germany for 310 days during the current tax year?
>
> The exclusion applies only to foreign earned income, so the interest income does not qualify for the exclusion. Her $130,000 salary from Germany plus her $85,000 U.S. income qualify for the exclusion, but the total cannot exceed ($101,300 * 310/365) or $86,035, so that is the income that she can exclude when filing her federal income taxes.

iii. **Foreign Currency Gains and Losses**
Foreign currency exchange gains and losses resulting from the normal course of business operations are ordinary gains and losses. The normal course of business is the buying and selling of goods and services. If they result from investment or non-business transactions, they are treated as capital gains and losses.

Multiple Choice

REG 5-Q67

Identify the federal filing requirements of cross border business investments.

The most common federal filing requirements for cross-border business investments are the following forms:
- Form 5471
- Form 8865
- Form 5472
- Form 926
- Form 8938
- FinCEN Form 114

Generally speaking, these are informational returns that must be filed with the IRS when transactions take place or a relationship exists between U.S. taxpayers or entities and foreign corporations and partnerships.

Form 5471:
- If a foreign corporation is a Controlled Foreign Corporation (CFC) for 30 consecutive days at any point during the tax year, every individual who owned 10% or more of the corporation's voting stock at any time during the year <u>and</u> who owns stock on the last day of its tax year must include in gross income the shareholder's pro rata share of the foreign corporation's Subpart F income for that year. In addition, the shareholder must report this amount on **Form 5471.**
- When any U.S. individual controls (i.e., owns more than 50% of the total vote or total value) a foreign corporation for at least 30 consecutive days during the shareholder's tax year, the shareholder must provide the IRS with information about the foreign corporation via **Form 5471**.
- Certain U.S. shareholders must report via Form 5471 the organization (or reorganization) or acquisition of stock in a foreign corporation.

Form 8865:
- Any U.S. partner that controls (i.e., directly or indirectly owns more than 50% interest in the partnership) a foreign partnership, must also provide certain information to the IRS. In this case, the partner must file Form 8865.
- The acquisition, disposal, or material change in the size of an interest in a foreign partnership must be reported on Form 8865 by any U.S. individual who controls a 10% or greater interest in the foreign partnership either before or after the transaction.
- Form 8865 must be filed by each U.S. person to report the transfer of property to a foreign partnership in certain tax-free exchanges or the distribution of property in complete liquidation to a non-U.S. person

Form 5472:
- A U.S. corporation which is 25% owned by one foreign person must file Form 5472 with the IRS to report transactions with related parties during the tax year.
- Similarly, any foreign corporation engaged in a U.S. trade or business must also file Form 5472 to report related party transactions that took place during the tax year.

Form 926:
- Form 926 must be filed by each U.S. person, domestic corporation and/or domestic estate/trust to report the transfer of property to a foreign corporation in certain tax-free exchanges or the distribution of property in complete liquidation to a non-U.S. person

Form 8938
- If a taxpayer has an interest in specified foreign financial assets which exceeds the applicable reporting threshold, that taxpayer must file Form 8938. Taxpayers with assets over the threshold must file Form 8938 even if the foreign assets have no effect on the taxpayer's tax liability for the year. One notable exception to this rule is the case in which no income tax return required. Taxpayers who are not required to file a tax return do not have to file Form 8938, even if the value of the specified foreign financial assets exceeds the appropriate reporting threshold.

FinCEN Form 114
- Taxpayers with a financial interest in or signature authority over a foreign financial account which exceeds certain thresholds may be required to report that account yearly to the Department of Treasury by electronically filing a Financial Crimes Enforcement Network (FinCEN) 114, Report of Foreign Bank and Financial Accounts (FBAR).

- Taxpayers are required to file an FBAR if:
    - The taxpayer is a United States person who had a financial interest in or signature authority over at least one financial account located outside of the United States; and
    - The aggregate value of all foreign financial accounts exceeded $10,000 at any time during the calendar year reported.
- A "United States person" includes U.S. citizens; U.S. residents; entities such as corporations, partnerships, or limited liability companies, created or organized in the United States or under the laws of the United States; and trusts or estates formed under the laws of the United States.
- A "foreign financial account" can include a bank account, brokerage account, mutual fund, trust, among others.
- Note that FinCEN Form 114 is <u>not filed</u> with the IRS. It must be filed directly with the office of Financial Crimes Enforcement Network (FinCEN), a bureau of the Department of the Treasury which is separate from the IRS.

Multiple Choice

REG 5-Q68

D. S Corporations

S corporations are so named because they are governed by Subchapter S of the IRC. S corporations follow, by default, the rules for C corporations. S corporations are similar to C corporations in that:
1. Shareholders are not liable for corporate debt
2. Shares can be freely transferred
3. A separation exists between ownership and management
4. When formed, they follow Section 351 rules like C Corporations

However, from a taxation perspective, S corporations are treated much more like partnerships. The S election allows an entity to avoid the double taxation imposed upon C corporations because, like partnerships, S corporations are not taxed at the entity level. Instead, income, loss, gain, deduction and credit items are passed through to shareholders, who are then taxed on these items at the individual level whether or not any distribution of cash or property is actually made. Any items that pass through as separately stated items retain their tax characteristics. Items that are not separately stated pass through from the S corporation to the shareholder as ordinary income or loss.

    a. Tax year
S corporations must generally use a calendar tax-year or adopt a fiscal year that aligns with the fiscal year used by shareholders owning more than 50% of the corporation.

While a calendar year is generally the default tax year for S corporations, an S corporation can elect a different fiscal year-end with IRS permission if there is a valid business reason

An S corporation may elect a different year-end so long as the election does not result in more than three months deferral. In this case, a deposit must be paid to the IRS to compensate for the deferral of benefits to shareholders if the income deferred exceeds $500.

    b. Reporting requirements
S corporations calculate taxable income in a manner similar to partnerships and report this income to the IRS on Form 1120S. S corporations report ordinary income and separately stated items for each shareholder on a Schedule K-1, regardless of whether any income was actually distributed to the shareholders.

    c. Accounting method
S corporations may use the cash basis of accounting as long as no shareholder is a tax shelter.

1. Eligibility and elections

Recall eligible shareholders for an S corporation for federal income tax purposes.

Not all entities can elect S corporation status. For an entity to be eligible for S corporation status, the shareholders themselves must be eligible. Specifically:
- Shareholders are limited to individuals, estates, certain qualified trusts and other such entities
  - Special stock voting trusts and qualified S trusts can be shareholders. In this case, all beneficiaries are qualified and electing shareholders.
  - Electing small business trusts and exempt entities are allowed as shareholders.
- Non-resident aliens, C corporations, and partnerships are **not** eligible.
- An S corporation can be a parent, but not a subsidiary, of any corporation except another S corporation.

Multiple Choice

REG 5-Q69

Recall S corporation eligibility requirements for federal income tax purposes.

To qualify for an S election, the corporation must be an eligible entity. Specifically:
- The entity must be incorporated.
- An S corporation can only have one class of stock outstanding. A few important special cases to consider and their effect on this requirement are:
    - If the S corporation has two or more separate types of stock which differ ONLY in voting rights, they are treated as one class of stock and are allowed.
    - Convertible debt is allowed unless and until it is converted into a second class of stock.
- An S corporation can have no more than 100 shareholders. In calculating the number of shareholders, keep in mind that:
    - Spouses and their estates are treated as a single shareholder.
    - All family members and estates can elect to be treated as a single shareholder.
    - Each benefactor of a shareholder trust is treated as a separate shareholder.
    - Co-owners of stock each count as one shareholder.
    - If a trust is considered to be owned by an individual, that individual is considered to be a shareholder.
- S corporations may own any amount of equity interest in a C corporation. However, the S corporation cannot file a consolidated return with an affiliated C corporation.
- S corporations may own a qualified subchapter S subsidiary (QSSS), which is a corporation that meets all requirements for Subchapter S status and is owned 100% by a parent S corporation. In this case the QSSS is not treated separately but is instead treated as part of the parent S corporation.
- Foreign corporations are **not eligible**.
- An existing C corporation cannot elect S corporation status if it has excessive amounts of passive income.

REG 5-Q70

Explain the procedures to make a valid S corporation election for federal income tax purposes.

Shareholders must make a qualifying election to obtain S status. **Unanimous consent** is required. All current shareholders and past shareholders for the current year up to the election date must consent for the election to be valid. In the case of stock which is jointly owned by spouses, both spouses must consent. Additionally, all eligibility requirements for S corporations must be met.

The election is valid for the current year if made on or before the 15th day of the third month (or March 15th for a calendar year entity).

In the initial year, the election must be made within 2 ½ months after starting the business.

> *Example:* A calendar year corporation is formed on February 1, 2016. To elect S corporation status for the 2016 tax year, the election must be made by April 15th 2016.

An election that is ineligible for the current year can still be valid for the next year if the issue causing the ineligibility (e.g. election deadline or unanimity) is corrected.

Once elected, the entity is treated as an S corporation until it elects to terminate its S corporation status.

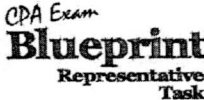

Identify situations in which S corporation status would be revoked or terminated for federal income tax purposes.

Termination of S corporation status can occur through various means. Note that regardless of the reason for the termination, once terminated, S corporation status generally cannot be elected without IRS permission for 5 years.

The S corporation status can be **voluntarily terminated** through a majority vote of all shareholders. If a prospective year is not specified as part of the revocation, the election is effective for the current year if made before the 15th day of the 3rd month of that year. If made after the 15th day of the third month, it is considered effective on day 1 of the following year.

If more than 50% of S corporation ownership changes, the new owners must affirm the S election.

> *Hint:* A unanimous vote is required to elect S corporation status, but only a simple majority is required to terminate S corporation status.

S corporation status can also be automatically **terminated involuntarily** if the entity violates any of the S corporation eligibility requirements. In this case, the termination is effective immediately on the date of the violation. The IRS can waive the termination if it was inadvertent. An involuntary termination caused by violation of eligibility requirements will cause the entity to convert from an S corporation to a C corporation, usually creating a short S corporation year and a short C corporation year.

Involuntary termination can also occur due to a special passive investment income limit which applies to S corporations that have E&P on their Balance Sheet from previous C corporation status. This limit requires that no more than 25% of gross receipts for three consecutive years can come from passive investments. In this case, the termination is effective on the first day of year 4.

2. Determination of ordinary business income (loss) and separately stated items

Calculate ordinary business income (loss) for an S corporation for federal income tax purposes.

Calculate separately stated items for an S corporation for federal income tax purposes.

Analyze components of S corporation income/deductions to determine classification as ordinary business income (loss) or separately stated items on federal Form 1120S – U.S. Income Tax Return for an S Corporation.

a. Calculating S corporation ordinary income and separately stated items
S corporations are treated similarly to partnerships in that they are pass-through entities. The S corporation is not itself taxed, but instead passes items of income, loss, etc. through to the individual shareholders. Even if income is not actually distributed to the shareholders, the shareholders are taxed on their pro-rata share of the S corporation's earnings.

Multiple Choice

REG 5-Q71

S corporation earnings or losses are reported to the IRS on Form 1120S, which must be filed by the 15th day of the third month after the close of the S corporation's tax year.

The S corporation must also report earnings or losses to shareholders through Schedule K-1. These forms list ordinary income as well as separately stated items. Each shareholder reports his/her distributive share of income consistent with the period in which the corporate stock was held. This distributive share of income allocated on a per-share, per-day basis to anyone who was a shareholder during the year.

All items of income, gain, loss, deduction or credit that must be separately stated because they have special tax characteristics or items that are specially allocated are removed from the S corporation's ordinary income or loss determination process.

Separately stated items are reported on any tax items that might be treated differently by any shareholder and therefore are reported separately to each shareholder. These items retain their tax characteristics as they are passed on to the shareholders. These items are reported to the shareholders on schedule K-1, which is given to each shareholder. The shareholders then report these items along with their other income and deduction items when filing their individual tax returns. Some common examples of separately stated items include:

- Dividend Income
- Charitable contributions
- Foreign income taxes
- Section 179 expenses
- Net income (loss) from rental real estate activity
- Section 1231 Gains/Losses (casualty or theft)
- Net Short-Term Capital Gains/Losses
- Interest expense on investment indebtedness

- Tax-exempt interest
- Royalty income
- Depletion
- Interest Income
- Net income (loss) from other rental activity
- Other Section 1231 Gains/Losses (casualty or theft)
- Net Long-Term Capital Gains/Losses
- Gains/Losses from sale of collectibles

All remaining items are lumped together to produce the S corporation's net ordinary income or loss which is also then proportionally reported to each shareholder.

- Ordinary business expenses including wages, rents, etc.
- Depreciation

- Amortization items (including amortization of start-up costs)
- Section 1245 and 1250 recapture

Multiple Choice

REG 5-Q72 through REG 5-Q75

Although they are technically corporations, S corporations receive unique tax treatment in several areas. S corporations are not entitled to most special corporate deductions (for example, the dividends received deduction), nor do S corporations pay special corporate taxes such as corporate AMT, PHC or accumulated earnings taxes.

S corporations, not shareholders, make most tax elections, including the election to amortize organization and start-up costs.

Employee-related expenses such as wages, insurance premiums and other fringe benefits paid by an S corporation are deductible as regular business expenses. When these expenses (which include health insurance and other fringe benefits) are incurred on behalf of a shareholder-employee who owns more than 2% of the S corporation, they are included in the shareholder's W-2 as income.

Shareholders who work for an S corporation are considered employees and are therefore subject to payroll taxes. The distributive share that is passed through to shareholders is not subject to self-employment taxes.

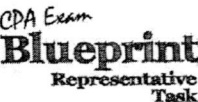

> **Analyze both the accumulated adjustment account and the other adjustments account of an S corporation for federal income tax purposes.**

> **Analyze the accumulated earnings and profits account of an S corporation that has been converted from a C corporation.**

Accumulated undistributed income generated while an entity has S corporation status is recorded at the corporate level in an accumulated adjustments account (AAA). The AAA tracks the cumulative total of undistributed net income items for S corporations (starting with tax years after 1982).

An AAA is adjusted in the same way as stock basis except that:
- No adjustment is made for tax-exempt income and related expenses. Another account, called the Other Adjustments Account (OAA) tracks the tax-exempt income and related expenses of the corporation.
- AAA can be negative. However, only losses can reduce AAA below zero. Distributions cannot create a deficit in AAA.

When distributions are made, they should be deducted in the following order:
1. Distributions are first made from the AAA. These distributions are tax-free to the extent of the AAA balance and represent reductions in stock basis. Remember that while losses can create a negative AAA balance, distributions cannot. Therefore, distributions can only reduce the AAA account to zero. If the AAA already has a zero or negative balance, this first step should be skipped.

2. Distributions from AAA and OAA reduce the adjusted basis of shareholder stock.
   Note that if multiple distributions occur throughout the year, a pro rata portion of each distribution is applied to the AAA.

   > **Example:** An S corporation had an AAA balance at year-end of $200. During the year, two distributions were made. The first distribution of $150 occurred on March 1st and the second distribution of $100 occurred on November 15th. Rather than deduct the distributions in chronological order, they must be treated on a pro-rata basis. Therefore, ($150/$250)*($200), or $120 of the first distribution came from AAA, with the remainder treated as a return of capital. ($100/$250)*($200), or $80 of the second distribution came from AAA with the remainder treated as a return of capital.

3. Next, distributions are made from the accumulated E&P account (AEP) and are treated as dividends until the AEP balance is exhausted.

   An S corporation will only have an AEP account if it has accumulated earnings and profits from a previous C corporation status. These amounts accumulated and were held in this account when the entity's status changed. However, since these amounts were never distributed to shareholders, they were never taxed to shareholders in that period.

   An S corporation that has always been an S corporation will not need to use an AEP unless and until the S election is terminated. In addition, an S corporation that was previously a C corporation will not need an AEP unless the corporation had E&Ps from this prior period.

4. Once AAA and (if it exists) AEP are exhausted, any additional distributions are considered to be made from the S corporation's stock basis (including the OAA and any paid-in capital) and represent a tax-free return of capital.

5. Any additional distributions are treated as capital gains to the shareholders.

> **Example:** At year-end, Mermaid Corp (an S corporation) has the following account balances: AAA: $200; E&P: $100; shareholder adjusted basis: $240. Mermaid Corp makes a distribution of $360 to its sole shareholder.
> - The first $200 is tax-free and comes from AAA and reduces stockholder basis.
> - The next $100 is treated as dividend income to the shareholder and comes from the E&P account (does not affect stockholder basis).
> - The final $60 is treated as a $40 return of capital, and $20 capital gain.
>
> Since the shareholder had an adjusted basis of $240, he recognizes two sources of income. The first is the $100 of dividend income. The second is a capital gain of $20, calculated as his $240 basis less $200 from AAA less $60 return of capital. Since basis can never dip below zero, the $20 is treated as a capital gain and the shareholder's resulting stock basis is $0.

3. Basis of shareholder's interest

CPA Exam Blueprint Representative Task
Calculate the shareholder's basis in S corporation stock for federal income tax purposes.
Analyze shareholder transactions with an S corporation to determine the impact on the shareholder's basis for federal income tax purposes.

Each S corporation shareholder has an adjusted basis in his S corporation stock that must be modified by contributions, income, distributions, and expenses.

Contributions of capital (cash and/or property) and S corporation income (including tax-exempt income) **increase** the shareholder's adjusted basis.

Multiple Choice

REG 5-Q76

If a shareholder contributes property with an attached liability and that liability is assumed by the S corporation, the shareholder will recognize a gain equal to the excess of liability assumed by S Corp over the basis of the property contributed.

Multiple Choice

REG 5-Q77

Distributions of capital (cash and/or property) and S corporation losses (including non-deductible expenses) **decrease** the shareholder's adjusted basis. Distributions of property should be applied to shareholder basis in this order:
1. Cash
2. Inventory and A/R
3. Other property

Shareholder basis is recalculated at year-end. Beginning basis is first increased by and income (including tax-exempt income), then any contributions of assets, and then decreases are applied, (distributions that are excluded from income, non-deductible expenses, and then deductible expenses and losses), remembering that basis can never fall below zero. In the case that distributions exceed the shareholder's adjusted basis in S corporation stock, the shareholder must recognize a gain on the excess. A shareholder can increase their basis by a debt owed to them by the S corporation.

Note that unlike a partnership, when an S corporation assumes debt, this debt assumption does not affect on the shareholder's basis since the shareholder is not personally liable for the S corporation's debt.

Multiple Choice
REG 5-Q78 through REG 5-Q83

4. Entity/owner transactions (including contributions, loans and distributions)

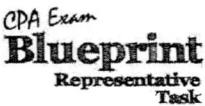

CPA Exam Blueprint Representative Task

Calculate the realized and recognized gain or loss to the shareholder of property contribution to an S corporation.

Calculate the allocation of S corporation income (loss) after the sale of a shareholder's share in the S corporation for federal income tax purposes.

Each shareholder reports income and separately stated items according to their ownership percentage of the stock in the S corporation and also the number of days of the year that the shareholder owned stock in the S corporation.

To calculate the shareholder's daily share of income when relative interests change during the tax year:

$$\frac{\text{S corporation's annual income and separately stated items}}{365} = \text{S corporation income (loss) per day}$$

S corporation income(loss) per day * # of days before the ownership % change * % ownership before change = Shareholder income before change

S corporation income or loss per day * # of days after the ownership % change * % ownership after change = Shareholder income after change

Shareholder income before change + Shareholder income after change = Total shareholder share of S corporation income

Example: An S corporation has ordinary income of $365,000, and there is a 365-day work year. The stockholder owned 60% of the stock before the change and held the stock for first 60 days of the year. The stockholder's ownership share decreased to 40% after the 60 days. The shareholder's income before and after the change is calculated as follows:

Shareholder basis before the change:

S corporation income (loss) per day	*	# of days before the ownership % change	*	% ownership before change	=	Shareholder income before change
$1,000	*	60	*	60%	=	$36,000

Shareholder basis after the change:

S corporation income or loss per day	*	# of days after the ownership % change	*	% ownership after change	=	Shareholder income after change
$1,000	*	305	*	40%	=	$122,000

The total shareholder share of S corporation income:

Shareholder income before change	+	Shareholder income after change	=	Total shareholder share of S corporation income
$36,000	+	$122,000	=	$158,000

Multiple Choice

REG 5-Q84

Hint: Contributions of property to an S corporation follow the same rules of C corporations under Section 351.

CPA Exam Blueprint Representative Task

Analyze the shareholder's impact of an S corporation's loss in excess of the shareholder's basis for federal income tax purposes.

The amount of shareholder losses related to an S corporation that can be deducted are limited in a number of ways.

Since the shareholder's adjusted basis can never decline below zero, the shareholder can only deduct losses up to his total adjusted basis in the S corporation.

Once the shareholder's adjusted stock basis is exhausted, if the shareholder has **debt basis**, additional losses can be deducted up to that amount. Debt basis is created when a shareholder loans his own funds to the S corporation or is personally responsible for S corporation debt. Only loans for which the shareholder is "at risk" can create debt basis for the shareholder. If the shareholder is not personally liable for the debt, it cannot be used to increase his debt basis in the S corporation.

Unused losses due to inadequate basis carry forward indefinitely until either the adjusted basis of the stock increases or the S election is revoked.

Later increases in basis (created, for example, by S corporation income (taxable as well as non-taxable), and shareholder contributions of capital) must first be used to restore debt basis up to its original amount. Once debt basis is restored, stock basis can begin to be restored.

> **Example:** Elijah owned 100% of an S corporation. At the beginning of the year, his adjusted basis in the S corporation was $25,000. During the year, the S corporation had $1,000 of ordinary income, a $3,000 long-term capital loss, and distributed $30,000 in cash to Elijah. What amount of this $30,000 distribution is taxable to Elijah?
>
> Elijah had $25,000 in basis and receives another $1,000 in basis for the S corporation's ordinary income, resulting in $26,000 in basis at year end. The distribution of $30,000 lowers Elijah's basis to $0, leaving $4,000 that must be taxed as a capital gain. The $3,000 capital loss is suspended indefinitely until Elijah has enough basis in the S corporation to deduct it.

The stock basis of the shareholder in an S corporation is **increased** by:
- All income items, whether taxable or not,
- Any additional contributions of assets, including cash.

The stock basis of the shareholder in an S corporation is **decreased** by:
- Distributions which are not part of gross income,
- All taxable losses and deductions,
- Nondeductible expenses that are not charged to capital. Non-deductible expenses on an S corporation and partnership return consist of expenses which were not deductible to arrive ordinary income (loss), but are reported on the schedule K and K-1. Guaranteed payments on a partnership return, do not reduce partner's basis.

> **Hint**: A shareholder cannot deduct a share of the ordinary loss on their individual tax return, unless it has basis before deduction the share of the ordinary loss. In other words, the loss that is deductible on Form 1040 is limited to the adjusted basis, before the loss deduction. Any ordinary loss that was not deductible on Form 1040 can be carried forward indefinitely or, until the taxpayer gets basis.

An S corporation shareholder's stock basis must be adjusted in the following order:
1) Increased for all income items, whether taxable or not.
2) Decreased for all distributions which are not part of gross income.
3) Decreased for capital items which are not deductible (withdrawal of assets).
4) Decreased for expenses and loss which are deductible or not, but losses and expenses cannot bring the adjusted basis of the taxpayer's stock below zero.

Deductions for S corporation losses can be further limited by the amount of the shareholder's at-risk basis and/or passive activity loss limitations. Remember that passive activity losses can be deducted only to the extent of the taxpayer's passive activity income. Income or losses from any S corporation in which If the shareholder does not materially participate will be considered passive. Also, any rental activity income or losses are always considered passive, unless the shareholder actively participates in the activity and owns 10% of the value of the S corporation's stock. In this case, up to $25,000 of rental losses can be deducted against non-passive income (for example, earned or portfolio income).

> **Analyze the federal income tax implication to the shareholders and the S corporation resulting from shareholder contributions and loans as well as S corporation distributions and loans to shareholders.**

a. Shareholder Contributions
The rules that govern contributions to an S corporation in exchange for corporate stock are the same as those that govern contributions to a C corporation.

S corporations do not recognize gain or loss on issuance of stock nor on the issuance of corporate debt.

Shareholders recognize no gain or loss when they contribute property to an S corporation in exchange for corporate stock so long as they are part of the control club (Section 351) immediately after the transaction and no boot is received. Instead, the shareholder's basis in the corporation is increased by the shareholder's basis in the contributed property. In the case where boot is received, a gain (but no loss) may be recognized by the shareholder.

When shareholders contribute property in exchange for corporate stock but are not part of the control club immediately after the transaction, the transaction is treated as a regular sale of property and the appropriate gain or loss would be recognized by the shareholder.

b. Shareholder Distributions
Distributions from an S corporation to a shareholder may trigger corporate gain, but usually represent a return of capital to the shareholder.

Distributions up to a shareholder's adjusted basis in the S corporation are treated as a return of capital. Any distributions in excess of the shareholder's adjusted basis must be treated as a gain (usually a capital gain).

Multiple Choice

REG 5-Q85

An S corporation can generate corporate gain by distributing appreciated property. This gain is then passed through to the shareholders similar to other S corporation income.

When an S corporation has no E&P, a distribution to shareholders creates gain to the shareholder if the distribution exceeds the shareholder's adjusted basis in the stock. The amount of the distribution is calculated as any cash plus the FMV of any distributed property. Distributions in excess of adjusted basis are taxed as gains from the sale of stock and usually treated as a capital gain since the stock will most likely be a capital asset in the hands of the shareholder. That is, an asset that was held for investment.

5. Built-in gains tax

> **Recall factors that cause a built-in gains tax to apply for federal income tax purposes.**

An S corporation, as a pass-through entity, generally is not taxed at the entity level. Some S corporations can, however, be subject to tax if the corporation sells property that contained a built-in gain at the time of the S election.

The built-in gains tax is **not imposed** on a corporation that has always been an S corporation. It only applies to entities that change their status from a C corporation to an S corporation. Additionally, the property must be sold after **5 years** from making the S election to avoid the S corporation from paying taxes on the gain at the highest corporate level (currently 35%); however, the income from the sale would flow-through and be taxed at the shareholder level. If the property is sold within 5 years, the S corporation would be required to calculate a corporate tax on the gain on the sale at the highest corporate rate.

> **New Exam Content:** Note that the time period for avoiding gain when sold used to be 10 years. For some time, it was temporarily reduced to 5 years, but this time period was permanently set to 5 years as part of the 2015 PATH act.

> **Example:** A C corporation elected S corporation status in 2010. In 2013, it sold property that had a built-in gain at the time of the S election. The S corporation must pay a built-in gain tax in 2010, when it became an S Corp. If the property was sold in 2014, which is within 5 years of the S election, there will be a tax on the gain on the sale to the S Corporation at the highest corporate level (currently 35%).

For the purposes of computing S corporation taxes, **built-in gain property** is property that has a fair value that exceeds its adjusted basis as of the beginning of the first year of the entity's S status. This property is also referred to as **appreciated property**.

Multiple Choice

> REG 5-Q86 through REG 5-Q88

The built-in gains tax is imposed at the highest corporate rate, which is currently 35%. The built-in gains tax is only imposed on property that was acquired before the S election, and the tax is imposed only on the built-in gain at the time of the S election.

The built-in gains tax is the lesser of the 35% of the built-in gain or 35% of the taxable income (ordinary income) of the S corporation.

If the built-in gain is due to a capital asset (or long-term capital gain), the built-in gains tax is treated as a capital loss to the shareholder and it reduces the built-in capital gain that occurred from the excess of the fair value of the asset over its adjusted basis, at the time the asset was transferred from the C Corporation to the S Corporation. The net amount reported by the shareholder is the recognized built-in gain if from a long-term capital asset less the built-in gains tax (which is treated as a long-term capital loss).

> **Example:** A C corporation elects S status. At the time of the election, the corporation owned an investment property with an adjusted basis of $50,000 and a FMV of $300,000, representing a built-in gain of $250,000.
>
> The corporation continued to hold the property for another 4 years, finally selling it for $375,000. In the year of the sale, the corporation had income of $500,000. The corporation itself will only be taxed on the built-in gain at the time of the S election ($250,000). And, also, it will be taxed on the gain from sale of the asset because the asset was sold within 5 years of the S election. Had the corporation's income in the year of the sale been $100,000, the corporation would have been taxed only on $100,000 of built-in gains. The remaining built-in gain is carried forward indefinitely to be taxed in a year when the corporation has eligible taxable income.

In the year of sale, if property is also sold that had built-in losses at the date of the S election, these built-in losses can offset the built-in gains.

In determining how these gains are passed through to the shareholders, the built-in gains tax paid by the S corporation is treated as a loss and is netted against the gain itself. The character of the gain and associated loss is determined by the character of the associated property.

> **Example:** Continuing the example from above, in the year of the sale, the corporation had income of $500,000 which included the built-in gain from the sale of investment property ($250,000). The S corporation, in the year it became an S Corp., pays a built-in gains tax equal to 35% times the lesser of the realized built-in gain of $250,000 or, the S corporation's taxable income of $500,000. This results in a built-in gains tax of $87,500 (35% x $250,000). Since the entire built-in gain of $250,000 was taxed in the year in the year of the sale, there is no suspended built-in gain to be taxed in future years. The $250,000 built-in gain deals with the transfer of a appreciated long-term capital asset. Therefore the built-in gain is a long-term capital gain. The associated built-in gains tax is treated as a long-term capital loss, which is netted against the built-in gain (long-term capital gain). This results in a net long-term capital gain of $162,500 ($250,000 - $87,500). The $162,500 passes through to the shareholders on K-1s.

> **Hint:** The built-in gain is calculated as an asset's FMV less its adjusted basis at the time the entity converts from C corp. to S corp. status. In the year of conversion, the S Corp pays a built-in gain equal to 35% x the lesser of the realized built-in gain or the S corp.'s taxable income. If the entire built-in gain is not taxed in the year of conversion, the remainder is suspended and taxed in future years when the S corp. has taxable income, until the entire suspended gain is exhausted. In these future years, take the suspended built-in gain and compare it to the taxable income for the respective year. The built-in gains tax is then equal to 35% x the lesser of the suspended built-in gain or the S corp.'s taxable income for that year.

6. Corporate reorganizations
    If a company is not solvent, it may want to reorganize, where the existing stockholders get stock in the acquired company in exchange for their stock that they presently own. If it is one of the 7 corporate reorganizations, there is no gain or loss to either the corporation or the stockholders of the corporation.

    a. Types of reorganizations
        1) Type A reorganization
            A **Type A** reorganization is a merger or consolidation under state law and sometimes referred to as a statutory merger. In this scenario, a Target Company exchanges its assets for

the Acquiring Company's stock. Once the Target Company dissolves, the shareholders of the Target Company now own Acquiring Company stock.

In a merger, the Target Company dissolves into another corporation, i.e., the Acquiring Corporation.

2) Type B reorganization
In a **Type B** reorganization, Target Company stock is acquired solely in exchange for the voting stock of Acquiring Company. Acquiring Company exchanges its own stock for stock in Target Company. Target Company remains in existence but is now owned by at least 80% of the Acquiring Company. Former Target company shareholders now own stock in Acquiring Company.

In a Type B reorganization, Acquiring Company must exchange its own voting stock, or that of its parent company, for stock in Target Company. Acquiring Company must own at least 80% of the stock of Target Company (voting and nonvoting stock) after the most recent stock acquisition.

3) Type C reorganization
In a **Type C** reorganization, "substantially all" of the assets of Target Company are acquired in exchange for voting stock in Acquiring Company. Essentially, Target Company is exchanging its assets for Acquiring Company stock. "**Substantially all assets**" is defined by the IRS as assets having a fair market value of at least 90% of the fair market value of all of Target Company's assets less liabilities AND at least 70% of the fair market value of all of Target Company's assets without regard to liabilities.

The stock that Acquiring Company transfers to Target Company can only be voting stock and must represent at least 80% of the consideration provided for the exchange. Other consideration provided (i.e., boot) cannot represent more than 20% of the total consideration given by Acquiring Company.

If liabilities are attached to Target Company's assets that are assumed by Acquiring Company, this liability relief is NOT considered boot.

Shareholders of Target Company own stock in Acquiring Company after the reorganization.

4) Type D reorganization
A Type D reorganization is a divisive, not acquisitive, reorganization in which the Parent Company divides by transferring assets to a Subsidiary Company in exchange for shares of the Subsidiary Company.

The Parent Company then distributes the Subsidiary Company shares to its shareholders (i.e., a spin-off), redeems Parent Company stock with Subsidiary Company stock (i.e., split-off), or liquidates into two new corporations (i.e., split-up). The main purpose is not for the reorganization to be an acquisition, but rather it used to divide a corporation.

In all events, the Parent Company must receive and distribute control (i.e., 80% of voting and all other classes of stock) of the Subsidiary Company in the exchange.

5) Other forms of reorganization
Type E is used for recapitalizations. For example, where bondholders exchange their old bonds for new bonds or stock.

Type F is used for nominal changes, such as name changes or changes in the state of incorporation.

Type G reorganizations are related to bankruptcy proceedings, where the former creditors often become owners in the corporation.

b. Additional requirements to qualify for tax-free treatment
In addition to meeting the specific reorganization rules defined for each type of reorganization, tax-free reorganizations must meet the following judicial principles:
- The transaction must be motivated by a valid business purpose.
- The continuity of business enterprise test must be passed. This test requires that the Acquiring Company must continue the historic business of the Target Company and must use a significant portion of the Target Company's assets in the continuing business of the Acquiring Company.
- The continuity of interest requirement must be met for the merger to qualify as a reorganization. This requires that a substantial amount of consideration given by Acquiring Company to Target Company must be Acquiring Company's stock. If 50% or more of the consideration given is made up of Acquiring Company's stock, the test is definitely met. The IRS has stated that 40% can be sufficient also in some circumstances.
- The step transaction doctrine permits multiple steps be collapsed into a single step when the steps are so interdependent that one step would not have occurred without the other. Collapsing the steps may lead to a tax result other than the result desired by the taxpayer.

c. Issues related to basis and deferral of gain and loss
Generally speaking, a reorganization does not require income to be recognized at the corporate level by either Target Company or the Acquiring Company.

1) Acquiring Company
In a corporate reorganization, the Acquiring Company does not recognize gain or loss on the transfer of its stock for ownership of the Target Company.

An exception occurs if the Acquiring Company distributes appreciated property in addition to stock. A distribution of appreciated property will trigger gain recognition for the Acquiring Company just as if the Acquiring Company had sold the assets.

2) Target Company
The Target Company generally does not recognize gain or loss as part of a corporate reorganization.

An exception occurs if the Target Company distributes appreciated property to its shareholders in connection with the acquisition. In this case, the Target Company will recognize gain as if the Target Company had sold the assets.

The Target Company takes on a basis for assets received in connection with the reorganization equal to:

Target Company basis in new assets = Basis in property to Target Company + Gain recognized by Target Company

> *Hint*: Whenever a corporation distributes appreciated property (i.e., property with a FMV that is greater than its adjusted basis), the corporation will recognize gain. This applies regardless of whether the distribution is related to a reorganization, redemption, or liquidation.

3) Shareholders
   No gain or loss is recognized by shareholders of either company involved in a tax-free reorganization if only stock is received in exchange for the Acquiring Company's property.

   If shareholders receive other property in addition to stock, this property is treated as boot and gain is recognized equal to the lower of:
   - Boot received
   - Realized Gain

   Any recognized gain will be treated as dividend income to the extent of the shareholder's proportionate share of the Target Company's E&P. Any remaining gain is treated as a capital gain.

   Basis to the shareholder in stock received is equal to:

   ```
        Basis in surrendered Target Company stock
   +    Recognized gain
   -    Boot received
   =    Shareholder basis in Acquiring Company stock
   ```

E. Partnerships

A business operated as a partnership is not taxed as a separate entity under tax laws. A partnership is a so-called pass-through entity in which the income and expenses of the business pass through to the partners, who then report these items as part of their individual tax returns.

Partnership income is taxed to each partner regardless of whether or not actual distributions of that income were made to the partners. Distributions, in turn, are treated as a return of the partner's capital.

A partnership is an association of two or more taxpayers created to operate a business with the objective of making a profit. Co-ownership and/or joint-use of property does not necessarily constitute a partnership. There must be an active conduct of business activity with the intent to earn and share profits.

1. Determination of ordinary business income (loss) and separately stated items

Calculate ordinary business income (loss) for a partnership for federal income tax purposes.
Calculate separately stated items for a partnership for federal income tax purposes.
Analyze components of partnership income/deductions to determine classification as ordinary business income (loss) or separately stated items on federal Form 1065 – U.S. Return of Partnership Income.

Items of income and expenses are allocated – or passed-through – from the partnership to the partners. Partners then include these items, known as their distributive share, on their individual tax return for the year that includes the partnership's year-end. The partners then modify the adjusted basis of their partnership for these allocations.

a. Allocation of partnership income
Profits and losses are allocated to each partner based on each partner's profit and loss sharing ratio as defined in the partnership agreement.

Special allocation agreements contained in the partnership agreement can stipulate a different allocation percentage for partnership income than partnership loss. Any special allocation agreement must pass a judgmental "substantial economic effect" test that ensures that partners with special allocations bear the economic burden or receive the economic benefit of the special allocation.

If no special allocation is provided in the partnership agreement, or if the allocation of an item does not meet the "substantial economic effect" test, then separately stated items and are distributed in the same proportion as income and loss.

b. Partnership income and separately-stated items
Partnerships themselves are pass-through entities and are therefore not subject to taxation. Partnerships are, however, required to file an informational return via Form 1065 to report taxable income to the IRS.

> *New Exam Content:* The Highway Trust Fund act directed the IRS to modify its regulations to allow a maximum extension of 6 months for Form 1065, effective for returns for tax years beginning after 12/31/15.

Partnerships must also report taxable income and separately stated items to the partnership on Schedule K, and each partner share of the items on Schedule K, are then reported to each partner on their Schedule K-1.

Measuring and reporting partnership income involves a two-step process:
1) All items of income, gain, loss, deduction or credit that must be separately stated because they have special tax characteristics or items that are specially allocated are removed from the partnership's ordinary income or loss determination process.

Separately stated items are any tax items that might be treated differently by each partner and therefore are reported separately (on the K-1s) to each partner. These items retain their tax characteristics as they are passed on to the partners. Some common examples include:

- Dividends
- Tax-exempt interest
- Charitable contributions
- Section 179 expenses
- Net income (loss) from rental real estate activity
- Royalty income
- Section 1231 Gains/Losses
- Interest Income
- Capital Gains/Losses
- Passive losses
- Investment Interest Expense
- Qualified dividends
- Tax-exempt interest income
- Foreign income taxes
- Interest expense on investment indebtedness
- Net income (loss) from other rental activity

2) All remaining items are lumped together to produce the partnership's net ordinary income or loss which is also then proportionally reported to each partner.

- Ordinary business expenses including wages, rents, etc.
- Depreciation (MACRS)
- Section 1245 and 1250 recapture
- Amortization items (including amortization of start-up costs and organization costs)
- Guaranteed payments to partners

Example: A partnership claims a Section 179 deduction for depreciated property purchased during the year on Sch. K. Should this deduction be stated separately on each partner's K-1? Yes. Section 179 expense is a separately stated item because the partner must combine Section 179 expenses passed through from the partnership with Section 179 expenses passed through from other businesses and the total cannot exceed the Section 179 annual limit.

Multiple Choice
REG 5-Q89

c. Self-employment tax on partnership income and guaranteed payments
A general partner's distributive share of partnership income is subject to self-employment tax. Limited partner's distributive share is generally not subject to self-employment tax.

Guaranteed payments, which are not considered a distributive share of income but rather payment for a service, is subject to self-employment tax for both general and limited partners.

d. Partnership start-up, organization, and syndication expenses
Similar to corporations, the first $5,000 of start-up and organizational costs can be expensed in the first year of operation up to $50,000 with remaining expenses able to be amortized over 180 months. Once the costs exceed $50,000, for every dollar over $50,000, the taxpayer loses $1 of the $5,000 immediate write-off in the first year.

Syndication expenses, which include any costs related to selling partnership interests, must be capitalized and cannot be amortized.

2. Basis of partner's interest and basis of assets contributed to the partnership

CPA Exam Blueprint Representative Task

> Calculate the partner's basis in the partnership for federal income tax purposes.

> Calculate the partnership's basis in assets contributed by the partner for federal income tax purposes.

> Analyze partner contributions to the partnership to determine the impact on the partner's basis for federal income tax purposes.

Each partner owns a "capital" interest and a "profits" interest in the partnership. The capital-sharing ratio represents each partner's share of partnership capital. Profit and loss sharing ratios determine each partner's share of the partnership's profits and losses. These interest percentages are determined and documented in the partnership agreement.

a. Contributions to a partnership
Contributions to a partnership in exchange for a partnership interest are usually not taxable events for either the partnership or the partners. No gain or loss is recognized by any party on contributions to a partnership, but the partners and the partnership are required to calculate a substituted basis for their partnership interest.

> *Hint:* The control club concept that is used for corporate contributions is not relevant for partnerships since partnerships are pass-through entities. Remember that the control club rule is the requirement that shareholders have 80% control immediately after the transaction in order to defer gain on contributions to a corporation.

No distinction is made between initial contributions to a partnership and later additional contributions. No deferral is available for contributions to a partnership that are made in exchange for any consideration other than an interest in the partnership. Deferral is only available when property is exchanged for partnership interest.

  1) Exceptions to the non-recognition rule
     - When a partner contributes **services in exchange for a partnership interest**, the value of the partnership interest received in exchange for partner services becomes the partner's adjusted basis in the partnership and the amount of compensation income that must be reported.

     > *Hint:* What the partner would normally charge for services is not relevant. The amount of income that must be reported and the partner's resulting partnership basis is solely based on the value of the partnership interest received by the partner in exchange for the services.

     > **Example:** The FMV of a partnership's assets equals $200,000, and a partner contributes services in exchange for a 10% interest in the partnership. Last week, the partner performed identical services for a client and charged $50,000. What is the partner's basis in the partnership?
     >
     > The partner's basis in the partnership is $20,000 ($200,000 * 10%). That same amount ($20,000) of ordinary income must be recognized by the taxpayer.

Multiple Choice

REG 5-Q90 through REG 5-Q93

- When a partner contributes property to a partnership that is subject to a liability and the resulting debt relief for the individual partner exceeds the partner's basis in the partnership, the excess of the % of the liability assumed by the other partners, over the adjusted basis of the property contributed is treated as a gain for the partner. The gain is generally capital in nature, but can be treated as ordinary income to the extent the property was subject to Section 1245 or Section 1250 depreciation recapture.

> **Example:** Upon formation of a partnership, Jackie contributes office furniture worth $15,000 and an adjusted basis of $3,000. She still owed $6,000 for the purchase of the furniture. This debt will be assumed by the partnership. In exchange for the furniture and the associated debt relief, Jackie will receive a 30% interest in the partnership. What if any gain will she recognize and what will her basis in the partnership be after the transaction?
>
> | | |
> |---|---:|
> | Jackie's Basis Before the Transaction | $0 |
> | Plus: adjusted basis of the contributed property | $3,000 |
> | Less: debt assumed by the partnership (70% x $6,000) | ($4,200) |
> | Jackie's Basis After the Transaction | $0 |
>
> As will be discussed in detail below, a partner's basis in a partnership can never fall below $0. Therefore, Jackie must recognize a gain equal to $1,200 on her property contribution ($3,000 - $4,200 = $1,200).

Multiple Choice

REG 5-Q94 through REG 5-Q97

b. Disposal of contributed property
Gain or loss on the disposition of property by the partnership is generally determined by how the partnership uses the asset. However, this is not always the case when the partnership disposes of property that was contributed to the partnership.

Property that had a built-in gain or loss at the time of its contribution to the partnership will be treated differently upon disposal by the partnership. **Built-in gain property** has a FMV that exceeds its adjusted basis at the time of contribution. **Built-in loss property** has a FMV lower than its adjusted basis at the time of contribution.

Built-in gains and losses are allocated back to the original contributing partner when the property is sold. Any gain or loss in excess of the built-in gain or loss is allocated among the individual partners as with any other asset.

The character of the built-in gain or loss is generally determined by the use of the property by the partnership with two exceptions:
1. Sales of contributed ordinary income or loss property (for example, inventory or A/R) generate ordinary income or loss to the contributing partner.
The characterization of income or loss as ordinary from the sale of **inventory** is limited to **five years** after the property was contributed to the partnership. There is **no time limit** for ordinary income characterization for **accounts receivable**.

If the above rule is met, all gain or loss on the sale is treated as ordinary. It is not limited to built-in gain or loss at the time of the contribution.

> *Hint:* There is no time limit on the allocation of the amount of built-in gain or loss from the sale of property. The time limit of five years applies to the **characterization** of these gains or losses as ordinary vs. capital.

> **Example:** Robert is a partner in a partnership and contributes to the partnership a capital asset which will be used as inventory. At the time of the contribution, the asset had a FMV of $20,000 and an adjusted basis of $25,000. The built-in loss at the time of contribution is $5,000. If the asset is sold within 5 years, the first $5,000 of recognized loss is allocated directly to Robert.
>
> For example, if the asset is sold three years later for $18,000, the recognized loss is $7,000($18,000-$25,000). $5,000 of this loss is allocated directly to Robert and treated as a capital loss. The remaining $2,000 is allocated among the partners. How the loss is characterized will depend on how the partnership used the asset. In this case, the asset was used as inventory, so the loss will be treated as an ordinary loss.

2. Sales of contributed capital assets with built-in capital losses generate capital losses to contributing partners if the gain or loss is realized within the 5 year period after the contribution. However, for built-in capital losses, the amount of loss that can be recharacterized as capital is limited to the build-in loss at the time of the contribution.

> **Example:** Partner A is an office-furniture salesman and a partner in Recruiting Partnership, a consulting firm. Partner A contributes a desk he was holding in inventory to the partnership to be used in the office (Section 1231 asset). The desk had a FMV of $200 and an adjusted basis of $60.
>
> If the partnership sells the desk within 5 years of the date of the contribution, any gain or loss up to the built-in gain or loss will be allocated to the asset and treated as an ordinary income or loss.
>
> For example, if the desk is sold 4 years later for $220. basis of $60, the $160 gain is Section 1231 gain. In both cases, the first $140 of gain ($200 less $60) is allocated to Partner A and the remaining $20 of gain is allocated between Partner A and the other partners based on the profit sharing ratios defined in the partnership agreement.

Multiple Choice
REG 5-Q98

c. Calculating outside and inside basis and holding period
Each partner calculates his personal adjusted basis (outside basis) in the partnership and the partnership calculates the adjusted basis of the assets held by the partnership (inside basis).

When a partner sells their interest in a partnership, the partner will compare the selling price of his interest to their basis in the partnership, which is known as the outside basis. If the partner does not keep track of their outside basis, the partner can use an alternate computation of their basis. The alternate computation is made up of the partner's capital account, plus the partner's share of liabilities (only recourse debt).

1) Partnership (Inside) Basis and Holding Period
The partnership takes a carryover **basis** for contributed property. In other words, the partnership takes on the adjusted basis that the contributor had in the property immediately before the contribution. The basis that the property, which is now owned by the partnership, is known as the partnership's inside basis. The inside basis of all contributed property is equal to the aggregate basis of assets transferred by in the partners to the partnership.

> **Example**: Assume Phil contributes an asset with a basis of $10,000 (this is the basis of the asset to Phil). If Phil transfers the asset to the partnership for a 20% interest in the partnership, the partnership will now have a basis in the contributed asset from Phil of $10,000. This basis to the partnership is known as the inside basis. The percentage that the partner receives in exchange for the asset transferred to the partnership is not relevant in the calculation of the inside basis.

Since the adjusted basis of contributed property carries over from the partner to the partnership, other tax attributes such as the asset **holding period** and the methods used for depreciation also continue unchanged.

2) Partner (outside) basis and holding period
Each partner would keep track of their basis by starting with their beginning basis in the partnership and increasing it for their share of all income items (both taxable and non-taxable), then reduce basis by any withdraws and distributions of assets, and then finally decreasing it for their share of loss items (limited to partner's basis). This amount is called the partner's outside basis.

The adjusted basis for partnership interests purchased from existing partners or interests received as gifts or inheritances are determined as they would be for other assets (cost or carryover basis, respectively).

The partner's **holding period** in the partnership interest includes the holding period of capital assets and Section 1231 assets that are contributed to the partnership. For other contributed assets, the holding period of the partner's interest starts when the partner contributes the asset.

> **Hint**:
> - The inside basis in the partnership is the basis of the property contributed by the partner to the partnership for an interest in the partnership.
> - The partner's outside basis is the partner's beginning basis in the partnership plus additional contributions and share of recourse debt, which is then adjusted each period by the partner's share of the partnership income, and the partner's withdrawals, and the losses (limited to basis). If a partner does not keep a record of his/her basis in the partnership (outside basis), an alternate computation can be used for basis. The alternate computation is the partner's capital account plus the partner's share of only recourse debt (e.g., debt that the partner is liable for). behalf of the partnership).

3) The partner's outside basis is adjusted in the following order
Beginning Basis
Partner's contribution of assets plus share of recourse debt
Partner's share of income, both taxable and tax-exempt income
(partner's distributions and withdrawals (not guaranteed payments))
(partner's share of non-deductible losses and expenses)
(partner's share of deductible losses)
The partner's interest can never be less than $0 (negative)

d. Partnership Income or Loss and Partner's Outside Basis
Partners must continually adjust their outside basis as a result of partnership transactions, including the deduction of their share of partnership losses.

The following transactions **increase** a partner's basis in the partnership, using outside basis:
- Contributions of property plus recourse debt
- The partner's proportionate share of income earned by the partnership, including capital gains and tax-exempt income

The following transactions **decrease** a partner's basis in the partnership, if using outside basis:
- Distributions from the partnership in the form of cash
- The adjusted basis of property distributions
- The partner's proportionate share of expenses, including deductions, losses, and non-deductible expenses. This does not include capital expenditures made by the partnership. Non-deductible expenses include all expenses that are not deducted to arrive at ordinary income(loss), but appear on the partner's K-1, except guaranteed payments.
- The partner's proportionate share of decreases in partnership liabilities, which are treated as a deemed distribution
- Any assumption by the partnership of a partner's individual liability (treated as if the partner received cash and used that cash to pay the liability)

> **Example:** A partner has basis in his partnership interest of $75. He receives a $90 cash distribution and is allocated a distributive share of ordinary partnership income of $5 and $20 of capital gain. How do these items affect the partner's outside basis in the partnership?
>
> | | |
> |---|---|
> | Starting Basis | $75 |
> | Increase for income items | $5 |
> | Increase for capital gain | $20 |
> | Decrease for distributions | ($90) |
> | Ending Basis | $10 |

> *Hint:* Withdrawals of capital, i.e., distributions, do not affect partnership income.

A partner's basis in a partnership **cannot be reduced below zero**. If the net change in a partner's adjusted basis due to debt being assumed by the partnership is greater than the partner's total basis of assets contributed, the partner must recognize a gain equal to that excess to prevent negative basis.

> **Example:** Jane has a 50% partnership interest in Tissue partnership. She contributes property to the partnership with an adjusted basis of $25, a FMV of $75 and associated liabilities of $60 which the partnership assumes. Because the liability assumed by the other partners is 50% of $60 or $30, which exceeds Jane's basis of $25, from the contribution of the property, Jane will recognize a capital gain of $5 and have basis in the partnership of zero ($25-$30).

Multiple Choice

REG 5-Q99 through REG 5-Q103

e. Loss Limitations
   Partners can only deduct losses if all three of the following hurdles are passed, in this order:
   1. The partner must have enough basis to deduct the loss
   2. Partners can deduct losses only to the extent of their at-risk basis. This amount is equal to the partner's adjusted basis plus the partner's share of recourse debt. Remember that nonrecourse liabilities are generally excluded from at-risk basis because the partner is not personally liable for nonrecourse debt.
   3. If the loss is passive, the partner can deduct the loss only to the extent of the partner's passive income. Note that a limited partner's losses are passive by definition. Passive

activities generally include any rental activities or any partnership or trade in which the partner does not materially participate.

> *Hint:* Remember that at least 10% of the value of the partnership interests must be owned by a partner (and spouse if applicable), in order to meet the criteria for the $25,000 exception for active participation in rental real estate activity.

Disallowed losses can be carried over indefinitely and can be used in future years when the remaining criteria are met.

> *Hint:* Passive income is not the same thing as portfolio income.

Multiple Choice
REG 5-Q104

3. Partnership and partner elections

Recall partner elections applicable to a partnership for federal income tax purposes.

Although partnership income and losses are not taxed at the partnership-level, but instead pass down to the partners, the partnership must make many of the elections as to the tax treatment of partnership items, which can differ from the methods used by the partners. Examples of elections that must be made by the partnership include accounting method, inventory accounting method, depreciation method and the election to expense depreciable assets under Section 179, election to amortize organizational costs, treatment of involuntary conversion gains/losses.

Multiple Choice
REG 5-Q105

a. Classification as a partnership
Under so-called check-the-box regulations, unincorporated entities may elect to be taxed as a corporation or a partnership. This choice is communicated to the IRS by the filing of Form 8832,

If an entity does not file this form, the IRS will classify the partnership according to default rules. The default entity is a partnership when the business has more than two owners. This default rule typically applies to partnerships and LLCs. If the entity does not prefer the default rule, it can elect to be taxed as a corporation.

b. Different types of partnership entities
In all partnership entities, income and losses are not taxed at the entity level, but are instead passed through to the partners where they are taxed as part of the individual taxpayer's return.
General Partnerships are partnerships in which two or more **general partners** each have joint and several liability for both the conduct and the liabilities of the partnership. General partners are assumed to actively participate in the management of the partnership.

Any general partner can be held responsible for partnership debt or malpractice judgments, whether or not that partner was personally involved in the malpractice or in incurring the liability. This liability can include taking possession of a general partner's personal assets by creditors to satisfy a partnership debt.

Limited Partnerships have at least one **general partner** and at least one **limited partner**. A general partner in a limited partnership is defined the same way as a general partner in a general partnership. A limited partner cannot actively participate in the daily operations of the partnership. However, a limited partner generally cannot be held responsible for any partnership liabilities (debt or malpractice) in excess of his capital contribution. Partnership losses are always passive losses to a limited partner.

Limited Liability Partnerships (LLPs) are formed when two or more partners form a partnership entity. An LLP is treated like a general partnership, except that LLP partners are not personally liable for the debts or obligations of the LLP. LLP partners are not responsible for damages resulting from the malpractice of other partners, but are still liable for damages resulting from their own malpractice. Firms that provide professional services such as accounting firms, law practices, and architecture firms are usually organized as LLPs.

Limited Liability Companies (LLCs) with two or more members are taxed as partnerships unless they elect to be taxed as a corporation (C Corp or S Corp). LLC owners are called members, and have the same limited liability treatment as limited partners in a limited partnership.

c. Partnership tax year
Since partnerships and partners may not necessarily have the same tax-year end, partners only report partnership income once the partnership closes its books at the end of the partnership tax year.

> **Example:** A partnership has a tax year end of July 31st. John is a partner who files his taxes on a calendar year basis. The partnership earned $44,000 for the fiscal year and an additional $10,000 from August 1 through December 31. If John is an equal partner with 3 other partners, he should report $11,000 of income from the partnership this year (25% of $44,000). John's share of partnership income earned from August through December will not be taxed until the partnership closes its books next year.

The required tax year is determined as follows:
- Partnerships must use the same year-end as its majority interest partner(s), that is, the partner(s) with more than 50% capital and profit and loss interest.
- If the majority owner(s) have no single year-end, the partnership uses the same year-end as ALL principal partners. A principal partner is a one with more than 5% profit and loss interest.

If the partnership does not want to use the required tax year, the partnership can elect a fiscal year end (with IRS permission) if there is a legitimate business purpose. A natural year-end can also be used. A **natural** business year is a year in which 25% or more of gross receipts occur in the last two months of the year. This test must be passed for three consecutive years to be considered a natural business year.

Under Section 444, partnerships may also elect to use a fiscal year end so long as the election does not result in a deferral period that is longer than three months. The **deferral period** is defined as the difference between the end of the elected fiscal year and the close of the year that would otherwise be required. A partnership that makes this election must pay a deposit to the IRS to compensate the government for the deferral of benefits to the partners (and therefore the postponement of tax payments), if the deferred benefit exceeds $500.

Multiple Choice

REG 5-Q106

d. Partnership accounting method
Generally, partnerships may use the cash basis of accounting. There are a few circumstances under which the cash basis is not allowed:
- No cash method can be used if inventories are necessary to clearly reflect income.
- No cash method can be used if the partnership is a "tax shelter" under any circumstances.
- No cash method can be used if at least one partner is a C corporation.

Hint: Any partnership (except a tax shelter) can use the cash method if it is a small business and does not have inventories for sale to companies. A small business is defined as one with average annual gross receipts at or under $5M for the prior three-year period ending with the current tax year. A small partnership with three-year average receipts under $1M can use the cash method even if it has inventories for sale to customers.

e. Partnership returns
Partnerships file Form 1065, which is an information return used to report the income, gains, losses, deductions, credits, etc., from the operation of a partnership.

4. Transactions between a partner and the partnership (including services performed by a partner and loans)

Calculate the tax implications of certain transactions between a partner and partnership (such as services performed by a partner or loans) for federal income tax purposes.

Analyze the tax implications of a partner transaction with the partnership (such as services performed by a partner or loans) to determine the impact on the partner's tax basis for federal income tax purposes.

a. Guaranteed payments
Partners are not employees of the partnership but might receive guaranteed payments for services rendered or for capital investments. Guaranteed payments are treated as payments to partners for services rendered and are not distributions of partnership income.

Guaranteed payments are treated as ordinary income to the recipient at the partnership's year-end. Guaranteed payments are considered to be paid on the last day of the partnership's tax year, regardless of when the payment is actually made to the partner. Guaranteed payments are also considered self-employment income.

A guaranteed payment to a partner does not have any **direct** effect on the partner's basis in the partnership interest because it is **not** a flow-through item, but instead a payment for services rendered. Guaranteed payments have an indirect impact on the basis of all partners in that they reduce partnership income and therefore reduce each partner's distributive share of such income.

Because the partner is not considered an employee, fringe benefit items that employees can exclude from gross income such as premiums for employer-provided health insurance or group term life insurance are not excluded from partner income. Any "employee" fringe benefits received by the partners are deductible by the partnership as guaranteed payments and should be reported by the partners as compensation income, and self-employment income.

Multiple Choice

REG 5-Q107

b. Related party rules
A partner may contract with a partnership at arm's length with "normal" consequences, but tax avoidance is strictly restricted.

1) Transactions with Controlling Partners
If a transaction involves a controlling partner (i.e., a partner or group that owns more than 50% of the partnership, directly and indirectly), special rules may apply. Constructive ownership rules apply in determining whether a transaction involves a controlling partner. As mentioned in the section on constructive ownership, a taxpayer's family includes siblings, spouse, ancestors and lineal descendants for this purpose. If the partner owns 50% directly, and his spouse owns 50%. Then the partner owns 50% directly, and another 50% indirectly through his spouse.

Losses on sales between a partnership and a partner who owns more than 50% interest in the partnership, either directly or indirectly, are disallowed. Gains are taxable. If later sold to a non-related party at a gain, the disallowed loss can reduce the gain.

> **Example:** A parent and three children are equal owners of a partnership. The partnership sells a building with an adjusted basis of $70,000 to one of the children for $50,000. No loss can be claimed since the purchaser constructively owns more than 50% of the partnership. If the purchaser later sells the building to an unrelated party for $85,000, he will only recognize a gain of $15,000. The $15,000 is determined by taking the $85,000 selling price minus the $50,000 basis in the building to arrive at gain of $35,000. The disallowed loss of ($20,000) will reduce the $35,000 gain to $15,000 recognized gain.

Sales of capital gain property by a controlling partner (i.e., a partner with a majority interest) will be deemed non-capital if the asset is not capital in the hands of the partnership. This rule also applies to sales between commonly controlled partnerships (i.e., brother-sister partnerships).

5. Impact of partnership liabilities on a partner's interest in a partnership

> **Calculate the impact of increases and decreases of partnership liabilities on a partner's basis for federal income tax purposes.**

> **Analyze the impact of partnership liabilities as they relate to the general partners and limited partners for federal income tax purposes.**

a. Recourse debt vs. non-recourse debt
Nonrecourse debt includes liabilities of the partnership in which the creditors of the partnership have no personal recourse against a partner if the debtor goes into default. Non-recourse liabilities are therefore generally excluded when calculating a partner's basis because the partner is not personally liable for nonrecourse debt.

Conversely, when a partnership takes on recourse debt, a creditor can hold the partner personally liable for the partnership's liabilities. For this reason, when a partnership takes on or disposes of recourse debt, the partner's basis in his partnership interest is directly affected.

b. Partner's share of partnership liabilities
A partner's basis in the partnership is **increased** by the partner's proportionate share of any **increases** in partnership liabilities (recourse debt), which are treated like a contribution from the partner.

A partner's basis in the partnership is also **increased** by any assumption of partnership debt (recourse debt) by the individual partner (treated as if the partner contributed cash and the partnership used that cash to pay the liability).

The partner's proportionate share of **decreases** in partnership liabilities (recourse debt), which are treated as a deemed distribution from the partnership, decrease a partner's basis in the partnership.

A partner's basis in the partnership is also **decreased** by any assumption by the partnership of a partner's individual liability (treated as if the partner received cash and used that cash to pay the liability). This only applies to recourse debt,

Multiple Choice

REG 5-Q108

6. Distribution of partnership assets

Calculate the realized and recognized gains (losses) by the partnership and partners of nonliquidating distributions from the partnership for federal income tax purposes.

Calculate the partner's basis of partnership assets received in a nonliquidating distribution for federal income tax purposes.

a. Partnership Gain/Loss Deferral
Partnerships generally do not recognize gain or loss on distributions, regardless of whether they are liquidating or non-liquidating, pro rata or non-pro rata.

b. **Pro Rata Non-Liquidating** (Current) Distributions
A pro rata non-liquidating or current distribution is a distribution to a continuing partner (including a draw by the partner) in accordance with the partner's ownership percentage. Current distributions do not terminate the partner's interest in the partnership. The basis of the property to the partner is the partnership's basis in the property.

Partners **can only recognize gain on non-liquidating distributions of cash which exceeds the partner's basis in the partnership.** No losses are allowed to the partner in a non-liquidating distribution.

Hot assets are inventory and unrealized receivables as defined under IRC Section 751. These are basically ordinary income-producing assets, such as accounts receivable not already recognized as income, and appreciated inventory (which is not a capital asset). Hot assets generate ordinary income, when the partner sells their interest in the partnership.

Multiple Choice

REG 5-Q109

Unrealized receivables generally are receivables of cash basis taxpayers.

Inventory is defined as any asset other than cash, capital assets or Section 1231 assets. Deemed distributions (decreases in liabilities) are treated as cash distributions. Distributions of marketable securities, up to the value of the securities less the partner's share of appreciation inherent in the securities, are treated as deemed distributions.

Multiple Choice

REG 5-Q110 through REG 5-Q111

Arm's length sales to partners are not considered distributions.

1) Effect on Basis and Holding Period
For partners, non-liquidating distributions are a return of capital that decrease outside basis and should be applied to outside basis in a specific order.
1. The partner's adjusted basis is first allocated to cash distributions and cash deemed distributed (such as a decrease in liabilities)
2. Next, the partner's adjusted basis is allocated to distributions of unrealized receivables and inventory in an amount equal to the partnership's basis in these assets.
3. Finally, the partner's adjusted basis is allocated to other assets distributed.

In a non-liquidating distribution, a partner's basis in non-cash property, when the partner receives cash and non-cash property, is calculated using the following steps:
1. Take the partner's beginning basis in the partnership.
2. Subtract any money distributed from the beginning basis, resulting in the remaining basis after subtracting the cash.
3. Compare the basis of the property to the partnership to the partner's basis in the partnership after the cash is withdrawn.
4. Take the lesser of the two(the partner's remaining basis in the partnership, or the basis of the property to the partnership), This amount is partner's basis in the property the partner receives, which is a reduction of the partner's basis in the partnership to arrive at the partner's ending basis in the partnership. The partner's basis cannot be less than zero.

Multiple Choice

REG 5-Q112 through REG 5-Q115

CPA Exam Blueprint Representative Task

Calculate the realized and recognized gains (losses) by the partnership and partners of liquidating distributions from the partnership for federal income tax purposes.

Calculate the partner's basis of partnership assets received in a liquidating distribution for federal income tax purposes.

c. Pro Rata Liquidating Distributions
A liquidating distribution occurs when the entire partnership is liquidated, or the interest of one partner is redeemed. The distribution can occur in one or multiple transfers.

Like non-liquidating distributions, partners can only recognize a gain on liquidating distributions if cash exceeds the partner's basis in the partnership. Similar to non-liquidating distributions, if a partner is relieved of a liability, it is treated as a cash distribution. A partner can recognize loss on liquidating distribution if the partner receives either cash, unrealized receivables, and or inventory. if these items received are less than basis.

Multiple Choice

REG 5-Q116 through REG 5-Q117

1) Effect on Basis
If cash and/or multiple properties are distributed in a liquidating distribution, the partner's basis for the partnership interest is allocated in the following order:
i. First, reduce the partner's basis in the partnership interest by any cash distributed, then the basis of the hot assets. After the cash and hot assets reduce the basis, any noncash property left in the partnership takes on the remaining partner's basis.

> **Example**: In a liquidating distribution, a partner receives $10,000 in cash, inventory with a FMV of $20,000 and an adjusted basis to the partnership of $12,000, and land with a FMV of $50,000 and an adjusted basis of $25,000. The land is used in a trade or business and held for more than one year. The partner's basis in the partnership was $25,000. What is the basis of these assets in the hands of the partner after the distribution is made and the partnership is dissolved?
>
> | | |
> |---|---:|
> | Partner's basis before liquidating distribution | $25,000 |
> | Cash | ($10,000) |
> | Inventory | ($12,000) |
> | Land (takes the basis of the remaining partner's interest to bring the partner's basis to zero) | ($3,000) |
> | BASIS IN PARTNERSHIP | $0 |

Cash and inventory items must be applied to the partner's basis first, leaving only $3,000 of basis left to be allocated to the land. Therefore, after the liquidating distribution, the partner's basis is $12,000 in the inventory and $3,000 in the land. The land's basis is merely adjusted down to equal the partner's remaining basis.

If the partner later sells the inventory for more than $12,000, he will recognize an ordinary gain. If he later sells the land for more than $3,000, he will recognize a capital gain, because the land is Section 1231 asset due the fact it was used in a trade or business and held for more than one year. A loss on a liquidating distribution is caused by the receipt of hot assets and cash that is less than the partner's basis in the partnership.

Multiple Choice

REG 5-Q118 through REG 5-Q123

7. Ownership changes

Recall the situations in which a partnership would be terminated for federal income tax purposes.

The partnership terminates for tax purposes if either occur:
- No part of the business continues to be carried on by any partner in the partnership form.

> **Example**: A 3 person partnership. Two partners sell their interest to the third partner. This transaction terminates the partnership for tax purposes because the partner no longer has more than one partner. It is now treated for tax purposes as a sole-proprietorship.

- The sale or exchange of at least 50% interest in both capital and profits occurs within a consecutive 12-month period. If the same partnership interest is sold twice in the same period, it is counted only once for this purpose.

> **Example**: A partner with a 30% stake in a partnership sells his interest to Jane who then sells it to Paul two months later. This only counts as a change in ownership of 30% of the partnership and therefore does not terminate the partnership.

Multiple Choice

REG 5-Q124

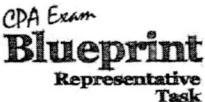

Calculate the allocation of partnership income (loss) after the sale of a partner's share in the partnership for federal income tax purposes.

The sale of a partnership interest usually results in a capital gain or loss for the partner. The gain is equal to the amount realized by the partner, less the partner's adjusted basis in the partnership.

During the year, if the ownership percentage changes in the partnership, the distributive shares of partnership income and expense must be allocated among partners appropriately.

The sale, exchange or liquidation of a partner's entire interest closes the partnership's tax year for that partner, but not for the other partners, nor for the partnership as a whole.

> **Example:** From January 1 through October 31, a cash-basis partnership had 4 equal partners and ordinary income to date for the current year of $15,000. On October 31st, one of the partners left the partnership and is replaced by a new partner.
>
> The old partner's portion of the year to date income of $15,000 is calculated as ($15,000/12)*10 months*25% = $3,125. At the end of the fiscal year, the new partner will be allocated his portion of any income earned from November 1st through December 31st.

The selling partner's amount realized includes the buyer's assumption of the selling partner's share of partnership liabilities.

> **Example:** A partner's adjusted basis in a partnership equals $40,000 (including a share of partnership liabilities of $25,000) and the partner sells his interest for $30,000 in cash and the new partner assumes the debt of the partner selling the interest.
>
> The partner received $30,000 in cash and rid himself of a $25,000 liability resulting in a total payment received of $55,000. This amount less his $40,000 basis in the partnership results in a capital gain of $15,000.

If a partnership has hot assets (unrealized receivables and inventory) at the time a partnership interest is sold, the selling partner must calculate the gain as either ordinary income or capital gain. The portion of the gain which is ordinary is the partner's percentage ownership in the hot assets, and any remaining gain is capital gain. allocate a portion of the sale proceeds to these assets and recognize ordinary income. Suppose that a cash basis partnership has a partner selling his interest for $100,000, and his basis is $40,000. This results in a gain of $60,000. If the partnership has unrealized receivables with a fair value of $30,000, and the partner selling owns a 30% interest. The amount of the gain that is ordinary is 30% of FMV of the unrealized receivables ($30,000) or $9,000. The balance of the gain of $51,000 is capital gain,

a. Withdrawal or Death of a Partner
When a partner dies or withdraws from the partnership, the partnership must compensate the partner for his basis in the partnership, plus a pro rata share of any partnership gain or loss up to the date of death or withdrawal. These payments to the partner or the partner's estate generally result in capital gain or loss to the retiring or deceased partner.

An exception to this rule occurs when payments are made from a partnership which is on a cash basis, but has unrealized receivables or inventory, known as hot assets. This will result in a portion of the gain being ordinary income.

Example: On September 30, 2015, a partner retires from a partnership. The partner's basis in the partnership was $95,000, comprised of $60,000 in capital assets and $35,000 in partnership liabilities. As a condition of leaving the partnership, the partner will receive $10,000 per month for 15 months, starting on October 1, 2015, and relief of the liabilities of $35,000. What gain should the partner report in 2015 and 2016 as a result of his departure from the partnership?

The partner should report income of $0 in 2015 and $90,000 in 2016.

In 2015, from October 1 through December 31, the partner receives 3 * $10,000 = $30,000 in cash payments plus $35,000 in relief of assumed liabilities. This reduces his basis by $95,000 – $65,000, or $30,000. Since the total receipts in 2015 are treated as a return of his basis in the partnership, $0 income is reported.

In 2016, the partner receives 12 * $10,000 or $120,000 in income. The first $30,000 is a return of basis with the remaining treated as income of $90,000.

Multiple Choice
REG 5-Q125

Calculate the revised basis of partnership assets when making a Section 754 election due to a transfer of a partnership interest for federal income tax purposes.

b. Section 754 election
When a partner sells his partnership interest, a partnership may make a Section 754 election. A Section 754 election attempts to make the <u>partnership's inside basis agree with that partner's tax basis (outside basis).</u>

When a partnership makes a Section 754 election, it is electing to adjust the **partnership's inside basis in partnership property** to more accurately reflect the gain or loss that occurred upon the sale of the partnership.

As a refresher, **inside basis** is the adjusted basis of an asset in the hands of the partnership. The partnership takes a carryover **basis** for any property or cash that is contributed to the partnership. In other words, the partnership takes on the adjusted basis that the contributor had in the property immediately before the contribution.

Example: Partner A contributes land with an adjusted basis of $75,000 to a partnership in exchange for a partnership interest. The partnership takes a carryover basis in the land, so the inside basis is now $75,000.

Outside basis is the partner's basis in the partnership interest. Each partner takes a substituted **basis** in the partnership interest from the assets contributed to the partnership.

Example: In the same example from above, Partner A contributes land with an adjusted basis of $75,000 to a partnership in exchange for a partnership interest. Partner A's outside basis in the partnership interest $75,000.

As illustrated in the example above, inside basis and outside basis are usually equal when a partnership is formed.

Example: Pip and Squeak form a partnership. Each contributes $50,000 to the partnership for a 50% stake. The partnership uses that money to purchase land worth $100,000. Since each partner contributed $50,000, each partner has an outside basis of $50,000. Since the partnership paid $100,000 for the land and each partner owns 50% of the partnership, the inside basis of the land is $100,000. The inside basis that is allocated to each partner, because they are equal partners is also $50,000.

	(Inside Basis)	Tax Basis (Outside Basis)	Partner's share of FMV of Partnership Assets
Pip	$50,000	$50,000	$100,000 x 50% = $50,000
Squeak	$50,000	$50,000	$100,000 x 50% = $50,000

When a partner sells his or her interest in a partnership, however, it can cause a disconnect between the purchasing partner's outside basis and the inside basis, which is the partnership's basis in the property.

Example: Continuing the example from above, a few years after forming the partnership, Squeak decides to sell his stake in the partnership. At this point, the land is now worth $150,000. Bubble purchases the 50% partnership interest for $75,000. Squeak recognizes a gain on the sale of $25,000, calculated as the $75,000 he received less the $50,000 outside basis he had in the partnership.

Bubble now has an outside basis in the partnership of $75,000 based on the price he paid for the partnership interest. If the partnership takes no action, Bubble will simply step into Squeak's shoes in terms of his outside basis. Squeak's inside basis in the partnership of $50,000 would simply be passed onto Bubble, and a discrepancy would arise between Bubble's outside basis, and the partnership's inside basis

	(Inside Basis)	Tax Basis (Outside Basis)	Partner's share of FMV of Partnership Assets
Pip	$50,000	$50,000	$150,000 x 50%=$75,000
~~Squeak~~ Bubble	$50,000	$75,000	$150,000 x 50%=$75,000

To avoid this disconnect between the purchaser's inside and outside basis, a partnership can make a Section 754 **election.** This election allows the partnership to increase or decrease their INSIDE BASIS to make it agree with that partner's OUTSIDE BASIS. The adjustment amount is equal to the difference between the basis of the purchaser's partnership interest ($75,000) over his share of the adjusted basis of partnership property ($50,000). In other words, the adjustment of $25,000 to the inside basis would make the inside basis equal to the outside basis, which is $75,000.

Example: Continuing the previous example, the partnership makes a Section 754 election at the time Squeak's partnership interest is sold.

Therefore, at the time of purchase, Bubble does NOT simply step into Squeak's shoes. Instead, the following basis adjustment is made:

$75,000   - $50,000   = $25,000
Purchase Price   -   Inside Basis   =   Section 754 Basis Adjustment

	Capital Account (Inside Basis)	Tax Basis (Outside Basis)
Pip	$50,000	$50,000
Bubble	$50,000 + **$25,000** = **$75,000**	$75,000

As a result, Bubble's inside and outside basis are in agreement.

Hint: If the partnership does not make the Section 754 election, the new partner steps into the old partner's shoes as far as their basis in the partnership. If the old partner had a basis of $50,000 in the partnership, the new partner would take on the same $50,000 basis. If the partnership DOES make the Section 754 election, the partnership will take on a basis in the partnership property of the FMV of the property contributed. Therefore, the FMV of the partnership's basis in the property would be $75,000. the FMV of the partnership's property.

Comprehensive Example: Alice and Betty form AB Partnership. Alice contributes $60,000 and receives a 60% share in the partnership. Betty contributes $40,000 and receives a 40% share in the partnership. The partnership purchases land for $100,000.

	Ownership %	Capital Account (Inside Basis)	Tax Basis (Outside Basis)	Partner's share of FMV of Partnership Assets
Alice	60%	$60,000	$60,000	$100,000 x 60% = $60,000
Betty	40%	$40,000	$40,000	$100,000 x 40% = $40,000

Two years later, the land still has a tax basis of $100,000 but a FMV of $200,000. In addition, the partnership has Accounts Receivable with a basis of $0 but a FMV of $25,000.

Partnership Assets	Tax Basis (Outside Basis)	FMV of Partnership Assets
A/R	$0	$25,000
Land	$100,000	$200,000
	$100,000	$225,000

	Partnership Assets	Capital Account (Inside Basis)	Tax Basis (Outside Basis)	Partner's share of FMV of Partnership Assets
Alice (60%)	A/R	(60%)($0) = $0	(60%)($0) = $0	(60%)($25,000) =$15,000
	Land	(60%)($100,000)= $60,000	(60%)($100,000)= $60,000	(60%)($200,000) =$120,000
		$60,000	$60,000	$135,000
Betty (40%)	A/R	(40%)($0) = $0	(40%)($0) = $0	(40%)($25,000) =$10,000
	Land	(40%)($100,000)= $40,000	(40%)($100,000)= $40,000	(40%)($200,000) =$80,000
		$40,000	$40,000	$90,000

At this point, Betty decides to sell her partnership interest to Carroll for $90,000, and the partnership makes a Section 754 election. Betty recognizes a gain of $50,000 on the sale and a Section 754 adjustment of the same amount must be applied:

$90,000	− $40,000	= **$50,000**
Purchase Price	− Selling Partner's Inside Basis	= Section 754 Basis Adjustment

		Capital Account (Inside Basis)	Tax Basis (Outside Basis)
Alice	A/R	$0	$0
	Land	$60,000	$60,000
~~Betty~~ Carroll	A/R	$0 + (40%)($25,000) = $10,000	(40%)($25,000) = $10,000
	Land	$40,000 + ($50,000 − $10,000) = $80,000	(40%)($200,000) = $80,000

In summary, the application of the Section 754 basis adjustment results in the following changes:
- Carroll's basis in partnership assets must be brought up by $50,000 ($90,000 − $40,000).
- Carroll's tax basis in the A/R should be increased by $10,000 ($25,000 × 40%)
- Carroll's tax basis in the land should be increased by $50,000 minus the $10,000 allocated to the A/R. Carroll's tax basis in the land is now $80,000.
- These two adjustments bring Carroll's basis in the partnership's assets in harmony with the amount he paid for his partnership interest:
    - $10,000 inside basis in A/R + $80,000 inside basis in land = inside basis $90,000
    - Purchase price (outside basis) of partnership interest = $90,000
- Note also that these adjustments do not affect Alice's basis in the partnership assets, which remains the same as it was prior to the sale of the partnership interest:
    - Alice still has $0 inside and outside basis in the A/R
    - Alice still has $60,000 inside and outside basis in the land

When the $25,000 of A/R is collected, income will be recognized as follows:
- Alice will recognize $15,000 income [($25,000 × 60%) − $0 basis].
- Carroll will recognize $0 income [($25,000 × 40%) − $10,000 basis].

The partnership decides to sell the land for $250,000. As a result, income is recognized as follows:
- Alice recognizes $90,000 income, computed as [($250,000 × 60%)] − $60,000 basis].
- Carroll recognizes $20,000 income, computed as [($250,000 × 40%)] − $80,000 basis].

The resulting capital account (inside basis) and tax basis (outside basis) totals for each partner after the A/R is collected and the land is sold are as follows:

	Partnership Assets	Capital Account (Inside Basis)	Tax Basis (Outside Basis)
Alice (60%)	A/R	$0+$15,000 gain = $15,000	$0+$15,000 gain = $15,000
	Land	$60,000+$90,000 gain = $150,000	$60,000+$90,000 gain = $150,000
		$165,000	$165,000
Betty (40%)	A/R	$10,000+$0 gain = $10,000	$10,000+$0 gain = $10,000
	Land	$80,000+$20,000 gain = $100,000	$80,000+$20,000 gain = $100,000
		$110,000	$110,000

Multiple Choice

REG 5-Q126 through REG 5-Q128

F. Limited Liability Companies

Recall the tax classification options for a limited liability company for federal income tax purposes.

Limited Liability Companies (LLCs) are technically not considered corporations. They are a hybrid of sorts, borrowing the limited liability of a corporation and the pass-through taxation treatment of a partnership. LLC owners are called members and have the same limited liability treatment as partners in an LLP.

However, note that partners in an LLP can participate actively in the management of the partnership. Members in an LLC can also actively participate in the management of the entity and still retain their limited liability.

LLCs with two or more members are taxed as partnerships and can file a Form 1065. Most LLCs can elect to be treated like a corporation for tax purposes. If they elect to be taxed as a corporation, they can be a C Corp and file Form 1120. They can instead elect to be like an S Corp, and file form 1120S.

A single member LLC is permitted and must file a Schedule C and compute self-employment tax.

Multiple Choice

REG 5-Q129

G. Trusts and Estates
  1. Types of trusts

Recall and explain the differences between simple and complex trusts for federal income tax purposes.

A trust is an entity that is created to allow a third party, or trustee, to hold assets on behalf of one or more beneficiaries. There are numerous different ways to structure a trust which specify exactly how and when the assets pass to the beneficiaries.

For taxation, the IRS divides trusts into two categories: simple and complex.
In a **simple trust**:
- All trust accounting income must be distributed to its beneficiaries annually
- No charitable contributions can be made from the trust
- No distributions of the trust principal, known as the corpus, can be made during the year

A simple trust can be **revocable** or **irrevocable**.

A revocable trust, known as a **living trust** or an **inter vivos** trust, allows the grantor to contribute assets into the trust throughout his lifetime. It also allows the grantor to make changes to the trust while he is living. The duration of a revocable trust is determined when the trust is created and can require the distribution of assets to the beneficiary during or after the trustor's lifetime.

The opposite of an inter vivos trust is a testamentary trust, which goes into effect upon the death of the grantor.

Unlike a revocable trust, which allows the grantor to change the terms of the trust and/or take the property back at any time, an irrevocable trust is a trust with terms and provisions that cannot be changed by the grantor.

A **complex trust** is simply any trust that cannot be classified as a simple trust. For example, a trust will be considered complex if it meets one or more of these conditions:
- Retains some current income within the trust.
- Provides for amounts to be set aside to be given as charitable gifts.
- Distributes monies allocated to the trust's corpus.

  2. Income and deductions

Calculate the total amount of income items reportable on a federal Form 1041 – U.S. Income Tax Return for Estates and Trusts.

Generally speaking, the gross income of an estate or trust is calculated in the same way as an individual taxpayer would calculate gross income. Income can be from various sources, including interest and dividend income, Schedule C income and loss, capital gains and losses, rents, royalties, income from partnerships, income from estates and trusts, farm income and loss, and other ordinary income.

Ordinary income can be distributed to the beneficiaries, who then pay taxes on the income, or it can stay inside the trust where it will be taxed. Capital gains and losses generally stay inside the trust until its expiration. A copy of the income section for Form 1041

	1	Interest income	1
	2a	Total ordinary dividends	2a
	b	Qualified dividends allocable to: (1) Beneficiaries _____ (2) Estate or trust _____	
Income	3	Business income or (loss). Attach Schedule C or C-EZ (Form 1040)	3
	4	Capital gain or (loss). Attach Schedule D (Form 1041)	4
	5	Rents, royalties, partnerships, other estates and trusts, etc. Attach Schedule E (Form 1040)	5
	6	Farm income or (loss). Attach Schedule F (Form 1040)	6
	7	Ordinary gain or (loss). Attach Form 4797	7
	8	Other income. List type and amount _____	8
	9	**Total income.** Combine lines 1, 2a, and 3 through 8 ▶	9

CPA Exam Blueprint Representative Task: Calculate the total amount of deductible expenses reportable on a federal Form 1041 – U.S. Income Tax Return for Estates and Trusts.

	10	Interest. Check if Form 4952 is attached ▶ ☐	10
	11	Taxes	11
	12	Fiduciary fees	12
	13	Charitable deduction (from Schedule A, line 7)	13
	14	Attorney, accountant, and return preparer fees	14
Deductions	15a	Other deductions **not** subject to the 2% floor (attach schedule)	15a
	b	Net operating loss deduction (see instructions)	15b
	c	Allowable miscellaneous itemized deductions subject to the 2% floor	15c
	16	Add lines 10 through 15c ▶	16
	17	Adjusted total income or (loss). Subtract line 16 from line 9 ... 17	
	18	Income distribution deduction (from Schedule B, line 15). Attach Schedules K-1 (Form 1041)	18
	19	Estate tax deduction including certain generation-skipping taxes (attach computation)	19
	20	Exemption	20
	21	Add lines 18 through 20 ▶	21

The deductions and credits available to trusts and estates are more or less the same deductions and credits allowed to individuals, such as deduction of business expenses or expenses incurred to manage income-producing property. Additionally, a deduction is allowed for all ordinary and necessary costs required administer the trust that would not have been incurred if the property were not held in the trust or estate.

Just as with individual taxpayers:
- Expenses incurred to produce tax-exempt income are not deductible.
- Capital losses can be used to offset capital gains and up to $3,000 of net capital losses are deductible per year. The remainder can be carried forward indefinitely.

a. 2% Miscellaneous Itemized Deductions
   The 2% miscellaneous deductions for an estate or trust are generally the same as those that would be allowed to an individual. However, some deductions that would be limited to the 2% floor for individuals are not subject to the floor when incurred by a trust. These include:
   - Tax return preparation costs not usually incurred by individuals
   - Investment advisory fees incurred by a non-grantor trust in excess of the amount that would be charged to an individual investor
   - Appraisal fees required to prepare tax returns or for the purposes of making distributions from the trust
   - Fiduciary expenses such as probate costs or publication costs for notices to creditors

b. Personal exemption
   A personal exemption is allowed and is calculated as follows:
   - Estates: $600
   - Simple trusts: $300
   - Complex trusts: $300 if required to distribute all annual income; $100 otherwise

c. Standard Deduction
   Estates and trusts are not permitted the option to take a standard deduction.

   Charitable Contributions
   Estates and complex trusts can make charitable contributions. These contributions are fully deductible so long as they are paid from income that is not tax-exempt. Charitable contributions that are made from tax-exempt income cannot be deducted.

d. Income Distribution Deduction
   The income distribution deduction is limited by the estate or trust's distributable net income (DNI). DNI is generally computed in the same way as the estate or trust's taxable income with some differences. The income distribution deduction will be **the lesser of**:
   - DNI
   - The amount actually distributed to beneficiaries

   To compute DNI, start with taxable income (gross income less deductions) and then:
   - Add back:
     - Personal exemption
     - Any deduction for distributions
     - Any net capital loss deductions
     - Any gain excluded on the sale of qualified small business stock
     - Tax exempt interest

     > *Hint:* In the case of a complex trust, tax-exempt interest can be included in DNI to the extent it is allocable to a charitable contribution.

   - Subtract:
     - Any extraordinary dividends and taxable stock dividends that are allocable to the corpus
     - Net capital gains that are allocable to the corpus

e. Net Operating Losses
   Trusts and estates are allowed the NOL deduction. The charitable deduction and deduction for distributions is disregarded when computing the trust or estate NOL.

Multiple Choice

REG 5-Q130

3. Determination of beneficiary's share of taxable income

Calculate the beneficiary's share of taxable income from a trust for federal income tax purposes.

Income received by a taxpayer from a trust must be included in gross income on the individual's tax return in the year it is received.

For a **simple trust**, the beneficiary is taxed on **the lower of**:
- The amount of trust income for the trust's tax year that is required to be distributed to the beneficiary (regardless of whether or not it is actually distributed)
- The beneficiary's proportionate share of the trust's DNI

The income that passes through retains all of its tax characteristics when reported by the beneficiary.
For a **complex trust**, the beneficiary is taxed on **the sum of**:
- The amount of income that is required to be distributed to the beneficiary (regardless of whether or not it is actually distributed). This amount would include any annuity that must be paid to the extent it is paid out of income for the current tax year.
- All other amounts that are properly paid (whether from income or principal, including income from in-kind property distributions.

The total amount of income reported by all beneficiaries cannot exceed the total of DNI of the trust or estate for the current tax year. To ensure this is the case, beneficiaries are divided into two tiers:
1. Tier 1: beneficiaries entitled to income that must be distributed currently (annually)
These beneficiaries report the amount of their current distributions, which, in the aggregate, total the amount of DNI for the tax year of the trust or estate without any charitable deduction. The result is that if the total of first-tier distributions is less than or equal to DNI without charitable deductions, each first-tier beneficiary reports his full share of the distributions. If the total of first-tier distributions exceeds DNI without charitable deductions, each beneficiary must compute his pro rata share of DNI and report that amount.
2. Tier 2: beneficiaries entitled to receive other "noncurrent" distributions
These beneficiaries report the amount of their second-tier distributions up to the trust's DNI after reducing it by first-tier distributions of current income. For this purpose, DNI is computed WITH an allowance of any charitable deduction. In other words, the maximum aggregate amount that all second-tier beneficiaries can report is DNI (including any charitable contribution deduction) less the total of first-tier distributions.
If the total of second-tier distributions is within this ceiling, each second-tier beneficiary reports the full amount of distributions he or she received. If it exceeds the ceiling, the second-tier beneficiaries must compute and report a pro rata share of the ceiling amount.

Multiple Choice

REG 5-Q131

a. Trust Filing Requirements
The fiduciary of a domestic decedent's estate, trust, or bankruptcy estate must file Form 1041 **by the 15th day of the 4th month** following the close of the tax year.

> *New Exam Content:* The Highway Trust Fund act directed the IRS to modify its regulations to allow a maximum extension of 5 ½ months for Form 1041, effective for returns for tax years beginning after 12/31/15.

H. Tax-Exempt Organizations
  1. Types of organizations

> Recall the different types of tax-exempt organizations for federal income tax purposes.

Tax-exempt organizations include charities, labor organizations, social clubs, pension and profit-sharing trusts, and private foundations among others.

Section 501(c) of the IRC designates which types of organizations can be granted tax-exempt status, and includes:

- 501(c)(1): Agencies organized under an Act of Congress which are federal and regulated, such as the FDIC or Federal Credit Unions
- 501(c)(2): Corporations which are organized to hold the title to property and collecting and remitting the corresponding income (less expenses) to an exempt organization; an example would include a corporation organized to hold the title to the buildings and land owned by a non-profit preschool
- 501(c)(3): Religious, charitable, scientific, literary and educational organizations, organizations testing for public safety, organizations that foster national or international amateur sports competition, those organized and operated for preventing cruelty to children or animals; examples include the Boy Scouts of America or the American Red Cross
- 501(c)(4): Civic leagues or organizations not organized for profit but operated exclusively for the promotion of social welfare, and local associations of employees the membership of which is limited to the employees of a designated person(s) in a particular municipality, and the net earnings of which are devoted exclusively to charitable, educational or recreational purposes; examples might include volunteer fire companies or homeowner's associations
- 501(c)(5): Labor, agricultural, or horticultural organizations; examples might include labor unions or flower societies
- 501(c)(6): Business leagues, chambers of commerce, real estate boards, boards of trade and professional football leagues; examples might include U.S. Chamber of Commerce or trade boards
- 501(c)(7): Social clubs or other entities organized for pleasure, recreation, and other non-profit purposes primarily supported by dues, fees, charges or other funds paid by their members; examples might include supper clubs, college fraternities or sororities, or country clubs
- 501(c)(8): Benefit societies, fraternal benefit societies or fraternal benefit orders; examples might include Knights of Columbus or the Royal Neighbors of America
- 501(c)(9): voluntary employees' beneficiary associations (VEBA) providing for the payment of life, sick, accident or other benefits to their members; an example is the United Auto Workers Retiree Medical Benefits Trust
- 501(c)(10): Domestic fraternal societies and associations, which devote its net earnings to charitable, fraternal and other specified purposes, but NOT to provide life, sickness, or accident benefits to its members;
- 501(c)(11): Teachers' retirement fund associations, which provide for the payment of teacher retirement benefits
- 501(c)(12): Benevolent life insurance associations, irrigation companies, telephone companies, etc., which have a mutually beneficial nature
- 501(c)(13): Cemetery companies or corporations chartered solely for the disposal of human bodies by burial or cremation
- 501(c)(14): State-chartered credit unions and mutual reserve funds
- 501(c)(15): Mutual insurance companies or associations which provide insurance to members substantially at cost
- 501(c)(16): Cooperative organizations to finance crop operations, also in conjunction with activities of marketing or purchasing associations
- 501(c)(17): Supplemental unemployment benefit trusts

- 501(c)(18): Employee funded pension trusts created before June 25, 1959
- 501(c)(19): Post or organization of past or present members of the armed forces; an example is the Veterans of Foreign Wars
- 501(d): Religious and apostolic associations which conduct business activities in a communal manner and where members include a portion of the organization's income in their gross income
- 501(e): Cooperative hospital service organizations which provide certain specified ancillary support services on a cooperative basis to two or more hospitals described in IRC 501(c)(3)
- 501(f): Amateur sports organizations that either conduct national or international sporting competitions or develop amateur athletes for national or international sporting competitions
- 501(k): Child care centers which provide child care, not in the child's home and which care for children while their parent or guardian is employed, seeking employment, or a full-time student

2. Obtaining and maintaining tax-exempt status

Recall the requirements to qualify as an IRC Section 501(c)(3) tax-exempt organization.

Section 501(c)(3) organizations are commonly referred to as "charitable organizations" and include religious, charitable, scientific, literary and educational organizations, organizations testing for public safety, organizations that foster national or international amateur sports competition, those organized and operated for preventing cruelty to children or animals.

To be eligible for tax-exempt status under Section 501(c)(3) of the IRC, an organization must:
- Be organized exclusively for exempt purposes outlined in Section 501(c)(3). In fact, the organization's articles of incorporation must explicitly limit the organization's activities to its tax-exempt purpose. This is referred to as the **organizational test**.
- Be operated exclusively for its exempt purpose by engaging only in activities that further its exempt purpose. If any meaningful part of the organization's activities does not further its exempt purpose, the organization will fail this **operational test**.
- Not be organized or operated for the benefit of private interests and none of its earnings may inure to any private shareholder or individual. This is referred to as the inurement test.
- The organization may not attempt to influence legislation as a substantial part of its activities nor may it participate in any campaign activity for or against political candidates. This is referred to as the **activities test**.

By default, Section 501(c)(3) organizations are treated as **private foundations** unless they prove to the IRS that they should be treated as a **public charity**.

a. Public Charities
Public charities include churches, educational organizations, hospitals or medical research organizations, and several other Section 501(c)(3) organizations.
There are certain advantages to classification as a public charity. Donors can exclude a larger amount of their donations when giving to a public charity. Also, public charities can attract support from both other public charities as well as private foundations.
To qualify for classification as a public charity, an organization must not only meet the tests described above (organizational, operational, inurement, and activities tests) but must also meet additional requirements.

More than 50% of a public charity's board of directors must be unrelated by blood, marriage, outside business co-ownership, nor compensated as employees of the organization. This requirement is meant to ensure that a majority of board members have an arms-length relationship with the organization.

Additionally, public charities must receive a significant amount of their revenue (33% minimum) from small donors who give less than 2% of the organization's income, from other public charities or the government.

b. Private Foundations
Section 501(c)(3) organizations that do not meet these requirements are automatically treated as private foundations. Private foundations are Section 501(c)(3) organizations other than churches, educational organizations, hospitals or medical research organizations, governmental units and publicly supported organizations.

Private foundation classification has several disadvantages:
- Donors can deduct a smaller amount of their contributions to private foundations as compared to public charities
- Private foundations must file Form 990-PF
- Private foundations must distribute a minimum of 5% of their assets annually

However, private foundations have more flexibility in terms of control. Private foundations can be controlled by related parties and, in some cases, even a single individual or family.

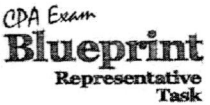

Summarize the federal filing and disclosure requirements to obtain tax-exempt status for an organization.

To qualify as an exempt organization, an organization must be specifically identified in the code and must operate exclusively for its tax-exempt purpose. To receive tax-exempt status, organizations must apply for and be granted an exemption by the IRS by filing Form 1023 within 15 months of organization.
Certain organizations do not need to file Form 1023 to receive tax-exempt status. These organizations include churches or organizations that meet the Section 501(c)(3) requirements and which have gross receipts totaling less than $5,000 annually.

Organizations with gross receipts totaling less than $50,000 annually and with assets totaling less than $250,000 can use Form 1023-EZ, which must be submitted electronically. Note that certain organizations such as churches, schools, hospitals, private foundations and foreign organizations cannot file Form 1023-EZ.

Summarize the annual federal filing and disclosure requirements for a tax-exempt organization.

Generally speaking, an exempt organization must file an informational return using Form 990 if its gross receipts exceed $50,000. This form reports the income, expenses and substantial contributors. It also must include the organization's lobbying and political expenditures.

> *Hint:* Certain organizations do not need to file Form 990. These organizations include churches, private foundations, federal agencies, and organizations with annual receipts under $50,000.

Most exempt organizations that are not required to file an informational return must still file an annual electronic notice (Form 990-N) with the IRS. This filing includes demographic information and justifies the continuing basis for the tax-exempt status. The exempt organization must also confirm that its annual gross receipts are still below the $50,000 threshold for filing a regular Form 990.

Form 990 must be filed on or before the 15th day of the 5th month after the close of the tax year. An automatic 3-month extension is available upon request.

> **New Exam Content:** The Highway Trust Fund act directed the IRS to modify its regulations to allow a maximum extension of 6 months for Form 990, effective for returns for tax years beginning after 12/31/15.

Form 990-EZ can be used unless gross receipts exceed $200,000 or the value of the organization's assets exceed $500,000.

> **Hint:** In summary, file:
> - Form 990 when annual revenue > $200,000
> - Form 990-EZ when annual revenue is between $50,000 and $200,000
> - Form 990-N e-postcard when annual revenue <$50,000

Private foundations must file Form 990-PF.
Most exempt organizations must make their last three years of tax returns and their tax-exempt application available to interested parties.

> **Hint:** Groups exempt from the electronic notice requirement include churches, state institutions and government units.

When an exempt organization has Unrelated Business Income for at least $1,000 (see below for more detail), it must file Form 990-T (whether or not Form 990 is also required).

Explain the requirements necessary for retaining tax-exempt status.

Exempt organizations must meet the filing requirements described above. Any organizations which do not make the required filings for three consecutive years will lose their tax-exempt status on the filing due date of the third missed year.

Explain the procedures and recall the time period required to obtain tax-exempt status once the status has been revoked.

The IRS automatically revokes tax-exempt status and publishes a list of organizations which have had their status revoked. An organization must apply to have its status reinstated, even if the organization was not originally required to file an application for exemption.

Generally, an organization can have its status retroactively reinstated if, within 15 months of revocation the organization:
- Submits Form 1023, Form 1023-EZ or Form 1024 as appropriate
- When necessary, provides a statement establishing that the organization had reasonable cause for its failure to file a required annual return for at least one of the three consecutive years in which it failed to file
- Files missed returns for all three years

In cases where the organization files to be reinstated after the 15-month period has passed, it can apply for reinstatement **effective from the postmark date of their application** if they complete and submit Form 1023, Form 1023-EZ or Form 1024 with the appropriate user fee.

3. Unrelated business income

| Calculate the unrelated business income for a tax-exempt organization for federal income tax purposes. |

Exempt organizations are still taxed on income generated by the organization that is unrelated to the organization's tax-exempt purpose. This income is called Unrelated Business Income or UBI.

To be considered UBI, income must:
- Be from a business regularly carried on by the organization
- Be unrelated to the exempt organization's tax-exempt purpose

Business is substantially related to the exempt organization's business purpose only if the activity contributes in an important way to the accomplishment of the exempt purpose of the organization.

Related business income which is therefore not subject to tax includes:
- Income from any activity where substantially all of the work is performed for no compensation
- Income from a business activity that is carried on for the convenience of students or members of a charitable, religious, or scientific organization (e.g., a college bookstore)
- Income from the sale of merchandise or stock received as contributions
- Investment income in general
- Rents from real property owned by the organization

Examples of UBI include:
- Income from debt-financed property that is unrelated to the organization's exempt function
- Income from advertising in journals or publications of the exempt organization

If UBI is $1,000 or more, the tax-exempt organization must file a Form 990T even if they are not required to file a Form 990. When calculating the taxable income from UBI, take the gross unrelated business income and subtract an exemption of $1,000, This is the Unrelated taxable income.

The unrelated taxable business income is taxed at regular corporate tax rates if the organization is a corporation. If the organization is a trust, the unrelated taxable business is taxed at trust tax rates. If UBI is lower than $1,000, no tax is assessed.

Multiple Choice

REG 5-Q132 through REG 5-Q135

Glossary: Federal Taxation for Entities

A

Accumulated earnings tax – tax imposed by the IRS if it determines that the corporation is trying to avoid paying dividends (and therefore helping its shareholders to avoid paying taxes on those dividends) by accumulating income in excess of reasonable business needs. Corporations can avoid this tax by either distributing income as dividends or by documenting the business reasons for accumulating income.

ACE adjustments – related to a C corporation's calculation of AMT and are required based on the recognition that the list of adjustments and preferences contained in the AMT formula is not all-inclusive. A positive ACE represents high pretax economic earnings. Therefore, a positive ACE increases AMTI and therefore can increase the company's AMT.

Affiliated group – exists when one corporation owns 80% or more of the voting power of another corporation **and** holds shares representing at least 80% of the owned corporation's value; this test must be met on **every single day** of the tax year

AMT preferences – increase taxable income, often represent economic income that is excluded from regular taxable income or deductions that are allowed when computing regular taxable income but which are not allowed when computing AMTI

B

Book income – income that is computed by applying GAAP to the corporations accounting records (i.e., its **books**) and communicated to the shareholders in the financial statements.

Boot – unlike property received in a transaction. Examples include the receipt of cash and non-qualified preferred stock in exchange for corporate stock.

Built-in gain property – property that has a value that exceeds its adjusted basis as of the beginning of the first year of the entity's S status. This property is also referred to as **appreciated property**

C

C corporations – so called because the rules governing corporate taxes are contained in Subchapter C of the IRC. Unlike partnerships, S corporations, or sole proprietorships, C corporations are subject to corporate income tax at the entity level.

Closely held – a corporation is if at any time during the last half of the taxable year more than 50% of the value of the corporation's outstanding shares is owned either directly or indirectly by five or fewer individuals.

Complex trust – any trust that cannot be classified as a simple trust. For example, a trust will be considered complex if it retains some current income within the trust, provides for amounts to be set aside to be given as charitable gifts, or distributes monies allocated to the trust's corpus

Constructive – (or indirect) ownership of stock is determined through stock attribution rules.

Constructive dividends – payments to shareholders that are not formally declared as dividends. Property distributions to shareholders are often treated as constructive dividends.

Controlled Foreign Corporation (CFC) – any foreign corporation for which more than 50% of the voting power or stock value is owned by U.S. shareholders on any day of the foreign corporation's tax year. For this purpose, **U.S. shareholders** are limited to those who directly or indirectly own 10% or more of combined voting power of the foreign corporation.

Controlled groups – parent-subsidiary corporations, brother-sister groups, and certain insurance companies.

D

E

F

G

General partnerships – partnerships in which two or more **general partners** each have joint and several liability for both the conduct and the liabilities of the partnership. General partners are assumed to actively participate in the management of the partnership.

Guaranteed payments – payment to partners for services rendered or for capital investments. Guaranteed payments are not considered distributions of partnership income, but are instead treated as ordinary income to the recipient.

H
Hot assets – inventory and unrealized receivables as defined under IRC Section 751. These are basically ordinary income producing assets, such as accounts receivable not already recognized as income, LIFO reserves, appreciated inventory, and depreciation recapture. Hot assets generate ordinary income or loss because the partner has not yet been taxed on accrued but unrealized income. For distributions, inventory has to be **substantially appreciated** (that is, the FMV of the asset has to exceed 120% of its adjusted basis) for it to be classified as a hot asset.

I
Inside basis – the aggregate basis of assets in the hands of the partnership
Inventory – defined as any asset other than cash, capital assets or Section 1231 assets.

J
K
L
Limited Liability Companies (LLCs) – two or more members are taxed as partnerships unless they elect to be taxed as a corporation. LLC partners are called members and have the same limited liability treatment as partners in an LLP.

Limited Liability Partnerships (LLPs) – formed when two or more limited partners form a partnership entity. There is no requirement that an LLP have a general partner. LLP partners are not responsible for damages resulting from the malpractice of other partners, but are still liable for damages resulting from their own malpractice. Firms that provide professional services such as accounting firms, law practices, and architecture firms are usually organized as LLPs.

Limited partner – partner that cannot actively participate in the daily operations of the partnership. However, a limited partner generally cannot be held responsible for any partnership liabilities (debt or malpractice) in excess of his capital contribution. Partnership losses are always passive losses to a limited partner.

Limited partnerships – at least one **general partner** and at least one **limited partner**. A general partner in a limited partnership is defined the same way as a general partner in a general partnership.

Liquidating distribution – a distribution from an entity to a shareholder that occurs in connection with the complete dissolution of the entity.

Liquidations – when a corporation completely dissolves and distributes all of its remaining assets. This is similar to a stock redemption in that shareholders receive assets in exchange for canceling their shares of stock.

M
N
Natural business year – one in which 25% of the entity's gross receipts occur in the last two months of the year for three consecutive years.

Net operating loss (NOL) – the excess of an entity's business deductions over its gross income during a particular tax year. A deduction is then allowed for this loss in other tax years when the entity's gross income exceeds its allowable business deductions.

Nexus – the degree of the relationship that must exist between a state and a foreign corporation for the state to have the right to impose a tax. Nexus is determined on a year by year basis.

Non-liquidating distribution – a regular distribution of cash or property to an entity's shareholders that is not associated with the termination (liquidation) of the entity.

Nonrecourse debt – liabilities of the partnership in which the creditors of the partnership have no personal recourse against a partner if the debtor goes into default. Non-recourse liabilities are therefore generally excluded when calculating a partner's basis because the partner is not personally liable for nonrecourse debt

O
Outside basis – equal to the adjusted basis of each partner's interest in a partnership.

P
Partial liquidations are treated as a sale by non-corporate shareholders. Partial liquidations are contractions of the corporation's business. The determination as to whether the transaction qualifies as for redemption treatment is made by looking for a contraction at the corporate level.

Permanent differences – in the context of reconciling book income to taxable income, arise from income items that are never taxable or expense items that are never deductible.

Personal holding company (PHC) tax is a penalty tax that is triggered by relatively high levels of investment income in a corporation. Like the Accumulated Earnings Tax, it imposes a penalty on undistributed income. The PHC tax can be avoided by keeping corporate investment levels low or distributing investment income to shareholders as dividends.

Personal service corporation – an incorporated service business with more than 10% of stock owned by shareholder-employees Principal partner

Private foundations – any Section 501(c)(3) organization that does not substantiate to the IRS that it should be treated as a **public charity**.

Public charities – churches, educational organizations, hospitals or medical research organizations, and several other Section 501(c)(3) organizations.

Q

R

Recourse debt – a creditor can hold the partner personally liable for the partnership's liabilities. For this reason, when a partnership takes on or disposes of recourse debt, the partner's basis in his partnership interest is directly affected.

Redemption of stock – when a corporation repurchases stock from shareholders. It is generally treated by the shareholder as a sale of stock that will trigger recognition of gain or loss by the shareholder.

S

S corporations – so named because they are governed by Subchapter S of the IRC. S corporations follow, by default, the rules for C corporations however they are pass-through entities and in this way are treated more like partnerships for taxation purposes.

Section 501(c)(3) organizations – commonly referred to as "charitable organizations" and include religious, charitable, scientific, literary and educational organizations, organizations testing for public safety, organizations that foster national or international amateur sports competition, those organized and operated for preventing cruelty to children or animals

Separately stated items – any tax items that might be treated differently by any shareholder and therefore are reported separately to each shareholder. These items retain their tax characteristics as they are passed on to the shareholders. The shareholders then report these items along with their other income and deduction items when filing their individual tax returns.

Simple trust – all trust accounting income must be distributed to its beneficiaries annually, no charitable contributions can be made from the trust, no distributions of the trust principal, known as the corpus, can be made during the year.

Sole proprietorship – the business and its owner are essentially one in the same from a taxation and legal perspective.

T

Taxable income – income that is used to compute a taxpayer's income tax liability.

Temporary differences – the context of reconciling book income to taxable income arise when GAAP rules dictate that income and expense to be recognized in one period, but tax accounting rules dictate that they be recognized in another period. Temporary differences will smooth out over time.

U

Uniform Division of Income for Tax Purposes (UDIPTA) – a model law that aims to minimize differences among state income tax laws. The act was adopted by the National Conference of Commissioners on Uniform State Laws and the American Bar Association to promote uniformity in state allocation and apportionment rules.

Unrealized receivables – generally are receivables of cash basis taxpayers. Potential Section 1245 and Section 1250 recapture are also included as an unrealized receivable.

Unrelated business income (UBI) – income that is generated by a tax-exempt organization through business regularly carried on by the organization but which is unrelated to the exempt organization's tax exempt purpose.

V

W

X

Y

Z

This page is intentionally left blank.

Multiple Choice – Questions

REG 5-Q1 R147. Quigley, Roberk, and Storm form a corporation. Quigley exchanges $25,000 of legal fees for 30 shares of stock. Roberk exchanges land with a basis of $10,000 and a fair market value of $100,000 for 60 shares of stock. Storm exchanges $10,000 cash for 10 shares of stock. What amount of income should each shareholder recognize?

	Quigley	Roberk	Storm
A.	$0	$0	$0
B.	$25,000	$90,000	$0
C.	$25,000	$90,000	$10,000
D.	$0	$90,000	$0

REG 5-Q2 R580. What type of business organization may generally be formed without filing an organizational document or certificate with a state government agency or office?

A. Corporation.
B. Limited liability Company.
C. A general partnership.
D. A limited partnership.

REG 5-Q3 R577. Berry, Drake, and Flanigan are partners in a general partnership. The partners made capital contributions as follows: Berry, $150,000; Drake, $100,000; and Flanigan, $50,000. Drake made a loan of $50,000 to the partnership. The partnership agreement specifies that Flanigan will receive a 50% share of profits, and Drake and Berry each will receive a 25% share of profits. Under the Revised Uniform Partnership Act and in the absence of any partnership agreement to the contrary, which of the following statements is correct regarding the sharing of losses?

A. The partners will share equally in any partnership losses.
B. The partners will share in losses on a pro rata basis according to the capital contributions.
C. The partners will share in losses on a pro rata basis according to the capital contributions and loans made to the partnership.
D. The partners will share in losses according to the allocation of profits specified in the partnership agreement.

REG 5-Q4 R583. Wilson and Thomas are partners. Wilson contributed $150,000 to the partnership, and Thomas contributed $50,000. Wilson does 40% of the work, and Thomas does 60%. They do not have a partnership agreement that addresses the sharing of profits and losses. By the end of the year, the partnership has earned a profit of $200,000. What is Wilson's share of the profit under the Revised Uniform Partnership Act?

A. $80,000
B. $100,000
C. $115,000
D. $150,000

REG 5-Q5 R605. If **no** provisions are made in an agreement, a general partnership allocates profits and losses based on the

A. Value of actual contributions made by each partner.
B. Number of partners.
C. Number of hours each partner worked in the partnership during the year.
D. Number of years each partner belonged to the partnership.

REG 5-Q6 R588. Under the Revised Uniform Limited Partnership Act, which of the following statements is correct regarding limited partnerships?

A. Limited partners may lose limited liability if they participate in management activities.
B. Limited partners may lose limited liability if they do not participate in management activities.
C. Limited partners have the same rights, responsibilities, and authority as general partners.
D. Limited partners may contribute cash only and may **not** contribute services as their capital contributions.

REG 5-Q7 R590. Fil and Breed are 50% partners in F&B Cars, a used-car dealership. F&B maintains an average used-car inventory worth $150,000. On January 5, National Bank obtained a $30,000 judgment against Fil and Fil's child on a loan that Fil had cosigned and on which Fil's child had defaulted. National sued F&B to be allowed to attach $30,000 worth of cars as part of Fil's interest in F&B's inventory. Will National prevail in its suit?

A. No, because the judgment was not against the partnership.
B. No, because attachment of the cars would dissolve the partnership by operation of law.
C. Yes, because National had a valid judgment against Fil.
D. Yes, because Fil's interest in the partnership inventory is an asset owned by Fil.

REG 5-Q8 R593. Under the Uniform Partnership Act, which of the following statements is(are) correct regarding the effect of the assignment of an interest in a general partnership?

I. The assignee is personally responsible for the assigning partner's share of past and future partnership debts.
II. The assignee is entitled to the assigning partner's interest in partnership profits and surplus on dissolution of the partnership.

A. I only.
B. II only.
C. Both I and II.
D. Neither I nor II.

REG 5-Q9 R582. What business entity can be voluntarily dissolved and terminated without filing a dissolution document with the state of organization?

A. A corporation.
B. A general partnership.
C. A limited liability limited partnership.
D. A limited partnership.

REG 5-Q10 R596. Under the Revised Uniform Limited Partnership Act and in the absence of a contrary agreement by the partners, which of the following events is most likely to dissolve a limited partnership?

A. A majority vote in favor by the partners.
B. A two-thirds vote in favor by the partners.
C. A withdrawal of a majority of the limited partners.
D. Withdrawal of the only general partner.

REG 5-Q11 R594. Which of the following parties generally has the most management rights?

A. Minority shareholder in a corporation listed on a national stock exchange.
B. Limited partner in a general partnership.
C. Member of a limited liability company.
D. Limited partner in a limited partnership.

REG 5-Q12 R585. The owners of a limited liability company (LLC) are known as which of the following?

A. Partners.
B. Members.
C. Stockholders.
D. Shareholders.

REG 5-Q13 R587. Two individuals are planning to form a business with equal ownership. The individuals would like to limit their personal liability, avoid double taxation, and be active in the business. Which of the following organizational structures would meet their requirements?

A. C corporation
B. Limited liability company (LLC)
C. Limited partnership
D. General partnership

REG 5-Q14 R561. Terry recently started a new business and is trying to decide what type of entity to form. Terry is part owner and is active in running the business. What type of entity would best protect Terry, as one of the owners, from personal liability?

A. General partnership.
B. Limited partnership.
C. Joint venture.
D. Limited liability Company.

REG 5-Q15 R569. Which form of business entity has the following attributes?

I. Limited liability for all its owners.
II. Can permit all its owners to participate in management and control of the entity.
III. Absent an agreement to the contrary, is dissolved on the death, withdrawal, or bankruptcy of an owner.

A. A limited partnership
B. A limited liability company
C. A general partnership
D. A corporation

REG 5-Q16 R591. Which of the following is a requirement for a small business corporation to elect S corporation status?

A. It has only one class of stock.
B. It has at least one partnership as a shareholder.
C. It has international ownership.
D. It has more than 75 shareholders.

REG 5-Q17 R604. Which of the following may **not** own shares in an S corporation?

A. Individuals
B. Estates
C. Trusts
D. Corporations

REG 5-Q18 R607. An S corporation must adhere to all of the following conditions **except** having

A. No more than 100 shareholders.
B. A nonresident alien as a shareholder.
C. An individual as a shareholder.
D. One class of stock.

REG 5-Q19 R857. Luba Corp. was organized in 1983 with the intention of operating an S corporation (Subchapter S). What is the maximum number of stockholders allowable for eligibility as an S corporation (Subchapter S)?

A. 50
B. 100
C. 75
D. 200

REG 5-Q20 R862. Which of the following is not a requirement for a corporation to elect S corporation status (Subchapter S)?

A. Must be a member of a controlled group.
B. Must confine stockholders to individuals, estates, and certain qualifying trusts.
C. Must be a domestic corporation.
D. Must have only one class of stock.

REG 5-Q21 R564. Which of the following disqualifies an entity from an S corporation election?

A. Seventy-seven individual shareholders (including four married couples).
B. An estate shareholder.
C. A 501 (c)(3) exempt organization shareholder.
D. A nonresident alien shareholder.

REG 5-Q22 R571. Which of the following forms of business generally provides all owners with limited liability while avoiding federal taxation of income at the entity level?

A. Subchapter C corporation
B. Subchapter S corporation
C. Partnership
D. Limited partnership

REG 5-Q23 R609. Which of the following statements describes the same characteristic for both an S corporation and a C corporation?

A. Both corporations can have more than 100 shareholders.
B. Both corporations have the disadvantage of double taxation.
C. Shareholders can contribute property into a corporation without being taxed.
D. Shareholders can be either citizens of the United States or foreign countries.

REG 5-Q24 R597. In which type of business organization are income taxes always required to be paid by the entity on profits earned as well as by the owners upon distribution thereof?

A. General partnership.
B. Limited liability company.
C. Subchapter C corporation.
D. Subchapter S corporation.

REG 5-Q25 R282. Which of the following items should be included on the Schedule M-1, *Reconciliation of Income (Loss) per Books With Income per Return,* of Form 1120, *U.S. Corporation Income Tax Return* to reconcile book income to taxable income?

A. Cash distributions to shareholders.
B. Premiums paid on key-person life insurance policy, where corporation is beneficiary.
C. Corporate bond interest income.
D. Ending balance of retained earnings.

REG 5-Q26 R44. Azure, a C corporation, reports the following:
Pretax book income of $543,000.
Depreciation on the tax return is $20,000 greater than depreciation on the financial statements.
Rent income reportable on the tax return is $36,000 greater than rent income per the financial statements.
Fines for pollution appear as a $10,000 expense in the financial statements.
Interest earned on municipal bonds is $25,000.

What is Azure's taxable income?

A. $528,000
B. $543,000
C. $544,000
D. $559,000

REG 5-Q27 R206. Jagdon Corp.'s book income was $150,000 for the current year, including interest income from municipal bonds of $5,000 and excess capital losses over capital gains of $10,000. Federal income tax expense of $50,000 was also included in Jagdon's books. What amount represents Jagdon's taxable income for the current year?

A. $185,000
B. $195,000
C. $205,000
D. $215,000

REG 5-Q28 R128. Which of the following entities must pay taxes for federal income tax purposes?

A. General partnership.
B. Limited partnership.
C. Joint venture.
D. C corporation.

REG 5-Q29 R129. Quail, Inc. manufactures consumer products and sells them to distributors. Quail advertises its products to increase sales and enhance the value of its trade name. What is the appropriate tax treatment for the advertising costs?

A. Amortize the costs over 15 years.
B. Amortize the costs over 36 months.
C. Amortize the costs over 60 months.
D. Deduct the costs currently as ordinary and necessary business expenses.

REG 5-Q30 R302. Which of the following entities may adopt any tax year end?

A. C corporation.
B. S corporation.
C. Limited liability company.
D. Trust.

REG 5-Q31 R68. The selection of an accounting method for tax purposes by a newly incorporated C corporation

A. Is made on the initial tax return by using the chosen method.
B. Is made by filing a request for a private letter ruling from the IRS.
C. Must first be approved by the company's board of directors.
D. Must be disclosed in the company's organizing documents.

REG 5-Q32 R170. An S corporation engaged in manufacturing has a year end of June 30. Revenue consistently has been more than $10 million under both cash and accrual basis of accounting. The stockholders would like to change the tax status of the corporation to a C corporation using the cash basis with the same year end. Which of the following statements is correct if it changes to a C corporation?

A. The yearend will be December 31, using the cash basis of accounting.
B. The yearend will be December 31, using the accrual basis of accounting.
C. The yearend will be June 30, using the accrual basis of accounting.
D. The yearend will be June 30, using the cash basis of accounting.

REG 5-Q33 R243. A C corporation must use the accrual method of accounting in which of the following circumstances?

A. The business had average sales for the past three years of **less** than $1 million.
B. The business is a service company and has over $1 million in sales.
C. The business is a personal service business with over $15 million in sales.
D. The business has more than $10 million in average sales.

REG 5-Q34 R443. In calculating the tax of a corporation for a short period, which of the following processes is correct?

A. Divide current-year income by prior-year income, then multiply the result by prior-year tax.
B. Compute tax on short-period income, then multiply the result by 12 divided by the number of months in the short period.
C. Determine the average taxable income for the past three years, then multiply the result by the number of months in the short period divided by 12.
D. Annualize income and calculate the tax on annualized income, then multiply the computed tax by the number of months in the short period divided by 12.

REG 5-Q35 R4. Nichol Corp. gave gifts to 15 individuals who were customers of the business. The gifts were not in the nature of advertising. The market values of the gifts were as follows:

　　5 gifts @ $15 each

　　9 gifts @ $30 each

　　1 gift @ $100

What amount is deductible as business gifts?

A. $0
B. $75
C. $325
D. $445

REG 5-Q36 R204. A C corporation has gross receipts of $150,000, $35,000 of other income, and deductible expenses of $95,000. In addition, the corporation incurred a net long-term capital loss of $25,000 in the current year. What is the corporation's taxable income?

A. $ 65,000
B. $ 87,000
C. $ 90,000
D. $115,000

REG 5-Q37 R45. Which of the following **cannot** be amortized for tax purposes?

A. Incorporation costs.
B. Temporary directors' fees.
C. Stock issuance costs.
D. Organizational meeting costs.

REG 5-Q38 R355. A corporation was completely liquidated and dissolved during the current year. The filing fees, professional fees, and other expenditures incurred in connection with the liquidation and dissolution are

A. Deductible in full by the dissolved corporation.
B. Deductible by the shareholders and **not** by the corporation.
C. Treated as capital losses by the corporation.
D. Not deductible by either the corporation or the shareholders.

REG 5-Q39 R3. For year 2, Quest Corp., an accrual-basis calendar-year C corporation, had an $8,000 unexpired charitable contribution carryover from year 1. Quest's year 2 taxable income before the deduction for charitable contributions was $200,000. On December 12, year 2, Quest's board of directors authorized a $15,000 cash contribution to a qualified charity, which was made on January 6, year 3. What is the maximum allowable deduction that Quest may take as a charitable contribution on its year 2 income tax return?

A. $23,000
B. $20,000
C. $15,000
D. $8,000

REG 5-Q40 R109. Robin, a C corporation, had revenues of $200,000 and operating expenses of $75,000. Robin also received a $20,000 dividend from a domestic corporation and is entitled to a $14,000 dividend-received deduction. Robin donated $15,000 to a qualified charitable organization in the current year. What is Robin's contribution deduction?

A. $15,000
B. $14,500
C. $13,900
D. $13,100

REG 5-Q41 R195. Pope, a C corporation, owns 15% of Arden Corporation. Arden paid a $3,000 cash dividend to Pope. Pope has a profit from operations of $10,000. What is the amount of Pope's dividend-received deduction?

A. $3,000
B. $2,400
C. $2,100
D. $0

REG 5-Q42 R235. Beta, a C corporation, reported the following items of income and expenses for the year:

Gross income	$600,000
Dividend income from a 30% owned domestic corporation	100,000
Operating expenses	400,000

What is Beta's taxable income for the year?

A. $200,000
B. $220,000
C. $230,000
D. $300,000

REG 5-Q43 R299. In the current year, Brown, a C corporation has gross income (before dividends) of $900,000 and deductions of $1,100,000 (excluding the dividends-received deduction). Brown received dividends of $100,000 from a Fortune 500 corporation during the current year. What is Brown's net operating loss?

A. $100,000
B. $130,000
C. $170,000
D. $200,000

REG 5-Q44 R434. Bent Corp., a calendar-year C corporation, purchased and placed into service residential real property during February 2016. No other property was placed into service during 2016. What convention must Bent use to determine the depreciation deduction for the alternative minimum tax?

A. Full-year.
B. Half-year.
C. Mid-quarter.
D. Mid-month.

REG 5-Q45 R326. Tan Corp. calculated the following taxes for the current year.

Regular tax liability $210,000
Tentative minimum tax 240,000
Personal holding company tax 65,000

What is Tan's total tax liability for the year?

A. $210,000
B. $240,000
C. $275,000
D. $305,000

REG 5-Q46 R336. Dole, the sole owner of Enson Corp., transferred a building to Enson. The building had an adjusted tax basis of $35,000 and a fair market value of $100,000. In exchange for the building, Dole received $40,000 cash and Enson common stock with a fair market value of $60,000. What amount of gain did Dole recognize?

A. $0
B. $5,000
C. $40,000
D. $65,000

REG 5-Q47 R161. Ames and Roth form Homerun, a C corporation and acquired 100% of the stock. Ames contributes several autographed baseballs to Homerun. Ames purchased the baseballs for $500, and they have a total fair market value of $1,000. Roth contributes several autographed baseball bats to Homerun. Roth purchased the bats for $5,000, and they have a fair market value of $7,000. What is Homerun's basis in the contributed bats and balls?

A. $0
B. $5,500
C. $6,000
D. $8,000

REG 5-Q48 R182. In April, A and B formed X Corp. A contributed $50,000 cash, and B contributed land worth $70,000 (with an adjusted basis of $40,000). B also received $20,000 cash from the corporation. A and B each receives 50% of the corporation's stock. What is the tax basis of the land to X Corp.?

A. $40,000
B. $50,000
C. $60,000
D. $70,000

REG 5-Q49 R175. Fox, the sole shareholder in Fall, a C corporation, has a tax basis of $60,000. Fall has $40,000 of accumulated positive earnings and profits at the beginning of the year and $10,000 of current positive earnings and profits for the current year. At year end, Fall distributed land with an adjusted basis of $30,000 and a fair market value (FMV) of $38,000 to Fox. The land has an outstanding mortgage of $3,000 that Fox must assume. What is Fox's tax basis in the land?

A. $38,000
B. $35,000
C. $30,000
D. $27,000

REG 5-Q50 R341. Aztec, a C corporation, distributed an asset to Burn, a shareholder. The asset had a fair market value of $30,000 and was subject to a $40,000 liability, assumed by Burn. The asset had an adjusted basis of $25,000. What amount of gain must Aztec recognize?

A. $0
B. $5,000
C. $10,000
D. $15,000

REG 5-Q51 R1. On January 1 of the current year, Locke Corp., an accrual-basis calendar-year C corporation, had $30,000 in accumulated earnings and profits. For the current year, Locke had current earnings and profits of $20,000, and made two $40,000 cash distributions to its shareholders, one in April and one in September. What amount of the distributions is classified as dividend income to Locke's shareholders?

A. $0
B. $20,000
C. $50,000
D. $80,000

REG 5-Q52 R92. Simon, a C corporation, had a deficit in accumulated earnings and profits of $50,000 at the beginning of the year and had current earnings and profits of $10,000. At year end, Simon paid a dividend of $15,000 to its sole shareholder. What amount of the dividend is reported as income?

A. $0
B. $ 5,000
C. $10,000
D. $15,000

REG 5-Q53 R158. Webster, a C corporation, has $70,000 in accumulated and no current earnings and profits. Webster distributed $20,000 cash and property with an adjusted basis and fair market value of $60,000 to its shareholders. What amount should the shareholders report as dividend income?

A. $20,000
B. $60,000
C. $70,000
D. $80,000

REG 5-Q54 R315. Bridge, a C corporation, had $15,000 in accumulated earnings and profits at the beginning of the current year. During the current year, Bridge reported earnings and profits of $10,000 and paid $20,000 in cash distributions to its shareholders in both March and July. What amount of the July distribution should be classified as dividend income to Bridge's shareholders?

A. $20,000
B. $15,000
C. $10,000
D. $ 5,000

REG 5-Q55 R389. At the beginning of the year, Westwind, a C corporation, had a deficit of $45,000 in accumulated earnings and profits. For the current year, Westwind reported earnings and profits of $15,000. Westwind distributed $12,000 during the year. What was the amount of Westwind's accumulated earnings and profits at year-end?

A. $30,000
B. $42,000
C. $45,000
D. $57,000

REG 5-Q56 R447. Brisk Corp. is an accrual-basis, calendar-year C Corporation with one individual shareholder. At year end, Brisk had $600,000 accumulated and current earnings and profits as it prepared to make its only dividend distribution for the year to its shareholder. Brisk could distribute either cash of $200,000 or land with an adjusted tax basis of $75,000 and a fair market value of $200,000. How would the taxable incomes of both Brisk and the shareholder change if land were distributed instead of cash?

	Brisk's taxable income	Shareholder's taxable income
A.	No change	No change
B.	Increase	Increase
C.	No change	Decrease
D.	Increase	Decrease

REG 5-Q57 R244. A corporation that has both preferred and common stock has a deficit in accumulated earnings and profits at the beginning of the year. The current earnings and profits are $25,000. The corporation makes a dividend distribution of $20,000 to the preferred shareholders and $10,000 to the common shareholders. How will the preferred and common shareholders report these distributions?

A. Preferred - $20,000 dividend income; common - $10,000 dividend income.
B. Preferred - $20,000 dividend income; common - $5,000 dividend income, $5,000 return of capital.
C. Preferred - $15,000 dividend income; common - $10,000 dividend income.
D. Preferred - $20,000 return of capital; common - $10,000 return of capital.

REG 5-Q58 R276. Wallace purchased 500 shares of Kingpin, Inc., 15 years ago for $25,000. Wallace has worked as an owner/employee and owned 40% of the company throughout this time. This year, Kingpin, which is not an S corporation, redeemed 100% of Wallace's stock for $200,000. What is the treatment and amount of income or gain that Wallace should report?

A. $0
B. $175,000 long-term capital gain.
C. $175,000 ordinary income.
D. $200,000 long-term capital gain.

REG 5-Q59 R191. Forrest Corp. owned 100% of both the voting stock and total value of Diamond Corp. Both corporations were C corporations. Forrest's basis in the Diamond stock was $200,000 when it received a lump sum *liquidating* distribution of property as a result of the redemption of all of Diamond stock. The property had an adjusted basis of $270,000 and a fair market value of $500,000. What amount of gain did Forrest recognize on the distribution?

A. $0
B. $ 70,000
C. $270,000
D. $500,000

REG 5-Q60 R354. Prin Corp., the parent corporation, and Strel Corp., both accrual-basis, calendar-year C corporations, file a consolidated return. During the year, Strel made dividend distributions to Prin as follows:

	Adjusted tax basis	Fair market value
Cash	$4,000	$4,000
Land	2,000	9,000

What amount of dividend income should be reported on Prin and Strel's consolidated income tax return for the current year?

A. $13,000
B. $11,000
C. $6,000
D. $0

REG 5-Q61 R130. On June 30, Gold and Silver are calendar-year C corporations. The corporations have merged, with Gold as a subsidiary of Silver. Silver owns 85% of Gold's voting stock and fair market value (FMV). Which of the following tax return filings would be appropriate for the two companies?

A. Two separate returns, because Silver owns at least 80% of both the voting stock and FMV of Gold.
B. Two separate returns, because the merger took place before the close of the second quarter.
C. A consolidated return, because Silver owns at least 80% of both the voting stock and FMV of Gold.
D. A consolidated return, because the merger took place before the close of the second quarter.

REG 5-Q62 R186. Which of the following groups may elect to file a consolidated corporate return?

A. A brother/sister-controlled group.
B. A parent corporation and all more-than-10%-controlled partnerships.
C. A parent corporation and all more-than-50%-controlled subsidiaries.
D. Members of an affiliated group.

REG 5-Q63 R274. ParentCo, SubOne, and SubTwo have filed consolidated returns since their inception. The members reported the following taxable income (losses) for the year.

ParentCo	$50,000
SubOne	($60,000)
SubTwo	($40,000)

No member reported a capital gain or loss or charitable contributions. What is the amount of the consolidated net operating loss?

A. $0
B. $ 30,000
C. $ 50,000
D. $100,000

REG 5-Q64 R1134. Which of the following factors are not commonly used when determining how to apportion the income of a multi-state corporation?

A. Sales
B. Cost of Goods Sold
C. Payroll
D. Property

REG 5-Q65 R1135. Spark Company is a Maine-based company and its headquarters are located very close to the New Hampshire border. Spark sells light fixtures and all of Spark's employees, assets, inventories, and property physically located in Maine. Spark is considering setting up an online store that would sell its products to customers all over the United States. Which factor taken individually will probably **not** play a role in determining if this new business will cause it to have nexus in states other than Maine:

A. Spark's sales staff will conduct an online sales campaign from Spark's headquarters to drive sales of light fixtures that will be shipped to customers nationwide.
B. The inventory will be stored in warehouses in Maine and on the west coast to facilitate quick delivery to customers.
C. Spark is considering offering a local installation service for nation-wide customers who purchase its products
D. Spark plans to send its sales staff to work in various hardware stores across the country to raise awareness of its new offering.

REG 5-Q66 R1137. At the beginning of 2015, all of the employees, inventory and operations of an Arizona-based online spice retailer were physically located in Arizona, but its spices, which it sold online, were shipped to customers in both Arizona and New Mexico. Four times per year, sales personnel travelled to Colorado to take part in a quarterly culinary festival where it accepts and approves orders for spices. The spices are then shipped from the Arizona warehouse. In the fourth quarter of 2015, the company moved some of its inventory to a warehouse in Utah where storage costs were much lower. In which states does the company most likely have nexus?

A. Arizona and Utah
B. Arizona, Colorado and Utah
C. Arizona, Colorado and New Mexico
D. Arizona, Colorado, New Mexico and Utah

REG 5-Q67 R1136. Rubber Band Corp earned $250,000 of U.S. source income and $72,000 of foreign source income. It paid $19,000 in foreign taxes and has a tax liability of $40,000 before the foreign tax credit. What amount of foreign tax credit can the company claim?

A. $0
B. $4,248
C. $8,944
D. $19,000

REG 5-Q68 R1149. Which of the following statements are false?

A. FinCEN Form 114 is required to be filed for taxpayers who have a financial interest in, or signature authority over a foreign financial account.
B. FinCEN Form 114 requires that the foreign financial account report must be electronically filed to the Department of Treasury.
C. A foreign financial account includes a bank account, brokerage account, and mutual funds.
D. FinCEN Form 114 must be filed with the IRS.

REG 5-Q69 R89. Which of the following statements about qualifying shareholders of an S corporation is correct?

A. A general partnership may be a shareholder.
B. Only individuals may be shareholders.
C. Individuals, estates, and certain trusts may be shareholders.
D. Nonresident aliens may be shareholders.

REG 5-Q70 R287. Jans, an individual, owns 80% and 100% of the total value and voting power of A and B Corps., respectively, which in turn own the following (both value and voting power):

Property	Ownership A Corp.	B Corp.
C Corp.	80%	-
D Corp.	-	100%

All companies are C corporations except B Corp., which as elected S status since inception. Which of the following statements is correct with respect to the companies' ability to file a consolidated return?

A. A, C, and D may file as a group.
B. A and C may **not** file as a group, and B and D may **not** file as a group.
C. A and C may file as a group, and B and D may file as a group.
D. A and C may file as a group, but B and D may **not** file as a group.

REG 5-Q71 R62. Carson owned 40% of the outstanding stock of a C corporation. During a tax year, the corporation reported $400,000 in taxable income and distributed a total of $70,000 in cash dividends to its shareholders. Carson accurately reported $28,000 in gross income on Carson's individual tax return. If the corporation had been an S corporation and the distributions to the owners had been proportionate, how much income would Carson have reported on Carson's individual return?

A. $28,000
B. $132,000
C. $160,000
D. $188,000

REG 5-Q72 R29. Which of the following items must be separately stated on Form 1120S, *U.S. Income Tax Return for a Corporation, Schedule K-1*?

A. Mark-to-market income.
B. Unearned revenue.
C. Section 1245 Gain.
D. Gain or loss from the sale of collectibles.

REG 5-Q73 R148. Tap, a calendar-year S corporation, reported the following items of income and expense in the current year:

Revenue	$44,000
Operating expenses	20,000
Long-term capital loss	6,000
Charitable contributions	1,000
Interest expense	4,000

What is the amount of Tap's ordinary income?

A. $13,000
B. $19,000
C. $20,000
D. $24,000

REG 5-Q74 R332. Boles Corp., an accrual-basis, calendar-year S corporation, has been an S corporation since its inception and is not subject to the uniform capitalization rules. In 2003, Boles recorded the following:

Gross receipts	$50,000
Dividend income from investments	5,000
Supplies expense	2,000
Utilities expense	1,500

On Boles' 2003 S corporation Form Schedule K, *Shareholders' Shares of Income, Credits, Deductions, etc.*, what amount of income should be separately stated from business income?

A. $50,000
B. $48,000
C. $5,000
D. $0

REG 5-Q75 R314. Boles Corp., an accrual-basis, calendar-year S corporation, has been an S corporation since its inception and is not subject to the uniform capitalization rules. In the current year, Boles recorded the following:

Gross receipts	$50,000
Dividend income from investments	5,000
Supplies expense	2,000
Utilities expense	1,500

What amount of business income should Boles report on its 2003 Form 1120S, *U.S. Income Tax Return for an S corporation*, Schedule K?

A. $53,500
B. $53,000
C. $48,000
D. $46,500

REG 5-Q76 R256. Evan, an individual, has a 40% interest in EF, an S corporation. At the beginning of the year, Evan's basis in EF was $2,000. During the year, EF distributed $100,000 and reported operating income of $200,000. What amount should Evan include in gross income?

A. $38,000
B. $40,000
C. $80,000
D. $118,000

REG 5-Q77 R60. The sole shareholder of an S corporation contributed equipment with a fair market value of $20,000 and a basis of $6,000 subject to $12,000 liability. What amount is the gain, if any, that the shareholder must recognize?

A. $0
B. $6,000
C. $8,000
D. $12,000

REG 5-Q78 R162. Sandy is the sole shareholder of Swallow, an S corporation. Sandy's adjusted basis in Swallow stock is $60,000 at the beginning of the year. During the year, Swallow reports the following income items:

Ordinary income	$30,000
Tax-exempt income	5,000
Capital gains	10,000

In addition, Swallow makes a nontaxable distribution to Sandy of $20,000 during the year. What is Sandy's adjusted basis in the Swallow stock at the end of the year?

A. $60,000
B. $70,000
C. $80,000
D. $85,000

REG 5-Q79 R107. Stone owns 100% of an S corporation and materially participates in its operations. The stock basis at the beginning of the year is $5,000. During the year, the corporation makes a distribution of $3,500 and passes through a loss from operations of $2,000 for the year. What loss can Stone deduct on Stone's personal tax return?

A. $0
B. $1,500
C. $2,000
D. $5,500

REG 5-Q80 R352. Packer Corp., an accrual-basis, calendar-year S corporation, has been an S corporation since its inception. Starr was a 50% shareholder in Packer throughout the current year and had a $10,000 tax basis in Packer stock on January 1. During the current year, Packer had a $1,000 net business loss and made an $8,000 cash distribution to each shareholder. What amount of the distribution was includible in Starr's gross income?

A. $8,000
B. $7,500
C. $4,000
D. $0

REG 5-Q81 R388. Stahl, an individual, owns 100% of Talon, an S corporation. At the beginning of the year, Stahl's basis in Talon was $65,000. Talon reported the following items from operations during the current year:

Ordinary loss	$10,000
Municipal interest income	6,000
Long-term capital gain	4,000
Short-term capital loss	9,000

What was Stahl's basis in Talon at year end?

A. $50,000
B. $55,000
C. $56,000
D. $61,000

REG 5-Q82 R392. Baker, an individual, owned 100% of Alpha, an S corporation. At the beginning of the year, Baker's basis in Alpha Corp. was $25,000. Alpha realized ordinary income during the year in the amount of $1,000 and a long-term capital loss in the amount of $3,000 for this year. Alpha distributed $30,000 in cash to Baker during the year. What amount of the $30,000 cash distribution is taxable to Baker?

A. $0
B. $ 5,000
C. $ 4,000
D. $30,000

REG 5-Q83 R25. For which of the following entities is the owner's basis increased by the owner's share of profits and decreased by the owner's share of losses but is **not** affected by the entity's bank loan increases or decreases?

A. S corporation.
B. C corporation.
C. Partnership.
D. Limited liability company.

REG 5-Q84 R90. Absent an election to close the books, the allocation of non-separately stated income or loss for an S corporation shareholder that changed his ownership interest during the year is computed based on which of the following ownership percentages?

A. Ownership percentage at the end of the S corporation year.
B. Ownership percentage computed on a per-share per-day basis.
C. Ownership percentage at the beginning of the S corporation year.
D. Ownership percentage determined as an average of the beginning and ending ownership percentages.

REG 5-Q85 R131. Stone Corp. has been an S corporation since inception. In each of year 1, year 2, and year 3, Stone made distributions in excess of each shareholder's basis. Which of the following statements is correct concerning these three years?

A. In year 1 and year 2 only, the excess distributions are taxed as capital gain.
B. In year 1 only, the excess distributions are tax free.
C. In year 3 only, the excess distributions are taxed as capital gain.
D. In all three years, the excess distributions are taxed as capital gains.

REG 5-Q86 R27. A sole proprietorship incorporated on January 1 and elected S corporation status. The owner contributed the following assets to the S corporation:

	Basis	Fair market value
Machinery	$ 7,000	$ 8,000
Building	11,000	100,000
Cash	1,000	1,000

Two years later, the corporation sold the machinery for $4,000 and the building for $110,000. The machinery had accumulated depreciation of $2,000, and the building had accumulated depreciation of $1,000. What is the built-in gain recognized on the sale?

A. $100,000
B. $ 99,000
C. $ 6,000
D. $0

REG 5-Q87 R219. Commerce a C Corporation, elects S corporation status as of the beginning of year 2000. At the time of Commerce's election, it held a machine with a basis of $20,000 and a fair market value of $30,000. In March of 2000, Commerce sells the machine for $35,000. What would be the amount subject to the built-in gains tax.

A. $0
B. $ 5,000
C. $10,000
D. $15,000

REG 5-Q88 R260. Magic Corp., a regular C corporation, elected S corporation status on Jan 2, 2001. It had an asset with a basis of $40,000 and a fair market value (FMV) of $85,000 on January 2. The asset was sold on Sept 2, 2001 for $95,000. Magic's corporate tax rate was 35%. What was Magic's tax liability as a result of the sale?

A. $0
B. $ 3,500
C. $15,750
D. $19,250

REG 5-Q89 R46. PDK, LLC had three members with equal ownership percentages. PDK elected to be treated as a partnership. For the tax year ending December 31, year 1, PDK had the following income and expense items:

Revenues	$120,000
Interest income	6,000
Gain on sale of securities	8,000
Salaries	36,000
Guaranteed payments	10,000
Rent expense	21,000
Depreciation expense	18,000
Charitable contributions	3,000

What would PDK report as non-separately stated income for year 1 tax purposes?

A. $30,000
B. $35,000
C. $43,000
D. $51,000

REG 5-Q90 R10. Turner, Reed, and Sumner are equal partners in TRS partnership. Turner contributed land with an adjusted basis of $20,000 and a fair market value (FMV) of $50,000. Reed contributed equipment with an adjusted basis of $40,000 and a FMV of $50,000. Sumner provided services worth $50,000. What amount of income is recognized as a result of the transfers?

A. $50,000
B. $60,000
C. $90,000
D. $150,000

REG 5-Q91 R215. Nolan designed Timber Partnership's new building. Nolan received an interest in the partnership for the services. Nolan's normal billing for these services would be $80,000 and the fair market value of the partnership interest Nolan received is $120,000. What amount of income should Nolan report?

A. $ 0
B. $ 40,000
C. $ 80,000
D. $120,000

REG 5-Q92 R231. Walker transferred property used in a sole proprietorship to the WXYZ partnership in exchange for a one-fourth interest. The property had an original cost of $75,000, an adjusted tax basis to Walker of $20,000, and fair market value of $50,000. The partnership has no liabilities. What is Walker's basis in the partnership interest?

A. $0
B. $20,000
C. $50,000
D. $75,000

REG 5-Q93 R339. Bailey contributed land with a fair market value of $75,000 and an adjusted basis of $25,000 to the ABC Partnership in exchange for a 30% interest. The partnership assumed Bailey's $10,000 recourse mortgage on the land. What is Bailey's basis for his partnership interest?

A. $15,000
B. $18,000
C. $65,000
D. $75,000

REG 5-Q94 R43. In return for a 20% partnership interest, Skinner contributed $5,000 cash and land with a $12,000 basis and a $20,000 fair market value to the partnership. The land was subject to a $10,000 mortgage that the partnership assumed. In addition, the partnership had $20,000 in recourse liabilities that would be shared by partners according to their partnership interests. What amount represents Skinner's basis in the partnership interest?

A. $27,000
B. $21,000
C. $19,000
D. $13,000

REG 5-Q95 R93. Campbell acquired a 10% interest in Vogue Partnership by contributing a building with an adjusted basis of $40,000 and a fair market value of $90,000. The building was subject to a $60,000 mortgage that was assumed by Vogue. The other partners contributed cash only. The basis of Campbell's partnership interest in Vogue is

A. $84,000
B. $34,000
C. $30,000
D. $0

REG 5-Q96 R300. Kerr and Marcus form KM Partnership with a cash contribution of $80,000 from Kerr and a property contribution of land from Marcus. The land has a fair market value of $80,000 and an adjusted basis of $50,000 at the date of the contribution. Kerr and Marcus are equal partners. What is Marcus's basis immediately after formation?

A. $0
B. $50,000
C. $65,000
D. $80,000

REG 5-Q97 R303. Smith received a one-third interest of a partnership by contributing $3,000 in cash, stock with a fair market value of $5,000 and a basis of $2,000, and a new computer that cost Smith $2,500. Which of the following amounts represents Smith's basis in the partnership?

A. $10,500
B. $ 7,500
C. $ 5,500
D. $ 3,000

REG 5-Q98 R57. When the AQR partnership was formed, partner Acre contributed land with a fair market value of $100,000 and a tax basis of $60,000 in exchange for a one-third interest in the partnership. The AQR partnership agreement specifies that each partner will share equally in the partnership's profits and losses. During its first year of operation, AQR sold the land to an unrelated third party for $160,000. What is the proper tax treatment of the sale?

A. Each partner reports a capital gain of $33,333.
B. The entire gain of $100,000 must be specifically allocated to Acre.
C. The first $40,000 of gain is allocated to Acre, and the remaining gain of $60,000 is shared equally by the other two partners.
D. The first $40,000 of gain is allocated to Acre, and the remaining gain of $60,000 is shared equally by all the partners in the partnership.

REG 5-Q99 R167. Dale was a 50% partner in D&P Partnership. Dale contributed $10,000 in cash upon the formation of the partnership. D&P borrowed $10,000 to purchase equipment. During the first year of operations, D&P had $15,000 net taxable income, $2,000 tax-exempt interest income, a $3,000 distribution to each partner, and a $4,000 reduction of debt. At the end of the first year of operation, what amount would be Dale's basis?

A. $16,500
B. $17,500
C. $18,500
D. $21,500

REG 5-Q100 R111. George and Martha are equal partners in G&M Partnership. At the beginning of the current tax year, the adjusted basis of George's partnership interest was $32,500, which included his share of $40,000 of partnership liabilities. During the tax year, the following information applied to G&M:

Operating loss	$30,000
Interest and dividend income	8,000
Partnership liabilities at end of year	24,000

What was the basis of George's partnership interest at year end?

A. $13,500
B. $21,500
C. $29,500
D. $43,500

REG 5-Q101 R193. Molloy contributed $40,000 in cash in exchange for a one-third interest in the RST Partnership. In the first year of partnership operations, RST had taxable income of $60,000. In addition, Molloy received a $5,000 distribution of cash and, at the end of the partnership year, Molloy had a one-third share in the $18,000 of partnership recourse liabilities. What was Molloy's basis in RST at year end?

A. $ 55,000
B. $ 61,000
C. $ 71,000
D. $101,000

REG 5-Q102 R279. A partnership had four partners. Each partner contributed $100,000 cash. The partnership reported income for the year of $80,000 and distributed $10,000 to each partner. What was each partner's basis in the partnership at the end of the current year?

A. $170,000
B. $120,000
C. $117,500
D. $110,000

REG 5-Q103 R390. Thompson's basis in Starlight Partnership was $60,000 at the beginning of the year. Thompson materially participates in the partnership's business. Thompson received $20,000 in cash distributions during the year. Thompson's share of Starlight's current operations was a $65,000 ordinary loss and a $15,000 net long-term capital gain. What is the amount of Thompson's deductible loss for the period?

A. $15,000
B. $40,000
C. $55,000
D. $65,000

REG 5-Q104 R248. The at-risk limitation provisions of the Internal Revenue Code may limit

I. A partner's deduction for his or her distributive share of partnership losses.
II. A partnership's net operating loss carryover.

A. I only.
B. II only.
C. Both I and II.
D. Neither I nor I

REG 5-Q105 R224. The individual partner rather than the partnership makes which of the following elections?

A. Election to amortize organizational costs.
B. Nonrecognition treatment for involuntary conversion gains.
C. Code Section 179 deductions for tangible personal property.
D. Whether to take a deduction or credit for taxes paid to foreign countries.

REG 5-Q106 R140. In the absence of an election to adopt an annual accounting period, the required tax year for a partnership is

A. A tax year that results in the greatest aggregate deferral of income.
B. A calendar year.
C. A tax year of one or more partners with a more than 50% interest in profits and capital.
D. A tax year of a principal partner having a 10% or greater interest.

REG 5-Q107 R112. As a general partner in Greenland Associates, an individual's share of partnership income for the current tax year is $25,000 ordinary business income and a $10,000 guaranteed payment. The individual also received $5,000 in cash distributions from the partnership. What income should the individual report from the interest in Greenland?

A.
B. $25,000
C. $35,000
D. $40,000

REG 5-Q108 R358. Acme and Buck are equal members in Dear, an LLC. Dear has elected to be treated as a partnership. Dear has not elected to be taxed as a corporation. Acme contributed $7,000 cash and Buck contributed a machine with an adjusted basis of $5,000 and a fair market value of $10,000, subject to a liability of $3,000, which is assumed by Dear. What is Acme's basis in Dear?

A. $ 4,000
B. $ 7,000
C. $ 8,500
D. $10,000

REG 5-Q109 R110. "Hot assets" of a partnership would include which of the following?

A. Cash.
B. Unrealized receivables.
C. Section 1231 assets.
D. Capital assets.

REG 5-Q110 R15. While preparing a partnership tax return, the accountant discovered that ABC Partnership distributed property to Anne, a partner, in a nonliquidating transfer. No money was distributed to Anne during the year, the property was in the partnership for over five years, and no debt was attached to the property. Anne had a basis in her partnership interest of $10,000. The partnership had an adjusted basis of $20,000 in the property distributed to Anne. Which of the following are the tax consequences to Anne?

A. $0 gain, basis in the partnership is reduced to $0, and basis in the property received is $10,000.
B. $0 gain, basis in the partnership is reduced to $0, and basis in the property received is $20,000.
C. $10,000 gain, basis in the partnership is reduced to $0, and basis in the property received is $20,000.
D. $10,000 gain, basis in the partnership is unchanged, and basis in the property received is $20,000.

REG 5-Q111 R132. Brown, a 50% partner in Brown & White, received a distribution of $12,500 in the current year. The partnership's income for the year was $25,000. What is the character of the payment that Brown received?

A. Partial liquidation.
B. Liquidating distribution.
C. Disproportionate distribution.
D. Current distribution.

REG 5-Q112 R318. Owen's tax basis in Regal Partnership was $18,000 at the time Owen received a non-liquidating distribution of $3,000 cash and land with an adjusted basis of $7,000 to Regal and a fair market value of $9,000. Regal did not have unrealized receivables, appreciated inventory, or properties that had been contributed by its partners. Disregarding any income, loss, or any other partnership distribution for the year, what was Owen's tax basis in Regal after the distribution?

A. $9,000
B. $8,000
C. $7,000
D. $6,000

REG 5-Q113 R357. Anderson's basis in the SBF Partnership is $80,000. Anderson received a nonliquidating distribution of $50,000 cash, and land with an adjusted basis of $40,000 and a fair market value of $50,000. What is Anderson's basis in the land?

A. $50,000
B. $40,000
C. $30,000
D. $20,000

REG 5-Q114 R351. Smith, a partner in Ridge Partnership, had a basis in the partnership interest of $100,000 at the time Smith received a nonliquidating distribution of land with an adjusted basis of $75,000 to Ridge and a fair market value of $135,000. Ridge had no unrealized receivables, appreciated inventory, or properties that had been contributed by its partners. Which of the following statements is(are) correct regarding the distribution?

I. Ridge recognized a $60,000 capital gain from the distribution.
II. Smith's holding period for the land includes the time it was owned by Ridge.

A. I only.
B. II only.
C. Both I and II.
D. Neither I nor II.

REG 5-Q115 R163. A $100,000 increase in partnership liabilities is treated in which of the following ways?

A. Increases each partner's basis in the partnership by $100,000.
B. Increases the partners' bases only if the liability is nonrecourse.
C. Increases each partner's basis in proportion to their ownership.
D. Does not change any partner's basis in the partnership regardless of whether the liabilities are recourse or nonrecourse.

REG 5-Q116 R113. In the current year, when Hoben's tax basis in Lynz Partnership interest was $10,000, Hoben received a *liquidating* distribution as follows:

	Adjusted tax basis	Fair market value
Marketable securities	$5,000	$5,000
Land	25,000	27,000

Lynz had no appreciated inventory, unrealized receivables, or properties that had been contributed by its partners. What was Hoben's recognized gain on the distribution?

A. $0
B. $15,000
C. $22,000
D. $32,000

REG 5-Q117 R253. Reid, Welsh, and May are equal partners in the RWM partnership. Reid's basis in the partnership interest is $60,000. Reid receives a liquidating distribution of $61,000 cash, in addition to land with a fair market value of $14,000 and an adjusted basis of $12,000. What gain must Reid recognize upon the liquidation of his partnership interest?

A. $0
B. $1,000
C. $13,000
D. $15,000

REG 5-Q118 R39. Gulde's tax basis in Chyme Partnership was $26,000 at the time Gulde received a liquidating distribution of $12,000 cash and land with an adjusted basis to Chyme of $10,000 and a fair market value of $30,000. Chyme did not have unrealized receivables, appreciated inventory, or properties that had been contributed by its partners. What was the amount of Gulde's basis in the land?

A. $0
B. $10,000
C. $14,000
D. $30,000

REG 5-Q119 R168. The adjusted basis of Smith's interest in EVA partnership was $230,000 immediately before receiving the following distribution in complete liquidation of EVA:

	Basis to EVA	Fair market value
Cash	$150,000	$150,000
Real estate	120,000	146,000

What is Smith's basis in the real estate?

A. $146,000
B. $133,000
C. $120,000
D. $80,000

REG 5-Q120 R194. Fern received $30,000 in cash and an automobile with an adjusted basis and market value of $20,000 in a proportionate liquidating distribution from EF Partnership. Fern's basis in the partnership interest was $60,000 before the distribution. What is Fern's basis in the automobile received in the liquidation?

A. $0
B. $10,000
C. $20,000
D. $30,000

REG 5-Q121 R213. Baker is a partner in BDT with a partnership basis of $60,000. BDT made a liquidating distribution of land with an adjusted basis of $75,000 and a fair market value of $40,000 to Baker. What amount of gain or loss should Baker report?

A. $35,000 loss.
B. $20,000 loss.
C. $0
D. $15,000 gain.

REG 5-Q122 R232. Olson, Wayne, and Hogan are equal partners in the OWH partnership. Olson's basis in the partnership interest is $70,000. Olson receives a liquidating distribution of $10,000 cash and land with a fair market value of $63,000, and a basis of $58,000. What is Olson's basis in the land?

A. $58,000
B. $60,000
C. $63,000
D. $70,000

REG 5-Q123 R216. The CSU partnership distributed to each partner cash of $4,000, inventory with a basis of $4,000 and a fair market value (FMV) of $6,000, and land with an adjusted basis of $5,000 and a FMV of $3,000 in a liquidating distribution. Partner Chang had an outside basis in Chang's partnership interest of $12,000. In the second year after receiving the liquidating distribution, Chang sold the inventory for $5,000 and the land for $3,000. What income must Chang report upon the sale of these assets?

A. $0 gain or loss.
B. $0 ordinary gain and $1,000 capital loss.
C. $1,000 ordinary gain and $1,000 capital loss.
D. $1,000 ordinary gain and $0 capital loss.

REG 5-Q124 R394. Stone and Frazier decided to terminate the Woodwest Partnership as of December 31. On that date, Woodwest's balance sheet was as follows:

Cash	$2,000
Equipment (adjusted basis)	2,000
Capital - Stone	3,000
Capital - Frazier	1,000

The fair market value of the equipment was $3,000. Frazier's outside basis in the partnership was $1,200. Upon liquidation, Frazier received $1,500 in cash. What gain should Frazier recognize?

A. $0
B. $250
C. $300
D. $500

REG 5-Q125 R249. On December 31, after receipt of his share of partnership income, Clark sold his interest in a limited partnership for $30,000 cash and relief of all liabilities. On that date, the adjusted basis of Clark's partnership interest was $40,000, consisting of his capital account of $15,000 and his share of the partnership liabilities of $25,000. The partnership has no unrealized receivables or substantially appreciated inventory. What is Clark's gain or loss on the sale of his partnership interest?

A. Ordinary loss of $10,000.
B. Ordinary gain of $15,000.
C. Capital loss of $10,000.
D. Capital gain of $15,000.

REG 5-Q126 R1138. Jack and Jill were equal partners in Hill Partnership. The partnership only had one asset: land with an adjusted basis of $80,000 and a FMV of $200,000. The capital accounts and tax bases for each partner were as follows:

	Capital Account (Inside Basis)	Tax Basis (Outside Basis)	Partner's share of FMV of Partnership Assets
Jack	$40,000	$40,000	$200,000*50% = $100,000
Jill	$40,000	$40,000	$200,000*50% = $100,000

Jill decides to sell her partnership interest to Peter for $100,000. After the sale, what will inside and outside basis of Jack and Peter look like if the partnership makes a Section 754 election?

A.
	(Inside Basis)	Tax Basis (Outside Basis)
Jack	$40,000	$40,000
Peter	$40,000	$40,000

B.
	(Inside Basis)	Tax Basis (Outside Basis)
Jack	$40,000	$40,000
Peter	$100,000	$100,000

C.
	(Inside Basis)	Tax Basis (Outside Basis)
Jack	$100,000	$100,000
Peter	$100,000	$100,000

D.
	(Inside Basis)	Tax Basis (Outside Basis)
Jack	$40,000	$40,000
Peter	$40,000	$100,000

REG 5-Q127 R1139. Peter and Piper were equal partners in Pepper Partnership. The partnership only had one asset: land with an adjusted basis of $30,000 and a FMV of $100,000. Piper decides to sell her partnership interest to Peck for $50,000 and the partnership makes a Section 754 election. How much gain will Peter and Peck each recognize when the land (one year later) is sold by the partnership for $200,000?

A. $0, the partnership (not the partners) will recognize the gain.

B.
	Gain
Peter	$85,000
Peck	$85,000

C.
	Gain
Peter	$85,000
Peck	$50,000

D.
	Gain
Peter	$50,000
Peck	$50,000

REG 5-Q128 R1140. When a partnership interest is sold and the partnership makes a Section 754 election, what exactly is the partnership electing to adjust and by what amount?

A. What is adjusted: The seller's inside basis is adjusted to partner's outside basis
B. What is adjusted: The seller's outside basis is adjusted to the partner's inside basis
C. What is adjusted: The partnership's inside basis is adjusted to the partner's outside basis,
D. What is adjusted: The continuing partner's inside basis is adjusted to the partner's outside basis.

REG 5-Q129 R306. Which of the following is an advantage of forming a limited liability company (LLC) as opposed to a partnership?

A. LLC may avoid taxation.
B. LLC may have any number of owners.
C. LLC owner(s) may participate in management while limiting personal liability.
D. LLC makes disproportionate allocations and distributions to members.

REG 5-Q130 R286. Which of the following types of entities is entitled to the net operating loss deduction?

A. Partnerships.
B. S corporations.
C. Trusts and estates.
D. Not-for-profit organizations.

REG 5-Q131 R353. Gardner, a U.S. citizen and the sole income beneficiary of a simple trust, is entitled to receive current distributions of the trust income. During the year, the trust reported:

Interest income from corporate bonds $5,000
Fiduciary fees allocable to income   750
Net long-term capital gain allocable to corpus 2,000

What amount of the trust income is includible in Gardner's gross income?

A. $7,000
B. $5,000
C. $4,250
D. $0

REG 5-Q132 R1130. For a tax-exempt organization, the unrelated business income is taxed at what rate?

A. Corporate tax rate
B. Trust tax rate
C. Estate tax rate
D. Either at corporate or trust rates, depending upon whether the tax-exempt organization is a corporation or a trust.

REG 5-Q133 R1131. Which of the following statements is true?

A. The amount of unrelated business income is determined by the IRS.
B. All of the unrelated business income is taxed either corporate or trust rates.
C. The unrelated business income that is taxed is the amount in excess of $1,000.
D. A church is not subject to unrelated business income tax, since they do not have to file a Form 990.

REG 5-Q134 R1132. Which of the following types of income is generally determined to be unrelated business income?

A. Rental income
B. Interest income
C. Dividend income
D. Advertising revenue

REG 5-Q135 R1133. If a tax-exempt organization is considered to be a charitable trust

A. The trust does not have to pay any unrelated business income tax.
B. The trust will pay corporate taxes on the unrelated business income in excess of $1,000.
C. The trust will pay trust taxes on the unrelated business income less than $1,000.
D. The trust will pay trust taxes on the unrelated business income in excess of $1,000.

Multiple Choice – Solutions

REG 5-Q1 R147. The correct answer is B. This question deals with the formation of a corporation and the tax consequences to the shareholders. There are three shareholders forming a corporation:
1) Quigley is receiving 30 shares for services rendered of $25,000.
2) Roberk is receiving 60 shares of stock for a transfer of land with a fair market value (FMV) of $100,000 and a basis of $10,000.
3) Storm is receiving 10 shares of stock in exchange for $10,000.

To prevent income to the shareholders, they must acquire 80% or more of the stock (or control) in exchange for property (rather than cash or services). Quigley will have taxable income for the 30 shares of stock received because he provided services of $25,000. Quigley doesn't qualify for a nontaxable event since contributed services (not property) and he only received 30% (30/100 shares) of the shares.

Roberk transferred property for 60 shares of stock. Roberk's income is the excess of the land FMV over the land basis ($100,000 - $10,000) or $90,000. While Roberk is the only stockholder that received shares for property transferred, he received only 60% (60/100 shares) rather than 80% or more.

Storm purchased 10 shares of stock for cash. Storm will not have taxable income because Storm simply purchased stock for cash contributed. Therefore, it doesn't cause Storm to have a taxable event.

REG 5-Q2 R580. The correct answer is C. A general partnership is created under contract law and not by filing an organizational document or certificate with a state government agency or office.
Answers A, B and D are incorrect because they are formed under an organizational document or certificate with a state government agency or office.

REG 5-Q3 R577. The correct answer is D. Partners will share in losses according to the allocation of profits specified in the partnership agreement. This makes answers A, B and C incorrect.

REG 5-Q4 R583. The correct answer is B. If a general partnership agreement does not address the sharing of profits and losses, the profits and losses are shared equally. Since the profits were $200,000, each partner would get $100,000 each because there were two partners. The percentage of work done by each partner has nothing to do with the distribution of profits. Also, the contribution of cash has nothing to do with the sharing of profits or losses.

REG 5-Q5 R605. The correct answer is B. Unless there is an agreement to the contrary, all partners have equal rights to share in the profits of the partnership.

Answers A, C, and D are incorrect because of the above explanation.

REG 5-Q6 R588. The correct answer is A. Limited partners may lose limited liability if they participate in management activities.

Answer B is incorrect because limited partners will not lose limited liability if they do not participate in management activities.

Answer C is incorrect because limited partners do not have the same rights, responsibilities, and authority as general partners. General partners can participate in management where limited partners cannot.

Answer D is incorrect because limited partners, in addition to cash, may also contribute property and services for their capital contributions.

REG 5-Q7 R590. The correct answer is A. National will not prevail in this lawsuit because National obtained a judgment against Fil and Fil's child, not against the partnership.

Answer B is incorrect because the judgment against Fil and Fil's child was not against the partnership, it would not cause a dissolution against the partnership by operation of law.

Answer C is incorrect because National would not prevail in its suit against the partnership because the judgment was against Fil alone.

Answer D is incorrect because National would not prevail because Fil's interest in the partnership inventory is not an asset owned by Fil. The property is owned by the partnership.

REG 5-Q8 R593. The correct answer is B. In a general partnership, a partner can assign their interest to a bank as collateral when obtaining a loan. The bank (assignee) is entitled to the assigning partner's interest in the partnership profits and surplus on dissolution of the partnership.

Answers A and C are incorrect because the bank (assignee) does not become a substitute partner and is not personally responsible for the debts of the partnership.

Answer D is incorrect because I is correct but II is not correct.

REG 5-Q9 R582. The correct answer is B. A general partnership can be voluntarily dissolved and terminated without filing a dissolution document with the state of organization. The dissolution occurs when a general partner withdraws from a partnership, the death of a general partner, bankruptcy of a general partner or the incapacity of a general partner.

Answers A, C and D are incorrect because they can be voluntarily dissolved and terminated by filing a dissolution document with the state of incorporation.

REG 5-Q10 R596. The correct answer is D. A limited partnership may be dissolved as a result of any of the following events:
1) The time or event specified in the limited partnership agreement occurs,
2) All the partners agree, in writing, to dissolve,
3) An event of withdrawal of the only general partner occurs, or
4) The limited partnership is dissolved by court order

The only event that is most likely to dissolve a limited partnership is the withdrawal of the only general partner. In order to have a limited partnership, there must be at least one general partner so that at least one of the partners is personally liable for the debts of the limited partnership.

REG 5-Q11 R594. The correct answer is C. All members of the LLC have a right to participate in management.

Answer A is incorrect because generally, they only have the right to elect directors and to vote on fundamental changes in the corporation.

Answer B is incorrect because in a general partnership, there are no limited partners. There are only general partners. With no limited partners, there are no management rights for limited partners.

Answer D is incorrect because limited partners in a limited partnership cannot take an active role in the management of the limited partnership.

REG 5-Q12 R585. The correct answer is B. The owners of a LLC are called members. Members have limited liability for the debts and obligations of the LLC.

Answer A is incorrect because partners are owners in a general partnership.

Answers C and D are incorrect because stockholders (also known as shareholders), are owners of a corporation by acquiring stock.

REG 5-Q13 R587. The correct answer is B. The two individuals want to limit liability, avoid double taxation, and be active in management. As limited liability members, they would have no liability beyond their investment. With a limited liability company, the entity would be taxed like a partnership with no double taxation. They would have the right to participate in the LLC management decisions.

Answer A is incorrect because a C corporation is subject to double taxation.

Answer C is incorrect because in a limited partnership, the general partners have unlimited liability and are active in the management of the business and the limited partners have liability only up to their investment and are not active in the management of the business. Therefore, the general partners cannot have limited liability and the limited partners do not have the right to manage in a limited partnership. Therefore, the general partners cannot have limited liability and the limited partners do not have the right to manage in a limited partnership.

Answer D is incorrect because a general partner in a general partnership has unlimited liability.

REG 5-Q14 R561. The correct answer is D. Terry should form a limited liability company because the members, not just Terry, have limited liability and are allowed to actively participate in running the business.

Answer A is incorrect because if Terry is a general partner, he has unlimited liability for the torts and contracts of the partnership.

Answer B is incorrect. Terry should not form a limited partnership and be a limited partner because Terry is taking an active role in running the business and will have unlimited liability for the contracts and torts of the limited partnership.

Answer C is incorrect because normally in a joint venture, the joint venture is entering into a single project and is treated as a partner generally, with unlimited liability.

REG 5-Q15 R569. The correct answer is B. In a limited liability company (LLC), all members have limited liability. All members of a limited liability company may participate in management, unless they choose otherwise. On the death, retirement, resignation, bankruptcy, etc. of a member, a limited liability company is dissolved.

Answer A is incorrect because a limited partnership has limited liability only for the limited partners and unlimited liability for the general partners. A limited partner cannot participate in the management of the business and has limited liability.

Answer C is incorrect because general partners in a general partnership have unlimited liability.

Answer D is incorrect because, although the shareholders are the owners of the corporation, they generally have no power to run the corporation. This is performed by the board and the officers of the LLC. Another reason D is incorrect is that death, withdrawal or bankruptcy of a stockholder does not dissolve a corporation.

REG 5-Q16 R591. The correct answer is A. An S corporation can only have one class of stock.

Answer B is incorrect because a partnership cannot be a shareholder in an S corporation. The shareholders can only be individuals, estates and trusts.

Answer C is incorrect because an S corporation is not required to have international ownership.

Answer D is incorrect because an S corporation cannot have more than 100 shareholders.

REG 5-Q17 R604. The correct answer is D. The only entities that can own stock in an S corporation are individuals, estates and trusts. Corporations cannot be stockholders in an S corporation.

Answers A, B, and C are incorrect because individuals can be stockholders in an S corporation.

REG 5-Q18 R607. The correct answer is B. Some of the requirements to be an S corporation are:
No more than 100 shareholders
Shareholders must be individuals, estates and trusts
No non-resident alien shareholders
Only one class of stock

Since answer B is not one of the conditions to be an S corporation, it is the correct answer.

REG 5-Q19 R857. The correct answer is B. An S corporation cannot have more than 100 shareholders. A husband and wife count as one shareholder.

REG 5-Q20 R862. The correct answer is A. In order to qualify for S corporation status, the following conditions must all be satisfied:

1. It must be a domestic corporation.
2. It cannot be a member of an affiliated group.
3. It has only individuals, estates and certain trusts as stockholders.
4. It does not have a nonresident alien as a stockholder.
5. It does not have more than 100 stockholders.
6. It does not have more than one class of stock.
7. It derives no more than 25% of its income from passive investments (including interest, dividends, rents, royalties, annuities, etc.).

REG 5-Q21 R564. The correct answer is D. Nonresident aliens cannot be shareholders in an S corporation.

Answers A, B and C are incorrect because to qualify as an S corporation, the corporation cannot have more than 100 shareholders. In this case, they only have 77. A shareholder can be an individual, an estate or a trust. A 501 (c)(3) tax exempt organization can be a shareholder.

REG 5-Q22 R571. The correct answer is B. A subchapter S corporation is a corporation by law but, is treated as a partnership for tax purposes. Because it is treated as a corporation by law, all the stockholders have limited liability. Since it is treated as a partnership for tax purposes, the S corporation generally pays no taxes on its income when filing the S corporation tax return (Form 1120S).

REG 5-Q23 R609. The correct answer is C. C corporations and S corporations can both have shareholders contributing property or cash into the corporation without being taxed.

Answer A is incorrect because an S corporation cannot have more than 100 shareholders. A C corporation has not limit on the number of shareholders it can have.

Answer B is incorrect because a C corporation is subject to double taxation where an S corporation is not subject to double taxation.

Answer D is incorrect because non-resident aliens cannot be shareholders in an S corporation, but there is no such requirement in a C corporation.

REG 5-Q24 R597. The correct answer is C. A subchapter C corporation files a Form 1120 and is subject to taxes on its taxable income. It is also taxed upon its owners when the owners receive dividends.

Answer A is incorrect because a general partnership files a Form 1065, which is an information return and does not pay taxes at the partnership level. The taxable income items and taxable deductions flow through to the individual partner's individual return Form 1040.

Answer B is incorrect because an LLC generally files a Form 1120S (S corporation return), which is like a partnership return. The LLC usually does not pay taxes but, all items on the Form 1120S flow through and are taxed or deducted on the individual member's Form 1040.

Answer D is incorrect because a subchapter S corporation files Form 1120S, which is like a partnership return. The S corporation usually does not pay taxes but, all items on the Form 1120S flow through and are taxed or deducted on the individual stockholder's Form 1040.

REG 5-Q25 R282. The correct answer is B. Schedule M-1 of Form 1120 for C corporations is Reconciliation of Income (Loss) per Books with Income per Return. This reconciles book income to taxable income. Premiums paid on key-person life insurance policies are deductible to arrive at book income, but are not deductible on the tax return if the corporation is the beneficiary. If the corporation is NOT the beneficiary, the premiums would be deductible on the corporate tax return. Therefore, the premiums may appear on the reconciliation if the corporation is the beneficiary.

Answer A is incorrect because cash distributions to shareholders are usually dividends and would appear in a reconciliation of retained earnings, schedule M-2 (reconciliation of beginning unappropriated retained earnings to ending unappropriated retained earnings).

Answer C is incorrect because corporate bond interest income is includable in both book income and taxable income and would not appear in the reconciliation. If an item is included in both, it does not have to be included in the reconciliation.

Answer D is incorrect because the ending balance of retained earnings would appear in Schedule M-2 (reconciliation of beginning unappropriated retained earnings to ending unappropriated retained earnings)

REG 5-Q26 R44. The correct answer is C.
Start with book income which includes all income minus all expenses. Reconcile book income to taxable income.

Pretax book income	$543,000
Subtract: Additional depreciation on the tax return	(20,000)
Add: Rental income reportable on the tax return not reportable on books	36,000
Add: Pollution expense on financial statements not deductible on tax return	10,000
Subtract: Interest on municipal bonds included on books but not on tax return	(25,000)
Total taxable income	$544,000

REG 5-Q27 R206. The correct answer is C. This question is testing the candidate's ability to reconcile book income to taxable income for the current year. Book income includes all income minus all expenses. When reconciling book to taxable income, add back any expenses to the book income which is not tax deductible and subtract any income from the book income that is not taxable income.

Start with book income of $150,000 and add back non-deductible expenses such as the excess capital loss of $10,000 and the federal income tax expense of $50,000. Subtract from book income items which are non-taxable income such as the interest income on municipal bonds of $5,000. Jagdon's taxable income for the current year would be: $150,000 + $10,000 + $50,000 - $5,000 = $205,000, answer C

REG 5-Q28 R128. The correct answer is D because a C corporation files Form 1120 to compute taxable income (loss). If there is taxable income, the C corporation must pay federal taxes.

Answers A, B and C are incorrect because the entities are partnerships, which file Form 1065 U.S. Partnership returns. Partnerships do not pay taxes.

REG 5-Q29 R129. The correct answer is D. Advertising expenses are deductible currently as ordinary and necessary business expenses.

Answers A, B and C are incorrect because advertising expenses are not amortized.

REG 5-Q30 R302. The correct answer is A. C corporations may elect to be on a fiscal year or a calendar year.

Answers B, C and D are incorrect because they must be a calendar year.

REG 5-Q31 R68. The correct answer is A. When filing the Form 1120 (corporate tax return for a C corporation), the Other Information section on Schedule K is where the accounting method is selected.

Answers B, C and D are incorrect because the selection of the accounting method for tax purposes is chosen on the initial tax return.

REG 5-Q32 R170. The correct answer is C. If a corporation changes from an S corporation having a year end of June 30th, to a C corporation, they must be on the accrual basis of accounting and can continue with the same fiscal year (June 30th). A small business taxpayer is a corporation that has more than $1,000,000 and less than $10,000,000 in annual gross receipts and if they meet certain requirements, they can be on a cash basis. Since this corporation has more than $10,000,000 in annual gross receipts, they must be on the accrual basis because they are not a small business taxpayer.

Answers A and D are incorrect because it says that they may be on a cash basis. They must be on an accrual basis as this corporation is not considered a small business taxpayer.

Answer B is incorrect because they would continue with the same year end of June 30th using the accrual basis as the stockholders wanted to keep the same year end of June 30th. However, even though the stockholders wanted the corporation to be on a cash basis, they are unable to be on a cash basis because they are not defined as a small business taxpayer as defined in the first paragraph above.

REG 5-Q33 R243. The correct answer is D. The accrual basis must generally be used by C corporations. C corporations with average annual sales over $5 million for previous three-year period that are not personal service corporations must use the accrual method.

Answer A is incorrect because a business that has average sales for the past three years of less than $1 million can use the cash method even if it has inventory which was purchased and is sold.

Answer B is incorrect because a small business taxpayer is eligible to use the cash method if they have average sales for the last three years of over $1 million and less than $10,000,000 and they meet any one of the following requirements:
1) The principal business activity is not retailing, wholesaling or manufacturing
2) The principal business activity is the provision of services

Since the business is a service company and has over $1 million in sales, they are not required to use the accrual method but, may elect the cash method.

Answer C is incorrect because if a business is a personal service business with over $15 million in sales is not required to use the accrual method as it performs a personal service and the amount of sales it has is irrelevant.

REG 5-Q34 R443. The correct answer is D. To calculate the tax of a corporation for a short period, the income must be annualized, follow these steps:
1) Multiple the short period taxable income by 12
2) Divide it the number of months in the short period
3) Compute the tax on the resulting taxable income
4) The amount of computed tax is multiplied by the number of months in the short period and then divide by 12 to derive the corporation's tax for the short period.

REG 5-Q35 R4. Correct answer is C. Business gifts are limited to $25 per recipient. The amount Nichol Corp can deduct as business gifts is:

5 gifts @ $15	$75
9 gifts @ $25	225
1 gift at $25	25
Total deduction	$325

REG 5-Q36 R204. The correct answer is C. To compute taxable income or loss of a C corporation, net capital losses cannot be deducted in the current year. However, net capital losses can be carried back 3 years and carried forward 5 years as short term. To calculate the answer, take the gross receipts of $150,000, add to it the other income of $35,000 and subtract deductible expenses of $95,000, resulting in taxable income of $90,000. Please note, the net capital loss is not deducted because capital losses of a corporation are only deductible against capital gains of the same corporation on Schedule D (Form 1120).

REG 5-Q37 R45. Answers A, B and D are incorrect because they can be amortized for tax purposes because they represent organization costs.

The correct answer is C. Stock issuance costs are never considered part of organization cost and it is not amortizable. Examples would be registration fees and underwriting costs.

REG 5-Q38 R355. The correct answer is A. If a corporation is completely liquidated and dissolved during the current year, filing fees, professional fees, and other expenditures incurred in connection with the liquidation and dissolution are a deductible in full by the dissolved corporation.

REG 5-Q39 R3. The correct answer is B. Corporations are limited on their charitable contributions to 10% of taxable income before the contribution deduction. The taxable income before charitable contribution was $200,000. The limit is 10% of $200,000, or $20,000.

Quest has a contribution carryover of $8,000. An accrual basis corporation can accrue a contribution and deduct it (subject to the 10% limitation) if paid by the due date of the tax return, March 15th of year 3. Since they paid the $15,000 on January 6th of year 3, they can deduct it (if they so elect) on the year 2 tax return. Therefore, the total of the carryover from year 1 and accrual for year 2 is $8,000 + $15,000 = $23,000. However, the limit as stated in the first paragraph is $20,000.

REG 5-Q40 R109. The correct answer is B. The charitable contribution deduction for a corporation is limited to 10% of taxable income before the deductions for charitable contributions and the dividend received deduction.

Revenues	$200,000
Gross dividends	20,000
Total gross income	$220,000
Operating expenses (exclude contributions dividend received deduction)	($75,000)
Taxable income before contribution and dividend received deductions	$145,000

The contribution deduction is the lesser the amount of contributions made of $15,000 or 10% of taxable income before contribution and dividend received deductions ($145,000 x 10%) which equals $14,500. The lesser of the two is the $14,500. The amount of the contribution not deducted of $500 can be carried forward for 5 consecutive five years.

REG 5-Q41 R195. The correct answer is C. The answer only applies to companies that receive dividends where they have a profit from operations. When a corporation receives a dividend distribution from another corporation, if the corporation who receives the dividend owns less than 20% of the corporation stock that paid the dividend; the corporation that receives the dividend can exclude

70% of the dividends received. In this case, Pope received $3,000 and can exclude 70% of the $3,000, which equals $2,100. If Pope owned 20% to 79% of Arden's stock, then Pope could exclude 80% of the dividends received.

REG 5-Q42 R235. The correct answer is B. To calculate Beta's taxable income for the year, start with the gross income of $600,000 and add the gross dividends of $100,000 which equals $700,000 total gross income. Then, subtract the operating expenses of $400,000, resulting in taxable income of $300,000 before the dividend received deduction. Next, calculate the dividend received deduction which will reduce the taxable income before the dividend received deduction to taxable income. When a corporation owns 20% to 79% of another company's stock, they may exclude 80% of the dividend received from the corporation they invested in. Take 80% of the dividends received of $100,000, which equals $80,000, the amount of dividends excludable from taxation (the dividend received deduction). Next, subtract $80,000 from the taxable income before the dividend received deduction of $300,000, resulting in taxable income (after the dividend received deduction) of $220,000.

REG 5-Q43 R299. The correct answer is C. When a corporation has a loss from operations which in this question is the gross income before dividends of $900,000 and deductions of $1,100,000 (before the dividends received deduction) equaling $200,000 loss from operations ($900,000 - $1,100,000). There is special rule for the dividends received deduction. Add in the gross dividend of $100,000 to the loss of $200,000 which equals taxable income (loss) before the dividend received deduction of $100,000 ($100,000 - $200,000).

This question does not state the percentage ownership that Brown owns of the Fortune 500 corporation. If no percentage ownership is stated, always assume ownership of less than 20% and therefore the 70% dividend received deduction.

Now go back to the taxable loss after inclusion of the gross dividends which equals $100,000. Apply the 70% dividend received deduction to the gross dividends of $100,000 which equals $70,000. If we subtract the $70,000 from the taxable loss and it either creates or adds to the loss, then the dividends received deduction is 70% of the dividends received. Take the taxable loss of $100,000 and add the $70,000 dividend received deduction to arrive at a taxable loss of $170,000. Because it adds to the loss, the dividend received deduction is 70% of dividends received.

What happens if we take the 70% of dividends received and it does not add to or create a loss, then the dividends received deduction would be 70% of the taxable income before the dividends received deduction. This special rule only applies when there is a loss from operations. If there is a profit from operations, the dividends received deduction would have been 70% of the gross dividends.

The net operating loss for the current year is the taxable loss including the dividend received deduction which is this case is $170,000.

REG 5-Q44 R434. The correct answer is D. The averaging convention methods are used to determine allowable deductions that can be taken in the first year on either tangible personal property used in a trade or business or real estate used in a trade or business. Because this asset is real estate, the averaging convention method is the mid-month method. For the first year, the mid-month method assumes that the real estate is placed in service in the middle of that month. For example, if the taxpayer placed the real estate in service April 28th for the first year, take the depreciation from April 15th of that first year to December 31st of that first year.

Answer A is incorrect because the taxpayer will never take a full year depreciation in the first year.

Answers B and C are incorrect because they are the averaging convention methods for personal property used in a trade or business for the first year and are either the half year or mid-quarter method.

REG 5-Q45 R326. The correct answer is D. If the tentative minimum tax of $240,000 is greater than the regular tax liability of $210,000, then the client owes alternative minimum tax (AMT). AMT is the excess of the tentative minimum tax over the regular tax liability, which equals $30,000. The Tan Corp total tax liability will be the AMT of $30,000 plus the regular tax liability of $210,000, plus the personal holding company tax of $65,000, resulting in a total tax liability of $305,000.

REG 5-Q46 R336. The correct answer is C. This question deals with transfers to a controlled corporation under IRC Section 351. Normally, if an individual, or a group of individuals, transfers property in exchange for 80% or more of the stock of that corporation, there is no taxable event to the incorporators or the corporation whose stock is being acquired.

There are two events that will cause gain recognition to the stockholders, even though they acquired 80% or more of the stock.

1) If the stockholder receives cash or investments in securities of another corporation, the cash or the investments, will cause gain recognition.
2) If the property transferred has a debt (mortgage), and the mortgage is assumed by the corporation, the excess of the liability assumed by the corporation over the basis of the property contributed to the corporation will cause recognition of gain.

Generally, there would be no recognized gain because Dole acquired 80% or more of the stock. However, because of exception #1 above (Dole received cash of $40,000 in addition to the stock); the cash received of $40,000 will cause recognition of gain. Therefore, the recognized gain is $40,000.

REG 5-Q47 R161. The correct answer is B. When stockholders form a corporation and contribute property to the corporation and acquire 80% or more of the stock, under Section 351 of the Internal Revenue Code, there is no tax consequences to the stockholders of the corporation or the corporation because the stockholders got control (control is acquiring 80% or more of the stock).

Ames and Roth acquired 100% of the stock of Homerun and have no taxable event with the corporation. When there is no taxable event, the stockholder's basis in the stock is equal to the basis of the property transferred in. The corporation's basis in the property is equal to the transferred basis of the shareholders. Ames's autographed baseballs have a basis of $500 and the corporation who now owns the baseballs takes on the basis of the baseballs from Ames which is $500. Roth contributed several autographed baseball bats to Homerun. Roth purchased the bats for $5,000 which is Roth's basis in the bats, and now Homerun Corporation takes the bats and also the takes the basis of $5,000. In conclusion, the basis of the balls and bats are $5,500 to Homerun Corporation. Correct answer is B.

REG 5-Q48 R182. The correct answer is C. No gain or loss is recognized if property is transferred to a corporation in exchange for stock and those persons transferring the property acquire at least 80% of the total combined voting power and 80% of each class of non-voting stock. The corporation's basis of the property is the transferor's basis plus the gain recognized to the transferor. If the transferor received cash, it will be a recognition of the gain. Therefore, the corporation's basis for the land is B's basis in the land ($40,000) plus B's gain ($20,000) for the cash received by B, or $60,000.

REG 5-Q49 R175. The correct answer is A. This question deals with a distribution of property by a corporation to its shareholders in a non-liquidating distribution. The amount of the basis of the property distributed to the stockholder is the fair market value (FMV) of $38,000 at date of distribution, not reduced by liabilities.

REG 5-Q50 R341. The correct answer is D. When a corporation distributes assets to its shareholders, the corporation will have a gain if the liability assumed by the shareholder ($40,000) exceeds the basis of the asset distributed to the shareholder ($25,000) and the fair market value (FMV) of the distributed property ($30,000) is less than the amount of the liability ($40,000). The gain is the excess of the liability of $40,000 over the basis of the asset of $25,000, which equals a gain to Aztec of $15,000.

REG 5-Q51 R1. Answer C is the correct answer. Dividends are taxable to the stockholders to the extent of current earnings and profits (E&P), if both the current and accumulated E&P are positive. The distribution was comprised of two $40,000 distributions for a total of $80,000. The amount of the distribution that is a dividend consists of current E&P, $20,000 and accumulated E&P, $30,000 for a total of $50,000. The remaining $30,000 of the distribution is first a return of stock basis (non-taxable) and if any distribution is left, it is a capital gain (taxable).

REG 5-Q52 R92. The correct answer is C. When a corporation makes a distribution, the distribution would be a dividend if the corporation has first current earnings and profits that are positive and then accumulated earnings and profits which are positive. In this question, Simon paid $15,000 to the shareholder. First go to the current earnings and profits and see if it is positive. The current earnings and profits are positive in the amount of $10,000. So, the first $10,000 is a dividend distribution because the current earnings and profits are positive. The remaining $5,000 of the distribution will be a dividend if there are positive accumulated earnings and profits of at least $5,000. The accumulated earnings and profits is a deficit, so the $5,000 is not a dividend. The total dividend of the $15,000 distribution is $10,000.

REG 5-Q53 R158. The correct answer is C. A dividend distribution is a taxable dividend if there are positive current earnings and profits, and positive accumulated earnings and profits. In a dividend distribution, the corporation always distributes its current earnings and profits first, if positive. Then, the accumulated earnings and profits are distributed if positive. The total distribution to the shareholder is the $20,000 cash and the fair market value (FMV) of the property of $60,000. Therefore, the total distribution is $20,000 + $60,000 = $80,000. Always use the FMV of the property, not the basis, as the amount of the distribution.

Since there are no current earnings and profits, none of the current earnings and profits would be dividends. Next, look at the accumulated current earnings and profits which is a positive $70,000. The amount of the distribution which is dividends is limited to the accumulated earnings and profits of $70,000. Since the total distribution was $80,000, we would only account for $70,000 as dividends. The remaining $10,000 would be a return of stock basis if there was a basis of at least $10,000 in the stock. If the stock basis was less than $10,000, the remaining amount of the distribution to the stockholder would be a capital gain.

REG 5-Q54 R315. The correct answer is D. In March, Bridge made a distribution of $20,000 which would be taxed as dividends to the shareholders first out of current earnings and profits of $10,000 and accumulated earnings and profits of $10,000. This would leave the accumulated earnings and profits with a balance of $5,000.

In July, Bridge made another distribution of $20,000. First, go to current earnings and profits. The balance in current earnings and profits is $0. Next, got to accumulated earnings and profits which has a balance of $5,000. So, the $20,000 distribution consists of a dividend distribution of $5,000 which is the remaining amount in the accumulated earnings and profits. The remaining $15,000 of the distribution is a return of stock basis which is non-taxable and if any distribution remains, it would be taxed as a capital gain.

REG 5-Q55 R389. The correct answer is B. When a corporation distributes cash to its stockholder, the amount of the distribution is a taxable dividend to the stockholder to the extent of positive current earnings and profits and then any positive accumulated earnings and profits left over from prior years.

In this question, Westwind distributed $12,000 during the year. Since the current earnings and profits are $15,000, the $12,000 distribution from Westwind is a taxable dividend to the stockholders because the current earnings and profits are positive. Since Westwind distributed $12,000 out of the $15,000 current earnings and profits, $3,000 of the current earnings and profits which are positive have not been distributed. Next step is to take the positive current earnings and profits of $3,000 and close it out to the accumulated earnings and profits with a deficit of $45,000. If you add a positive current earnings and profits of $3,000 to a deficit of $45,000, which is the beginning accumulated earnings and profits, the ending earnings and profits will equal a $42,000 deficit [($45,000) deficit + $3,000 positive earnings = ($42,000) deficit]

REG 5-Q56 R447. The correct answer is B. If Brisk distributes land which has appreciated in value as a property dividend, Brisk would treat the transaction as though they sold the land to the shareholder. To determine Brisk's gain, take the fair market value of the land ($200,000) over the basis of the land ($75,000), which would result in a gain on the distribution to Brisk of $125,000 which would increase Brisk's taxable income by $125,000. If Brisk distributes cash as a cash dividend, there is no gain or loss on the distribution of cash. If land was distributed instead of cash, Brisk would have an increase in taxable income of $125,000 because a distribution of appreciated property in a property dividend is treated as though the corporation is selling the property to the shareholders at a gain.

The shareholder would take the fair market value of the property which is $200,000 and would have a taxable dividend for the lesser of the FMV of the property ($200,000) or the earnings and profits ($600,000). $200,000 is the lesser amount which is a taxable dividend to the shareholder. If the shareholder received cash instead of property, the taxable dividend would be the lesser of the cash distributed of $200,000 or the current and accumulated earnings and profits of $600,000. The lesser amount is a cash dividend of $200,000. So, whether the shareholder receives a property dividend or a cash dividend, the total dividend would be $200,000.

REG 5-Q57 R244. The correct answer is B. The total distribution is $30,000. The amount of current earnings and profits that is positive is $25,000. The amount of accumulated earnings and profits is negative and therefore cannot be taxable dividends to the shareholders. When there is a distribution, the amount that is dividends to the shareholder first comes out of the current earnings and profits if positive. So, the distribution of $30,000 goes to the preferred stockholders, who are paid first. The preferred stockholders would get a $20,000 dividend distribution of the current earnings and profits and common stockholders would receive $5,000 dividend distribution, the balance of the current earnings and profits. Since the distribution of $30,000 exceeds the current earnings and profits of $25,000, the remaining $5,000 is a return of capital.

REG 5-Q58 R276. The correct answer is B. In a total redemption, the usual result of the transaction to the stockholder is a capital gain if the amount received exceeds the shareholder's basis in the stock. In this question, Wallace's basis in the shares of Kingpin, which he acquired 15 years ago, has a basis of $25,000 and Wallace redeemed 100% of the stock for $200,000 resulting in a long-term capital gain of $175,000 ($200,000 - $25,000).

REG 5-Q59 R191. The correct answer is A. When a corporation owns 80% of more of both the voting stock and the total value of that stock in another corporation, we have a parent-subsidiary relationship. When there is a parent-subsidiary relationship, there is a no gain or loss on the distribution of property to the parent or the subsidiary. Forrest is the parent company and Diamond is the subsidiary.

REG 5-Q60 R354. The correct answer is D. Any dividend income that occurs on a consolidated tax return is neither taxable to the parent or the subsidiary.

REG 5-Q61 R130. The correct answer is C. If the parent company (Silver) owned 80% or more (which is control) of a subsidiary (Gold) voting stock and fair market value (FMV), then they may file a consolidated return.

Answer A is incorrect because two separate returns are not required to be filed if the parent owns at least 80% of both the voting stock and FMV of Gold. They may elect to file separate returns if they want to.

Answer B and D are incorrect because filing does not have anything to do with the timing of the merger.

REG 5-Q62 R186. The correct answer is D. Members of an affiliated group, which is defined as combining of a parent company owning 80% or more of its subsidiary's stock, may elect to file a consolidated tax return. This relationship of a parent owning at least 80% of the stock of a subsidiary companies is the only relationship where they may elect to file a consolidated tax return.

Answer A is incorrect because brother/sister controlled groups do not own stock in each other and therefore cannot elect to file a consolidated return.

Answer B is incorrect because a parent corporation cannot elect to file a consolidated return with any partnership.

Answer C is incorrect because the definition of filing a consolidated financial statement is: if the parent owns more 50% of the stock of the sub, they must file consolidated financial statements under GAAP. For tax purposes, a parent corporation may elect to file consolidated returns if they own at least 80%-controlled subsidiaries.

REG 5-Q63 R274. The correct answer is C. To arrive at the correct answer, combine the Parent taxable income of $50,000 and subtract the subsidiary taxable losses of ($60,000) and ($40,000), to arrive at a consolidated net operating loss of ($50,000).

REG 5-Q64 R1134. The correct answer is B. Sales, Payroll and Property are the three common factors used by states to determine what percentage of a multi-state corporation's business income must be reported to and taxed in a particular state.

REG 5-Q65 R1135. The correct answer is A. The only scenario that probably does NOT create nexus is scenario A because the sales staff will continue to work in their current location to generate sales. They will not physically be located in a state other than Maine. Soliciting sales of tangible personal property that are approved and shipped outside the state

Answer B is incorrect because the company will most likely have nexus in whatever states it stores inventory.

Answer C is incorrect because installation of a product usually generates nexus in the state in which the installation occurs.

Answer D is incorrect because the company's sales staff would be physically located and performing their work duties in another state, nexus would probably be created in the states in which they are working.

REG 5-Q66 R1137. The correct answer is B. The company is likely to have nexus in:
- Arizona because its employees, operations, and inventory are located in Arizona.
- Colorado, because it sends sales staff there who make and approve the sales on site in the state.
- Utah, because the company has inventory physically located in the state.

The company likely does NOT have nexus in New Mexico. Even though it sells to customers in New Mexico and ships its product there, it does not have any personnel or inventory there, nor does it approve the sales orders there.

REG 5-Q67 R1136. The answer is C. The company can claim the lower of the $19,000 in foreign taxes paid or, $8,944 foreign tax credit limit, calculated as follows:

$$\text{Foreign tax credit limitation} = \text{U.S. tax on worldwide income} * \frac{\text{Foreign source taxable income}}{\text{Worldwide taxable income}}$$

$$= \$40,000 * \frac{\$72,000}{\$250,000 + \$72,000}$$

$$= \$8,944$$

Therefore, the company can claim a foreign tax credit of $8,944.

REG 5-Q68 R1149. The correct answer is D. FinCEN stands for Financial Crimes Enforcement Network. FinCEN Form 114 must be filed directly with the office of Financial Crimes Enforcement Network (FinCEN), a bureau of the Department of the Treasury which is separate from the IRS.

Answers A, B and C are incorrect because each of them is true statements regarding FinCEN.

REG 5-Q69 R89. The correct answer is C. The following can be shareholders in an S corporation: Individuals, estates, and certain trusts may be shareholders.

Answers A and D are incorrect because a partnership and non-resident aliens cannot be shareholders in an S corporation.

Answer B is incorrect because it states only individuals may be shareholders. Estates and certain trusts also may be shareholders.

REG 5-Q70 R287. The correct answer is D. Not all corporations are allowed the right to file a consolidated return, which include:
1) S Corporations
2) Foreign corporations
3) Most real estate investment trusts (REITs)
4) Some insurance companies
5) Most exempt organizations

A and C may file a as a group (consolidated return) because neither of them are S corporations. B and D may **not** file as a group (consolidated return) because D is owned by B, an S corporation which does not have the right to file a consolidated return. Therefore, the correct answer is D.

Answer A is incorrect because B (an S corporation) owns 100% of D, D cannot be included in the consolidated return as they are owned by an S corporation, which are not allowed to consolidate.

Answer B is incorrect because A and C MAY file a consolidated return as they have no relationship to an S corporation.

Answer C is incorrect because D cannot file a consolidated return with B, which is an S corporation.

REG 5-Q71 R62. The correct answer is C. If the corporation had been an S corporation, the taxpayer would prepare Form 1120S and calculate ordinary income on the front of the return (taxable income). The shareholder, Carson, would have picked up 40% of the ordinary income resulting in $160,000 ($400,000 x 40%). This amount would have been reported to Carson on Form K-1 from the Form 1120S return. The distribution to Carson of $70,000 would be non-taxable because it would have been a distribution of previously taxed ordinary income. The $70,000 is not taxed because S corporations are not subject to double taxation.

REG 5-Q72 R29. The correct answer is D because the gain or loss from sale of collectibles is a separate line item on Schedule K-1, Form 1120S.

A is incorrect because mark-to-market income is the method used by dealers in securities for calculating gain or loss for sales in the ordinary course of business. It is therefore used in the calculation of ordinary income and ordinary loss.

Answer B is incorrect because unearned revenue is income that has not yet been earned.

Answer C is incorrect because a Section 1245 gain is the amount of gain from a sale of personal property and real property used in a trade or business held for more than one year which is recaptured as ordinary income. There is no separate line item on Schedule K-1 for Section 1245 gains.

REG 5-Q73 R148. The correct answer is C. Ordinary income of an S corporation is calculated in much the same way as a partnership return. Look at the revenue of $44,000, which is ordinary income and subtract the ordinary and necessary expenses. The ordinary and necessary expenses are the operating expenses of $20,000 and the interest expense of $4,000. The only interest expense that is not deductible to arrive at ordinary income is investment interest expense. When you take the $44,000 and subtract the $20,000 and the $4,000, the ordinary income is $20,000.

The long-term capital loss of $6,000 and the charitable contribution of $1,000 are not used to arrive at ordinary income, but are shown on the Schedule K, Form 1120S.

REG 5-Q74 R332. The correct answer is C. Items that are used in the calculation of ordinary income (loss) on the front of Form 1120S are considered to be ordinary income used in a trade or business and ordinary expenses that are subtracted from the gross ordinary business income to arrive at ordinary income (loss). If an item on Form 1120S is not ordinary in nature then the individual shareholder will be taxed on those income items that are not ordinary in nature. If the S corporation has deductions that are not ordinary in nature, they will not be deductible on the front of the Form 1120S to arrive at ordinary income (loss).

The deductions and income which are not ordinary in nature will flow through to the shareholder's individual tax return. They are first reported on Schedule K and K-1, Form 1120S. Examples of this are portfolio income, which include dividends, royalties, interest and capital gains/losses. Passive income and loss items such as rental income (loss) also appear on the Schedule K and K-1, Form 1120S. Certain deductions which are not ordinary in nature are reported on Schedule K and K-1, Form 1120S. Examples of these deductions include Section 179 expense write-offs, charitable contributions, investment interest expense and foreign taxes paid.

Gross receipts are used in the determination of ordinary income (loss). Dividend income from investments is considered to be portfolio income which is not used in the calculation of ordinary income (loss) and appears on Schedule K and K-1, Form 1120S.

Supplies expense and utilities expense are ordinary expenses of the corporation which occur during the normal, everyday operation of the business. Therefore, the one item that is not used to arrive at ordinary income (loss) is the $5,000 dividend income from investments, which is considered to be portfolio income and goes directly to Schedule K and K-1, Form 1120S.

REG 5-Q75 R314. The correct answer is D. The question asks for the ordinary income (loss) that is calculated on the front of Form 1120S and brought over to the line on Schedule K, ordinary income (loss). To calculate ordinary income, take the gross receipts of $50,000, then subtract the supplies expense of $2,000 and subtract the utilities expense of $1,500, resulting in $46,500. Do not include dividend income from investments of $5,000 because dividend income is portfolio income that is not used in calculating ordinary income since it goes directly to Schedule K.

REG 5-Q76 R256. The correct answer is C. This question deals with how much a stockholder in an S corporation has to report on their individual tax return as income. Evan, who is a 40% stockholder in an S corporation, would have to report 40% of the $200,000 operating income as his share of ordinary income which equals $80,000 on Evans Schedule E. When the S corporation makes any distribution, the shareholder would not be taxed again, as there is no double taxation for an S corporation.

REG 5-Q77 R60. The correct answer is B. A shareholder will recognize a gain when transferring in property to the corporation. The shareholder would recognize a gain if the liability assumed by the corporation exceeds the total basis of the property transferred by the shareholder. Liability assumed ($12,000) exceeds the basis of the property ($6,000) by $6,000 which represents the gain recognized by the shareholder.

REG 5-Q78 R162. The correct answer is D. This question deals with determining a stockholder's basis in an S corporation. To calculate Sandy's ending basis in the stock of the S corporation, do the following:
1) Start with Sandy's beginning basis.
2) Increase Sandy's beginning basis in the corporation by Sandy's share of all taxable and nontaxable income for the year.
3) Decrease Sandy's basis in the stock by any distributions. However, the basis of Sandy's stock cannot be reduced below zero.
4) Add steps 1 and 2 and subtract step 3.

Calculation:
1) $60,000 (beginning basis)
2) Increase basis by Sandy's share all taxable and non-taxable income: 100% x [ordinary income of $30,000 + tax-exempt income of $5,000 + capital gains of $10,000] = $45,000
3) Reduce basis by distribution of $20,000
4) $60,000 + $45,000 - $20,000 = $85,000 (Answer D)

REG 5-Q79 R107. The correct answer is B. This question deals with how much loss a taxpayer can deduct from an S corporation on their personal return. Like a partnership return, an S corporation will allow a taxpayer to deduct a loss from the S corporation up to the basis. Whatever loss is deductible on the personal return reduces the shareholder's basis but not below zero.

We first calculate the stock basis. The beginning basis of the stock is $5,000. Next, deduct the distribution of $3,500 from the beginning basis, leaving the taxpayer with a net basis of $1,500. The remaining item that is deducted from the stockholder's basis is the loss from operations of the S corporation that the stockholder will deduct on their personal return. The stockholder can deduct ordinary loss by taking the lesser of the remaining basis of $1,500 or the actual loss of $2,000. The lesser of the two is $1,500 which is the amount of ordinary loss the stockholder can deduct on their personal return. This $1,500 loss is a reduction of stock basis. The stock basis was $1,500 before the loss deduction. Now we deduct the $1,500 loss from the stock basis of $1,500, giving the stockholder a basis in the stock of $0. We took the lesser of the ordinary loss or the basis before the deduction of the loss as the amount of the loss we can deduct so that the taxpayer would not have a negative basis.

REG 5-Q80 R352. The correct answer is D. Starr's beginning basis in Packer Corp, an S corp, is $10,000. Next step is to reduce Starr's basis by Starr's share of the loss of Packer. Total loss of Packer is $1,000. Starr's share is 50% of $1,000 or $500, which reduces Starr's basis to $9,500. There will be a gain to Starr if the cash that Starr receives exceeds Starr's basis of $9,500. Starr received $8,000, which does not cause a gain because the cash received of $8,000 does not exceed Starr's basis in the S corp. of $9,500. Therefore the $8,000 distribution is not included in Starr's gross income. However, Starr's basis in the S corp. of Packer will be reduced by the $8,000 cash distribution leaving Starr's basis in Packer at $1,500 ($9,500 - $8,000).

REG 5-Q81 R388. The correct answer is C. To determine Stahl's basis in Talon at year end, start with Stahl's basis at the beginning of the year and increase Stahl's basis by his share of all income of the S corporation, and reduce his basis in the stock by his share of all losses. When Stahl's basis is reduced by his share of loss items, he cannot reduce his basis in the stock below zero.

Stahl's beginning basis is $65,000. Add his 100% share of all income items, whether taxable or not, which includes municipal interest income of $6,000 and long-term capital gain of $4,000 which equals $10,000. Stahl's basis now equals beginning basis of $65,000 plus $10,000 or $75,000. From the $75,000, deduct 100% of the short-term capital loss of $9,000 and the 100% of the ordinary loss of $10,000. This results is an ending stock basis of $75,000 - $9,000 - $10,000 = $56,000.

REG 5-Q82 R392. The correct answer is C. The shareholder's basis of the stock in an S corp. is calculated in this priority order:
1) Beginning basis
2) Add: Shareholder's share of income, both taxable and non-taxable
3) Add: Additional contributions of assets
4) Subtract: Distributions to shareholders
5) Subtract: Losses of S corp., <u>but only up to the basis after subtracting step "4" distributions.</u>

Baker, an individual tax payer, owns 100% of the stock of an S corp. At the beginning of the year, Baker's beginning basis in the stock was $25,000. Increase Baker's basis in the stock of the S corp. by 100% of the ordinary income of $1,000. This now gives Baker a basis of $26,000. The next item that reduces Baker's basis, is the distribution of $30,000. Because the distribution of $30,000 is greater than Baker's basis of $26,000, Baker will have a gain of $4,000 and Baker's basis will be $0. This is because the distribution reduces Baker's basis and gives Baker a negative basis of $4,000. A shareholder in an S corp. cannot have a basis of less than $0. The next item to look at is the long-term capital loss of $3,000. Losses can be deducted on the shareholder's tax return up to their basis. Since Baker's basis is $0, none of the $3,000 loss can be deducted on Baker's individual tax return. The $3,000 loss will be carried forward and deductible when Baker has some basis in the stock of the S corp.

REG 5-Q83 R25. The correct answer is A. An S corporation is a corporation that wants to be treated like a partnership for tax purposes. Like a partnership, income and losses of the S corporation increase or decrease the basis of the stock. However, an S Corporation cannot add the liabilities of the corporation to the stockholder's basis because the stockholder is not personally liable for the debt of the corporation. A partner in a partnership can increase their basis in the partnership for the partner's share of partnership liabilities because a partner is personally liable for his or her share of partnership liabilities (recourse debt). A stockholder in an S Corporation can increase his or her basis in the stock by the amount of any debt the S corporation owes to the stockholder.

REG 5-Q84 R90. The correct answer is B. Absent an election to close the books, the allocation of non-separately stated income or loss for S corporation shareholders is based on the ownership percentage of the stock in the S corporation and also the number of days of the year that the shareholder owned stock in the S corporation.

REG 5-Q85 R131. The correct answer is D. When an S corporation makes distributions to its shareholders in excess of their basis, which occurred in years one, two and three, the excess distributions are taxed as capital gains. Please note, that this corporation was an S corporation from its inception and would not have any earnings or profits. If no earnings or profits, then distributions will never be dividends.

REG 5-Q86 R27. The correct answer is D. The built-in gains tax applies when a C corporation becomes an S corporation. At the inception of the S corporation, the assets transferred in from the C corporation will be subject to a built-in gains tax. The S corporation will take the excess of the fair market value (FMV) over the basis of the asset and the excess of the FMV over the basis for those appreciated assets will give the S corporation the built-in gain on each of the appreciated assets.

There is no built-in gains tax because this entity is going from a sole proprietor to an S corporation. The built-in gains tax is only calculated when the company goes from a C corporation to an S corporation.

REG 5-Q87 R219. The correct answer is C. When a corporation elects S corporation status, the S corporation has to pay a built-in gains tax on the excess of the machine's fair market value (FMV) of $30,000 over the machine's basis of $20,000. The built-in gain is $10,000 ($30,000 - $20,000). This $10,000 built-in gain is subject to the built-in gains tax to be paid by the S corporation.

REG 5-Q88 R260. The correct answer is C. This question deals with the built-in gains tax. When a C corporation elects to be an S corp at the beginning of the calendar year, the S corp has to pay a built-in gains tax on appreciated property transferred by the C corp to the S corp. To calculate the tax, take the excess the fair market value (FMV) of the asset ($85,000) over the asset's adjusted basis ($40,000) resulting in a gain of $45,000. Multiply the $45,000 gain by the corporate tax rate of 35% which give the corporation a built-in gains tax of $15,750.

REG 5-Q89 R46. The correct answer is B. The nonseparately stated items are the items used to arrive at ordinary income (loss). These items are shown on front of Form 1065 U.S. Partnership return.

The separately stated items are the amounts that appear on schedule K and K1 of the U.S. Partnership return.

The correct answer is B which is the ordinary income of the partnership. The calculation of ordinary income is as follows:

Revenues		$120,000
Subtract:		
Salaries	$36,000	
Guaranteed payments	10,000	
Rent expense	21,000	
Depreciation expense	18,000	(85,000)
Ordinary Income		$35,000

Interest income, gain on sale of securities, guaranteed payments and charitable contributions are all considered schedule K items.

REG 5-Q90 R10. Correct answer is A. Sumner provided services worth $50,000 for a partnership interest. Therefore, when a partner provides services for an interest in a partnership, that partner will have taxable income, which in this case is $50,000.

Turner and Reed provided property for their interest in the partnership. When a partner provides property for an interest in a partnership, there is no taxable event to the incoming partner or the partnership.

REG 5-Q91 R215. The correct answer is D. When an individual receives in interest in a partnership for services rendered, the individual will recognize income to the extent of the fair market value of the partnership interest that the individual receives for the services rendered. The fair market value of the partnership interest Nolan received is $120,000.

REG 5-Q92 R231. The correct answer is B. A partner's basis in the partnership where the partner contributes property will not lead to any taxable event to either the partner or the partnership. The partner's basis in the partnership is equal to the basis of the property transferred in. The basis of the property is $20,000 which gives the partner a basis in the partnership of $20,000.

REG 5-Q93 R339. The correct answer is B. When a partner contributes property to a partnership for an interest there is generally not a taxable event to the partner or the partnership. This question asks for Bailey's basis for his partnership interest. To determine partnership interest, take the basis of the land contributed by Bailey ($25,000) and since the partnership is assuming the recourse mortgage of $10,000, subtract from the $25,000 the percentage of the debt which is being assumed by the other partners. Bailey is getting a 30% interest, the other partners are getting a 70% interest. Bailey's basis for his partnership interest is $25,000 minus the percentage of the debt assumed by the other partners of $7,000 (70% x $10,000), which equals $18,000. The other partners will increase their basis by their percentage interest of the debt assumed by the partnership.

REG 5-Q94 R43. The correct answer is D. An incoming partner who contributes property and cash generally has no taxable event coming into a partnership.

Skinner's basis is equal to the cash contributed of $5,000 and his basis is increased by the basis of the property contributed of $12,000. The basis of the property contributed of $12,000 is reduced by the percentage of the mortgage assumed by the partnership. Since Skinner is getting a 20% interest, the other partners represent the remaining 80%.

Reduce Skinner's basis by 80% of the mortgage (80% x $10,000 = $8,000). When the basis of the property is reduced by the mortgage assumed by the other partners, it cannot be reduced the below zero. The last thing that effects Skinner's basis is the existing recourse debt (debt that partners or liable for). Any debt assumed by Skinner or any other partner increases the partner's basis. In this case, the recourse debt of $20,000 is shared by all partners. Skinner must increase his basis by 20% of the $20,000 recourse debt, which will increase his basis by $4,000 ($20,000 x 20% = $4,000).

In conclusion, Skinner's basis would be as follows:

Cash contributed	$5,000
Property ($12,000 – (80% x $10,000 = $8,000))	4,000
Assumption of recourse debt ($20,000 x 20%)	4,000
Total basis	$13,000

REG 5-Q95 R93. The correct answer is D. Normally, the basis of a partner's interest in a partnership is equal to the basis of the property contributed. Campbell contributes a building with a basis of $40,000 for a 10% interest in Vogue Partnership. Usually, the $40,000 would be Campbell's basis in the partnership. However, if the property had a mortgage which is assumed by the partnership, you reduce the $40,000 by the percentage interest of the other partners (90% interest) multiplied by the debt which is $60,000. When you subtract the percentage of the debt assumed by the other partners, there cannot be a negative basis. So, the basis cannot be less than zero. Take the $40,000 basis in the partnership and subtract 90% of the $60,000 mortgage which is $54,000. This results in a negative basis of $14,000. Don't forget, the minimum basis a partner can have is zero! If the liability assumed by the other partners of $54,000 exceeds the basis of the property contributed of $40,000, the incoming partner will have a capital gain of $14,000.

REG 5-Q96 R300. The correct answer is B. When a partner contributes property for a partnership interest, there is no gain or loss to the partner or the partnership. Marcus contributed property having a basis of $50,000, therefore, Marcus's basis in the partnership is a transferred basis, which means that his basis in the partnership is equal to the basis of the property contributed of $50,000.

REG 5-Q97 R303. The correct answer is B. A partner and the partnership have no taxable event when a partner gets an interest in a partnership for property contributed. The basis of the partnership interest is equal to the basis of the property contributed. In this question, Smith contributed cash ($3,000), stock with a basis of $2,000 and a new computer with a basis of $2,500 resulting in Smith's basis of $7,500 ($3,000 + $2,000 + $2,500).

REG 5-Q98 R57. The correct answer is D. When a new partner enters a partnership and transfers in appreciated property for the partnership interest, the new partner will be taxed on the built-in gain. In this question, the fair market value of the property transferred in is $100,000 and the basis is $60,000. Because the fair market value exceeds the basis of the property, the built-in gain is $40,000 ($100,000 - $60,000) and the incoming partner will be taxed on the $40,000. When the fair market value exceeds the basis of the property, the basis of the property to the partnership is always fair market value ($100,000).

If the partnership sells the property to an unrelated third party for $160,000 with a basis of $100,000, the gain of $60,000 ($160,000 - $100,000) is shared equally by all partners. The gain is shared equally because the question states that profits and losses are shared equally.

REG 5-Q99 R167. The correct answer is C. This question deals with determining a partner's basis in the partnership at the end of the year. To calculate initial basis, take Dale's contribution of $10,000. If the partnership borrowed $10,000, each partner can increase their basis by their share of the $10,000. Since Dale is a 50% partner, Dale would increase his basis for the debt of $5,000 (50% x $10,000). Next, the partner's basis is increased by the partner's share (in this case 50%) of taxable and non-taxable income. The taxable income is $15,000 and the tax-exempt interest income is $2,000 for a total income of $17,000. Take 50% of $17,000 which is $8,500 and increase Dale's basis. The next item which effect Dale's basis is the $3,000 distribution. A distribution to a partner decreases that partner's basis. And the last item, the partnership had a $4,000 reduction of debt and Dale's share of that reduction of debt is 50% of $4,000 or $2,000 which will reduce Dale's basis.

To summarize, Dale's basis equals $10,000 + $5,000 + $8,500 - $3,000 - $2,000 which results in an ending basis of $18,500, answer C.

REG 5-Q100 R111. The correct answer is A. This question deals with calculating the partner's basis at the end of the year. We take the beginning basis of the partner's interest and increase that basis by the partner's share of income items whether taxable or not. Reduce the partner's basis by the partner's share of the operating loss of the partnership, not to exceed the basis. If the liabilities of the partnership decrease we will reduce the partner's basis by the partner's percentage ownership multiplied by the decrease in partnership liabilities. If the liabilities of the partnership increase, we will increase the partner's basis by the partner's percentage ownership multiplied by the increase in the partnership liabilities.

Beginning basis	$32,500
Add: Partner's share of interest and dividend income (50% x $8,000)	4,000
Subtract: Partner's share of decrease in liabilities	
Beginning liabilities	$40,000
Ending liabilities	24,000
Decrease $16,000 x 50%	(8,000)
Ending basis before loss deduction	$28,500
Partner's share of operating loss ($30,000 x 50%)	(15,000)
Ending basis	$13,500

REG 5-Q101 R193. The correct answer is B. To calculate the partner's basis, start with the beginning basis ($40,000), increase the basis by the partner's share of taxable income (one-third of $60,000 = $20,000) and reduce the partner's basis by the withdrawal of the cash of $5,000. Do not forget that a partner's share of the partnership's recourse liabilities increases the partner's basis (one-third of $18,000 = $6,000). Therefore, Molloy's basis in RST at year end is $40,000 + $20,000 -$5,000 + $6,000 = $61,000. Also, keep in mind a partner's share of the partnership's non-recourse liabilities do not affect the partner's basis.

REG 5-Q102 R279. The correct answer is D. Each partner would start with a beginning basis of $100,000. A partner's beginning basis is equal to any asset contributed, which in this case would be $100,000 cash per partner.

Each partner's share of partnership income which would increase that partner's beginning basis and any distributions of assets such as cash, decrease that partner's basis. To compute each partner's basis in the partnership at the end of the current year, take the beginning basis of $100,000 and add each partner's share of partnership income which in this case would be 1/4 of $80,000 or $20,000 and subtract the withdrawal of cash of $10,000 to arrive at $110,000 ($100,000 + $20,000 - $10,000).

REG 5-Q103 R390. The correct answer is C. To determine the amount of Thompson's deductible loss for the period to be shown on his individual return, take Thompson's beginning basis of $60,000, add Thompson's share of net long-term capital gain of $15,000 which equals $75,000. Next reduce Thompson's basis by the $20,000 cash distribution, which equals $55,000 and now deduct Thompson's share of ordinary loss, which is the lesser of $65,000 ordinary loss or his basis before taking his share of loss of $55,000. Reduce his basis by $55,000 which is the amount of ordinary loss that Thompson can deduct on his individual return. Thompson's ending basis is now zero and Thompson has a $10,000 ordinary loss that he can deducted in the future when he obtains additional basis.

REG 5-Q104 R248. The correct answer is A. The partner's at-risk rules deal with how much of the partnership debts can be added to the partner's basis. The partner's share of recourse debt of the partnership increases the partner's basis because it is considered a contribution of capital. For example, if the partnership's recourse debt is $100,000 and a specific partner has a 20% interest in the partnership, that partner can increase his basis by 20% of the $100,000, or $20,000. If the partner's share of recourse debt, increases the partner's basis, it will allow the partner to deduct a greater amount of losses because a partner can deduct losses on his individual return up to his amount of basis in the partnership. The at-risk limitation provisions of the internal revenue code have nothing to do with a partnership's net operating loss carryover. Therefore, the correct answer is A.

REG 5-Q105 R224. The correct answer is D. The individual partner, rather than the partnership, makes the decision whether to take a deduction or a tax credit for taxes paid to foreign countries. Answers A, B and C are incorrect because the partnership decides what actions to take in these areas.

REG 5-Q106 R140. The correct answer is C. A newly formed partnership is required to adopt the same taxable year as its one or more partners owning more than 50% interest in the profits and capital.

REG 5-Q107 R112. The correct answer is C. This question deals with what income should the individual report from the interest in Greenland partnership.

Partner's share of ordinary business income	$25,000
Guaranteed payment to partner	10,000
Total income reported on partner's return	$35,000

The partner is not taxed on the $5,000 cash distribution because the $5,000 is a distribution of the previously taxed ordinary income and to tax it again would be double taxation.

REG 5-Q108 R358. The correct answer is C. In this question, Acme and Buck are equal members in Dear, an LLC. Dear has decided to be treated as a partnership, and Dear has decided not to be taxed as a corporation. Therefore, Dear has to be treated like a partnership for tax purposes. When a member contributes cash or property, there is generally no tax consequences either to the member or the LLC. In this question, they are asking for Acme's basis in Dear LLC. Since Acme contributed $7,000 in cash, it would normally be considered his basis in Dear. However, since the LLC. assumed a liability of Buck, the other member, Acme, who is a 50% member, will increase their basis in Dear for the cash of $7,000 plus the 50% of the debt of $3,000 ($1,500), which is being assumed by Acme. Acme's basis is cash of $7,000 plus assumption of debt of $1,500 which equals $8,500.

When a partnership assumes the liability of a partner, the other partners, other than the incoming partner will increase their basis by the percentage of the debt assumed by the other partners. The incoming partner whose debt is assumed by the partnership will reduce his/her basis by the percentage of the debt assumed by the other partners.

REG 5-Q109 R110. The correct answer is B. Section 751 of the Internal Revenue Code provides that upon the sale of a partnership interest, the selling partner is required to look to the partnership and determine which items – if sold directly by the partnership – would generate ordinary income.

These items are commonly referred to as "hot assets," and generally fall into three categories:
1. Unrealized accounts receivables of a cash basis partnership (i.e., the partnership has no basis in the receivables because they have not been included in income pursuant to the cash method);
2. Inventory; and
3. Depreciable assets that if sold, would generate ordinary income recapture if sold under Sections 1245 or 1250.

REG 5-Q110 R15. Correct answer is A. There is no gain on a non-liquidating distribution in a partnership unless the cash distributed to the partner exceeds the partner's basis in the partnership. Since there was no cash distributed, there is no gain. Therefore, C and D are incorrect.

To calculate the basis of the property received by the partner, take the partner's basis in the partnership and subtract any cash received. Anne's basis in the partnership is $10,000. Since there is no cash distributed to Anne, her basis is simply $10,000 minus $0 = $10,000. Compare Anne's basis of $10,000 to the basis of the partnership's property ($20,000). The basis of the property to Anne is the lesser of $10,000 (Anne's basis in the partnership minus any money distributed to her) and $20,000 (partnership's basis in the property), which results in a correct answer of a zero gain and a $10,000 basis in the property received by Anne.

REG 5-Q111 R132. The correct answer is D. The distribution of $12,500 was a current distribution of a non-liquidation distribution. In a current distribution (non-liquidation distribution), the $12,500 is a return of basis which is non-taxable and the partner remains in the partnership. A liquidation distribution is a distribution to a partner in order to pay off the partner and terminate the partner from the partnership.

REG 5-Q112 R318. The correct answer is B. In a non-liquidating distribution, the partner's basis in non-cash property, when the partner receives cash and non-cash property is calculated in the following manner: First take the partner's beginning basis in the partnership which is $18,000. Next, subtract any money distributed ($3,000) from the beginning basis of 18,000, resulting in $15,000, or the remaining basis after subtracting the cash.

The final step is to compare the $15,000 to the partnership's basis in the property which is $7,000 and take the lesser of the $15,000 or the $7,000 to arrive at the basis of the property taken by the partner. The lesser of the two is $7,000, which is a reduction of the partner's basis in the partnership.

To arrive at the Owen's basis after the distributions, start with the beginning basis of $18,000, subtract the withdrawals of both the $3,000 cash and the property with a basis to the partner of $7,000, resulting in an ending basis of $8,000.

REG 5-Q113 R357. The correct answer is C. In a non-liquidating distribution of cash and property to a partner, to determine the partner's basis in the land, do the following calculation. When there are multiple distributions of cash and non-cash property, subtract the cash ($50,000) from the $80,000 beginning basis, which results in a remaining basis in the partnership of $30,000. To determine the basis of the property to Anderson, the partner, take the lesser of the $30,000 (remaining basis of Anderson after the cash is subtracted) or the basis of the land to the partnership which is $40,000. The lesser amount of $30,000 is the basis of the land to the partner in a non-liquidating distribution.

REG 5-Q114 R351. The correct answer is B. In a non-liquidating distribution, the partner who transfers property to the partnership will transfer both his basis and his holding period for the asset transferred. Smith's holding period for the land includes the time it was owned by Ridge.

Answer A is incorrect because a partner only has a gain in a non-liquidating distribution if the partner receives cash in excess of the partner's basis. The partner did not receive any cash.

Answer C is incorrect because only II is correct.

Answer D is incorrect because II is correct.

REG 5-Q115 R163. The correct answer is C. This question deals with the treatment of an increase in partnership liabilities. Each partner will increase his basis in the partnership by the increase of partnership liabilities multiplied by that partner's percentage ownership in the partnership. If there is a decrease in partnership liabilities, the reduction in partnership liabilities will reduce the partner's basis in the partnership. To determine this basis decreases, multiple the reduction of partnership liabilities by the partner's percentage ownership in the partnership.

Answer A is incorrect because you don't increase each partner's basis by $100,000. You increase the partner's basis in the partnership by the increase of $100,000 times the percentage ownership of that partner.

Answer B is incorrect because you do not increase the partner's basis if the liability is nonrecourse. Nonrecourse debt is liabilities of the partnership in which the creditors of the partnership have no personal recourse against a partner if the debtor goes into default. You only increase the partner's basis if the debt is recourse debt.

Answer D is incorrect because it does change the partner's basis in the partnership, but only recourse debt.

REG 5-Q116 R113. The correct answer is A. This question deals with a recognized gain on liquidating distributions from a partnership to a partner. A gain to the partner in a liquidating distribution to a partner can only be caused by cash being distributed to the partner in excess of the partner's basis. Since no cash was distributed to the partner, there is no gain recognized.

REG 5-Q117 R253. The correct answer is B. In liquidation of a partnership interest where there are multiple distributions, take the following steps to calculate the basis of the property distributed to the partner. First, take the partner's basis in the partnership ($60,000) and subtract the cash ($61,000). Gain to a partner upon the liquidation of his partnership interest occurs only if the money received by the partner exceeds his beginning basis. As stated earlier, the partner received $61,000 in cash which is greater than his beginning partnership interest of $60,000 which give the partner a gain of $1,000. These gains are usually capital gains and after the cash of $61,000 is subtracted from the beginning basis of $60,000, the partner's basis is zero because a partner can never have a negative basis in taxation.

REG 5-Q118 R39. The correct answer is C. With a total liquidation of a partnership interest, the basis of the property is the partner's beginning basis ($26,000) less the money distributed ($12,000). This equals $14,000 which is the basis of the land to the partner.

REG 5-Q119 R168. The correct answer is D. In a total liquidation of a partnership, to determine the basis of the property, take the partner's basis before receiving the distribution and always subtract the cash first, and the remaining basis will be the basis of the real estate to Smith, the partner. A total liquidation is where the partner is completely leaving the partnership. Where there are multiple distributions to the partner who is leaving, always subtract the cash first from the partner's basis and whatever is left of the partner's basis after subtracting the cash is always the basis of the non-cash property.

Partner's basis before distribution	$230,000
Cash distributed	(150,000)
Basis of real estate	$80,000

REG 5-Q120 R194. The correct answer is D. In a total liquidation of a partner's basis in a partnership where there are multiple distributions of cash and property and the question asks for the basis of the non-cash property; to arrive at the basis of the non-cash property (automobile) do the following: Start with the partner's beginning basis of $60,000 and reduce the beginning basis by the amount of money distributed ($30,000). After the cash is distributed, the remaining basis would be the basis of the automobile which is $30,000.

In a total liquidation and a non-liquidating distribution of a partner's basis in a partnership, gain is recognized to the partner if the cash received exceeds the partner's beginning basis in the partnership. Loss is recognized to the partner in a total liquidation if the partner receives unrealized receivables, appreciated inventory and cash which is less than his beginning basis in the partnership. Loss is never recognized when there is a non-liquidating distribution.

REG 5-Q121 R213. The correct answer is C. Gain in a liquidating distribution is recognized if the partner receives cash in excess of his basis. Since there was no cash received, there can be no gain. Loss can be recognized in a liquidating distribution of a partner's interest through the receipt of only money, unrealized receivables and inventory. These items must be less than the partner's basis in the partnership to have a recognized loss in total liquidation of a partner's interest. Loss is not recognized on the non-liquidation of a partner's interest.

REG 5-Q122 R232. The correct answer is B. In a total liquidation of a partner's interest, there could be multiple distributions given to the partner to eliminate his basis in the partnership. In this question, the partner is receiving cash and property to liquidate the partner's interest. To calculate the basis of the property to the partner, start with the partner's beginning basis in the partnership and subtract the cash first. Whatever basis is left over, it becomes the basis in the property to the partner. For example, take the partner's beginning basis of $70,000, subtract the cash of $10,000 which leaves a basis of $60,000. Whatever basis is left over, which the $60,000, becomes the basis in the property to the partner.

REG 5-Q123 R216. The correct answer is C. In a liquidating distribution, the partner's basis in the partnership is going to be reduced to zero. When a partner received multiple distributions of assets, they are distributed in the following order:
1) Cash
2) Unrealized receivables
3) Inventories
4) Other assets

Start with the partner's basis in the partnership and first reduce the partner's basis by the cash. The beginning partner's basis is $12,000; subtract the cash of $4,000, leaving a basis of $8,000. Next subtract the basis of the inventory which is the partnership's basis of $4,000 from the $8,000 leaving a basis of $4,000. The partner's basis in the inventory is the same basis that the partnership was carrying the inventory at ($4,000). The remaining basis of $4,000 will become the basis of the land to the partner. Subtract the $4,000 basis in the land from the partner's basis of $4,000 and now the partner's basis is zero.

The question is asking what is the gain or loss on the inventory and the land. Because the land was used in a trade or business, and is no longer used in a trade or business due to being distributed to the partner as investment property, the land is considered now a capital asset. The inventory is a non-capital asset per the IRS code.

To calculate the gain or loss on the inventory, take the basis of the inventory, which is $4,000 to the former partner and subtract the selling price of $5,000, resulting in a $1,000 ordinary gain.

To calculate the gain or loss on the land, which is a capital asset, take the selling price of $3,000 and subtract the former partner's basis in the land of $4,000, resulting in a $1,000 capital loss.

REG 5-Q124 R394. The correct answer is C. When Frazier calculates his gain, Frazier will use his outside basis in the partnership which is his tax basis. If a partner does not keep track of his outside basis, the partner's basis will be his inside basis which is his capital account increased by his share of partnership liabilities. These liabilities must be liabilities which the partner is personally liable for. In the question, we are given Frazier's outside basis of $1,200. Upon liquidation, Frazier received $1,500 in cash in excess of his outside basis of $1,200 resulting in a gain of $300. In a total liquidation of a partner's interest, gain is recognized if the cash received by the partner exceeds his basis.

REG 5-Q125 R249. The correct answer is D. To determine the gain on the sale of the partnership interest, take the amount realized from the sale and subtract from that amount realized the partner's basis in the partnership. If the amount realized exceeds the partner's basis, this will provide the partner with a gain. Gains on sales of partnership interest are generally capital gains. The amount realized from the sale is defined as the cash received by the partner plus any liabilities that the new partner assumes of the old partner. To calculate amount realized from the sale, take the cash received ($30,000) and add the liabilities that the new partner assumes of the old partner ($25,000), which total $55,000. Then, subtract from the $55,000, the seller's basis in the partnership of $40,000 which results in a $15,000 capital gain.

If the question does not give you the partner's basis in the partnership, calculate the basis by taking the partner's capital account and adding the selling partner's share of partnership liabilities.

REG 5-Q126 R1138. The correct answer is B. When a partnership interest is sold the purchasing partner has an outside basis equal to the purchase price of the partnership interest (in this example, the partner paid $100,000 and therefore has an outside basis of $100,000 in his partnership interest. When the partnership makes a Section 754 election, it is electing to adjust the inside basis of the purchasing partner as follows:

$100,000	-	$40,000	=	**$60,000**
Purchase Price	-	Selling Partner's Inside Basis	=	Section 754 Basis Adjustment

Therefore, the result is that the partnership will have an inside basis of $100,000 – equal to the partner's outside basis.

REG 5-Q127 R1139. The correct answer is C. When a partnership interest is sold the purchasing partner has an outside basis equal to the purchase price of the partnership interest (in this example, Peck paid $50,000 and therefore has an outside basis of $50,000 in his partnership interest. When the partnership makes a Section 754 election, it is electing to adjust the inside basis of the purchasing partner as follows:

$50,000	-	$15,000	=	**$35,000**
Purchase Price	-	Selling Partner's Inside Basis	=	Section 754 Basis Adjustment

Therefore, the result is that the new partner will have an inside basis of $50,000 – equal to his outside basis in the partnership interest.

When the partnership later sells the land for $200,000:
Peter's gain = ($200,000)(50%) - $15,000 = $85,000
Peck's gain = ($200,000)(50%) - $50,000 = $50,000

REG 5-Q128 R1140. The correct answer is C. When a partnership interest is sold the purchasing partner has an outside basis equal to the purchase price of the asset transferred to the partnership.. When the partnership makes a Section 754 election, it is electing to adjust the inside basis of the partnership's basis in the property transferred in by the partner.

REG 5-Q129 R306. The correct answer is C. An LLC owner(s), known as a member, may participate in management while limiting personal liability. In a partnership, the partner(s) may participate in management but has unlimited personal liability.

Answer A is incorrect because both an LLC and a partnership can avoid taxation. An LLC can elect to be taxed as either a partnership or an S corporation. Therefore, an LLC and a partnership are flow-through entities and are both taxed at the ownership level (either the partner's or the stockholder's individual tax return).

Answer B is incorrect because both an LLC and a partnership may have any number of owners.

Answer D is incorrect because both an LLC and a partnership may make disproportionate allocations and distributions to the partners in a partnership.

REG 5-Q130 R286. The correct answer is C. A net operating loss (NOL) occurs when business deductions exceed business income and it can also occur when certain non-business deductions exceed taxable income for the year. Tax law allows individuals, C corporations, in addition to trusts and estates to carryback NOLs to prior years to claim a refund or to carry forward a loss for no more than 20 years to reduce taxable income in each of the years in which the NOL can be carried. Pass-through entities cannot claim NOLs. Trusts and estates file a Form 1041 US fiduciary return and in many respects are treated much like individual tax returns. A NOL can be taken as a deduction on Form 1041 as long as it is not deductible on Form 1040.

Answers A and B are incorrect because a partnership and S corporations are pass-through entities and cannot claim NOLs.

Answer D is incorrect because a net operating loss deduction is allowed for a business that pays taxes on taxable income. Not-for-profit organizations are not considered businesses that are profit making organizations that pay taxes therefore, a net operating loss cannot be used as a business deduction for not-for-profit organizations.

REG 5-Q131 R353. The correct answer is C. The amount of trust income that is included in Gardner's (sole income beneficiary of the trust) is calculated by taking the interest income of $5,000 minus any fees incurred to earn the $5,000 interest income. The fiduciary fee is allocable to the income, which means it was a cost incurred to earn the interest income of $5,000. The $750 fee is subtracted from the interest income of $5,000, so that the sole beneficiary will be taxed on his individual return of $4,250 ($5,000 - $750). The net long-term capital gain is not taxed to the income beneficiary because it is allocable to the corpus (body of the trust).

In a question, if an item states that it is allocable to the corpus, it is not taxable to the income beneficiary.

REG 5-Q132 R1130. The correct answer is D. A tax-exempt organization that has unrelated business income (UBI), is taxed at either corporate or trust rates, depending upon whether the tax-exempt organization is a corporation or a trust.

REG 5-Q133 R1131. The correct answer is C. For unrelated business income (UBI), a tax-exempt organization is allowed an exemption of $1,000 against the total UBI. This means that the first $1,000 of UBI is not taxable.

Answer A is incorrect because the amount of UBI is determined by the tax-exempt organization and not the IRS.

Answer B is incorrect because not all of the UBI is taxed at either corporate or trust rates. It is the amount in excess of $1,000.

Answer D is incorrect because even though a church does not have to file an annual return Form 990, they are still required to file a Form 990T (tax on UBI), if the church has UBI in excess of $1,000.

REG 5-Q134 R1132. The correct answer is D. Choices A, B and C are deemed to be related income of a tax-exempt organization. If a tax-exempt organization publishes a program for an annual dinner benefit and sells advertising space, the advertising revenue is considered to be unrelated business income.

REG 5-Q135 R1133. The correct answer is D. A trust will pay trust taxes on the unrelated business income in excess of $1,000.

Answers A and C are incorrect because a trust will pay trust taxes on the unrelated business income in excess of $1,000.

Answer B is incorrect because a trust will pay trust taxes and not corporate taxes on unrelated business income in excess of $1,000.

This page is intentionally left blank.

Forms

Form 1120 – U.S. Corporation Income Tax Return

Form 1120 — U.S. Corporation Income Tax Return (2016)

Department of the Treasury, Internal Revenue Service
For calendar year 2016 or tax year beginning _____, 2016, ending _____, 20 ___
OMB No. 1545-0123
▶ Information about Form 1120 and its separate instructions is at www.irs.gov/form1120.

A Check if:
1a Consolidated return (attach Form 851) ☐
b Life/nonlife consolidated return ☐
2 Personal holding co. (attach Sch. PH) ☐
3 Personal service corp. (see instructions) ☐
4 Schedule M-3 attached ☐

TYPE OR PRINT — Name; Number, street, and room or suite no. If a P.O. box, see instructions.; City or town, state, or province, country, and ZIP or foreign postal code

B Employer identification number
C Date incorporated
D Total assets (see instructions) $

E Check if: (1) ☐ Initial return (2) ☐ Final return (3) ☐ Name change (4) ☐ Address change

Income

1a	Gross receipts or sales	1a
b	Returns and allowances	1b
c	Balance. Subtract line 1b from line 1a	1c
2	Cost of goods sold (attach Form 1125-A)	2
3	Gross profit. Subtract line 2 from line 1c	3
4	Dividends (Schedule C, line 19)	4
5	Interest	5
6	Gross rents	6
7	Gross royalties	7
8	Capital gain net income (attach Schedule D (Form 1120))	8
9	Net gain or (loss) from Form 4797, Part II, line 17 (attach Form 4797)	9
10	Other income (see instructions—attach statement)	10
11	**Total income.** Add lines 3 through 10 ▶	11

Deductions (See instructions for limitations on deductions.)

12	Compensation of officers (see instructions—attach Form 1125-E) ▶	12
13	Salaries and wages (less employment credits)	13
14	Repairs and maintenance	14
15	Bad debts	15
16	Rents	16
17	Taxes and licenses	17
18	Interest	18
19	Charitable contributions	19
20	Depreciation from Form 4562 not claimed on Form 1125-A or elsewhere on return (attach Form 4562)	20
21	Depletion	21
22	Advertising	22
23	Pension, profit-sharing, etc., plans	23
24	Employee benefit programs	24
25	Domestic production activities deduction (attach Form 8903)	25
26	Other deductions (attach statement)	26
27	**Total deductions.** Add lines 12 through 26 ▶	27
28	Taxable income before net operating loss deduction and special deductions. Subtract line 27 from line 11	28
29a	Net operating loss deduction (see instructions)	29a
b	Special deductions (Schedule C, line 20)	29b
c	Add lines 29a and 29b	29c

Tax, Refundable Credits, and Payments

30	Taxable income. Subtract line 29c from line 28. See instructions	30
31	Total tax (Schedule J, Part I, line 11)	31
32	Total payments and refundable credits (Schedule J, Part II, line 21)	32
33	Estimated tax penalty. See instructions. Check if Form 2220 is attached ▶ ☐	33
34	**Amount owed.** If line 32 is smaller than the total of lines 31 and 33, enter amount owed	34
35	**Overpayment.** If line 32 is larger than the total of lines 31 and 33, enter amount overpaid	35
36	Enter amount from line 35 you want: Credited to 2017 estimated tax ▶ _____ Refunded ▶	36

Sign Here: Under penalties of perjury, I declare that I have examined this return, including accompanying schedules and statements, and to the best of my knowledge and belief, it is true, correct, and complete. Declaration of preparer (other than taxpayer) is based on all information of which preparer has any knowledge.

Signature of officer | Date | Title

May the IRS discuss this return with the preparer shown below? See instructions. ☐ Yes ☐ No

Paid Preparer Use Only: Print/Type preparer's name | Preparer's signature | Date | Check ☐ if self-employed | PTIN
Firm's name ▶
Firm's address ▶
Firm's EIN ▶
Phone no.

For Paperwork Reduction Act Notice, see separate instructions. Cat. No. 11450Q Form **1120** (2016)

Form 1120X – Amended U.S. Corporation Income Tax Return

Form 1120X
(Rev. November 2016)
Department of the Treasury
Internal Revenue Service

Amended U.S. Corporation Income Tax Return

▶ Information about Form 1120X and its instructions is at www.irs.gov/form1120x.

OMB No. 1545-0123

For tax year ending ▶
(Enter month and year.)

Please Type or Print

- Name
- Number, street, and room or suite no. If a P.O. box, see instructions.
- City or town, state, and ZIP code

Employer identification number

Telephone number (optional)

Enter name and address used on original return. If same as above, write "Same."

Internal Revenue Service Center where original return was filed ▶

Fill in applicable items and use Part II on the back to explain any changes

Part I — Income and Deductions (see instructions)

			(a) As originally reported or as previously adjusted	(b) Net change — increase or (decrease) — explain in Part II	(c) Correct amount
1	Total income	1			
2	Total deductions	2			
3	Taxable income. Subtract line 2 from line 1	3			
4	Total tax	4			

Payments and Credits (see instructions)

5a	Overpayment in prior year allowed as a credit	5a	
b	Estimated tax payments	5b	
c	Refund applied for on Form 4466	5c	
d	Subtract line 5c from the sum of lines 5a and 5b	5d	
e	Tax deposited with Form 7004	5e	
f	Credit from Form 2439	5f	
g	Credit for federal tax on fuels and other refundable credits	5g	
6	Tax deposited or paid with (or after) the filing of the original return	6	
7	Add lines 5d through 6, column (c)	7	
8	Overpayment, if any, as shown on original return or as later adjusted	8	
9	Subtract line 8 from line 7	9	

Tax Due or Overpayment (see instructions)

10	Tax due. Subtract line 9 from line 4, column (c). If paying by check, make it payable to the "United States Treasury" ▶	10	
11	Overpayment. Subtract line 4, column (c), from line 9 ▶	11	
12	Enter the amount of line 11 you want: Credited to 20___ Estimated tax ▶ Refunded ▶	12	

Sign Here

Under penalties of perjury, I declare that I have filed an original return and that I have examined this amended return, including accompanying schedules and statements, and to the best of my knowledge and belief, this amended return is true, correct, and complete. Declaration of preparer (other than taxpayer) is based on all information of which preparer has any knowledge.

Signature of officer | Date | Title

Paid Preparer Use Only

| Print/Type preparer's name | Preparer's signature | Date | Check ☐ if self-employed | PTIN |

Firm's name ▶ | Firm's EIN ▶
Firm's address ▶ | Phone no.

For Paperwork Reduction Act Notice, see instructions.   Cat. No. 11530Z   Form **1120X** (Rev. 11-2016)

Form 1120 Schedule PH – U.S. Personal Holding Company (PHC) Tax

SCHEDULE PH (Form 1120)
(Rev. November 2015)
Department of the Treasury
Internal Revenue Service

U.S. Personal Holding Company (PHC) Tax

► Attach to tax return.
► Information about Schedule PH (Form 1120) and its separate instructions is at www.irs.gov/form1120.

OMB No. 1545-0123

Name | Employer identification number

Part I — Undistributed Personal Holding Company Income (see instructions)

Additions

1. Taxable income before net operating loss deduction and special deductions. Enter amount from Form 1120, line 28 .... **1**
2. Contributions deducted in figuring line 1. Enter amount from Form 1120, line 19 . **2**
3. Excess expenses and depreciation under section 545(b)(6). Enter amount from Part V, line 2 .... **3**
4. Total. Add lines 1 through 3 .... **4**

Deductions

5. Federal and foreign income, war profits, and excess profits taxes not deducted in figuring line 1 (attach schedule) **5**
6. Contributions deductible under section 545(b)(2). See instructions for limitation . . . **6**
7. Net operating loss for the preceding tax year deductible under section 545(b)(4) **7**
8a. Net capital gain from Schedule D (Form 1120), line 17 . . | **8a**
   b. Less: Income tax on this net capital gain (see section 545(b)(5)) (attach computation) . . . . | **8b** | **8c**
9. Deduction for dividends paid (other than dividends paid after the end of the tax year). Enter amount from Part VI, line 5 .... **9**
10. Total. Add lines 5 through 9 .... **10**
11. Subtract line 10 from line 4 .... **11**
12. Dividends paid after the end of the tax year (other than deficiency dividends defined in section 547(d)), but not more than the smaller of line 11 or 20% of Part VI, line 1 . . . **12**
13. Undistributed PHC income. Subtract line 12 from line 11 .... **13**

Note: If the information in Part II and Part IV is not submitted with the return, the limitation period for assessment and collection of the PHC tax is any time within 6 years after the return is filed. See section 6501(f).

Part II — Personal Holding Company Income (see instructions)

14a. Dividends . . . . | **14a**
   b. Less: Dividends excluded (under section 543(a)(1)(C)) . . . . . | **14b** | **14c**
15a. Interest . . . . | **15a**
   b. Less: Amounts excluded (attach schedule) . . . . | **15b** | **15c**
16. Royalties (other than mineral, oil, gas, or copyright royalties) . . . . | **16**
17. Annuities . . . . | **17**
18a. Rents . . . . | **18a**
   b. Less: Adjustments to rents (attach schedule) . . . . | **18b** | **18c**
19a. Mineral, oil, and gas royalties . . . . | **19a**
   b. Less: Adjustments to mineral, oil, and gas royalties (attach schedule) . . . . | **19b** | **19c**
20. Copyright royalties . . . . | **20**
21. Produced film rents . . . . | **21**
22. Compensation received for use of corporation property by 25% or more shareholder . . . | **22**
23. Amounts received under personal service contracts and from their sale . . . . | **23**
24. Amounts includible in taxable income from estates and trusts . . . . | **24**
25. PHC income. Add lines 14 through 24 . . . . | **25**

Part III — Tax on Undistributed Personal Holding Company Income (see instructions)

26. PHC tax. Multiply the amount on line 13 by 20%. Enter the result here and on Schedule J (Form 1120), line 8, or on the proper line of the appropriate tax return . . . . | **26**

For Paperwork Reduction Act Notice, see the Instructions for Form 1120. Cat. No. 11465P Schedule PH (Form 1120) (Rev. 11-2015)

Form 1139 – Corporation Application for Tentative Refund

Form 1139 (Rev. November 2014)
Department of the Treasury
Internal Revenue Service

Corporation Application for Tentative Refund

► Information about Form 1139 and its separate instructions is at www.irs.gov/form1139.
► Do not file with the corporation's income tax return—file separately.
► Keep a copy of this application for your records.

OMB No. 1545-0123

Name	Employer identification number
Number, street, and room or suite no. If a P.O. box, see instructions.	Date of incorporation
City or town, state, and ZIP code	Daytime phone number

1 Reason(s) for filing. See Instructions—attach computation
- **a** Net operating loss (NOL) ► $
- **b** Net capital loss ► $
- **c** Unused general business credit ► $
- **d** Other ► $

2 Return for year of loss, unused credit, or overpayment under section 1341(b)(1) ►
- **a** Tax year ended
- **b** Date tax return filed
- **c** Service center where filed

3 If this application is for an unused credit created by another carryback, enter ending date for the tax year of the first carryback ►

4 Did a loss result in the release of a foreign tax credit, or is the corporation carrying back a general business credit that was released because of the release of a foreign tax credit (see instructions)? If "Yes," the corporation must file an amended return to carry back the released credits . . . . ☐ Yes ☐ No

5a Was a consolidated return filed for any carryback year or did the corporation join a consolidated group (see instructions)? ☐ Yes ☐ No
b If "Yes," enter the tax year ending date and the name of the common parent and its EIN, if different from above (see instructions) ►

6a If Form 1138 has been filed, was an extension of time granted for filing the return for the tax year of the NOL? ☐ Yes ☐ No
b If "Yes," enter the date to which extension was granted ►
c Enter the date Form 1138 was filed ►
d Unpaid tax for which Form 1138 is in effect . . . . ► $

7 If the corporation changed its accounting period, enter the date permission to change was granted . . . . ►

8 If this is an application for a dissolved corporation, enter date of dissolution . . . . ►

9 Has the corporation filed a petition in Tax Court for the year or years to which the carryback is to be applied? . . . ☐ Yes ☐ No

10 Is any part of the decrease in tax due to a loss or credit resulting from a reportable transaction required to be disclosed? If Yes, attach Form 8886 . . . . ☐ Yes ☐ No

Computation of Decrease in Tax See Instructions.	preceding tax year ended ►		preceding tax year ended ►		preceding tax year ended ►	
	(a) Before carryback	(b) After carryback	(c) Before carryback	(d) After carryback	(e) Before carryback	(f) After carryback

Note: If only filing for an unused general business credit (line 1c), skip lines 11 through 15.

11	Taxable income from tax return						
12	**Capital loss carryback** (see instructions)						
13	Subtract line 12 from line 11						
14	**NOL deduction** (see instructions) . . .						
15	Taxable income. Subtract line 14 from line 13						
16	Income tax						
17	Alternative minimum tax						
18	Add lines 16 and 17						
19	General business credit (see instructions)						
20	Other credits (see instructions)						
21	Total credits. Add lines 19 and 20 . .						
22	Subtract line 21 from line 18						
23	Personal holding company tax (Sch. PH (Form 1120))						
24	Other taxes (see instructions)						
25	Total tax liability. Add lines 22 through 24						
26	Enter amount from "After carryback" column on line 25 for each year . . .						
27	Decrease in tax. Subtract line 26 from line 25						
28	Overpayment of tax due to a claim of right adjustment under section 1341(b)(1) (attach computation)						

Sign Here Under penalties of perjury, I declare that I have examined this application and accompanying schedules and statements, and to the best of my knowledge and belief, they are true, correct, and complete.

► Signature of officer   Date   ► Title

Paid Preparer Use Only

Print/Type preparer's name	Preparer's signature	Date	Check ☐ if self-employed	PTIN
Firm's name ►			Firm's EIN ►	
Firm's address ►			Phone no.	

For Paperwork Reduction Act Notice, see separate instructions.   Cat. No. 11170F   Form **1139** (Rev. 11-2014)

Form 8938 – Statement of Specified Foreign Financial Assets

Form 8938 — Statement of Specified Foreign Financial Assets
Department of the Treasury
Internal Revenue Service

▶ Information about Form 8938 and its separate Instructions is at www.irs.gov/form8938.
▶ Attach to your tax return.

OMB No. 1545-2195
2016
Attachment Sequence No. 175

For calendar year 20___ or tax year beginning ___, 20___ and ending ___, 20___

If you have attached continuation statements, check here ☐ Number of continuation statements _____

1 Name(s) shown on return

2 TIN

3 Type of filer
  a ☐ Specified individual b ☐ Partnership c ☐ Corporation d ☐ Trust

4 If you checked box 3a, skip this line 4. If you checked box 3b or 3c, enter the name and TIN of the specified individual who closely holds the partnership or corporation. If you checked box 3d, enter the name and TIN of the specified person who is a current beneficiary of the trust. (See instructions for definitions and what to do if you have more than one specified individual or specified person to list.)
  a Name   b TIN

Part I Foreign Deposit and Custodial Accounts Summary

1 Number of Deposit Accounts (reported in Part V) . . . . ▶
2 Maximum Value of All Deposit Accounts . . . . $
3 Number of Custodial Accounts (reported in Part V) . . . . ▶
4 Maximum Value of All Custodial Accounts . . . . $
5 Were any foreign deposit or custodial accounts closed during the tax year? . . . . . . ☐ Yes ☐ No

Part II Other Foreign Assets Summary

1 Number of Foreign Assets (reported in Part VI) . . . . ▶
2 Maximum Value of All Assets (reported in Part VI) . . . . $
3 Were any foreign assets acquired or sold during the tax year? . . . . ☐ Yes ☐ No

Part III Summary of Tax Items Attributable to Specified Foreign Financial Assets (see instructions)

(a) Asset Category	(b) Tax item	(c) Amount reported on form or schedule	Where reported	
			(d) Form and line	(e) Schedule and line
1 Foreign Deposit and Custodial Accounts	1a Interest	$		
	1b Dividends	$		
	1c Royalties	$		
	1d Other income	$		
	1e Gains (losses)	$		
	1f Deductions	$		
	1g Credits	$		
2 Other Foreign Assets	2a Interest	$		
	2b Dividends	$		
	2c Royalties	$		
	2d Other income	$		
	2e Gains (losses)	$		
	2f Deductions	$		
	2g Credits	$		

Part IV Excepted Specified Foreign Financial Assets (see instructions)

If you reported specified foreign financial assets on one or more of the following forms, enter the number of such forms filed. You do not need to include these assets on Form 8938 for the tax year.

1. Number of Forms 3520 _____ 2. Number of Forms 3520-A _____ 3. Number of Forms 5471 _____
4. Number of Forms 8621 _____ 5. Number of Forms 8865 _____

Part V Detailed Information for Each Foreign Deposit and Custodial Account Included in the Part I Summary (see instructions)

If you have more than one account to report in Part V, attach a continuation statement for each additional account (see instructions).

1 Type of account ☐ Deposit ☐ Custodial   2 Account number or other designation

3 Check all that apply
  a ☐ Account opened during tax year   b ☐ Account closed during tax year
  c ☐ Account jointly owned with spouse d ☐ No tax item reported in Part III with respect to this asset

4 Maximum value of account during tax year . . . . $
5 Did you use a foreign currency exchange rate to convert the value of the account into U.S. dollars? . . ☐ Yes ☐ No
6 If you answered "Yes" to line 5, complete all that apply.

(a) Foreign currency in which account is maintained	(b) Foreign currency exchange rate used to convert to U.S. dollars	(c) Source of exchange rate used if not from U.S. Treasury Department's Bureau of the Fiscal Service

For Paperwork Reduction Act Notice, see the separate Instructions.   Cat. No. 37753A   Form **8938** (2016)

Form 1120F Schedules M-1 and M-2 – Reconciliation of Income (Loss) and Analysis of Unappropriated Retained Earnings per Books

SCHEDULES M-1 and M-2 (Form 1120-F)
Department of the Treasury
Internal Revenue Service

Reconciliation of Income (Loss) and Analysis of Unappropriated Retained Earnings per Books
▶ Go to www.irs.gov/Form1120F for the latest information.
▶ Attach to Form 1120-F.

OMB No. 1545-0123

2017

Name of corporation | Employer identification number

Schedule M-1 — Reconciliation of Income (Loss) per Books With Income per Return
Note: The corporation may be required to file Schedule M-3 (see instructions).

1. Net income (loss) per books
2. Federal income tax per books
3. Excess of capital losses over capital gains
4. Income subject to tax not recorded on books this year (itemize):
5. Expenses recorded on books this year not deducted on this return (itemize):
   a. Depreciation $
   b. Charitable contributions $
   c. Travel and entertainment $
   d. Other (itemize):
6. Add lines 1 through 5
7. Income recorded on books this year not included on this return (itemize):
   a. Tax-exempt interest $
   b. Other (itemize):
8. Deductions on this return not charged against book income this year (itemize):
   a. Depreciation $
   b. Charitable contributions $
   c. Other (itemize):
9. Add lines 7 and 8
10. Income—line 6 less line 9

Schedule M-2 — Analysis of Unappropriated Retained Earnings per Books

1. Balance at beginning of year
2. Net income (loss) per books
3. Other increases (itemize):
4. Add lines 1, 2, and 3
5. Distributions: a. Cash
   b. Stock
   c. Property
6. Other decreases (itemize):
7. Add lines 5 and 6
8. Balance at end of year (line 4 less line 7)

Who Must File

Generally, any foreign corporation that is required to complete Form 1120-F, Section II must complete Schedules M-1 and M-2 (Form 1120-F). However, the following rules apply.

Do not complete Schedules M-1, M-2, and M-3 if total assets at the end of the tax year (Schedule L, line 17, column (d)) are less than $25,000.

Complete Schedule M-3 in lieu of Schedule M-1 if total assets at the end of the tax year that are reportable on Schedule L are $10 million or more.

A corporation filing Form 1120-F that is not required to file Schedule M-3 may voluntarily file Schedule M-3 instead of Schedule M-1. See the Instructions for Schedule M-3 (Form 1120-F) for more information.

Foreign corporations that (a) are required to file a Schedule M-3 (Form 1120-F) and have less than $50 million in total assets at the end of the tax year or (b) are not required to file a Schedule M-3 (Form 1120-F) and voluntarily file a Schedule M-3 (Form 1120-F) must either (1) complete Schedule M-3 (Form 1120-F) entirely or (2) complete Schedule M-3 (Form 1120-F) through Part I and complete Schedule M-1 instead of completing Parts II and III of Schedule M-3 (Form 1120-F). If the foreign corporation chooses (2), then Schedule M-1, line 1 must equal Schedule M-3 (Form 1120-F), Part I, line 11. See the Instructions for Schedule M-3 (Form 1120-F) for more information.

Note: If Schedule M-3 is completed in lieu of Schedule M-1, the corporation is still required to complete Schedule M-2.

Specific Instructions

Schedule M-1

Line 1. Net income (loss) per books. The foreign corporation must report on line 1 of Schedule M-1 the net income (loss) per the set or sets of books taken into account on Schedule L.

Line 5c. Travel and entertainment expenses. Include any of the following:

- Meal and entertainment expenses not deductible under section 274(n).
- Expenses for the use of an entertainment facility.
- The part of business gifts over $25.
- Expenses of an individual over $2,000 that are allocable to conventions on cruise ships.
- Employee achievement awards over $400.
- The cost of entertainment tickets over face value (also subject to the 50% limit under section 274(n)).
- The cost of skyboxes over the face value of nonluxury box seat tickets.
- The part of luxury water travel expenses not deductible under section 274(m).
- Expenses for travel as a form of education.
- Other nondeductible travel and entertainment expenses.

Line 7a. Tax-exempt interest. Report any tax-exempt interest received or accrued, including any exempt-interest dividends received as a shareholder in a mutual fund or other regulated investment company. Also report this same amount in item P at the top of page 2 of Form 1120-F.

Schedule M-2

Line 1. Beginning balance of unappropriated retained earnings. Enter the beginning balance of unappropriated retained earnings per the set(s) of books taken into account on Schedule L.

Note: For additional information for Schedule M-2 reporting, see the Instructions for Schedule M-3 (Form 1120-F).

For Paperwork Reduction Act Notice, see the Instructions for Form 1120-F. Cat. No. 49678K Schedules M-1 and M-2 (Form 1120-F) 2017

Form 1120 Schedule M-3 – Net Income (Loss) Reconciliation for Corporations with Total Assets of $10 Million or More

SCHEDULE M-3 (Form 1120)
Department of the Treasury
Internal Revenue Service

Net Income (Loss) Reconciliation for Corporations With Total Assets of $10 Million or More
► Attach to Form 1120 or 1120-C. ► Information about Schedule M-3 (Form 1120) and its separate instructions is available at www.irs.gov/form1120.

OMB No. 1545-0123

2016

Name of corporation (common parent, if consolidated return) | Employer identification number

Check applicable box(es): (1) ☐ Non-consolidated return (2) ☐ Consolidated return (Form 1120 only)
(3) ☐ Mixed 1120/L/PC group (4) ☐ Dormant subsidiaries schedule attached

Part I — Financial Information and Net Income (Loss) Reconciliation (see instructions)

1a Did the corporation file SEC Form 10-K for its income statement period ending with or within this tax year?
  ☐ Yes. Skip lines 1b and 1c and complete lines 2a through 11 with respect to that SEC Form 10-K.
  ☐ No. Go to line 1b. See instructions if multiple non-tax-basis income statements are prepared.
b Did the corporation prepare a certified audited non-tax-basis income statement for that period?
  ☐ Yes. Skip line 1c and complete lines 2a through 11 with respect to that income statement.
  ☐ No. Go to line 1c.
c Did the corporation prepare a non-tax-basis income statement for that period?
  ☐ Yes. Complete lines 2a through 11 with respect to that income statement.
  ☐ No. Skip lines 2a through 3c and enter the corporation's net income (loss) per its books and records on line 4a.
2a Enter the income statement period: Beginning MM/DD/YYYY Ending MM/DD/YYYY
b Has the corporation's income statement been restated for the income statement period on line 2a?
  ☐ Yes. (If "Yes," attach an explanation and the amount of each item restated.)
  ☐ No.
c Has the corporation's income statement been restated for any of the five income statement periods immediately preceding the period on line 2a?
  ☐ Yes. (If "Yes," attach an explanation and the amount of each item restated.)
  ☐ No.
3a Is any of the corporation's voting common stock publicly traded?
  ☐ Yes.
  ☐ No. If "No," go to line 4a.
b Enter the symbol of the corporation's primary U.S. publicly traded voting common stock . . . .
c Enter the nine-digit CUSIP number of the corporation's primary publicly traded voting common stock . . . .

4a Worldwide consolidated net income (loss) from income statement source identified in Part I, line 1 . | **4a**
b Indicate accounting standard used for line 4a (see instructions):
  (1) ☐ GAAP (2) ☐ IFRS (3) ☐ Statutory (4) ☐ Tax-basis (5) ☐ Other (specify) _____
5a Net income from nonincludible foreign entities (attach statement) . . . . | **5a** (   )
b Net loss from nonincludible foreign entities (attach statement and enter as a positive amount) . . . | **5b**
6a Net income from nonincludible U.S. entities (attach statement) . . . . | **6a** (   )
b Net loss from nonincludible U.S. entities (attach statement and enter as a positive amount) . . . | **6b**
7a Net income (loss) of other includible foreign disregarded entities (attach statement) . . . . . | **7a**
b Net income (loss) of other includible U.S. disregarded entities (attach statement) . . . . . | **7b**
c Net income (loss) of other includible entities (attach statement) . . . . | **7c**
8 Adjustment to eliminations of transactions between includible entities and nonincludible entities (attach statement) . . . . | **8**
9 Adjustment to reconcile income statement period to tax year (attach statement) . . . . | **9**
10a Intercompany dividend adjustments to reconcile to line 11 (attach statement) . . . . | **10a**
b Other statutory accounting adjustments to reconcile to line 11 (attach statement) . . . . | **10b**
c Other adjustments to reconcile to amount on line 11 (attach statement) . . . . . | **10c**
11 Net income (loss) per income statement of includible corporations. Combine lines 4 through 10 . | **11**
  Note: Part I, line 11, must equal Part II, line 30, column (a) or Schedule M-1, line 1 (see instructions).
12 Enter the total amount (not just the corporation's share) of the assets and liabilities of all entities included or removed on the following lines.

	Total Assets	Total Liabilities
a Included on Part I, line 4 ►		
b Removed on Part I, line 5 ►		
c Removed on Part I, line 6 ►		
d Included on Part I, line 7 ►		

For Paperwork Reduction Act Notice, see the Instructions for Form 1120. Cat. No. 37961C Schedule M-3 (Form 1120) 2016

Form 1120S – U.S Income Tax Return for an S Corporation

Form **1120S**	**U.S. Income Tax Return for an S Corporation**	OMB No. 1545-0123
Department of the Treasury Internal Revenue Service	▶ Do not file this form unless the corporation has filed or is attaching Form 2553 to elect to be an S corporation. ▶ Information about Form 1120S and its separate instructions is at www.irs.gov/form1120s.	**2016**

For calendar year 2016 or tax year beginning , 2016, ending , 20

A	S election effective date				D	Employer identification number
B	Business activity code number (see instructions)	TYPE OR PRINT	Name Number, street, and room or suite no. If a P.O. box, see instructions.		E	Date incorporated
C	Check if Sch. M-3 attached ☐		City or town, state or province, country, and ZIP or foreign postal code		F	Total assets (see instructions) $

G Is the corporation electing to be an S corporation beginning with this tax year? ☐ Yes ☐ No   If "Yes," attach Form 2553 if not already filed
H Check if: (1) ☐ Final return (2) ☐ Name change (3) ☐ Address change (4) ☐ Amended return (5) ☐ S election termination or revocation
I Enter the number of shareholders who were shareholders during any part of the tax year . . . . ▶

Caution: Include only trade or business income and expenses on lines 1a through 21. See the instructions for more information.

Income
1a	Gross receipts or sales	1a	
b	Returns and allowances	1b	
c	Balance. Subtract line 1b from line 1a	1c	
2	Cost of goods sold (attach Form 1125-A)	2	
3	Gross profit. Subtract line 2 from line 1c	3	
4	Net gain (loss) from Form 4797, line 17 (attach Form 4797)	4	
5	Other income (loss) (see instructions—attach statement)	5	
6	Total income (loss). Add lines 3 through 5 . . . . ▶	6	

Deductions (see instructions for limitations)
7	Compensation of officers (see instructions—attach Form 1125-E)	7	
8	Salaries and wages (less employment credits)	8	
9	Repairs and maintenance	9	
10	Bad debts	10	
11	Rents	11	
12	Taxes and licenses	12	
13	Interest	13	
14	Depreciation not claimed on Form 1125-A or elsewhere on return (attach Form 4562)	14	
15	Depletion (**Do not deduct oil and gas depletion.**)	15	
16	Advertising	16	
17	Pension, profit-sharing, etc., plans	17	
18	Employee benefit programs	18	
19	Other deductions (attach statement)	19	
20	Total deductions. Add lines 7 through 19 . . . . ▶	20	
21	Ordinary business income (loss). Subtract line 20 from line 6	21	

Tax and Payments
22a	Excess net passive income or LIFO recapture tax (see instructions) . .	22a		
b	Tax from Schedule D (Form 1120S)	22b		
c	Add lines 22a and 22b (see instructions for additional taxes)		22c	
23a	2016 estimated tax payments and 2015 overpayment credited to 2016	23a		
b	Tax deposited with Form 7004	23b		
c	Credit for federal tax paid on fuels (attach Form 4136)	23c		
d	Add lines 23a through 23c		23d	
24	Estimated tax penalty (see instructions). Check if Form 2220 is attached . . . . ▶ ☐		24	
25	Amount owed. If line 23d is smaller than the total of lines 22c and 24, enter amount owed . .		25	
26	Overpayment. If line 23d is larger than the total of lines 22c and 24, enter amount overpaid		26	
27	Enter amount from line 26 Credited to 2017 estimated tax ▶ Refunded ▶		27	

Sign Here
Under penalties of perjury, I declare that I have examined this return, including accompanying schedules and statements, and to the best of my knowledge and belief, it is true, correct, and complete. Declaration of preparer (other than taxpayer) is based on all information of which preparer has any knowledge.

Signature of officer   Date   Title

May the IRS discuss this return with the preparer shown below (see instructions)? ☐ Yes ☐ No

Paid Preparer Use Only
Print/Type preparer's name	Preparer's signature	Date	Check ☐ if self-employed	PTIN
Firm's name ▶			Firm's EIN ▶	
Firm's address ▶			Phone no.	

For Paperwork Reduction Act Notice, see separate instructions.   Cat. No. 11510H   Form **1120S** (2016)

Form 1120 Schedule K-1 – Shareholder's Share of Income, Deductions, Credits, etc.

		671113
☐ Final K-1	☐ Amended K-1	OMB No. 1545-0123

Schedule K-1 (Form 1120S)
Department of the Treasury
Internal Revenue Service

2016

For calendar year 2016, or tax year beginning _____, 2016 ending _____, 20 ___

Shareholder's Share of Income, Deductions, Credits, etc. ► See back of form and separate instructions.

Part I Information About the Corporation

A Corporation's employer identification number

B Corporation's name, address, city, state, and ZIP code

C IRS Center where corporation filed return

Part II Information About the Shareholder

D Shareholder's identifying number

E Shareholder's name, address, city, state, and ZIP code

F Shareholder's percentage of stock ownership for tax year .... %

For IRS Use Only

Part III Shareholder's Share of Current Year Income, Deductions, Credits, and Other Items

1	Ordinary business income (loss)	13	Credits
2	Net rental real estate income (loss)		
3	Other net rental income (loss)		
4	Interest income		
5a	Ordinary dividends		
5b	Qualified dividends	14	Foreign transactions
6	Royalties		
7	Net short-term capital gain (loss)		
8a	Net long-term capital gain (loss)		
8b	Collectibles (28%) gain (loss)		
8c	Unrecaptured section 1250 gain		
9	Net section 1231 gain (loss)		
10	Other income (loss)	15	Alternative minimum tax (AMT) items
11	Section 179 deduction	16	Items affecting shareholder basis
12	Other deductions		
		17	Other information

* See attached statement for additional information.

For Paperwork Reduction Act Notice, see Instructions for Form 1120S.   IRS.gov/form1120s   Cat. No. 11520D   Schedule K-1 (Form 1120S) 2016

Form 1065 – U.S. Return of Partnership Income

Form **1065** Department of the Treasury Internal Revenue Service	**U.S. Return of Partnership Income** For calendar year 2016, or tax year beginning _____, 2016, ending _____, 20 ___ ▶ Information about Form 1065 and its separate instructions is at www.irs.gov/form1065.	OMB No. 1545-0123 **2016**
A Principal business activity	Name of partnership	D Employer identification number
B Principal product or service	Number, street, and room or suite no. If a P.O. box, see the instructions.	E Date business started
C Business code number	City or town, state or province, country, and ZIP or foreign postal code	F Total assets (see the instructions) $

G Check applicable boxes: (1) ☐ Initial return (2) ☐ Final return (3) ☐ Name change (4) ☐ Address change (5) ☐ Amended return
(6) ☐ Technical termination - also check (1) or (2)
H Check accounting method: (1) ☐ Cash (2) ☐ Accrual (3) ☐ Other (specify) ▶ _____
I Number of Schedules K-1. Attach one for each person who was a partner at any time during the tax year ▶ _____
J Check if Schedules C and M-3 are attached . . . . ☐

Caution. Include only trade or business income and expenses on lines 1a through 22 below. See the instructions for more information.

Income
1a	Gross receipts or sales	1a	
b	Returns and allowances	1b	
c	Balance. Subtract line 1b from line 1a	1c	
2	Cost of goods sold (attach Form 1125-A)	2	
3	Gross profit. Subtract line 2 from line 1c	3	
4	Ordinary income (loss) from other partnerships, estates, and trusts (attach statement) . .	4	
5	Net farm profit (loss) (attach Schedule F (Form 1040))	5	
6	Net gain (loss) from Form 4797, Part II, line 17 (attach Form 4797)	6	
7	Other income (loss) (attach statement)	7	
8	**Total income (loss).** Combine lines 3 through 7	8	

Deductions (see the instructions for limitations)
9	Salaries and wages (other than to partners) (less employment credits)	9	
10	Guaranteed payments to partners	10	
11	Repairs and maintenance	11	
12	Bad debts	12	
13	Rent	13	
14	Taxes and licenses	14	
15	Interest	15	
16a	Depreciation (if required, attach Form 4562)	16a		
b	Less depreciation reported on Form 1125-A and elsewhere on return	16b		16c
17	Depletion (Do not deduct oil and gas depletion.)	17	
18	Retirement plans, etc.	18	
19	Employee benefit programs	19	
20	Other deductions (attach statement)	20	
21	**Total deductions.** Add the amounts shown in the far right column for lines 9 through 20 .	21	
22	**Ordinary business income (loss).** Subtract line 21 from line 8	22	

Sign Here
Under penalties of perjury, I declare that I have examined this return, including accompanying schedules and statements, and to the best of my knowledge and belief, it is true, correct, and complete. Declaration of preparer (other than general partner or limited liability company member manager) is based on all information of which preparer has any knowledge.

▶ _____   ▶ _____
Signature of general partner or limited liability company member manager   Date

May the IRS discuss this return with the preparer shown below (see instructions)? ☐ Yes ☐ No

Paid Preparer Use Only
Print/Type preparer's name	Preparer's signature	Date	Check ☐ if self-employed	PTIN
Firm's name ▶			Firm's EIN ▶	
Firm's address ▶			Phone no.	

For Paperwork Reduction Act Notice, see separate instructions.   Cat. No. 11390Z   Form **1065** (2016)

Form 1065 Schedule K – Partners' Distributive Share Items

			Schedule K — Partners' Distributive Share Items		Total amount
Income (Loss)	1		Ordinary business income (loss) (page 1, line 22)	1	
	2		Net rental real estate income (loss) (attach Form 8825)	2	
	3a		Other gross rental income (loss)	3a	
		b	Expenses from other rental activities (attach statement)	3b	
		c	Other net rental income (loss). Subtract line 3b from line 3a	3c	
	4		Guaranteed payments	4	
	5		Interest income	5	
	6	a	Dividends: Ordinary dividends	6a	
		b	Qualified dividends	6b	
	7		Royalties	7	
	8		Net short-term capital gain (loss) (attach Schedule D (Form 1065))	8	
	9a		Net long-term capital gain (loss) (attach Schedule D (Form 1065))	9a	
		b	Collectibles (28%) gain (loss)	9b	
		c	Unrecaptured section 1250 gain (attach statement)	9c	
	10		Net section 1231 gain (loss) (attach Form 4797)	10	
	11		Other income (loss) (see instructions) Type ▶	11	
Deductions	12		Section 179 deduction (attach Form 4562)	12	
	13a		Contributions	13a	
		b	Investment interest expense	13b	
		c	Section 59(e)(2) expenditures: (1) Type ▶ (2) Amount ▶	13c(2)	
		d	Other deductions (see instructions) Type ▶	13d	
Self-Employment	14a		Net earnings (loss) from self-employment	14a	
		b	Gross farming or fishing income	14b	
		c	Gross nonfarm income	14c	
Credits	15a		Low-income housing credit (section 42(j)(5))	15a	
		b	Low-income housing credit (other)	15b	
		c	Qualified rehabilitation expenditures (rental real estate) (attach Form 3468, if applicable)	15c	
		d	Other rental real estate credits (see instructions) Type ▶	15d	
		e	Other rental credits (see instructions) Type ▶	15e	
		f	Other credits (see instructions) Type ▶	15f	
Foreign Transactions	16a		Name of country or U.S. possession ▶		
		b	Gross income from all sources	16b	
		c	Gross income sourced at partner level	16c	
			Foreign gross income sourced at partnership level		
		d	Passive category ▶ e General category ▶ f Other ▶	16f	
			Deductions allocated and apportioned at partner level		
		g	Interest expense ▶ h Other ▶	16h	
			Deductions allocated and apportioned at partnership level to foreign source income		
		i	Passive category ▶ j General category ▶ k Other ▶	16k	
		l	Total foreign taxes (check one): ▶ Paid ☐ Accrued ☐	16l	
		m	Reduction in taxes available for credit (attach statement)	16m	
		n	Other foreign tax information (attach statement)		
Alternative Minimum Tax (AMT) Items	17a		Post-1986 depreciation adjustment	17a	
		b	Adjusted gain or loss	17b	
		c	Depletion (other than oil and gas)	17c	
		d	Oil, gas, and geothermal properties—gross income	17d	
		e	Oil, gas, and geothermal properties—deductions	17e	
		f	Other AMT items (attach statement)	17f	
Other Information	18a		Tax-exempt interest income	18a	
		b	Other tax-exempt income	18b	
		c	Nondeductible expenses	18c	
	19a		Distributions of cash and marketable securities	19a	
		b	Distributions of other property	19b	
	20a		Investment income	20a	
		b	Investment expenses	20b	
		c	Other items and amounts (attach statement)		

Form 1065 Schedule K-1 – Partner's Share of Income, Deductions, Credits, etc.

Schedule K-1 (Form 1065) — 2016

651113
☐ Final K-1   ☐ Amended K-1   OMB No. 1545-0123

Department of the Treasury
Internal Revenue Service

For calendar year 2016, or tax year beginning _____, 2016 ending _____, 20 ____

Partner's Share of Income, Deductions, Credits, etc. ► See back of form and separate instructions.

Part I Information About the Partnership

A Partnership's employer identification number

B Partnership's name, address, city, state, and ZIP code

C IRS Center where partnership filed return

D ☐ Check if this is a publicly traded partnership (PTP)

Part II Information About the Partner

E Partner's identifying number

F Partner's name, address, city, state, and ZIP code

G ☐ General partner or LLC member-manager   ☐ Limited partner or other LLC member

H ☐ Domestic partner   ☐ Foreign partner

I1 What type of entity is this partner? _____

I2 If this partner is a retirement plan (IRA/SEP/Keogh/etc.), check here ☐

J Partner's share of profit, loss, and capital (see instructions):

	Beginning	Ending
Profit	%	%
Loss	%	%
Capital	%	%

K Partner's share of liabilities at year end:
- Nonrecourse . . . . $ _____
- Qualified nonrecourse financing . $ _____
- Recourse . . . . $ _____

L Partner's capital account analysis:
- Beginning capital account . . . $ _____
- Capital contributed during the year $ _____
- Current year increase (decrease) $ _____
- Withdrawals & distributions . . $ (_____)
- Ending capital account . . . . $ _____

☐ Tax basis   ☐ GAAP   ☐ Section 704(b) book
☐ Other (explain)

M Did the partner contribute property with a built-in gain or loss?
☐ Yes   ☐ No
If "Yes," attach statement (see instructions)

Part III Partner's Share of Current Year Income, Deductions, Credits, and Other Items

1	Ordinary business income (loss)	15	Credits
2	Net rental real estate income (loss)		
3	Other net rental income (loss)	16	Foreign transactions
4	Guaranteed payments		
5	Interest income		
6a	Ordinary dividends		
6b	Qualified dividends		
7	Royalties		
8	Net short-term capital gain (loss)		
9a	Net long-term capital gain (loss)	17	Alternative minimum tax (AMT) items
9b	Collectibles (28%) gain (loss)		
9c	Unrecaptured section 1250 gain		
10	Net section 1231 gain (loss)	18	Tax-exempt income and nondeductible expenses
11	Other income (loss)		
		19	Distributions
12	Section 179 deduction		
13	Other deductions	20	Other information
14	Self-employment earnings (loss)		

*See attached statement for additional information.

For IRS Use Only

For Paperwork Reduction Act Notice, see Instructions for Form 1065.   IRS.gov/form1065   Cat. No. 11394R   Schedule K-1 (Form 1065) 2016

Form 8832 – Entity Classification Election

Form 8832
(Rev. December 2013)
Department of the Treasury
Internal Revenue Service

Entity Classification Election

▶ Information about Form 8832 and its Instructions is at www.irs.gov/form8832.

OMB No. 1545-1516

Type or Print

Name of eligible entity making election

Employer identification number

Number, street, and room or suite no. If a P.O. box, see instructions.

City or town, state, and ZIP code. If a foreign address, enter city, province or state, postal code and country. Follow the country's practice for entering the postal code.

▶ Check if: ☐ Address change   ☐ Late classification relief sought under Revenue Procedure 2009-41
☐ Relief for a late change of entity classification election sought under Revenue Procedure 2010-32

Part I Election Information

1 Type of election (see instructions):

a ☐ Initial classification by a newly-formed entity. Skip lines 2a and 2b and go to line 3.
b ☐ Change in current classification. Go to line 2a.

2a Has the eligible entity previously filed an entity election that had an effective date within the last 60 months?

☐ Yes. Go to line 2b.
☐ No. Skip line 2b and go to line 3.

2b Was the eligible entity's prior election an initial classification election by a newly formed entity that was effective on the date of formation?

☐ Yes. Go to line 3.
☐ No. Stop here. You generally are not currently eligible to make the election (see instructions).

3 Does the eligible entity have more than one owner?

☐ Yes. You can elect to be classified as a partnership or an association taxable as a corporation. Skip line 4 and go to line 5.
☐ No. You can elect to be classified as an association taxable as a corporation or to be disregarded as a separate entity. Go to line 4.

4 If the eligible entity has only one owner, provide the following information:

a Name of owner ▶ _____
b Identifying number of owner ▶ _____

5 If the eligible entity is owned by one or more affiliated corporations that file a consolidated return, provide the name and employer identification number of the parent corporation:

a Name of parent corporation ▶ _____
b Employer identification number ▶ _____

For Paperwork Reduction Act Notice, see Instructions.   Cat. No. 22598R   Form **8832** (Rev. 12-2013)

Form 8832 (Rev. 12-2013) Page **2**

Part I Election Information (Continued)

6 Type of entity (see instructions):

- a ☐ A domestic eligible entity electing to be classified as an association taxable as a corporation.
- b ☐ A domestic eligible entity electing to be classified as a partnership.
- c ☐ A domestic eligible entity with a single owner electing to be disregarded as a separate entity.
- d ☐ A foreign eligible entity electing to be classified as an association taxable as a corporation.
- e ☐ A foreign eligible entity electing to be classified as a partnership.
- f ☐ A foreign eligible entity with a single owner electing to be disregarded as a separate entity.

7 If the eligible entity is created or organized in a foreign jurisdiction, provide the foreign country of organization ▶ _____

8 Election is to be effective beginning (month, day, year) (see instructions) . . . . ▶ _____

9 Name and title of contact person whom the IRS may call for more information | 10 Contact person's telephone number

Consent Statement and Signature(s) (see instructions)

Under penalties of perjury, I (we) declare that I (we) consent to the election of the above-named entity to be classified as indicated above, and that I (we) have examined this election and consent statement, and to the best of my (our) knowledge and belief, this election and consent statement are true, correct, and complete. If I am an officer, manager, or member signing for the entity, I further declare under penalties of perjury that I am authorized to make the election on its behalf.

Signature(s)	Date	Title

Form **8832** (Rev. 12-2013)

Form 1041 – U.S Income Tax Return for Estates and Trusts

Form 1041 — Department of the Treasury — Internal Revenue Service
U.S. Income Tax Return for Estates and Trusts — 2016
OMB No. 1545-0092

▶ Information about Form 1041 and its separate instructions is at www.irs.gov/form1041.

For calendar year 2016 or fiscal year beginning _____, 2016, and ending _____, 20 ___

A Check all that apply:
- ☐ Decedent's estate
- ☐ Simple trust
- ☐ Complex trust
- ☐ Qualified disability trust
- ☐ ESBT (S portion only)
- ☐ Grantor type trust
- ☐ Bankruptcy estate-Ch. 7
- ☐ Bankruptcy estate-Ch. 11
- ☐ Pooled income fund

Name of estate or trust (If a grantor type trust, see the instructions.)

Name and title of fiduciary

Number, street, and room or suite no. (If a P.O. box, see the instructions.)

City or town, state or province, country, and ZIP or foreign postal code

C Employer identification number

D Date entity created

E Nonexempt charitable and split-interest trusts, check applicable box(es), see instructions.
- ☐ Described in sec. 4947(a)(1). Check here if not a private foundation ▶ ☐
- ☐ Described in sec. 4947(a)(2)

B Number of Schedules K-1 attached (see instructions) ▶

F Check applicable boxes:
- ☐ Initial return
- ☐ Final return
- ☐ Amended return
- ☐ Net operating loss carryback
- ☐ Change in trust's name
- ☐ Change in fiduciary
- ☐ Change in fiduciary's name
- ☐ Change in fiduciary's address

G Check here if the estate or filing trust made a section 645 election . . . ▶ ☐ Trust TIN ▶

Income
1. Interest income **1**
2a. Total ordinary dividends **2a**
 b. Qualified dividends allocable to: (1) Beneficiaries _____ (2) Estate or trust _____
3. Business income or (loss). Attach Schedule C or C-EZ (Form 1040) . . . **3**
4. Capital gain or (loss). Attach Schedule D (Form 1041) **4**
5. Rents, royalties, partnerships, other estates and trusts, etc. Attach Schedule E (Form 1040) . **5**
6. Farm income or (loss). Attach Schedule F (Form 1040) **6**
7. Ordinary gain or (loss). Attach Form 4797 . . . . **7**
8. Other income. List type and amount _____ **8**
9. **Total income.** Combine lines 1, 2a, and 3 through 8 . . . . ▶ **9**

Deductions
10. Interest. Check if Form 4952 is attached ▶ ☐ **10**
11. Taxes **11**
12. Fiduciary fees **12**
13. Charitable deduction (from Schedule A, line 7) **13**
14. Attorney, accountant, and return preparer fees **14**
15a. Other deductions not subject to the 2% floor (attach schedule) **15a**
 b. Net operating loss deduction. See instructions **15b**
 c. Allowable miscellaneous itemized deductions subject to the 2% floor . **15c**
16. Add lines 10 through 15c . . . . ▶ **16**
17. Adjusted total income or (loss). Subtract line 16 from line 9 . . . **17**
18. Income distribution deduction (from Schedule B, line 15). Attach Schedules K-1 (Form 1041) . **18**
19. Estate tax deduction including certain generation-skipping taxes (attach computation) . **19**
20. Exemption **20**
21. Add lines 18 through 20 . . . . ▶ **21**

Tax and Payments
22. Taxable income. Subtract line 21 from line 17. If a loss, see instructions . **22**
23. **Total tax** (from Schedule G, line 7) **23**
24. Payments: a 2016 estimated tax payments and amount applied from 2015 return . **24a**
 b. Estimated tax payments allocated to beneficiaries (from Form 1041-T) . **24b**
 c. Subtract line 24b from line 24a **24c**
 d. Tax paid with Form 7004. See instructions **24d**
 e. Federal income tax withheld. If any is from Form(s) 1099, check ▶ ☐ . **24e**
 Other payments: f Form 2439 _____ ; g Form 4136 _____ ; Total ▶ **24h**
25. **Total payments.** Add lines 24c through 24e, and 24h . . . . ▶ **25**
26. Estimated tax penalty. See instructions **26**
27. **Tax due.** If line 25 is smaller than the total of lines 23 and 26, enter amount owed . **27**
28. **Overpayment.** If line 25 is larger than the total of lines 23 and 26, enter amount overpaid . **28**
29. Amount of line 28 to be: a Credited to 2017 estimated tax ▶ _____ ; b Refunded ▶ **29**

Sign Here
Under penalties of perjury, I declare that I have examined this return, including accompanying schedules and statements, and to the best of my knowledge and belief, it is true, correct, and complete. Declaration of preparer (other than taxpayer) is based on all information of which preparer has any knowledge.

Signature of fiduciary or officer representing fiduciary | Date | EIN of fiduciary if a financial institution

May the IRS discuss this return with the preparer shown below (see instr.)? ☐ Yes ☐ No

Paid Preparer Use Only
Print/Type preparer's name | Preparer's signature | Date | Check ☐ if self-employed | PTIN
Firm's name ▶
Firm's address ▶
Firm's EIN ▶
Phone no.

For Paperwork Reduction Act Notice, see the separate instructions. Cat. No. 11370H Form **1041** (2016)

Form 1041 Schedule K-1 – Beneficiary's Share of Income, Deductions, Credits, etc.

Schedule K-1 (Form 1041) — 2016

Department of the Treasury, Internal Revenue Service

For calendar year 2016, or tax year beginning _____, 2016, and ending _____, 20 ___

Beneficiary's Share of Income, Deductions, Credits, etc. ► See back of form and instructions.

☐ Final K-1 ☐ Amended K-1 OMB No. 1545-0092

Part I — Information About the Estate or Trust

- A. Estate's or trust's employer identification number
- B. Estate's or trust's name
- C. Fiduciary's name, address, city, state, and ZIP code
- D. ☐ Check if Form 1041-T was filed and enter the date it was filed _____
- E. ☐ Check if this is the final Form 1041 for the estate or trust

Part II — Information About the Beneficiary

- F. Beneficiary's identifying number
- G. Beneficiary's name, address, city, state, and ZIP code
- H. ☐ Domestic beneficiary ☐ Foreign beneficiary

Part III — Beneficiary's Share of Current Year Income, Deductions, Credits, and Other Items

1. Interest income
2a. Ordinary dividends
2b. Qualified dividends
3. Net short-term capital gain
4a. Net long-term capital gain
4b. 28% rate gain
4c. Unrecaptured section 1250 gain
5. Other portfolio and nonbusiness income
6. Ordinary business income
7. Net rental real estate income
8. Other rental income
9. Directly apportioned deductions
10. Estate tax deduction
11. Final year deductions
12. Alternative minimum tax adjustment
13. Credits and credit recapture
14. Other information

*See attached statement for additional information.

Note. A statement must be attached showing the beneficiary's share of income and directly apportioned deductions from each business, rental real estate, and other rental activity.

For Paperwork Reduction Act Notice, see the Instructions for Form 1041. IRS.gov/form1041 Cat. No. 11380D Schedule K-1 (Form 1041) 2016

Form 1023 – Application for Recognition of Exemption

Form 1023
(Rev. December 2013)
Department of the Treasury
Internal Revenue Service

Application for Recognition of Exemption Under Section 501(c)(3) of the Internal Revenue Code

OMB No. 1545-0056

Note: If exempt status is approved, this application will be open for public inspection.

Use the instructions to complete this application and for a definition of all **bold** items. For additional help, call IRS Exempt Organizations Customer Account Services toll-free at 1-877-829-5500. Visit our website at www.irs.gov for forms and publications. If the required information and documents are not submitted with payment of the appropriate user fee, the application may be returned to you.

Attach additional sheets to this application if you need more space to answer fully. Put your name and EIN on each sheet and identify each answer by Part and line number. Complete Parts I - XI of Form 1023 and submit only those Schedules (A through H) that apply to you.

Part I Identification of Applicant

1. Full name of organization (exactly as it appears in your **organizing document**)
2. c/o Name (if applicable)
3. **Mailing address** (Number and street) (see instructions) — Room/Suite
4. Employer Identification Number (EIN)
5. Month the annual accounting period ends (01 – 12)
6. Primary contact (officer, director, trustee, or **authorized representative**)
   a Name:
   b Phone:
   c Fax: (optional)
7. Are you represented by an authorized representative, such as an attorney or accountant? If "Yes," provide the authorized representative's name, and the name and address of the authorized representative's firm. Include a completed Form 2848, Power of Attorney and Declaration of Representative, with your application if you would like us to communicate with your representative. ☐ Yes ☐ No
8. Was a person who is not one of your officers, directors, trustees, employees, or an authorized representative listed in line 7, paid, or promised payment, to help plan, manage, or advise you about the structure or activities of your organization, or about your financial or tax matters? If "Yes," provide the person's name, the name and address of the person's firm, the amounts paid or promised to be paid, and describe that person's role. ☐ Yes ☐ No
9. a Organization's website:
   b Organization's email: (optional)
10. Certain organizations are not required to file an information return (Form 990 or Form 990-EZ). If you are granted tax-exemption, are you claiming to be excused from filing Form 990 or Form 990-EZ? If "Yes," explain. See the instructions for a description of organizations not required to file Form 990 or Form 990-EZ. ☐ Yes ☐ No
11. Date incorporated if a corporation, or formed, if other than a corporation. (MM/DD/YYYY) __/__/__
12. Were you formed under the laws of a **foreign country**? If "Yes," state the country. ☐ Yes ☐ No

For Paperwork Reduction Act Notice, see page 24 of the Instructions. Cat. No. 17133K Form **1023** (Rev. 12-2013)

Form 1023-EZ – Streamlined Application for Recognition of Exemption under Section 501(c)(3) of the Internal Revenue Code

Form 1024 – Application for Recognition of Exemption under Section 501(a)

Form 1024 (Rev. September 1998)
Department of the Treasury
Internal Revenue Service

Application for Recognition of Exemption Under Section 501(a)

OMB No. 1545-0057

If exempt status is approved, this application will be open for public inspection.

Read the Instructions for each Part carefully. **A User Fee must be attached to this application.** If the required information and appropriate documents are not submitted along with Form 8718 (with payment of the appropriate user fee), the application may be returned to the organization. **Complete the Procedural Checklist on page 6 of the Instructions.**

Part I. Identification of Applicant (Must be completed by all applicants; also complete appropriate schedule.) Submit only the schedule that applies to your organization. Do not submit blank schedules.

Check the appropriate box below to indicate the section under which the organization is applying:

- a ☐ Section 501(c)(2)—Title holding corporations (Schedule A, page 7)
- b ☐ Section 501(c)(4)—Civic leagues, social welfare organizations (including certain war veterans' organizations), or local associations of employees (Schedule B, page 8)
- c ☐ Section 501(c)(5)—Labor, agricultural, or horticultural organizations (Schedule C, page 9)
- d ☐ Section 501(c)(6)—Business leagues, chambers of commerce, etc. (Schedule C, page 9)
- e ☐ Section 501(c)(7)—Social clubs (Schedule D, page 11)
- f ☐ Section 501(c)(8)—Fraternal beneficiary societies, etc., providing life, sick, accident, or other benefits to members (Schedule E, page 13)
- g ☐ Section 501(c)(9)—Voluntary employees' beneficiary associations (Parts I through IV and Schedule F, page 14)
- h ☐ Section 501(c)(10)—Domestic fraternal societies, orders, etc., not providing life, sick, accident, or other benefits (Schedule E, page 13)
- i ☐ Section 501(c)(12)—Benevolent life insurance associations, mutual ditch or irrigation companies, mutual or cooperative telephone companies, or like organizations (Schedule G, page 15)
- j ☐ Section 501(c)(13)—Cemeteries, crematoria, and like corporations (Schedule H, page 16)
- k ☐ Section 501(c)(15)—Mutual insurance companies or associations, other than life or marine (Schedule I, page 17)
- l ☐ Section 501(c)(17)—Trusts providing for the payment of supplemental unemployment compensation benefits (Parts I through IV and Schedule J, page 18)
- m ☐ Section 501(c)(19)—A post, organization, auxiliary unit, etc., of past or present members of the Armed Forces of the United States (Schedule K, page 19)
- n ☐ Section 501(c)(25)—Title holding corporations or trusts (Schedule A, page 7)

1a Full name of organization (as shown in organizing document)

2 Employer identification number (EIN) (If none, see **Specific Instructions** on page 2)

1b c/o Name (if applicable)

3 Name and telephone number of person to be contacted if additional information is needed

1c Address (number and street) | Room/Suite

1d City, town or post office, state, and ZIP + 4. If you have a foreign address, see **Specific Instructions** for Part I, page 2.

1e Web site address | **4** Month the annual accounting period ends | **5** Date incorporated or formed

6 Did the organization previously apply for recognition of exemption under this Code section or under any other section of the Code? ☐ Yes ☐ No
If "Yes," attach an explanation.

7 Has the organization filed Federal income tax returns or exempt organization information returns? ☐ Yes ☐ No
If "Yes," state the form numbers, years filed, and Internal Revenue office where filed.

8 Check the box for the type of organization. **ATTACH A CONFORMED COPY OF THE CORRESPONDING ORGANIZING DOCUMENTS TO THE APPLICATION BEFORE MAILING.**

- a ☐ Corporation—Attach a copy of the Articles of Incorporation (including amendments and restatements) showing approval by the appropriate state official; also attach a copy of the bylaws.
- b ☐ Trust—Attach a copy of the Trust Indenture or Agreement, including all appropriate signatures and dates.
- c ☐ Association—Attach a copy of the Articles of Association, Constitution, or other creating document, with a declaration (see instructions) or other evidence that the organization was formed by adoption of the document by more than one person. Also include a copy of the bylaws.

If this is a corporation or an unincorporated association that has not yet adopted bylaws, check here ▶ ☐

PLEASE SIGN HERE ▶

I declare under the penalties of perjury that I am authorized to sign this application on behalf of the above organization, and that I have examined this application, including the accompanying schedules and attachments, and to the best of my knowledge it is true, correct, and complete.

_____ (Signature) | _____ (Type or print name and title or authority of signer) | _____ (Date)

For Paperwork Reduction Act Notice, see page 5 of the instructions.

Form 990 – Return of Organization Exempt From Income Tax

Form **990**	**Return of Organization Exempt From Income Tax**	OMB No. 1545-0047
Department of the Treasury Internal Revenue Service	Under section 501(c), 527, or 4947(a)(1) of the Internal Revenue Code (except private foundations) ▶ Do not enter social security numbers on this form as it may be made public. ▶ Information about Form 990 and its instructions is at www.irs.gov/form990.	**2016** Open to Public Inspection

A For the 2016 calendar year, or tax year beginning _____, 2016, and ending _____, 20____

B Check if applicable:
☐ Address change
☐ Name change
☐ Initial return
☐ Final return/terminated
☐ Amended return
☐ Application pending

C Name of organization _____
Doing business as _____
Number and street (or P.O. box if mail is not delivered to street address) _____ Room/suite _____
City or town, state or province, country, and ZIP or foreign postal code _____
F Name and address of principal officer: _____

D Employer identification number
E Telephone number
G Gross receipts $ _____
H(a) Is this a group return for subordinates? ☐ Yes ☐ No
H(b) Are all subordinates included? ☐ Yes ☐ No
If "No," attach a list. (see instructions)

I Tax-exempt status: ☐ 501(c)(3) ☐ 501(c) ( ) ◀ (insert no.) ☐ 4947(a)(1) or ☐ 527
J Website: ▶
K Form of organization: ☐ Corporation ☐ Trust ☐ Association ☐ Other ▶
L Year of formation: _____ **M** State of legal domicile: _____
H(c) Group exemption number ▶

Part I Summary

Activities & Governance
1. Briefly describe the organization's mission or most significant activities: _____
2. Check this box ▶ ☐ if the organization discontinued its operations or disposed of more than 25% of its net assets.
3. Number of voting members of the governing body (Part VI, line 1a) . . . . . | 3 |
4. Number of independent voting members of the governing body (Part VI, line 1b) . . . | 4 |
5. Total number of individuals employed in calendar year 2016 (Part V, line 2a) . . . | 5 |
6. Total number of volunteers (estimate if necessary) . . . . | 6 |
7a. Total unrelated business revenue from Part VIII, column (C), line 12 . . . . | 7a |
 b. Net unrelated business taxable income from Form 990-T, line 34 . . . . . | 7b |

		Prior Year	Current Year
Revenue	8. Contributions and grants (Part VIII, line 1h)		
	9. Program service revenue (Part VIII, line 2g)		
	10. Investment income (Part VIII, column (A), lines 3, 4, and 7d) . . .		
	11. Other revenue (Part VIII, column (A), lines 5, 6d, 8c, 9c, 10c, and 11e) . .		
	12. Total revenue—add lines 8 through 11 (must equal Part VIII, column (A), line 12)		
Expenses	13. Grants and similar amounts paid (Part IX, column (A), lines 1–3) . . .		
	14. Benefits paid to or for members (Part IX, column (A), line 4)		
	15. Salaries, other compensation, employee benefits (Part IX, column (A), lines 5–10)		
	16a. Professional fundraising fees (Part IX, column (A), line 11e)		
	b. Total fundraising expenses (Part IX, column (D), line 25) ▶ _____		
	17. Other expenses (Part IX, column (A), lines 11a–11d, 11f–24e)		
	18. Total expenses. Add lines 13–17 (must equal Part IX, column (A), line 25) .		
	19. Revenue less expenses. Subtract line 18 from line 12		
		Beginning of Current Year	End of Year
Net Assets or Fund Balances	20. Total assets (Part X, line 16)		
	21. Total liabilities (Part X, line 26)		
	22. Net assets or fund balances. Subtract line 21 from line 20		

Part II Signature Block

Under penalties of perjury, I declare that I have examined this return, including accompanying schedules and statements, and to the best of my knowledge and belief, it is true, correct, and complete. Declaration of preparer (other than officer) is based on all information of which preparer has any knowledge.

Sign Here
▶ Signature of officer _____ Date _____
▶ Type or print name and title _____

Paid Preparer Use Only
Print/Type preparer's name _____ Preparer's signature _____ Date _____ Check ☐ if self-employed PTIN _____
Firm's name ▶ _____ Firm's EIN ▶ _____
Firm's address ▶ _____ Phone no. _____

May the IRS discuss this return with the preparer shown above? (see instructions) . . . . ☐ Yes ☐ No

For Paperwork Reduction Act Notice, see the separate instructions. Cat. No. 11282Y Form **990** (2016)

Form 990 Schedule PF – Return of Private Foundation

Form 990T – Exempt Organization Business Income Tax Return

Form 990-T — Exempt Organization Business Income Tax Return
(and proxy tax under section 6033(e))

OMB No. 1545-0687

2016

For calendar year 2016 or other tax year beginning _____, 2016, and ending _____, 20 ___.

Department of the Treasury
Internal Revenue Service

▶ Information about Form 990-T and its instructions is available at *www.irs.gov/form990t*.
▶ Do not enter SSN numbers on this form as it may be made public if your organization is a 501(c)(3).

Open to Public Inspection for 501(c)(3) Organizations Only

- **A** ☐ Check box if address changed
- **B** Exempt under section
  - ☐ 501( )( )
  - ☐ 408(e) ☐ 220(e)
  - ☐ 408A   ☐ 530(a)
  - ☐ 529(a)
- **C** Book value of all assets at end of year

Print or Type
- Name of organization (☐ Check box if name changed and see instructions.)
- Number, street, and room or suite no. If a P.O. box, see instructions.
- City or town, state or province, country, and ZIP or foreign postal code

- **D** Employer identification number (Employees' trust, see instructions.)
- **E** Unrelated business activity codes (See instructions.)

- **F** Group exemption number (See instructions.) ▶
- **G** Check organization type ▶ ☐ 501(c) corporation ☐ 501(c) trust ☐ 401(a) trust ☐ Other trust
- **H** Describe the organization's primary unrelated business activity. ▶
- **I** During the tax year, was the corporation a subsidiary in an affiliated group or a parent-subsidiary controlled group? . . ▶ ☐ Yes ☐ No
  If "Yes," enter the name and identifying number of the parent corporation. ▶
- **J** The books are in care of ▶   Telephone number ▶

Part I — Unrelated Trade or Business Income

		(A) Income	(B) Expenses	(C) Net
1a	Gross receipts or sales			
b	Less returns and allowances ____ c Balance ▶ 1c			
2	Cost of goods sold (Schedule A, line 7) 2			
3	Gross profit. Subtract line 2 from line 1c 3			
4a	Capital gain net income (attach Schedule D) . . 4a			
b	Net gain (loss) (Form 4797, Part II, line 17) (attach Form 4797) 4b			
c	Capital loss deduction for trusts 4c			
5	Income (loss) from partnerships and S corporations (attach statement) 5			
6	Rent income (Schedule C) 6			
7	Unrelated debt-financed income (Schedule E) . . 7			
8	Interest, annuities, royalties, and rents from controlled organizations (Schedule F) 8			
9	Investment income of a section 501(c)(7), (9), or (17) organization (Schedule G) 9			
10	Exploited exempt activity income (Schedule I) . . 10			
11	Advertising income (Schedule J) 11			
12	Other income (See instructions; attach schedule) . 12			
13	**Total.** Combine lines 3 through 12 13			

Part II — Deductions Not Taken Elsewhere
(See instructions for limitations on deductions.) (Except for contributions, deductions must be directly connected with the unrelated business income.)

14	Compensation of officers, directors, and trustees (Schedule K)	14	
15	Salaries and wages	15	
16	Repairs and maintenance	16	
17	Bad debts	17	
18	Interest (attach schedule)	18	
19	Taxes and licenses	19	
20	Charitable contributions (See instructions for limitation rules)	20	
21	Depreciation (attach Form 4562) 21		
22	Less depreciation claimed on Schedule A and elsewhere on return . . 22a	22b	
23	Depletion	23	
24	Contributions to deferred compensation plans	24	
25	Employee benefit programs	25	
26	Excess exempt expenses (Schedule I)	26	
27	Excess readership costs (Schedule J)	27	
28	Other deductions (attach schedule)	28	
29	**Total deductions.** Add lines 14 through 28	29	
30	Unrelated business taxable income before net operating loss deduction. Subtract line 29 from line 13	30	
31	Net operating loss deduction (limited to the amount on line 30)	31	
32	Unrelated business taxable income before specific deduction. Subtract line 31 from line 30 . .	32	
33	Specific deduction (Generally $1,000, but see line 33 instructions for exceptions)	33	
34	**Unrelated business taxable income.** Subtract line 33 from line 32. If line 33 is greater than line 32, enter the smaller of zero or line 32.	34	

For Paperwork Reduction Act Notice, see instructions.   Cat. No. 11291J   Form **990-T** (2016)

Form 5471 – Information Return of U.S. Persons with respect to Certain Foreign Investments

Form 5472 – Information Return of a 25% Foreign-Owned U.S. Corporation or a Foreign Corporation Engaged in a U.S. Trade or Business

Form 8938 – Statement of Specified Foreign Financial Assets

Form 8938
Department of the Treasury
Internal Revenue Service

Statement of Specified Foreign Financial Assets
▶ Information about Form 8938 and its separate instructions is at www.irs.gov/form8938.
▶ Attach to your tax return.
For calendar year 20___ or tax year beginning _____, 20___ and ending _____, 20___

OMB No. 1545-2195
2016
Attachment Sequence No. 175

If you have attached continuation statements, check here ☐   Number of continuation statements _____

1	Name(s) shown on return	2 TIN

3 Type of filer
    a ☐ Specified individual   b ☐ Partnership   c ☐ Corporation   d ☐ Trust

4 If you checked box 3a, skip this line 4. If you checked box 3b or 3c, enter the name and TIN of the specified individual who closely holds the partnership or corporation. If you checked box 3d, enter the name and TIN of the specified person who is a current beneficiary of the trust. (See instructions for definitions and what to do if you have more than one specified individual or specified person to list.)
    a Name   b TIN

Part I — Foreign Deposit and Custodial Accounts Summary

1. Number of Deposit Accounts (reported in Part V) . . . . ▶
2. Maximum Value of All Deposit Accounts . . . . $
3. Number of Custodial Accounts (reported in Part V) . . . . ▶
4. Maximum Value of All Custodial Accounts . . . . $
5. Were any foreign deposit or custodial accounts closed during the tax year? . . . . ☐ Yes   ☐ No

Part II — Other Foreign Assets Summary

1. Number of Foreign Assets (reported in Part VI) . . . . ▶
2. Maximum Value of All Assets (reported in Part VI) . . . . $
3. Were any foreign assets acquired or sold during the tax year? . . . . ☐ Yes   ☐ No

Part III — Summary of Tax Items Attributable to Specified Foreign Financial Assets (see instructions)

(a) Asset Category	(b) Tax item	(c) Amount reported on form or schedule	Where reported	
			(d) Form and line	(e) Schedule and line
1 Foreign Deposit and Custodial Accounts	1a Interest	$		
	1b Dividends	$		
	1c Royalties	$		
	1d Other income	$		
	1e Gains (losses)	$		
	1f Deductions	$		
	1g Credits	$		
2 Other Foreign Assets	2a Interest	$		
	2b Dividends	$		
	2c Royalties	$		
	2d Other income	$		
	2e Gains (losses)	$		
	2f Deductions	$		
	2g Credits	$		

Part IV — Excepted Specified Foreign Financial Assets (see instructions)

If you reported specified foreign financial assets on one or more of the following forms, enter the number of such forms filed. You do not need to include these assets on Form 8938 for the tax year.

1. Number of Forms 3520 _____
2. Number of Forms 3520-A _____
3. Number of Forms 5471 _____
4. Number of Forms 8621 _____
5. Number of Forms 8865 _____

Part V — Detailed Information for Each Foreign Deposit and Custodial Account Included in the Part I Summary (see instructions)

If you have more than one account to report in Part V, attach a continuation statement for each additional account (see instructions).

1 Type of account   ☐ Deposit   ☐ Custodial   **2** Account number or other designation

3 Check all that apply
    a ☐ Account opened during tax year   b ☐ Account closed during tax year
    c ☐ Account jointly owned with spouse   d ☐ No tax item reported in Part III with respect to this asset

4 Maximum value of account during tax year . . . . $

5 Did you use a foreign currency exchange rate to convert the value of the account into U.S. dollars? . . ☐ Yes   ☐ No

6 If you answered "Yes" to line 5, complete all that apply.

(a) Foreign currency in which account is maintained	(b) Foreign currency exchange rate used to convert to U.S. dollars	(c) Source of exchange rate used if not from U.S. Treasury Department's Bureau of the Fiscal Service

For Paperwork Reduction Act Notice, see the separate instructions.   Cat. No. 37753A   Form **8938** (2016)

Form 926 – Return by a U.S. Transferor of Property to a Foreign Corporation

Form 926 (Rev. December 2013)
Department of the Treasury
Internal Revenue Service

Return by a U.S. Transferor of Property to a Foreign Corporation
► Information about Form 926 and its separate instructions is at www.irs.gov/form926.
► Attach to your income tax return for the year of the transfer or distribution.

OMB No. 1545-0026
Attachment Sequence No. 128

Part I — U.S. Transferor Information (see instructions)

Name of transferor _____ Identifying number (see instructions) _____

1. If the transferor was a corporation, complete questions 1a through 1d.
   a. If the transfer was a section 361(a) or (b) transfer, was the transferor controlled (under section 368(c)) by 5 or fewer domestic corporations? ☐ Yes ☐ No
   b. Did the transferor remain in existence after the transfer? ☐ Yes ☐ No
   If not, list the controlling shareholder(s) and their identifying number(s):

Controlling shareholder	Identifying number

   c. If the transferor was a member of an affiliated group filing a consolidated return, was it the parent corporation? ☐ Yes ☐ No
   If not, list the name and employer identification number (EIN) of the parent corporation:

Name of parent corporation	EIN of parent corporation

   d. Have basis adjustments under section 367(a)(5) been made? ☐ Yes ☐ No

2. If the transferor was a partner in a partnership that was the actual transferor (but is not treated as such under section 367), complete questions 2a through 2d.
   a. List the name and EIN of the transferor's partnership:

Name of partnership	EIN of partnership

   b. Did the partner pick up its pro rata share of gain on the transfer of partnership assets? ☐ Yes ☐ No
   c. Is the partner disposing of its entire interest in the partnership? ☐ Yes ☐ No
   d. Is the partner disposing of an interest in a limited partnership that is regularly traded on an established securities market? ☐ Yes ☐ No

Part II — Transferee Foreign Corporation Information (see instructions)

3. Name of transferee (foreign corporation) _____
4a. Identifying number, if any _____
5. Address (including country) _____
4b. Reference ID number (see instructions) _____
6. Country code of country of incorporation or organization (see instructions) _____
7. Foreign law characterization (see instructions) _____
8. Is the transferee foreign corporation a controlled foreign corporation? ☐ Yes ☐ No

For Paperwork Reduction Act Notice, see separate instructions.   Cat. No. 16982D   Form **926** (Rev. 12-2013)

REG 6 – Task-based Simulations

Task-based Simulation – Questions   **TBS 6-1 – 6-8**

    REG 6-SIMQ1 SIM2   1

    REG 6-SIMQ2 SIM4   2

    REG 6-SIMQ3 SIM7   3

    REG 6-SIMQ4 DRS1   4

    REG 6-SIMQ5 SIM30   7

Task-based Simulation – Solutions   **TBS 6-8 – TBS 6-16**

    REG 6-SIMQ1 SIM2   8

    REG 6-SIMQ2 SIM4   9

    REG 6-SIMQ3 SIM7   10

    REG 6-SIMQ4 DRS1   12

    REG 6-SIMQ5 SIM30   15

Task-based Simulations – Questions

Remember: The icons and buttons below are *not* functional. The formatting in this chapter mirrors the CPA exam. It is intended to familiarize you with the look and feel of the exam.

REG 6-SIMQ1 SIM2

[🖉 Professional and Legal Responsibilities]   [Help]   Authoritative Literature      Submit Testlet

There are many rules and regulations governing the accounting profession and specifically Certified Public Accountants. Regarding these rules and regulations, for each of the following items, indicate whether it is either correct or incorrect in the shaded area.

List of abbreviations used:
- American Institute of Certified Public Accountants (AICPA)
- Joint Ethics Enforcement Program (JEEP)
- National Association of State Boards of Accountancy (NASBA)
- Professional Ethics Executive Committee (PEEC)
- Statement on Standards for Accounting and Review Services (SSARS)
- Securities and Exchange Commission (SEC)
- Uniform Accountancy Act (UAA)

Item	Correct	Incorrect
The SEC does not have the authority to penalize a CPA with civil fines for violations of securities laws and regulations.		
A member of the AICPA must drop their membership in the AICPA if they belong to more than one individual state society.		
The only services performed by a CPA that requires a license are compilation of financial statements under SSARS and attest services.		
Development of the UAA was joint effort between the AICPA, NASBA and every individual state board of accountancy.		
The AICPA Code of Processional Conduct is applicable only to AICPA members in public practice.		
A member of the AICPA may be expelled or suspended if the member intentionally fails to file their own required individual tax return.		
NASBA is responsible for regulating and enforcing the accounting practice in every state.		
PEEC is a committee of Chief Financial Officers (CFO) from each of the 30 public companies in the Dow Jones Industrial Average charged with interpreting and enforcing the AICPA Code of Professional Conduct.		
Competitive bidding is excluded from enforcement of the rules of the JEEP program.		

⌕ = Reminder   Directions | 1 | 2 | 3 | 4 | 5 | 6 | 7 | 8   ◀ Previous | Next ▶

Remember: The icons and buttons below are **not** functional. The formatting in this chapter mirrors the CPA exam. It is intended to familiarize you with the look and feel of the exam.

REG 6-SIMQ2 SIM4

| Corporate Taxation | Help |

Authoritative Literature   Submit Testlet

Crown Corporation is an accrual basis, calendar year public company that has been in business making farm tractors for 20 years. Crown's average gross sales each year over the last three years were $18,000,000. Crown's tax department has compiled the following items related to 2014:

- Regular taxable income before net operation loss (NOL) deduction. $955,000
- Dividend received deduction (70% limitation) on dividend income from 10% owned corporation. $130,000
- MACRS depreciation in excess of straight line method on building placed in service in 1998. $67,000
- Increase in LIFO recapture. (Crown uses LIFO for costing inventory. $38,000
- Gain on sale of land at the end of 2014. ($30,000 was reported for regular tax purposes in 2014 using the installment method. Crown is not in the business as a dealer of property. $100,000
- Interest income on tax-exempt private activity bonds issued in 2012 (net of expenses). $85,000
- Interest income on tax-exempt municipal bonds issued in 2008 (net of expenses). $60,000
- Life insurance policy proceeds from the death of a key executive in 2014 in which Crown is the owner and beneficiary. (Premiums paid during 2014 were $50,000 and the cash surrender value at the date of death was $40,000. $300,000

Given the selected financial information, calculate the following alternative minimum tax (AMT) related amounts for 2014 for each shaded area:

Total preference items

Total adjustments other than adjusted current earnings (ACE) and NOL

Total of all items included in adjusted current earnings (ACE) used in calculating ACE adjustment.

▷ = Reminder   Directions | 1 | 2 | 3 | 4 | 5 | 6 | 7 | 8   ◀ Previous | Next ▶

REG 6-SIMQ3 SIM7

Individual Taxation | Help | Authoritative Literature | Submit Testlet

The following scenarios are about Frank, a single, 56-year-old taxpayer with no dependents. For each scenario, determine the appropriate gain or loss for each shaded area. Each scenario is independent of the others except where stated.

A. Frank's brother Jacob gave him a gift of 1,000 shares of ABC Corporation common stock in February, 2013, when Jacob's basis in the stock was $10,000. At the gift date, the stock's fair market value (FMV) was $8,000. Frank sold the 1,000 shares of ABC Corporation in June, 2014 for $8,200. How much should Frank report as a gain or loss in 2014?

B. In 2014, Frank traded an office building he owned (purchased in 2006, straight line depreciation and basis of $450,000) for an apartment building that had a fair market value (FMV) of $950,000. What is Frank's recognized gain or loss?

C. Same facts as "B." except that Frank also received $200,000 in cash as part of the exchange. What is Frank's recognized gain or loss?

D. Same facts as "B", except that Frank's office building he exchanged was subject to a mortgage of $125,000 in addition to receiving $100,000 in cash. What is Frank's recognized gain or loss?

E. Frank sold his principal residence, a townhouse, in 2014 for $525,000, net of selling expenses. On the sales date, the townhouse had a basis of $280,000. Frank bought the townhouse in 2002 and had occupied it until he sold it. What is the maximum amount of exclusion on the gain from the sale that Frank can claim on his 2014 tax return?

F. Frank's taxable income in 2014 was $90,000, exclusive of any capital gains and losses. For 2014, he had a net long-term capital loss of $2,500. How much can Frank offset this capital loss against his 2014 ordinary income?

Remember: The icons and buttons below are not functional. The formatting in this chapter mirrors the CPA exam. It is intended to familiarize you with the look and feel of the exam.

REG 6-SIMQ4 DRS1

| ✏ Document Review | Exhibits | Help |

Authoritative Literature

Submit Testlet

Scroll down to complete all parts of the task.

Cool Beans, CPA accounting firm is updating its website. A staff associate prepared a draft of the website's "About Us" page. Ms. Beans, a partner in charge of this engagement, has asked you to review the document and revise the website content, correcting any errors.

To revise the document, click on each segment of underlined text below and select the best choice for needed correction, if any, from the list provided. If the underlined text is already correct in the context of the document, select [Original text] from the list. If removal of the entire underlined text is the best revision to the document as a whole, select [Delete text] from the list.

(DRAFT) Web Page Content – About Us

Cool Beans was founded by Mrs. Beans in 1997. She holds an M.S. in Accounting from the prestigious "Costs a Lot of Beans" University. Mrs. Beans possesses an active CPA license issued by the <u>State of California Board of Accountancy</u>.

1. Choose an option below:
- ○ [Original text] State of California Board of Accountancy
- ○ [Delete text]
- ○ Security and Exchange Commission (SEC)
- ○ Public Accounting Oversight Board (PCAOB)
- ○ American Institute of Certified Public Accountants (AICPA)

Cool Beans is registered with the <u>Public Company Accounting Oversight Board (PCAOB)</u>

2. Choose an option below:
- ○ [Original text] Public Company Accounting Oversight Board (PCAOB)
- ○ [Delete text]
- ○ Security and Exchange Commission (SEC)
- ○ American Institute of Certified Public Accountants (AICPA)
- ○ State CPA Society

and provides auditing services to publicly traded companies. Often, our auditing clients enjoy working with us so much that they also recruit us for assistance with their <u>bookkeeping</u>.

3. Choose an option below:
- ○ [Original text] bookkeeping
- ○ [Delete text]
- ○ appraisal and valuation
- ○ human resources
- ○ tax services.

Although, we can only accommodate this request when we have prior approval from the client's audit committee. Clients, for whom audits are not conducted by Cool Beans, can freely choose from the menu of services provided by Cool Beans.

We pride ourselves on our tax expertise. Tax returns are usually prepared by our highly qualified registered tax return preparers (RTRP).

4. Choose an option below:
- *[Original text]* registered tax return preparers (RTRP).
- *[Delete text]*
- Mr. Beans
- Mrs. Beans
- Enrolled Agents (EAs)

Depending on your particular situation, your tax planning questions can be quickly answered by registered tax return preparers (RTRP).

5. Choose an option below:
- *[Original text]* registered tax return preparers (RTRP).
- *[Delete text]*
- enrolled agents (EA).
- Mr. Beans.
- Mrs. Beans.

Audit representation is usually provided by registered tax return preparers (RTRP).

6. Choose an option below:
- *[Original text]* registered tax return preparers (RTRP).
- *[Delete text]*
- Mr. Beans.
- Mrs. Beans herself.
- our highly competent office staff

We reserve the right to change our fees no sooner than 60 days

7. Choose an option below:
- *[Original text]* 60 days
- *[Delete text]*
- 30 days
- 1 year
- 15 days

after the date the current rates are published. Contingent fees can be charged depending on the outcome of your company's IRS examination.

8. Choose an option below:
- *[Original text]* outcome of your company's IRS examination.
- *[Delete text]*
- outcome of your company's public audit conducted by us.
- amount of your tax refund due with the original return we prepare.

Please note that we can🚩

9. Choose an option below:
○ *[Original text]* can
○ *[Delete text]*
○ cannot

endorse your refund checks. Copy of completed returns will be provided to you no later than the due date of your returns.🚩

10. Choose an option below:
○ *[Original text]* due date of your returns
○ *[Delete text]*
○ date we file your tax return
○ date we present your returns for your signature
○ date your payment has cleared our bank

🚩 = Reminder   Directions | 1 | 2 | 3 | 4 | 5 | 6 | 7 | 8   ◀ Previous | Next ▶

Remember: The icons and buttons below are not functional. The formatting in this chapter mirrors the CPA exam. It is intended to familiarize you with the look and feel of the exam.

REG 6-SIMQ5 SIM30

A client received a Form 1099-DIV showing only a portion of the total distribution as qualified dividends. Which section and subsection of the Internal Revenue Code defines the tax rates to be imposed on qualified dividends?

Enter your response in the answer fields below. Guidance on correctly structuring your response appears above and below the answer fields.

Type the subsection here.
A correctly formatted IRC subsection is a lower case letter shown within the parenthesis.

IRC § [ ] ([ ])

Type the section here.
Examples of correctly formatted sections are shown below.

Examples of correctly formatted IRC responses are IRC§1(a), IRC§56(a), IRC§54A(a), IRC§162(a), IRC§54AA(a), IRC§263A(a), IRC§1245(a), IRC§2032A(a) and IRC§1400U-1(a)

Task-based Simulations – Solutions

REG 6-SIMQ1 SIM2

Item	Correct	Incorrect	
The SEC does not have the authority to penalize a CPA with civil fines for violations of securities laws and regulations.		✓	A.
A member of the AICPA must drop their membership in the AICPA if they belong to more than one individual state society.		✓	B.
The only services performed by a CPA that requires a license are compilation of financial statements under SSARS and attest services.	✓		C.
Development of the UAA was joint effort between the AICPA, NASBA and every individual state board of accountancy.		✓	D.
The AICPA Code of Processional Conduct is applicable only to AICPA members in public practice.		✓	E.
A member of the AICPA may be expelled or suspended if the member intentionally fails to file their own required individual tax return.	✓		F.
NASBA is responsible for regulating and enforcing the accounting practice in every state.		✓	G.
PEEC is a committee of Chief Financial Officers (CFO) from each of the 30 public companies in the Dow Jones Industrial Average charged with interpreting and enforcing the AICPA Code of Professional Conduct.		✓	H.
Competitive bidding is excluded from enforcement of the rules of the JEEP program.	✓		I.

Explanations:
- A. The SEC does have the authority to penalize a CPA with civil fines for violations of securities laws and regulations.
- B. A member of the AICPA can belong to one or more individual state CPA societies.
- C. A CPA license is required by CPAs performing compilation of financial statements under SSARS and attest services.
- D. Development of the UAA was joint effort between both the AICPA and NASBA in the early 1980s.
- E. The AICPA Code of Processional Conduct is applicable to all AICPA members and not just those in public practice.
- F. A member of the AICPA may be expelled or suspended if the member intentionally fails to file their own required tax return.
- G. Individual state boards are responsible for regulating and enforcing the accounting practice in their particular state.
- H. PEEC is a committee within the AICPA charged with interpreting and enforcing the AICPA Code of Professional Conduct.
- I. Competitive bidding is excluded from enforcement of the rules of the JEEP program.

REG 6-SIMQ2 SIM4

Given the selected financial information, calculate the following alternative minimum tax (AMT) related amounts for 2014 for each shaded area:

Total preference items	**$85,000**

Interest income on tax-exempt private activity bonds issued in 2012 (net of expenses).

Total adjustments other than adjusted current earnings (ACE) and NOL	**$67,000**

MACRS depreciation in excess of straight line method on building placed in service in 1998

Dividend received deduction (70% limitation) on dividend income from 10% owned corporation. — $130,000

Increase in LIFO recapture. — $38,000

Gain on sale of land at the end of 2014.

Gain on sale	$100,000	
Reported for tax purposes	30,000	
		$70,000

Interest income on tax-exempt municipal bonds issued in 2008 (net of expenses) — $60,000

Life insurance policy proceeds from the death of a key executive in 2014 in which Crown is the owner and beneficiary.

Gain on sale	$300,000	
Cash surrender value	40,000	
		$260,000

Total of all items included in adjusted current earnings (ACE) used in calculating ACE adjustment.	**$558,000**

REG 6-SIMQ3 SIM7

A. Frank's brother Jacob gave him a gift of 1,000 shares of ABC Corporation common stock in February, 2013, when Jacob's basis in the stock was $10,000. At the gift date, the stock's fair market value (FMV) was $8,000. Frank sold the 1,000 shares of ABC Corporation in June, 2014 for $8,200. How much should Frank report as a gain or loss in 2014?

$0

No recognized gain or loss. No gain or loss is recognized on the sale of property (stock) from a gift if the calculation for the gain results in a loss and the calculation for the loss results in a gain.

Calculation of gain (use donor's (Jacob's) basis at gift date):
Sales price	$	8,200
Basis		10,000
Loss	$	(1,800) (gain calculation results in a loss)

Calculation of gain (use lower of donor's (Jacob's) basis or FMV at gift date):
Sales price	$	8,200
FMV		8,000
Loss	$	200 (loss calculation results in a gain)

B. In 2014, Frank traded an office building he owned (purchased in 2006, straight line depreciation and basis of $450,000) for an apartment building that had a fair market value (FMV) of $950,000. What is Frank's recognized gain or loss?

$0

No recognized gain or loss. This is a like-kind exchange as the same class of property (i.e., investment real estate for investment real estate) where no gain or loss is recognized. The "realized" gain, because there was no money (boot) received, would be:

$	950,000	FMV of property received
	450,000	Basis of property exchanged
$	500,000	Realized gain

C. Same facts as "B." except that Frank also received $200,000 in cash as part of the exchange. What is Frank's recognized gain or loss?

$200,000

$200,000 recognized gain. In this like-kind exchange scenario, the realized gain of $500,000 is recognized only to the extent of the boot received of $200,000. This is because in like-kind exchanges, gains are recognized to the extent of the lesser of boot received or the realized gain.

$	950,000	FMV of property received
	450,000	Basis of property exchanged
$	500,000	Realized gain (only recognized to extent of boot received)
$	200,000	Recognized gain (boot received)

D. Same facts as "B", except that Frank's office building he exchanged was subject to a mortgage of $125,000 in addition to receiving $100,000 in cash. What is Frank's recognized gain or loss?

$225,000

$225,000 recognized gain. In like-kind exchanges, gains are recognized to the extent of the lesser of boot received or the realized gain. The assumption of the mortgage is treated as if it was boot received for a total of $225,000 ($125,000 mortgage + $100,000 cash).

$	950,000	FMV of property received
	100,000	Cash received
	125,000	Assumed mortgage
	1,175,000	Amount realized
	450,000	Basis of property exchanged
$	725,000	Realized gain (only recognized to extent of boot received)
$	225,000	Recognized gain ($125,000 mortgage + $100,000 cash)

E. Frank sold his principal residence, a townhouse, in 2014 for $525,000, net of selling expenses. On the sales date, the townhouse had a basis of $280,000. Frank bought the townhouse in 2002 and had occupied it until he sold it. What is the maximum amount of exclusion on the gain from the sale that Frank can claim on his 2014 tax return?

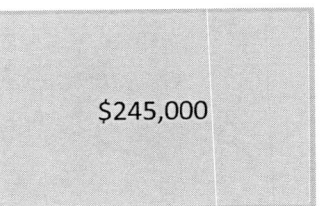

$245,000

$245,000. Frank meets requirements to exclude up to $250,000 of gain that is realized on the sale of a primary residence. The requirements are that Frank had to own and occupy the residence as a principal residence for an aggregate of at least two of the five years preceding the sale. Frank can exclude the entire $245,000 realized gain ($525,000 - $280,000) as it is within the $250,000 limit.

F. Frank's taxable income in 2014 was $90,000, exclusive of any capital gains and losses. For 2014, he had a net long-term capital loss of $2,500. How much can Frank offset this capital loss against his 2014 ordinary income?

$2,500

$2,500. For individuals, any net capital loss can be offset against ordinary income up to a maximum of $3,000. Frank's net capital loss is $2,500, so the entire amount of that loss can be taken as a net capital loss deduction in 2014.

REG 6-SIMQ4 DRS1

(DRAFT) Web Page Content – About Us

Cool Beans was founded by Mrs. Beans in 1997. She holds an M.S. in Accounting from the prestigious "Costs a Lot of Beans" University. Mrs. Beans possesses an active CPA license issued by the <u>State of California Board of Accountancy</u>.

- ⊙ *[Original text]* **State of California Board of Accountancy**

  State Boards of Accountancy have the sole power to license Certified Public Accountants.

  The selection *Securities and Exchange Commission (SEC)* is incorrect because the SEC has a primary responsibility of enforcing the federal securities laws and regulations and securities industry.

  The selection *Public Company Accounting Oversight Board (PCAOB)* is incorrect because the PCAOB is an organization that was created to oversee over the audits of public companies.

  The selection *American Institute of Certified Public Accountants (AICPA)* is incorrect because the AICPA can only sanction and discipline its members, not grant or revoke the licenses.

Cool Beans is registered with the <u>Public Company Accounting Oversight Board (PCAOB)</u>

- ⊙ *[Original text]* **Public Company Accounting Oversight Board (PCAOB)**

  All companies engaged in auditing of the SEC issuers are required to be registered with Public Company Accounting Oversight Board (PCAOB).

  The selection *Security and Exchange Commission (SEC)* incorrect because the SEC oversees Public Company Accounting Oversight Board (PCAOB), which in turn registers and regulates the issuers of public securities.

  The selection *American Institute of Certified Public Accountants (AICPA)* is incorrect because the AICPA deals mostly with setting standards for its CPA members and advocating on their behalf.

  The selection *State CPA Society* is incorrect because membership in the state CPA society is not required for auditing SEC issuers.

and provides auditing services to publicly traded companies. Often, our auditing clients enjoy working with us so much that they also recruit us for assistance with their ~~bookkeeping~~.

- ⊙ **tax services.**

  Tax services are the only services that the firm is allowed to provide to its SEC issuing auditing clients. Note that performance of tax services is only allowed with the prior approval from the board of directors.

  The selection *bookkeeping* is incorrect because the firm would end up auditing its own bookkeeping work.

  The selection *appraisal and valuation* is incorrect because providing appraisal and valuation services to auditing clients is specifically prohibited under the Sarbanes-Oxley Act.

  The selection *human resources* is incorrect because providing human resource services to auditing clients is specifically prohibited under the Sarbanes-Oxley Act.

Although, we can only accommodate this request when we have prior approval from the client's audit committee. Clients, for whom audits are not conducted by Cool Beans, can freely choose from the menu of services provided by Cool Beans.

We pride ourselves on our tax expertise. Tax returns are usually prepared by our highly qualified registered tax return preparers (RTRP).

- ⊙ *[Original text]* **registered tax return preparers (RTRP).**

    Registered Tax Preparer's scope of practice before the IRS includes tax return preparation. They also have the cheapest rate, as provided in the exhibits tab.

    The selection *Mr. Beans* is incorrect because while Mr. Beans, as an attorney, can practice before the IRS, at his billing rate he is not the most cost-efficient choice for tax preparation.

    The selection *Mrs. Beans* is incorrect because while Mrs. Beans, as a CPA, can practice before the IRS, a Registered Tax Return Preparer (RTRP) hired by her will perform this job in a more cost-efficient way.

    The selection *Enrolled Agents (EAs)* is incorrect because while Enrolled Agent (EA) has unlimited rights to practice before the IRS, a Registered Tax Return Preparer (RTRP) hired by the firm can perform this job in a more cost-efficient way

Depending on your particular situation, your tax planning questions can be quickly answered by ~~registered tax return preparers (RTRP)~~.

- ⊙ **enrolled agents (EA).**

    Enrolled Agents (EAs), like attorneys and CPAs, have unlimited practice rights before the IRS. Taking into consideration their billing rates, EAs become the most cost-efficient choice in this case.

    The selection *registered tax return preparers (RTRP)* is incorrect because practice as a Registered Tax Return Preparer (RTRP) is limited to preparing and siging tax returns, refund claims, and other documents submitted to the IRS. The scope of RTRP practice should not include providing tax advice besides that which is necessary to prepare the tax return.

    The selection *Mr. Beans* is incorrect because while Mr. Beans, as an attorney, has unlimited practice rights before the IRS, at his billing rate he is not the most cost-efficient choice in this case.

    The selection *Mrs. Beans* is incorrect because while Mrs. Beans, as a CPA, has unlimited practice rights before the IRS, at her billing rate she is not the most cost-efficient choice in this case.

Audit representation is usually provided by ~~registered tax return preparers (RTRP)~~.

- ⊙ **Mrs. Beans herself.**

    CPAs have unlimited practice rights before the IRS.

    The selection *registered tax return preparers (RTRP)* is incorrect because practice as a Registered Tax return Preparer (RTRP) is limited to preparing and siging tax returns, refund claims, and other documents submitted to the IRS. Only when RTRP prepared the return or claim for refund for the year in question, can she or he represent taxpayer during the IRS examination.

    The selection *Mr. Beans* is incorrect because while Mr. Beans, as an attorney, has unlimited practice rights before the IRS, at his billing rate he is not the most cost-efficient choice in this case.

    The selection *our highly competent office staff* is incorrect because office staff without CPA, EA, or attorney credentials is not allowed to provide IRS audit representation.

We reserve the right to change our fees no sooner than ~~60 days~~.

- ⊙ **30 days**

  According to Circular 230, the practitioner must not increase the rates for at least 30 days after the fee schedule is published.

  The other selections are incorrect because according to Circular 230, the practitioner must not increase the rates for at least 30 (**not** 15 days, 60 days, or 1 year) days after the fee schedule is published.

after the date the current rates are published. Contingent fees can be charged depending on the outcome of your company's IRS examination.

- ⊙ *[Original text]* **outcome of your company's IRS examination.**

  According to Circular 230, contingent fees may only be charged in connection with the IRS examination of the original or amended returns or claims for refund, or any judicial proceedings arising under the Code.

  The selection *outcome of your company's public audit conducted by us* is incorrect because it is unethical to guarantee positive outcomes of the audit to the company.

  The selection *amount of your tax refund due with the original return we prepare* is incorrect because According to Circular 230, contingent fees may only be charged in connection with the IRS examination of the original or amended returns or claims for refund, or any judicial proceedings arising under the Code.

Please note that we ~~can~~

- ⊙ **cannot**

  Under IRC § 6695(g), tax preparer who endorses or negotiates federal tax refund checks issued to a client is subject to $500 penalty.

  The selection *can* is incorrect because no federal tax refund checks issued to a client by the government may be endorsed or negotiated by the practitioner.

endorse your refund checks. Copy of completed returns will be provided to you no later than the ~~due date of your returns.~~

- ⊙ **date we present your returns for your signature**

  Tax preparer must provide a copy of the return or claim for refund to the taxpayer no later than when the preparer presents a copy of those documents for the taxpayer's signature.

  The selection *due date of your returns* is incorrect because tax preparer must provide a copy of the return or claim for refund to the taxpayer no later than when the preparer presents a copy of the return to the taxpayer for signing. This might happen before or after the due date of the return.

  The selection *date we file your tax return* is incorrect because tax preparer must provide a copy of the return or claim for refund to the taxpayer no later than when the preparer presents a copy of the return to the taxpayer for signing. Because taxpayer is required to sign the return before it can be filed, answer C is a better answer.

  The selection *date your payment has cleared our bank* is incorrect because payment for tax work can occur before or after the return is signed and filed by the taxpayer.

REG 6-SIMQ5 SIM30

IRC § [1] ([h])

Keywords: Qualified dividends